September 18–20, 2012
San Jose, California, USA

I0054880

**Association for
Computing Machinery**

Advancing Computing as a Science & Profession

ICAC'12

Proceedings of the 9th ACM

International Conference on Autonomic Computing

Sponsored by:
ACM SIGARCH and University of Arizona

Supported by:
IEEE

**Association for
Computing Machinery**

Advancing Computing as a Science & Profession

The Association for Computing Machinery
2 Penn Plaza, Suite 701
New York, New York 10121-0701

Notice to Past Authors of ACM-Published Articles

ISBN: 978-1-4503-1520-3

Additional copies may be ordered prepaid from:

ACM Order Department
PO Box 30777
New York, NY 10087-0777, USA

Phone: 1-800-342-6626 (USA and Canada)
+1-212-626-0500 (Global)
Fax: +1-212-944-1318
E-mail: acmhelp@acm.org
Hours of Operation: 8:30 am – 4:30 pm ET

ACM Order Number: 102121

Printed in the USA

Chairs' Welcome

It is our great pleasure to welcome you to the *9th ACM International Conference on Autonomic Computing (ICAC'12)* in San Jose, California, the heart of Silicon Valley. In the past nine years, ICAC has established itself as a premier venue that attracts strong technical papers addressing the multiple aspects of self-management in computing infrastructures, systems, services, and applications. It has also created a valuable tradition of synergistic interactions between academia and industry, reflected by the composition of its program committee, authorship of technical papers, and affiliation of attendees. This year's ICAC continues that tradition and presents a strong, exciting technical program that covers a spectrum of core and emerging topics such as resource management, control, diagnosis, virtualization, clouds, and big data.

The call for papers attracted 67 submissions (including 62 full papers and 5 posters) from academia and industry around the world. Each full paper submission received an average of four reviews and each poster submission was reviewed by two PC members. After a period of online reviewing and discussions, a face-to-face PC meeting was held on May 11, 2012, at HP Labs (Palo Alto, CA). A full day's discussion (from 9am to 6pm) resulted in the acceptance of 15 full papers and 9 short papers from the 62 full submissions. The accepted papers will be presented in five regular sessions and two short paper sessions, with a corresponding poster on each paper to be presented during the poster session. We would like to thank all authors – regardless of the review results – for their valuable contribution to the conference. We would also like to thank all PC members for their dedicated, rigorous work throughout the paper review/selection process.

This year we are excited to present three distinguished Keynote Speakers, Dr. Amin Vahdat from UCSD/Google, Dr. Subutai Ahmad from Numenta, and Dr. Eitan Frachtenberg from Facebook.

In addition to the regular conference, there are four workshops taking place the day before and the day after conference. The workshops cover new and exciting areas of managing big data systems, self-aware Internet of things, federated Clouds, and feedback computing. We thank Fred Douglis, the workshop chair, and all workshop organizers for putting this exciting agenda together.

The organization of ICAC 2012 is a team effort, and we would like to extend our thanks to all involved in making this event successful: our steering committee for their guidance; our program committee for paper selection; our workshops chair, Fred Douglis; our publicity team, led by Ming Zhao, who effectively managed the ICAC-2012 Web presence; Ioan Raicu, our social networking chair; regional publicity chairs, Daniel Macêdo Batista, Vartan Padaryan, and Jianfeng Zhan; our sponsorships chair, Xiaoyun Zhu, who took the leadership in attracting sponsors to the conference during trying economic times; and Eno Thereska, who has coordinated the posters/demo/exhibits session. Budgets and expenses were carefully planned and accounted for by Michael Kozuch, our finance chair. Our sincere thanks go to Jessica Blaine, the local arrangements chair, without whom the event would not have taken place. Last but not least, we thank our industry sponsors for their generous support.

Dejan S. Milojicic
ICAC'12 General Chair
HP Labs, USA

Dongyan Xu and Vanish Talwar
ICAC'12 Program Co-Chairs
Purdue University, USA   HP Labs, USA

Table of Contents

Keynote Address I

Session 1: Virtualization

Session 2: Performance and Resource Management

Session 3: Short Papers I

Keynote Address II

Session 4: Control-Based Approaches

Session 5: Energy

Session 6: Short Papers II

Keynote Address III

Session 7: Diagnosis and Monitoring

Author Index

ICAC'12 Conference Organization

General Chair: Dejan Milojicic, HP Labs

Program Co-chairs: Dongyan Xu, Purdue University
Vanish Talwar, HP Labs

Finance Chair: Michael Kozuch, Intel

Publicity Chairs: Ming Zhao, Florida International University (Web Presence)
Ioan Raicu, Illinois Institute of Technology (Social Networking)
Daniel Macêdo Batista, IME/USP (Region Chair: South America)
Vartan Padaryan, Russian Academy of Sciences (Region Chair: Russia)
Jianfeng Zhan, Chinese Academy of Sciences (Region Chair: China)

Steering Committee: Salim Hariri, University of Arizona (Co-Chair)
Jeffrey Kephart, IBM Research (Co-Chair)
Tarek Abdelzaher, University of Illinois at Urbana-Champaign
Renato Figueiredo, University of Florida
Emre Kiciman, Microsoft Research
Manish Parashar, Rutgers University
Hartmut Schmeck, Karlsruhe Institute of Technology
Karsten Schwan, Georgia Tech
John Wilkes, Google

Program Committee: Tarek Abdelzaher, UIUC, USA
Umesh Bellur, IIT, Bombay, India
Ken Birman, Cornell University, USA
Rajkumar Buyya, The University of Melbourne, Australia
Rocky Chang, Hong Kong Polytechnic University, Hong Kong
Yuan Chen, HP Labs, USA
Alva Couch, Tufts University, USA
Peter Dinda, Northwestern University, USA
Fred Douglis, EMC, USA
Renato Figueiredo, University of Florida, USA
Mohamed Hefeeda, Qatar Computing Research Institute, Qatar
Joe Hellerstein, Google, USA
Geoff Jiang, NEC Labs, USA
Jeff Kephart, IBM Research, USA
Emre Kiciman, Microsoft Research, USA
Fabio Kon, University of São Paulo, Brazil
Michael Kozuch, Intel, USA
Dejan Milojicic, HP Labs, USA
Klara Nahrstedt, UIUC, USA
Priya Narasimhan, CMU, USA

ICAC 2012 Sponsors & Supporters

Sponsors: SIGARCH   THE UNIVERSITY OF ARIZONA. Arizona's First University.

Technical Supporters: acm

Gold Level Partner: IBM

Conference Partners: vmware   neustar   hp

PhD Student Sponsor: Google

NEC Laboratories America
Relentless passion for innovation

Symbiosis in Scale Out Networking and Data Management

Amin Vahdat

Google and University of California, San Diego

vahdat@cs.ucsd.edu

ABSTRACT

This talk highlights the symbiotic relationship between data management and networking through a study of two seemingly independent trends in traditionally separate communities: large-scale data processing and software defined networking. First, data processing at scale increasingly runs across hundreds or thousands of servers. We show that balancing network performance with computation and storage is a prerequisite to both efficient and scalable data processing. We illustrate the need for scale out networking in support of data management through a case study of TritonSort, currently the record holder for several sorting benchmarks, including GraySort and JouleSort. Our TritonSort experience shows that disk-bound workloads require 10 Gb/s provisioned bandwidth to keep up with modern processors while emerging flash workloads require 40 Gb/s fabrics at scale.

We next argue for the need to apply data management techniques to enable Software Defined Networking (SDN) and Scale Out Networking. SDN promises the abstraction of a single logical network fabric rather than a collection of thousands of individual boxes. In turn, scale out networking allows network capacity (ports, bandwidth) to be expanded incrementally, rather than by wholesale fabric replacement. However, SDN requires an extensible model of both static and dynamic network properties and the ability to deliver dynamic updates to a range of network applications in a fault tolerant and low latency manner. Doing so in networking environments where updates are typically performed by timer-based broadcasts and models are specified as comma-separated text files processed by one-off scripts presents interesting challenges. For example, consider an environment where applications from routing to traffic engineering to monitoring to intrusion/anomaly detection all essentially boil down to inserting, triggering and retrieving updates to/from a shared, extensible data store.

Categories and Subject Descriptors

C.0 [**Computer Systems Organization**]: General

Keywords

Scale out, Data Management, Networking

BIO

Amin Vahdat is a Distinguished Engineer at Google working on data center and wide-area networking. He is also a Professor and holds the Science Applications International Corporation Chair in the Department of Computer Science and Engineering at the University of California San Diego. Vahdat's research focuses broadly on computer systems, including distributed systems, networks, and operating systems. He received a PhD in Computer Science from UC Berkeley under the supervision of Thomas Anderson after spending the last year and a half as a Research Associate at the University of Washington. Vahdat is an ACM Fellow and a past recipient of the the NSF CAREER award, the Alfred P. Sloan Fellowship, and the Duke University David and Janet Vaughn Teaching Award.

Net-Cohort: Detecting and Managing VM Ensembles in Virtualized Data Centers

Liting Hu[1], Karsten Schwan[1], Ajay Gulati[2], Junjie Zhang[1], Chengwei Wang[1]

[1]College of Computing
Georgia Institute of Technology
Atlanta, GA 30332

{foxting, schwan, jjzhang,
flinter}@cc.gatech.edu

[2]Resource Management Team
VMware, Inc.
Palo Alto, CA 94304

agulati@vmware.com

ABSTRACT

Bi-section bandwidth is a critical resource in today's data centers because of the high cost and limited bandwidth of higher-level network switches and routers. This problem is aggravated in virtualized environments where a set of virtual machines, jointly implementing some service, may run across multiple L2 hops. Since data center administrators typically do not have visibility into such sets of communicating VMs, this can cause inter-VM traffic to traverse bottlenecked network paths. To address this problem, we present 'Net-Cohort', which offers lightweight system-level techniques to (1) discover VM ensembles and (2) collect information about intra-ensemble VM interactions. Net-Cohort can dynamically identify ensembles to manipulate entire services/applications rather than individual VMs, and to support VM placement engines in co-locating communicating VMs in order to reduce the consumption of bi-section bandwidth. An implementation of Net-Cohort on a Xen-based system with 15 hosts and 225 VMs shows that its methods can detect VM ensembles at low cost and with about 90.0% accuracy. Placements based on ensemble information provided by Net-Cohort can result in an up to 385% improvement in application throughput for a RUBiS instance, a 56.4% improvement in application throughput for a Hadoop instance, and a 12.76 times improvement in quality of service for a SIPp instance.

Categories and Subject Descriptors

D.4.1 [**Operating Systems**]: Process Management – *scheduling*; D.4.7 [**Operating Systems**]: Organization and Design – *distributed systems.*

General Terms

Algorithms, Management, Design.

Keywords

Virtualization, Clustering, Dependency Analysis.

1. INTRODUCTION

Virtualization is being deployed in data centers at a rapid pace to consolidate workloads for improved server utilization, for ease of provisioning, configuration management, and more generally, for flexible use of data center resources. A typical application running in a virtualized environment consists of a set of virtual machines (VMs) – a VM ensemble – that cooperate and communicate to jointly provide a certain service or accomplish a task. A multi-tier web application, for instance, may be structured as an ensemble with certain VMs implementing its front end service, other VMs running application servers, and backend VMs running databases or network file systems.

VM ensembles can be configured and mapped to data center machines to scale throughput by partitioning tasks across multiple machines, to obtain high availability by mapping VMs to different nodes or racks, or to improve power consumption by minimizing the number of machines used by an ensemble, while still meeting performance and reliability requirements [18].

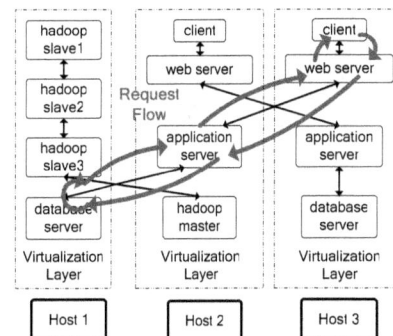

Figure 1. VM ensemble consisting of a multi-tier application mapped across multiple hosts in a data center.

Figure 1 shows one such configuration for a multi-tier e-commerce web application represented by RUBiS. In this case, client requests arrive at the VM running the web server front end and are then forwarded to one of the VMs running application servers, which in turn may request data from a backend VM hosting a database.

Bi-section bandwidth of the network infrastructure is a critical, scarce, and expensive resource in data centers today. Recent studies [11] [20] [21] have shown that servers in different racks have to share the up-links from top of rack switches (ToRs). Since these are typically 5:1 to 20:1 oversubscribed, this can result in a worst-case available bi-section bandwidth as low as 125Mbps [17]. Furthermore, higher level switches in the network topology cost much more, due to the amount of network bandwidth and numbers of ports they have to support.

Limited bi-section bandwidth places constraints on the mapping of VM ensembles to underlying hosts. As illustrated in Figure 2, an ensemble of frequently communicating, 'chatty' VMs is placed across multiple racks. Such a placement can negatively affect the services provided by the ensemble [26]. First, as the shared up-links from ToRs become saturated, intra-ensemble communications may be delayed. Such delays can be further exacerbated by message retransmissions due to time-outs. Second, the use of scarce, shared bandwidth can affect other services and ensembles, as evident in applications like Hadoop that experience slowdown due to file system-level data reorganization. This is also demonstrated in one of our experiments, where a RUBiS benchmark experiences a 79.4% performance loss in application throughput when placed across a bandwidth-constrained set of machines (see Section 6). Finally, a link failure can cause severe imbalances across paths and may require relocation of some of the VMs in order to reduce over-subscription.

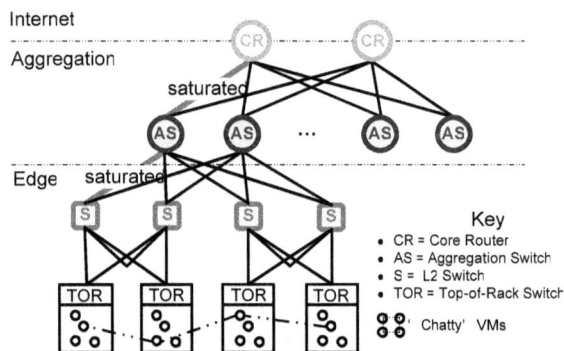

Figure 2. Example of shared up-links from TORs crash, causing performance degradation for many VMs.

This paper presents 'Net-Cohort', a lightweight system that (1) continuously monitors a system to identify potential VM ensembles, (2) assesses the degree of 'chattiness' among the VMs in these potential ensembles, thereby (3) enabling optimized VM placement to reduce the stress on bi-section bandwidth of the data center's network. 'Net-Cohort' has the following unique properties:

- *scalable* – it accurately identifies 'chatty' VMs using commonly available runtime statistics and a two-step method for increased precision when needed;
- *actionable* – insights derived from running Net-Cohort can help management software better co-locate VM ensembles on underlying hosts;
- *privacy-preserving* – its black-box methods do not require any VM (guest-OS) level changes or any information about the VM ensemble being run from the user.

Discovering VM ensembles and their inter-VM dependencies is quite challenging. A naïve method that continuously gathers statistics about all communicating VM-pairs is prohibitively expensive. First, it would require introspection of all packets sent and received by the VMs; this would induce notable CPU overheads and additional per packet latencies of the tens of microseconds. Second, additional memory resources would be required to maintain statistics for every pair of IP addresses.

Net-Cohort uses a two-step approach to limit runtime overheads in terms of metric collection and per packet analysis. The first step acquires VM-level statistics commonly available in virtualized systems, such as the total numbers of packet in/out over time. It then computes the correlation coefficients among these statistics and divides the corresponding VMs into subsets (also called ensembles) using correlation values and a hierarchical clustering algorithm.

The second step uses a statistical packet sniffer only on the VMs identified as members of a misplaced ensemble, i.e., an ensemble with VMs placed across remote racks. The packet sniffer maintains information about outgoing packets, their destination IP addresses and corresponding counters, which are then used to determine the actual communication intensity among VMs. To optimize memory consumption, only the top-k destinations are tracked in an online manner using the statistical algorithm proposed by Lukasz and David in [16]. Finally, this information about VM level communications is used to drive new VM placement decisions.

Determining a new placement of VMs to physical servers is similar to multi-dimensional bin-packing problem. Placement requires evaluation of multiple criteria such as balancing of CPU, memory and I/O resources on each host. Existing solutions like VMware DRS, use weighted mechanisms to combine the standard deviation across multiple dimensions. Different policies can also influence the placement. For example, power savings would give priority to consolidating VMs on fewer servers whereas load-balancing would redistribute VMs across all servers. Net-Cohort can supplement any placement system by providing network communication cost as another dimension. However, designing a placement solution just based on network communication would not be very useful and designing a complete solution is out of scope of this paper. As suggested in the Section 4, Net-Cohort can suggest soft or hard affinity rules between VMs and the placement engine (e.g. VMware DRS) can enforce them during load-balancing.

We have implemented Net-Cohort on Xen hypervisor, and evaluated its effectiveness on a virtualized infrastructure consisting of 15 hosts and 225 VMs. These VMs run a diverse mix of business, web, Internet services, and batch workloads. Experimental results show that Net-Cohort can identify VM ensembles with 90.0% accuracy, and improved placements due to its use can increase application performance in terms of throughput and latency. In particular, we observe an up to 385% improvement in application throughput for a RUBiS instance, a 56.4% improvement in application throughput for a Hadoop instance, and a 12.76 times improvement in quality of service for a SIPp instance.

The remainder of this paper is organized as follows. Section 2 discusses background and related work. Section 3 describes the Net-Cohort design and implementation. Section 4 discusses the support and integration with VM placement engines. Sections 5 and 6 present the experimental setup and performance evaluation, respectively. We conclude with some directions for future work in Section 7.

2. BACKGROUND AND RELATED WORK

We first explain the dominant design pattern for today's data centers [2] and why an inappropriate placement of VMs on data center machines can incur substantial performance penalties. We then discuss the related literature.

2.1 Data Center Background

As shown in Figure 2, data center networks are based on a proven layered approach, including a layer of servers in racks at the bottom (access layer), a layer of aggregation 10 Gigabit Ethernet switches at the middle (aggregation layer), and a layer of core routers at the top (core layer). There are typically 20 to 40 servers per rack, each singly connected to a Top of Rack (ToR) switch with a 1 Gbps link. ToRs connect to End of Row (EoR) switches via 1-4 of the available 10 GigE uplinks, and these switches manage traffic into and out of the rack. At the top of the hierarchy, core routers carry traffic between aggregation switches and manage traffic into and out of the data center.

As traffic moves up through the layers of switches and routers, the over-subscription ratio, which is the ratio of the allocated bandwidth per host to the worst-case guaranteed bandwidth per host, increases rapidly. For example, for servers in the same rack, they can communicate at the full rate of their interfaces (e.g., 1Gbps) with 1:1 over-subscription ratio. Unfortunately, servers in different racks have to share the up-links from ToRs, which are typically 5:1 to 20:1 oversubscribed, resulting in 125Mbps as the worst-case available bi-section bandwidth [17].

Network latencies may not vary much, but the bandwidth available within a rack, across racks, and across rows can vary substantially. Therefore, inappropriate placement of VMs can have dire consequences. An example is the placement of heavily communicating VMs across multiple racks, thereby consuming the bandwidth available to a QoS-sensitive VM ensemble. Based on anecdotal evidence, users deploy multiple VMs in a public cloud to finally find a group with low ping latency between them and then hold on to them. Such scenarios motivate us to develop Net-Cohort's runtime methods to identify VM ensembles, as once identified, they can better place VMs onto data center machines.

2.2 Related Work

We classify related literature into four different categories: manual techniques, trace-based and middleware-based techniques, and techniques using explicit perturbation.

2.2.1 Manual Techniques

Some sophisticated network management systems, e.g., Mercury MAM [3] and Microsoft MOM [4], rely on application designers or owners to specify dependency models. This restricts these approaches to particular applications or vendors and requires significant updates or changes when applications evolve. This is not very practical both for public clouds like Amazon EC2 or for private cloud deployments to run the IT for large enterprises like those reported in a survey conducted by the Wall Street Journal'08, which states that a single company, Citigroup, operates over 10,000 line-of-business applications [15].

2.2.2 Trace-based Techniques

Project5 [9] and WAP5 [23] infer causal path patterns from offline network traces, using messages at hosts recorded with both sent and received timestamps. Project5 infers causal relationships between two message streams by computing their cross correlation. WAP5 generates timelines and causal trees, based on the assumption that causal delays follow an exponential distribution. The project's purpose is to isolate performance bottlenecks, e.g., to detect which nodes are sources of latency. Their primary concern, therefore, is to resolve which incoming message triggers which outgoing message. In contrast, Net-Cohort operates at a larger scale and requires less information about the underlying system.

E2Eprof [8] reconstructs causal paths based on kernel-level network tracing. Compared to Net-Cohort, E2EProf has higher runtime overheads due to capturing the end-to end latencies of all requests in multi-tier systems and applying cross correlation analysis to all network flows.

Orion [15] discovers dependencies for enterprise applications by using the 'time correlation' of messages between different services, meaning that if service A depends on service B, the message delay between A and B should be close to a "typical" value. Applying this rule to VM platforms may be difficult, because a "typical" spike could be distorted by noise, e.g., the domain running service A or B may lose its processor and spend some uncertain amount of time waiting to be scheduled.

Our earlier workshop paper [10], called LWT, is not sufficiently accurate or flexible: they are based only on CPU metrics; their use of k-means clustering requires parameters settings to be customized to the applications being run.

Pinpoint [14] collects end-to-end traces of client requests travelling through a distributed system, by tagging each J2EE call with a unique request-ID. These traces enable automated statistical analyses. Pinpoint requires all distributed applications to run on homogeneous platforms with logging capabilities, but real-life large enterprise data centers are almost heterogeneous with a plethora of operating systems from different vendors.

2.2.3 Middleware-Based Techniques

vPath [24] provides path discovery by monitoring and recording thread and network activities at runtime, such as which thread performs a *send* or *recv* system call over certain TCP connection. vPath can be implemented in either the OS kernel or a virtual machine monitor (VMM). Although the implementation is agnostic to user-space code, it requires changes to the VMM code and the guest OS.

Aurora [1] is targeted at flow-based network traffic analysis for large networks to provide anomaly and virus detection/mitigation, BGP/OSPF/RIP monitoring, and traffic network maps. It discovers communication dependencies among servers through detailed network traffic reports from NetFlow, which a network protocol developed by Cisco Systems. However, it requires an installation of a netflow collector and works specifically on Cisco routers. The cost and overhead of generating the traffic report can be quite high in large datacenters.

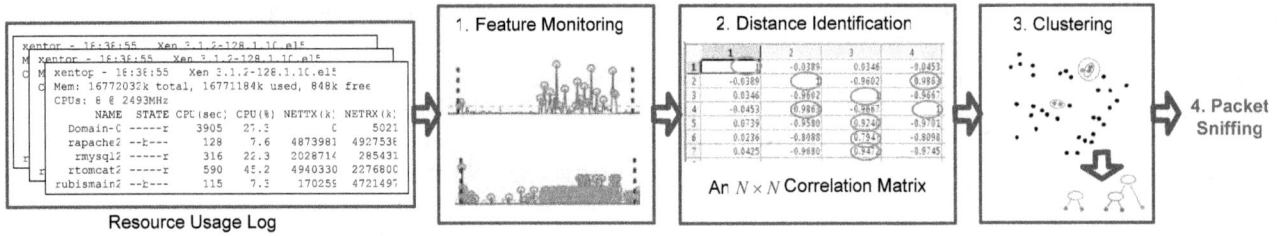

Figure 3. Workflow of Net-Cohort.

2.2.4 Perturbation-Based Techniques

Resource dependencies are uncovered using an active approach in [12] – using fault injection. In [13], cross-domain dependencies are identified by explicitly perturbing system components while monitoring the system's response, e.g., by locking a particular database table to deny the queries from certain component. Pip [22] can obtain a high rate of accuracy for extracting causal paths by modifying, or at least recompiling the applications. The generality of all these approaches is limited by that fact that they require expert knowledge about the systems and applications being evaluated.

3. NET-COHORT DESIGN

Net-Cohort's uses a three-step approach to discover VM ensembles and make use of them. These include (1) monitoring of some basic statistics, (2) computing potential ensembles using correlation techniques and creating hierarchical clusters, and (3) collecting more precise communication statistics between the VMs in each ensemble. Figure 3 shows these steps at a high level, with additional detail presented next.

3.1 Data Collection

The basic monitor module captures the following universally available system-level metrics about each VM:

- *CPU*: CPU usage per second in percentage terms (%)
- *PacketOut*: Packets transmitted per second (KByte/sec),
- *PacketIn*: Packets received per second (KByte/sec)

These periodic measurements result in three time series signals per VM. Before explaining the actual analysis being applied, we illustrate the utility of taking these measurements with a simple example.

Multi-tier applications (e.g., RUBiS) typically use a request-response architecture, in which a client node sends a request to the front end (e.g., Apache), which does load balancing and assigns the work to an appropriate server (e.g., Tomcat) running the application logic. The application logic services the request by querying the backend (e.g., a database server like MySQL) to produce the necessary output, and sending the response back to the client.

Therefore, given the nature of multitier applications, we can expect correlations between one or more of "*CPU*", "*PacketOut*", and "*PacketIn*" statistics for interacting nodes. Figure 4 shows these measurements for Client, Apache, Tomcat and MySQL VMs for one instance of RUBiS. Here we find that the "spikes" and "valleys" of their packet flows consistently occur together. The reason is that an instant rise of CPU usage or packet flow rate

in one VM directly or indirectly triggers activities in other VMs, thereby creating the correlations among these statistics.

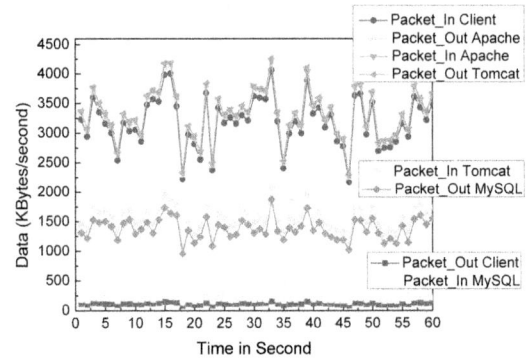

Figure 4. Example of a multi-tier RUBiS application showing correlation on packet flowrate.

Although "*PacketOut*" and "*PacketIn*" are more intuitive metrics to do correlation analysis among communicating VMs, we also used "*CPU*" metric for the analysis because it provides extra information in certain scenarios. For example, a bunch of VMs doing many-to-many but infrequent large data exchanges. It gets even harder to detect these using only packet-based metrics if the interval between exchanges is larger than the sampling window. In these cases, CPU correlation provided better results as compared to others. We found one such example during our evaluation as well (see Section 6.1, Figure 9).

3.2 Distance Identification

For each pair of VMs in the data center, we calculate the correlation coefficient value, denoted as corr(V_i, V_j), to identify the dependency strength between them. In statistics, the correlation coefficient indicates the strength and direction of a linear relationship between two random variables. We choose the pearson product-moment correlation coefficient (PMCC) to measure the degree of correlation, giving a value between +1 and −1 inclusive.

Let $X = \{X_1, X_2, ..., X_n\}$ and $Y = \{Y_1, Y_2, ..., Y_n\}$ be the vectors of two random variables, then the strength of the dependence between X and Y is:

$$corr(X,Y) = \frac{\sum_{i=1}^{n}(X_i - \bar{X})(Y_i - \bar{Y})}{\sqrt{\sum_{i=1}^{n}(X_i - \bar{X})^2}\sqrt{\sum_{i=1}^{n}(Y_i - \bar{Y})^2}} \quad \ldots\ldots \quad \ldots\ldots (1)$$

Here $\bar{X}$ and $\bar{Y}$ denote the sample means of X and Y, respectively. We expect to see a large, positive correlation coefficient between certain statistics of the interacting VMs.

3.3 Compute Pair-wise Distance among VMs

Let w be the size of observation window in seconds. Let $V = \{VM_1, VM_2, ..., VM_N\}$ be the set of all VMs in the data center. For each observation window, let $CPU_i = \{CPU_1, CPU_2, ..., CPU_w\}_i$ denote the set of CPU usage readings collected for VM_i; let $PacketOut_i = \{PacketOut_1, PacketOut_2, ..., PacketOut_w\}_i$ be the set of $PacketOut$ readings collected for VM_i; let $PacketIn_i = \{PacketIn_1, PacketIn_2, ..., PacketIn_w\}_i$ be the set of $PacketIn$ readings collected for VM_i.

The readings interval is few seconds. For each pair of VMs (denoted as V_i, V_j), we calculate the correlation coefficients for the following three combinations of statistics using Equation (1):

- $corr_1 = corr(CPU_i, CPU_j)$
- $corr_2 = corr(PacketOut_i, PacketIn_j)$
- $corr_3 = corr(PacketIn_i, PacketOut_j)$

Next as illustrated in Figure 5, a $N \times N$ correlation matrix for the set of all VMs is generated, in which the correlation coefficient between V_i and V_j, (denoted as $corr(V_i, V_j)$) is set as the maximum value of the three combinations, $Max(corr_1, corr_2, corr_3)$. The above process is repeated for each observation window. Finally, we have ρ $N \times N$ correlation matrices (ρ refers to the number of observation windows).

	Nbench	Iperf Client	Rubis SQL	Iperf Server	Rubis Client	Rubis Tomcat	Rubis Apache
Nbench	1.0000	0	0	0	0	0	0
Iperf Client	0	1.0000	-0.97238	0.999435	-0.96725	-0.96309	-0.96269
Rubis Sql	0	-0.97238	1.0000	-0.97231	0.941962	0.931968	0.932395
Iperf Server	0	0.999435	-0.97231	1.0000	-0.96969	-0.96617	-0.96522
Rubis Client	0	-0.96725	0.941962	-0.96969	1.0000	0.992994	0.999513
Ruis Tomcat	0	-0.96309	0.931968	-0.96617	0.992994	1.0000	0.993191
Rubis Apache	0	-0.96269	0.932395	-0.96522	0.999513	0.993191	1.0000

Figure 5. Example of a $N \times N$ correlation matrix.

Given the ρ observation windows, we need to handle the noise and outliers in incoming data. Two negative situations have to be excluded: (1) unrelated VMs showing "similar" resource usage features lasting for μ observation windows ($\mu \ll \rho$); (2) two correlated VMs showing "diverse" resource usage features lasting for μ observation windows ($\mu \ll \rho$). To avoid these abnormal samples from affecting our result, we calculate the average value for $corr(V_i, V_j)$ based on ρ windows. We further define the distance between V_i and V_j as:

$$Dist(V_i, V_j) \begin{cases} 1/corr(V_i, V_j) & if\ corr(V_i, V_j) > 0 \\ \infty & if\ corr(V_i, V_j) \leq 0 \end{cases}$$

The distance indicates the strength of dependency between two VMs, meaning that the closer the distance, the stronger the correlation. We then calculate a $N \times N$ distance matrix for all VMs, which will be used in the next step.

3.4 Hierarchical Clustering

Given a set of N VMs with a $N \times N$ distance matrix, Net-Cohort uses an unobtrusive black-box approach to cluster them into ensembles. The black-box clustering requires only VM-level's external observations like CPU usage over time, packet

transmitted over time, to indicate which VMs may be interacting with each other. Such observations are commonly available from any data center's monitoring system or hypervisors and thus collecting the source data is easy and lightweight.

Two commonly used clustering algorithms are hierarchical clustering and k-means clustering. Net-cohort uses hierarchical clustering for the following reasons:

- Hierarchical clustering does not require the number of clusters in advance.
- It works well with both globular and non-globular clusters, while k-means fails to handle non-globular data.
- k-means clustering is sensitive to initial centroids. If the user does not have adequate knowledge about the data set, this may lead to erroneous results.

The process of hierarchical clustering is shown in Figure 6:

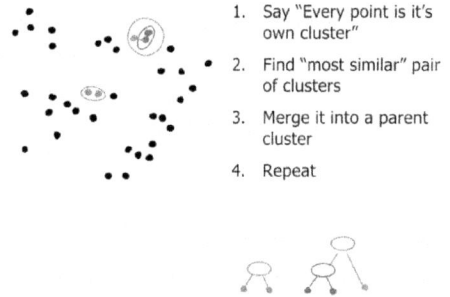

1. Say "Every point is it's own cluster"
2. Find "most similar" pair of clusters
3. Merge it into a parent cluster
4. Repeat

Figure 6. Example of hierarchical clustering.

- Step 1: initially assign each VM to a cluster, so that there are N initial cluster for N VMs.
- Step 2: find the closest (most similar) pair of clusters and merge them into a single cluster.
- Step 3: compute distances (similarities) between the new cluster and each of the old clusters.
- Step 4: repeat Steps 2 and Step 3 until all items are clustered into a single cluster of size N.

Concerning Step 4, of course, there is no point in having all N items grouped into a single cluster, but doing so results in the construction of the complete hierarchical tree, which can be used to obtain k clusters by just cutting its $k-1$ longest links. K can be based on the number racks in the datacenter, or it can be chosen to make the inter-cluster distance is less than a certain threshold.

3.5 Statistical Packet Sniffing

Based on the ensembles information from Section 3.3 and the initial known VM/PM mappings, Net-Cohort detects the ensemble whose components might be misplaced, e.g., a RUBiS ensemble but its components (Apache, Tomcat, Database) are placed across remote racks. Then packet sniffing is enabled only on such misplaced VMs to determine the actual communication intensity among them. Calculating the communication intensity is important because a bunch of VMs that do frequent, synchronized exchanges would appear to be an ensemble by the first step, but their communication volume transferred might be trivial and will have little impact on bi-section bandwidth.

Net-cohort uses a lightweight packet sniffer inside domain0 to log the destination IPs and communication frequency for a VM.

Note that not all VMs with high correlation are suitable for being placed close to each other. Informally, the VMs whose communication exceed a certain threshold and occur for a "sustained" period are better candidates for co-location. After all, there is no need to co-locate VMs that have only lightweight "ping pong" packet communications. However, the hierarchical clustering tree lacks information about how much data has been exchanged between dependent VMs. By contrast, the packet sniffer can provide a better estimate of data transmission.

In order to make the data collection more efficient, only *top-K* destinations in terms of network communication are collected. Consider a data center with large number of VMs, the overhead for maintaining data structures of all distinct IP addresses might be costly. We therefore adapt well-known techniques from data mining, as proposed by Lukasz and David in [16], to compute *top-K* destination IP addresses and an approximate packet count. This algorithm identifies frequent items in sliding windows defined over real-time packet streams with limited memory. More details can be found in [16]. Packet sniffer is not completely transparent and introduces some CPU and memory overhead (see Section 6.3), so we only apply it to the misplaced ensembles and run it for a short period.

4. SUPPORT FOR PLACEMENT ENGINE

Based on VM ensemble discovery and fine-grained statistics, Net-Cohort can supplement any VM placement engine to identify collocation opportunities for VM that are communicating heavily.

A VM placement engine is responsible for managing the mappings of VMs onto physical machines (PMs) in accordance with criteria specified by users or administrators. For example, if the optimization criterion is to minimize power usage, the VM placement engine might consolidate VMs onto fewer hosts and power off unneeded hosts during periods of low resource utilization (e.g., VMware DPM); if the optimization criterion is to achieve high levels of QoS, VM placement engine might perform load-balancing of VMs between physical hosts when specific thresholds are exceeded, such as transactions per second, CPU utilization, etc. (e.g., Microsoft's Performance and Resource Optimization (PRO) [5], VMware DRS and DPM [7]).

With Net-Cohort, a VM placement engine can be enhanced to consider VM level communication in its decisions. One way for Net-Cohort to interact with a placement engine is to provide it with a list of candidates for VM movement, ranked by the potential benefits accrued in terms of reduced use of network bi-section bandwidth. The engine, then, considers those facts along with other migration criteria, such as load balancing and VM migration costs, to make migration decisions. Another alternative is to set soft affinity rules among VMs that are communicating heavily, which is then considered by the placement engine when it decides on VM relocations. If the VM level communications are known in advance or from historical records, the VM placement engine can co-locate them from the very beginning.

Regardless of how an engine leverages Net-Cohort's information, however, it is the engine's task to resolve conflicts between different rules and the movements they suggest.

Placement engine design and details are beyond the scope of this paper, for our analysis we assume that we have enough resources in terms of CPU and memory to do collocation of VMs based on their communication intensity and there is not interfering rule regarding separating them for higher availability.

5. EXPERIMENTAL SETUP
This section validates Net-Cohort with experiments performed with representative applications in a virtualized infrastructure.

5.1 Testbed
Experiments are run on 15 dual-core dual-socket servers, each of which has two Intel Xeon 5150 processors, 16GB of memory, and 80GB hard drives. The 15 servers are distributed across 4 edge switches, with 4, 4, 4, and 3 servers/switch. All switch and NIC ports run at 1Gbps. Switches are connected to each other, with an oversubscription ratio of at most 4:1.

Applications are embedded in a total of 225 virtual machines, each of which is configured to use 128MB of RAM. Xen 3.1.2 is used as the virtual machine monitor on each host, and the host kernel for XenoLinux is a modified version of Linux 2.6.18.

5.2 Workload and Metrics
Experiments employ 6 instances of RUBiS (24 VMs), 3 instances of Hadoop (48 VMs), 6 instances of Iperf (12 VMs), 6 instances of N-bench (6 VMs), 6 instances of SIPp (12 VMs) and 3 instance of MalGen (123VMs), resulting in a total of 225 VMs running a mix of business, internet services, and batch workloads.

RUBiS is an eBay-like benchmark. We use a PHP-based configuration of RUBiS, with a web server front end (Apache) and an application server (Tomcat) connected to a database backend (MySQL). Workload generation uses a fourth client VM.

SIPp is a traffic generator for the SIP protocol. It can establish actual client and server sessions and initiate/release thousands of calls with given rate. We use call rates (calls per second) starting from 800, increased by 10 every second, and a maximum rate of 3000, with total calls set to 1000K.

Hadoop is a Map/Reduce-like framework in which the application is divided into many small fragments of work, each of which may be executed or re-executed on any node in the cluster.

N-bench is a CPU benchmark measuring CPU performance, such as integer operations and floating point arithmetic.

Iperf is a commonly used network workload generation tool. We continuously run Iperf pairs to generate interference traffic, thereby causing the bandwidth bottleneck.

MalGen is a set of scripts that generate a large, distributed data set across multiple nodes in a cluster. One MalGen instance consists of one seed and a dozen workers.

6. EXPERIMENTAL EVALUATION
We first evaluate the basic functionality of Net-cohort (Section 6.1) in finding the right set of ensembles. We then evaluate the benefit of these findings for better VM placement on hosts through the comparison of application throughput and response time between initial VM placement and final VM placement (Section 6.2). Finally we evaluate the overhead, if any, induced by Net-Cohort (Section 6.3).

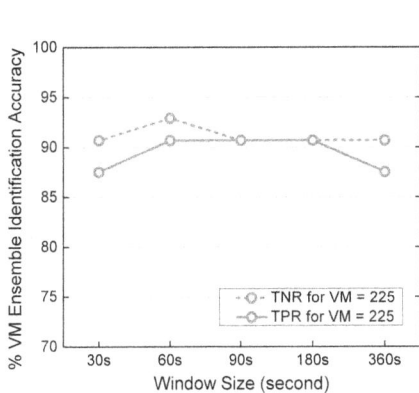

Figure 7. VM ensemble identification accuracy (in percentage) over 225 VMs with an increasing window size.

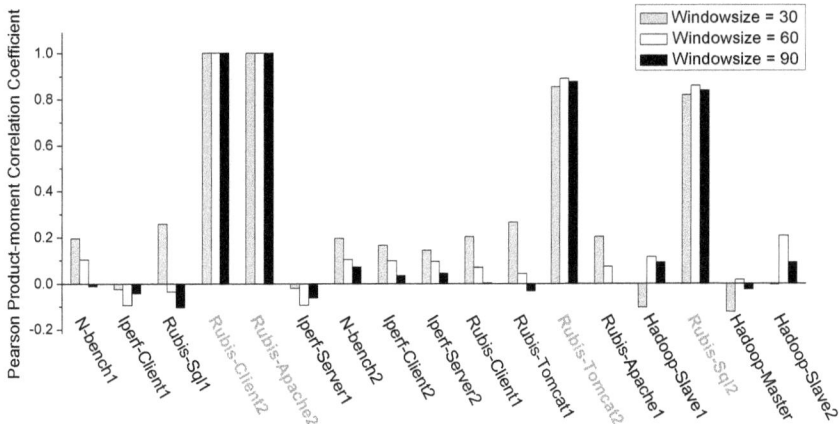

Figure 8 . Intra-cluster/Inter-cluster correlation coefficient among RUBiS2-Client and other VMs.

6.1 Net-Cohort's Functionality Evaluation

The following metrics are used to evaluate Net-Cohort's functionality: (1) *true positive rate* (TPR) and *true negative rate* (TNR). TPR is defined as the ratio of the VMs that have been grouped into the right ensembles to the total set of VMs, denoted as $|V_{TP}|/|V|$. TNR is defined as the ratio of the VMs that have not been grouped into the wrong ensemble to the total set of VMs, denoted as $|V_{NP}|/|V|$. (2) The *intra-cluster correlation coefficient* is defined as the representative correlation coefficient value for pairs of VMs within one particular ensemble. The (3) *hierarchical tree structure* is comprised of the VM ensembles determined by the hierarchical clustering algorithm.

Figure 7 presents the accuracy of VM ensemble identification by Net-Cohort over 225 VMs with an increasing window size. The TPRs are 87.5%, 90.0%, 90.0%, 90.0%, and 87.5% for window sizes 30 seconds, 60 seconds, 90 seconds, 180 seconds, and 360 seconds, respectively. The TNRs are 90.0%, 92.5%, 90.0%, 90.0%, and 90.0% for window sizes 30 seconds, 60 seconds, 90 seconds, 180 seconds, and 360 seconds, respectively.

The results shows that: (1) without relying on any knowledge of the configuration of the test system, Net-Cohort can correctly classify around 90% of virtual machines; (2) there is not much difference between the results for different window sizes, indicating that Net-Cohort is relatively insensitive to the size of the observation window and thus user-friendly for system administrators to set its parameters.

To better understand the above results, we look at correlation coefficients among various VMs within and across ensembles that are calculated by Net-Cohort. For the sake of clarity, we have selected a few representative VMs and presented their correlation with a random subset of all the 225 VMs. The subset includes 7 instances ((N-bench$_1$, N-bench$_2$, Iperf$_1$, Iperf$_2$, RUBiS$_1$, RUBiS$_2$ and Hadoop) out of all 30 instances, where N-bench$_1$ denotes the first instance of N-bench, Iperf$_2$ denotes the second instance of Iperf, etc. The figures show the intra-cluster/inter-cluster correlation coefficient for a representative VM and 17 VMs, where X-axis represents certain VM's name and Y-axis represents PMCC value between the representative VM and that VM. We

find that the VMs belonging to the same application have relatively strong correlations and thus shorter distances.

Figure 8 shows the correlation coefficient between among RUBiS$_2$-Client and RUBiS$_2$-Apache, RUBiS$_2$-Tomcat, RUBiS$_2$-Sql. Note that the *intra-cluster correlation coefficients* among RUBiS$_2$-Client and RUBiS$_2$-Apache, RUBiS$_2$-Tomcat, RUBiS$_2$-Sql are all close to 1.0, while the *inter-cluster correlation coefficients* between RUBiS$_2$-Client and other VMs are less than 0.2. We have evaluated the correlation values for window sizes of 30, 60, and 90. These results demonstrate that the correlation detection mechanism based on the three metrics of CPU utilization, PacketsIn and PacketsOut can correctly identify VM groups that communicate with each other.

Net-Cohort is also able to differentiate the same classes of instances that run different tasks. This is because different tasks typically show different resource usage patterns which can then be used by Net-Cohort to identify the *intra-cluster correlations* within the ensemble and the *inter-cluster correlations* outside of the ensemble. For example, Figure 9 (a) and (b) show the CPU usage patterns of two Hadoop instances respectively. The first Hadoop instance reads text files and counts how often words occur. The second Hadoop instance computes exact binary digits of the mathematical constant π. From Figure 9 (a) and (b), we learn that the "CPU spikes" and "CPU valleys" of the slaves that belongs to the same ensemble consistently occur together, thereby creating the correlations needed by Net-Cohort.

For intuition about the ensemble identification process, we also look at how the correlation-based hierarchical tree is built by Net-Cohort.

Figure 10 shows the hierarchical trees constructed using the decreasing level of dependency strength. We first determine a $N \times N$ correlation strength matrix, and then run the hierarchical clustering algorithm over the distance matrix for the cases without packet sniffing. The hierarchical trees generated by **R** [6], which shows the calculated dependent links between the VMs being observed. This demonstrates that Net-Cohort can effectively expose most of the underlying dependencies between the VMs within our testbed.

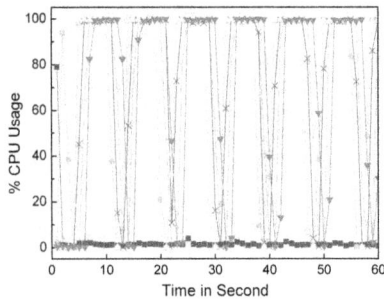

Figure 9 (a). CPU pattern of Hadoop instance of word

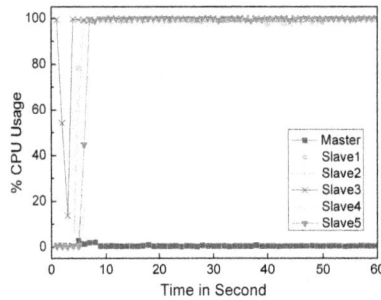

Figure 9 (b). CPU pattern of Hadoop instance of computing PI.

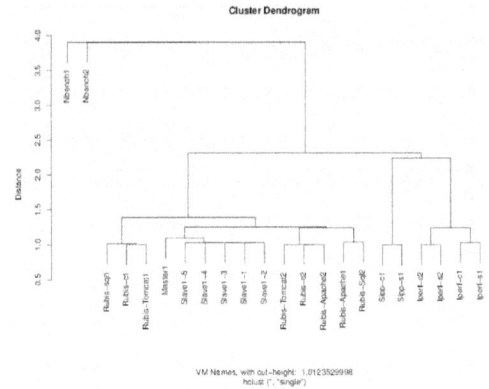

Figure 10. Hierarchical tree generated by R with window size = 90.

6.2 Net-Cohort Benefit Evaluation

After determining the VM ensembles and hierarchical clustering of VM groups, we next evaluate the benefit of these inputs for better VM placement on hosts. In doing so, we first look into the impact of available bi-section bandwidth on applications. To study this impact, we set the crossover bandwidth among RUBiS components from 1Mbps to 100Mbps to reveal how bandwidth changes influence RUBiS performance.

Figure 11 (a) reports the throughput in requests per second as a function of available bandwidth among components. Bandwidth is varied from 1Mbps to 100Mbps. Every RUBiS workload includes three stages: up ramp, runtime session, and down ramp. This shows that the throughput of all three stages of RUBiS are quite sensitive to the available bandwidth, since the throughput corresponding to 100Mbps bandwidth is more than that of the 1Mbps available network bandwidth by about 20 times. Figure 11 (b) reports the response time in millisecond per request as the available bandwidth among components. Bandwidth is varied from 1Mbps to 100Mbps. It shows that as bandwidth increases, the average response time of all three stages of RUBiS is significantly reduced by over 1000 times.

To test VM placement, we deploy the RUBiS components (Apache server, Tomcat server, database server and client), SIPp components (SIPp server, SIPp client) to domains with 100Mbps limited bi-section bandwidth. The incoming and outgoing bandwidth is capped by Linux control groups and traffic shaping tools at VMM's layer. To aggravate competition for bi-section bandwidth, we simultaneously run the Iperf instance, the mapping of VMs to hosts and racks is shown in Figure 12. We apply Net-Cohort black-box methods to determine the VM ensembles, use that input to come up with the moves through VM placement engine, and remap VMs onto hosts. We then compare application performance results for initial and final placements. Here, we assume that CPU and memory resources are not a bottleneck.

Figure 13(a) shows that RUBiS throughput increases from 27 request/second, 20 request/second, and 19 request/second to 68 request/second, 97 request/second, and 41 request/second for up ramp, runtime session, and down ramp, respectively. Figure 13(b) shows that RUBiS response time per request decreases from 6787 millisecond, 15245 millisecond, and 28037 millisecond to 468

millisecond, 31 millisecond, and 25 millisecond for up ramp, runtime session, and down ramp, respectively.

Figure 14 shows that compared to the initial placement, the throughput of the first Hadoop instance increases from 735.5 Kbyte/second to 1103.3 Kbyte/second, and the throughput of the second Hadoop instance increases from 1180.5 Kbyte/second to 1609.9 byte/second.

Figure 15 shows that SIPp's quality of service in terms of number of failed calls is improved significantly. Calls failed due to the co-located VMs saturate the limited bandwidth. The average number of failed calls decreases from 250.62 to 19.64.

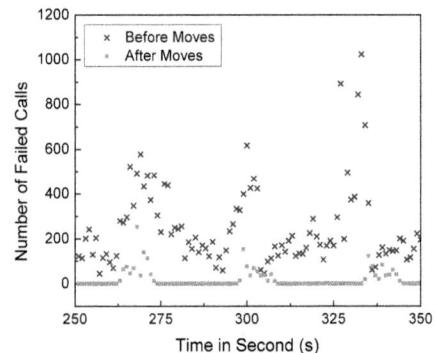

Figure 15. Comparison of SIPp performance in number of failed calls for initial vs final VM placements.

Experimental results clearly indicate the benefits of bandwidth-aware VM placement, thereby demonstrating that information obtained using Net-Cohort can help improve placement and migration actions while reducing utilization of network resources in virtualized data centers. These potential improvements are motivation for future work in which we are integrating Net-cohort with existing management utilities. (e.g., see vManage [19]).

6.3 Packet Sniffer Overheads

The first phase of correlation detection has no extra overhead because basic VM level statistics are already reported by management systems. The second phase of distance identification has a complexity of $O(N^2)$ where N equals to number of VMs, costing several seconds. The third phase of clustering has a complexity of $O(N^2)$ costing several seconds. Packet sniffing is turned on a very selective set of hosts and VMs.

10

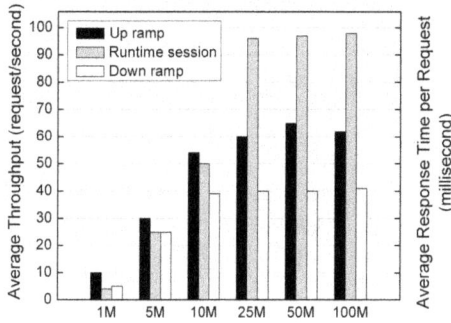

Figure 11 (a). RUBiS throughput changes as a function of available bandwidth.

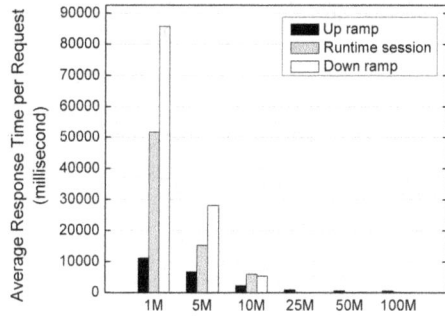

Figure 11 (b). RUBiS response time changes as a function of available bandwidth.

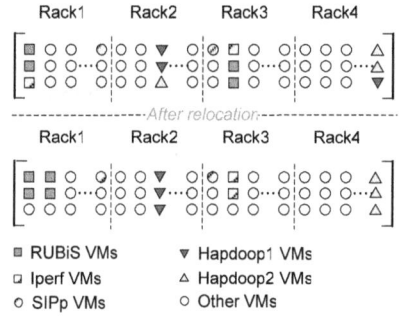

Figure 12. Before and after VM/PM mappings.

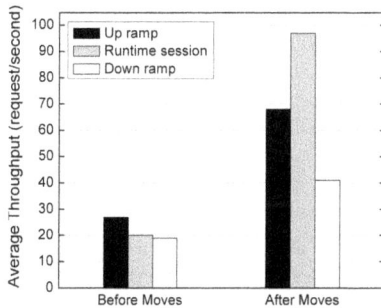

Figure 13 (a). Comparison of RUBiS throughput for initial vs. final VM placements.

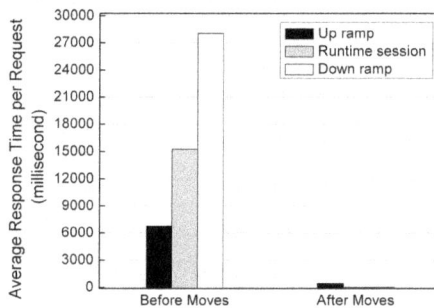

Figure 13 (b). Comparison of RUBiS response time for initial vs. final VM placements.

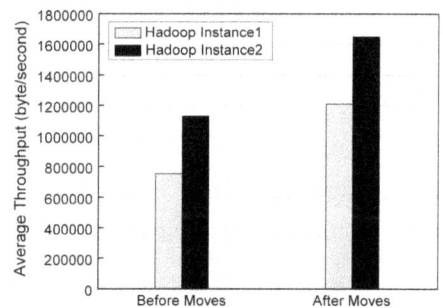

Figure 14. Comparison of Hadoop throughput for initial vs. final VM placements.

We empirically estimate the CPU and memory overheads due to the packet sniffer running in Domain0. Figure 16 shows the additional CPU usage when using the packet sniffer for 5VMs and 10VMs as a function of time. Note that the CPU overhead can be negligible if the transferred traffic is not heavy and the number of VMs monitored is small. However, the packet sniffing technique may trigger irregular fluctuations in CPU usage when capturing large amount of packets, switching among interfaces or periodically flushing I/O buffers of logs to disks. Effects would worsen for larger numbers of VMs on a host or when moving from 1Gbps to 10 Gbps NICs. Latency per packet would also be higher if the packet sniffer is being run in a separate VM due to multiple context switches.

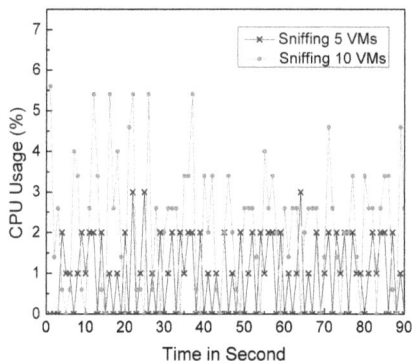

Figure 16. CPU overhead of packet sniffer when sniffing different number of VMs.

In summary, since the packet sniffer is not transparent to users in that its use may introduce heavy CPU overheads, we apply it only when the black-box methods require additional information to accurately cluster VMs.

7. CONCLUSIONS

Net-Cohort presents a set of lightweight, non-intrusive techniques for identifying communicating VMs so as to enable VM placements and migrations that reduce the pressure on bi-section bandwidth in consolidated data centers.

Net-Cohort benefits data center administrators in several ways. In general, it informs them about the VM ensembles currently being run in the data center, thereby enabling them to manage their systems for entire applications rather than individual VMs. More specifically, it makes it possible to place communicating VMs in ways that preserve scarce bi-section bandwidth, which can improve application performance and reduce effects on other bandwidth-sensitive services. Net-cohort's simple design can be realized with available statistics and in a scalable fashion, without requiring changes to data center facilities. It has three unique characteristics:

- It does not require knowledge about application semantics, the implementation of the platform, or a priori information about communication paths.
- There is no need to modify applications, middleware, workloads, or platforms.
- It has extremely low impact on system performance.

Net-Cohort's methods are fully implemented, but additional work is required for using it to continuously monitor and manage data center systems at scale [25]. This includes practical steps like the efficient correction for time series correlation calculation due to potential lack of synchronization among VMs' clocks, and the efficient runtime construction and deployment of monitoring and analysis 'overlays' with data center systems and applications. Moreover, we are working on a pre-clustering module that is capable of filtering out background traffic (i.e., management traffic), since such traffic might otherwise be interpreted as intra-ensemble communications. Further, it would be interesting to understand how methods like Net-Cohort can be integrated with management solutions like VMware's DRS and Hyper-V's PRO. Finally, we note that future 'flat' data center networks, like those developed by companies like Brocade, HP, and Juniper Networks, may shift the utility of Net-Cohort from providing a means to reducing the use of network bi-section bandwidth to instead, serving as a management tool that enables administrators to recognize and manipulate entire applications or properties rather than individual VMs.

8. REFERENCES

[1] Aurora. http://www.zurich.ibm.com/aurora/.

[2] Cisco Data Center Infrastructure 2.5 Design Guide. www.cisco.com/application/pdf/en/us/guest/netsol/ns107/c649/ccmigration_09186a008073377d.pdf.

[3] Mercury MAM. http://www.mercury.com/us/products/business-availability-center/application-mapping.

[4] Microsoft MOM. http://technet.microsoft.com/en-us/systemcenter/om/bb498244.aspx.

[5] Microsoft's Performance and Resource Optimization (PRO). http://technet.microsoft.com/en-us/library/cc764283.aspx.

[6] R Project. http://www.r-project.org/.

[7] VMware Distributed Resource Scheduler (DRS). http://www.vmware.com/products/drs/.

[8] S. Agarwala, F. Alegre, K. Schwan, J. Mehalingham, "E2EProf: Automated End-to-End Performance Management for Enterprise Systems", In the 37th Annual IEEE/IFIP International Conference on Dependable Systems and Networks (DSN'07), June 2007.

[9] M. K. Aguilera, J. C. Mogul, J. L. Wiener, P. Reynolds, and A. Muthitacharoen, "Performance Debugging for Distributed Systems of Black Boxes," In Proceedings of SOSP, 2003.

[10] R. Apte, L. Hu, K. Schwan, A. Ghosh, "Look Who's Talking: Discovering Dependencies between Virtual Machines Using CPU Utilization," In the 2nd USENIX Workshop on Hot Topics in Cloud Computing (HotCloud' 10), June 2010.

[11] M. Al-Fares, S. Radhakrishnan, B. Raghavan, N. Huang, and A. Vahdat. "Hedera: Dynamic Flow Scheduling for Data Center Networks," In USENIX NSDI, April 2010.

[12] S. Bagchi, G. Kar, and J. L. Hellerstein, "Dependency analysis in distributed systems using fault injection: Application to problem determination in an e-commerce environment," In Proc. 12th Intl. Workshop on Distributed Systems: Operations & Management, Nancy, France, Oct. 2001.

[13] A. Brown, G. Kar, and A. Keller, "An active approach to characterizing dynamic dependencies for problem

determination in a distributed environment," In Proc. 7th IFIP/IEEE Intl. Symp. on Integrated Network Management, Seattle,WA, May 2001.

[14] M. Chen, E. Kiciman, E. Fratkin, A. Fox, and E. Brewer, "Pinpoint: Problem determination in large, dynamic systems," In Proc. 2002 Intl. Conf. on Dependable Systems and Networks, pages 595–604, Washington, DC, June 2002.

[15] X. Chen, M. Zhang, Z. M. Mao, and P. Bahl, "Automating network application dependency discovery: Experiences, limitations, and new solutions," In OSDI, San Diego, California, Dec. 2008.

[16] L. Golab, D. DeHaan, E. D. Demaine, "Identifying. Frequent Items in Sliding Window over On-line Packet Streams," Proceedings of the 3rd ACM SIGCOMM conference on Internet measurement (IMC '03), Florida, USA.

[17] A. Greenberg, J. R. Hamilton, N. Jain, S. Kandula, C. Kim, P. Lahiri, D. A. Maltz, P. Patel, S. Sengupta, "VL2: A Scalable and Flexible Data Center Network," ACM SIGCOMM 2009, August 2009.

[18] G. Jung, K. Joshi, M. Hiltunen, R. Schlichting, and C. Pu. "Performance and Availability Aware Regeneration for Cloud Based Multitier Applications," In the 40th IEEE/IFIP International Conference on Dependable Systems and Network (DSN 2010) Performance and Dependability Symposium, Illinois, Chicago, June 2010.

[19] S. Kumar, V. Talwar, V. Kumar, P. Ranganathan, K. Schwan: "vManage: loosely coupled platform and virtualization management in data centers," ICAC 2009, 127-136.

[20] J. Mudigonda, P. Yalagandula, M. Al-Fares, and J.C. Mogul, "SPAIN: COTS Data center Ethernet for Multipathing over Arbitrary Topologies," In Proc. NSDI, 2010, pp.265-280.

[21] S. Radhakrishnan, H. Bazzaz, V. Subramanya, Y. Fainman, G. Papen, and A. Vahdat, "Helios: A Hybrid Electrical/Optical Switch Architecture for Modular Data Centers", In Proceedings of the ACM SIGCOMM Conference, New Delhi, India, August 2010.

[22] P. Reynolds, C. Killian, J. L. Wiener, J. C. Mogul, M. A. Shah, and A. Vahdat, "Pip: Detecting the unexpected in distributed systems," In Proc. NSDI, San Jose, CA, May 2006.

[23] P. Reynolds, J. L. Wiener, J. C. Mogul, M. K. Aguilera, and A. Vahdat, "WAP5: black-box performance debugging for widearea systems," In WWW, 2006.

[24] B.C. Tak, C. Tang, C. Zhang, S. Govindan, B. Urgaonkar, and R. N. Chang, "vPath: Precise Discovery of Request Processing Paths from Black-Box Observations of Thread and Network Activities," In USENIX ATC, 2009.

[25] C. Wang, K. Schwan, V. Talwar, G. Eisenhauer, L. Hu, M. Wolf, "A Flexible Architecture Integrating Monitoring and Analytics for Managing Large-Scale Data Centers," In ICAC, 2011.

[26] Y. Zhang, A. Su and G. Jiang, "Understanding Data Center Network Architectures in Virtualized Environments: A View from Multi-Tier Applications," Elsevier Computer Networks, Vol. 55, No. 9, 2011.

Application-aware Cross-layer Virtual Machine Resource Management

Lixi Wang   Jing Xu   Ming Zhao

School of Computing and Information Sciences
Florida International University, Miami, FL, USA
{lwang007,jxu,ming}@cs.fiu.edu

ABSTRACT

Existing resource management solutions in datacenters and cloud systems typically treat VMs as black boxes when making resource allocation decisions. This paper advocates the cooperation between VM host- and guest-layer schedulers for optimizing the resource management and application performance. It presents an approach to such cross-layer optimization upon fuzzy-modeling-based resource management. This approach exploits guest-layer application knowledge to capture workload characteristics and improve VM modeling, and enables the host-layer scheduler to feedback resource allocation decision and adapt guest-layer application configuration. As a case study, this approach is applied to virtualized databases which have challenging dynamic, complex resource usage behaviors. Specifically, it characterizes query workloads based on a database's internal cost estimation and adapts query executions by tuning the cost model parameters according to changing resource availability. A prototype of the proposed approach is implemented on Xen VMs and evaluated using workloads based on TPC-H and RUBiS. The results show that with guest-to-host workload characterization, resources can be efficiently allocated to database VMs serving workloads with changing intensity and composition while meeting Quality-of-Service (QoS) targets. For TPC-H, the prediction error for VM resource demand is less than 3.5%; for RUBiS, the response time target is met for 92% of the time. Both significantly outperform the resource allocation scheme without workload characterization. With host-to-guest database adaptation, the performance of TPC-H-based workloads is also improved by 17% when the VM's available I/O bandwidth is reduced due to contention.

Categories and Subject Descriptors

C.4 [**Performance of System**]: Modeling techniques; I.5.1 [**Pattern Recognition**]: Models – *fuzzy set*

Keywords

Autonomic computing, Fuzzy modeling, Resource management, Virtualization

1. INTRODUCTION

With the rapid growth of computational power on compute servers and the fast maturing of x86 virtualization technologies, virtual machines (VMs [1][2]) are becoming increasingly important in supporting efficient and flexible application and resource provisioning. Virtualization is the key enabling technology for building agile datacenters and emerging cloud systems [3][4]. It allows a single physical server to be carved into multiple virtual resource containers, each delivering a powerful, secure, customizable, and portable execution environment for applications. As the level of VM-based consolidation continues to grow, there is an increasingly urgent need for virtualized systems to deliver better Quality-of-Service (QoS) guarantees, so that users are comfortable in running their applications on the shared infrastructure. However, currently such systems cannot meet stringent performance requirements, particular not for applications with dynamic and complex behaviors. Consequently, examples such as cloud systems cannot support QoS-based Service Level Agreements (SLA), whereas users often have to purchase unnecessary resources for their VMs.

Existing resource management solutions typically treat VMs as black boxes when making resource allocation decisions. The host-layer VM scheduler is agnostic of the guest-layer application-specific resource scheduling, whereas a guest-layer application scheduler is unaware of the host-layer VM resource allocation. Although such transparency is important for reasons such as portability and legacy support, it also prevents the resource management effectively providing application-desired QoS. On one hand, the knowledge of an application's workload characteristics can help the host-layer resource management to better understand the VM's resource demand and meet the application's QoS target. On the other hand, the knowledge of the host's VM allocation decision can help the guest-layer resource management understand the actual resource availability and adapt its scheduling to improve application performance.

Therefore, this paper proposes cross-layer optimization in VM resource management which allows certain awareness and cooperation between host and guest in order to improve application performance and meet its QoS target. Specifically, this paper studies two aspects of such cross-layer optimization. First, *guest-to-host optimization* exploits guest-layer application knowledge to capture dynamic workload characteristics and improve the modeling of VM resource usage. Second, *host-to-guest optimization* enables the host-layer scheduler to feedback resource allocation decision and adapt guest-layer application configuration. These two aspects of cross-layer optimization are integrated into a fuzzy-modeling-based resource management system [5] which uses fuzzy logic to model VM resource demand online and allocate resource dynamically according to application QoS requirement.

This paper considers virtualized databases as an interesting and challenging case study. Databases often serve complex and dynamic workloads which consist of a variety of queries with different types and amounts of resource demand. Moreover, databases typically employ sophisticated optimization schemes which adapt query executions according to their resource availability. Hence, applying cross-layer optimization to the resource management of virtualized databases can be a convincing showcase of our proposed approach. Specifically in this case study, the proposed cross-layer optimization approach performs workload characterization based on database's internal cost model and adapts query executions by tuning the cost model parameters according to changing resource availability.

This proposed system is prototyped on Xen-based VM environments and evaluated by experiments using typical database workloads created based on TPC-H [6] and RUBiS [7] benchmarks. The results show that the fuzzy-modeling-based resource allocation with guest-to-host workload characterization can accurately predict the resource needs for complex application workloads. For TPC-H, it achieves less than 3.5% error for predicting VM resource demand; for RUBiS, it meets the response time target for 92% of the time. Both substantially outperform the resource allocation scheme without workload characterization, in terms of both application QoS and resource efficiency. Moreover, the results also show that our proposed approach of host-to-guest application adaptation effectively optimizes the database's query execution when the VM's resource availability changes due to I/O contention. The performance of a TPC-H workload is improved by about 17% compared to the scheme without such adaptation.

To the best of our knowledge, this paper is the first to study cross-layer optimization in VM resource management, considering both guest-to-host workload characterization and host-to-guest application adaptation. The case study demonstrates the effectiveness of this approach and provides an experimental evaluation. Compared to existing VM resource management solutions, this approach can accurately capture complex resource usage behavior for virtualize applications, timely adapt to dynamic changes in workloads, and optimize their performance under varying resource availability. In the rest of the paper, Section 2 presents the motivating examples, Section 3 introduces the background on fuzzy-modeling-based resource management, Section 4 and 5 present the general approach of cross-layer optimization and its case study on virtualized databases, Section 6 discusses the evaluation, Section 7 examines the related work, and Section 8 concludes the paper.

2. MOTIVATING EXAMPLES

In this section, we use several examples to motivate the need of cross-layer optimization in VM resource management, including both guest-to-host workload characterization and host-to-guest application adaptation.

2.1 Guest-to-Host Workload Characterization

For the first aspect of cross-layer resource management, we use an example to demonstrate that it is necessary for the host-layer VM scheduler to use the knowledge from guest-layer for workload characterization. Coarse-grained workload information such as the request rate or number of concurrent users can be easily obtained without knowledge about application internals. However, this information is no longer sufficient when the application workload consists of different types of requests with diverse usage of multiple types of resources. Here we use a concrete example based on a typical multi-tier OLTP benchmark, RUBiS [7] to demonstrate this limitation (Figure 1 and 2).

We fix the RUBiS' database tier's query workload intensity by running 300 concurrent client sessions in RUBiS. But we vary the composition of the query workload by increasing the ratio between bidding and browsing requests to the web tier, which corresponds to the ratio between read and write queries to the

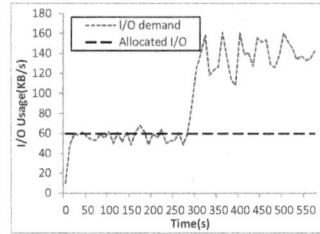

Figure 1 I/O Allocation for a changing mix in RUBiS

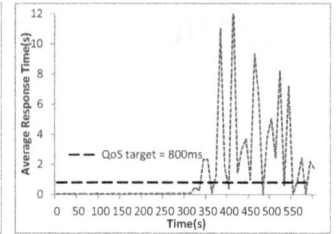

Figure 2 Performance for a changing mix in RUBiS

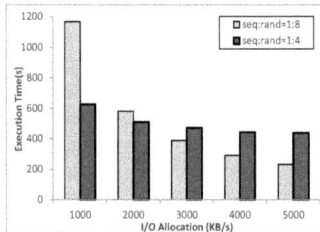

Figure 3 Execution time of TPC-H Q8 with varying I/O allocation

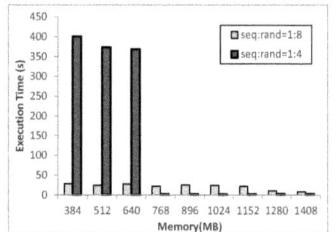

Figure 4 Execution time of TPC-H Q8 with varying memory allocation

database tier. The entire experiment lasts for 600 seconds, starting with a browsing-only mix and then shifting to a 30%-bidding mix from the 300th second. The QoS target for this workload is set to 800ms. Without being aware of the changes in workload composition, the amount of resources needed by the RUBiS VM is estimated based solely on the workload intensity. Hence only 60KB/s I/O bandwidth is allocated to the RUBiS VM throughout the entire experiment (Figure 1). This allocation is enough for the workload to meet the QoS target in the first 300 seconds when the workload is not I/O intensive; but it leads to many QoS violations in the second 300 seconds due to the under-provisioning of I/O bandwidth (Figure 2). To address this problem, this paper proposes to exploit application-specific knowledge of workload characteristics in terms of different types of requests in order to make more accurate allocation decisions.

2.2 Host-to-Guest Application Adaptation

We use other examples from virtualized databases to show the advantage of feeding back the information of resource availability from host- to guest-layer. We run a workload consisting of single copy of TPC-H query Q8 on a 3GB database VM, and manually set the database cost model parameters given different resource capacity. Figure 3 and 4 compare the query performance using two representative settings of the cost model parameters, *seq_page_cost* and *random_page_cost*. Both parameters characterize the database's execution environment: the former defines the cost of fetching a page from disk using sequential reads whereas the latter, usually more costly, defines the cost of a non-sequential disk page fetch. Changing these parameters affects the database performance indirectly by influencing the database's internal query cost estimation. Lower value of *seq_page_cost* reduces the cost of a plan with more sequential scans on the tables; lower value of *random_page_cost* reduces the cost of a plan with more random scans, e.g., index scans. Therefore, changing the ratio between these two parameters affects the database's preference on different execution plans.

In the first example (Figure 3), Q8 runs on a cold database VM, as the I/O bandwidth allocated to the VM is reduced from 5000 to 1000 KB/s. Both database configurations suffer from performance degradation with reduced available I/O bandwidth. However, when the available I/O bandwidth is high, the configuration that

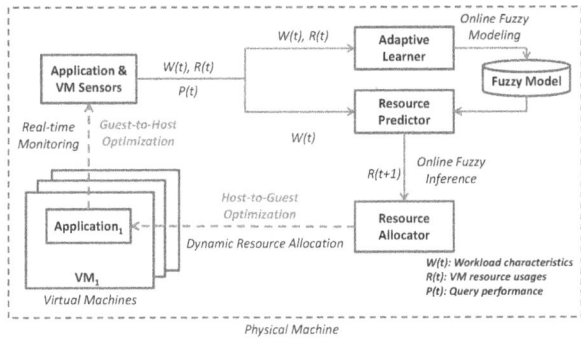

Figure 5 Architecture of cross-layer optimization on fuzzy-modeling-based resource management system

favors sequential scan outperforms that favors random scan (by 89% at 5000KB/s). When the I/O bandwidth is throttled, the latter's performance is only slightly affected and as a result it is 1.9 times better than the former at 1000 KB/s. The second example performed in a warm database VM shows similar behavior of Q8 performance but with respect to changing memory availability (Figure 4). When the available memory is low, the sequential-preferable DBMS configuration is drastically faster (by 14 times) because only a small amount of indices or tables can be cached in memory. As the memory allocation increases from 640 to 768MB, the indices can be effectively cached and consequently the index-preferable configuration's performance substantially outperforms the sequential-preferable configuration (by 3 times).

The above examples show strong evidence of the importance of host-to-guest optimization. If the database cost parameters can be adjusted dynamically to reflect the actual resource availability to the VM, the database performance can be further improved.

3. Fuzzy-modeling-based VM Resource Management

The main challenges to VM resource management are how to efficiently allocate resources to VMs and how to do so automatically and continuously. To address these challenges, our previous work [5][8] proposed fuzzy-modeling-based resource management to learn a VM's resource demand and allocate resources according to its QoS target in an autonomic manner. Fuzzy logic is used to create a VM's resource usage model automatically from data observed from the system without assuming any *a priori* knowledge about the system's structure. It is shown to be able to effectively capture complex, nonlinear resource usage behaviors in a virtualized system.

Figure 5 illustrates the architecture of our fuzzy-modeling-based resource management system. It consists of four key modules. As a workload executes on the VM, the *Application and VM Sensors* monitor the workload $W(t)$, its performance $P(t)$, and the VM's resource usage $R(t)$. The *Adaptive Learner* creates and updates a fuzzy model that represents the relationship between a workload and its VM's resource needs. With this model and the current workload $W(t)$, the *Resource Predictor* estimates the resource needs for time $t+1$ and the *Resource Allocator* adjusts the allocation accordingly. Together, these modules form a closed-loop for the VM's resource control and optimization.

Fuzzy logic is employed to build the model based on the qualified input-output data pairs, $<W(t), R(t)>$ whose workload performance $P(t)$ meet the desired QoS target. Both the workload input $W(t)$ and the resource usage output $R(t)$ can be vectors with multiple dimensions. This model captures the relationship between the application's workload and the VM's resource demand for meeting the QoS target. With the fuzzy model created by the

Adaptive Learner, the *Resource Predictor* performs fuzzy inference to generate an estimate of the resource needs R given the workload input W. This estimation is then sent to the *Resource Allocator* to guide the VM's resource allocation. More details on fuzzy modeling can be found in our previous work [5][8].

In this paper we propose to further improve this existing fuzzy-modeling-based resource management system by incorporating cross-layer optimization between the VM host and guest, which is discussed in detail in the rest of this paper.

4. GENERAL APPROCAH TO CROSS-LAYER OPTIMIZATION

The goal of cross-layer optimization is to enable VM host- and guest-layer resource schedulers to communicate scheduling-related information and collaboratively improve the performance of a virtualized application and satisfy its QoS requirement. Existing resource management solutions typically treat VMs as black boxes when making resource allocations. The host-layer VM scheduler is agnostic of the guest-layer application-specific resource scheduling, whereas a guest-level application scheduler is also unaware of the host-layer VM resource allocation. Such transparency is important for reasons such as portability and legacy support, but for applications requiring strong QoS guarantees, a tradeoff can be made to allow certain awareness and cooperation between host and guest for meeting the QoS target.

Such cross-layer optimization is two-fold. First, the host-layer scheduler can leverage the guest-layer application-specific knowledge to improve the VM resource allocation decisions. Second, the guest-layer scheduler can adapt its application-specific scheduling based on the host-layer VM resource allocation to improve the application performance under changing resource availability. We will describe the general approach to both of these aspects of cross-layer optimization in this section.

4.1 Guest-to-Host Optimization

The guest-to-host aspect of our proposed cross-layer optimization is to exploit the guest-layer application-specific information to improve the understanding of the VM workload's resource usage patterns. Such knowledge will enable the host-layer resource scheduler to more accurately estimate the VM's resource demands and more agilely adapt to its workload changes. We propose to analyze an application's workload by describing it in terms of the characteristics that are relevant to its VM resource usage behaviors. Such characteristics provide important inputs to the effective modeling and prediction of the VM's resource needs. A commonly used workload characteristic is its overall intensity such as the total request rate or total number of online users. As shown in the motivating examples (Section 2.1), this characteristic alone is not sufficient for a real-world workload that consists of requests with diverse use of resources. As another example, a web workload consisting of only static web page has distinct resource needs versus one containing also considerable dynamic web page requests, even if their total request rates are exactly the same (the former consumes mainly CPU while the latter requires also substantial I/O bandwidth). Hence, it is important to characterize a workload's composition of different types of requests in terms of their resource usage patterns. But such characterization is difficult to do in existing resource management solutions which treat VMs as black boxes where application-specific knowledge is hidden.

To address this problem, we propose cross-layer optimization which allows a host-layer scheduler to exploit a guest-layer application's knowledge to understand the resource usage patterns of its received requests in the workload. For example, for web

15

workloads, the web server's knowledge can be exploited to understand whether the received HTTP requests are targeting static or dynamic content. Such characterization of workload composition is key to understanding the VM's demands of CPU and I/O resources. For the workloads that contain more complex requests, such as in Online Analytical Processing (OLAP), more sophisticated application knowledge is required to analyze their resource usage patterns. We propose to characterize such workloads by leveraging the application's internal cost model, which is discussed in detail in Section 5.

The characterization of each individual request's resource usage pattern can be aggregated to describe the entire workload's resource usage characteristics. However, for workloads containing vast diversity of requests, it is impractical to describe all requests in the workload characterization. A concise representation is needed to effectively compress the information of all requests, which is critical to ensure low overhead and high robustness of the characterization. We propose to use data clustering techniques to group a workload's queries into clusters, so that those within a cluster are more similar in terms of their resource requirements to each other than the ones from different clusters. Assuming after the clustering a workload consists of m different groups of requests ($r_1, \ldots r_m$), the entire workload can then be characterized by the request rates of all these groups ($W_{r1}, \ldots, W_{rm}$), where each group represents a distinct resource usage pattern.

Many well established offline clustering algorithms are available for use, such as K-means, hierarchical clustering, subtractive clustering, etc. However, because of the dynamic nature of real-world workloads, the request cluster analysis should be carried out in an online fashion. To achieve this, we propose online, adaptive request clustering for an online, dynamic VM system, in which the clustering is performed in a way that is self-learning and self-adapting, without needing the number of clusters to be pre-specified. The basic idea is to perform one-pass, non-iterative clustering of a stream of requests using a method such as subtractive clustering. The procedure starts with an empty set of clusters and creates the first cluster with the first request sample assumed to be the cluster center. As more request samples come in, either a new cluster is added with the center based on the new data, or an existing cluster is removed or updated based on certain criteria (e.g., the radius set in subtractive clustering [9]). Such a clustering approach has the ability to gradually adapt to the changing data patterns. It can be applied to the data set of any size and allows flexible clustering with an evolving shape so that it can better match the current data distribution.

The above proposed workload characterization process will be performed online periodically (e.g., every 10s), in which the recently received requests will be used to update the workload's current clustering results. In this way, the characterization does not need *a priori* knowledge about all the queries that compose the workload, and it can dynamically adapt to the changing workload composition.

4.2 Host-to-Guest Optimization

The host-to-guest aspect of our proposed cross-layer optimization is to feed back the host-layer VM resource allocation decision and enable the guest-layer application-specific scheduling to adapt for better performance. Many applications need to be tuned to optimize their performance based on the resource availability of the hosting system. For example, a web server needs to tune parameters such as the number of concurrent threads based on its host's available memory. A database needs to tune its internal cost model (e.g., the CPU and I/O costs of processing a tuple) based on

its host's resource availability so that it can correctly estimate the costs of different query execution plans and select the most efficient one to use. A web search engine may change its crawling, indexing, or searching strategies as the resource availability varies. When resource is constrained, it may crawler over only a portion of available web pages, restrict the depth of parsing and indexing on the searched contents, and return a limited number of best matching results to the users. Another example application is a simulator that can tune the modeling resolution based on its host's resource availability to increase the simulation accuracy or speed up the simulation progress [10].

When such an application is hosted on a physical machine, it needs to be tuned only once during the initial deployment. However, on a VM, the resource availability can vary over time, because of *1)* changing resource contention from other co-hosted VMs as they come and go dynamically and their workloads vary over time; *2)* changing resource allocation policy such as VM priorities or Service-level Agreements (SLAs). Nonetheless, the changing resource availability to a VM is hidden to the application in existing VM resource management solutions. As a result, the application is stuck with the initial configuration assuming a resource availability that is no longer valid. It cannot adapt itself to use a configuration that is more efficient in application performance and/or resource utilization when the VM's resource becomes either under pressure or abundant.

To address this problem, we propose cross-layer optimization for the host-layer scheduler to feedback the resource allocation decision to the guest-layer and automatically adapt the latter's configuration for improved performance given the current resource availability. The general approach to this host-to-guest optimization can be formally described as follows. Assuming that there are M different types of resources, such as memory, CPU capacity, or I/O bandwidth, $R_i=[R_{i1}, \ldots R_{iM}]$ represents the amount of resource of different types available for workload W_i of application i. The goal of the optimization is to find a feasible set of configuration parameters, denoted as C_i, of the application i that the performance of the workload P_i is optimized, given the VM's current resource availability R_i. In order to enable such adaption, we need to have a means of mapping different recourse allocations to the corresponding optimal parameter settings. Although this mapping is application specific, there are some general steps.

1) Find out the set of possible parameters $C_i = [c_{i1}, \ldots c_{ik}, c_{in}]$ that contributes to the application i's performance. For each parameters c_{ik}, we need to determine a function that defines c_{ik} as a function of R_i, i.e., $f_{ik}(R_i)$.
2) Given a certain resource allocation, run a general workload of the virtualized application for the mapping process. Iterate a variety of settings for c_{ik} over its value range and measure the application performance. Collect the setting c_{ik_opt} with the best performance.
3) Repeat Step 2 under different candidate resource allocations over the possible range.
4) Collect the data pairs $<c_{ik\_opt}, R_i>$ for each allocation, and perform regression analysis on the set of the data to fit the function $c_{ik\_opt} = f_{ik}(R_i)$.

Once such a mapping is built for an application, the resource availability to the VM can be directly fed back to enable the application's adaptation.

The aforementioned two aspects of cross-layer optimization are integrated with our existing fuzzy-modeling-based VM resource management middleware. For guest-to-host optimization, the workload is characterized by *Application Sensor* based on application-specific knowledge, which is used by the *Adaptive Learner* for better modeling and predicting the VM's resource usage behavior. For host-to-guest optimization, as *Resource Allocator* adjusts the allocation based on the prediction given by the fuzzy model, it also feeds back this decision to the VM for the application to tune its parameters for better performance. The resulting autonomic resource management system can not only automatically allocate resources to VMs based on their dynamic workload demand but also adaptively improve application performance even when the system is overloaded.

5. CASE STUDY

In this section, we take virtualized databases as an interesting and challenging case study of our proposed cross-layer resource management approach. Traditionally, databases are hosted on dedicated physical servers that have sufficient hardware resources to satisfy their expected peak workloads with desired QoS. However, this is often inefficient for the real-world situations in many application domains such as e-business [11] and stream data management[12], where the workloads are intrinsically dynamic in terms of their bursty arrival patterns and ever-changing unit processing costs. Using VMs to host databases can effectively address this limitation. It allows a database to transparently share the consolidated resources with other applications, where a database's resource usage can elastically grow and shrink based on the dynamic demand of its workload.

The cross-host-guest cooperation for a virtualized database is implemented as follows. For guest-to-host optimization, a database proxy served as the *Application Sensor* is deployed on the host to intercept the incoming query requests to the database VM and characterize the workload composition by classifying the queries. For host-to-guest optimization, a daemon running on the guest periodically obtains resource allocation decision from the *Resource Allocator*, looks up the corresponding optimal database parameters, and sends an administrative query to the database to change the parameters accordingly.

5.1 Guest-to-Host Workload Characterization

Databases are a challenging application because of their highly complex and dynamic resource usage behaviors. Database queries can be both CPU and I/O intensive and a typical database workload can have a diverse variety of such queries with dynamically changing composition. Nonetheless, a database's internal query optimizer has intimate knowledge of a query resource usage pattern. Such knowledge can be extracted from the database and used to classify queries for characterizing the entire workload in terms of its resource demands. The result of the workload characterization can be then used as input to the VM's fuzzy model to improve its accuracy and adaptability under dynamic changes of the workload. Typically, the query cost is defined as a function of the amount of resource usages estimated by the database, which can be extracted as a vector of different resource costs. Note that the database's cost estimation cannot be directly used to infer its VM's resource needs because, first, its accuracy is often limited [13], and second, it does not capture the entire VM's resource needs.

Specifically, we use PostgreSQL database system as an example to demonstrate our proposed guest-to-host optimization on workload characterization. The internal cost model in PostgreSQL is defined as a function of a set of database cost parameters, denoted as $Cost_D(C)$ where $C=[c_1, c_2,.., c_m]$. Each cost parameter represents the unit cost of either CPU or I/O usage associated with

an operation in the database. For example, *sequential_page_cost* and *random_page_cost* represent the overhead of a single sequential and non-sequential I/O to fetch a page from disk, respectively; *cpu_tuple_cost* estimates the CPU cost of processing each row in a table. The total cost that aggregates the costs of all operations in a query plan can be broken down into two parts: the total CPU cost and the total I/O cost. Each query can be expressed as a 2-dimention cost vector $<Cost_{CPU}, Cost_{I/O}>$.

To characterize a workload, the *Application Sensor* first extracts the cost vector for all unique queries in a workload from database and then performs subtractive clustering [9] on the set of query cost vectors collected. By setting the radius of a cluster r, any pair of the query vectors with distance $d<r$ will fall into the same cluster indicating queries with similar resource usage patterns. Finally, as the workload runs, the *Application Sensor* measures query intensity online by counting the request rate for each individual cluster. For example, a workload mix W consists of N queries, and after clustering only K clusters are generated where $K<<N$. The workload can be abstracted as a vector of arrival rates of these clusters $<C_1, C_2, ..., C_K>$. Then the above arrival rate vector that reflects the current characteristics of the workload is periodically fed to the *Adaptive Learner* as an input for modeling the VM's current usage behavior. At the same time, the workload characterization of current time t is also used as the input for the *Resource Predictor* to estimate the resource demand of the next time step $t+1$ based on the assumption that no abrupt change happens to the workload within one period of time.

5.2 Host-to-Guest Database Adaptation

Databases are a typical application that has a complex internal self-scheduling and self-optimization mechanism which can optimize its performance based on its knowledge about the outside environment. Based on the given resource capacity, a database's query optimizer can automatically evaluate different query execution plans and choose the most efficient one to execute queries. As the availability of resources changes, critical parameters on which the query optimizer depends on for cost evaluation should also be updated accordingly, which will lead to better resource utilization and more efficient query executions. Specifically, a database usually uses the aforementioned cost model $Cost_D(C)$, defined as a function of a set of parameters C, to estimate the costs for all possible query execution plans. Each parameter c_k in the cost model serves as a cost factor related to a certain type of operation in query processing such as table scanning and tuple processing. Appropriate values on these parameters that reflect the actual VM resource availability will help the query planner choose the most efficient operations. Taking PostgreSQL as an example, as shown in Section 2.2, the query optimizer will switch from a sequential scan to an index scan for processing the TPC-H query Q8 as the relative value of *rand_page_cost* to *sequential_page_cost* decreases. Such tuning is necessary when the I/O contention happens and more efficient scanning method is desired given the limited I/O bandwidth.

To tune the cost parameters given changing resource availability, we need to find the mapping from the resource allocation to the optimal parameter values. Because all the cost parameters in a cost model are factors normalized on the same scale, only the changes in their relative values will result in alternative query execution plan. Therefore we focus on building the mapping between the ratio of those cost parameters and the resource allocation to the VM. For example, to investigate the impact of I/O allocation on the scanning methods, the ratio of the aforementioned two I/O cost parameters is considered. We generate a simple query that needs to read all the rows from a large table. The query is executed by different plans using sequential scan vs. random scan iteratively with different amount of I/O allocation. The performance obtained from the changing I/O allocation is observed for each scanning plan. Since the total cost of each plan is mainly resulted from the scanning operations, other types of processing overhead can be ignored. We then normalize the performance of different plans and consider them as the estimation of the I/O cost parameters for different I/O allocation. In this way, a mapping is built between the I/O allocation and I/O cost parameters, which is consistent with the actual performance observed with the corresponding plans.

In addition to those parameters that reflect the knowledge about the database's execution environment, there are also other types of parameters used in database-level scheduling that defines the database's own limit for certain type of resource usage. For instance in PostgreSQL, the parameter *shared_buffers* changes the amount of memory that the database uses for caching data. A reasonable setting value of *shared_buffers* should be proportional to (e.g., ¼) the amount of memory allocated to its VM.

6. EVALUATION
6.1 Setup
This section evaluates our approach using representative database workloads hosted on a typical VM environment. The testbed is a Dell PowerEdge 2970 server equipped with two six-core 2.4GHz AMD Opteron CPUs, 32GB of RAM, and one 500GB 7.2 RPM SAS disk. Xen 3.3.1 is installed to provide the VMs, where the operating system for both Dom0 and DomU VMs is Ubuntu Linux 8.10 with paravirtualized kernel 2.6.18.8. The evaluated databases are hosted on DomUs, while our resource management system is hosted on Dom0. In all experiments, the management system monitors and controls the database VM's usage of both CPU cycles and disk I/O bandwidth every 10 seconds. In the *VM Sensor*, resource monitoring is done using xentop and iostat, where the I/O bandwidth usage is considered as the sum of reads and writes per period of time. In the *Application Sensor*, a database proxy deployed on Dom0 is used to measure the performance of the database VM. The *Resource Allocator* uses Xen's credit CPU scheduler to assign CPU allocations and Linux's dm-ioband I/O controller to set the cap for disk I/O bandwidth [14].

Two typical database benchmarks, TPC-H and RUBiS, are used in our experiments for different purposes. Experiments designed on TPC-H are aimed to show the accuracy of our approach in modeling resource consumption behaviors for highly complex workloads. For RUBiS, it is to show the effectiveness of our solution in adapting to more random changes in the system. The performance metrics is average query response time measured every 10s. Three different resource allocation schemes are compared: 1) The fuzzy-modeling-based allocation with cross-layer optimization which includes guest-to-host workload characterization and host-to-guest database tuning; 2) The fuzzy-modeling-based allocation without cross-layer optimization; 3) The traditional peak-load-based allocation which statically allocates a fixed amount of resources based on the peak workload demand. By comparing the VM's resource usage and the benchmark's performance between these cases, we evaluate whether our proposed cross-layer optimization approach can allocate resources more efficiently while meeting the desired QoS target or improving its performance.

6.2 Guest to Host Optimization
6.2.1 TPC-H Experiments
TPC-H provides 22 representative queries of business decision support systems, which involve the processing of large volumes of data with a high degree of complexity. Based on these queries, we construct synthetic workloads with varying demands of different types of resources. With peak-load based allocation, 100% CPU and 10MB/s I/O are allocated to the database VM statically. With fuzzy-modeling-based allocation, there are two phases involved. In the training phase, the fuzzy model is learned without resource restrictions, while in the testing phase the model is applied to predict the resource demand and control the resource allocation. The evaluation of more realistic workloads with online training is discussed in Section 6.2.2. The database used here is PostgresSQL 8.1.3 with 2GB of data on a VM with one CPU and 1GB RAM.

To characterize the TPC-H workload, subtractive clustering is performed on all the 22 queries based on their cost vectors, where a small radius of 0.1 is used in the clustering to derive tight clusters. The result identifies four clusters. Cluster I containing single query Q1 and Cluster II containing single query Q18 represent highly and moderately CPU-intensive queries, respectively. Cluster III including Q4, Q6, Q15, and Q12 represents highly I/O-intensive queries. Cluster IV including most of the remaining queries represents simple queries which are neither CPU nor I/O intensive. This result is experimentally verified by the actual resource usages when running the queries separately on the database VM. The only exception is Q22 which is identified as another single-query cluster and estimated by the database's cost model as both CPU and I/O intensive. However, its actual usage of CPU and I/O is very low, similarly to the queries in Cluster III, which confirms our discussion in Section 5.1 that the database's query cost estimation cannot be used directly to infer the VM's resource needs.

6.2.1.1 CPU-intensive Workload
The first experiment is based on a CPU-intensive workload consisting of Cluster I and II queries, Q1 and Q18. The workload's total request rate is varied from 20 to 50 request/minute while the percentage of Cluster I is also varied from 0% to 80%. About 20 data points with different combinations of request rate and cluster ratio evenly selected from both input ranges are used to train the VM's fuzzy model. With workload characterization (*fuzzy modeling w/ char*), both the request rate and cluster ratio are considered as the input for the CPU usage modeling. In contrast, without workload characterization (*fuzzy modeling w/o char*), only the request rate is used for the input and the ratio factor is ignored. To evaluate these two models, the workload is run with a different set of request rate and cluster ratio combinations (totally 60 data points) while the models are used to control the VM's resource allocation.

Figure 6(a) compares the VM CPU allocations given by these two models against the actual CPU usage of the VM when the resource is allocated based on peak load. Figure 6(b) compares the workload performance under these two CPU allocation schemes against the ideal performance under peak-load-based allocation. The result shows that the CPU allocation given by the fuzzy model created with workload characterization closely follows the VM's actual demand; the average error is below 2.3%. The model created without workload characterization can lead to significant under- or over-provision; the average error is about 36.7%. The difference in CPU allocation accuracy leads to significant difference in the query workload's performance. When using the

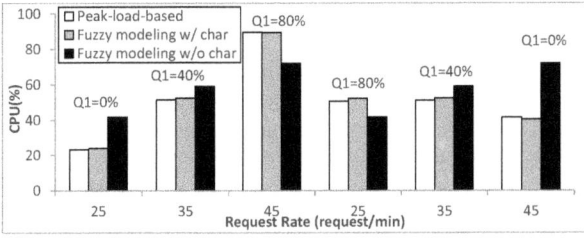

Figure 6(a) CPU allocations for a CPU-intensive TPC-H workload

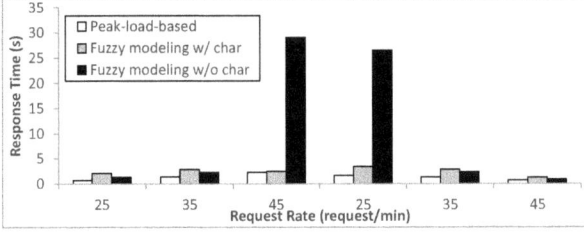

Figure 6(b) Performance for a CPU-intensive TPC-H workload

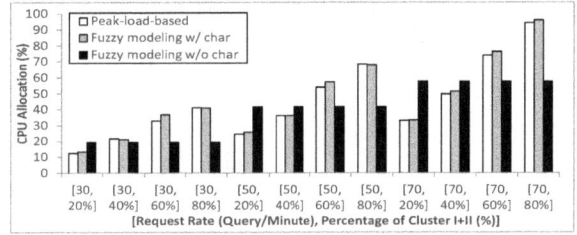

Figure 7(a) CPU allocations for a CPU/IO-intensive TPC-H workload

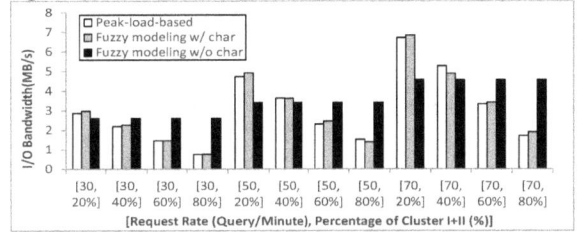

Figure 7(b) I/O allocations for a CPU/IO-intensive TPC-H workload

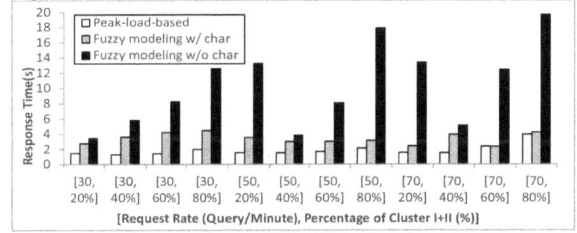

Figure 7(c) Performance for a CPU/IO-intensive TPC-H workload

model created with workload charactrization, the query response time is always at the same level as the peak-load-based allocation; the difference is less than 2s. When using the model created without workload characterization, in some case it leads to up to 27s delay in response time with a 15% under-provision of CPU; in another case, it results in an over-provision of CPU by 15.7% but achieves a response time only 0.6s better than the former scheme.

6.2.1.2 CPU/IO-intensive Workload

In the second experiment, we study a more interesting and challenging workload which includes not only CPU-intensive (Q1 from Cluster I) but also I/O-intensive queries (Q18 from Cluster II and Q6 from Cluster III). As the workload runs, the total percentage of Cluster I+II in the entire workload is varied from 0.1 to 0.9 (the ratio between Cluster I and Cluster II is fixed) and the total request rate also varies from 20 to 80 request/minute. Similarly, different sets of data points are evenly taken from these data ranges for training (450 data points) and testing (120 data points). The experiment is performed separately using fuzzy-modeling-based resource allocation w/ and w/o characterization. The former captures the workload using a vector [*Request rate*, *Percentage of Cluster I+II*] as the input, while the latter considers only the total request rate of the workload. Both CPU and I/O are controlled in the two cases.

Figure 7(a) and (b) compare the VM CPU and I/O allocations in these two cases against the actual CPU and I/O usages of the VM when the resource is allocated based on peak load. Figure 7(c) compares the workload performance of these two allocation schemes against the ideal performance under peak-load-based allocation. The results show that the fuzzy modeling with workload characterization method can predict the VM's actual demand with an average error of 3.5% for both CPU and I/O allocations. It is more accurate than the case without characterization in which the average error is about 37% for CPU and 73% for I/O. As a result, in the former case it always achieves the same level of performance as the peak-load-based allocation, with only a 1.5s delay in average response time; while in the latter case, the response time is always worse than the peak-load-based case. In the worst case, it produces either a 36% under-provision of CPU which causes a 15s delay or a 27% under-provision of I/O for 11s additional delay. Noticed that the performance in the without characterization case is always worse than the other two cases due to the misprediction of VM resource demand: although

over-provision of either CPU or I/O does happen, the demands for CPU and I/O cannot be both met at the same time.

6.2.2 RUBiS Experiments

RUBiS models an online auction site that supports the core functionalities such as browsing, selling, and bidding [7]. A typical two-tier setup is used to set up RUBiS, where the web tier and database tier are deployed on separated VMs. The web-tier VM hosts Apache Tomcat 4.1.40 with RUBiS and its clients while the database-tier VM hosts MySQL 5.0 with 1.1 GB of data. Both VMs are configured with one CPU and 1GB RAM.

Compared to the synthetic workloads used in the above TPC-H experiments, here we constructed more realistic workloads, based on real traces from the 1998 World Cup site [15], one of the public traces widely used in related research for creating realistic workloads [16][17]. In order to emphasize of the variation in workload composition, the workload's intensity is kept constant (the number of concurrent client sessions to the web tier is fixed at 800) while its composition is varied based on the pattern in a typical one-day hourly trace from the World Cup site. We identify the read and write requests in the World Cup trace based on the "Get" and "Post" methods, respectively, used in each request. The ratio of the read and write requests in this trace is then mapped to the ratio of the browsing and bidding requests in the RUBiS workload (Figure 8(a)), which corresponds to the SELECT to INSERT/UPDATE ratio of its database workload.

We compare the performance of the fuzzy model created with workload characterization versus without it. The former considers both the workload's intensity and composition as the input to the modeling whereas the latter considers only the intensity. The composition can be captured by the ratio of two types of queries, the SELECT queries, which are read-only, and the INSERT and

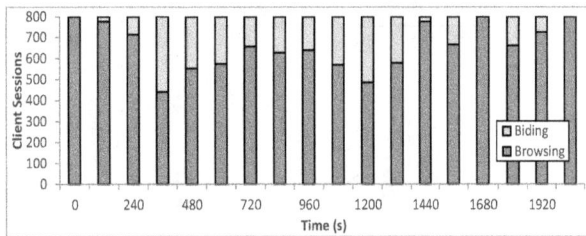

Figure 8(a). Trace for RUBiS with changing composition

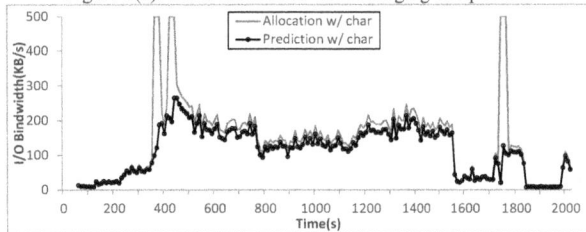

Figure 8(b). I/O allocations with workload characterization

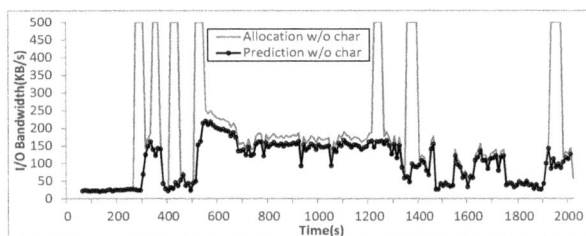

Figure 8(c). I/O allocations without workload characterization

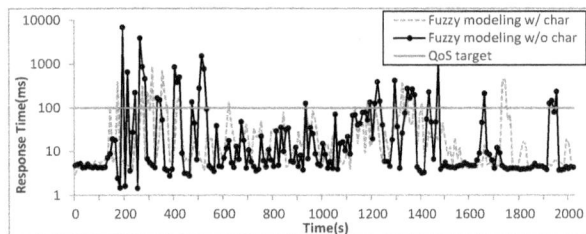

Figure 8(d). Performance comparisons for RUBiS workload

UPDATE queries, which are writes to the database. These characteristics are captured by interposing a MySQL proxy before the database tier. Since this experiment is performed completely online, only the first 10 data points collected are used to initialize the VM's fuzzy model. Afterwards the model is used to allocate resources right away and in the meantime it is updated with new observed data every 10s.

The desired QoS target for these workloads is defined according to the performance of the database VM under the peak-load-based resource allocation which statically assigns 70% CPU and 320KB/s disk I/O bandwidth. In the experiment, the QoS target is set to 100ms for the average response time within each period. A 10% margin is added to the resource allocation predicted by the fuzzy model. When the QoS target cannot be met due to inaccuracy in the model, a backup policy is invoked to allocate a fixed amount of I/O bandwidth (500KB/s) to the VM temporarily. This backup mechanism allows the performance loss to be quickly recovered and ensures that the model can be timely updated to reflect the VM's current resource needs. It is invoked when two consecutive QoS violations occur and revoked after the QoS target are met again for three consecutive periods of time.

Afterwards, the fuzzy model updated with the new measurements is used again for guiding the resource allocation.

Figure 8(b) and (c) show the I/O predictions and allocations using a fuzzy model created with/without workload characterization, respectively, for the changing composition RUBiS workload. Figure 8(d) compares the corresponding performance in both cases with the pre-set QoS target. For the fuzzy modeling with workload characterization, it is able to predict the VM's resource needs throughout most of the experiment and require only a few (3 times) invocations of the backup allocation policy. It can quickly react to the changes in workload composition and deliver the desired QoS for 92% of the time; the average response time is 44.9ms throughout the entire experiment. However, without characterization, the QoS target is violated for 15% of the time, and the backup policy is triggered twice more often (7 times). The resulting average response time of 119.5ms cannot meet the QoS target, almost 3 times worse than the one with characterization.

6.3 Combining both Guest-to-Host and Host-to-Guest Optimizations

This experiment demonstrates the effectiveness of our cross-layer resource management by combining guest-to-host workload characterization and host-to-guest database tuning for an OLAP-like database workload.

To construct a more interesting workload, we mix multiple copies of Q1, Q4, Q6, and Q14 from TPC-H queries. To make these queries more diverse in resource usage patterns, distinct query copies are derived from Q4, Q6, and Q14 by modifying the condition in the *where* cause in the original query statements. Each copy touches a different section of the involved tables and the data accessed by different copies is evenly distributed within the range of a table. In this way, the intensity in I/O can be easily varied by changing the total number of these copies, while the CPU intensity is varied by changing the number of copies of original Q1. The experiment is performed in two phases. In *Phase 1*, the workload intensity is fixed by running 18 copies of queries in total but the composition is varied by changing the percentage of Q1's copies from 17% then to 50% and finally to 83%. In *Phase 2*, an I/O cap from 3000 to 1000KB/s is set to the VM to simulate different levels of I/O contention from other VMs while the workload composition is kept constant with 83% of Q1.

Using our proposed approach with cross-layer optimization, during Phase 1, it models the VM's resource demand using the workload characterization result, [*Request rate*, *Percentage of Cluster 1*], as the input (two types of queries are classified: Q1 as the CPU-intensive query and the others as the I/O intensive). This model is then used to allocate resources to the VM in the absence of contention. When the experiment transits to Phase 2 and I/O contention is introduced into the system, our approach feeds the I/O bandwidth pressure back to the guest layer by tuning the database parameters according to the resource availability as discussed in Section 5.2. In comparison, we repeat the experiment using fuzzy-modeling-based resource allocation without cross-layer optimization. In this case, during Phase1, only the workload intensity is used to create the fuzzy model; during Phase 2, the database configuration is not adapted and kept static as in Phase 1.

Figure 9 compares the database performance under fuzzy-modeling-based resource allocation with cross-layer optimization (*Cross-layer Opt*) and without it (*Non-Opt*) versus the ideal performance under peak-load-based resource allocation (*Peak-load-based*). From the result we can see that in Phase 1, the

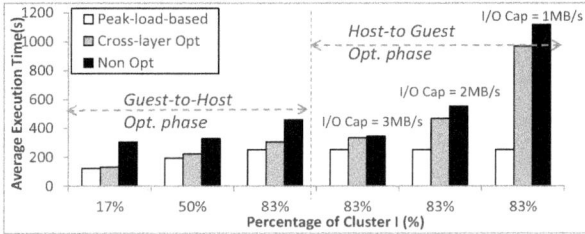

Figure 9 Performance of a TPC-H workload with both guest-to-host and host-to-guest optimizations

performance in *Cross-layer Opt* closely follows the one under peak-load-based allocation. It is as much as seven times better than that in *Non-Opt* which results in a 98% average performance degradation. In Phase 2, both approaches suffer from the reduced I/O bandwidth. However, the *Cross-layer Opt* case still achieves about 17% performance improvement than the *Non-Opt* case. The host-to-guest feedback enables the database query optimizer to switch from a bitmap-scan preferable plan to an index-scan preferable plan for all I/O intensive queries by tuning the I/O cost parameters *sequential_page_cost* vs. *random_page_cost* from the original 1:4 ratio to 1:1 as the I/O cap decreases from 3MB/s to 1MB/s. This adaptation improves the query performance significantly because the index-scan preferable query plan requires less I/O bandwidth than the bitmap-scan preferable one.

7. RELATED WORK

Various solutions have been studied in the literature to address the problem of automatically deciding a VM's resource allocation based on its hosted application's demand and QoS requirement. In particular, different machine learning algorithms have been considered to model VM resource usages. For example, a simple regression method is used to predict the performance impact of VM memory allocation [18]; Reinforcement learning is used to automatically tune VM resource configuration [19]; Artificial neural networks are used to model the nonlinear behaviors for a variety of applications when their VMs are under I/O contention [20]; our previous work [5][8] proposed to use *fuzzy logic* to model the relationship between application workload and VM resource demand, which is shown to be both fast and accurate for modeling systems with complex behaviors. Unlike the traditional solutions which treat VM as a black box, this paper's application-aware approach takes advantage of application-specific knowledge to capture the workload patterns so that the VM model can accurately predict its demand and quickly adapt to the changes in application workload.

Classical feedback control theory has also been used to adjust VM resource allocations according to the application's performance requirement. Linear multi-input-multi-output (MIMO) models are often used for performance modeling, for example, to allocate CPU resource for Web servers [21][22], to manage the performance interference of competing VMs [25], and in more complicated cases, to allocate multiple types of resources to multi-tier applications [23][24]. Although such linear models can be updated adaptively as the system moves from one operating point to another, their accuracy and speed are limited for capturing complex nonlinear behaviors existing in VMs. In contrast, the fuzzy-modeling-based approach proposed in this paper can effectively capture such behaviors and the modeling is shown to be fast. In fact, our previous work as well as others [26] proposed a fuzzy-model-based predictive controller, which embeds fuzzy-modeling into a predictive control system, shows promising

results for both effectively capturing complex system behaviors and quickly adapting to changes in the system [27].

In the related research on workload-aware resource management, R. Singh *et al.* proposed a mix-aware provisioning solution for allocating server capacity to the bottleneck-tier in datacenters serving workloads with changes in both volume and mix [28]. It employs *k-means* clustering to characterize workload mix and queuing models for predicting server capacity. In comparison, our proposed approach exploits application-specific knowledge to effectively characterize workloads, employs fuzzy modeling to accurately capture VM resource usage, and supports finer-grained allocations of multiple types of resources including both CPU and I/O. Furthermore, in addition to extracting knowledge from the guest to host for better understanding of application resource demand, our approach also delivers the allocation decisions from host to guest for the application to better adapt to resource availability changes.

In the related work on virtualized database resource management, Soror *et al.* proposed using calibrated database query cost model to estimate the VM resource demand [29]. It considers a workload as a static entity consisting of a fixed set of queries, so the resource allocation decision is made for the entire workload according to the overall performance requirement. To deal with the inaccuracy in database cost models, it employs online refinement by assuming a linear VM resource usage model. In contrast, our proposed approach uses database cost model only as a tool to discover workload composition, but not for directly estimating VM resource demand, thereby avoiding the well-known inaccuracy inherent to database cost models. Our approach also more realistically treats a workload as a non-stationary time series and considers fine-grained query performance needs. The VM's complex resource usage model is automatically learned and adapted online without any *a priori* assumption.

Other related autonomous database work [30][31][32] focuses only on a database's internal tuning and query optimization, but not the resource allocation to an entire database VM. Previous work [33][34] points out workload characterization as the key to understanding the resource intensity of a database workload. This paper incorporates both of the two aspects of work in the fuzzy-modeling-based resource management of virtualized databases. It improves the static workload characterization method by allowing online and adaptive characterization and optimizes the performance of virtualized databases by further tuning database parameters according to the adjustment in resource allocations.

8. CONCLUSION AND FUTURE WORK

This paper proposes a new VM resource management approach based on fuzzy modeling and cross-host-guest optimization. It enables the communication between VM host- and guest-layer schedulers and allows them to collaboratively optimize the resource allocation and application performance. The host-layer scheduler exploits guest-layer application-specific information to characterize VM workload and model its resource demand. The guest-layer scheduler uses the host-layer feedback to understand the changing resource availability and adapt its configuration accordingly. As a challenging case study, this cross-layer optimization approach is applied to the resource management of virtualized databases. It uses a database's cost estimation for workload characterization and adapts the database by tuning its cost model parameters according to its resource availability.

A prototype of this approach is implemented on Xen-based VMs and evaluated using typical database workloads based on TPC-H and RUBiS. The results demonstrate that the cross-layer optimization approach significantly outperforms the application-unaware one which treats VMs as black boxes. It can efficiently allocate both CPU and I/O resources to database VMs serving workloads with dynamically changing intensity and composition while meeting QoS targets or improving the performance when under resource pressure.

The proposed cross-layer optimization requires certain awareness between virtualization software and virtualized application. Such awareness breaks the transparency offered by traditional full virtualization, but we advocate that this tradeoff is necessary for business- and mission-critical applications to achieve their desired QoS on virtualized systems. The benefit of this tradeoff is demonstrated by our initial results reported in this paper. The underlying argument is the same as that drives the success of paravirtualization [2] which sacrifices complete transparency for lighter-weight and more efficient virtualization. Although not every virtualized application is capable of adapting its behavior according to changing resource availability, we believe it will become a necessity for critical applications as virtualization becomes pervasive. In our future work, we will study how to create a concise and generic interface for cross-layer optimization that can support diverse guest OSes and applications.

9. ACKNOWLEDGMENTS

This research is sponsored by National Science Foundation under grant CCF-0938045 and Department of Homeland Security grant 2010-ST-062-000039. The authors are also thankful to the anonymous reviewers for their useful comments to improve the quality of the paper.

REFERENCES

[1] VMware, URL: http://www.vmware.com.

[2] P. Barham, Dragovic, B., Fraser, K., Hand, S., Harris, T., Ho, A., Neugebauer, R., Pratt, I. and Warfield, A, "Xen and the Art of Virtualization", SOSP, 2003.

[3] Amazon Elastic Compute Cloud, URL: http://aws.amazon.com/ec2/.

[4] Windows Azure, URL: http://www.microsoft.com/windowsazure/.

[5] L. Wang, J. Xu, M. Zhao, Y. Tu and J. A.B. Fortes, "Fuzzy Modeling Based Resource Management for Virtualized Database Systems", MASCOTS, 2011.

[6] TPC-H Benchmark Specification, URL: http://www. tcp. org.

[7] C. Amza, A. Chanda, A. Cox, S. Elnikety, R. Gil, K. Rajamani and W. Zwaenepoel, "Specification and Implementation of Dynamic Web Site Benchmarks", WWC-5, 2002.

[8] J. Xu, M. Zhao and J. Fortes, "Autonomic Resource Management in Virtualized Data Centers Using Fuzzy-logic-based Control", Cluster Computing, 2008.

[9] S. Chiu, "Fuzzy Model Identification Based on Cluster Estimation", Journal of Intelligent and Fuzzy Systems, 1994.

[10] J. Liu, R. Rangaswami, and M. Zhao, "Model-Driven Network Emulation With Virtual Time Machine", Winter Simulation Conference, December 2010.

[11] A. Chen, P. Goes, A. Gupta and J. Marsden, "Heuristics for Selecting Robust Database Structures with Dynamic Query Patterns", EJOR, 2006.

[12] M. Wang, T. Madhyastha, N. Chan, S. Papadimitriou and C. Faloutsos, "Data Mining Meets Performance Evaluation: Fast Algorithms for Modeling Bursty Traffic", ICDE, 2002.

[13] S. Chaudhuri, "Relational Query Optimization – Data Management Meets Statistical Estimation", Communications of ACM, 2009.

[14] dm-ioband, URL: http://sourceforge.net/apps/trac/ioband.

[15] M. Arlitt and T. Jin, "Workload Characterization of the 1998 World Cup Web Site," in HP Technical Report, 1999.

[16] Z. Gong and X. Gu, "PAC: Pattern-driven Application Consolidation for Efficient Cloud Computing", MASCOTS, 2010.

[17] G. Jung, M. Hiltunen, K. Joshi, R. Schlichting and C. Pu, "Mistral: Dynamically Managing Power, Performance, and Adaptation Cost in Cloud Infrastructures", ICDCS, 2010.

[18] J. Wildstrom, P. Stone and E. Witchel, "CARVE: A Cognitive Agent for Resource Value Estimation", ICAC, 2008.

[19] J. Rao, X. Bu, C. Xu, L. Wang and G. Yin, "VCONF: A Reinforcement Learning Approach to Virtual Machines Auto-configuration", ICAC, 2009.

[20] S. Kundu, R. Rangaswami, K. Dutta and M. Zhao, "Application Performance Modeling in a Virtualized Environment," HPCA, 2010.

[21] X. Liu, X. Zhu, S. Singhal and M. Arlitt, "Adaptive Entitlement Control of Resource Containers on Shared Servers", IM, 2005.

[22] Z. Wang, X. Zhu and S. Singhal, "Utilization and SLO-Based Control for Dynamic Sizing of Resource Partitions", DSOM, 2005.

[23] P. Padala, K. Hou, K. Shin, X. Zhu, M. Uysal, Z. Wang, S. Singhal and A. Merchant, "Automated Control of Multiple Virtualized Resources", SIGOPS/EuroSys, 2009.

[24] X. Liu, X. Zhu, P. Padala, Z. Wang and S. Singhal,"Optimal Multivariate Control for Differentiated Services on a Shared Hosting Platform", CDC, 2007.

[25] R.Nathuji and A. Kansal, "Q-Clouds: Managing Performance Interference Effects for QoS-Aware Clouds", Eurosys, 2010.

[26] P. Lama and X. Zhou, "PERFUME: Power and Performance Guarantee with Fuzzy MIMO Control in Virtualized Servers", IWQoS, 2011.

[27] L.Wang, J. Xu, M. Zhao and J. A.B. Fortes, "Adaptive Virtual Resource Management with Fuzzy Model Predictive Control" FeBID, 2011.

[28] R. Singh, U. Sharma, E. Cecchet, and P.J. Shenoy, "Autonomic Mix-Aware Provisioning for Non-Stationary Data Center Workloads", ICAC. 2010A.

[29] Soror, U. Minhas, A. Aboulnaga, K. Salem, P. Kokosielis and S. Kamath, "Automatic Virtual Machine Configuration for Database Workloads", SIGMOD, 2008

[30] G. Weikum, A. Moenkeberg, C. Hasse and P. Zabback, "Self-tuning Database Technology and Information Services: From Wishful Thinking to Viable Engineering", VLDB, 2002.

[31] S. Chaudhuri and G. Weikum, "Foundations of Automated Database Tuning", ICDE, 2006.

[32] B. Schroeder, M. Harchol-Balter, A. Iyengar and E. Nahum, "Achieving Class-based QoS for Transactional Workloads", ICDE, 2006.

[33] P. Martin, S. Elnaffar and T. Wasserman, "Workload Models for Autonomic Database Management Systems", ICAS, 2006.

[34] T. Wasserman, P. Martin and D. Skillicorn, "Developing a Characterization of Business Intelligence Workloads for Sizing New Database Systems", DOLAP, 2004.

Shifting GEARS to Enable Guest-context Virtual Services

Kyle C. Hale
Dept. of EECS
Northwestern University
Evanston, IL 60208
kh@u.northwestern.edu

Lei Xia
Dept. of EECS
Northwestern University
Evanston, IL 60208
lxia@northwestern.edu

Peter A. Dinda
Dept. of EECS
Northwestern University
Evanston, IL 60208
pdinda@northwestern.edu

ABSTRACT

We argue that the implementation of VMM-based virtual services for a guest should extend into the guest itself, even without its cooperation. Placing service components directly into the guest OS or application can reduce implementation complexity and increase performance. In this paper we show that the set of tools in a VMM required to enable a broad range of such guest-context services is fairly small. Further, we outline and evaluate these tools and describe their design and implementation in the context of Guest Examination and Revision Services (GEARS), a new framework within the Palacios VMM. We then describe two example GEARS-based services—an MPI communication accelerator and an overlay networking accelerator—that illustrate the benefits of allowing virtual service implementations to span across the VMM, guest, and application. Other VMMs could employ the ideas and tools in GEARS.

Categories and Subject Descriptors

D.4.4 [**Software**]: OPERATING SYSTEMS

Keywords

virtual machines, services, code transformation

1. INTRODUCTION

The virtualization layer is commonplace in cloud/data center computing, well attested to in adaptive/autonomic computing, and increasingly common even in high performance computing. In each of these areas, the capability to augment guests with VMM-based virtual services that can enhance their functionality, security, or performance, and can better match a user's VMs with a provider's hardware resources, is one of the key benefits of virtualization.

This project is made possible by support from the United States National Science Foundation (NSF) via grant CNS-0709168 and the Department of Energy (DOE) via grant DE-SC0005343.

To expedite the creation and deployment of virtual services, it would be beneficial to provision the VMM with the ability to implant parts of the service implementations directly in the guest. VMM code *running directly within the context of the guest OS or application without its cooperation* has the potential to considerably simplify the design and implementation of services because the services could then directly manipulate aspects of the guest from within the guest itself. Furthermore, these kinds of services could eliminate many overheads associated with costly exits to the VMM, improving their performance. Finally, extending a service into the guest would enable new classes of services that are not possible, or are extremely difficult to implement solely within the VMM context. We refer to virtual services that can span the VMM, the guest kernel, and the guest application, as *guest-context virtual services*.

We present the Guest Examination and Revision Services (GEARS), a novel framework that aims to enable guest-context virtual services. The tools in GEARS have been carefully selected as those sufficient to implement a wide range of such services, and their abstractions are independent of our implementation. We also present the design, implementation, and performance evaluation of the GEARS tools in the context of the Palacios VMM, an effort that demonstrates that the tools can be made available in a VMM with only a modest increase in its code size and with very low overhead (and zero overhead when not used). Finally, we demonstrate how we built two guest-context virtual services using the tools, and how they can enhance overlay networking and MPI performance without significant implementation complexity. The overlay service improves latency by 3–20%, while the MPI service approaches the native memory copy throughput limit for co-located VMs.

The GEARS implementation also attempts to broaden the community of virtual service developers by eliminating the need for programmers to be intimately familiar with VMM internals. While basic knowledge of the guest is required, the GEARS framework provides the necessary tools to transform standard code into a guest-context service. Guest-specific information can then remain mostly opaque to the service developer, and how these services are used to affect guest operation is entirely at his or her discretion. GEARS also allows the VMM to transparently *mutate* guest applications and OSes into VMM-aware entities. Thus, we believe that frameworks like GEARS have the potential to beget adaptive applications that reap the benefits of virtualization while retaining the performance available to those aware of the underlying software and hardware stack.

2. RELATED WORK

Adaptive or autonomic computing in virtualized computing environments is an area of considerable current interest and promise (e.g., [21, 24, 19]). Autonomic computing in this context extends new services to the guest, typically without guest knowledge. This has much in common with the virtual service model in other contexts.

Virtual services need to be cognizant of the guest, but there exists a *semantic gap* [4] between the VMM and the guest. Some have shown that the VMM can infer a great deal of information about the guest (both the applications and the kernel) through indirect means [8, 7]. These techniques have particularly useful applications in security, where trust can be placed in the VMM to detect attacks and malicious processes [5, 9, 18, 15].

While these methods glean useful information about the guest, the information only flows in one direction. Further, the guest cannot assist in providing the information, limiting the VMM to coarse-grained observations and decisions. In contrast, *Paravirtualization* makes the guest OS aware of the underlying VMM, allowing it to provide information directly to the VMM [2]. However, the paravirtualized interface can only be utilized directly by the guest. The VMM sees this interface as an extension to its existing event-driven model.

Symbiotic virtualization allows information to flow both ways between the VMM and guest [11], where the guest OS optionally exposes a software interface directly to the VMM. The VMM can then call into guest-context code. This approach also requires that the guest be aware of the VMM and implies modifications to the guest OS. It would certainly be beneficial to have a two-way interface that requires no *a priori* modification to the guest. With GEARS, we aspire to extend service implementations into the guest itself, even without guest knowledge or cooperation.

Secure in-VM monitoring, or SIM [20], also utilizes guest-context code execution, but it is aimed primarily at security applications, not virtual services. Further, SIM requires some degree of guest modification. Namely, it assumes that a paravirtualized driver is present in the guest. This driver is necessary for running VMM-trusted code in guest context. GEARS requires no such preconditions in order to forcefully and transparently affect guest execution.

One of the tools that GEARS employs is system call interposition. This technique has been explored in the context of several hypervisors, including Xen [3], KVM [17], and QEMU [13]. Onoe et al. present a method to filter system calls based on security policies [16]. MAVMM, a custom, lightweight VMM designed for malware detection [15] also utilizes system call interception. Ether [6] uses the same interception mechanism, but focuses on keeping its presence undetectable by malware. While system call interposition is an important technique in the GEARS tool set, it alone does not afford the ability to spread virtual services across virtualization layers. Ether and VAMPiRE [22] have the interesting capability to insert breakpoints into guest processes to implement instruction stepping, but they do not enable the broad range of services offered by the code injection facilities in the GEARS framework.

3. EXAMPLE SERVICES

When a VMM utilizes its higher privilege level to enable or enhance functionality, optimize performance, or otherwise modify the behavior of the guest in a favorable manner, it is said to provide a service to the guest. VMM-based services are usually provided transparently to the guest without its knowledge (e.g. via a virtual device). We now consider several example services that could profit from GEARS.

Overlay networking acceleration An important service for many virtualized computing environments is an overlay networking system that provides fast, efficient network connectivity among a group of VMs and the outside world, regardless of where the VMs are currently located. Such an overlay can also form the basis of an adaptive/autonomic environment, as described in Section 2. A prominent challenge for overlay networks in this context is achieving low latency and high throughput, even in high performance settings, such as supercomputers and next-generation data centers. We show in Section 7.3 how GEARS can enhance an existing overlay networking system with a guest-context component.

MPI acceleration MPI is the most widely used communication interface for distributed memory parallel computing. In an adaptive virtualized environment, two VMs running an application communicating using MPI may be co-located on a single host. Because the MPI library has no way of knowing this, it will use a sub-optimal communication path between them. An MPI acceleration service would detect such cases and automatically convert message passing into memory copies and/or memory ownership transfers. Section 7.4 outlines the design of this service.

Procrustean services While administrators can install services or programs on guests already, this task must be repeated many times. Furthermore, because the administrators of guests and those of provider hosts may not be the same people, providers may execute guests that are not secure. GEARS functionality would permit the creation of services that would automatically deploy security patches and software updates on a provider's guests.

4. GUEST-CONTEXT VIRTUAL SERVICES

Services that reside within the core of the VMM have the disadvantage of relying on the mechanism by which control is transferred to the VMM. A VMM typically does not run until an exceptional situation arises, such as the execution of a privileged instruction (a direct call to the VMM in the case of paravirtualization) or the triggering of external or software interrupts. Much like in an operating system, the transition to the higher privilege level, called an *exit*, introduces substantial overhead. Costly exits remain one of the most prohibitive obstacles to achieving high-performance virtualization.

Eliminating these exits can, thus, improve performance considerably. The motivation is similar to minimizing costly system calls to OS code in user-space processes. Modern Linux implementations, for example, provide a mechanism called *virtual system calls*, in which the OS maps a read-only page into every process's address space on start-up. This page contains code that implements commonly used services and obviates the need to switch into kernel space. If the implementation of a VMM service could be pushed up into the guest in a similar manner, more time would be spent in direct execution of guest code rather than costly invocations of the VMM. This is precisely what GEARS seeks to achieve, and this ability to eliminate exits will, perhaps, become most clear as we discuss our fast system call exiting utility in Sections 6 and 7.

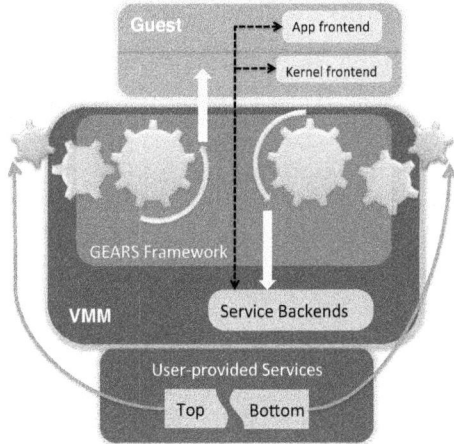

Figure 1: GEARS services are broken into two parts; one exists in the guest and the other in the VMM. GEARS takes both parts provided as source code and uses several utilities to register and manage execution of the service.

Moving components of a service implementation into the guest can not only improve performance, but also enable services that would otherwise not be feasible. In particular, guest-context services have a comprehensive view of the state of the guest kernel and application. These services can make more informed decisions than those implemented in a VMM core, which must make many indirect inferences about guest state. The VMM must reconstruct high-level operations based on the limited information that the guest exposes architecturally. Moreover, in order to manipulate the state of a guest kernel or application, the VMM must make many transformations from the low-level operations that the guest exposes to high-level operations that affect guest execution. While services certainly exist that can accomplish this transformation, their implementation would, perhaps, become more elegant operating at the same semantic level as the guest components they intend to support.

These services are also easier for the developer to design. Rather than having to effectively reverse engineer a particular execution path in the guest from the VMM's limited perspective, the developer can reason about the service at a high level, avoiding the intricacies introduced by the semantic gap.

GEARS employs a tiered approach, which involves both the host and the VMM, to inject and run services in guest context. The process is outlined in Figure 1. Users (service developers) provide standard C code for the VMM without needing extensive knowledge of VMM internals. This makes the procedure of implementing a service straight-forward, enabling rapid development. The code provided is a service implementation, split into two clearly distinguishable parts. We refer to these as the *top-half* and the *bottom-half*. The top-half is the portion of the service that will run in the guest-context. The bottom-half, which may not always be present, resides within a host kernel module readily accessible to the VMM. The top-half will call into its respective bottom-half if it requires its functionality. The bottom-half can similarly invoke the top-half, allowing for a two-way interaction between the service components.

The code for the top-half must adhere to a guest-specific format. However, GEARS provides host-resident utilities that transform the code appropriately. Hence, from the user's perspective, writing the top-half of a guest-context

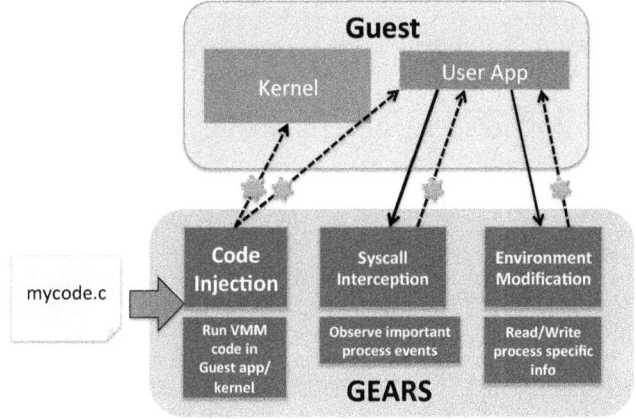

Figure 2: GEARS tools used to implement guest-context services. Each tool is shown with a box indicating its primary function. Dashed lines with gears indicate the ability to modify control flow in the guest. Solid lines show that a tool is used for passively extracting information from the guest. Note that all of these tools can be used in different ways to alter the guest execution path.

service implies little more requisite knowledge than the ability to write a normal program or kernel module for the guest in question. GEARS must simply provide the transformation utilities appropriate for that guest. If the service requires access to, or assistance from the VMM core, the developer can design a bottom half by writing a host kernel module that implements the relevant interface. We outline how this module connects with the VMM in Section 6.5.

The notion of leaving service implementations entirely up to the user allows a clean separation between the framework and the services that it enables. GEARS provides the necessary tools to create cross-layer services, and users are responsible for using this platform to design innovative guest-VMM interactions.

5. GEARS

We now provide a high-level description of the specific tools used in the GEARS framework. These tools allow for a broad range of feasible services, some of which we illustrated in Section 3.

To enable guest-context services, the VMM must provide a mechanism that can place components directly within the guest. GEARS implements this mechanism with the code injection tool. Further, the VMM must have a way to select an appropriate time at which to perform this placement. The GEARS system call interception utility provides one way of accomplishing this. Finally, in order for the VMM to control guest execution paths at a higher level, e.g. for library calls, it must have the ability to modify the environment passed to the process. GEARS does this with process environment modification. Because these three conditions alone can facilitate the creation of guest-context services, we claim that GEARS provides the necessary and sufficient tools to accomplish this task.

5.1 System call interception

System call interception allows a VMM to monitor the activity of the guest at a fine granularity. Normally, system calls are not exceptional events from the standpoint of the VMM. However, system calls are commonly triggered using software interrupts, which modern hardware allows VMM interception of. Once the VMM can track the execution of system calls, it can provide a wide range of services to the guest, such as sanity checking arguments to sensitive kernel code or matching system call patterns as in [13].

5.2 Process environment modification

System call interception enables the VMM to essentially see the creation of every process in the guest through calls to `execve`, for example. The interception is done before the system call even starts, so the VMM has the option to modify the guest's memory at this point. One useful thing it can do is modify the environment variables that the parent process passes on to its child.

There are certain environment variables that are particularly useful. One is the `LD_PRELOAD` variable, which indicates that a custom shared library should be given precedence over the one originally indicated. This variable gives the VMM an opportunity to directly modify the control flow of a guest application. Other interesting environment variables affecting control flow include `LD_BIND_NOW` and `LD_LIBRARY_PATH`. The very fact that the Linux kernel itself uses the environment to pass information to the process (e.g. with the `AT_SYSINFO` variable) opens up a broad range of interesting possibilities.

Environment variables can not only be modified, but also, with careful treatment of memory, added or removed. This introduces the potential for the VMM to provide information directly to the guest application without the need for paravirtualization. The guest OS would not need to be aware of the underlying VMM. Instead, VMM-awareness could vary on an application by application basis. This would allow developers to make rapid optimizations to utilize VMM services. As we will later discuss in detail, these developers could even implement their own VMM service with minimal effort. Notice that this is a marked divergence from the usual reliance of user space applications on the operating system's ABI.

5.3 Code injection

Code injection is perhaps the most unique mechanism in the GEARS framework. Because it allows the VMM to run arbitrary code in the context of the guest without any cooperation or knowledge on the part of the guest OS or application, it is the core tool enabling guest-context services.

We employ two types of code injection—user-space and kernel-space. User-space injection allows the VMM to map a piece of trusted code into the address space of a user-space process. On exits, the VMM can invoke this code manually or redirect user-space function calls to it by patching the process binary image. The latter requires more complex techniques that we are currently developing.

GEARS can also inject code into a guest that will dynamically link with the libraries mapped into the applications' address spaces. Our current example services do not utilize this GEARS feature and we leave its detailed description to future work.

The other type of injection is kernel-space code injection, which relies on the ability to inject code into a user-space process. Injected kernel code must currently be implemented in a kernel module compiled for the guest. We use user-space code injection to write the module into the guest file system and subsequently insert it into the guest kernel.

Figure 2 shows the GEARS tools and outlines how they are used together to control and modify guest execution.

Component	Lines of Code
System Call Interception	833
Environment Modification	683
Code Injection	915
Total	2431

Figure 3: Implementation complexity for GEARS and its constituent components.

These particular tools are the fundamental components that allow a VMM to push service implementations into the guest and affect its operation using guest semantics.

6. IMPLEMENTATION

We now outline the implementation of the tools comprising the GEARS framework. GEARS is implemented within the Palacios Virtual Machine Monitor, an open-source, embeddable VMM actively developed and maintained by researchers at several institutions [10, 12]. Its source code is available for free online at `v3vee.org`, and will soon include the latest GEARS framework.

While the current GEARS implementation is targeted at Linux guests, it consists of relatively few components, each of which rely on features provided almost universally by modern OSes and architectures. This means that porting GEARS for other kinds of guests entails no great effort. Figure 3 shows the size of the GEARS codebase. Each component is relatively compact. GEARS is currently implemented as a set of extensions to the Palacios VMM, and would likely become even more compact if integrated into the hypervisor core.

GEARS currently focuses on AMD hardware, and the port to Intel hardware is a work in progress. There are no fundamental limitations that will make the implementation of GEARS on Intel any more challenging since the hardware virtualization extensions that we utilize are provided by both vendors. While the current GEARS framework has many simplifications to ease implementation, we note that the purpose of this paper is to demonstrate its ability to enable transparent guest-context services—there is no loss of general applicability of GEARS to hypervisor software.

6.1 Hooking system calls

Both Intel VT and AMD-V hardware virtualization support hypervisor interception of software interrupts (`INTn` instructions). This provides a fairly simple way to catch the execution of system calls in guests by looking specifically for `INT 0x80` instructions. Once this instruction is intercepted and handled in the VMM, the original software interrupt can be injected back into the guest.

Most modern 64-bit software uses AMD's more recently introduced `SYSCALL` instruction to invoke system routines, but hardware support for its interception is not yet provided. Several have worked around this issue by intercepting the write to the model-specific register (MSR) containing the system call target address (named LSTAR in the case of AMD) [3, 13, 16, 15, 6].

GEARS supports both of these implementations. However, there are some limitations because of the simplicity of our current implementation. In the case of `INT 0x80` on AMD hardware, situations can arise where the system call invoked with this instruction causes another faulting condition that triggers an exit to the VMM—namely, a page fault. This is particularly noticeable with `fork()`. Normally, the system call is restarted by the kernel, but the VMM implementation will have already incremented the instruction pointer, so it will return to the next instruction, and behave as if the system call were skipped. Thus, without hardware support, the VMM must support full emulation of the software interrupt instruction. However, this problem can be avoided if the hardware supports nested paging, as these page faults will not trap to the VMM. We therefore only support the `INT 0x80` instruction on machines supporting nested paging. Without hardware support for `INTn` interception, the VMM can overwrite the appropriate entry in the IDT with either an illegal instruction or a `VMMCALL`. When intercepting `INT 0x80`, GEARS currently assumes the necessary hardware support.

Interception of the `SYSCALL` instruction can be achieved by guaranteeing that the register containing the system call entry point (LSTAR on AMD hardware) points to an unmapped memory address, causing a trap to the VMM by page fault. However, finding an address that will trap under nested paging is more difficult, as the VMM is invoked much less frequently on page faults. We currently only intercept `SYSCALL` instructions when the machine is using shadow paging. The VMM can also unset the SCE bit in the EFER MSR, causing an illegal instruction exception when a `SYSCALL` instruction is executed. This exception will cause a trap to the VMM, at which point the instruction at the RIP is checked against the `SYSCALL` opcode. GEARS currently only supports the method using page faults.

While these methods of interception are certainly viable, they introduce substantial performance overhead. These techniques require that *every* system call trigger an exit to the VMM. We have developed a mechanism using GEARS that can virtually eliminate this overhead. We call this the Fast System Call Exiting Utility. This mechanism bears some resemblance to the *exit-gates* presented in SIM [20], but requires no guest cooperation. During guest boot, GEARS records the address written to the appropriate STAR register by the guest kernel and subsequently emulates the write. After the guest has booted, GEARS can use code injection to insert a kernel module into the guest. This kernel module contains a compact stub intended to compare every system call number to a bit vector mapped into the kernel address space by the VMM. During module initialization, the VMM is provided the address of this stub, which it writes to the STAR register. All system calls invoked by the guest are then redirected to this stub. GEARS can dynamically update the system call bit-vector, indicating which system calls should trap to the VMM. At any time, this module can be forcefully removed from the guest kernel, completely disabling system call exiting when not required.

6.2 Process monitoring

With the system call interception facility, we can easily track the creation of new processes by looking for calls to `fork` and `execve`. For our purposes in this paper, `execve` is of particular interest because it represents the moment when a process receives a new address space and begins executing code independent of that in its parent's address space. In Linux, this call takes an executable object as an argument and runs it within the new process. We allow the VMM to hook the execution of specified binaries by comparing the arguments to `execve` to binaries registered dynamically within the VMM.

6.3 Modifying process environments

Along with the binary to execute, and arguments passed to the new process, `execve` passes a pointer to an array of environment variables. Since the system call is intercepted before process creation, the VMM sees the state of the parent process. This allows the VMM to change the environment that the parent passes to the child process.

We analyze environment variables by tracing the environment pointer, given as an argument, back to all of the strings that it points to. The VMM can then modify these strings at will. However, more work must be done if a modification results in a string larger than the original. The VMM shifts the preceding components up past the stack pointer to make room for the overlap and repairs pointers by the appropriate offsets. This is essentially a form of code relocation, and also allows for the addition of an arbitrary number of environment variables to a child process's environment.

In this paper, we utilize this facility to redirect library calls in targeted binaries to custom library wrappers using the `LD_PRELOAD` environment variable.

6.4 Code injection

GEARS uses two modes of code injection—immediate injection and *exec-hooked* injection. When using immediate injection, the VMM, after receiving code to inject at run-time, will inject the code into any user-space process as soon as it can. There are many ways of tracking user-space events, but GEARS currently uses system calls for this purpose. Thus, the code will be injected at the subsequent system call intercepted by the VMM.

Exec-hooked injection allows a means by which to inject at more specific points. With this method, a user specifies a binary file in the guest, which, upon execution, will trigger the injection of the provided code. While this provides more control, the injection actually happens in the parent process, as the interception of the system call happens before the new process is created. One potential way of addressing this issue is to correlate CR3 values with calls to `execve`, and looking for future user-space events matching the recorded value.

The VMM injects code into a process using several steps of binary patching. We outline the steps comprising immediate code injection below:

1 Intercept next system call
2 Inject `mmap()` call into process. This will allocate space for code in a mapped region marked as `rwx`.
3 Touch every page in the region to ensure guest kernel allocates pages
4 Inject a page fault for a page in the region
5 Subsequently copy a page of code into the faulted page
6 Continue steps 4 and 5 until all code is copied
7 Finally, set RIP to start of injected code

Once the code has been copied, the VMM can immediately set the instruction pointer to the code's entry point so that it begins executing on guest entry. The common way that code is compiled in Linux directs the loader to map the ELF binary into memory twice, once read-only for code, and once read-write for data. The linked code will take into account the fixed offset between the mapped locations of code and data. However, we cannot guarantee the address at which `mmap` will allocate memory, so the presence of two mappings would require dynamic relocation of references from the code segment to data segment. To avoid this complication, we currently use custom linker scripts for injected code to ensure that it is mapped into memory only once. For the same reason, the injected code must be compiled to be position-independent.

We can use GEARS to modify the behavior of the guest kernel as well. Given user-space code injection, we can inject code that will forcefully write out a file to the guest file system. One kind of file that we can write out is a kernel module. This presents an opportunity to affect the operation of the guest kernel. Once GEARS writes out a module, it can subsequently insert it into the kernel. The entire process ensues without any cooperation from the guest. While GEARS could also potentially inject code into the kernel address space directly using a technique similar to that employed by user-space injection, kernel modules represent the simplest and safest way to inject service components into the guest kernel. Note that we do not claim the guest cannot *detect* the effects of the injection. We are concerned with the case in which the VMM is simply providing a beneficial service to the guest. While creating invisible guest-context services is paramount to preventing exploits, it is outside the scope of this paper. We direct the interested reader to the security-related projects outlined in Section 2.

6.5 Bottom-half interface

The bottom half of a GEARS-based VMM service can be implemented either directly in the VMM itself or as a separate kernel module for the Linux host OS. In the latter case, the kernel module can be implemented without detailed knowledge of Palacios. The module hooks to Palacios through a new *host hypercall* interface that allows hypercall implementations to be created outside of the Palacios codebase. This host interface provides the hypercall implementations with a *constrained guest access* interface that enables them to inspect and modify guest state, such as general purpose and control registers, guest address translation, and read/write access to guest physical and virtual memory. Since Palacios is host OS-independent, the implementation of these two interfaces is split between the general logic within Palacios, and a host-specific component. The host-independent logic in Palacios comprises 274 lines of C, while the host-specific component, for Linux, consists of 165 lines of C.

7. EVALUATION

In this section we evaluate the performance-sensitive component of GEARS and the prototype example services we have built.

7.1 Experimental setup

We perform all experiments on AMD 64-bit hardware. We primarily use two physical machines for our testbed:

- 2GHz quad-core AMD Opteron 2350 with 2GB memory, 256KB L1, 2MB L2, and 2MB L3 caches. We refer to this machine as *vtest*.

- 2.3GHz 2-socket, quad-core (8 cores total) AMD Opteron 2376 with 32GB of RAM, 512KB L1, 2MB L2, and 6MB L3 caches, called *lewinsky*.

Both of these machines have Fedora 15 installed, with Linux kernel versions 2.6.40 and 2.6.42, respectively. The guests we use in our testbed are Linux kernel versions 2.6.38. All experiments were run using the Palacios VMM configured for nested paging.

Strategy	Latency (μs)
guest	4.83
guest+intercept	10.24

Figure 4: Average system call latency for getpid system call using INT 80 exiting. Because getpid is such a simple system call, the latency difference represents the fixed cost of system call exiting. This form of exiting roughly doubles the fixed cost of all system calls.

7.2 System call interception

The primary performance issue associated with GEARS is the cost of intercepting system calls. As we mentioned in Section 6, we must use either `INT 0x80` interception or `SYSCALL` interception until the machine is booted. GEARS can then forcibly inject the fast system call exiting utility into the guest to all but eliminate the overhead of system call exiting. Since our main concern is the effect of this overhead on applications, we present the performance of the fast system call exiting utility.

Our system call micro-benchmark suite consists of two timing programs that measure the time to completion for a single system call. Each timing run essentially consists of the following sequence of instructions:

```
time:
    cpuid
    rdtsc
    mov $SYSCALL_NR, %rax
    syscall
    cpuid
    rdtsc
```

The `cpuid` instructions enforce serialized execution, avoiding situations in which `rdtsc` instructions might be rearranged by the instruction scheduler. Each experiment consists of 1000 trial runs. We take the minimum of these runs to ignore any intermittent influences such as context switches.

Figures 4 and 5 show the latency associated with the `getpid` system call for software interrupt interception and selective system call exiting, respectively. This particular call is one of the simpler system calls in Linux, so these numbers represent the fixed cost introduced by system call interception. The row labeled *guest* represents a standard guest with no GEARS extensions. The *guest+intercept* row indicates a GEARS-enabled guest using system call exiting. For `INT 0x80` exiting, every system call results in a VMM exit, so this technique has a significant effect on the latency of the system call path. In the case of selective exiting, all system calls are routed through the injected kernel module, but do not cause an exit to the VMM unless marked to do so. In this experiment, no system calls were marked for exiting. Thus, this figure shows the overhead introduced to the system call path only by this rerouting process. Whether or not any particular system call is marked to trigger a VMM invocation, this shows the bare minimum cost that must be paid for system call exiting. Selective system call exiting adds only about 6% latency overhead to a standard guest— less than one microsecond.

Figure 6 shows the *bandwidth* cost of selective system call exiting. For this experiment, we chose a system call that varies in performance according to the amount of data handled. We measured the bandwidth of the `write` system call with varying buffer sizes. Notice that the difference in bandwidth is virtually negligible. Figure 7 displays this difference

Strategy	Latency (μs)
guest	4.26
guest+intercept	4.51

Figure 5: Average system call latency for getpid system call using selective exiting. The overhead is significantly smaller than INT 80 exiting.

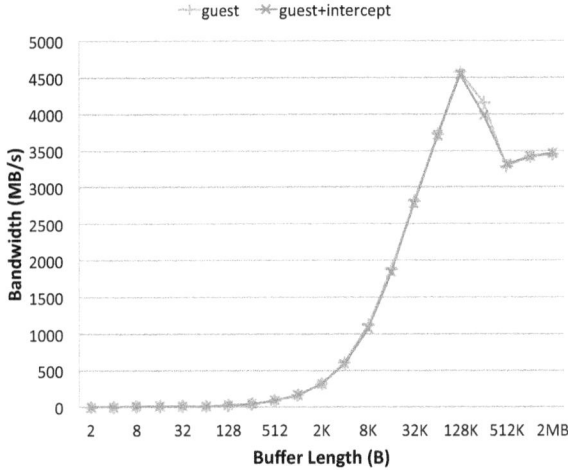

Figure 6: Bandwidth (MB/s) vs. bytes transferred for a write system call. These lines track very closely, demonstrating how little selective system call exiting affects the bandwidth of a data-intensive system call.

more clearly with the ratio of bandwidth with a standard guest over the bandwidth of a GEARS-provisioned guest. The ratio approaches one as the fixed overhead cost of system call exiting is amortized over the amount of data being written.

7.3 VNET/P accelerator

VNET/P [23] is an overlay networking system with a layer 2 abstraction implemented inside the Palacios VMM. It currently achieves near-native performance in the 1 Gbps and 10 Gbps switched networks common in clusters today, and we intend for it to work at native speeds on even faster networks, such as InfiniBand, in the future. At the time of this writing, VNET/P can achieve, with a fully encapsulated data path, 75% of the native throughput with 3-5x the native latency between directly connected 10 Gbps machines. We use GEARS tools to further improve this performance.

The throughput and latency overheads of VNET/P are mostly due to guest/VMM context switches, and data copies or data ownership transfers. We can potentially reduce the number of context switches, and the volume of copies or transfers, by shifting more of the VNET/P data path into the guest itself. In the limit, the entire VNET/P data path could execute in the guest with guarded privileged access to the underlying hardware. In this paper, we explore an initial step towards this goal that does not involve privileged access and aims at reducing the latency overhead as a proof-of-concept.

Figure 8 illustrates this initial proof-of-concept implementation of the VNET/P Accelerator Service. In the baseline VNET/P data path, shown on the left, raw Ethernet packets sent from a VM through a virtual NIC are encapsulated and forwarded within the VMM and sent via a physical NIC. In the VNET/P Accelerator data path, shown on the right, the

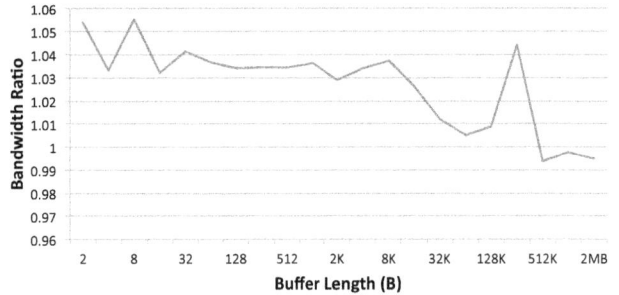

Figure 7: Bandwidth ratio of standard guest to guest with GEARS. This ratio approaches unity as the fixed system call exiting cost is amortized.

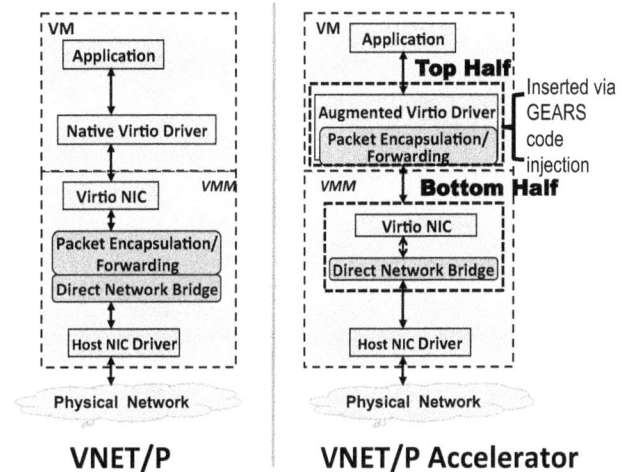

Figure 8: Implementation of the prototype VNET/P Accelerator.

encapsulation and forwarding functionality of VNET/P resides within the guest as part of the guest's device driver for the virtual NIC. This augmented device driver kernel module is uncooperatively inserted into the guest kernel using the GEARS code injection tool. The augmented driver then delivers Ethernet frames containing the encapsulated packets to the virtual NIC. In our implementation, the driver that has been augmented is the Linux virtio NIC driver. The backend virtio NIC implementation in Palacios has no changes; it is simply bridged to the physical NIC.

The implementation complexity of the proof-of-concept VNET/P accelerator is shown in Figure 9, which illustrates that few changes are needed to split VNET/P functionality into a top half and a bottom half. The control plane of VNET/P remains in the bottom half in the VMM; only the encapsulation and forwarding elements move into the top half that GEARS injects into the guest.

Figure 10 depicts the performance of the initial, proof-of-concept VNET/P Accelerator. Here, the round-trip latency and throughput is measured between a VM running on the *vtest* machine and a VM running on an adjacent machine that does not use the accelerator. We measure latency using ping with 1000 round-trips. The throughputs are measured using ttcp, where both TCP and UDP throughput are reported. We run ttcp with a 6400 byte buffer, 10000 packets sent, and a standard 1500 byte MTU. We compare accelerated VNET/P with standard VNET/P and native performance between the two host machines without virtualization or overlays.

Component	Lines of Code
vnet-virtio kernel module (Top Half)	329
vnet bridge (Bottom Half)	150
Total	479

Figure 9: Implementation complexity of prototype VNET/P Accelerator Service. The complexity given is the total number of lines of code that were changed. The numbers indicate that few changes are necessary to port VNET/P functionality into a Linux virtio driver module

Benchmark	Native	VNET/P	VNET/P Accel
Latency			
min	0.082 ms	0.255 ms	0.205 ms
avg	0.204 ms	0.475 ms	0.459 ms
max	0.403 ms	2.787 ms	2.571 ms
Throughput			
UDP	922 Mbps	901 Mbps	905 Mbps
TCP	920 Mbps	890 Mbps	898 Mbps

Figure 10: VNET/P accelerator results.

The VNET/P Accelerator achieves the same bandwidth as VNET/P, and both are as close to native as possible given that encapsulation is used. The VNET/P Accelerator achieves a modest improvement in latency compared to VNET/P (20% minimum, 3% average, 8% maximum). It is important to note that this accelerator is a proof-of-concept of using GEARS to build a guest-context service. Our next step will require guarded privileged execution of injected code, which is in progress. We should note, however, that the implementation complexity (Figure 9) will not change significantly, since guarded privileged execution is GEARS-level functionality, not service-level.

7.4 MPI accelerator

Consider an MPI application executing within a collection of VMs that may migrate due to decisions made by an administrator, an adaptive computing system, or for other reasons. The result of such migrations, or even initial allocation, may be that two VMs are co-located on the same host machine. However, the MPI application and the MPI implementation itself are oblivious to this, and will thus employ regular network communication primitives when an MPI process located in one VM communicates with an MPI process in the other. VNET/P will happily carry this communication, but performance will be sub-optimal.

Fundamentally, the communication performance in such cases is limited to the main memory copy bandwidth. Ideally, matching MPI send and receive calls on the two VMs would operate at this bandwidth. We assume here that the receiver touches all of the data. If that is not the case, the performance limit could be even higher because copy-on-write techniques might apply. The goal of the MPI Accelerator service is to do precisely this transformation of MPI sends and receives between co-located VMs into memory copy operations.

Building such an MPI Accelerator purely within the VMM would be extremely challenging because MPI send and receive calls are *library routines* that indirectly generate system calls and ultimately cause guest device driver interactions with the virtual hardware the VMM provides. It is these virtual hardware interactions that the VMM sees. In order to implement an MPI Accelerator service, it would be necessary to reconstruct the lost semantics of MPI operation. The ability to discern the MPI semantics *from the*

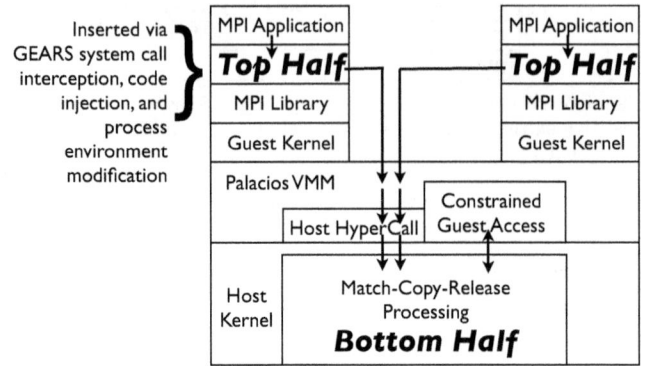

Figure 11: Implementation of the MPI Accelerator service for co-located VMs. This illustrates the fast path between an MPI_Send and its matching MPI_Recv.

guest application is the key enabler of our MPI Accelerator implementation.

GEARS provides two essential tools that the MPI Accelerator service leverages: (a) user space code injection, and (b) process environment modification. At any point during VM execution, the service uses (a) to inject and run a program that creates a file in the VM. The file contains a shared library that is an `LD_PRELOAD` wrapper for MPI. The system then uses (b) to force `exec()`s of processes to use the `LD_PRELOAD` wrapper. This can be limited to specific executables by name if desired. The wrapper installs itself between the processes and the MPI shared library such that MPI calls bind to the wrapper. The wrapper, which constitutes the top half of the service can then decide how to process each MPI call in coordination with the bottom half of the service that resides in the VMM. The top and bottom halves communicate using service-specific hypercalls.

In our prototype implementation, illustrated in Figure 11, we focus on the blocking MPI_Send and MPI_Recv calls. The top half intercepts the appropriate MPI calls as follows:

- MPI_Init() : After normal initialization processing in MPI, this call also notifies the bottom half of this MPI process, including its name, arguments, and other parameters. It registers the process for consideration with the service.
- MPI_Finalize(): Before normal de-initialization in MPI, this call notifies the bottom half that the process can be unregistered.
- MPI_Comm_rank(): After a normal ranking in MPI, this call notifies the bottom half of the process's rank.
- MPI_Send(): The wrapper checks to see if this is an MPI_Send() that the bottom half can implement. If it is not, it hands it to the MPI library. If it is, it touches each page of the data to assure it is faulted in, and then hands the send request to the bottom half and waits for it to complete the work. If the bottom half asserts that it cannot, the wrapper defaults to the MPI library call.
- MPI_Recv(): This is symmetric to MPI_Send().

The hypercalls also implicitly carry a pointer to Palacios's structures that represent the VM and the current virtual core's state, allowing ready access to the CR3 register, which contains a pointer to the current page table. This information is used to identify a guest process. It should be clear that this model can readily be extended to support a wider range of MPI functionality.

The bottom half of the service is implemented as a Linux kernel module that supplies the hypercall implementations. This module is relatively straightforward. It maintains a table of registered processes, as well as their current rank,

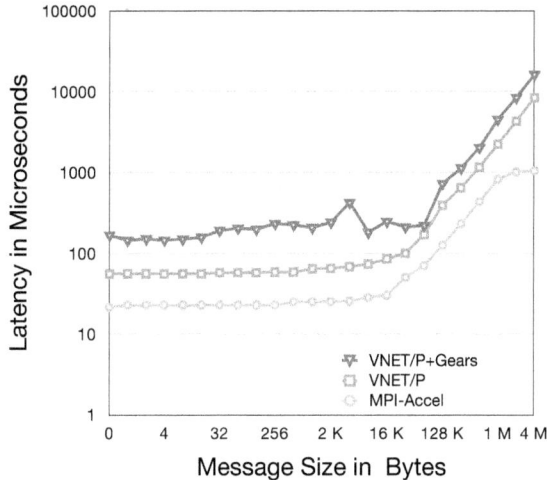

Figure 12: Performance of MPI Accelerator Service on OSU MPI Latency Benchmark running in two co-located VMs on *lewinsky* test machine. For small messages, it achieves a 22 μs latency, limited by system call interception and hypercall overheads. For large messages, the MPI accelerator approaches the maximum possible performance given the memory copy bandwidth of the machine (4.6 GB/s).

Component	Lines of Code
Preload Wrapper (Top Half)	345
Kernel Module (Bottom Half)	676
Total	1021

Figure 13: Implementation complexity of MPI Accelerator.

send state, and receive state. The table can be queried by the VM/virtual core/CR3/executable name combination that uniquely identifies registered MPI processes across all of the co-located VMs on the host. When an MPI process initiates an applicable MPI_Send, the guest exists due to the top half's hypercall, and Palacios redirects execution into the kernel module's handler. The handler attempts to find a matching pending receive. If it can, it copies the data from the guest virtual addresses in the sending VM to the guest virtual addresses in the receiving VM. It then writes the appropriate return code to the receiving thread, which waits in the kernel module as well, and subsequently releases it. Both hypercalls return to their respective guests, and the transfer is seen as complete by both of them. If the receive is not pending or no matching receive is yet available, the sender saves the send side state into its own entry in the table, marks itself as pending, and waits for the receiver. In this instance, the receiver will perform the copy operation when it arrives and then release the sender. Note that if the copy operation fails, for example, due to a guest virtual address that is not currently paged in on the guest, the copy simply stops and the error is signaled to the top half, which falls back on the MPI library to complete the transfer.

Our implementation is intended as a proof of concept demonstrating the utility of GEARS tools and advancing the overall argument of this paper. Nonetheless, it also performs quite well. We have run the OSU MPI Latency benchmark [1] (osu_latency) between two co-located VMs using VNET/P, VNET/P with the GEARS tools enabled in Palacios, and with the MPI Accelerator active. We use the MPICH2 MPI library [14] for our measurements. Our performance measurements are taken on the *lewinsky* machine, previously described. The results are shown in Figure 12. It is important to note that for larger message sizes, the message transfer time is dominated by the machine's memory bandwidth. According to the STREAM benchmark, the machine has a main memory copy bandwidth of 4.6 GB/s. Our results suggest that we approach this—specifically, the MPI latency for 4 MB messages implies a bandwidth of 4

GB/s has been achieved. For small messages the MPI latency is approximately 22 μs (about 50,000 cycles). The small message latency is limited by system call interception, exit/entry, and hypercall overheads. Here, GEARS selective system call interception is not enabled. Using it would further reduce the overhead for small messages.

The figure also shows the performance of using VNET/P for this co-located VM scenario. The "VNET/P" curve illustrates the performance of VNET/P without any GEARS features enabled. Without system call interception overheads, we see that VNET/P achieves a 56 μs latency for small messages and the large message latency is limited due to a transfer bandwidth of a respectable 500 MB/s. The "VNET/P+Gears" curve depicts VNET/P with the GEARS features enabled and illustrates the costs of non-selective system call interception. The small message latency grows to 150 μs, while the large message latency is limited due to a transfer bandwidth of 250 MB/s. In contrast to these, the MPI Accelerator Service, based on GEARS, is achieving 1/3 the latency and 8 times the bandwidth, approaching the latency limits expected due to the hypercall processing and the bandwidth limits expected due to the system's memory copy bandwidth. Note that the impact of GEARS system call interception on the MPI Accelerator's small message latency is much smaller than its impact on VNET/P. This is not a discrepancy. With the MPI Accelerator, far fewer system calls are made per byte transfered because the injected top-half intercepts each MPI library call before it can turn into multiple system calls.

Figure 13 illustrates that the service implementation is quite compact. The GEARS tools are the primary reason for the service's feasibility and compactness.

8. CONCLUSIONS AND FUTURE WORK

GEARS is a set of tools that enable the creation of *guest-context services* which span the VMM, the guest kernel and the guest application. We have shown through an implementation within the Palacios VMM that the complexity of these tools is tractable, suggesting that they could be implemented in other VMMs without great effort. GEARS in Palacios allows developers to write VMM services with relatively little knowledge of VMM internals. Further, we have shown that the implementations of the services themselves can remain relatively compact while still delivering substantial performance or functionality improvements.

We are currently investigating several aspects of guest-context services, including boundaries between guest code and code injected by the VMM. This includes the ability to safely run trusted components of a service in the guest while providing them with fully privileged hardware access. Finally, we intend to explore interfaces that provide a direct connection between the VMM and guest application.

The source code for GEARS is available as part of the open-source Palacios VMM from **v3vee.org**.

9. REFERENCES

[1] Osu micro-benchmarks. http://mvapich.cse.ohio-state.edu/benchmarks/.

[2] BARHAM, P., DRAGOVIC, B., FRASER, K., HAND, S., HARRIS, T., HO, A., NEUGEBAUER, R., PRATT, I., AND WARFIELD, A. Xen and the art of virtualization. In *ACM Symposium on Operating Systems Principles (SOSP)* (2003).

[3] BECK, F., AND FESTOR, O. Syscall interception in xen hypervisor. Technical report, Institut National Polytechnique de Lorraine (INPL), 2009.

[4] CHEN, P. M., AND NOBLE, B. D. When virtual is better than real. In *Proceedings of the Eighth Workshop on Hot Topics in Operating Systems (HotOS 2001)* (May 2001).

[5] CHEN, X., GARFINKEL, T., LEWIS, E. C., SUBRAHMANYAM, P., WALDSPURGER, C. A., BONEH, D., DWOSKIN, J., AND PORTS, D. R. Overshadow: a virtualization-based approach to retrofitting protection in commodity operating systems. In *Proceedings of the 13th international conference on Architectural support for programming languages and operating systems (ASPLOS 2008)* (March 2008).

[6] DINABURG, A., ROYAL, P., SHARIF, M., AND LEE, W. Ether: malware analysis via hardware virtualization extensions. In *Proceedings of the 15th ACM conference on Computer and communications security (CCS 2008)* (October 2008).

[7] JONES, S. T., ARPACI-DUSSEAU, A. C., AND ARPACI-DUSSEAU, R. H. Antfarm: tracking processes in a virtual machine environment. In *Proceedings of the USENIX Annual Technical Conference (USENIX ATC 2006)* (June 2006).

[8] JONES, S. T., ARPACI-DUSSEAU, A. C., AND ARPACI-DUSSEAU, R. H. Geiger: monitoring the buffer cache in a virtual machine environment. In *Proceedings of the 12th international conference on Architectural support for programming languages and operating systems (ASPLOS 2006)* (October 2006).

[9] KING, S. T., CHEN, P. M., WANG, Y.-M., VERBOWSKI, C., WANG, H. J., AND LORCH, J. R. Subvirt: Implementing malware with virtual machines. In *Proceedings of the 2006 IEEE Symposium on Security and Privacy* (May 2006).

[10] LANGE, J., PEDRETTI, K., HUDSON, T., DINDA, P., CUI, Z., XIA, L., BRIDGES, P., GOCKE, A., JACONETTE, S., LEVENHAGEN, M., AND BRIGHTWELL, R. Palacios and kitten: New high performance operating systems for scalable virtualized and native supercomputing. In *Proceedings of the 24th IEEE International Parallel and Distributed Processing Symposium (IPDPS 2010)* (April 2010).

[11] LANGE, J. R., AND DINDA, P. Symcall: symbiotic virtualization through vmm-to-guest upcalls. In *Proceedings of the 7th ACM SIGPLAN/SIGOPS international conference on Virtual execution environments (VEE 2011)* (March 2011).

[12] LANGE, J. R., DINDA, P., HALE, K. C., AND XIA, L. An introduction to the palacios virtual machine monitor—version 1.3. Tech. Rep. NWU-EECS-11-10, Department of Electrical Engineering and Computer Science, Northwestern University, November 2011.

[13] LI, B., LI, J., WO, T., HU, C., AND ZHONG, L. A vmm-based system call interposition framework for program monitoring. In *16th IEEE International Conference on Parallel and Distributed Systems (ICPADS 2010)* (December 2010).

[14] LUSK, E., DOSS, N., AND SKJELLUM, A. A high-performance, portable implementation of the mpi message passing interface standard. *Parallel Computing 22* (1996), 789–828.

[15] NGUYEN, A., SCHEAR, N., JUNG, H., GODIYAL, A., KING, S., AND NGUYEN, H. Mavmm: Lightweight and purpose built vmm for malware analysis. In *Proceedings of the Annual Computer Security Applications Conference (ACSAC 2009)* (December 2009).

[16] ONOUE, K., OYAMA, Y., AND YONEZAWA, A. Control of system calls from outside of virtual machines. In *Proceedings of the 2008 ACM symposium on Applied computing (SAC 2008)* (March 2008).

[17] PFOH, J., SCHNEIDER, C., AND ECKERT, C. Nitro: Hardware-based system call tracing for virtual machines. In *Proceedings of the International Workshop on Security (IWSEC 2011)* (November 2011).

[18] RILEY, R., JIANG, X., AND XU, D. Guest-transparent prevention of kernel rootkits with vmm-based memory shadowing. In *Proceedings of the 11th international symposium on Recent Advances in Intrusion Detection (RAID 2008)* (September 2008).

[19] RUTH, P., RHEE, J., XU, D., KENNELL, R., AND GOASGUEN, S. Autonomic live adaptation of virtual computational environments in a multi-domain infrastructure. In *Proceedings of the 3rd International Conference on Autonomic Computing (ICAC 2006)* (June 2006).

[20] SHARIF, M. I., LEE, W., CUI, W., AND LANZI, A. Secure in-vm monitoring using hardware virtualization. In *Proceedings of the ACM Conference on Computer and Communications Security (CCS 2009)* (November 2009).

[21] SUNDARARAJ, A., GUPTA, A., AND DINDA, P. Increasing application performance in virtual environments through run-time inference and adaptation. In *Proceedings of the 14th IEEE International Symposium on High Performance Distributed Computing (HPDC)* (July 2005).

[22] VASUDEVAN, A., AND YERRABALLI, R. Stealth breakpoints. In *Proceedings of the 21st Annual Computer Security Applications Conference (ACSAC)* (December 2005).

[23] XIA, L., CUI, Z., LANGE, J., TANG, Y., DINDA, P., AND BRIDGES, P. VNET/P: Bridging the cloud and high performance computing through fast overlay networking. In *Proceedings of 21st International ACM Symposium on High-Performance Parallel and Distributed Computing (HPDC 2012)* (June 2012).

[24] XU, J., AND FORTES, J. A multi-objective approach to virtual machine management in datacenters. In *Proceedings of the 8th International Conference on Autonomic Computing (ICAC 2011)* (June 2011).

When Average is Not Average: Large Response Time Fluctuations in n-Tier Systems

Qingyang Wang[1], Yasuhiko Kanemasa[2], Motoyuki Kawaba[2], Calton Pu[1]
[1]College of Computing, Georgia Institute of Technology
[2]Cloud Computing Research Center, FUJITSU LABORATORIES LTD.
[1]{qywang, calton}@cc.gatech.edu, [2]{kanemasa, kawaba}@jp.fujitsu.com

ABSTRACT

Simultaneously achieving both good performance and high resource utilization is an important goal for production cloud environments. Through extensive measurements of an n-tier application benchmark (RUBBoS), we show that the response time of an n-tier system frequently presents large scale fluctuations (e.g., ranging from tens of milliseconds up to tens of seconds) during periods of high resource utilization.

Except the factor of bursty workload from clients, we found that the large scale response time fluctuations can be caused by some system environmental conditions (e.g., L2 cache miss, JVM garbage collection, inefficient scheduling policies) that commonly exist in n-tier applications. The impact of these system environmental conditions can largely amplify the end-to-end response time fluctuations because of the complex resource dependencies in the system. For instance, a 50ms response time increase in the database tier can be amplified to 500ms end-to-end response time increase. We evaluate three heuristics to stabilize response time fluctuations while still achieving high resource utilization in the system. Our results show that large scale response time fluctuations should be taken into account when designing effective autonomous self-scaling n-tier systems in cloud environments.

Categories and Subject Descriptors

C.2.4 [**Computer-Communication Networks**]: Distributed Systems-Distributed Applications; C.4 [**Performance of Systems**]: Reliability, availability, and serviceability; H.3.4 [**Performance evaluation (efficiency and effectiveness)**]: Metrics—*complexity measures, performance measures*

Keywords

N-tier system, Web-facing applications, Performance evaluation, scalability, Soft resources, burstiness.

1. INTRODUCTION

Simultaneously achieving good performance and high resource utilization is an important goal for production cloud environments. High utilization is essential for high return on investment for cloud providers and low sharing cost for cloud users [9]. Good performance is essential for mission-critical applications, e.g., web-facing e-commerce applications with Service Level Agreement (SLA) guarantees such as bounded response time. Unfortunately, simultaneously achieving both objectives for applications that are *not* embarrassingly parallel has remained an elusive goal. Consequently, both practitioners and researchers have encountered serious difficulties in predicting response time in clouds during periods of high utilization. A practical consequence of this problem is that enterprise cloud environments have been reported to have disappointingly low average utilization (e.g., 18% in [17]).

In this paper, we describe concrete experimental evidence that shows an important contributing factor to the apparent unpredictability of cloud-based application response time when under high utilization conditions. Using extensive measurements of an n-tier benchmark (RUBBoS [1]), we found the presence of large scale response time fluctuations. These fluctuations, ranging from tens of milliseconds up to tens of seconds, appear when workloads become bursty [13], as expected of web-facing applications. The discovery of these large scale response time fluctuations is important as it will have significant impact on the autonomous performance prediction and tuning of n-tier application performance, even for moderately bursty workloads. Specifically, a distinctly bi-modal distribution with two modes (that span a spectrum of 2 to 3 orders of magnitude) can cause significant distortions on traditional statistical analyses and models of performance that assume uni-modal distributions.

One of the interesting facts that made this research challenging is that the long queries (that last several seconds) are not inherently complex in their nature, i.e., they are normal queries that would finish within tens of milliseconds when run by themselves. Under a specific (and not-so-rare) set of system environmental conditions, these queries take several seconds. The detailed analysis to reveal these system environmental conditions in an n-tier system is non-trivial considering that classical performance analysis techniques that assume uni-modal distributions are inapplicable. Our approach recorded both application level and system level metrics (e.g., response time, throughput, CPU, and disk I/O) of each tier in an n-tier system at fine-grained time granularity (e.g., 100ms). Then we analyzed the relationship

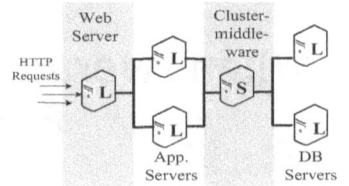

Function	Software
Web Server	Apache 2.0.54
Application Server	Apache Tomcat 5.5.17
Cluster middleware	C-JDBC 2.0.2
Database server	MySQL 5.0.51a
Sun JDK	jdk1.6.0_14
Operating system	RHEL Server 5.7 (Tikanga)
System monitor	Sysstat 10.0.02, Collectl 3.5.1
Transaction monitor	Fujitsu SysViz

(a) Software setup

Hardware	Processor			Memory	Disk	Network
	# cores	Freq.	L2 Cache			
Large (L)	2	2.27GHz	2M	2GB	200GB	1Gbps
Medium (M)	1	2.4 GHz	4M	2GB	200GB	1Gbps
Small (S)	1	2.26GHz	512k	1GB	80GB	1Gbps

(b) Hardware node setup

(c) 1L/2L/1S/2L sample topology

Figure 1: Details of the experimental setup.

of these metrics among each tier to identify the often shifting and sometimes mutually dependent bottlenecks. The complexity of this phenomenon is illustrated by a sensitivity study of soft resource allocation (e.g., number of threads in the web and application servers and DB connection pool) on system performance and resource utilization.

The first contribution of the paper is an experimental illustration of the large scale response time fluctuations of systems under high resource utilization conditions using the n-tier RUBBoS benchmark. Due to the large fluctuations, the average system response time is not representative of the actual system performance. For instance, when the system is under a moderately bursty workload and the average utilization of the bottleneck resource (e.g., MySQL CPU) is around 90%, the end-to-end response time shows a distinctly bi-modal distribution (Section 2.2).

The second contribution of the paper is a detailed analysis of several system environmental conditions that cause the large scale response time fluctuations. For instance, some transient events (e.g., CPU overhead caused by L2 cache miss or Java GC, see Section 4.1) in the tier under high resource utilization conditions significantly impact the response time fluctuations of the tier. Then the in-tier response time fluctuations is amplified to the end-to-end response time due to the complex resource dependencies across tiers in the system (Section 4.2). We also found that the operating system (OS) level "best" scheduling policy in each individual tier of an n-tier system may not achieve the best overall application level response time (Section 4.3).

The third contribution of the paper is a practical solution for stabilizing the large scale response time fluctuations of systems under high resource utilization conditions (Section 5). For instance, our experimental results show that the CPU overhead caused by transient events can be reduced by limiting the concurrency of request processing in the bottleneck tier (heuristic ii) while the limitations of OS level scheduling policies can be overcome through application level transaction scheduling (heuristic i).

The rest of the paper is organized as follows. Section 2 shows the large scale response time fluctuations using a concrete example. Section 3 illustrates our fine-grained monitoring analysis. Section 4 shows some system environmental conditions for the large scale response time fluctuations. Section 5 explains three heuristics in detail. Section 6 summarizes the related work and Section 7 concludes the paper.

2. BACKGROUND AND MOTIVATION

2.1 Background Information

In our experiments we adopt the RUBBoS n-tier benchmark, based on bulletin board applications such as Slashdot [1]. RUBBoS can be configured as a three-tier (web

server, application server, and database server) or four-tier (addition of clustering middleware such as C-JDBC [11]) system. The workload includes 24 different interactions such as "register user" or "view story". The benchmark includes two kinds of workload modes: browse-only and read/write interaction mixes. We use browse-only workload in this paper.

Mi et al. [13] proposed a *bursty workload generator* which takes into account the Slashdot effect, where a web page linked by a popular blog or media site suddenly experiences a huge increase in web traffic. Unlike the original workload generator which generates a request rate that follows a Poisson distribution parameterized by a number of emulated browsers and a fixed user think time E[Z], the bursty workload generator generates request rates in two modes: a fast mode with short user think time and a slow mode with long user think time. The fast mode simulates the Slashdot effect where the workload generator generates traffic surges for the system. The bursty workload generator uses one parameter to characterize the intensity of the traffic surges: *index of dispersion*, which is abbreviated as I. The larger the I is, the longer the duration of the traffic surge. In this paper, we use both the original workload generator (with $I = 1$) and the bursty workload generator (with $I = 100, 400$, and 1000) to evaluate the system performance.

Figure 1 outlines the details of the experimental setup. We carry out the experiments by allocating a dedicated physical node to each server. A four-digit notation $\#W/\#A/\#C/\#D$ is used to denote the number of web servers, application servers, clustering middleware servers, and database servers. We have three types of hardware nodes: "L", "M", and "S", each of which represents a different level of processing power. Figure 1(c) shows a sample 1L/2L/1S/2L topology. Hardware resource utilization measurements are taken during the runtime period using collectl at different time granularity. We use Fujitsu SysViz [3], a prototype tool developed by Fujitsu laboratories, as a transaction monitor to precisely measure the response time and the number of concurrent requests in each short time window (e.g., every 100ms) with respect to each tier of an n-tier system.

2.2 Motivation

In this section, we give one example to show that the average of measured performance metrics may not be representative of the actual system performance perceived by clients when the system is under high utilization conditions. The results shown here are based on 10-minute runtime experiments of RUBBoS benchmark running in a four-tier system (see Figure 1(c)) with different burstiness levels of workload.

Figure 2 shows the system response time distribution with four different burstiness levels of workload. The sum of the value of each bar in a subfigure is the total system throughput. We note that in all these four cases, the CPU utilization

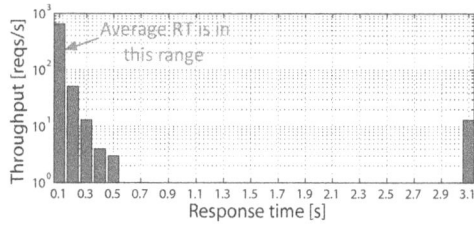

(a) $I = 1$ (original workload generator); average RT = 0.068s

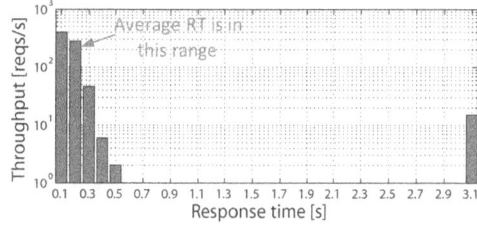

(b) $I = 100$; average RT = 0.189s

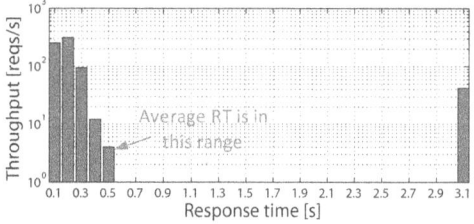

(c) $I = 400$; average RT = 0.439s

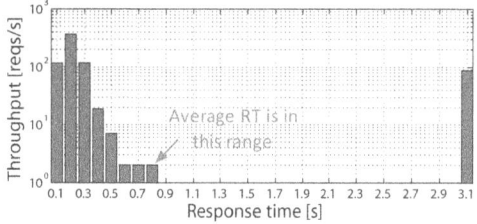

(d) $I = 1000$; average RT = 0.776s

Figure 2: End-to-end response time distribution of the system in workload 5200 with different burstiness levels; the average CPU utilization of the bottleneck server is 90% in 10 minutes runtime experiments for all the four cases.

of the bottleneck server (the CJDBC server) of the system is 90%. This figure shows that the response time distribution in each of these four cases has a distinctly bi-modal characteristic; while majority of requests from clients finish within a few hundreds of milliseconds, a few percentage finish longer than three seconds. Furthermore, this figure shows the more bursty the workload, the more requests there will be with response time longer than 3 seconds.

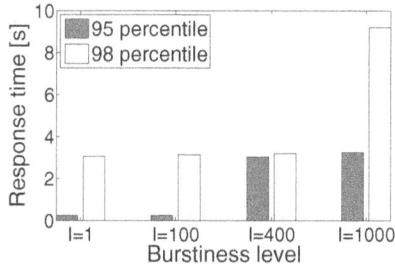

Figure 3: The percentiles of system response time in workload 5200 with different burstiness levels.

Large scale response time fluctuations have significant negative impact on the performance of a system requiring strict Service Level Agreement (SLA) guarantees such as bounded response time. Figure 3 shows the 95- and 98-percentiles of the end-to-end response time under different levels of bursty workload. For the original workload ($I = 1$) case and the bursty workload ($I = 100$) case, the 95th percentile is very low (less than 200ms) while the 98th percentile is over 3 seconds. As the burstiness level of workload increases, even the 95-percentile's response time is beyond 3 seconds, and the 98-percentile's for bursty workload ($I = 1000$) case exceeds 9 seconds. Some web-facing applications have strict response time requirement, for example, Google requires clients' requests to be processed within one second [2]. Thus, response time with large scale fluctuations may lead to severe SLA violations though the average response time is small.

3. FINE-GRAINED ANALYSIS FOR LARGE RESPONSE TIME FLUCTUATIONS

In this section we show the cause of the distinctly bi-modal response time distribution as introduced in the motivation case through fine-grained analysis. The results here are based on the same configuration as shown in the motivation case. We use the original workload generator ($I = 1$), which is an extension analysis for the case as shown in Figure 2(a).

Figure 4(a) shows the average throughput and response time of the system from workload 5000 to 5800. The response time distribution shown in Figure 2(a) is based on the result of workload 5200, where the average response time is 0.068s and the average CPU utilization of CJDBC server is about 90% (see Figure 4(d)). Next, we zoom in the highly aggregated average of the application/system metrics measured in workload 5200 through fine-grained analysis.

Figure 4(b) and 4(c) show the average system response time and throughput aggregated at 100ms and 10s time granularities respectively. Figure 4(b) shows both the system response time and throughput present large fluctuations while such fluctuations are highly blurred when 10 second time granularity is used (Figure 4(c)). Figure 4(e) and 4(f) show the similar graphs for the CJDBC (the bottleneck server) CPU utilization. Figure 4(e) shows the CJDBC CPU frequently reaches 100% utilization if monitored at 100ms granularity while such CPU saturation disappears if 10s time granularity is used [1].

Figure 4(h) and 4(i) show the number of concurrent requests on the Apache web server aggregated at 100ms and 10s time granularity in workload 5200. Concurrent requests on a server refer to the requests that have arrived, but have not departed from the server; these requests are being processed concurrently by the server due to the multi-threading architecture adopted by most modern internet server designs (e.g., Apache, Tomcat, and MySQL). We note that the

---

[1] 10 seconds or even longer control interval is frequently used in automatic self-scaling systems [5, 12, 15, 20].

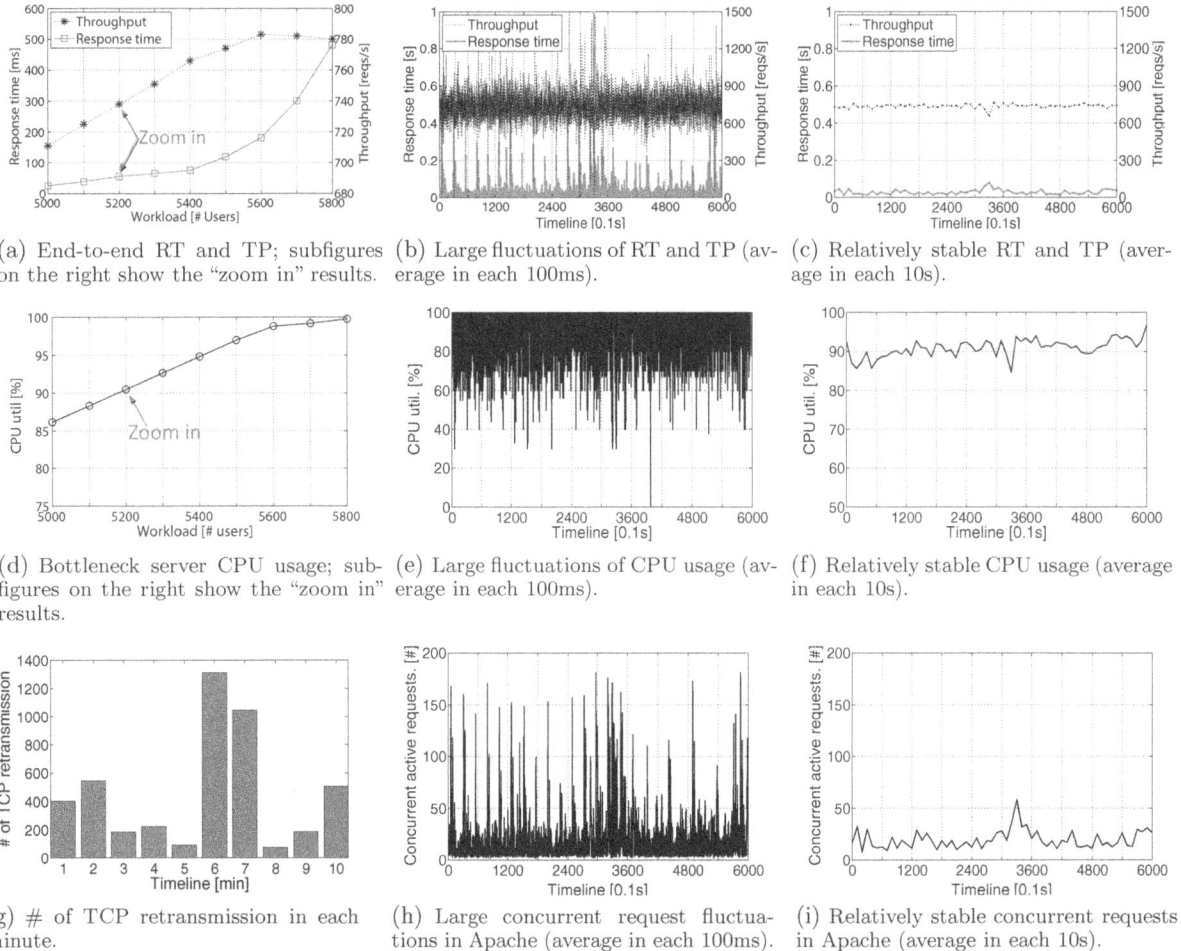

(a) End-to-end RT and TP; subfigures on the right show the "zoom in" results.

(b) Large fluctuations of RT and TP (average in each 100ms).

(c) Relatively stable RT and TP (average in each 10s).

(d) Bottleneck server CPU usage; subfigures on the right show the "zoom in" results.

(e) Large fluctuations of CPU usage (average in each 100ms).

(f) Relatively stable CPU usage (average in each 10s).

(g) # of TCP retransmission in each minute.

(h) Large concurrent request fluctuations in Apache (average in each 100ms).

(i) Relatively stable concurrent requests in Apache (average in each 10s).

Figure 4: Analysis of system/application level metrics for the large response time fluctuations of the system (1L/2L/1S/2L config.). Requests with long response time are caused by TCP transmissions as shown in subfigure (g), which are caused by the large fluctuations of concurrent requests in Apache web tier as shown in subfigure (h).

thread pool size we set for the Apache web server in this set of experiments is 50; considering the underlying operating system has a buffer (TCP backlog, the default size is 128) for incoming TCP connection requests from clients, the maximum number of concurrent requests the Apache web server can handle is 178. Once the server reaches the limit, the new incoming requests will be dropped and TCP retransmission happens, which causes the long response time perceived by a client [2]. Figure 4(h) shows that the concurrent requests, if aggregated at 100ms time granularity, frequently present high peaks which are close to the limit. Such high peaks cause large number of TCP retransmissions as shown in Figure 4(g), which counts the number of TCP retransmissions in every minute during the 10-minute runtime experiment.

3.1 Sensitivity Analysis of Large Fluctuations with Different Bursty Workloads

System administrators may want to know under which workload(s) the large scale response time fluctuations happen. Table 1 shows the minimum workload (with different

---

[2] TCP retransmission is transparent to clients; the waiting time is three seconds for the first time and is exponentially increased for the consecutive retransmissions (RFC 2988).

Burstiness level	Threshold WL	Bottleneck server CPU util.
$I = 1$	5000	88.1%
$I = 100$	4800	86.3%
$I = 400$	4400	80.4%
$I = 1000$	3800	74.6%

Table 1: Workload (with different burstiness levels) beyond which more than 1% TCP retransmission happens.

burstiness levels) under which the system has at least 1% requests that encounter TCP retransmissions. This table shows that both the threshold workload and the corresponding average CPU utilization of the bottleneck server decrease as the burstiness level of workload increases. This further justifies that the evaluation of the large scale response time fluctuations using fine-grained monitoring is an important and necessary step in autonomic system design.

4. SYSTEM CONDITIONS FOR LARGE RESPONSE TIME FLUCTUATIONS

Understanding the exact causes of large scale response time fluctuations of an n-tier system under high utilization conditions is important to efficiently utilize the system resources while achieving good performance. In this section we will discuss some system environmental conditions that cause large scale response time fluctuations even under the moderately bursty workload from clients. We note that all the experimental results in this section are based on the original RUBBoS browse-only workload ($I = 1$).

4.1 Impact of Transient Events

Transient events are events that are pervasive but only happen from time to time in computer systems, such as L2 cache miss, JVM GC, page fault, etc. In this section we will show two types of transient events, L2 cache miss (the last level cache) and JVM GC, that cause significant overhead to the bottleneck resource in the system, especially when the bottleneck tier is in high concurrency of request processing.

4.1.1 CPU overhead caused by L2 cache misses

For modern computer architectures, caching effectiveness is one of the key factors for system performance [8, 14]. We found that the number of L2 cache misses of the bottleneck server in an n-tier system increases *nonlinearly* as workload increases, especially when the system is under high utilization conditions. Thus the CPU overhead caused by L2 cache misses significantly impacts the large scale response time fluctuations of the system.

The hardware configuration of the experiments in this section is 1L/2L/1M (one Apache and two Tomcats on the type "L" machine, and one MySQL on the type "M" machine). Under this configuration, the MySQL server CPU is the bottleneck of the system. We choose the "M" type machine for MySQL as the corresponding Intel $Core^{TM}2$ CPU has two CPU performance counters which allow us to monitor the L2 cache misses during the experiment.

Figure 5(a) shows the MySQL CPU utilization as workload increases from 1200 to 4600 at a 200 increment per step. Ideally the MySQL CPU should increase linearly as workload increases until saturation if there is no CPU overhead. However, this figure clearly shows that the CPU overhead increases nonlinearly as workload increases, especially in high workload range. In order to quantify the CPU overhead and simplify our analysis, we make one assumption here: MySQL has no CPU overhead for request processing from workload 0 to workload 1200 (our starting workload). Under this assumption, we can quantify the CPU overhead for the following increasing workloads by measuring the distance between the actual CPU utilization and the ideal CPU utilization. For instance, under workload 4600, the MySQL CPU overhead reaches 45%.

Figure 5(b) shows the correlation between the number of L2 cache misses of MySQL and the corresponding CPU overhead from workload 1200 to 4600. The CPU overhead is calculated as shown in Figure 5(a) and the number of L2 cache misses in MySQL is recorded using the CPU performance counter [3] during the runtime experiments. This figure shows that the L2 cache misses and the corresponding CPU overhead are almost linearly correlated; thus higher L2 cache misses indicate higher CPU overhead.

One more interesting phenomenon we found is that the CPU overhead caused by L2 cache misses can be effectively reduced by limiting the concurrency level of request processing in the bottleneck server. Table 2 shows the comparison of CPU utilization and L2 cache misses under two different DB

---

[3] The CPU performance counter increases by 1 for 6000 L2 cache misses in our environmental settings.

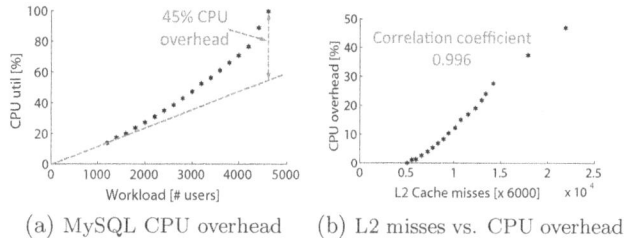

(a) MySQL CPU overhead (b) L2 misses vs. CPU overhead

Figure 5: CPU overhead caused by L2 cache misses.

WL	DBconn12			DBconn2		
	TP (req/s)	CPU util (%)	L2 miss (×6000)	TP (req/s)	CPU util (%)	L2 miss (×6000)
1200	168	13.8	5036	169	13.6	4704
2400	340	34.9	8320	340	34.6	8153
3600	510	61.0	12304	510	60.2	11233
3800	538	66.1	12963	536	64.5	11968
4200	595	76.6	14204	595	74.8	13053
4600	642	99.6	21868	650	86.2	14133

Table 2: Comparison of MySQL CPU utilization and L2 cache misses between DBconn12 and DBconn2 with 1L/2L/1M configuration; higher concurrency leads to more L2 cache misses in the bottleneck tier (MySQL).

connection pool sizes in Tomcat: DBconn12 and DBconn2. In the current RUBBoS implementation, each Servlet has its own local DB connection pool; DBconn12 means the DB connection pool size for each Servlet is 12 while DBconn2 means 2. This table shows that although the throughputs of these two cases are similar under different workloads, the DBconn2 case has less CPU utilization and less L2 cache misses in MySQL than the DBconn12 case, especially in the high workload range. We note that the DB connection pools in Tomcat controls the number of active threads in MySQL. In the DBconn12 case under high workload more concurrent requests are sent to the MySQL server, thus more concurrently active threads are created in MySQL and contend for the limited space of L2 cache causing more cache misses and CPU overhead than those in the DBconn2 case.

4.1.2 CPU overhead caused by Java GC

For Java-based servers like Tomcat and CJDBC, the JVM garbage collection process impacts the system response time fluctuations in two ways: first, the CPU time used by the garbage collector cannot be used for request processing; second, the JVM uses a synchronous garbage collector and it waits during the garbage collection period, only starting to process requests after the garbage collection is finished [4]. This delay significantly lengthens the pending requests and causes fluctuations in system response time.

Our measurements show that when a Java-based server is highly utilized, the JVM GCs of the server increase *nonlinearly* as workload increases. The hardware configuration of the experiments in this section is 1L/2L/1S/2L (see Figure 1(c)). Under this configuration, the CJDBC CPU is the bottleneck of the system. We note that the CJDBC server is a Java-based DB clustering middleware; each time a Tomcat server establishes a connection to the CJDBC server, which balances the load among the DB servers, a thread is created by CJDBC to route the SQL query to a DB server.

Table 3 compares the CPU utilization and the total GC time of the CJDBC server during the runtime experiments

WL	DBconn24			DBconn2		
	TP (req/s)	CPU util (%)	GC (s)	TP (req/s)	CPU util (%)	GC (s)
3000	428	49.6	0.05	428	49.2	0.05
4000	572	69.0	0.07	571	68.8	0.07
5000	721	**86.1**	**1.06**	719	**84.8**	0.19
5200	738	**91.2**	**1.51**	737	**87.4**	0.37
5400	759	**94.3**	**1.72**	767	**91.1**	0.40
5600	779	**98.8**	**2.15**	795	**96.6**	0.45

Table 3: Comparison of CJDBC CPU utilization and JVM GC time between DBconn24 and DBconn2 with 1L/2L/1S/2L configuration; higher concurrency leads to longer JVM GC time in the bottleneck tier (CJDBC).

between the cases DBconn24 and DBconn2 from workload 3000 to 5600. This table shows that the total GC time for both the two cases increases nonlinearly as workload increases, especially when the CJDBC CPU approaches saturation. One reason is that when the CJDBC CPU approaches saturation, the available CPU for GC shrinks; thus cleaning the same amount of garbage takes longer time than in the non-saturation situation. Accordingly, the impact of JVM GC on system response time fluctuations is more significant when CJDBC approaches saturation.

Table 3 also shows that the total GC time of the CJDBC server in the DBconn24 case is longer than that in the DBconn2 case from workload 5000 to 5600. The reason is similar to the L2 cache miss case as introduced in Section 4.1.1. Compared to the DBconn2 case, the Tomcat App tier in the DBconn24 case is able to send more concurrent requests to the CJDBC server under high workload, which in turn creates more concurrent threads for query routing and consumes more memory. Thus the CJDBC server performs more GCs for cleaning garbage in memory in the DBconn24 case than that in the DBconn2 case.

4.2 Fluctuation Amplification Effect in n-Tier Systems

Unlike some embarrassingly parallel "web indexing" applications using MapReduce and Hadoop, an n-tier application is unique in its amplification effect among different tiers due to the complex resource dependencies in the system. For instance, small request rate fluctuations from clients can be amplified to a bottom tier (e.g., DB tier), which causes significant response time fluctuation in the bottom tier; on the other hand, response time fluctuations in the bottom tier can be amplified to the front tiers.

4.2.1 Top-down request rate fluctuation amplification

The traffic for an n-tier system is, by nature, bursty [13]. One interesting phenomenon we found is that the bursty request rate from clients can be amplified to the bottom tier of the system. Except for the impact of transient events such as JVM GC, the complexity of inter-tier interactions of an n-tier system contributes most to the amplification effect. For example, a client's HTTP request may trigger multiple interactions between the application server tier and the DB tier to retrieve all the dynamic content to construct the web page requested by the client (We define the entire process as a client *transaction*).

Figure 6 shows the approximately instant request rate (aggregate at every 100ms) received by the Apache web tier and the MySQL DB tier of a three tier system (1L/2L/1L) in

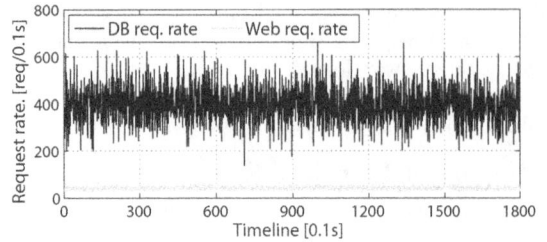

Figure 6: Amplified request rate fluctuation from the web tier to the DB tier with 1L/2L/1L configuration in WL 3000.

Req. Rate (req/0.1s)	Web	App	DB
Mean	42.88	41.12	397.40
Std. Deviation	6.71	6.53	77.70
Coefficient of Variance.	**0.16**	0.16	**0.20**

Table 4: Statistic analysis of top-down request rate fluctuation amplification (corresponds to Figure 6).

workload 3000. This figure shows that the request rate fluctuation in the MySQL tier is significantly larger than that in the Apache web tier. Table 4 shows the statistical analysis result of the amplification effect corresponding to Figure 6. This table shows three values related to the request rate for each tier: mean, standard deviation, and coefficient of variation (CV) [4]. Comparing the mean request rate between the web tier and the DB tier, one HTTP request can trigger 9.3 database accesses on average, which explains why the instant DB request rate is much higher than the instant Web request rate; second, the CV of the request rate in the DB tier (0.20) is larger than that in the web tier (0.16), which shows the effect of request rate fluctuation amplification from the web tier to the DB tier.

4.2.2 Bottom-up response time fluctuation amplification

Due to the top-down request rate fluctuation amplification and also the interference of transient events, the response time of the bottom tier in an n-tier system naturally fluctuates. We found that even small response time fluctuations in the bottom tier can be amplified to the front tiers due to the following two reasons.

First, the complex soft resource dependencies among tiers may cause requests to queue in front tiers before they reach the bottom tier, which increases the waiting time of transaction execution. Soft resources refer to system software components such as threads, TCP connections, and DB connections [19]. In an n-tier system, every two consecutive tiers in an n-tier system are connected through soft resources during the long invocation chain of transaction execution in the system. For example, the Tomcat App tier connects to the MySQL tier through DB connections. Such connections are usually limited soft resources; once soft resources in a tier run out, the new requests coming to the tier have to queue in the tier until they get the released soft resources by other finished requests in the same tier. We note that for a RPC-style n-tier system, a request in a front tier releases soft resources (e.g., a processing thread) in the tier until

---

[4]Coefficient of variation means normalized standard deviation, which is standard deviation divided by mean.

Browse–only mix transactions

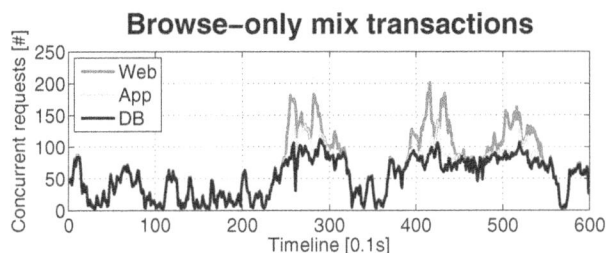

(a) Approximately instant # of concurrent requests in each tier

ViewStory transactions

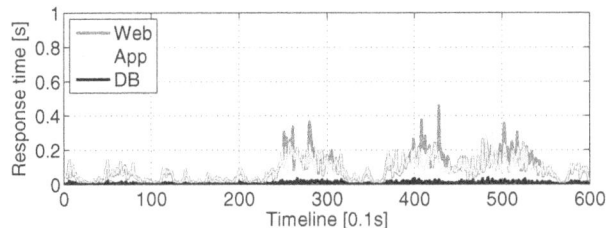

(b) Approximately instant # of concurrent ViewStory requests in each tier

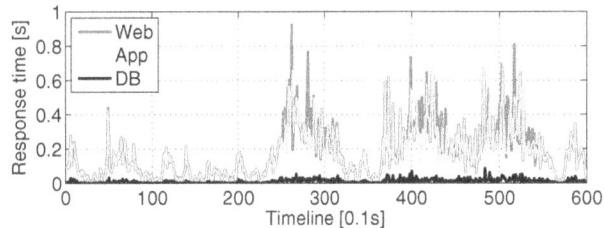

(c) Approximately instant response time in each tier

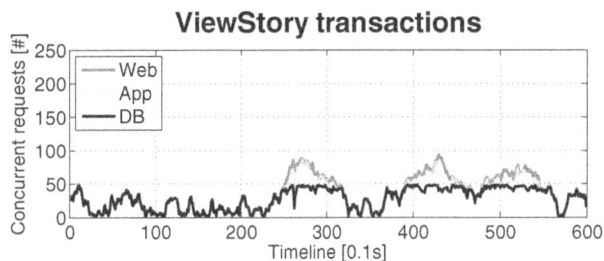

(d) Approximately instant response time for ViewStory requests in each tier

Figure 7: Amplified response time fluctuations from the DB tier to the web tier with 1L/2L/1L (DBconn24) configuration in WL 5400.

the downstream tiers finish all the processing for the corresponding transaction. Accordingly, long response times in the bottom tier may lead to the saturation of soft resources (and thus a large number of queued requests) in front tiers.

Figure 7(a) shows the approximately instant number of concurrent requests (aggregated every 100ms) in each tier of a three-tier system (1L/2L/1L, MySQL is the bottleneck tier) under workload 5400. This figure shows that when the number of concurrent requests in MySQL reaches about 90, requests start to queue in the front tiers due to the scarcity of DB connections in Tomcat. Figure 7(c) shows the approximately instant response time in each tier. This figure shows that very small response time fluctuations (within 50ms) in MySQL lead to large response time fluctuations in Tomcat and Apache; the high peaks of response time in Figure 7(c) match well with the high peaks of queued requests in front tiers as shown in Figure 7(a). This indicates the waiting time of requests in front tiers largely contributes to the long response time of transaction execution.

Second, multi-interactions between tiers of an n-tier system amplify the bottom-up response time fluctuations. In an n-tier system it is natural that some transactions involve more interactions between different tiers than the other transactions. For example, in the RUBBoS benchmark, a ViewStory request triggers an average of twelve interactions between Tomcat and MySQL; a small response time increment in MySQL leads to a largely amplified response time in Tomcat and thus longer occupation time of soft resources in Tomcat. In such case, soft resources such as DB connections in Tomcat are more likely to run out, which leads to longer waiting time of the queued requests in Tomcat.

Figure 7(b) and 7(d) show the similar graphs as shown in Figure 7(a) and 7(c), but only for ViewStory transactions. Compared to Figure 7(c), Figure 7(d) shows that the response time of ViewStory requests in the Apache tier fluctuates more significantly. This is because ViewStory requests involve more interactions between Tomcat and MySQL than

the average and run out their local DB connections earlier than the other types of requests; thus new incoming ViewStory requests have to wait longer in the Tomcat App tier (or in the Apache web tier if the connection resources between Apache and Tomcat also run out).

4.3 Impact of Mix-Transactions Scheduling in n-Tier Systems

Scheduling polices impacting web server performance have been widely studied [10, 16]. These previous works mainly focus on a single web server and show that the performance can be dramatically improved via a kernel-level modification by changing the scheduling policy from the standard FAIR (processor-sharing) scheduling to SJF (shortest-job-first) scheduling. However, for more complex n-tier systems where a completion of a client transaction involves complex interactions among tiers, the best OS level scheduling policy may increase the overall transaction response time.

The main reason for this is because the operating system of each individual server in an n-tier system cannot distinguish heavy transactions from light transactions without application level knowledge. A transaction being heavier than a light transaction can be caused by the heavy transaction having more interactions between different tiers than the light one. However, in each individual interaction the processing time of the involved tiers for a heavy transaction can be even smaller than that for a light transaction. Since the operating system of a tier can only schedule a job based on the processing time of the current interaction, applying SJF scheduling policy to the operating system of each tier may actually delay the application level light transactions.

Figure 8 shows sample interactions between a Tomcat App tier and a MySQL tier for a ViewStory transaction (heavy) and a StoryOfTheDay transaction (light) specified in the RUBBoS benchmark. A ViewStory transaction involves multiple interactions between Tomcat and MySQL (see Figure 8(a)) while a StoryOfTheDay transaction in-

(a) A sample ViewStory (heavy) transaction processing

(b) A sample StoryOfTheDay (light) transaction processing

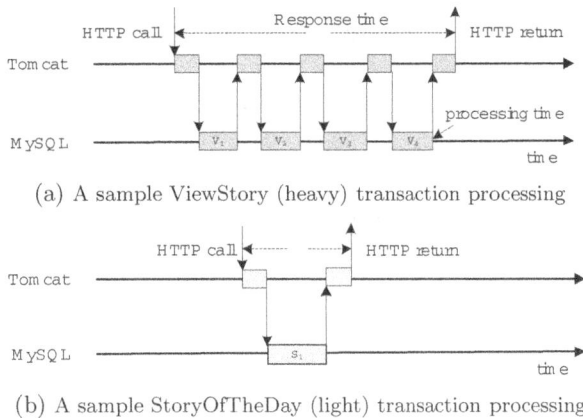

Figure 8: ViewStory vs. StoryofTheDay, different interaction pattern between Tomcat and MySQL.

volves only one interaction (see Figure 8(b)). Suppose MySQL is the bottleneck tier. Our measurements show that a single query from a ViewStory transaction has similar execution time in MySQL as a query from a StoryOfTheDay transaction. During each interaction, a thread in the MySQL tier receives a query from Tomcat and returns a response after the query processing, regardless of which servlet sends the query. From MySQL's perspective, MySQL cannot distinguish which transaction is heavy and which transaction is light. Thus either FAIR or SJF scheduling in the MySQL tier can delay the processing of the light transactions.

We note that once the waiting time of queries from light transactions increases in MySQL, the total number of queued light requests in upper tiers also increases. Since each queued request (regardless if entailing heavy or light transactions) in upper tiers occupies soft resources such as threads and connections, soft resources in upper tiers are more likely to run out under high workload. In this case, the response time fluctuations in a bottom tier are more likely to amplified to upper tiers (see Section 4.2.2).

5. SOLUTION AND EVALUATION

So far we have discussed some system environmental conditions causing the large scale response time fluctuations under high utilization conditions and explained the unique amplification effect inside an n-tier system. In this section we will evaluate three heuristics to help stabilizing the large scale response time fluctuations.

Heuristic (i): *We need to give higher priority to light transactions than heavy transactions to minimize the total amount of waiting time in the whole n-tier system. We need to schedule transactions in an upper tier which can distinguish light transactions from heavy transactions.*

Heuristic (i) is essentially an extension of applying the SJF scheduling policy in the context of n-tier systems. Suppose the MySQL tier is the bottleneck tier; as explained in section 4.3, applying SJF scheduling policy to MySQL through the kernel-level modification may not reduce the overall system response time because MySQL cannot distinguish application level heavy transactions and light transactions. Thus we need to schedule transactions in an upper tier that can make such distinction in order to apply SJF scheduling policy properly in an n-tier system. We define such scheduling as cross-tier-priority (CTP) based scheduling.

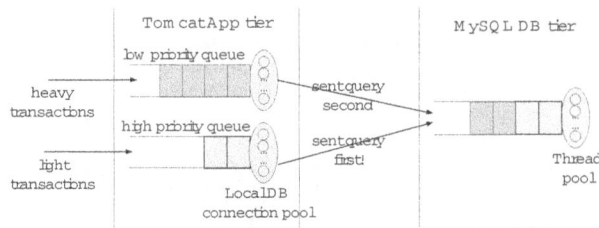

Figure 9: Illustration of applying CTP scheduling policy across tiers (only 2 servlets shown).

Figure 9 illustrates how to apply the CTP scheduling to a simple two-tier system. This figure shows only requests for two servlets (the RUBBoS browse-only workload consists of requests for eight servlets): ViewStory (heavy) and StoryOfTheDay (light). Once ViewStory requests and StoryOfTheDay requests reach the Tomcat App tier at the same time, we give StoryOfTheDay requests higher priority to send queries to MySQL. In this case the waiting time of the light StoryOfTheDay transactions can be reduced and the overall waiting time for all transactions is reduced [5].

Figure 10 shows the response time stabilization by applying the CTP scheduling to a three-tier system (1L/2L/1L with DBconn2) in workload 5800. Under this configuration, the MySQL CPU is the bottleneck in the system. Figure 10(a) and 10(c) show the results of the original RUBBoS implementation (using the default OS level scheduling) and Figure 10(b) and 10(d) show the results after the CTP scheduling is applied to the Tomcat App tier and the MySQL DB tier (see Figure 9).

Figure 10(a) and Figure 10(b) show the number of concurrent requests in each tier of the three-tier system for these two cases. Although in both cases the number of concurrent requests in the MySQL tier is very small (around eight), the fluctuations of the number of concurrent requests in the Tomcat App tier and the Apache web tier are much higher in the original case than those in the CTP scheduling case. This is because in the original case more light requests are queued in the upper tiers due to the increased waiting time of light requests in the MySQL tier.

Figure 10(c) and Figure 10(d) show that the approximately instant response time in the Apache web tier in the original case has much larger fluctuations than that in the CTP scheduling case, which validates that CTP scheduling actually reduces the overall waiting time of all transactions in the system. In fact the high peaks of response time in these two figures perfectly matches the high peaks of the number of queued requests in upper tiers as shown in Figure 10(a) and Figure 10(b).

Heuristic (ii): *We need to restrict the number of concurrent requests to avoid overhead caused by high concurrency in the bottleneck tier.*

Heuristic (ii) is illustrated by Figure 11. The hardware configuration is 1L/2L/1S/2L where the CJDBC server CPU is the bottleneck of the system. We choose DBconn24 and DBconn2 for each servlet in Tomcat; the CPU utilization and JVM GC time of the CJDBC server under different workloads are shown in Table 3.

Figure 11(a) and 11(b) show the approximately instant

---

[5]Heavy transactions are only negligibly penalized or not penalized at all as a result of SJF-based scheduling [10].

Original DBconn2 Case

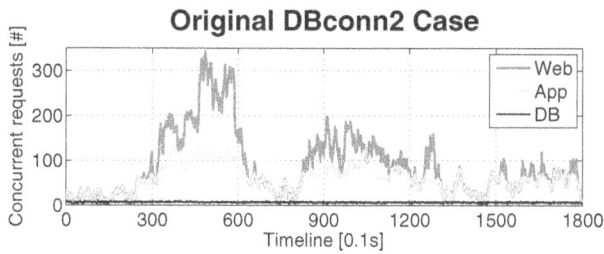

(a) Approximately instant # of concurrent requests in each tier

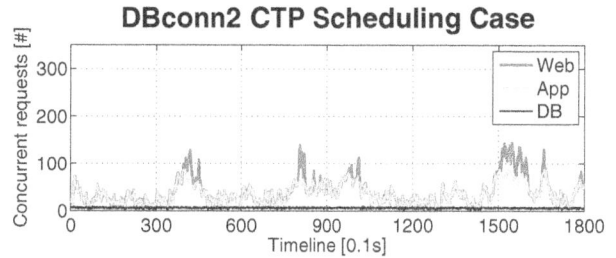

DBconn2 CTP Scheduling Case

(b) Approximately instant # of concurrent requests in each tier

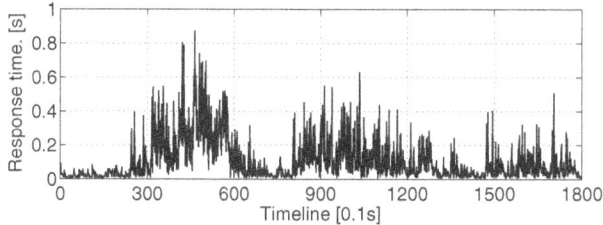

(c) Approximately instant response time in Apache web tier

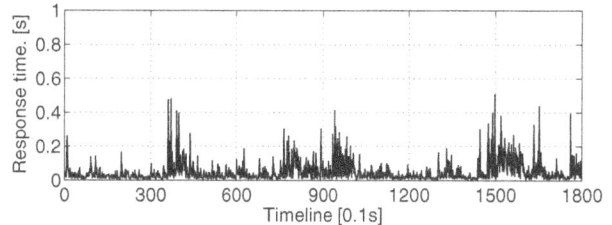

(d) Approximately instant response time in Apache web tier

Figure 10: Response time stabilization by applying CTP scheduling in 1L/2L/1L configuration in WL 5800.

response time in the Apache web tier for the DBconn24 case and the DBconn2 case in workload 5600 respectively. These two figures show that the response time in the DBconn24 case present much larger fluctuations than that in the DB-conn2 case. As shown in Table 3, the DBconn24 case in workload 5600 has significantly longer JVM GC and high CPU utilization in CJDBC than those in the DBconn2 case. This set of results clearly shows that higher concurrency in the bottleneck tier causes many more transient events such as JVM GC, which in turn cause more CPU overhead in the tier and lead to large end-to-end response time fluctuations.

We note that lower concurrency in the bottleneck tier is not always better; too low concurrency in the bottleneck tier may under-utilize the hardware resource in the tier and degrade the overall system performance. Interested readers can refer to [19] for more information.

Heuristic (iii): *We need to allocate enough amount of soft resources in front tiers (e.g., web tier) to buffer large fluctuations of concurrent requests and avoid TCP retransmission.*

This heuristic is illustrated in the motivation case. Though the average concurrent requests over a long time window is low (see Figure 4(i)), the approximately instant concurrent requests may present high peaks that can be 10 times higher than the average (see Figure 4(h)) due to the impact of system environmental conditions discussed in this paper. Thus, allocating a large number of soft resources in front tiers is necessary to buffer such high peaks of concurrent requests and avoid TCP retransmission. A reasonable allocation should also be hardware dependent since soft resources consume hardware resources such as memory.

6. RELATED WORK

Autonomic self-scaling n-tier systems based on elastic workload in cloud for both good performance and resource efficiency has been studied intensively before [12, 15, 20, 21]. The main idea of these previous works is to propose adaptive control to manage application performance in cloud by combining service providers' SLA specifications (e.g., bounded

response time) and virtual resource utilization thresholds. Based on the average of the monitored metrics (e.g., response time, CPU) over a period of time (a control interval), the controller of the system allocates necessary hardware resources to the bottleneck tier of the system once the target threshold is violated. However, how long a proper control interval should be is an open question and sometimes difficult to determine. As shown in this paper, the average of monitored metrics based on inappropriately long control intervals may blur the large performance fluctuations caused by factors such as bursty workload or JVM GC.

The performance impact of bursty workloads for the target n-tier system has been studied before. The authors in [6, 13] observed that while the system CPU utilization may be low at a coarse time granularity, it fluctuates significantly if observed at a finer time granularity, and such large fluctuation significantly impacts the n-tier system response time. Different from the previous works which mainly focus on bursty workload, we focus more on system aspects such as JVM GC, scheduling policy, and fluctuation amplification effects in n-tier systems. As shown in this paper, system response time presents large scale fluctuations due to these factors even under the moderately bursty workload.

Analytical models have been proposed for performance prediction and capacity planning of n-tier systems. Chen et al. [7] present a multi-station queuing network model with regression analysis to translate the service providers' SLA specifications to lower-level policies with the purpose of optimizing resource usage of an n-tier system. Thereska et al. [18] propose a queuing modeling architecture for clustered storage systems which constructs the model during the system design and continuously refines the model during operation for better accuracy due to the changes of system. Though these models have been shown to work well for particular domains, they are constrained by rigid assumptions such as normal/exponential distributed service times, disregard of some important factors inside the system which can cause significant fluctuations of both application level and system level metrics.

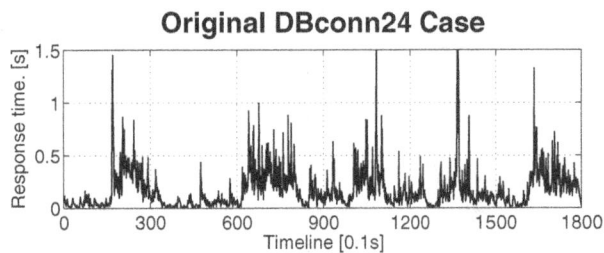

(a) Approximately instant response time in Apache web tier (b) Approximately instant response time in Apache web tier

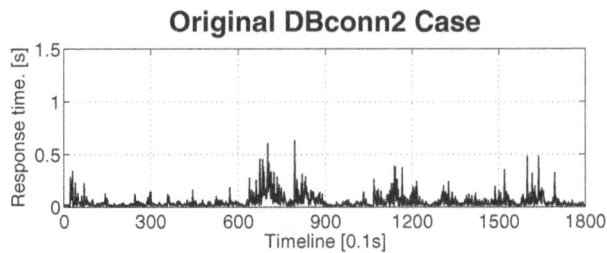

Figure 11: Response time stabilization by limiting bottleneck tier concurrency in 1L/2L/1S/2L config. in WL 5600.

7. CONCLUSIONS

We studied the large scale response time fluctuations of n-tier systems in high resource utilization using the n-tier benchmark RUBBoS. We found that the large scale response time fluctuations can be caused by some system environmental conditions such as L2 cache miss, JVM GC, and limitations of OS level scheduling policies in the system, in addition to the bursty workload from clients. We showed that because of the complex resource dependencies across tiers, a small response time fluctuation in a bottom tier can be amplified to front tiers and eventually to clients. To mitigate the large scale response time fluctuations, we evaluated three heuristics to stabilize the response time fluctuations while still achieving efficient resource utilization. Our work is an important contribution to design more effective autonomous self-scaling n-tier systems in cloud to achieve both good performance and resource efficiency under elastic workloads.

8. ACKNOWLEDGMENTS

This research has been partially funded by National Science Foundation by IUCRC/FRP (1127904) , CISE/CNS (1138666), RAPID (1138666), CISE/CRI (0855180), NetSE (0905493) programs, and gifts, grants, or contracts from DARPA/I2O, Singapore Government, Fujitsu Labs, Wipro Applied Research, and Georgia Tech Foundation through the John P. Imlay, Jr. Chair endowment. Any opinions, findings, and conclusions or recommendations expressed in this material are those of the author(s) and do not necessarily reflect the views of the National Science Foundation or other funding agencies and companies mentioned above.

9. REFERENCES

[1] *Rice University Bulletin Board System.* "http://jmob.ow2.org/rubbos.html", 2004.

[2] *What is the average response time for displaying results.* "http://support.google.com/mini/bin/answer.py?hl=en&answer=15796", 2004.

[3] *Fujitsu SysViz: System Visualization.* "http://www.google.com/patents?id=OpGRAAAAEBAJ&zoom=4&pg=PA1#v=onepage&q&f=false", 2010.

[4] *Java SE 6 Performance White Paper.* http://java.sun.com/performance/reference/whitepapers/6_performance.html, 2010.

[5] T. Abdelzaher, Y. Diao, J. Hellerstein, C. Lu, and X. Zhu. Introduction to control theory and its application to computing systems. SIGMETRICS Tutorial, 2008.

[6] P. Bodik, A. Fox, M. J. Franklin, M. I. Jordan, and D. A. Patterson. Characterizing, modeling, and generating workload spikes for stateful services. SoCC'10.

[7] Y. Chen, S. Iyer, X. Liu, D. Milojicic, and A. Sahai. Translating service level objectives to lower level policies for multi-tier services. *Cluster Computing*, 2008.

[8] S. Cho and L. Jin. Managing distributed, shared l2 caches through os-level page allocation. MICRO'06.

[9] T. Forell, D. Milojicic, and V. Talwar. Cloud management: Challenges and opportunities. In *IPDPSW'11*.

[10] M. Harchol-Balter, B. Schroeder, N. Bansal, and M. Agrawal. Size-based scheduling to improve web performance. *ACM Trans. Comput. Syst.*, 2003.

[11] E. C. Julie, J. Marguerite, and W. Zwaenepoel. *C-JDBC: Flexible Database Clustering Middleware.* 2004.

[12] H. C. Lim, S. Babu, and J. S. Chase. Automated control for elastic storage. ICAC'10.

[13] N. Mi, G. Casale, L. Cherkasova, and E. Smirni. Injecting realistic burstiness to a traditional client-server benchmark. ICAC'09.

[14] K. S. Min Lee. Region scheduling: Efficiently using the cache architectures via page-level affinity. ASPLOS'12.

[15] P. Padala, K.-Y. Hou, K. G. Shin, X. Zhu, M. Uysal, Z. Wang, S. Singhal, and A. Merchant. Automated control of multiple virtualized resources. EuroSys'09.

[16] B. Schroeder, A. Wierman, and M. Harchol-Balter. Open versus closed: a cautionary tale. NSDI'06.

[17] B. Snyder. Server virtualization has stalled, despite the hype. *InfoWorld*, 2010.

[18] E. Thereska and G. R. Ganger. Ironmodel: robust performance models in the wild. SIGMETRICS'08.

[19] Q. Wang, S. Malkowski, Y. Kanemasa, D. Jayasinghe, P. Xiong, M. Kawaba, L. Harada, and C. Pu. The impact of soft resource allocation on n-tier application scalability. IPDPS'11.

[20] P. Xiong, Z. Wang, S. Malkowski, Q. Wang, D. Jayasinghe, and C. Pu. Economical and robust provisioning of n-tier cloud workloads: A multi-level control approach. ICDCS'11.

[21] X. Zhu, M. Uysal, Z. Wang, S. Singhal, A. Merchant, P. Padala, and K. Shin. What does control theory bring to systems research? *SIGOPS Oper. Syst. Rev.*, 2009.

Provisioning Multi-tier Cloud Applications Using Statistical Bounds on Sojourn Time

Upendra Sharma, Prashant Shenoy, Don Towsley
Dept. of Computer Science, University of Massachussetts
Amherst, MA, USA
{upendra,shenoy,towsley}@cs.umass.edu

ABSTRACT

In this paper we present a simple and effective approach for resource provisioning to achieve a percentile bound on the end to end response time of a multi-tier application. We, at first, model the multi-tier application as an open tandem network of M/G/1-PS queues and develop a method that produces a near optimal application configuration, i.e, number of servers at each tier, to meet the percentile bound in a homogeneous server environment – using a single type of server. We then extend our solution to a K-server case and our technique demonstrates a good accuracy, independent of the variability of service-times. Our approach demonstrates a provisioning error of no more than 3% compared to a 140% worst case provisioning error obtained by techniques based on an M/M/1-FCFS queue model. In addition, we extend our approach to handle a heterogenous server environment, i.e., with multiple types of servers. We find that fewer high-capacity servers are preferable for high percentile provisioning. Finally, we extend our approach to account for the rental cost of each server-type and compute a cost efficient application configuration with savings of over 80%. We demonstrate the applicability of our approach in a real world system by employing it to provision the two tiers of the java implementation of TPC-W – a multi-tier transactional web benchmark that represents an e-commerce web application, i.e. an online bookstore.

Categories and Subject Descriptors

C.4 [**Performance of Systems**]: Modeling techniques

Keywords

Performance modeling, cloud computing, multi-tier applications

1. INTRODUCTION

Cloud computing platforms are becoming increasingly popular for hosting enterprise applications due to their ability to support dynamic provisioning of virtualized resources to handle workload fluctuations and also because of usage based pricing. Enterprise applications are known to observe dynamic workload and provisioning correct capacity for these applications remains an important and challenging problem. High variability in workload is caused by a variety of reasons, such as flash crowds, short term sustained surges, or long-term fluctuations based on change in business or underlying IT infrastructure etc. Predicting these workload fluctuations or the peak workload is challenging. Erroneous predictions often lead to under-utilized systems or in some situations cause temporarily outage of an otherwise well provisioned web-site; e.g. in November 2000 Amazon.com site suffered a forty-minute outage due to overload. Consequently, rather than provisioning server capacity to handle infrequent (and hard to predict) peak workloads, an alternate approach of dynamically provisioning capacity on-the-fly in response to workload fluctuations has become popular. Dynamic provisioning is especially well suited to the cloud due to the ability of cloud platforms to provision capacity when needed and charge for usage on pay-per-use basis.

There have been numerous efforts that have addressed the issue of dynamic provisioning of server capacity to distributed applications [8, 11, 20, 19] . These efforts fall into two categories - *proactive*, where a model of the application is used to compute the capacity needed to service a particular workload at a certain performance level, or *reactive*, where additional capacity is allocated *after* a workload spike arrives and causes significant performance degradation.

In case of proactive approaches, application models have been derived to predict how much capacity is needed to provide a certain *mean* response time for a given workload [19, 20]. However, typical service level agreement (SLAs) for the application are specified in terms of the worst case (or peak) response times [7] (e.g. 99% of the requests should see no more than a 1-sec response time). Consequently, there is a mismatch between the provisioning models which allocate capacity for a target mean response, time and the SLA, which dictates that the capacity should be allocated based on a high percentile (peak) response time.

Second, many enterprise applications are distributed or replicated with multi-tier architecture. Typically SLAs are specified on an end-to-end basis for the entire application. The few provisioning efforts that focus on allocating capacity for the tail of the work translate it to per-tier SLA metrics [20]; provisioning for per-tier SLA can result in large errors in provisioning the capacity if the tier response time estimates are incorrect.

Third, most provisioning techniques to-date are cost oblivious – they can determine *how much* server capacity to allocate but do not consider the *cost* of allocating the server capacity. In cloud platform, different server configurations are available at different prices. The capacity does not scale linearly across configurations and nor does the price. Since multiple combinations of servers can provision a certain capacity C for an application, a cloud specific provisioning scheme must take the cloud costs into account when making provisioning decisions.

In this work we present a new model driven provisioning approach targeted for cloud platforms. Our approach focuses on i.) allocating capacity based on peak (high percentile) of the workload, ii) takes a holistic view of the entire multi-tier application by considering bounds on on end to end response times while making provisioning decisions and iii) takes cloud server configs and pricing models when determining the most cost effective config to provision a certain amount of capacity.

1.1 Research Contributions

The contributions of this paper are the following:

Cost aware provisioning subject to a percentile response time SLA. We present an algorithm for resource provisioning for a multi-tier cloud application, subject to an SLA expressed in terms of high percentile of end to end response time, that minimizes the total cost of compute resources required by the application. Our formulation models the application as an open tandem queue network of M/G/1-PS queues.

Service time and response-time approximations. We present an approximation of the response time distribution of the M/G/1 processor sharing queue based on the distribution of conditional expected response times given the service times and show it to be accurate for our purposes. In addition, we present a new service time characterization based on a mixture of shifted exponential distributions.

Cost-efficient configuration with heterogeneous servers subject to percentile SLA. We extend the above approach to account for the presence of multiple types of servers with different costs and computational capabilities. This is achieved by formulating an integer optimization problem with the constraint that per-tier capacity should be at least as much as that computed by the queueing theoretic model.

Prototype implementation and experimentation. We have implemented our analytical model in MATLAB and tested it using a multi-tier application, i.e. java implementation of TPC-W, over a private cloud. For comparison, we also implemented a baseline case using M/M/K-FCFS queues. Our experimental results show that our approach is able to provision the application to meet the SLA specified on 99 percentile of end-to-end response time with less than 3% provisioning error, while the baseline techniques provisioned with an error as large as 140%. In the case of heterogeneous provisioning, our approach shows, as high as, 81% savings in server cost as compared to that of the corresponding optimal homogeneous configuration. In case of private cloud experiments we found that heterogeneous approach showed around 11% cost saving (using Amazon EC2 pricing) over homogenous configurations.

2. BACKGROUND AND PROBLEM FORMULATION

In this section, we present the system model and a high level problem description. We describe the SLA performance metric, and thereafter formulate the provisioning problem that we address in this work.

Multi-tier Application: Modern large scale web applications are developed as multiple tiers for reasons pertaining to scalability. A multi-tier architecture offers flexibility for development as well as deployment of applications. Each application tier, typically, provides a specific functionality and the various tiers form a processing pipeline. In a typical multi-tier application various tiers participate in the processing of an incoming request; each of the participating tier receives partially processed requests from the previous tier and feeds these requests into the next tier after local processing (see Figure 1). The tiers are replicated to scale according to the processing demand; a load balancer is used to distribute the load over all replicas of such a tier. Figure 1 depicts a two-tier application where both tiers are replicated. This is a commonly employed architecture by e-commerce web applications where, both, web-server and database tiers are clustered to scale up according to increase in the incoming workload.

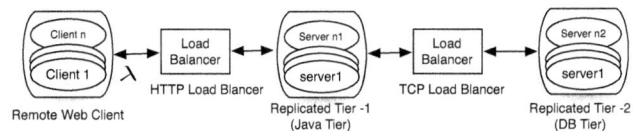

Figure 1: Topological configuration of a typical replicated two-tier web application

We assume that each tier is placed on a dedicated server and that replicating a tier essentially means replicating the server. Each clustered tier is also assumed to employ a protocol-session aware load balancer responsible for distributing requests to replicas in that tier. It is assumed that the each tier's capacity (number of servers), can be varied dynamically without disturbing the application's normal functioning, and that each tier can be independently provisioned for capacity.

Cloud Platforms: Cloud computing has emerged as a new IT delivery model. Infrastructure as a Service (IaaS) cloud-model is being seriously evaluated by enterprises to deploy their web applications that support dynamic capacity resizing. In this model, an organization/client can rent remote compute and storage resources to host networked applications and resources can be dynamically added or removed on an as-needed basis. We consider a cloud computing platform that allows compute servers to run hosted applications. We assume that the platform offers N heterogeneous server configurations for rent, each with a different rental-cost and configuration.

We assume that the cloud platform has an infinite pool of servers and that servers can be provisioned by invoking server-instance creation APIs; servers may be requested and terminated at any time and billing is based on the amount of time for which each server is used (e.g., based on the number of hours for which each server is used). We also assume that the cloud platform employs virtualization—each physical server is assumed to run a hypervisor that controls the allocation of physical resources on the machine and offers performance isolation to each of its virtual servers.

2.1 Problem Formulation

Let N and M denote the number of tiers and server-types respectively. Let tier j be jointly served by $\sum_{i=1}^{M} n_{ij}$ servers, where n_{ij} denotes the number of servers of type i present at tier j. Let $\overline{n}_j = [n_{1j}, n_{2j}, \ldots n_{Mj}]$ be a vector representing the server configuration of tier j and $\overline{p} = [p_1, p_2, \ldots p_M]$, where p_k denotes the cost of a server of type k. Let T be the end-to-end response time of requests to the multi-tier application and F_T be its CDF, i.e. $F_T(t) = P(T \leq t)$. Then for a given percentile bound θ, and response-time threshold T_D, the cost minimization problem becomes:

$$\text{minimize} \sum_{j=1}^{N} \sum_{i=1}^{M} n_{ij} p_i, \qquad (1)$$

subject to the constraint

$$F_T(T_D) \geq \theta. \tag{2}$$

It should be noted that F_T, also depends on n_{ij}, since n_{ij} specifies the application configuration that determines the end-to-end response time of the application. In the next section we present a model of a multi-tier application which enables us to capture the effect of n_{ij} on F_T.

3. APPLICATION MODEL

In this section we model the multi-tier application as a network of queues. Our first model of multi-tier application is a chain of tiers where each tier is modeled as single M/G/1-PS queue (see Figure 2). Each tier carries out a specific function, for instance, a web-application server or a database server etc. In this work we assume single customer class.

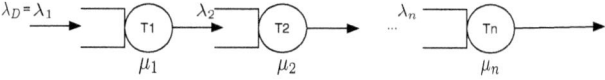

Figure 2: Multi-tier application model

Let A_i denote the ith tier of the application, λ_i the average arrival rate of incoming requests at the ith tier, and μ_i the average service rate $\forall i = 1 \ldots N$. We define the total response time of a request as the time between when it enters the first tier and the time when it leaves the last tier. Note that different λ_i for each tier handles the case where one tier issues multiple requests to the lower tier.

Let T_j be a random variable representing the response time for tier j, then the end-to-end response time of a request is

$$T = \sum_{j=1}^{N} T_j. \tag{3}$$

Let $f_T(t)$ be the probability density function (PDF) of the response time T and $L_T(s) = \mathcal{L}(f_T(t))$ be the Laplace transform of the PDF of response time T then

$$L_T(s) = \prod_{j=1}^{N} L_{T_j}(s), \tag{4}$$

where $L_{T_j}(s)$ is the Laplace transform of the PDF of T_j. Thus the PDF of end-to-end response time, $f_T(t)$, can be computed by taking the Laplace inverse of (4)

$$f_T(t) = \mathcal{L}^{-1} \left(\prod_{j=1}^{N} L_{T_j}(s) \right). \tag{5}$$

To solve (5) we require the PDF of the random variable T_j. Unfortunately there are no exact formulas for response time distributions of an M/G/1-PS queue. We, therefore, present an approximation for the same in the next section.

4. ESTIMATING END-TO-END RESPONSE TIMES

In this section we describe our approach to estimate the PDF of end-to-end response time of a chain of M/G/1-PS queues. In order to do that we estimate the PDF of response time of a single M/G/1-PS queue and then leverage (5) to compute the end to end response time.

Section 4.1 describes our method of approximating the response time distribution of a M/G/1-PS queue. The result depends of the definition of the PDF of service-time distribution of the queue and we describe a mechanism to approximate the same for any real-life system in section 4.2. Section 4.3 provides a closed form equation of the end-to-end response time of the chain of queues.

4.1 Approximate Response Time Distribution

The exact form of the response time distribution for the M/G/1-PS is not generally known [23]. Thus we approximate it with the expected conditional response time distribution as described below. Let T denote the job response time, and X its service time; then the expected conditional response time, conditioned on the service time being x is

$$\tau = E[T|X = x] = \frac{x}{1 - \rho}, \tag{6}$$

where $\rho = \lambda/\mu$ is the average load.

We approximate T by τ. Since τ is a function of X,

$$F_\tau(t) = P[\tau \leq t] = P[\tfrac{X}{1-\rho} \leq t] = P[X \leq t(1 - \rho)],$$
$$F_T(t) \approx F_\tau(t) = F_X(t(1 - \rho)), \tag{7}$$

It has been observed in real-life systems that job service time distributions exhibit heavy tailed behavior [6]. Heavy tailed distributions have very high variance; high variance in service time distribution of jobs makes it a dominant factor in determining the behavior of response time distribution. Approximation proposed in (7) captures the variability of service time and will be particularly useful in such situations. We discuss the impact of variability of service time in section 7 and demonstrate that our approach shows significant improvement.

4.2 Approximate Service Time Distribution

In real systems, like computer clusters and web servers, there is a strong evidence that job service times are highly variable [6]. Some heavy tailed distributions do not have a closed-form Laplace transforms, e.g., the Pareto distribution, while those possessing convenient Laplace transforms might lead to an intractable complex function after undergoing an Nth order convolution in (4). We, thus, need a distribution function, which can closely approximate a service time distribution observed by a real world application and leads to an easily invertible Laplace transform even after undergoing higher order convolutions. In this section we describe such a distribution function and also present an algorithm to approximate the service time distribution from the service-time histogram; service time histograms can be easily collected from the server either through logs or through off-line profiling.

We express the service time distribution as a mixture of K shifted exponentials, as shown in (8). The motivation behind this is two fold: i.) the web application workload is a mix of different job types [12, 5]. Capturing the service time distribution as sum of shifted exponentials, essentially, means that job-size of each job-type is exponentially distributed but each job-type has a different mean job-size. ii.) The formulation leads to a Laplace transform that is easy to invert.

Formally, we want to fit a mixture of shifted exponentials,

$$f_X(x) = \sum_{k=1}^{K} \alpha_k \mathbf{1}\{x \geq t_k\} \mu_k e^{-\mu_k(x - t_k)}, \quad x \geq 0 \tag{8}$$

to data $x_1, x_2, \ldots, x_n$, where $\mathbf{1}\{P\}$ is one if predicate P is true and zero otherwise. This involves inferring the number of shifted exponentials, K, the shifts of each exponential, $\{t_k\}$, the mix proportion of the shifted exponential, $\{\alpha_k\}$, and their average rates $\{\mu_k\}$ from the data. Let us begin by assuming that K and $t_1, \ldots, t_K$ are already known. In other words we want to find the best fit for $\{\mu_k\}$ and $\{\alpha_k\}$; we perform maximum likelihood estimation using the expectation-maximization algorithm (EM).

4.2.1 EM algorithm for estimating mixture parameters

Suppose we know which shifted exponential distribution each observation x_i belongs to, in other words suppose we have $y_i \in \{1, \ldots, K\}$ available to us where $y_i \in \{1 \ldots K\}$ represents the particular shifted exponential distribution. Then the parameter values that maximize the log likelihood function can be computed as:

$$\alpha_k = \frac{1}{n} \sum_{i=1}^{n} \mathbf{1}\{y_i = k\}/n, \quad k = 1, \ldots, K \qquad (9)$$

$$1/\mu_k = \frac{\sum_{i=1}^{n} \mathbf{1}\{y_i = k\} x_i}{\sum_{i=1}^{n} \mathbf{1}\{y_i = k\}}, \quad k = 1, \ldots, K \qquad (10)$$

EM is an iterative algorithm that infers y_i as needed. Suppose μ_k^j and α_k^j are the estimates at the end of the j-th iteration. The next iteration consists of an expectation step followed by a maximization step as given below.

Expectation. Let $y_{i,k}$ denote the probability (expectation) that sample x_i belongs to the k-th shifted exponential. It is given as

$$y_{i,k} = P[Y_i = k | X = x_i]$$

$$= \frac{\alpha_k^j \mathbf{1}\{x_i \geq t_k^j\} \mu_k e^{-\mu_k^j(x_i - t_k^j)}}{\sum_{l=1}^{K} (\alpha_l^j \mathbf{1}\{x_i \geq t_l^j\} \mu_l e^{-\mu_l^j(x_i - t_l^j)})} \qquad (11)$$

$\forall i = i, \ldots, n$ and $k = 1, \ldots K$. Note that $y_{i,k} = 0$ when $x_i < t_k^j$.
Maximization. Having computed $y_{i,k}$, we now update our estimates of α_k and μ_k. This is done by using modified versions of (9) and (10).

$$\alpha_k^{j+1} = \frac{1}{n} \sum_{i=1}^{n} y_{i,k}, \quad k = 1, \ldots, K \qquad (12)$$

$$1/\mu_k^{j+1} = \frac{\sum_{i=1}^{n} y_{i,k} x_i}{\sum_{i=1}^{n} y_{i,k}}, \quad k = 1, \ldots, K \qquad (13)$$

This is referred to as the maximization step because the above estimates maximize the likelihood given the current values of $\{y_{i,k}\}$.

These steps are repeated until the parameters converge; $\{\alpha_k^0\}$ and $\{\mu_k^0\}$ are the initial values, which can be computed as mentioned in the section below.

4.2.2 Algorithm for approximating service-time distribution

We use an iterative approach to determine the best number of exponentials K, and then determine t_k, μ_k^0, and α_k^0, to initialize the EM algorithm, (11), (12) and (13).

The basic idea underlying the algorithm, as outlined in as mentioned in [12], is to iteratively run a *k-means* clustering algorithm for every value of $k = 1 \ldots K_{max}$ and compute the following three metrics[1]: coefficient of variation[2] of intra-cluster distance (C_{intra}), coefficient of variation of inter-cluster distance (C_{inter}), and ratio of intra-cluster to inter-cluster coefficient of variation (β_{cv}). The

value of β_{cv} drops as number of clusters increase and will be minimum (i.e. zero) when number of clusters is equal to the total number of points. We find that K, where the rate of decrease of β_{cv} falls below a threshold (or the slope goes above a negative threshold value).

Having computed K, and the cluster centers e_k, we compute initial estimates of the mean service rate $\{\mu_k^0\}$ and mixture fraction (α_k^0) as follows:

$$\mu_k^0 = \frac{1}{e_k - t_k}, \quad \alpha_k^0 = \frac{\text{number of points in cluster}}{\text{total number of points}}. \qquad (14)$$

We set the shifts to be equidistant from from two neighboring cluster centers, i.e., $t_i = (\mu_{i-1} + \mu_i)/(2\mu_{i-1}\mu_i), \forall i = 2 \ldots K$. However, $t_1 = 0$, i.e., the shift for the first exponential is zero (details of the algorithm can be found in [17].

4.3 Approximate Application Response Time Distribution

The PDF of the end to end response time of N-tier application is obtained using (8) and (7) in (5) as

$$f_\tau(t) = \mathcal{L}^{-1} \left(\prod_{j=1}^{N} \sum_{k=1}^{K_j} \frac{\alpha_{jk} \mu_{jk}' e^{-st_j'}}{(s + \mu_{jk}')} \right), \qquad (15)$$

where for each tier $j = 1, \ldots, N$, service times are modeled as mixtures of K_j shifted exponentials and their density functions are expressed using (8); we rewrite the result for the jth tier for the sake of completeness:

$$f_{X_j}(x) = \sum_{k=1}^{K_j} \alpha_{jk} \mathbf{1}\{x \geq t_{jk}\} \mu_{jk} e^{-\mu_{jk}(x - t_{jk})}. \qquad (16)$$

After inverting (15), the final expression of $f_\tau(t)$ takes the following form:

$$f_\tau(t) = \sum_{i_1=1}^{K_1} \ldots \sum_{i_N=1}^{K_N} \left(\mathbf{1}\{t \geq t'\} \prod_{j=1}^{N} \alpha_{ji_j} \mu_{ji_j}' \times \right.$$
$$\left. \sum_{l=1}^{N} r_l e^{-\mu_{li_l}'(t - t')} \right), \qquad (17)$$

where $\mu_{ji_j}' = \mu_{ji_j}(1 - \rho_j)$, $t' = \sum_{j=1}^{N} t_{j,i_j}/(1 - \rho_j)$, and $r_l = 1/\left(\prod_{k \neq l}^{N} (\mu_{ki_k}' - \mu_{li_l}') \right)$.

Note that α_{ji_j} and μ_{ji_j} are the parameters of the kth shifted exponential of the jth-tier (as shown in (16)); ρ_j is the average utilization of the jth tier, and r_j is the jth residue, where $j = 1, \ldots, N$.

Note that the expression in (15) does not involve higher order poles[3] because none of the rates μ_{li_l} is ever equals any of the μ_{ji_j}. This becomes especially helpful in inverting the Laplace transform as absence of higher order terms in denominator leads to a simple computation of partial fractions.

The final expression of $f_\tau(t)$ in (17) is, essentially, a product of sums of the shifted exponentials, which is easily readable in (15). This means that the $f_\tau(t)$ will be expressed, in total, by $\prod_{j=1}^{N} K_j$ terms; for example let $K_j = a, \forall j = 1 \ldots N$, then $f_\tau(t)$ will be expressed as a sum of a^N terms. It is easy to see that number of terms grow exponentially with number of tiers. Fortunately, real

---

[1] the metrics are computed as mentioned in [12]

[2] Coefficient of variation or variation coefficient is defined as a ratio of the standard deviation to the mean, i.e. $C_v = \sigma/\mu$;

[3] If for some l, j, $\mu_{li_l} = \mu_{ji_j}$, we slightly perturb the starting $\mu_{li_l}^0$ for tier-l by adding a small random number and re-run the EM algorithm for that tier-l

life systems do not have more than three or at most four tiers and thus $f_\tau(t)$ is easily computable.

5. FINDING NEAR OPTIMAL HOMOGENEOUS CONFIGURATION

In this section we present a solution to the the resource optimization problem, as expressed by (1) and (2), but with only one type of server, $M = 1$ (homogeneous setting).

We substitute the approximate response time of an M/G/1-PS queue, i.e. $f_\tau(t)$ as shown in (17), in (2) to obtain:

$$F_\tau(T_D) = \sum_{i_1=1}^{K_1} \cdots \sum_{i_N=1}^{K_N} \left(\mathbf{1}\{T_D \geq t'\} \prod_{j=1}^{N} \alpha_{ji_j}\mu'_{ji_j} \right.$$
$$\left. \sum_{l=1}^{N} \frac{r_l(1-e^{-\mu'_{li_l}(T_D-t')})}{\mu'_{li_l}} \right) \geq \theta, \quad (18)$$

where μ'_{jk_j} and r_j are the same as in (17) while $t' = \sum_{j=1}^{N} t_{j,i_j}/(1-\rho_j)$.

Thus the problem of minimizing (1) reduces to the problem of maximizing ρ_j ($\forall j = 1, \ldots, N$) such that $F_\tau(T_D) \geq \theta$, where $F_\tau(T_D)$ is given by (18). As this is an N-dimensional non-linear maximization problem, it is not easy to solve. However, the problem complexity is significantly reduced by assuming same utilization at each tier[4], i.e.,

$$\rho_1 = \rho_2 = \ldots = \rho_N = \rho.$$

It should be noted that it is desirable to have a balanced utilization at each tier in real-life systems. In practice, administrators often use a rule of thumb to bound the max utilization of servers of all tiers to avoid performance problems and outages [15].

Consequently, (18) reduces to an inequality in a single variable, namely ρ.

$$F_\tau(T_D) = \sum_{i_1=1}^{K_1} \cdots \sum_{i_N=1}^{K_N} \left(\mathbf{1}\{T_D \geq t'\} \prod_{j=1}^{N} \alpha_{ji_j}\mu_{ji_j} \right.$$
$$\left. \sum_{l=1}^{N} \frac{r'_l(1-e^{-\mu'_{li_l}(T_D-t')})}{\mu_{li_l}} \right) \geq \theta, \quad (19)$$

where, $t' = \sum_{j=1}^{N} t_{j,i_j}/(1-\rho)$, and $r'_l = 1/\prod_{k\neq n}^{N}(\mu_{ki_k} - \mu_{li_l})$. We solve for the maximum value of ρ, say ρ^*, by numerically solving (19) as an equality.

5.1 Computing the Application Configuration

In practice, large scale applications have each of their tier replicated for scalability as depicted in Figure 3. The idea is to be able to handle increasing number of requests while conforming to the SLA. In an ideal situation an application-tier's ability to process the number of requests increases linearly with number of its replicas, which means that if an application or application-tier with a single replica had a service rate of μ then K replica version of application-tier will have a request rate of $K\mu$. We have assumed a linear scaling in this work but that is not a limitation and any kind of scaling function can used in the technique to obtain the number of replicas at each application-tier. We have used replicas and servers interchangeably because we have assumed dedicated hosting model.

We use ρ^* to compute the number of servers at each tier, i.e. n_{ij}. In the homogenous setup $i = 1$ and thus we solve for n_j, $j = 1 \ldots N$. Let λ_j and μ_j be arrival and service rates respectively, at

[4]The constraint reduces the solution search space and thus the final solution is not guaranteed to be an optimal solution as it could result into a slightly over-provisioned system.

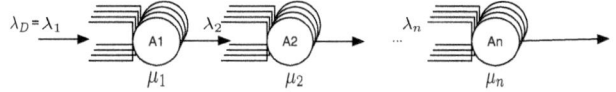

Figure 3: Multi-tier application model

tier j then $n_j = \lceil \lambda_j/(\zeta\rho^*\mu_j) \rceil$, where ζ is the scale factor, which can be chosen heuristically and

$$\mu_j = \sum_{i=1}^{K_j} \alpha_{ji} \frac{(1+\mu_{ji}t_{ji})e^{-\mu_{ji}t_{ji}}}{\mu_{ji}}. \quad (20)$$

The pseudo code of the algorithm for finding the application configuration in homogenous setup is outlined in [17].

6. COST EFFICIENT HETEROGENOUS CONFIGURATION

We extend the solution approach described in Section 5 to be able to generate a cost efficient configuration in a heterogenous setting.

The basic idea underlying our approach is to greedily search for a low cost configuration which has a high utilization. At a high level the algorithm is iterative involving the following three steps at each iteration: 1.) creating a single hybrid-server from a given hybrid-configuration for each tier, 2.) solve the homogeneous configuration problem for the hybrid-server, 3.) translate the solution for hybrid-server into a heterogenous configuration, and the iterations are used to search for new hybird-configuration with lower cost and higher utilization. Figure 4 shows the block diagrammatic representation of the cost effective heterogeneous configuration algorithm.

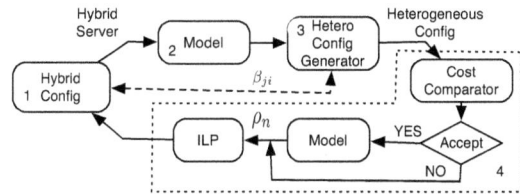

Figure 4: Functional block diagram of heterogeneous configuration algorithm

Hybrid server: Inorder to reuse our methodology for finding the near optimal number of servers in homogeneous setting, it is imperative that we approximate each hybrid configuration at each tier by a single server; we call it a hybrid-server. We construct the service time distribution of the hybid-server for each tier as a proportional mixture of the service time distributions of the servers involved in the heterogeneous configuration. Let $\overline{n} = \{n_i\}$ denote the hybrid-configuration where n_i, $i = 1, \ldots, M$, is the number of servers of type i. Then the hybrid-server's service-time distribution function for tier-j is expressed as

$$f'_j = \sum_{m=1}^{M} \beta_{jm} f_{jm}, \quad (21)$$

where f_{jm} is the service-time probability density function (PDF) of the mth-server-type at j^{th}-tier and f'_j is the PDF of the hybrid-server for tier-j; β_{jm} is the mixing proportion of the component server m for tier-j and is computed using the formula

$$\beta_{jm} = \frac{n_m\mu_{jm}}{\sum_{j=1}^{M} n_m\mu_{jm}}. \quad (22)$$

We explain our procedure of creating a hybrid-server with the following example: suppose we have two servers, say s_1 and s_2, with corresponding average service rates at tier-j as $\mu_{j1} = 50$ and $\mu_{j2} = 100$, respectively. We construct a single hybrid-server, say s_h, by proportionally mixing the component shifted-exponentials of each s_1 and s_2. Let the configuration be one-server of each type, i.e. $\overline{n} = [1, 1]$; then the mixing proportions using (22) is $\beta_{j1} = 1/3$ and $\beta_{j2} = 2/3$, and the final service-time distribution of the hybrid-server for the jth tier is $f'_j = \left(\frac{f_{j1}}{3} + \frac{2f_{j2}}{3} \right)$.

Heterogeneous configuration: Once we obtain the optimal configuration for a given hybrid-server, and given workload and percentile, we translate this solution configuration to the corresponding heterogenous server configuration; this is done by reversing the steps of creating the hybrid-server. Let us assume that the servers are indexed in increasing order of their average service rate; i.e. $\mu_1 \leq \mu_2 \leq \ldots \leq \mu_M$; let n'_j be the number of hybrid-servers at tier-j, then the number of servers of type-i for tier-j is $n_{ji} = \beta_{ji} n'_j / (\mu_i / \mu_1)$.

Searching for a new hybrid-configuration: The cost of the new heterogenous configuration, computed in the step above, is evaluated using the prices of the servers. If the cost is less than that of the current solution configuration, then this new configuration is accepted else it is dropped. The new configuration is again fed to the model, and its utilization ρ^* is evaluated for the desired arrival rate λ_D. We then try to search for a new hybrid-configuration which has higher utilization but lower cost then the current-configuration; the new utilization $\rho_n = (\rho_{max} + \rho_l)/2$, where ρ_{max} is maximum utilization of the hybrid-server and $\rho_l = \rho^*$. The new hybrid configuration is searched for using the following ILP solved for each tier:

$$\text{minimize} \sum_{i=1}^{M} n_{ji} p_i, \qquad (23)$$

subject to the constraint

$$\sum_{i=1}^{M} n_{ji} \mu_{ji} > \lambda_D / \rho_n. \qquad (24)$$

Note that if the currently suggested configuration is not accepted we continue to search for higher ρ^*. The algorithm stops when $\rho_n - \rho_{max}$ is less than a pre-decided threshold; the pseudo code is outlined in [17].

7. EXPERIMENTAL EVALUATION

In this section we demonstrate the efficacy of our approach. We have implemented our analytical method using MATLAB®. For solving the ILP, we have used lpsolve version 5.5.2.0 and have used mxlpsolve MATLAB Interface version 5.5.0.6 for calling lpsolve from within the MATLAB environment.

We begin by showing the effectiveness of the service-time approximation algorithm on lognormal[5] distribution with different coefficient of variations (C_v). Thereafter we evaluate the goodness of the approximation of the response-time distribution for a 1-tier and a 2-tier system by comparing the response times computed using (17) with those obtained using a multi-tier application-simulator described below. Finally we do a case-study of provisioning of a two-tier application for a SLA specified as a threshold on the 99th percentile of response time. We evaluate the effectiveness of our approach by computing the 99 percentile of response

---

[5]PDF of a log normal distribution is expressed as $f(x, \mu, \sigma) = \frac{1}{x\sigma\sqrt{2\pi}} e^{-((ln(x)-\mu)/(\sqrt{2}\sigma))^2}$, where mean is $e^{\mu + \sigma^2/2}$

times obtained using a two-tier application-simulator configured according to the capacity decisions provided by our approach; note that the simulator depicts an ideal version of a multi-tier application which we analytically model as a chain of M/G/1-PS queues. We also evaluate the effectiveness of our approach, using a metric called provisioning error (described in Section 7.4), by comparing against the two other baseline approaches, which model the multi-tier application as an open tandem network of M/M/K-FCFS queues.

7.1 Multi-tier Application Simulator

We implemented a simulator for the PS queue in MATLAB®. It takes as input an array of request arrival instants and size of each request (in terms of service time) and outputs the request departure instants. We used this queue simulator to simulate a multi-tiered application by feeding the output of first queue to the input of the next queue.

To simulate an application with replicated tiers, we have implemented a loadbalancer, as shown in Figure 1, which takes the incoming requests from the previous tier and distributes it to the next tier according to a specific load distribution policy. It also does the necessary book-keeping to track each request across various tiers for computing the end-to-end response time. We have implemented a random loadbalancing policy, i.e. loadbalancer distributes the requests at random but ensures that each server gets the same load, i.e. $\rho*$ as computed in section 5. We have assumed an ideal loadbalancer, which means that it introduces no queueing and processing delay. Note that this is not a limitation of our approach, as our approach can easily account for loadbalancer by considering it as another tier and its capacity can also be computed, which is often needed in a real setup.

7.2 Service Time Approximation

We have implemented the EM algorithm (in MATLAB) for finding the parameters of mixture of shifted exponentials, namely α_i, μ_i in (8), using the E and M steps mentioned in Section 4.2.1. The shifts and initial values of parameters are estimated using the algorithm outlined in Section 4.2.2. We use MATLAB's implementation of KMeans and have kept $K_{max} = 20$ in all our experiments, which means that we search for the number of shifted exponents from 3 till 20. We evaluate the accuracy of CDF approximation using relative percentage error defined as $\epsilon(x) = (F_{aprx}(x) - F_{sim}(x))/(F_{sim}(x))$, where $F_{aprx}(x)$ and $F_{sim}(x)$ are the values of approximate and actual CDFs, respectively, evaluated at x.

To evaluate the effectiveness of our approach in approximating highly variable distribution, we approximated the PDF a lognormal distribution with same mean rate of 20 but with a coefficient of variation of 100 ($C_v = 100$); it was expressed using 10 shifted exponentials. Figure 5a shows the CCDF of the actual distribution in red while our approximated distribution is shown in blue.

The CCDF in Figure 5 highlight the approximation of the tail of the distribution by plotting the $1 - F(x)$ in a log log scale. We observed that the approximation shows a relatively high error at low percentiles (as high as 21%) but displays low errors at the tail, with errors less than 1% at 95 percentile. This is because, that at low percentiles the number of exponentials available to approximate the distribution are less but as we approach the tail of the distribution a large number of exponentials contribute towards the approximation of the PDF and thus we observe much greater accuracy.

Another aspect of our algorithm is K, i.e. the number of exponentials required to approximate a distribution. We conducted a large number of experiments on various data sets with C_v ranging from 1 to 100. In our experiments we found that K its average values starts at 14 for $C_v = 1$ and slightly decreases to an average value of 10 for $C_v = 100$. It should be noted that we are testing our approximation scheme for a smooth distribution function, but the scheme has been designed keeping a web application in vision, which has only a limited number of request types at each tier and our approach is tuned to estimate this number as K.

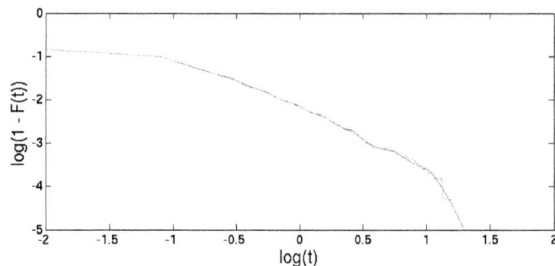

(a) Lognormal with $C_v = 100$

Figure 5: Figure shows the log log plot of 20,000 data points sampled from lognormal distribution with $C_v = 100$; the simulated CDF is shown in red and approximate in blue.

In summary, the service time approximation approach offers very low errors, i.e. less than 1%, in estimating the tail of a distribution.

7.3 Response Time Approximation

In this section we describe the effectiveness of our approach of approximating the end to end response time of an application modeled as a chain of M/G/1-PS queues.

We evaluated the goodness of the response-time approximation we compare the response time computed by our approach with that obtained from the simulator described above. We show the results for for a 2-tier setup by plotting the response time CDFs for our approximation and simulation. We have sampled service times from a lognormal distribution with a $C_v = 10$.

We generate the workload which has exponential inter-arrival times with $\lambda = 25$ and service times sampled from a lognormal distribution with $\mu = 50$ at each tier. The simulation results are considered exact since the simulation model is an exact representation of the queueing network under study.

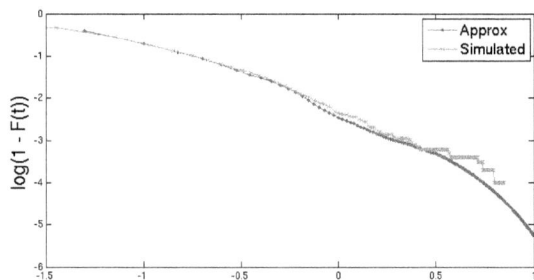

(a) CDF RT of 2-tier app

Figure 6: Figure shows the CDF plot of actual response time distribution in red and approximated using our approach in blue for a heavy-tailed service-time distribution with $\mu = 50$ and $c_v = 10$

The approximated response time, using our approach, exhibits high accuracy, as can be seen from Figure 6. The jagged tail of simulation result is because of less number of data points.

7.4 Provisioning in a Homogenous Setup

In this section we evaluate the effectiveness of our approach, outlined in section-5, in finding the homogenous configuration for a two-tier application, where each tier is replicated using same type of servers.

For a given SLA, expressed as a cutoff threshold T_D on the 99th percentile of end to en response time, we fix a service time distribution and for different arrival rates compute the number of servers required at each tier of the application. We, then, run the replicated application simulator with these number of servers and obtain the end to end response time distribution for the provisioned application. To evaluate the goodness of provisioning decisions made, we define a metric called *provisioning error*, which essentially calculates the error in the 99th percentile response time observed from the simulator, i.e. T_{scheme}, and T_D. Formally, $\epsilon_{scheme} = (T_{scheme} - T_D) * 100 / T_D$. To do a comparative evaluation of our technique, we have implemented two baseline provisioning algorithms based on M/M/1-FCFS queues, namely *per-tier-exp* and *end-to-end-exp*. The schemes are described below:

per-tier-exp (pte) : In this scheme we assume the knowledge of average proportion of time spent by a request at each tier. In other words, let T be the total time spent by a request in the system and T_i be the time spent at tier i; then, *pte* assumes the knowledge of $E[\delta_i]$, where $\delta_i = T_i / T$. We model each tier as an M/M/K-FCFS queue and again approximate multiple servers by a single server, thus each tier can be approximated by an M/M/1-FCFS queue. For this system the response time is exponentially distributed with parameter $\mu(1 - \rho)$. Finally, as in Section 5, for each tier j, we solve for ρ^* with $T_D = \delta_j T$ and compute $n_j = \lceil \lambda_j / (\rho^* \mu_j) \rceil$

end-to-end-exp (ete): We developed this scheme completely along the lines of our scheme, however assuming an M/M/K-FCFS queue based model instead of an M/G/K-PS queue based model. The corresponding version of (19) is:

$$F_T(t') = \sum_{j=1}^{N} r_j (1 - e^{-\mu_j' t'}) \geq \theta, \qquad (25)$$

where $t' = T_D$, $r_j = 1 / \prod_{k \neq j}^{N} (\mu_k' - \mu_j')$ and $\mu_j' = \mu_j(1 - \rho)$. The provisioning algorithm for homogenous setting is outlined in [17].

We ran the experiment with $T_D = 0.4s$, $\mu = 50$ and $C_v = 3$. We increased the workload from $\lambda = 40$ rps to 240 rps and for each λ we computed application capacity using each of the three algorithms. For *pte* we used $\delta_1 = \delta_2 = 0.5$. The results are shown in Table 1.

λ	% ϵ_{our}	% ϵ_{ete}	% ϵ_{pte}	Config$_{our}$	Config$_{ete}$	Config$_{pte}$
40	-3.63	16	15.2	[3;3]	[2;2]	[2;2]
80	-6.17	48.1	27.9	[5;5]	[3;3]	[4;3]
120	-0.235	94.3	38.5	[8;7]	[4;4]	[5;5]
160	-2.25	91.6	49.9	[9;9]	[5;5]	[6;6]
200	-2.17	140	40.7	[12;12]	[6;6]	[8;8]
240	2.57	91.3	53.7	[15;15]	[8;8]	[9;9]

Table 1: Homogeneous configuration suggested by the three schemes and their provisioning errors. Note that, unlike the positive error, negative value of ϵ is not an SLA violation.

A Positive value of ϵ means that some or all of the tiers of the application were provisioned with fewer servers than required (we call it under-provisioning); however, a negative value means the opposite (we call it over-provisioning). Thus a positive ϵ is an SLA violation, while a negative ϵ is not. However, a negative ϵ does suggests a possibility of finding a more cost efficient solution.

Note that our scheme reports a worst case provisioning error of 2.57% as opposed to the worst case under-provisioning of 140% by ete and 53.7% by pte.

In summary: for a single server type scenario (i.e. homogeneous setup), application provisioned by our scheme reports worst case provisioning error of 2.57%, while the baseline approaches shows as high as 140% provisioning error

7.5 Cost Efficient Server Configuration in a Multiple Server-type Environment

Here we demonstrate the effectiveness of our heterogenous provisioning algorithm in finding a cost-efficient solution when multiple types of servers are available. We have kept the time threshold $T_D = 0.4$-sec and varied the desired load from $\lambda = 40$-rps to $\lambda = 240$-rps. We have considered four types of servers, namely small (S), medium (M), large (L), and extra-large (XL), with their corresponding average service rates being 50, 100, 150 and 200 rps, respectively. The coefficient of variation of service times for requests at each of the tiers is $C_v = 9$.

ServerType	Small	Medium	Large	XLarge
Price	0.02	0.04	0.06	0.08

(a) server prices

λ	% ϵ_{homo}	% ϵ_{hetro}	Config$_{homo}$	Config$_{hetro}$	%Saving
40	1.63	-40.9	[9;9]	[0 1 0 0;0 1 0 0]	77.78
80	1.01	-35.7	[17;15]	[0 0 0 1;0 0 1 0]	78.13
120	1.16	-22.9	[26;23]	[0 0 2 0;0 1 1 0]	77.55
160	1.06	-23.5	[34;30]	[0 0 1 1;0 0 2 0]	79.69
200	1.09	-21.5	[43;47]	[0 0 3 0;0 1 2 0]	81.11
240	1.04	-9.82	[51;45]	[0 0 2 1;0 0 3 0]	80.21

(b) 99-percentile provisioning and cost benefit

Table 2: Heterogeneous configuration suggested by the three schemes and provisioning error of each scheme. Note that a negative ϵ only means over-provisioning and is not an SLA violation

We assume linear pricing as depicted in Table 2a. The results of provisioning algorithms in homogenous and heterogenous settings are shown in Table 2b. We call the computed capacity configurations in the homogenous and heterogeneous settings as $Config_{homo}$ and $Config_{hetro}$, respectively. Only the "small" server-types were used in $Config_{homo}$, while all the available server types we used to obtain $Config_{hetro}$. As in previous evaluations, we again test the computed configuration using the multi-tier application simulator.

Each configuration is $N \times M$ dimensional matrix depicting the number of servers of each type; each row j depicts the configuration of the jth tier, while each column tells the number of servers for each type: for e.g. Config$_{homo}$ = [9;9] means 9-small servers at both the tiers, while Config$_{hetro}$ = [0 1 0 0;0 1 0 0] means 0-small, 1-Medium, 0-large and 0-x-large server at both the tiers. The "%Cost Saving" is computed as a percentage of cost of homogenous configuration, i.e. $\frac{Cost(Config_{homo}) - Cost(Config_{hetro})}{Cost(Config_{homo})}$.

We make following important observations: 1) the percentage provisioning error for the heterogeneous scheme is as low as -41%, which means that not-only is this configuration cost-efficient but it also provides low average response-times (because negative provisioning error means the system is probably over-provisioned). The small positive error in the case of homogeneous configurations is because of approximation used in section 5.1 and can be easily corrected by setting $\zeta < 1$, i.e. a sublinear scaling. 2) it is better to use larger servers that fit the same cost and average service-rate; in

other words its better to use a small number of large servers instead of a large number of small servers.

In summary, it is better to use a small number of large servers instead of a large number of small servers for high percentile provisioning ii) Cost efficient heterogenous algorithm offers server configurations with cost savings as high as 81% and also offer a configurations with lower average response-times.

8. EVALUATION ON PRIVATE CLOUD

In this section we describe an experimental investigation for provisioning for a percentile SLA in a private cloud setup. Our goal is to evaluate our provisioning algorithm under situations which are typical to multi-tier web applications deployed in a datacenter or private/public cloud environment.

8.1 Private Cloud Setup

In this section we provide the necessary details of our experimental testbed, i.e private cloud, and necessary steps before we can perform server provisioning.

Web Application: We used TPC-W for our experiments. TPC-W is a multi-tier transactional web benchmark that represents an e-commerce web application – an online bookstore – comprising of a web server tier and a database tier. It simulates the activities of a retail store website using 14 different type of pages for web interactions; each of these pages are created dynamically by the web server using differing amounts of data stored in the database tables. TPC-W benchmark defines three different mixes of web interactions, namely browsing, shopping and ordering, each varying the ratio of inventory browsing related web pages and ordering related web pages. It applies the workload mixes via remote browser emulator (RBE).

We used the Java implementation of TPC-W [3]. The web application has following two-tiers: i.) Web server tier based on Apache Tomcat servlet container 5.5.26 ii.) database tier based on MySQL 5.0.77. We deployed each of the tiers on separate dedicated servers. We performed round robin load balancing between replicas of web server tier using a dedicated loadbalancer server on HAProxy [9] on a server as a dedicated load balancer. We used round robin load balancing at the database tier by setting up a master-slave replication configuration of MySQL servers; we instrumented TPC-W to use the replication aware MySQL JDBC connector version 3.1.12.

Private Cloud: We constructed private cloud using OpenNebula [14] on Xen/linux-based cluster consisting of two types of servers: 8-core 2GHz AMD Opteron 2350 servers and 4-core 2.4 GHz Intel Xeon X3220 systems. All machines run Xen 3.3 and Linux 2.6.18 (64bit kernel). Our platform is assumed to support *small* and *large* servers, comprising 1 and 4 cores, respectively. These are constructed by deploying a Xen VM on the above mentioned servers and dedicating the corresponding number of cores to the VM (by pinning the VM's VCPUs to the cores)

Profiling servers for web server tier: For profiling the servers for the first tier, i.e. web-server tier, we instrumented Tomcat such that it reports per-request service times, along with the other default stats. We profile each server type (e.g. *small* and *large*) by provisioning an instance of that server-type and deploying the first tier of TPC-W on it. We then connect it to an already installed TPC-W database installed on a *large* server type instance. We then issue the browsing workload using the TPC-W clients (i.e. RBEs) for a duration of 35 mins and collect the service times from the tomcat server logs.

Profiling servers for database server tier: Profiling the servers for the second tier of TPC-W (i.e. the database tier) was in two steps: firstly, we collect the 35-min query logs from MySQL server, executing the TPC-W workload; then for each server type we slowly replay each of the SQL query and record their execution time as service times.

8.2 Percentile Based Capacity Provisioning on Private Cloud

Given λ_D and T_D, we outline the high level steps required to compute application capacities for both homogenous and heterogenous setup. In both the cases we assume to require an SLA where 99th percentile of the end-to-end response time must be less than 0.5 seconds. We follow the following sequence of steps

Step 1: Estimating service time distributions: We use the service times collected during the offline profiling step and use the service time approximation algorithm – as outlined in [17].

Step 2: Estimating capacity in a homogenous/Heterogenous setup: We used the single core virtual machines (i.e. *small*) in our homogenous setup. Load across multiple web-server replicas was distributed using a HAProxy based load-balancer, however, in the case of database tier, we used the master-slave setup. In this setup all the wites are sent to the master, whereas the reads are load-balanced.

We test our approach for both homogenous and heterogeneous environment. For homogenous setup, we choose *small* server type for this case and assume $T_D = 0.5$sec. To test the provisioning setup for large change in workload, we varied λ_D from 15 rps to 90 rps. For each λ_D, using our approach, we computed server capacities for each of the tier of TPC-W. We ran the setup for 35-mins and in the end we collected the end-to-end response times from the first tier (i.e. web-server tier). We ran our heterogeneous provisioning algorithm on the same setup and found that it gave a different configuration, only for $\lambda_D = 90$. Table 3a provides the details of the final configuration and also the 99th-percentile of the end-to-end response time details of the experiment. We compute the percentage provisioning error, ϵ_{our}, as mentioned in 7.4.

λ_D	99th %	% ϵ_{our}	Config$_{our}$
15	0.361	-27.8	[1;1]
30	0.459	-8.2	[1;2]
45	0.488	-2.4	[1;3]
90	0.512	2.4	[2;7]
90	0.46	-8.0	[2,0;2,1]

(a) Server Provisioning

Server Type	*small*	*large*
Prices ($)	0.085	0.34

(b) Server prices

Table 3: Homogenous and heterogeneous provisioning decisions. Note that a -ve ϵ_{our} only means that the system is over-provisioned and thus SLA will not be violated

We found that server provisioning by our approach keeps provisioning error below 3%. The positive 2.4% error at $\lambda = 90$ for homogenous setup could be because database tier does not scale linearly as the master database server gets overloaded by replicating the updates to each of the 6 slaves. We see that the server provisioning for the heterogenous environment, is not only 11.11% cheaper than the corresponding homogenous server setup but also has a lower 99th response time.

In summary, our algorithm effectively accurately captures the service time distributions and provisions the two-tier implementation of TPC-W with the worst provisioning error of 3%. Also, we, again, find that its better to use bigger server for high percentile provisioning.

9. RELATED WORK

A number of efforts have modeled internet applications. Modeling single tier has gotten much of the attention. Doyle *et al.* propose a queuing model for static content [8], Menasce uses a queuing model to model the web servers [11], while Abdelzaher *et al.* in [1] use classical feedback control theory to model the bottleneck tier for providing performance guarantees for web applications serving static content, while Chen *et al.* in [4] use a machine learning technique for provisioning the database tier.

Ranjan *et al.* [16] use a G/G/N queuing model to compute the number of servers necessary to maintain a target utilization level. This strategy is shown to be effective for sudden increases in request arrival rate. Other efforts have employed M/G/1 queuing models in conjunction with offline profiling to model service delay and predict performance [18] but they do not provision for response time percentile and neither do they address the problem in heterogenous environment. The approach in [21] formulates the application tier server provisioning as a profit maximization problem and models application servers as M/G/1/PS queuing systems; the approach only considers the impact of different number of end-clients (and thus, request volumes)

Benanni *et al.* in [2] employ approximate mean-value analysis (MVA) to develop an online provisioning technique for multiple request classes. Urgaonkar *et al.* in [19] develop a queuing network model for multi-tier Internet applications having request classes with differentiated QoS. Zhang et. al. [24] use a multi-class model to capture the dynamics of workload by employing a fixed set of 14 predefined transactions-types and leverage it to predict the performance of a multi-tier system.

There has been some work for finding the pdf of response time, for e.g. Muppula *et al.* in [13] derive the response time for a closed queuing network using pteri-nets and sojourn time distribution was calculated for large Markov chains in [10]. The approach leads to an inversion of a complex Laplace transform. Xiong *et al.* in [22] perform the provisioning of a multi-station setup for a given percentile bound. The model the system as a open tandem network of M/M/1-FCFS queues and compute the response time PDF by numerical inversion of its Laplace transform; they assume that each station is serviced by same type of servers.

In contrast to these efforts, our work automatically characterizes service time distribution as a mixture of shifted exponentials and leverages this to estimate the response time distribution. The estimated distribution is used to estimate the capacity of the system which assists in finding a near optimal solution to the provisioning problem in homogeneous environment. Further, while most of these efforts have focused on a single server type environment (i.e. homogeneous), we extend our approach for a cloud specific heterogenous environment as well. We developed a full prototype implementation and our experiments were conducted on an actual private cloud.

10. CONCLUSION

Multi-tier architecture is a preferred architecture for enterprise web applications and high response time percentile provisioning is the more meaningful than mean response time based ones. We present an approach of optimizing server allocation for a multi-tier application to achieve a percentile bound on the end to end response time. We model the application as an open tandem network of queues and model each tier as an M/G/1-PS queue. We have developed an approximate model to compute the response time distribution and have also developed a technique to estimate the service time distribution from the service time histograms. We have developed an algorithm to compute per tier server allocation of the application and in a homogenous setup. We also have extended the homogenous setup solution to solve the server allocation problem in a heterogenous setup. We have tested the efficacy of our approach using a multi-tier application simulator and also compared it against two other baseline approaches developed using models based on M/M/K-FCFS queue. We have demonstrated superior performance of our approach as compared to the baseline approaches. Our experiments indicated that its better to use small number of large servers than large number of small servers. Finally we tested our approach using the multi-tier implementation of TPC-W benchmark over private cloud created using Xen over Linux.

11. ACKNOWLEDGMENTS

We would like to thank our anonymous reviewers. This research was supported in part by NSF grants CNS-1117221, CNS-0916972, CNS-0855128 and OCI-1032765. Upendra Sharma was supported by an IBM PhD fellowship.

12. REFERENCES

[1] T. F. Abdelzaher, K. G. Shin, and N. Bhatti. Performance Guarantees for Web Server End-Systems: A Control-Theoretical Approach. *IEEE Transactions on Parallel and Distributed Systems*, 13(1):80–96, 2002.

[2] M. N. Bennani and D. A. Menasce. Resource allocation for autonomic data centers using analytic performance models. In *ICAC '05*, pages 229–240, Washington, DC, USA, 2005. IEEE Computer Society.

[3] H. W. Cain and R. Rajwar. An architectural evaluation of Java TPC-W. In *In Proceedings of the Seventh International Symposium on High-Performance Computer Architecture*, pages 229–240, 2001.

[4] J. Chen, G. Soundararajan, and C. Amza. Autonomic Provisioning of Backend Databases in Dynamic Content Web Servers. In *ICAC*, pages 231–242, June 2006.

[5] L. Cherkasova and P. Phaal. Session based admission control: a mechanism for peak load management of commercial web sites. *IEEE Transactions on Computers*, 51(6), June 2002.

[6] M. Crovella. Performance evaluation with heavy tailed distributions. In *Proceedings of the 11th International Conference on Computer Performance Evaluation: Modelling Techniques and Tools*, TOOLS '00, pages 1–9, London, UK, 2000. Springer-Verlag.

[7] G. DeCandia, D. Hastorun, M. Jampani, G. Kakulapati, A. Lakshman, A. Pilchin, S. Sivasubramanian, P. Vosshall, and W. Vogels. Dynamo: amazon's highly available key-value store. *SIGOPS Oper. Syst. Rev.*, 41:205–220, October 2007.

[8] R. Doyle, J. Chase, O. Asad, W. Jin, and A. Vahdat. Model-based resource provisioning in a web service utility. In *Proceedings of Fourth USENIX Symposium on Internet Technologies and Systems (USITS '03), Seattle, WA*, March 2003.

[9] Haproxy the reliable, high performance tcp/http load balancer. http://haproxy.1wt.eu/.

[10] P. G. Harrison and W. J. Knottenbelt. Passage time distributions in large markov chains. In *SIGMETRICS '02: Proceedings of the 2002 ACM SIGMETRICS international conference on Measurement and modeling of computer systems*, pages 77–85, New York, NY, USA, 2002. ACM.

[11] D. Menasce. Web Server Software Architectures. In *IEEE Internet Computing*, volume 7, November/December 2003.

[12] D. A. Menascé, V. A. F. Almeida, R. Fonseca, and M. A. Mendes. A methodology for workload characterization of e-commerce sites. In *EC '99: Proceedings of the 1st ACM conference on Electronic commerce*, pages 119–128, New York, NY, USA, 1999. ACM.

[13] J. K. Muppala, K. S. Trivedi, V. Mainkar, and V. G. Kulkarni. Numerical computation of response time distributions using stochastic reward nets. In *Annals of Operations Research*, pages 155–184, 1994.

[14] Opennebula. http://www.opennebula.org.

[15] G. Pacifici, W. Segmuller, M. Spreitzer, M. Steinder, A. Tantawi, and A. Youssef. Managing the response time for multi-tiered web applications. In *IBM, Technical Report*, January 2005.

[16] S. Ranjan, J. Rolia, H. Fu, and E. Knightly. Qos-driven server migration for internet data centers. In *Proceedings of the Tenth International Workshop on Quality of Service (IWQoS 2002)*, May 2002.

[17] U. Sharma, P. Shenoy, and D. F. Towsley. Provisioning Multi-tier Cloud Applications Using Statistical Bounds on Sojourn Time. Technical Report UM-CS-2012-009, Dept. of Computer Science, Univ. of Massachusetts, March 2012.

[18] C. Stewart and K. Shen. Performance Modeling and System Management for Multi-component Online Services. In *Proc. USENIX Symp. on Networked Systems Design and Implementation (NSDI)*, May 2005.

[19] B. Urgaonkar, G. Pacifici, P. Shenoy, M. Spreitzer, and A. Tantawi. An Analytical Model for Multi-tier Internet Services and Its Applications. In *Proc. of the ACM SIGMETRICS Conf.*, Banff, Canada, June 2005.

[20] B. Urgaonkar, P. Shenoy, A. Chandra, P. Goyal, and T. Wood. Agile dynamic provisioning of multi-tier internet applications. *ACM Transactions on Adaptive and Autonomous Systems (TAAS), Vol. 3, No. 1*, pages 1–39, March 2008.

[21] D. Villela, P. Pradhan, and D. Rubenstein. Provisioning Servers in the Application Tier for E-commerce Systems. In *Proceedings of the 12th IWQoS*, June 2004.

[22] K. Xiong and H. Perros. Qrp01-6: Resource optimization subject to a percentile response time sla for enterprise computing. In *Global Telecommunications Conference, 2006. GLOBECOM '06. IEEE*, pages 1 –6, 27 2006-dec. 1 2006.

[23] S. F. Yashkov. Processor-sharing queues: some progress in analysis. *Queueing Syst. Theory Appl.*, 2(1):1–17, 1987.

[24] Q. Zhang, L. Cherkasova, N. Mi, and E. Smirni. A regression-based analytic model for capacity planning of multi-tier applications. *Cluster Computing*, 11(3):197–211, 2008.

Automated Profiling and Resource Management of Pig Programs for Meeting Service Level Objectives*

Zhuoyao Zhang
University of Pennsylvania
zhuoyao@seas.upenn.edu

Ludmila Cherkasova
Hewlett-Packard Labs
lucy.cherkasova@hp.com

Abhishek Verma
University of Illinois at
Urbana-Champaign
verma7@illinois.edu

Boon Thau Loo
University of Pennsylvania
boonloo@cis.upenn.edu

ABSTRACT

An increasing number of MapReduce applications associated with live business intelligence require completion time guarantees. In this paper, we consider the popular Pig framework that provides a high-level SQL-like abstraction on top of MapReduce engine. Programs written in this framework are compiled into directed acyclic graphs (DAGs) of MapReduce jobs. There is a lack of performance models and analysis tools for automated performance management of such MapReduce jobs. We offer a performance modeling environment for Pig programs that automatically profiles jobs from the past runs and aims to solve the following inter-related problems: (i) estimating the completion time of a Pig program as a function of allocated resources; (ii) estimating the amount of resources (a number of map and reduce slots) required for completing a Pig program with a given (soft) deadline. For solving these problems, initially, we optimize a Pig program execution by enforcing the *optimal schedule* of its concurrent jobs. For DAGs with concurrent jobs, this optimization helps reducing the program completion time: 10%-27% in our experiments. Moreover, it eliminates possible non-determinism of concurrent jobs' execution in the Pig program, and therefore, enables a more accurate performance model for Pig programs. We validate our approach using a 66-node Hadoop cluster and a diverse set of workloads: PigMix benchmark, TPC-H queries, and customized queries mining a collection of HP Labs' web proxy logs. The proposed scheduling optimization leads to significant resource savings (20%-40% in our experiments) compared with the original, unoptimized solution. Predicted program completion times are within 10% of the measured ones.

Categories and Subject Descriptors: C.4 [Computer System Organization] Performance of Systems, D.2.6.[Software] Programming Environments.

General Terms: Algorithms, Design, Performance, Measurement, Management

*This work was originated and largely completed during Z. Zhang's and A. Verma's internship at HP Labs. B. T. Loo and Z. Zhang are supported in part by NSF grants (CNS-1117185, CNS-0845552 , IIS-0812270). A. Verma is supported in part by NSF grant CCF-0964471.

Keywords: Hadoop, Pig, Resource Allocation, Scheduling

1. INTRODUCTION

The amount of enterprise data produced daily is exploding. This is partly due to a new era of automated data generation and massive event logging of automated and digitized business processes; new style customer interactions that are done entirely via web; a set of novel applications used for advanced data analytics in call centers and for information management associated with data retention, government compliance rules, e-discovery and litigation issues that require to store and process large amount of historical data. Many companies are following the new wave of using MapReduce [4] and its open-source implementation Hadoop to quickly process large quantities of new data to drive their core business. MapReduce offers a scalable and fault-tolerant framework for processing large data sets. However, a single input dataset and simple two-stage dataflow processing schema imposed by MapReduce model is low level and rigid. To enable programmers to specify more complex queries in an easier way, several projects, such as Pig [6], Hive [15], Scope [3], and Dryad [9], provide high-level SQL-like abstractions on top of MapReduce engines. These frameworks enable complex analytics tasks (expressed as high-level declarative abstractions) to be compiled into *directed acyclic graphs* (DAGs) of MapReduce jobs.

Another technological trend is the shift towards using MapReduce and the above frameworks for supporting *latency-sensitive* applications, e.g., personalized advertising, sentiment analysis, spam and fraud detection, real-time event log analysis, etc. These MapReduce applications are deadline-driven and typically require completion time guarantees and achieving service level objectives (SLOs). While there have been some research efforts [17, 19, 14] towards developing performance models for MapReduce jobs, these techniques do not apply to complex queries consisting of MapReduce DAGs. To address this limitation, our paper studies the popular Pig framework [6], and aims to design a performance modeling environment for Pig programs to offer solutions for the following problems:

- Given a Pig program, estimate its completion time as a function of allocated resources (i.e., allocated map and reduce slots);

- Given a Pig program with a completion time goal, estimate the amount of resources (a number of map and reduce slots) required for completing the Pig program with a given (*soft*) deadline.

The designed performance framework enables an SLO-driven job scheduler for MapReduce environments that given a Pig program with a completion time goal, it could allocate the appropriate amount of resources to the program that it completes within the desired deadline. This framework utilizes an automated profiling tool and past Pig program runs to extract performance profiles of the MapReduce jobs that constitute a given Pig program. We focus on Pig, since it is quickly becoming a popular and widely-adopted system for expressing a broad variety of data analysis tasks. With Pig, the data analysts can specify complex analytics tasks without directly writing Map and Reduce functions. In June 2009, more than 40% of Hadoop production jobs at Yahoo! were Pig programs [6].

While our paper is based on the Pig experience, we believe that the proposed models and optimizations are general and can be applied for performance modeling and resource allocations of complex analytics tasks that are expressed as an ensemble (DAG) of MapReduce jobs.

The paper makes the following key contributions:

Pig scheduling optimizations. For a Pig program defined by a DAG of MapReduce jobs, its completion time might be approximated as the sum of completion times of the jobs that constitute this Pig program. However, such model might lead to a higher time estimate than the actual measured program time. The reason is that unlike the execution of sequential jobs where due to data dependencies the next job can only start after the previous one is completed, for concurrent jobs in the DAG, they might be executed in arbitrary order and their map (and reduce) phases might be pipelined. That is, after one job completes its map phase and begins its reduce phase, the other concurrent job can start its map phase execution with the released map resources in a pipelined fashion. The performance model should take this "overlap" in executions of concurrent jobs into account. Moreover, this observation suggests that the chosen execution order of concurrent jobs may impact the "amount of overlap" and the overall program processing time. Using this observation, we first, optimize a Pig program execution by enforcing the *optimal schedule* of its concurrent jobs. We evaluate optimized Pig programs and the related performance improvements using TPC-H queries and a set of customized queries mining a collection of HP Labs' web proxy logs (both sets are presented by the DAGs with concurrent jobs). Our results show 10%-27% decrease in Pig program completion times.

Performance modeling framework. The proposed Pig optimization has another useful outcome: it eliminates existing non-determinism in Pig program execution of concurrent jobs, and therefore, it enables better performance predictions. We develop an accurate performance model for completion time estimates and resource allocations of optimized Pig programs. The accuracy of this model is validated using the PigMix benchmark [2] and a combination of TPC-H and web proxy log analysis queries on a 66-node Hadoop cluster. Our evaluation shows that the predicted completion times are within 10% of the measured ones. For Pig programs with concurrent jobs, we demonstrate that the proposed approach leads to significant resource savings (20%-40% in our experiments) compared with the original, non-optimized solution.

This paper is organized as follows. Section 2 provides a background on MapReduce processing and the Pig framework. Section 3 discusses subtleties of concurrent jobs execution in Pig, introduces optimized scheduling of concurrent jobs, and offers a novel performance modeling framework for Pig programs. Section 4 describes the experimental testbed and three workloads used in the performance study. The models' accuracy is evaluated in Section 5. Section 6 describes the related work. Section 7 presents a summary and future directions.

Acknoledgements: Many thanks to our HPL colleagues Hernan Laffitte for his help with the Hadoop testbed and Ken Burden for offering the HP Labs proxy logs.

2. BACKGROUND

This section provides a basic background on the MapReduce framework [4] and its extension, the Pig system [6].

2.1 MapReduce Jobs

In the MapReduce model, computation is expressed as two functions: map and reduce. The map function takes an input pair and produces a list of intermediate key/value pairs. The reduce function then merges or aggregates all the values associated with the same key.

MapReduce jobs are automatically parallelized, distributed, and executed on a large cluster of commodity machines. The map and reduce stages are partitioned into map and reduce tasks respectively. Each map task processes a logical split of input data. The map task reads the data, applies the user-defined map function on each record, and buffers the resulting output. The reduce stage consists of three phases: shuffle, sort and reduce phase. In the shuffle phase, the reduce tasks fetch the intermediate data files from the already completed map tasks, thus following the "pull" model. After all the intermediate data is shuffled (i.e., when the entire map stage with all the map tasks is completed), a final pass is made to merge all these sorted files, hence interleaving the shuffle and sort phases. Finally, in the reduce phase, the sorted intermediate data is passed to the user-defined reduce function. The output from the reduce function is generally written back to the distributed file system.

Job scheduling in Hadoop is performed by a master node, which manages a number of worker nodes in the cluster. Each worker has a fixed number of *map slots* and *reduce slots*, which can run map and reduce tasks respectively. The number of map and reduce slots is statically configured (typically, one per core or disk). Slaves periodically send heartbeats to the master to report the number of free slots and the progress of tasks that they are currently running. Based on the availability of free slots and the scheduling policy, the master assigns map and reduce tasks to slots in the cluster.

2.2 Pig Programs

There are two main components in the Pig system:

- The *language*, called Pig Latin, that combines high-level declarative style of SQL and the low-level procedural programming of MapReduce. A Pig program is similar to specifying a query execution plan: it represent a sequence of steps, where each one carries a single data transformation using a high-level data manipulation constructs, like *filter*, *group*, *join*, etc. In this way, the Pig program encodes a set of explicit dataflows.

- The *execution environment* to run Pig programs. The Pig system takes a Pig Latin program as input, compiles it into a DAG of MapReduce jobs, and coordinates their execution on a given Hadoop cluster. Pig relies on underlying Hadoop execution engine for scalability and fault-tolerance properties.

The following specification shows a simple example of a Pig program. It describes a task that operates over a table *URLs* that stores data with the three attributes: (url, category, pagerank). This program identifies for each category the url with the highest pagerank in that category.

```
URLs = load 'dataset' as (url, category, pagerank);
groups = group URLs by category;
result = foreach groups generate group, max(URLs.pagerank);
store result into 'myOutput'
```

The example Pig program is compiled into a single MapReduce job. Typically, Pig programs are more complex, and can be compiled into an execution plan consisting of several stages of MapReduce jobs, some of which can run concurrently. The structure of the execution plan can be represented by a DAG of MapReduce jobs that could contain both concurrent and sequential branches. Figure 1 shows a possible DAG of five MapReduce jobs $\{j_1, j_2, j_3, j_4, j_5\}$, where each node represents a MapReduce job, and the edges between the nodes represent *data dependencies* between jobs.

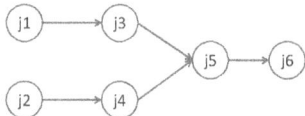

Figure 1: Example of a Pig program' execution plan represented as a DAG of MapReduce jobs.

To execute the plan, the Pig engine first submits all the *ready* jobs (i.e., the jobs that do not have data dependency on the other jobs) to Hadoop. After Hadoop has processed these jobs, the Pig system deletes them and the corresponding edges from the processing DAG, and identifies and submits the next set of ready jobs. This process continues until all the jobs are completed. In this way, the Pig engine partitions the DAG into multiple stages, each containing one or more independent MapReduce jobs that can be executed concurrently.

For example, the DAG shown in Figure 1 is partitioned into the following four stages for processing:

- first stage: $\{j_1, j_2\}$;
- second stage: $\{j_3, j_4\}$;
- third stage: $\{j_5\}$;
- fourth stage: $\{j_6\}$.

In Section 5, we will show some examples based on TPC-H and web log analysis queries that are representative of such MapReduce DAGs. Note that for stages with concurrent jobs, there is no specifically defined ordering in which the jobs are going to be executed by Hadoop.

3. PERFORMANCE MODELING FRAME-WORK FOR PIG PROGRAMS

This section introduces our modeling framework for Pig programs. First, we outline the profiling and modeling technique for a single MapReduce job. Then we analyze subtleties in execution of concurrent MapReduce jobs and demonstrate that the job order has a significant impact on the program completion time. We optimize a Pig program by enforcing the *optimal schedule* of its concurrent jobs, and it enables more accurate Pig program performance modeling.

3.1 Performance Model of a Single MapReduce Job

As a building block for modeling Pig programs defined as DAGs of MapReduce jobs, we apply a slightly modified approach introduced in [17] for performance modeling of a single MapReduce job. The proposed MapReduce performance model [17] evaluates lower and upper bounds on the job completion time. It is based on a general model for computing performance bounds on the completion time of a given set of n tasks that are processed by k servers, (e.g., n map tasks are processed by k map slots in MapReduce environment). Let $T_1, T_2, \ldots, T_n$ be the duration of n tasks in a given set. Let k be the number of slots that can each execute one task at a time. The assignment of tasks to slots is done using an online, *greedy* algorithm: assign each task to the slot which finished its running task the earliest. Let *avg* and *max* be the *average* and *maximum* duration of the n tasks respectively. Then the completion time of a greedy task assignment is proven to be at least:

$$T^{low} = avg \cdot \frac{n}{k}$$

and at most

$$T^{up} = avg \cdot \frac{(n-1)}{k} + max.$$

The difference between lower and upper bounds represents the range of possible completion times due to task scheduling non-determinism (i.e., whether the maximum duration task is scheduled to run last). Note, that these provable lower and upper bounds on the completion time can be easily computed if we know the average and maximum durations of the set of tasks and the number of allocated slots. See [17] for detailed proofs on these bounds.

As motivated by the above model, in order to approximate the overall completion time of a MapReduce job J, we need to estimate the *average* and *maximum* task durations during different execution phases of the job, i.e., *map*, *shuffle/sort*, and *reduce* phases. These measurements can be obtained from the job execution logs. By applying the outlined bounds model, we can estimate the completion times of different processing phases of the job. For example, let job J be partitioned into N_M^J map tasks. Then the lower and upper bounds of the duration of the entire map stage in the **future** execution with S_M^J map slots (denoted as T_M^{low} and T_M^{up} respectively) are estimated as follows:

$$T_M^{low} = M_{avg}^J \cdot N_M^J / S_M^J \tag{1}$$

$$T_M^{up} = M_{avg}^J \cdot (N_M^J - 1)/S_M^J + M_{max}^J \tag{2}$$

where M_{avg} and M_{max} are the average and maximum of the map task durations of the past run respectively. Similarly, we can compute bounds of the execution time of other processing phases of the job. As a result, we can express the estimates for the entire job completion time (lower bound T_J^{low} and upper bound T_J^{up}) as a function of allocated map/reduce slots (S_M^J, S_R^J) using the following equation form:

$$T_J^{low} = \frac{A_J^{low}}{S_M^J} + \frac{B_J^{low}}{S_R^J} + C_J^{low}. \tag{3}$$

The equation for T_J^{up} can be written in a similar form (see [17] for details and exact expressions of coefficients in these equations). Typically, the average of lower and upper bounds (T_J^{avg}) is a good approximation of the job completion time.

Once we have a technique for predicting the job completion time, it also can be used for solving the inverse problem: finding the appropriate number of map and reduce slots that could support a given job deadline D (e.g., if D is used instead of T_J^{low} in Equation 3). When we consider S_M^J and S_R^J as variables in Equation 3 it yields a hyperbola. All integral points on this hyperbola are possible allocations of map and reduce slots which result in meeting the same deadline D. There is a point where the sum of the required map and reduce slots is minimized. We calculate this minima on the curve using Lagrange's multipliers [17], since we would like to conserve the number of map and reduce slots required for the minimum resource allocation per job J with a given deadline D. Note, that we can use D for finding the resource allocations from the corresponding equations for upper and lower bounds on the job completion time estimates. In Section 5, we will compare the outcome of using different bounds for estimating a completion time of a Pig program.

3.2 Modeling Concurrent Jobs' Executions

Our goal is to design a model for a Pig program that can estimate the number of map and reduce slots required for completing a Pig program with a given (soft) deadline. These estimates can be used by the SLO-based scheduler like ARIA [17] to tailor and control resource allocations to different applications for achieving their performance goals. When such a scheduler allocates a recommended amount of map/reduce slots to the Pig program, it uses a FIFO schedule for jobs within the DAG (see Section 2.2 for how these jobs are submitted by the Pig system).

There is a subtlety in how concurrent jobs in the DAG of MapReduce jobs might be executed. In the explanations below, we use the following useful abstraction. We represent any MapReduce job as a composition of *non-overlaping map* and *reduce stages*. Indeed, there is a barrier between map and reduce stages and any reduce task may start its execution only after all map tasks complete and all the intermediate data is shuffled. However, the shuffle phase (that we consider as a part of the reduce stage) overlaps with the map stage. Note, that in the ARIA performance model [17] that we use for estimating a job completion time, the shuffle phase measurements include only non-overlapping portion of the latency. These measurements and the model allow us to estmate the duration of map and reduce stages (as a function of allocated map and reduce slots) and support a simple abstraction where the job execution is represented as a composition of *non-overlaping map* and *reduce stages*.

Let us consider two concurrent MapReduce jobs J_1 and J_2. Let us also assume that there are no data dependencies among the concurrent jobs. Therefore, unlike the execution of sequential jobs where the next job can only start after the previous one is entirely finished (shown in Figure 2 (a)), for concurrent jobs, once the previous job completes its map stage and begins reduce stage processing, the next job can start its map stage execution with the released map resources in a pipelined fashion (shown in Figure 2 (b)). The Pig performance model should take this "overlap" in executions of concurrent jobs into account.

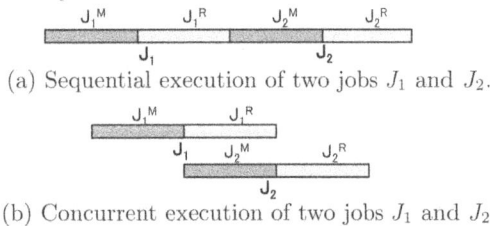

(a) Sequential execution of two jobs J_1 and J_2.

(b) Concurrent execution of two jobs J_1 and J_2.

Figure 2: Difference in executions of (a) two sequential MapReduce jobs; (b) two concurrent MapReduce jobs.

We find one more interesting observation about concurrent jobs' execution of the Pig program. The original Hadoop implementation executes concurrent MapReduce jobs from the same Pig program in a random order. Some ordering may lead to inefficient resource usage and an increased processing time. As a motivating example, let us consider two concurrent MapReduce jobs that result in the following map and reduce stage durations:

- Job J_1 has a map stage duration of $J_1^M = 10s$ and the reduce stage duration of $J_1^R = 1s$.
- Job J_2 has a map stage duration of $J_2^M = 1s$ and the reduce stage duration of $J_2^R = 10s$.

There are two possible executions shown in Figure 3:

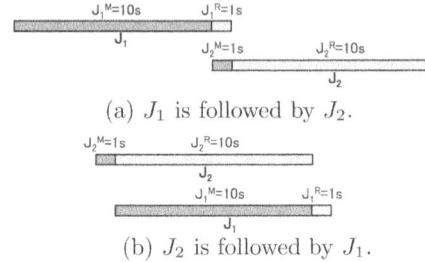

(a) J_1 is followed by J_2.

(b) J_2 is followed by J_1.

Figure 3: Impact of concurrent job scheduling on their completion time.

- J_1 is followed by J_2 shown in Figure 3(a). The reduce stage of J_1 overlaps with the map stage of J_2 leading to overlap of only $1s$. The total completion time of processing two jobs is $10s + 1s + 10s = 21s$.
- J_2 is followed by J_1 shown in Figure 3(b). The reduce stage of J_2 overlaps with the map stage of J_1 leading to a much better pipelined execution and a larger overlap of $10s$. The total makespan is $1s + 10s + 1s = 12s$.

There is a significant difference in the job completion time (75% in the example above) depending on the execution order of the jobs. We optimize a Pig program execution by enforcing the optimal schedule of its concurrent jobs. We apply the classic Johnson algorithm for building the optimal two-stage jobs' schedule [10]. The optimal execution of concurrent jobs leads to improved completion time. Moreover, this optimization eliminates possible non-determinism in Pig program execution, and enables more accurate completion time predictions for Pig programs.

3.3 Completion Time Estimates for Pig Programs

Using the model of a single MapReduce job as a building block, we consider a Pig program P that is compiled into a DAG of $|P|$ MapReduce jobs $P = \{J_1, J_2, ...J_{|P|}\}$.

Automated profiling. To automate the construction of all performance models, we build an automated profiling tool that extracts the MapReduce job profiles[1] of the Pig program from the past program executions. These job profiles represent critical performance characteristics of the underlying application during all the execution phases: map, shuffle/sort, and reduce phases.

For each MapReduce job $J_i (1 \leq i \leq |P|)$ that constitutes Pig program P, in addition to the number of map ($N_M^{J_i}$) and reduce ($N_R^{J_i}$) tasks, we also extract metrics that reflect the durations of map and reduce tasks (note that shuffle phase measurements are included in the reduce task measurements) [2]:

$$(M_{avg}^{J_i}, M_{max}^{J_i}, AvgSize_M^{J_i\,input}, Selectivity_M^{J_i})$$

---

[1] To differentiate MapReduce jobs in the same Pig program, we modified the Pig system to assign a unique name for each job as follows: *queryName-stageID-indexID*, where *stageID* represents the stage in the DAG that the job belongs to, and *indexID* represents the index of jobs within a particular stage.

[2] Unlike prior models [17], we normalize all the collected measurements per record and per input dataset to reflect the processing cost of a single record of a given data input. These normalized costs are used to approximate the duration of map and reduce tasks when the

$$(R_{avg}^{J_i}, R_{max}^{J_i}, Selectivity_R^{J_i})$$

- $AvgSize_M^{J_i input}$ is the average amount of input data per map task of job J_i (we use it to estimate the number of map tasks to be spawned for processing a new dataset).

- $Selectivity_M^{J_i}$ and $Selectivity_R^{J_i}$ refer to the ratio of the map (and reduce) output size to the map input size. It is used to estimate the amount of intermediate data produced by the map (and reduce) stage of job J_i. This allows to estimate the size of the input dataset for the next job in the DAG.

As a building block for modeling a Pig program defined as a DAG of MapReduce jobs, we apply the approach introduced in ARIA [17] for performance modeling of a single MapReduce job. We extract performance profiles of all the jobs in the DAG from the past program executions. Using these job profiles we can predict the completion time of each job (and completion time of map and reduce stages) as a function of allocated map and reduce slots. We can compute the completion time using a lower or upper bound estimates as described in Section 2. For the rest of this section, we use the completion time estimates based on the average of the lower and upper bounds.

Let us consider a Pig program P that is compiled into a DAG of MapReduce jobs and consists of S stages.

Note that due to data dependencies within a Pig execution plan, the *next stage* cannot start until the *previous stage* finishes. Let T_{S_i} denote the completion time of stage S_i. Thus, the completion of a Pig program P can be estimated as follows:

$$T_P = \sum_{1 \le i \le S} T_{S_i}. \qquad (4)$$

For a stage that consists of a single job J, the stage completion time is defined by the job J's completion time.

For a stage that contains concurrent jobs, the stage completion time depends on the jobs' execution order. Suppose there are $|S_i|$ jobs within a particular stage S_i and the jobs are executed according to the order $\{J_1, J_2, ...J_{|S_i|}\}$. Note, that given a number of allocated map/reduce slots (S_M^P, S_R^P) to the Pig program P, we can compute for any MapReduce job $J_i (1 \le i \le |S_i|)$ the duration of its map and reduce phases that are required for the Johnson's algorithm [10] to determine the optimal schedule of the jobs $\{J_1, J_2, ...J_{|S_i|}\}$.

Let us assume, that for each stage with concurrent jobs, we have already determined the optimal job schedule that minimizes the completion time of the stage. Now, we introduce the performance model for predicting the Pig program P completion time T_P as a function of allocated resources (S_M^P, S_R^P). We use the following notations:

$timeStart_{J_i}^M$	the start time of job J_i's map phase
$timeEnd_{J_i}^M$	the end time of job J_i's map phase
$timeStart_{J_i}^R$	the start time of job J_i's reduce phase
$timeEnd_{J_i}^R$	the end time of job J_i's reduce phase

Then the stage completion time can be estimated as

$$T_{S_i} = timeEnd_{J_{|S_i|}}^R - timeStart_{J_1}^M \qquad (5)$$

We now explain how to estimate the start/end time of each job's map/reduce phase[3].

Let $T_{J_i}^M$ and $T_{J_i}^R$ denote the completion times of map and reduce phases of job J_i respectively. Then

$$timeEnd_{J_i}^M = timeStart_{J_i}^M + T_{J_i}^M \qquad (6)$$

$$timeEnd_{J_i}^R = timeStart_{J_i}^R + T_{J_i}^R \qquad (7)$$

Figure 4 shows an example of three concurrent jobs execution in the order J_1, J_2, J_3.

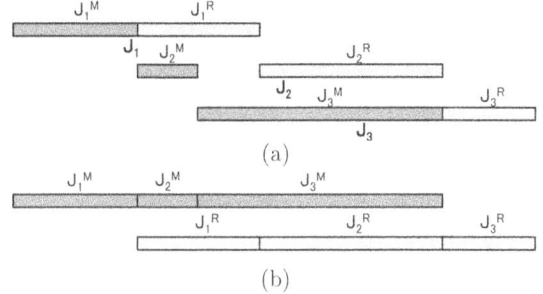

Figure 4: Execution of Concurrent Jobs

Note, that Figure 4 (a) can be rearranged to show the execution of jobs' map/reduce stages separately (over the map/reduce slots) as shown in Figure 4 (b). It is easy to see that since all the concurrent jobs are independent, the map phase of the next job can start immediately once the previous job's map stage is finished, i.e.,

$$timeStart_{J_i}^M = timeEnd_{J_{i-1}}^M = timeStart_{J_{i-1}}^M + T_{J_{i-1}}^M \qquad (8)$$

The start time $timeStart_{J_i}^R$ of the reduce stage of the concurrent job J_i should satisfy the following two conditions:

1. $timeStart_{J_i}^R \ge timeEnd_{J_i}^M$

2. $timeStart_{J_i}^R \ge timeEnd_{J_{i-1}}^R$

Therefore, we have the following equation:

$$timeStart_{J_i}^R = max\{timeEnd_{J_i}^M, timeEnd_{J_{i-1}}^R\} =$$
$$= max\{timeStart_{J_i}^M + T_{J_i}^M, timeStart_{J_{i-1}}^R + T_{J_{i-1}}^R\} \qquad (9)$$

Finally, the completion time of the entire Pig program P is defined as the *sum of its stages* using eq. (4).

3.4 Resource Allocation Estimates for Optimized Pig Programs

Let us consider a Pig program P with a given deadline D. The optimized execution of concurrent jobs in P may significantly improve the program completion time. Therefore, P may need to be assigned a smaller amount of resources for meeting a given deadline D compared to its non-optimized execution. First, we explain how to approximate the resource allocation of a non-optimized execution of a Pig program. The completion time of non-optimized P can be represented as a sum of completion time of the jobs that comprise the DAG of this Pig program. Thus, for a Pig

---

Pig program executes on the new dataset(s) with a larger/smaller number of records. To reflect a possible skew of records per task, we collect an average and maximum number of records per task. The task durations (average and maximum) are computed by multiplying the measured per-record time by the number of input records (average and maximum) processed by the task.

[3]These computations present the main, typical case when the number of allocated slots is smaller than the number of tasks that jobs need to process, and therefore, the execution of concurrent jobs is pipelined. There are some corner cases with small concurrent jobs when there are enough resources for processing them at the same time. In this case, the designed model over-estimates the stage completion time. We have an additional set of equations that describes these corner cases in a more accurate way. We omit them here for presentation simplicity.

program P that contains $|P|$ jobs, its completion time can be estimated as a function of assigned map and reduce slots (S_M^P, S_R^P) as follows:

$$T_P(S_M^P, S_R^P) = \sum_{1 \leq i \leq |P|} T_{J_i}(S_M^P, S_R^P) \qquad (10)$$

The unique benefit of this model is that it allows us to express the completion time D of a Pig program P via a special form equation shown below (similar to eq. (3)):

$$D = \frac{A^P}{S_M^P} + \frac{A^P}{S_R^P} + C^P \qquad (11)$$

This equation can be used for solving the inverse problem of finding resource allocations (S_M^P, S_R^P) such that P completes within time D. This equation yields a hyperbola if (S_M^P, S_R^P) are considered as variables. We can directly calculate the minima on this curve by using Lagrange's multipliers for finding the resource allocation of a single MapReduce job with a given deadline.

The model introduced in Section 3.3 for accurate completion time estimates of an optimized Pig program is more complex. It requires computing a function *max* for stages with concurrent jobs, and therefore, it cannot be expressed as a single equation for solving the inverse problem of finding the appropriate resource allocation. However, we can use the "over-provisioned" resource allocation defined by eq. (11) as an initial point for determining the solution required by the optimized Pig program P. The hyperbola with all the possible solutions according to the "over-sized" model is shown in Figure 5 as the red curve, and $A(M, R)$ represents the point with a minimal number of map and reduce slots (i.e., the pair (M, R) results in the minimal sum of map and reduce slots). We designed the following algorithm described below that determines the minimal resource allocation pair (M_{min}, R_{min}) for an optimized Pig program P with deadline D. This computation is illustrated by Figure 5.

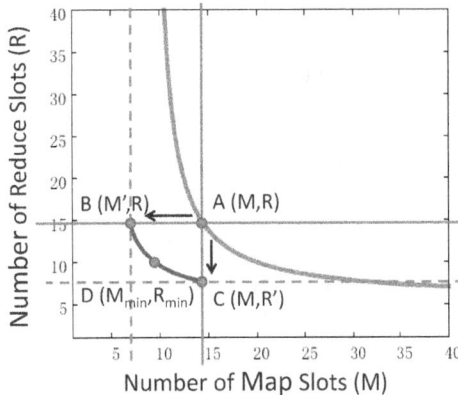

Figure 5: Resource allocation estimates for an optimized Pig program.

First, we find the minimal number of map slots M' (i.e., the pair (M', R)) such that deadline D can still be met by the optimized Pig program with the enforced optimal execution of its concurrent jobs. We do it by fixing the number of reduce slots to R, and then step-by-step reducing the allocation of map slots. Specifically, Algorithm 1 sets the resource allocation to $(M-1, R)$ and checks whether program P can still be completed within time D (we use T_P^{avg} for completion time estimates). If the answer is positive, then it tries $(M-2, R)$ as the next allocation. This process continues until point $B(M', R)$ (see Figure 5) is found such that the number M' of map slots cannot be further reduced for meeting a given deadline D (lines 1-4 of Algorithm 1).

Algorithm 1 Determining the resource allocation for a Pig program

---

Input:
Job profiles of all the jobs in $P = \{J_1, J_2, ...J_{|S_i|}\}$
$D \leftarrow$ a given deadline
$(M, R) \leftarrow$ the minimum pair of map and reduce slots obtained for P and deadline D by applying the *basic* model
Optimal execution of jobs $J_1, J_2, ...J_{|S_i|}$ based on (M, R)
Output:
Resource allocation pair (M_{min}, R_{min}) for optimized P

1: $M' \leftarrow M$, $R' \leftarrow R$
2: **while** $T_P^{avg}(M', R) \leq D$ **do**   // From A to B
3:     $M' \Leftarrow M' - 1$
4: **end while**
5: **while** $T_P^{avg}(M, R') \leq D$ **do**   // From A to C
6:     $R' \Leftarrow R' - 1$,
7: **end while**
8: $M_{min} \leftarrow M, R_{min} \leftarrow R$, $Min \leftarrow (M + R)$
9: **for** $\hat{M} \leftarrow M' + 1$ **to** M **do**   // Explore purple curve B to C
10:     $\hat{R} = R - 1$
11:     **while** $T_P^{avg}(\hat{M}, \hat{R}) \leq D$ **do**
12:         $\hat{R} \Leftarrow \hat{R} - 1$
13:     **end while**
14:     **if** $\hat{M} + \hat{R} < Min$ **then**
15:         $M_{min} \Leftarrow \hat{M}, R_{min} \Leftarrow \hat{R}, Min \leftarrow (\hat{M} + \hat{R})$
16:     **end if**
17: **end for**

In the second step, we apply the same process for finding the minimal number of reduce slots R' (i.e., the pair (M, R')) such that the deadline D can still be met by the optimized Pig program P (lines 5-7 of Algorithm 1).

In the third step, we determine the intermediate values on the curve between (M', R) and (M, R') such that deadline D is met by the optimized Pig program P. Starting from point (M', R), we are trying to find the allocation of map slots from M' to M, such that the minimal number of reduce slots $\hat{R}$ should be assigned to P for meeting its deadline (lines 10-12 of Algorithm 1).

Finally, (M_{min}, R_{min}) is the pair on this curve such that it results in the the minimal sum of map and reduce slots.

4. EXPERIMENTAL TESTBED AND WORKLOADS

All experiments are performed on 66 HP DL145 GL3 machines. Each machine has four AMD 2.39GHz cores, 8 GB RAM and two 160GB hard disks. The machines are set up in two racks and interconnected with gigabit Ethernet. We used Hadoop 0.20.2 and Pig-0.7.0 with two machines dedicated as the JobTracker and the NameNode, and remaining 64 machines as workers. Each worker is configured with 2 map and 1 reduce slots. The file system blocksize is set to 64MB. The replication level is set to 3. We disabled speculative execution since it did not lead to significant improvements in our experiments.

In our case studies, we use three different workload sets: the PigMix benchmark, TPC-H queries, and customized queries for mining web proxy logs from an enterprise company. We briefly describe each dataset and our respective modifications:

PigMix. We use the well-known PigMix benchmark [2] that was created for testing Pig system performance. It consists of 17 Pig programs (L1-L17), which uses datasets generated by the default Pigmix data generator. In total, 1TB of data across 8 tables are generated. The PigMix programs

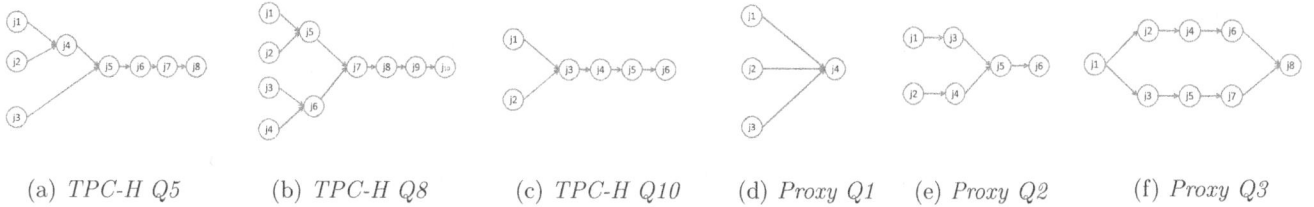

(a) *TPC-H Q5* (b) *TPC-H Q8* (c) *TPC-H Q10* (d) *Proxy Q1* (e) *Proxy Q2* (f) *Proxy Q3*

Figure 6: DAGs of Pig programs in the TPC-H and HP Labs Proxy query sets.

cover a wide range of the Pig features and operators, and the data set are generated with similar properties to Yahoo's datasets that are commonly processed using Pig. With the exception of L11 (that contains a stage with 2 concurrent jobs), all PigMix programs involve DAGs of sequential jobs. Therefore, with the PigMix benchmark we mostly evaluate the accuracy of the proposed performance model for completion time estimates and resource allocation decisions,. The efficiency of the designed optimization technique for concurrent job execution is evaluated with the next two workloads in the set.

TPC-H. This workload is based on TPC-H [1], a standard database benchmark for decision-support workloads. We select three queries $Q5, Q8, Q10$ out of existing 22 SQL queries and express them as Pig programs.

For each query, we select a logical plan that results in a DAG of concurrent MapReduce jobs shown in Fig. 6 (a),(b),(c) respectively[4]:

- The *TPC-H Q5* query joins 6 tables, and its dataflow results in 3 concurrent MapReduce jobs.
- The *TPC-H Q8* query joins 8 tables, and its dataflow results in two stages with 4 and 2 concurrent jobs.
- The *TPC-H Q10* query joins 4 tables, and its dataflow results in 2 concurrent MapReduce jobs.

HP Labs' Web Proxy Query Set. This workload consists of a set of Pig programs for analyzing HP Labs' web proxy logs. It contains 6 months access logs to web proxy gateway at HP Labs. The fields include information such as *date, time, time-taken, c-ip, cs-host*, etc. We intend to create realistic Pig queries executed on real-world data.

- The *Proxy Q1* program investigates the dynamics in access frequencies to different websites per month and compares them across different months. The Pig program results in 3 concurrent MapReduce jobs with the DAG of the program shown in Figure 6 (d).
- The *Proxy Q2* program discovers the co-relationship between two websites from different sets (tables) of popular websites: the first set is created to represent the top 500 popular websites accessed by web users within the enterprise. The second set contains the top 100 popular websites in US according to Alexa's statistics[5]. The program DAG is shown in Figure 6 (e).
- The *Proxy Q3* program presents the intersection of 100 most popular websites (i.e., websites with highest access frequencies) accessed both during work and after work hours. The DAG of the program is shown in Figure 6 (f).

To perform the validation experiments, we create two different datasets for each of the three workloads above:

---
[4]While more efficient logical plans may exist, our goal here is to create a DAG with concurrent jobs to stress test our model.
[5]http://www.alexa.com/topsites

1. A **test dataset**: It is used for extracting the job profiles of the corresponding Pig programs.
   - For PigMix benchmark, the *test dataset* is generated by the default data generator. It contains 125 million records for the largest table and has a total size around 1 TB.
   - For TPC-H, the *test dataset* is generated with scaling factor 9 using the standard data generator. The dataset size is around 9 GB.
   - For HP Labs' Web proxy query set, we use the logs from February, March and April as the *test dataset* with the total input size around 9 GB.

2. An **experimental dataset**: It is used to validate our performance models using the profiles extracted from the Pig programs that were executed with the *test dataset*. Both the *test* and *experimental* datasets are formed by the tables with the same layout but with different input sizes.
   - For PigMix benchmark, the input size of the *experimental dataset* is 20% larger than the *test dataset* (with 150 million records for the largest table).
   - For TPC-H, the *experimental dataset* is around 15 GB (scaling factor 15 using the standard data generator).
   - For HP Labs' Web proxy query set, we use the logs from May, June and July as the *experimental dataset*, the total input size is around 9 GB.

5. PERFORMANCE EVALUATION

This section presents the performance evaluation of the proposed models and optimizations. Since PigMix benchmark mostly consists of the Pig programs with sequential DAGs, we use PigMix only for validating the accuracy of the proposed performance models. Because TPC-H and HP Labs' proxy log queries represent Pig programs that are defined by the DAGs with concurrent jobs, we use these two workloads for evaluating the performance benefits of introduced Pig program optimization as well as the models' validation.

5.1 PigMix Case Study

This section aims to evaluate the accuracy of the proposed models: i) the bound-based model for estimating the completion time of Pig programs as a function of allocated resources, and ii) the accuracy of the recommended resource allocation for meeting the completion time goals.

First, we run the Pigmix benchmark on the *test dataset*, and the job profiles of the corresponding Pig programs are built from these executions. By using the extracted job profiles and the designed Pig model we compute the completion time estimates of Pig programs in the PigMix benchmark for processing these two datasets (*test and experimental*) as a function of allocated resources. Then we validate the predicted completion times against the measured ones.

Figure 7 shows the predicted vs measured results for the PigMix benchmark that processes the *test dataset* with 128 map and 64 reduce slots. Given that the completion times of different programs in PigMix are in a broad range of 100s – 2000s, for presentation purposes and easier comparison, we **normalize** the predicted completion times with respect to the measured ones. The three bars in Figure 7 represent the predicted completion times based on the lower (T^{low}) and upper (T^{up}) bounds, and the average of them (T^{avg}). We observe that the actual completion times (shown as the straight *Measured-CT* line) of all 17 programs fall between the lower and upper bound estimates. Moreover, the predicted completion times based on the average of the upper and lower bounds are within 10% of the measured results for most cases. The worst prediction (around 20% error) is for the Pig query L11.

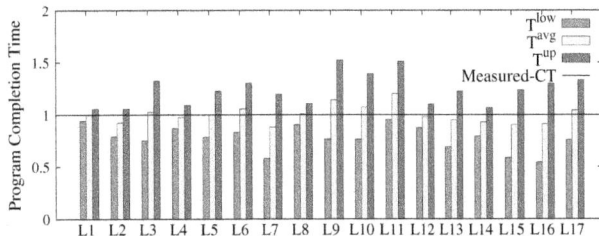

Figure 7: Predicted and measured completion time for PigMix executed with *test dataset* **and 128x64 slots.**

Figure 8 shows the results for the PigMix benchmark that processes the *test dataset* with 64 map and 64 reduce slots. Indeed, our model accurately computes the program completion time estimates as a function of allocated resources: the actual completion times of all 17 programs are between the computed lower and upper bounds. The predicted completion times based on the average of the upper and lower bounds provide the best results: 10-12% of the measured results for most cases.

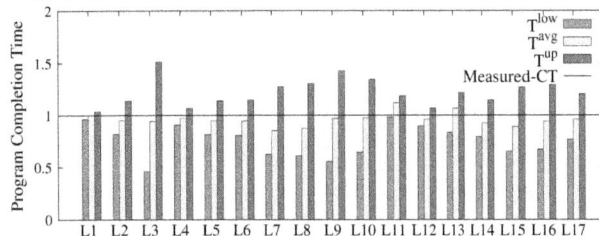

Figure 8: Predicted and measured completion time for PigMix executed with *test dataset* **and 64x64 slots.**

Figure 9 shows the predicted vs measured completion times for the PigMix benchmark that processes the larger, *experimental dataset* with 64 map and 64 reduce slots.

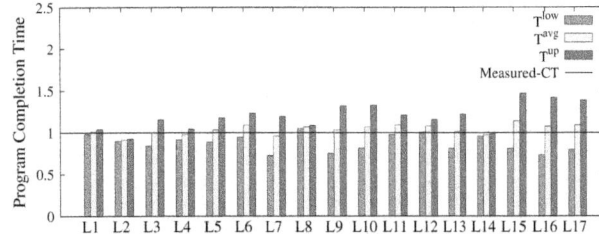

Figure 9: Predicted and measured completion time for PigMix executed with *experimental dataset* **and 64x64 slots.**

As shown in Figure 9, our model and computed estimates are quite accurate. The measured completion time of all

programs is between the low and upper bounds. The predicted completion times that are based on the average of the upper and lower bounds provide the best results: they are within 10% of the measured results for most cases.

In Figures 7, 8, 9 we execute PigMix benchmark three times and report the measured completion time averaged across 3 runs. A variance for most programs in these three runs is within 1%-2%, with the largest variance being around 6%. Because the variance is so small, we have omitted the error bars in Figures 7, 8, 9.

Our second set of experiments aims to evaluate the solution of the inverse problem: the accuracy of a resource allocation for a Pig program with a completion time goal, often defined as a part of Service Level Objectives (SLOs).

In this set of experiments, let T denote the Pig program completion time when the program is processed with maximum available cluster resources (i.e., when the entire cluster is used for program processing). We set $D = 3 \cdot T$ as a completion time goal. Using the approach described in Section 3.4 we compute the required resource allocation, i.e., a tailored number of map and reduce slots that allow the Pig program to be completed with deadline D on a new *experimental dataset*. We compute resource allocations when D is targeted as either a lower bound, or upper bound or the average of lower and upper bounds on the completion time. Figure 10 shows the measured program completion times based on these three different resource allocations. Similar to our earlier results, for presentation purposes, we **normalize** the achieved completion times with respect to the given deadline D.

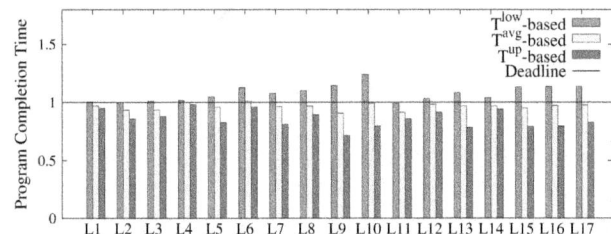

Figure 10: PigMix executed with the *experimental dataset*: **do we meet deadlines?**

In most cases, the resource allocation that targets D as a lower bound is insufficient for meeting the targeted deadline (e.g., the L10 program misses deadline by more than 20%). However, when we compute the resource allocation based on D as an upper bound – we are always able to meet the required deadline, but in most cases, we over-provision resources, e.g., L16 and L17 finish more than 20% earlier than a given deadline.

The resource allocations based on the average between lower and upper bounds result in the closest completion time to the targeted program deadlines.

5.2 Optimal Schedule of Concurrent Jobs

Figure 11 shows the impact of concurrent jobs scheduling on the completion time of TPC-H and Proxy queries when each program is processed with **128** map and **64** reduce slots. Figures 11 (a) and (c) show two extreme measurements: the best program completion time (i.e., when the optimal schedule of concurrent jobs is chosen) and the worst one (i.e., when concurrent jobs are executed in the "worst" possible order based on our estimates). For presentation purposes, the best (optimal) completion time is **normalized** with respect to the worst one. The choice of optimal

(a) Job completion time (b) Stage completion time

(c) Job completion time (d) Stage completion time

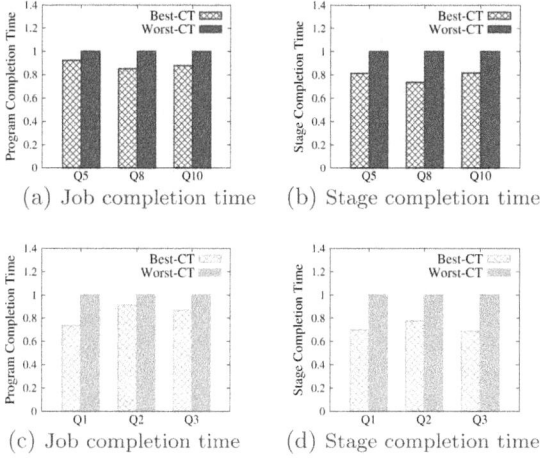

Figure 11: Normalized completion time for different schedules of concurrent jobs: (a-b) TPC-H, (c-d) HP Labs proxy queries.

schedule of concurrent jobs reduces the completion time by 10%-27% compared with the worse case ordering.

Figures 11 (b) and (d) show completion times of stages with concurrent jobs under different schedules for the same TPC-H and Proxy queries. Performance benefits at the stage level are even higher: they range between 20%-30%.

5.3 Predicting Completion Time and Resource Allocation of Optimized Pig Programs

Figure 12 shows the Pig program completion time estimates (we use T_P^{avg} in these experiments) based on the proposed performance model for TPC-H and Proxy queries with the *experimental datasets*. Figure 12 shows the results when each program is processed with **64x64** and **32x64** map and reduce slots respectively.

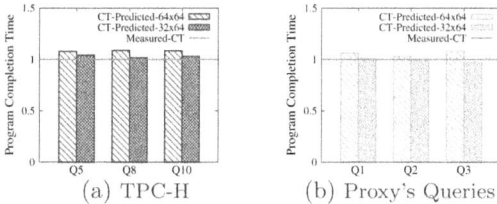

(a) TPC-H (b) Proxy's Queries

Figure 12: Predicted Pig programs completion times executed with the *experimental dataset*.

In all cases, the predicted completion times are within 10% of the measured ones.

Let T denote the Pig program completion time when program P is processed with maximum available cluster resources. We set $D = 2 \cdot T$ as a completion time goal (we use different deadlines for different experiments on purpose, in order to validate the accuracy of our models for a variety of parameters). Then we compute the required resource allocation for P executed with the *experimental dataset* to meet the deadline D. Figure 13 (a) shows measured completion times achieved by the TPC-H and Proxy's queries respectively when they are assigned the resource allocations computed with the designed resource allocation model. All the queries complete within 10% of the targeted deadlines.

Figure 13 (b) compares the amount of resources (the sum of map and reduce slots) for non-optimized and optimized executions of TPC-H and Proxy's queries respectively. The optimized executions are able to achieve targeted deadlines with much smaller resource allocations (20%-40% smaller) compared to resource allocations for non-optimized Pig pro-

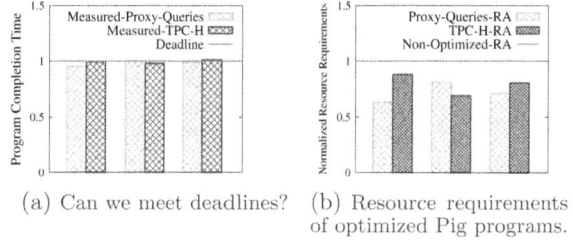

(a) Can we meet deadlines? (b) Resource requirements of optimized Pig programs.

Figure 13: Resource allocations for optimized Pig programs executed with the *experimental dataset*.

grams. Therefore, the proposed optimal schedule of concurrent jobs leads to significant resource savings for deadline-driven Pig programs.

6. RELATED WORK

While performance modeling in the MapReduce framework is a new topic, there are several interesting research efforts in this direction.

Polo et al. [14] introduce an online job completion time estimator which can be used in their new Hadoop scheduler for adjusting the resource allocations of different jobs. However, their estimator tracks the progress of the map stage alone, and use a simplistic way for predicting the job completion time, while skipping the shuffle/sort phase, and have no information or control over the reduce stage.

FLEX [19] develops a novel Hadoop scheduler by proposing a special slot allocation schema that aims to optimize some given scheduling metric. FLEX relies on the speedup function of the job (for map and reduce stages) that defines the job execution time as a function of allocated slots. However, it is not clear how to derive this function for different applications and for different sizes of input datasets. The authors do not provide a detailed MapReduce performance model for jobs with targeted job deadlines.

ARIA [17] introduces a deadline-based scheduler for Hadoop. This scheduler extracts the job profiles from the past executions, and provides a variety of bounds-based models for predicting a job completion time as a function of allocated resources and a solution of the inverse problem. However, these models apply only to a single MapReduce job.

Tian and Chen [16] aim to predict performance of a single MapReduce program from the test runs with a smaller number of nodes. They consider MapReduce processing at a fine granularity. For example, the map task is partitioned in 4 functions: read a block, map function processing of the block, partition and sort of the processed data, and the combiner step (if it is used). The reduce task is decomposed in 4 functions as well. The authors use a *linear regression technique* to approximate the cost (duration) of each function. These functions are used for predicting the larger dataset processing. There are a few simplifying assumptions, e.g., a single wave in the reduce stage. The problem of finding resource allocations that support given job completion goals are formulated as an optimization problem that can be solved with existing commercial solvers.

There is an interesting group of papers that design a detailed job profiling approach for pursuing a different goal: to optimize the configuration parameters of both a Hadoop cluster and a given MapReduce job (or workflow of jobs) for achieving the improved completion time. *Starfish* project [8, 7] applies *dynamic instrumentation* to collect a detailed runtime monitoring information about job execution at a fine granularity: data reading, map processing, spilling, merging, shuffling, sorting, reduce processing and writing. Such a detailed job profiling information enables the authors to analyze and predict job execution under different configuration parameters, and automatically derive an optimized configuration. One of the main challenges outlined by the authors is a design of an efficient searching strategy through the high-dimensional space of parameter values. The authors offer a workflow-aware scheduler that correlate data (block) placement with task scheduling to optimize the workflow completion time. In our work, we propose complementary optimizations based on optimal scheduling of concurrent jobs within the DAG to minimize overall completion time.

Kambatla et al [11] propose a different approach for optimizing the Hadoop configuration parameters (number of map and reduce slots per node) to improve MapReduce program performance. A signature-based (fingerprint-based) approach is used to predict the performance of a new MapReduce program using a set of already studied programs. The ideas presented in the paper are interesting but it is a position paper that does not provide enough details and lacking the extended evaluation of the approach.

Ganapathi et al. [5] use Kernel Canonical Correlation Analysis to predict the performance of *Hive queries*. However, they do not attempt to model the actual execution of the MapReduce job: the authors discover the feature vectors through statistical correlation.

CoScan [18] offers a special scheduling framework that merges the execution of Pig programs with common data inputs in such a way that this data is only scanned once. Authors augment Pig programs with a set of *(deadline, reward)* options to achieve. Then they formulate the schedule as an optimization problem and offer a heuristic solution.

Morton et al. [12] propose *ParaTimer*: the progress estimator for parallel queries expressed as Pig scripts [6]. In their earlier work [13], they designed *Parallax* – a progress estimator that aims to predict the completion time of a limited class of Pig queries that translate into a sequence of MapReduce jobs. In both papers, instead of a detailed profiling technique that is designed in our work, the authors rely on earlier debug runs of the same query for estimating throughput of map and reduce stages on the input data samples provided by the user. The approach is based on precomputing the expected schedule of all the tasks, and therefore identifying all the pipelines (sequences of MapReduce jobs) in the query. The approach relies on a simplified assumption that map (reduce) tasks of the same job have the same duration. This work is closest to ours in pursuing the completion time estimates for Pig programs. However, the usage of the FIFO scheduler and simplifying assumptions limit the approach applicability for progress estimation of multiple jobs running in the cluster with a different Hadoop scheduler, especially if the amount of resources allocated to a job varies over time or differs from the debug runs that are used for measurements.

7. CONCLUSION

Design of new job profiling tools and performance models for MapReduce environments has been an active research topic in industry and academia during past few years. Most of these efforts were driven by design of new schedulers to satisfy the job specific goals and to improve cluster resource management. In our work, we have introduced a novel performance modeling framework for processing Pig programs with deadlines. Our job profiling technique is not intrusive, it does not require any modifications or instrumentation of either the application or the underlying Hadoop/Pig execution engines. The proposed approach enables automat-

ed SLO-driven resource sizing and provisioning of complex workflows defined by the DAGs of MapReduce jobs. Moreover, our approach offers an optimized scheduling of concurrent jobs within a DAG that allows to significantly reduce the overall completion time.

Our performance models are designed for the case without node failures. We see a natural extension for incorporating different failure scenarios and estimating their impact on the application performance and achievable "degraded" SLOs. We intend to apply designed models for solving a broad set of problems related to capacity planning of MapReduce applications (defined by the DAGs of MapReduce jobs) and the analysis of various resource allocation trade-offs for supporting their SLOs.

8. REFERENCES
[1] TPC Benchmark H (Decision Support), Version 2.8.0, Transaction Processing Performance Council (TPC), http://www.tpc.org/tpch/, 2008.
[2] Apache. PigMix Benchmark, http://wiki.apache.org/pig/PigMix, 2010.
[3] R. Chaiken, B. Jenkins, P.-A. Larson, B. Ramsey, D. Shakib, S. Weaver, and J. Zhou. Easy and Efficient Parallel Processing of Massive Data Sets. *Proc. of the VLDB Endowment*, 1(2), 2008.
[4] J. Dean and S. Ghemawat. MapReduce: Simplified Data Processing on Large Clusters. *Communications of the ACM*, 51(1), 2008.
[5] A. Ganapathi, Y. Chen, A. Fox, R. Katz, and D. Patterson. Statistics-driven workload modeling for the cloud. In *Proc. of 5th International Workshop on Self Managing Database Systems (SMDB)*, 2010.
[6] A. Gates, O. Natkovich, S. Chopra, P. Kamath, S. Narayanam, C. Olston, B. Reed, S. Srinivasan, and U. Srivastava. Building a High-Level Dataflow System on Top of Map-Reduce: The Pig Experience. *Proc. of the VLDB Endowment*, 2(2), 2009.
[7] H. Herodotou and S. Babu. Profiling, What-if Analysis, and Costbased Optimization of MapReduce Programs. In *Proc. of the VLDB Endowment, Vol. 4, No. 11*, 2011.
[8] H. Herodotou, H. Lim, G. Luo, N. Borisov, L. Dong, F. Cetin, and S. Babu. Starfish: A Self-tuning System for Big Data Analytics. In *Proc. of 5th Conf. on Innovative Data Systems Research (CIDR)*, 2011.
[9] M. Isard, M. Budiu, Y. Yu, A. Birrell, and D. Fetterly. Dryad: Distributed Data-Parallel Programs from Sequential Building Blocks. *ACM SIGOPS OS Review*, 41(3), 2007.
[10] S. Johnson. Optimal Two- and Three-Stage Production Schedules with Setup Times Included. *Naval Res. Log. Quart.*, 1954.
[11] K. Kambatla, A. Pathak, and H. Pucha. Towards optimizing hadoop provisioning in the cloud. In *Proc. of the First Workshop on Hot Topics in Cloud Computing*, 2009.
[12] K. Morton, M. Balazinska, and D. Grossman. ParaTimer: a progress indicator for MapReduce DAGs. In *Proc. of SIGMOD*. ACM, 2010.
[13] K. Morton, A. Friesen, M. Balazinska, and D. Grossman. Estimating the progress of MapReduce pipelines. In *Proc. of ICDE*, 2010.
[14] J. Polo, D. Carrera, Y. Becerra, J. Torres, E. Ayguadé, M. Steinder, and I. Whalley. Performance-Driven Task Co-Scheduling for MapReduce Environments. In *Proc. of the 12th IEEE/IFIP Network Operations and Management Symposium*, 2010.
[15] A. Thusoo, J. S. Sarma, N. Jain, Z. Shao, P. Chakka, S. Anthony, H. Liu, P. Wyckoff, and R. Murthy. Hive - a Warehousing Solution over a Map-Reduce Framework. *Proc. of VLDB*, 2009.
[16] F. Tian and K. Chen. Towards Optimal Resource Provisioning for Running MapReduce Programs in Public Clouds. In *Proc. of IEEE Conference on Cloud Computing (CLOUD 2011)*.
[17] A. Verma, L. Cherkasova, and R. H. Campbell. ARIA: Automatic Resource Inference and Allocation for MapReduce Environments. *Proc. of the 8th ACM International Conference on Autonomic Computing (ICAC'2011)*, 2011.
[18] X. Wang, C. Olston, A. Sarma, and R. Burns. CoScan: Cooperative Scan Sharing in the Cloud. In *Proc. of the ACM Symposium on Cloud Computing,(SOCC'2011)*, 2011.
[19] J. Wolf, D. Rajan, K. Hildrum, R. Khandekar, V. Kumar, S. Parekh, K.-L. Wu, and A. Balmin. FLEX: A Slot Allocation Scheduling Optimizer for MapReduce Workloads. *Proc. of the 11th ACM/IFIP/USENIX Middleware Conference*, 2010.

AROMA: Automated Resource Allocation and Configuration of MapReduce Environment in the Cloud

Palden Lama
Department of Computer Science
University of Colorado at Colorado Springs
Colorado Springs, CO 80918
plama@uccs.edu

Xiaobo Zhou
Department of Computer Science
University of Colorado at Colorado Springs
Colorado Springs, CO 80918
xzhou@uccs.edu

ABSTRACT

Distributed data processing framework MapReduce is increasingly deployed in Clouds to leverage the pay-per-usage cloud computing model. Popular Hadoop MapReduce environment expects that end users determine the type and amount of Cloud resources for reservation as well as the configuration of Hadoop parameters. However, such resource reservation and job provisioning decisions require in-depth knowledge of system internals and laborious but often ineffective parameter tuning. We propose and develop AROMA, a system that automates the allocation of heterogeneous Cloud resources and configuration of Hadoop parameters for achieving quality of service goals while minimizing the incurred cost. It addresses the significant challenge of provisioning ad-hoc jobs that have performance deadlines in Clouds through a novel two-phase machine learning and optimization framework. Its technical core is a support vector machine based performance model that enables the integration of various aspects of resource provisioning and auto-configuration of Hadoop jobs. It adapts to ad-hoc jobs by robustly matching their resource utilization signature with previously executed jobs and making provisioning decisions accordingly. We implement AROMA as an automated job provisioning system for Hadoop MapReduce hosted in virtualized HP ProLiant blade servers. Experimental results show AROMA's effectiveness in providing performance guarantee of diverse Hadoop benchmark jobs while minimizing the cost of Cloud resource usage.

Categories and Subject Descriptors

C.4 [**Computer System Organization**]: Performance of Systems;
D.2.6 [**Software**]: Programming Environments

Keywords

MapReduce, resource allocation, auto-configuration

1. INTRODUCTION

Large-scale distributed data processing in enterprises is increasingly facilitated by software frameworks such as Google MapReduce and its open-source implementation Hadoop, which paral-

lelize and distribute jobs across large clusters [1, 5, 27]. There are growing interests in deploying such a framework in the Cloud to harness the unlimited availability of virtualized resources and pay-per-usage cost model of cloud computing. For example, Amazon's Elastic MapReduce provides data processing services by using Hadoop MapReduce framework on top of their compute cloud EC2, and their storage cloud S3.

Existing MapReduce environments for running Hadoop jobs in a cloud platform aim to remove the burden of hardware and software setup from end users. However, they expect end users to determine the number and type of resource sets to be allocated and also provide appropriate Hadoop parameters for running a job. A resource set is a set of virtualized resources rented as a single unit, e.g., virtual machines rented by Amazon web services. Here, we use the term resource set and virtual machine interchangeably. In the absence of automation tools, currently end users are forced to make job provisioning decisions manually using best practices. As a result, customers may suffer from a lack of performance guarantee and increased cost of leasing the cloud resources.

In this paper, we propose to enable automated allocation of heterogeneous cloud resource sets and configuration of Hadoop parameters for meeting job completion deadlines while minimizing the incurred cost at the same time. There are significant challenges in achieving the goal. First, the heterogeneity of available resource sets in terms of hardware configurations and different pricing schemes complicate the resource allocation decision for various jobs and different input data sizes. Second, Hadoop has over 180 configuration parameters that have varying impact on job performance. Examples include the number of reducers to be launched, the size of memory buffer to use while sorting map output, the number of concurrent connections a reducer should use when fetching its input from mappers etc. Furthermore, the optimal configuration of Hadoop parameters is tightly coupled with hardware configuration of selected resource sets as well as the type of jobs submitted.

There are techniques that each addresses resource allocation and parameter configuration in a Hadoop MapReduce framework separately [10, 12, 23]. However, in practice the effectiveness and cost efficiency of those techniques are often inter-dependent. For instance, a Hadoop parameter such as $mapred \cdot tasktracker \cdot map \cdot tasks \cdot maximum$ (the maximum number of parallel mappers) is optimal at different values when the number of virtual CPU cores of a Hadoop node is different [12]. It is important to consider a holistic approach that integrates various aspects of resource provisioning and auto-configuration for Hadoop jobs.

We propose and develop AROMA, a system that automates the allocation of heterogeneous Cloud resources and auto-configuration of Hadoop MapReduce parameters. It can be applied as a Cloud service that manages the provisioning of Hadoop jobs. One challenge in automating the resource allocation and configuration of jobs in Hadoop is a lack of performance model for such a complex distributed processing framework. A recent study focused on intensive profiling of routinely executed jobs in the Hadoop environment in order to estimate their performance for various input data sizes [23]. However, such an approach is not feasible for ad-hoc jobs submitted to the system, which have unpredictable execution characteristics. One possible workaround for ad-hoc jobs is to perform intensive job profiling by running them in a staging cluster that is similar to the target Hadoop cluster in size and configuration. However, there are overheads in terms of resources usage and the time spent in job profiling. Hence, it is not suitable for ad-hoc jobs that have deadlines.

AROMA addresses the challenges of Hadoop job provisioning with a novel two-phase machine learning and optimization framework. It exploits an important observation that jobs with similar resource consumption pattern would face similar bottlenecks and as a result they would exhibit similar performance behavior in relation to the changes in resource allocation and Hadoop configuration. In the first offline phase, it groups the information about past jobs into different clusters using the classic k-medoid clustering technique. Each cluster consists of jobs that exhibit similar CPU, network and disk utilization patterns. Then for each cluster, it trains a support vector machine (SVM) model that is able to make accurate and fast prediction of a job's performance for various combinations of resource allocation, configuration parameters and input data sizes.

In the second online phase, it obtains the resource utilization pattern of a newly submitted job by running it in a staging cluster of small VMs with default configuration parameters and using only a fraction of input data to capture its resource utilization signature. This is a lightweight process both in terms of resource usage and the time spent in capturing the signature. AROMA matches the resource utilization signature to those job clusters and identifies the performance model to use for finding the best configuration and resource allocation. Finally, AROMA applies a pattern search based optimization technique on the selected job cluster's performance model to find close to optimal resource allocation and configuration parameters that meet a Hadoop job's completion deadline at the minimal resource cost.

While it sounds intuitive, our approach is non-trivial mainly due to two reasons. First, it is difficult to define a resource utilization pattern in a shared multi-tenant cloud environment. The contention of underlying resources shared between different applications introduces non-negligible disturbance in the resource utilization pattern of the VMs. AROMA addresses this challenge by applying a Longest Common Subsequence (LCSS) based distance metric. Unlike a commonly used Euclidean Distance metric, LCSS is robust against noise and outliers in a resource utilization pattern. It is also effective in comparing the similarity between patterns that are out of phase and of different lengths.

Second, jobs with similar resource utilization signatures show similar changes in the performance in response to the same adjustment in resource allocation and configuration. However in absolute terms, the job execution times may be different. Hence, a performance model for one job can not directly predict the absolute execution time of another similar job for a given resource allocation and configuration. AROMA addresses this challenge by utilizing the concept of relative performance. For instance, assume that two jobs A and B have similar resource utilization patterns. Given the difference between the performance of the two jobs for the same resource allocation R, we can utilize the performance model of job A to predict the performance of job B for various resource allocations. We then evaluate AROMA's adaptiveness to ad-hoc jobs.

We implement AROMA on a testbed of HP ProLiant BL460C G6 blade servers hosting Hadoop MapReduce framework. The testbed uses VMware ESX 4.1 to create a pool of virtual machines which are run as Hadoop nodes. Experimental results show that AROMA makes effective and automated job provisioning decisions to achieve performance guarantee of diverse Hadoop benchmark jobs while minimizing the cost of Cloud resource usage.

To our best knowledge, AROMA is the first automated job provisioning system that meets all the challenges discussed above for MapReduce framework in Clouds. The main contributions of AROMA are as follows:

1. It enables automated job provisioning of Hadoop MapReduce framework in the Cloud so that end users can utilize cloud services without acquiring in-depth knowledge of system internals or going through laborious and time consuming manual but ineffective configuration tuning.

2. It provides a holistic job provisioning facility that integrates resource allocation and parameter configuration to meet the completion deadline guarantee and to improve the cost efficiency of MapReduce jobs.

3. It is able to make effective provisioning decisions for ad-hoc jobs while avoiding extensive and time-consuming job profiling. It does so through innovative and practical techniques that combine machine learning and optimization.

In the following, Section 2 discusses related work. Section 3 gives a case study of the cost and performance impact of resource allocation and parameter configuration in MapReduce. The AROMA architecture and design is presented in Section 4. Section 5 provides the system implementation. Section 6 presents experimental results and analysis. We conclude with future work in Section 7.

2. RELATED WORK

Recently distributed data processing framework MapReduce and its open source implementation Hadoop have gained much research [7, 11, 15, 16, 18, 21]. The pay-per-use utility model of Cloud computing introduces new opportunities as well as challenges in deploying a MapReduce framework [24]. Lee *et al.* designed an architecture to allocate resources to a data analytics cluster in the cloud, and proposed a metric of share in a heterogeneous cluster to realize a scheduling scheme that achieves high performance and fairness [15]. However, their approach allocates resources based on a simple criteria of job storage requirement without considering any performance guarantee.

There are a few studies focusing on performance estimation and guarantee of MapReduce jobs. Polo *et al.* [18] proposed an online job completion time estimator that can be used for adjusting the resource allocations of different jobs. However, their job estimator tracks the progress of the map stage alone and has no information or control over the reduce stage. An interesting approach recently designed by Verma *et al.* uses job profiles of routinely executed Hadoop jobs and a MapReduce performance model to determine the amount of resources required for job completion within a given deadline [23]. However, such an approach does not guarantee the performance of ad-hoc jobs submitted to the system. More importantly, it does not consider the impact of Hadoop configuration parameters on the effectiveness and efficiency of resource allocation. Resource allocation efficiency in datacenters is very important from the economical perspective [8, 25].

Kambatla *et al.* [12] proposed to select the optimal Hadoop configuration parameters for improving the performance of jobs using a given set of resources. However, there is no guidance on deciding the appropriate number and type of resources to be allocated. There is a need for a holistic system that considers the inter-dependence of various job provisioning decisions in providing performance guarantee in a cost efficient manner.

There are simulation based approaches to systematically understanding the performance of MapReduce setups [9] and tuning the MapReduce configuration parameters [10]. However, designing an accurate simulator that can comprehensively capture the internal dynamics of such complex systems is potentially error-prone.

There are recent studies that address the important issue of improving MapReduce query performance [4, 6]. For example, Lee *et al.* proposed and developed YSmart, a correlation aware SQL-to-MapReduce query translator [16]. Those studies are complimentary to our research in this paper.

AROMA's technical core is based on a novel two-phase statistical machine learning and optimization framework. Statistical machine learning techniques have been used for measuring the capacity of multi-tier Internet sites [20], for online application and virtual machine auto-configuration [2, 19] and for resource allocation for performance and power control in datacenters [13, 14, 17, 22]. AROMA automates resource allocation and configuration of MapReduce environment in the Cloud in a novel and practical way. It is able to provision ad-hoc MapReduce jobs for achieving performance guarantee in a cost-efficient manner.

3. A CASE STUDY

An interesting artifact of the utility nature of the cloud paradigm is that the cost of using 1000 virtual machines (VMs) for one hour is the same as using one virtual machine (VM) of the same capacity for 1000 hours. Thus, a MapReduce job can potentially improve its performance while incurring the same currency cost by acquiring several machines and executing in parallel. However, a user submitting jobs to a Cloud service has to choose from a variety of virtual machines, which have different hardware configurations and corresponding pricing policies usually expressed as $per hour. For a given MapReduce job with the certain input data set, it is challenging to determine how many and what type of virtual machines should be allocated to meet the job completion deadline while minimizing the incurred cost.

Furthermore, the configuration parameters of the Hadoop MapReduce framework for each virtual machine can significantly affect the performance of a running job. There is no single MapReduce configuration that can optimize the performance of all types of VMs and all types of jobs. To illustrate this, we conduct a case study in a testbed of virtualized Hadoop nodes based on VMware vSphere 4.1. A MapReduce benchmark job Sort, which does a partial sort of its input, is executed with 20 GB input data on a cluster of six VMs. We measure the job execution time for various combinations of resource type and configuration parameters as shown in Table 1. For the sake of clarity we use only one configuration parameter and two types of VMs in this case study. We allocate 1 CPU core with 2 GB RAM to a small VM and 2 CPU cores with 4 GB RAM to a medium VM. The usage costs of small and medium VMs are assumed to be 0.85per hour and 1.275per hour, respectively. We assume that the maximum number of parallel mappers and reducers are fixed to 1 slot per node for small VMs and 2 slots per node for medium VMs.

The results in Table 1 illustrate the impact of resource allocation and configuration on both performance and cost of running a Hadoop job. We observe that the performance impact of MapReduce parameters significantly varies with resource allocation. For example when six small VMs are allocated, the optimal configu-

Table 1: Cost and performance impact of resource allocation and parameter configuration.

	Hadoop MapReduce Configuration		
small VMs	mapred.reduce.tasks	Exec.time	Cost (cents)
Case 1	7	17.2min	146.2
Case 2	35	14min	119.0
Case 3	70	13min	110.5
medium VMs	mapred.reduce.tasks	Exec. time	Cost (cents)
Case 4	7	11.5min	146.6
Case 5	35	7.36min	93.8
Case 6	70	8min	102.0

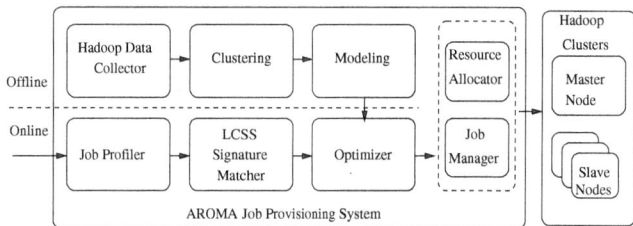

Figure 1: The system architecture of AROMA.

ration is given by case 3 with $mapred \cdot reduce \cdot tasks$ equal to 70. However for six medium VM allocation, the optimal configuration is Case 5 with $mapred \cdot reduce \cdot tasks$ equal to 35. In this particular study, we have a counter intuitive observation that it may be cheaper to run a Hadoop job using six medium VMs instead of six small VMs. However, the situation can be further complicated by the fact that cost and performance impact can also vary with the different number of VMs and different input size of jobs running in a Hadoop cluster. Hence, it is important to consider all these factors for making a cost efficient and effective job provisioning decision.

4. AROMA ARCHITECTURE AND DESIGN

AROMA is an automated job provisioning system that integrates resource allocation and parameter configuration to meet job deadline guarantee and improve the cost efficiency of Hadoop MapReduce in Clouds. Figure 1 shows the architecture of AROMA. End users submit jobs as input to AROMA through a command line interface. AROMA first calculates the number and type of VMs to be allocated, and assigns appropriate MapReduce configuration parameters to meet its completion deadline at minimal cost. Then, its resource allocator powers on a pool of dormant VMs pre-installed with Hadoop software. Finally, the job manager submits the job to the Hadoop master node along with its configuration parameters. Here, the key challenges lie in making fast and effective decisions at job submission time, allocating the right amount of resources and finely tuning the MapReduce configuration settings for an ad-hoc job with unpredictable input data size and completion deadline.

The core components of AROMA work in two phases. First the data collector, clustering and performance modeling components process Hadoop log files and resource utilization data to learn the performance models for various types of Hadoop jobs in the offline phase. Next in the online phase, the job profiler, resource signature matcher and optimizer select the appropriate performance model for an incoming job based on its resource utilization signa-

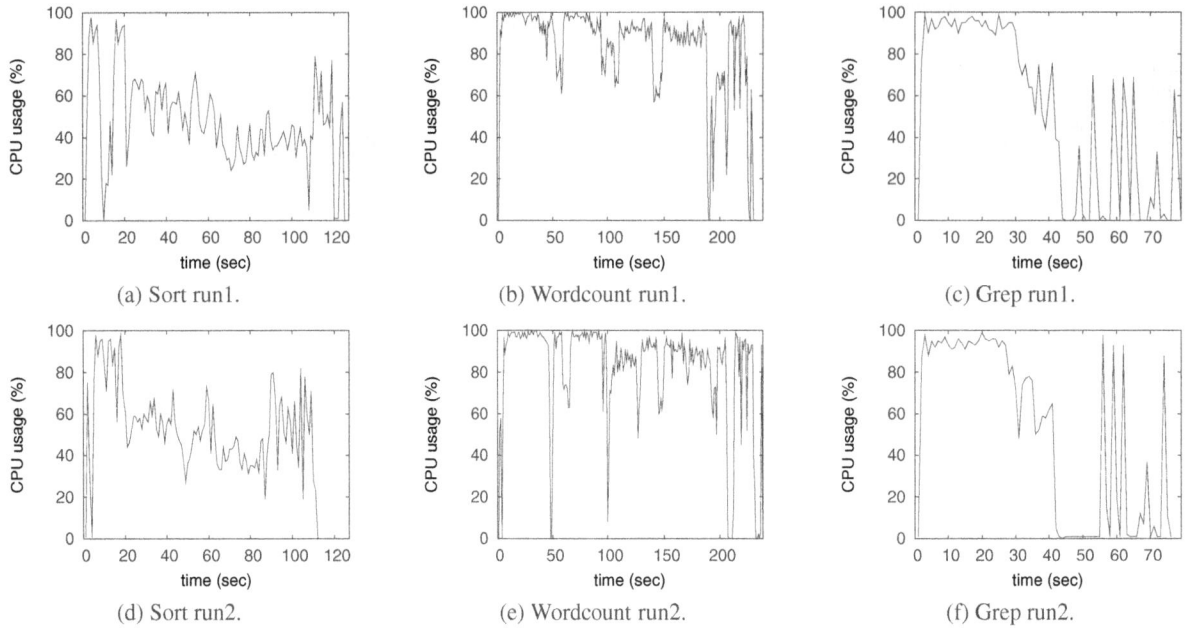

Figure 2: CPU utilization of Sort, Wordcount and Grep jobs during different runs.

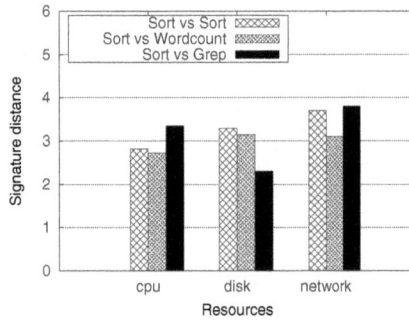

Figure 3: Euclidean Signature Distances for CPU, Network and Disk resources for (i) Sort vs Sort;(ii) Sort vs Wordcount;(iii) Sort vs Grep.

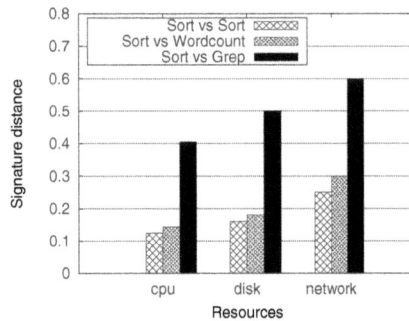

Figure 4: LCSS Signature Distances for CPU, Network and Disk resources for (i) Sort vs Sort;(ii) Sort vs Wordcount;(iii) Sort vs Grep.

ture and calculate the optimal resource allocation and configuration that meet the job completion deadline.

4.1 Machine Learning Performance Modeling

The first challenge for making optimal job provisioning decisions is the lack of the performance models for different Hadoop jobs. AROMA learns the performance models of various types of jobs in the offline phase.

4.1.1 Data collection and clustering

The data collector component extracts the execution time, input data size, resource allocation and MapReduce configuration parameters of various past jobs from the Hadoop JobTracker log files. For each job, it fetches the corresponding series of resource utilization data of the slave VM nodes. We use *dstat* tool at each slave VM to measure CPU usage (in terms of User, System, Idle and Wait percentages), disk usage (number of blocks in and out) and network usage (bytes/sec into and out of network card) every second. All the usage measurements are normalized using their respective maximum values. In our testbed, the JobTracker and slave VM logs are saved in a repository when a Hadoop cluster is decommissioned after job completion.

A core principle that enables AROMA's adaptiveness to ad-hoc jobs is based on the observation that jobs with similar resource utilization pattern exhibit similar performance behavior. As a result, AROMA needs to learn only a single performance model for a group of similar jobs. The resource utilization signature of each job is a combination of time series data of average CPU usage, average memory usage and average disk usage rate. However, it is difficult to compare the resource signatures of two jobs accurately in a multi-tenant cloud environment. It is due to the fact that the contention of shared resources between multiple applications introduces noise and outliers in the resource utilization patterns.

We examine the variability of resource utilization patterns of various Hadoop jobs running on a small cluster of 2 small VMs and using 1 GB input data. The Hadoop configuration parameters are set to the default value. To simulate a multi-tenant cloud environ-

Table 2: Feature Selection for SORT performance model.

Features	t-statistic	p-value
io.sort.factor	-3.6306	0.0211
mapred.job.shuffle.merge.percent	0.9613	0.3423
io.sort.spill.percent	2.13	0.2014
mapred.job.shuffle.input.buffer.percent	-1.5352	0.1328
io.sort.record.percent	-1.0588	0.0191
mapred.job.reduce.input.buffer.percent	1.4043	0.1682
mapred.reduce.parallel.copies	4.3869	0.0342
io.sort.mb	-3.3465	0.0312
mapred.reduce.tasks	-6.4583	0.0101
input size	10.8	0.0011
VM type	8.5	0.0045
number of VMs	-4.2	0.0021

Table 3: Feature Selection for GREP performance model.

Features	t-statistic	p-value
io.sort.factor	-1.1324	0.2682
mapred.job.shuffle.merge.percent	-1.4953	0.1474
io.sort.spill.percent	-1.4527	0.1587
mapred.job.shuffle.input.buffer.percent	-0.8069	0.4273
io.sort.record.percent	3.8211	0.0007
mapred.job.reduce.input.buffer.percent	3.8016	0.0008
mapred.reduce.parallel.copies	-0.1715	0.8652
io.sort.mb	9.487	0.0112
mapred.reduce.tasks	-0.7814	0.4419
input size	9.3	0.0033
VM type	7.5	0.0056
number of VMs	-4.5	0.0011

ment, we host another group of VMs in the same physical server cluster of our testbed and execute Hadoop jobs in them. Figures 2 (a) and 2(d) compare the CPU utilization patterns of a VM node when a Sort job is executed twice. Similarly, the CPU utilization patterns of Wordcount and Grep jobs are also compared. We observed variations in the utilization patterns of the same job when it is executed at different times.

It is challenging to accurately identify the degree of similarity between different jobs due to the disturbance in the resource utilization pattern of VMs. We demonstrate this challenge by measuring the difference between the utilization patterns of various job combinations using a straightforward Euclidean distance metric. Figure 3 shows the Euclidean distance between the resource utilization signatures of different job combinations. We observe that the Euclidean distance based resource utilization signature comparison is misleading. For instance according to this metric, the signature distance of CPU and network utilization between two executions of the same Sort job is found to be greater than that of Sort vs Wordcount job executions.

AROMA addresses this challenge by applying a Longest Common Subsequence (LCSS) based distance metric. Unlike a commonly used Euclidean Distance metric, LCSS is robust against noise and outliers in a resource utilization pattern. It is also effective in comparing the similarity between patterns that are out of phase and of different lengths. Figure (4) shows LCSS distance between the resource utilization signatures of different job combinations. The distances between the CPU, disk and network utilization patterns of two Sort jobs is the smallest and the distances between the utilization patterns of Sort and Grep jobs are the largest.

AROMA applies the classic k-medoid based clustering technique along with LCSS distance metric to group jobs with similar utilization patterns of CPU, network and disk resources. According to the resource utilization patterns of the three jobs, AROMA groups Sort and Wordcount jobs in the same cluster and the Grep job belongs to a different cluster. Resource signatures implicitly capture the potential impact of input data content on a job's behavior.

4.1.2 Performance modeling

AROMA applies a powerful supervised machine learning technique to learn the performance model for each cluster of jobs. It constructs a support vector machine (SVM) regression model to estimate the completion time of jobs belonging to a cluster for different input data sizes, resource allocations and configuration parameters. SVM methodology is known to be robust for estimating real-valued functions (regression problem) from noisy and sparse train-

ing data having many attributes. This property of SVM makes it a suitable technique for performance modeling of complex Hadoop jobs in the Cloud environment.

It is important to create a model that utilizes only the statistically significant features and avoids "overfitting" the data. For each job cluster, we apply a stepwise regression technique to determine which set of features are the best predictors for the job performance. It is a systematic method for adding and removing terms from a model based on their statistical significance in a regression. The method begins with an initial model and then compares the explanatory power of incrementally larger and smaller models. At each step, the p value of a t-statistic is computed to test models with and without a potential term. If a term is not currently in the model, the null hypothesis is that the term would have a zero coefficient if added to the model. If there is sufficient evidence to reject the null hypothesis, the term is added to the model. Conversely, if a term is currently in the model, the null hypothesis is that the term has a zero coefficient. If there is insufficient evidence to reject the null hypothesis, the term is removed from the model.

We conduct stepwise regression on the data sets collected from our testbed of virtualized Hadoop nodes. For data collection, we measured the execution times of various Hadoop jobs with different input data sizes in the range 5 GB to 50 GB, using different Hadoop configuration parameters and running on different cluster sizes of Hadoop nodes comprising of small and medium VMs. Tables 2 and 3 show the results of stepwise regression for two different Hadoop jobs, Sort and Grep respectively. Note that the features whose *p-values* are smaller than or equal to the significance level of 0.05 are selected for performance modeling using SVM regression.

The idea of SVM regression is based on the computation of a linear regression function in a high dimensional feature space where the input data are mapped via a nonlinear function. The linear model in an M dimensional feature space $f(x, \omega)$ is given by

$$f(x, \omega) = \sum_{m=1}^{M} \omega_m g_m(x) + b \qquad (1)$$

where $g_m(x)$ denotes a set of nonlinear transformations and b is the bias term. The input data x for AROMA's performance model consists of the features selected by the stepwise regression method.

AROMA applies $\varepsilon - SV$ regression technique [3] that aims to find a function $f(x, \omega)$ that has at most ε deviation from the actual output values y for all the training data points. In this case, the output values of the performance model are the job execution times. At the same time, it also tries to reduce model complexity by min-

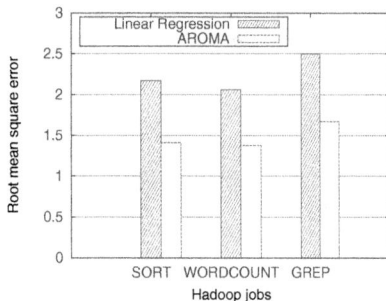

Figure 5: Prediction accuracy of AROMA performance model.

imizing the term $||\omega||^2$. We apply the LIBSVM [3] library to find suitable kernel functions and train the SVM regression model.

SVM regression has a good generalization and prediction power due to the fact that unlike other learning techniques, it attempts to minimize a generalized error bound so as to achieve generalized performance. This error bound is the combination of the training error and a regularization term that controls the complexity of the model. One approach for assessing how accurately a predictive model will perform in practice is to perform *cross-validation*. We apply leave-one-out cross-validation (LOOCV), which involves using a single observation from the original data sample as the validation data, and the remaining observations as the training data. This is repeated such that each observation in the sample is used once as the validation data. Figure 5 shows the results of cross validation performed for three Hadoop jobs in terms of the root mean square error in prediction. AROMA's SVM regression based performance model is able to achieve significantly better prediction accuracy than a linear regression model.

4.2 Online Job Profiling and Signature Match

A MapReduce environment needs to run ad-hoc jobs with unpredictable resource utilization patterns that make it difficult to apply performance models. AROMA addresses this challenge by first running a new job in a small set of Hadoop nodes and using a small chunk of input data. It collects the resource utilization signature of the job using *dstat* tool. Then the signature is compared with the resource utilization signatures of various job clusters' centroid. We observe that signature matching with the cluster centroid rather than each data point is sufficient since the data points within the same cluster are similar. As a result, this process can be executed with less overhead.

However, a straightforward comparison of resource utilization signatures may cause misleading results due to the presence of noise and outliers. AROMA applies the LCSS distance metric to match the signatures corresponding to each resource type for a sequence of measurement samples. It is able to make accurate comparison between the resource utilization patterns of two jobs.

4.3 Cost Efficient Performance Guarantee

It is important but challenging to make effective job provisioning decisions to meet performance guarantee in terms of job completion deadlines and to minimize the cost of resource allocation. AROMA's job provisioning decision is based on a non-linear constrained optimization problem formulated for a given job with input size s and completion deadline D as follows:

$$\text{Minimize} \quad \sum_{i=1}^{N} n_i * rate_i * t_s \qquad (2)$$

Subject to Constraints:

$$t_s \leq D \qquad (3)$$

$$\forall j \in [1, C], \quad lb_j \leq conf_j \leq ub_j \qquad (4)$$

Eq. (2) gives the optimization objective to minimize the total cost of allocating VMs to the Hadoop cluster. Here, n_i is the number of VMs of type i (small,medium) that is charged a cost of $rate_i$ at $\$perhour$ and t_s is the execution time of the given job with input data size s. Eq. (3) defines a constraint that the job execution time must be less than its completion deadline D. Eq. (4) defines the lower bound lb and upper bound ub values of each MapReduce configuration parameter under consideration.

In this optimization problem, the relationship between the decision variables $(n_i, conf_j)$ and the dependent variable t_s is given by the SVM regression model corresponding to a given job type. We solve the optimization problem by applying a pattern search algorithm, the generating set search. It is a direct search method that can optimize complex objective functions that are not differentiable.

It computes a sequence of points that approach an optimal point. At each step, the algorithm searches a set of points, called a mesh, around the current point computed at the previous step of the algorithm. The mesh is formed by adding the current point to a scalar multiple of a set of vectors called a pattern. If the pattern search algorithm finds a point in the mesh that improves the objective function at the current point, the new point becomes the current point at the next step of the algorithm.

4.4 Resource Allocator and Job Manager

AROMA's optimizer sends its solutions to the resource allocator and the job manager components. The resource allocator is responsible for powering on the appropriate number and types of VMs with pre-installed Hadoop software. It uses VMware vSphere API 4.1 to issue commands for VM management. Note that a VM in its powered off state poses negligible infrastructure cost. Once the VMs are started up, the job manager submits the given job to the Hadoop master node along with the optimized MapReduce configuration parameters. It does so by issuing commands to the hadoop master node using a java *ssh* library.

5. SYSTEM IMPLEMENTATION

5.1 The Testbed

We implement AROMA on a testbed consisting of seven HP Pro-Liant BL460C G6 blade server modules and a HP EVA storage area network with 10 Gbps Ethernet and 8 Gbps Fibre/iSCSI dual channels. Each blade server is equipped with Intel Xeon E5530 2.4 GHz quad-core processor and 32 GB PC3 memory. Virtualization of the cluster is enabled by VMware ESX 4.1. We create a pool of VMs with different hardware configurations from the virtualized blade server cluster and run them as Hadoop nodes. There are small VMs with 1 vCPU, 2 GB RAM and 50 GB hard disk space. Medium VMs have 2 vCPUs, 4 GB RAM and 80 GB hard disk space. Each VM uses Ubuntu Linux version 10.04 and Hadoop 0.20.2.

We designate one blade server to host the master VM node and use rest of the servers to host the slave VM nodes. The single master node runs the JobTracker and the NameNode, while each slave node runs both the TaskTracker and the DataNode. A small slave VM is configured with one Map slot, one Reduce slot and 200 MB memory per task. Whereas, a medium type slave VM is configured with two Map slots, two Reduce slots and 300 MB memory per task. The data block size is set to 64 MB. The AROMA job provisioning system can be run either on a separate VM or a standalone machine as it manages the Hadoop nodes remotely.

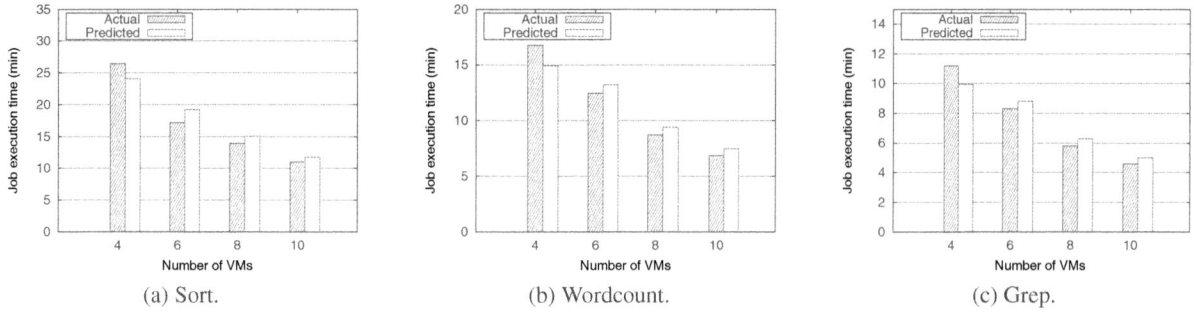

(a) Sort.　　　　　　(b) Wordcount.　　　　　　(c) Grep.

Figure 6: Actual and predicted running times of MapReduce jobs for various VM resource allocations (small VMs).

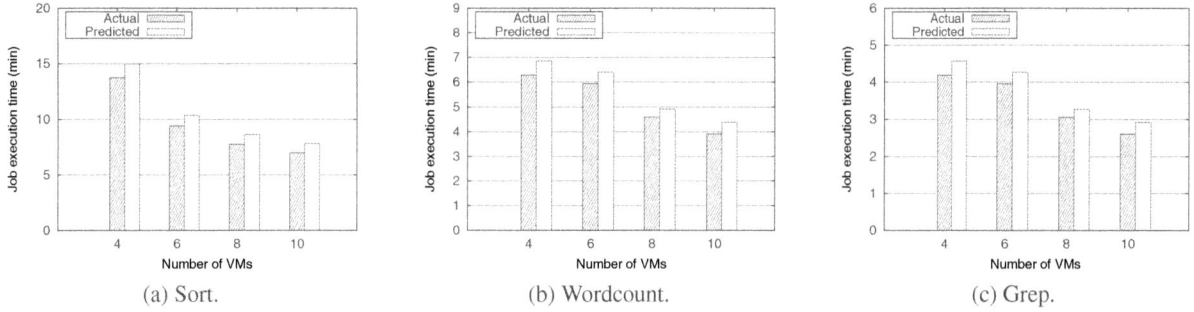

(a) Sort.　　　　　　(b) Wordcount.　　　　　　(c) Grep.

Figure 7: Actual and predicted running times of MapReduce jobs for various VM resource allocations (medium VMs).

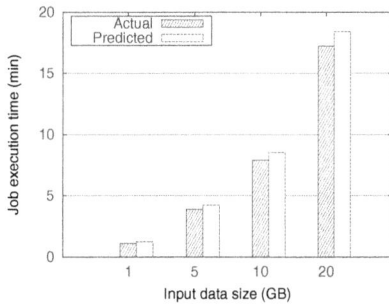

Figure 8: Actual and predicted running times of Sort for various input data sizes.

As related studies [12, 23], we use a number of benchmark jobs that come with the Hadoop distribution for performance evaluation, i.e., Sort, Grep, and Wordcount. We use the RandomWriter and RandomTextWriter tools in the Hadoop package to generate data of various sizes for the Sort, WordCount and Grep programs.

6. PERFORMANCE EVALUATION

We evaluate AROMA's capability for predicting the performance of Hadoop jobs, auto-configuration of Hadoop MapReduce parameters, joint resource allocation with configuration, and adaptiveness to ad-hoc Hadoop jobs for improving job performance and reducing the incurred cost. For our experiments, the costs of using a small VM and a medium VM are assumed to be $0.85 per hour and $1.275 per hour respectively.

6.1 AROMA Performance Model Accuracy

First, we evaluate AROMA's ability to predict the completion times of Hadoop jobs when they are executed with different num-

ber of VM nodes of different types and different input data sizes. We use the default Hadoop configuration for this experiment. Figures 6 (a), (b) and (c) show the actual and predicted running times of Sort, Wordcount and Grep jobs respectively as the number of Hadoop slave nodes are varied. In this case, we use small VMs as Hadoop nodes and fix the input data to be 20 GB. Figures 7 (a), (b) and (c) show the results of a similar study using medium VMs. We observe that AROMA's SVM regression based performance model is able to predict the speedup achieved for each job as we increase the number of VMs. The relative error between the actual and predicted job completion time is less than 12% on all the cases. We observed similar prediction accuracy when the input data size is varied while keeping the number of VMs fixed as shown in Figure 8. Here, we use six small VMs to run a Sort job.

6.2 Auto-Configuration

We evaluate AROMA's capability to automatically configure the Hadoop environment parameters according to variations in the resource allocation. We execute the Hadoop Sort benchmark. The jobs are executed for an input data of 10 GB. Figures 9 (a), (b) and (c) compare the impact of using the default Hadoop configuration with AROMA's auto-tuned configuration on the job execution time and the incurred cost. AROMA's auto-configuration significantly outperforms the default configuration for various allocations of small VMs. The improvement in job performance and cost due to AROMA increases from 17% to 30% when using more number of VMs. It is due to the fact that there are more opportunities for configuration tuning in case of using more VMs. Figures 10 (a), (b) and (c) show the job execution results when medium VMs are used. We observe that using more than six medium VMs shows little improvement in performance and hence increases the cost. It is due to the fact that for a moderately small input data of 10 GB, the overhead of managing a large number of Map/Reduce slots in the cluster can be significant.

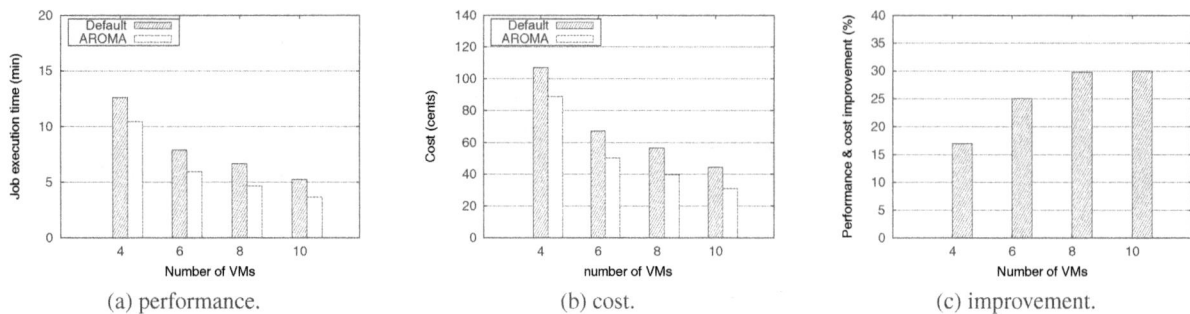

(a) performance.   (b) cost.   (c) improvement.

Figure 9: Impact of AROMA's auto-configuration on job performance and cost for various VM resource allocations (small VMs).

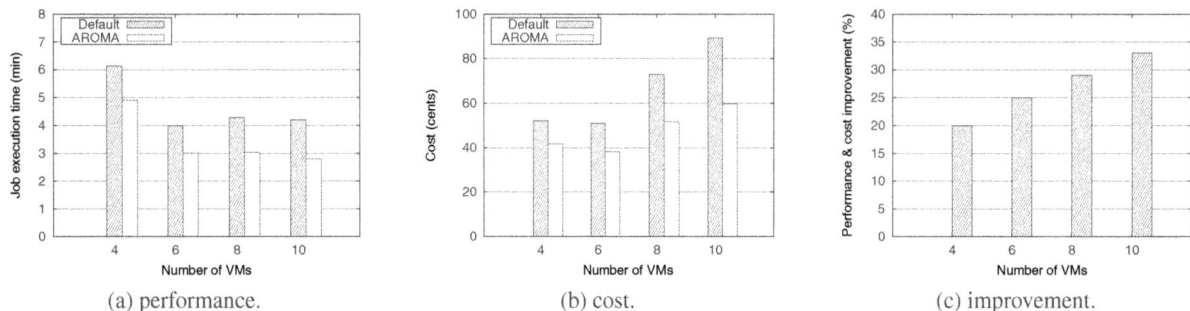

(a) performance.   (b) cost.   (c) improvement.

Figure 10: Impact of AROMA's auto-configuration on job performance and cost for various VM resource allocations (medium VMs).

Note that in Figure 9(c) and Figure 10(c), the improvement percentage in performance and in cost are the same since the cost of using a VM depends on how long a job runs.

Table 4 compares the Hadoop configurable parameter values due to AROMA's auto-configuration with the default Hadoop values. AROMA uses this configuration for running Sort benchmark with six small VMs and input data of 20 GB. We can observe that there are many differences between two settings. In particular, parameters $io \cdot sort \cdot factor$, $mapred \cdot reduce \cdot tasks$, and $mapred \cdot reduce \cdot parallel \cdot copies$ have significantly different values. Hadoop Sort benchmark sets the default value of $mapred \cdot reduce \cdot tasks$ to 0.9 times the total number of reduce slots in the cluster.

Please note that for the Sort job even if an end user is able to come up with the same parameter configuration as that of AROMA based on best practices, such a parameter configuration is not effective when the Hadoop environment and the submitted jobs change dynamically. For instance, Table 5 shows the parameter configuration differences for running the Sort job with six medium VM and input data of 20 GB. It shows there are a few important differences between two parameter configurations by AROMA.

Next, we evaluate the auto-configuration capability of AROMA when the input data size is varied. Figures 11(a),(b) and (c) show the performance improvement due to AROMA for running the Sort benchmark by using six small VMs.

6.3 Efficient Resource Allocation and Configuration

A key feature of AROMA is its holistic job provisioning approach with optimization for joint resource allocation and auto-configuration. We demonstrate the merit of this feature by comparing the cost efficiency in achieving the job completion deadline by AROMA with and without the integration of resource allocation with auto-configuration of Hadoop parameters.

Tables 6 and 7 show the execution time and cost of complet-

Table 4: Hadoop configuration parameters for Sort benchmark (six small VMs and 20 GB input data).

Hadoop parameters	AROMA	Default
io.sort.factor	300	10
mapred.job.shuffle.merge.percent	0.66	0.66
io.sort.spill.percent	0.8	0.8
mapred.job.shuffle.input.buffer.percent	0.7	0.7
io.sort.record.percent	0.15	0.05
mapred.job.reduce.input.buffer.percent	0	0
mapred.reduce.parallel.copies	12	5
io.sort.mb	130	100
mapred.reduce.tasks	120	5

Table 5: Hadoop configuration parameters for Sort benchmark (six medium VMs and 20 GB input data).

Hadoop parameters	AROMA	Default
io.sort.factor	100	10
mapred.job.shuffle.merge.percent	0.66	0.66
io.sort.spill.percent	0.8	0.8
mapred.job.shuffle.input.buffer.percent	0.7	0.7
io.sort.record.percent	0.3	0.05
mapred.job.reduce.input.buffer.percent	0	0
mapred.reduce.parallel.copies	8	5
io.sort.mb	160	100
mapred.reduce.tasks	120	10

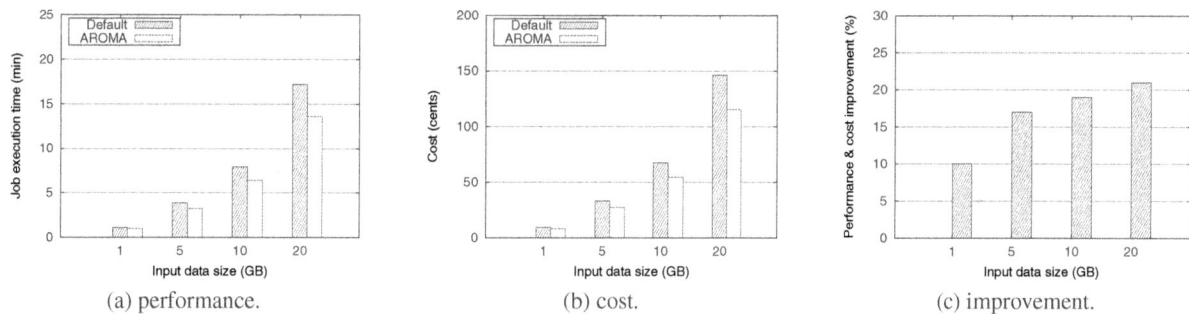

(a) performance.	(b) cost.	(c) improvement.

Figure 11: Impact of AROMA auto-configuration on job performance and cost for various input data sizes.

Table 6: Cost of meeting job execution deadline (360 sec).

AROMA w/o auto-configuration			
Data input	VMs (number and type)	Execution time (sec)	Cost (cents)
5 GB	3 small	300	21
10 GB	6 medium	240	51
20 GB	12 medium	358	152

Table 7: Cost of meeting job execution deadline (360 sec).

AROMA w auto-configuration			
Data input	VMs (number and type)	Execution time (sec)	Cost (cents)
5 GB	3 small	210	14.8
10 GB	5 medium	205	36
20 GB	10 medium	357	126

ing a Hadoop Sort job for various input data sizes by AROMA without and with the integration of resource allocation with auto-configuration respectively. Results show that both approaches can complete the job within the completion deadline 360 seconds. However, AROMA with auto-configuration is much more cost efficient for meeting the job completion deadline for all different input data sizes. For example, for the Sort benchmark job with data size 10 GB, AROMA without auto-configuration costs 51 cents to finish the job within the given deadline using 6 medium VMs. On the other hand, AROMA with auto-configuration uses only 5 medium VMs to meet the deadline while incurring the total cost of 36 cents.

The main reason for the cost efficiency of AROMA is two-fold. First, AROMA is able to fine tune the Hadoop configuration parameters corresponding to various resource allocations. As a result, a job running with AROMA's optimized configuration can finish faster than a job using the default Hadoop configuration for the same set of resource allocations. We have observed similar performance improvement results for other job completion deadlines but omitted here due to the space limit.

Second, it performs a cost-aware optimization for the allocation of heterogeneous resources. As shown in Table 7, when the input data is 5 GB, AROMA allocates three small VMs that complete the job in 210 seconds. We note that using two small VMs could still be able to meet the job completion deadline that is 360 seconds. This kind of counter intuitive behavior of AROMA is in fact advantageous. This is due to the fact that running three small VMs for 210 seconds is cheaper than running two VMs of the same capacity for a much longer time, while still meeting the job completion deadline. The cost saving is 12% in this case. On average, AROMA shows cost efficiency of 25%.

6.4 Adaptiveness to Ad-hoc Jobs

We evaluate AROMA's ability to predict the performance of ad-hoc jobs. Assuming that an ad-hoc Wordcount job with 10 GB input data is submitted to the system, AROMA first captures the resource utilization signature of the job by executing it in a staging cluster of two small VMs using 1 GB input data and default

Hadoop configuration. As discussed in Section 4.1.1, the resource utilization signature of Wordcount job is found to be similar to that of a Sort job. We assume that the performance model of Sort job is available due to offline data clustering and modeling. AROMA calculates the difference between the measured execution time of Wordcount in the staging cluster and the execution time predicted by the SVM performance model of the Sort job. It applies this difference value to scale the predictions made by the performance model for different resource allocations and configurations.

The accuracy of AROMA's resource signature matching and the performance of ad-hoc jobs depend on the diversity of existing job clusters. Job clustering is initially performed offline based on past data. It can be repeated at regular time intervals to accommodate diverse new jobs.

Figure 12 demonstrates the accuracy of AROMA's performance prediction of Wordcount job for various VM resource allocations. In this case, we use small VMs with default Hadoop configuration for performance evaluation. AROMA is able to achieve a very accurate prediction of job execution time with a relative error of less than 12.5%. Next, we compare the actual and predicted execution times of Wordcount job running on 4 small VMs with 20 various Hadoop configurations as shown in Figure 13.

7. CONCLUSIONS

The software framework MapReduce and its open-source implementation Hadoop are increasingly deployed in the Cloud to harness the unlimited availability of virtualized resources and pay-per-usage cost model of cloud computing. However, currently end users have to make job provisioning decisions manually at the Hadoop environment using best practices. They suffer from a lack of performance guarantee and increased cost of leasing the Cloud resources.

AROMA is proposed and developed to enable automated allocation of heterogeneous cloud resource sets and configuration of Hadoop parameters for meeting job completion deadlines while minimizing the incurred cost. It addresses the significant challenges of automated and efficient Hadoop job provisioning with a novel two-phase machine learning and optimization framework.

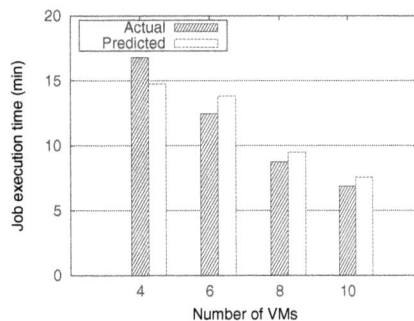

Figure 12: Prediction accuracy for an ad-hoc job for various VM resource allocations.

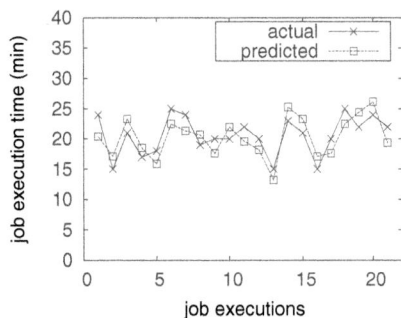

Figure 13: Prediction accuracy for an ad-hoc job for 20 Hadoop configurations.

It is able to make optimal job provisioning decisions with respect to resource allocation efficiency in the face of unpredictable input data sizes and performance expectations. The significance also lies in the fact that it enables automated job provisioning of Hadoop MapReduce framework in the Cloud so that end users can utilize cloud services without acquiring in-depth knowledge about the system internals or going through laborious and time consuming manual but ineffective configuration tuning.

AROMA is developed upon the popular Hadoop MapReduce environment. It is ready to be tailored for other MapReduce running environments. In the future work, we will extend AROMA for running multi-stage job workflows.

Acknowledgement

This research was supported in part by NSF CAREER award CNS-0844983. The authors thank the NISSC for providing HP blade server equipments for conducting the experiments.

8. REFERENCES

[1] A. Abouzid, K. Bajda-Pawlikowski, D. Abadi, A. Silberschatz, and A. Rasin. Hadoopdb: an architectural hybrid of MapReduce and DBMS technologies for analytical workloads. In *Proc. of the VLDB*, 2009.

[2] X. Bu, J. Rao, and C.-Z. Xu. A reinforcement learning approach to online web system auto-configuration. In *Proc. IEEE Int'l Conference on Distributed Computing Systems (ICDCS)*, 2009.

[3] C. Chang and C. Lin. LIBSVM: A library for support vector machines. *ACM Transactions on Intelligent Systems and Technology*, 2, 2011.

[4] T. Condie, N. Conway, P. Alvaro, J. M. Hellerstein, K. Elmeleegy, and R. Sears. MapReduce online. In *Proc. USENIX NSDI*, 2010.

[5] J. Dean and S. Ghemawat. MapReduce: simplified data processing on large clusters. *Communications of the ACM*, 51(1), 2008.

[6] J. Dittrich, J.-A. Quiané-Ruiz, A. Jindal, Y. Kargin, V. Setty, and J. Schad. Hadoop++: making a yellow elephant run like a cheetah (without it even noticing). *Proc. of the VLDB*, 3:515–529, 2010.

[7] Y. Geng, S. Chen, Y. Wu, R. Wu, G. Yang, and W. Zheng. Location-aware MapReduce in virtual cloud. In *Proc. IEEE Int'l Conference on Parallel Processing (ICPP)*, 2011.

[8] F. Goiri, K. Le, J. Guitart, J. Torres, and R. Bianchini. Intelligent placement of datacenters for internet services. In *Proc. IEEE Int'l Conference on Distributed Computing Systems (ICDCS)*, 2011.

[9] W. Guanying, A. Butt, P. Pandey, and K. Gupta. A simulation approach to evaluating design decisions in MapReduce setups. In *Proc. IEEE Int'l Symposium on Modeling, Analysis, and Simulation of Computer and Telecommunication Systems (MASCOTS)*, 2009.

[10] H. Herodotou and S. Babu. Profiling, what-if analysis, and cost-based optimization of MapReduce programs. In *Proc. of the VLDB*, 2011.

[11] b. Hindman, A. Konwinski, M. Zaharia, A. Ghodsi, A. D. Joseph, R. Katz, S. Shenker, and I. Stoica. Mesos: A platform for fine-grained resource sharing in the data center. In *Proc. USENIX NSDI*, 2011.

[12] K. Kambatla, A. Pathak, and H. Pucha. Towards optimizing hadoop provisioning in the cloud. In *HotCloud Workshop in conjunction with USENIX Annual Technical Conference*, 2009.

[13] P. Lama and X. Zhou. Autonomic provisioning with self-adaptive neural fuzzy control for end-to-end delay guarantee. In *Proc. IEEE/ACM Int'l Symposium on Modeling, Analysis, and Simulation of Computer and Telecommunication Systems (MASCOTS)*, 2010.

[14] P. Lama and X. Zhou. PERFUME: Power and performance guarantee with fuzzy mimo control in virtualized servers. In *Proc. IEEE Int'l Workshop on Quality of Service (IWQoS)*, 2010.

[15] G. Lee, B. Chun, and H. K. Randy. Heterogeneity-aware resource allocation and scheduling in the cloud. In *HotCloud Workshop in conjunction with USENIX Annual Technical Conference*, 2011.

[16] R. Lee, T. Luo, F. Wang, Y. Huai, Y. He, and X. Zhang. Ysmart: Yet another SQL-to-MapReduce translator. In *Proc. IEEE Int'l Conference on Distributed Computing Systems (ICDCS)*, 2011.

[17] X. Meng, C. Isci, J. Kephart, L. Zhang, and E. Bouillet. Efficient resource provisioning in compute clouds via vm multiplexing. In *Proc. Int'l Conference on Autonomic Computing (ICAC)*, 2010.

[18] J. Polo, D. Carrera, Y. Becerra, J. Torres, E. Ayguade, M. Steinder, and I. Whalley. Performance-driven task co-scheduling for MapReduce environments. In *Proc. of the IEEE/IFIP Network Operations and Management Symposium (NOMS)*, 2010.

[19] J. Rao, X. Bu, C. Xu, L. Wang, and G. Yin. Vconf: A reinforcement learning approach to virtual machines auto-conguration. In *Proc. IEEE Int'l Conference on Autonomic Computing Systems (ICAC)*, 2009.

[20] J. Rao and C. Xu. CoSL: a coordinated statistical learning approach to measuring the capacity of multi-tier Websites. In *Proc. IEEE Int'l Parallel and Distributed Processing Symposium (IPDPS)*, 2008.

[21] L. Shi, X. Li, and K. L. Tan. S3: An efficient shared scan scheduler on MapReduce framework. In *Proc. IEEE Int'l Conference on Parallel Processing (ICPP)*, 2011.

[22] R. Singh, U. Sharma, E. Cecchet, and P. Shenoy. Autonomic mix-aware provisioning for non-stationary data center workloads. In *Proc. IEEE Int'l Conference on Autonomic Computing (ICAC)*, 2010.

[23] A. Verma, L. Cherkasova, and R. Campbell. ARIA: automatic resource inference and allocation for MapReduce environments. In *Proc. IEEE/ACM Int'l Conference on Autonomic Computing (ICAC)*, 2011.

[24] D. Warneke and O. Kao. Exploiting dynamic resource allocation for efficient parallel data processing in the cloud. *IEEE Trans. on Parallel and Distributed Systems*, 22(6), 2011.

[25] P. Xiong, Z. Wang, S. Malkowski, D. Jayasinghe, Q. Wang, and C. Pu. Economical and robust provisioning of n-tier cloud workloads: A multi-level control approach. In *Proc. IEEE Int'l Conference on Distributed Computing Systems (ICDCS)*, 2011.

[26] J. Xu and J. Fortes. A multi-objective approach to virtual machine management in datacenters. In *Proc. of IEEE/ACM Int'l Conference on Autonomic computing (ICAC)*, 2011.

[27] M. Zaharia, A. Konwinshi, A. D. Josepj, R. Katz, and I. Stoica. Improving MapReduce performance in heterogeneous environments. In *Proc. the USENIX OSDI*, 2008.

Locomotion@Location: When the Rubber hits the Road

Gerold Hoelzl, Marc Kurz,
Peter Halbmayer, Juergen Erhart,
Michael Matscheko, Alois Ferscha
Institute for Pervasive Computing
Johannes Kepler University Linz, Austria
surname@pervasive.jku.at

Susanne Eisl, Johann Kaltenleithner
Energie AG Vertrieb, Energie AG Data,
Energie AG Oberösterreich
Böhmerwaldstrasse 3, 4040-Linz, Austria
service@energieag.at

ABSTRACT

Contextual information of persons can be comprised of a variety of different fragments. The sensor-based recognition of activities, which is one very important part of contextual information, is very well evaluated in laboratory surroundings with different sensor configurations. This paper presents the utilization of locomotion and location information inferred from sensor-readings in a real-world setting by applying a system that operates in an opportunistic and unobtrusive way. We let the rubber hit the road by exploiting locomotion and (in-door) location information in private households to optimize the energy consumption in terms of autonomous and implicit control of electronic appliances. By using on-body and environmental sensor devices, that are not presumably fixed, thus are accessed in an opportunistic manner, our system is able to safely control devices in terms of implicitly optimizing the energy consumption. We have conducted a field study in 15 households, where we have used the location and locomotion information of the residents to decide with a rule-based background intelligence, which electronic appliances can be safely turned off.

Categories and Subject Descriptors

D.0 [**Software**]: General

Keywords

Implicit Power Management, Activity and Context Recognition, Opportunistic Sensing

1. INTRODUCTION

Energy efficiency has gained increased awareness in the public over the last years, due to the rising prices of energy and the fact, that it is a scarce resource. The European Union Action Plan for Energy Efficiency (COM(2006)545) unveils on an EU wide scale, energy saving potentials of more than 20% by 2020, achievable without loss of economic strength or quality of life.

Basically, this concept is based on a more efficient use of available energy. Today's electronic equipment, machines and appliances, as a matter of convenience, provide features to be explicitly switched to reduced energy consumption modes (so called "stand-by" modes), when not in active use (but to be instantly ready for use upon explicit user invocation). Through bearing potentials as an energy saving solution, the analysis of behavioral patterns in several user studies reports effects towards the exact opposite; with the ability to just put an appliance in standby mode when not in use, devices are no longer switched (totally) "off" which causes surprisingly high so called "stand-by losses".

As a result, the user behavior needs to change towards a more economical usage of energy, which gained increased awareness in the public during the last years, but is also a long term process, or to be more precise, an evolution. To support the user in this task, we present an energy management system based on the opportunistic sensing approach presented in [6]. Using this approach, we are able to reduce the standby losses based on the *location information* of the user within the household, in combination with his/her current *locomotions*, but without forcing the user to explicitly switch a device on or off. This enables the unobtrusive control of electrical power consumers, in terms of automatically turning them on and off and thus reducing stand-by losses, without reducing the convenience, the level of living, and the habits of the user.

The sensor and computer based recognition of user's *locomotion* and *location* were well studied and evaluated in laboratory settings and can be identified in three areas of research, namely (i) activity and context recognition [1, 7, 10, 11], (ii) (in-door) localization [2, 4], and (iii) energy/power management in households and smart homes [3, 5, 9]. Summarizing, the best sensor modality for on body activity recognition are accelerometers [8] due to their high accuracy and their unobtrusiveness. Ubisense is identified as a robust and *off-the-shelf* solution for indoor localization [2].

Main contribution of this paper is the fact that we put the developed methods of this research out in the field. We do not assume a fixed and static sensing infrastructure to unobtrusively control electrical power consumers, as it can be found in laboratory settings. We utilize sensors in dynamic, varying environments to infer locomotion and location information. Using the opportunistic approach [6] allows us to break the chain of predefining a fixed sensing infrastructure at design time of the system. This is especially useful for the purpose of saving energy in households as the available sensing infrastructure changes over time. Relating locomotion to different locations enables the possibility to give locomotion different meaning in different locations and react accordingly. A vast heterogeneity of already deployed sensors in the surrounding environment is available in today's homes. These body or infrastructure based multi-sensor platforms, like mobile phones or smart watches, can be utilized without stressing the user to wear or install new sensors that have to be deployed, maintained and consume additional electrical power. Households are highly dynamic and heterogeneous environments in terms of sensing infrastructure. Not only the sensing infrastructure itself varies in different households, also over the time period of a day, the presence of persons changes and thus the availability of sensor devices. A robust and flexible system (described in Section 2) is needed to deal with the varying, dynamic sensing infrastructure to handle multiple sources of information for locomotion and location to effectively manage energy consumers in an unobtrusive and convenient way.

The remaining paper is structured as follows; based on the opportunistic sensing approach described in [6], we have implemented an energy management system as a use case of an opportunistic system. The system utilizes users' location and locomotion information to reduce stand-by losses, and is described in detail in Section 2. To empirically underpin the developed technology we have conducted a field study (be referred to Section 3) in fifteen domestic households with a total of 58 participating persons over a period of nine months. Results show an average energy saving potential of 17% in implicit power management controllable energy consumption (see Section 4). Finally, we summarize and conclude the presented work in Section 5.

2. A ROBUST SYSTEM SETTING

The main purpose of this paper is to investigate and develop a robust and flexible system for daily use in real life situations. In a real-world setting the system has to cope with (i) different users, (ii) different sensors and (iii) different environmental conditions. The requirements for the developed system were identified to (i) be able to detect locomotion and location of the present residents in a dynamic way and to (ii) combine this information in a rule like form to control the electrical power consumers in the household.

To design and implement the locomotion and location recognition system, we utilized our approach of an opportunistic activity and context recognition system as presented in [6]. Using the opportunistic sensing approach has the benefit that our system is not pinned to a fixed and static sensing infrastructure to infer locomotion and location information. This is an extremely important fact, as households are of highly dynamic and heterogeneous nature in terms of the available sensing infrastructure (e.g., smart phones and smart watches). The presence of people and thus the available (on-body) sensing infrastructure changes over time. Furthermore also the environmental sensors can fail due to e.g., power loss or physical damage over time.

So we have to separate different layers when we talk of an opportunistic system: (i) we have to find a way to describe and utilize the available sensors from whatever kind they are and (ii) we have to find a way to handle the dynamic sensing infrastructure. In the following we utilize the solutions proposed in [6] to build a robust system that can handle a heterogeneous and varying sensing infrastructure over time. We use *Sensor Abstractions* and *Sensor-Self-Descriptions* in

combination with *Experience Items* [6]. Each sensor is abstracted and describes its capabilities in terms of inferring locomotion and location information using *Experience Items*. The experience item itself encapsulates the complete recognition chain needed to detect the labels it is capable of, containing all steps necessary to infer context information out of the raw sensor data and a qualitative value, the so called *Degree of Fulfillment* [6] estimating the accuracy of the recognition process. By using the *Experience Items* we can dynamically instantiate the recognition chains dependent on the recognition purpose and the available sensing infrastructure. So from the systems viewpoint, we see a sensor as a label (locomotion and location) delivering entity that can be queried for its capabilities and be utilized.

The opportunistic sensing approach allows for the dynamic configuration of sensor ensembles [6]. A sensor ensemble is the set of available sensors that is best suited in a certain situation to achieve the highest recognition accuracy according to a recognition purpose. This is an important feature of an opportunistic system as it makes it flexible against changes in the sensing infrastructure, as sensors can spontaneously become available or unavailable (e.g., a person turns his/her smart phone on or off, or leaves the house).

We use the opportunistic sensing approach [6] to recognize locomotion and location. This allows us to implement a robust and flexible system that can handle the dynamic and varying sensing infrastructure of a household to recognize the locations and locomotions of persons.

To effectively control the electrical power consumers of a household in an implicit, user centered way, it is necessary, to capture the manageable devices and control them according to their actual status and the activities of the residents. Therefore, a model has to be developed that generates the control actions out of the current locomotions and locations of present house residents and the status of the captured and monitored electrical power consumers. It was necessary to develop the concept of *Symbolic Locations* as shown in Figure 1 that directly relate the locomotion and location of a user to the needed or used electrical devices in the corresponding zone.

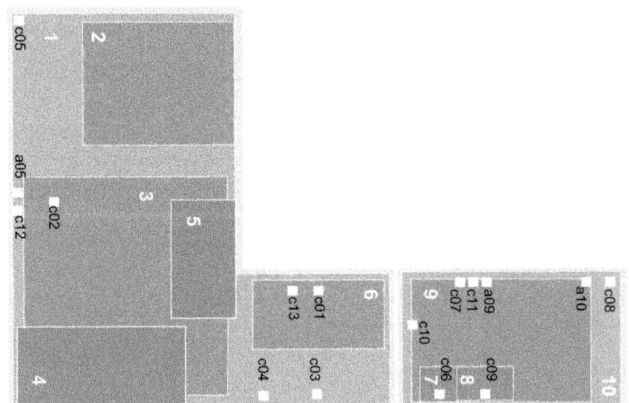

Figure 1: Exemplarily household of the field study and its segmentation into energy consumption zones named *Symbolic Locations* that directly relate the locomotion and location of a user to the the assigned electrical power consumers e.g., *Symbolic Location 9 "kitchen"*→$c07$ (toaster), $c11$ (water boiler); *Symbolic Location 8 "sink"*→$c09$ (dishwasher).

Based on the model we implemented a *background intelligence*, that manages the knowledge about which devices are needed according to the location and locomotion of present residents, which devices will be needed in the future according to the general behavior characteristics of the residents, and which devices can be turned off safely. The schematics of the developed system components and their interplay are shown in Figure 2.

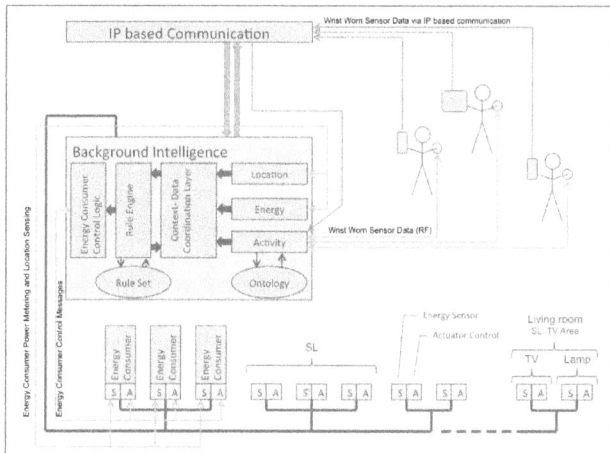

Figure 2: Schematics of the developed system components and their interplay. Body-worn sensors are used for activity recognition, in our case the modes of locomotion (used sensors are described in Section 3) and in combination with the energy measurements to detect the location of the residents. The two dimensional information of *Locomotion* and *Location* is passed into the *Background Intelligence* where it is further processed and events are generated based on a defined *Rule Set* to switch power consumers on and off.

An implicit system used for energy management, as it is described here, may never overrule the user. It has to be an extension and enrichment to the user's life. It has to act as unobtrusively as possible in the best case without user's notice. But, the users always have to understand what and why the system is doing something. Only in this case they will use the system without getting afraid of losing control over its behavior. In consideration of this fact, we gave the users the option to read and manage the rule base in a simple way. Therefore we used a GUI that displayed the ruleset in a table like form and allowed the users to manually add, modify and delete rules. This approach puts the user in the center as it allows to control and alter the rules on which decisions are based on. So users can adapt the behavior of the implicit energy management system to their own needs and their changing lifestyle. The users have, at each point in time, control over the events generated from the implicit energy management system. They are in the "center" of the system and can control its behavior if necessary.

Summarizing, we have utilized the opportunistic sensing approach to detect locomotion and location as presented in [6]. We can deal with a vast heterogeneity of different sensors having different modalities using sensor abstractions. Furthermore, we can handle the dynamic varying sensing infrastructure where sensors can appear and disappear spontaneously. We can dynamically instantiate the required machine learning techniques (recognition chains) using *Experience Items* to infer locomotion and location data out of the raw sensor data streams. So we have a robust system for the detection of locomotion and location that can utilize different sensors during runtime of the system to infer the needed information for implicit energy management. On top of that robust fundament we put a user controllable engine in a rule based form that generates the action events necessary to turn electrical power consumers on and off safely (as shown in Figure 2). Both, the locomotion and the location information of users, are used to trigger the corresponding action events. During the design of the background intelligence we focused on the user as the ultimate control instance of the system. The human always has to be in the center to make such a system successful. So, at each point in time the user has the possibility to "overrule" the decisions made by the implicit energy management control system.

The setup of the presented system used during a field study to underpin the suitability for daily use is shown in Section 3.

3. EXPERIMENT DESIGN

The main contribution of this paper is the real world utilization of *locomotion* combined with *location* information to implicitly reduce standby losses caused by electrical power consumers. We described a robust system (see Section 2) operating in an opportunistic way capable of utilizing the best available set of sensors in terms of recognition accuracy at each point in time to get locomotion and location information of the residents. By utilizing this two-dimensional information, a background intelligence generates the necessary action events to turn energy consumers on and off safely and thus avoid energy losses.

We show that such a system can be used in the field with different people, different sensing hardware and different settings. We designed an experimental setup in form of a field study to show (i) that our system is applicable in a real world setting and (ii) it can be used to increase the efficiency of energy usage. To highlight the flexibility of the opportunistic sensing approach, the field study consisted of 15 households with a total of 58 participating persons. Having a high diversity between the households and the participating persons, we can not assume a common, fixed and static sensing infrastructure. This made it the ideal scenario to show the flexibility of the opportunistic sensing approach in the "real-world" used to implicitly control electrical power consumers.

The first design issue was to decide which sensing systems should be used during the field study. As we abstract and self describe each sensor (as explained in Section 2), we could have used each sensing device capable of inferring the needed locomotion an location information. To have a comparable result, that is not affected by different hardware components, we decided to take a subset of the possible available sensors as the "pool" for the opportunistic sensing approach. We decided, for the on body worn sensors used to detect locomotion, to use a wrist worn 3-axis-acceleration sensor and a smartphone as a multi sensor platform. Our system decided during runtime which is the most accurate sensing ensemble (one of the two sensors, or both combined) in terms of achieving the highest recognition accuracy, and configured it accordingly for each user.

Inferring location information is not a trivial task especially in indoor environments. Again, we abstract the location sensors and could have used any available technology.

We decided to use the *Ubisense* Location system as this is an *off-the-shelf* and highly accurate technology [2].

Summarizing, the sensor setup in each household consisted of a Ubisense system to gather location information in the defined *Symbolic Locations* of each (present) resident, a smart phone and a wrist worn 3-axis-acceleration sensor per person to infer locomotion information. The availability of all three sensor systems (if a Ubisense tag is accounted as being a sensor) varied over time. Our system decided opportunistically which sensors to utilize to infer locomotion and location information depended on the available sensors to achieve the highest possible recognition accuracy at each point in time.

To measure the energy consumption of each observed device and the possibility to turn it on and off remotely, we utilized a "simple" adapter that is plugged between the device and the power outlet. This adapter can act on the one hand as a sensor, measuring the power consumption of the attached device and on the other hand, as an actuator to remotely turn the attached device on and off. Measuring the consumed electrical power of the attached device is highly important as it ensures on the one hand to measure the consumed electrical power and on the other hand to only switch off devices that are not used at the moment. Nobody wants the microwave oven for example to be turned off while warming the food for dinner.

To get a reliable and comprehensive dataset for further offline analysis, we extended the system setting explained in Section 2. Beside the described realtime capabilities we added a software component capable of recording the transmitted data from the sensing ensembles and the energy consumed by the individual electrical appliances. This allows to operate our system in two different modes, namely (i) the real-time mode were we implicitly control electrical power consumers and have the ability to capture the data of the sensors and the actuators, and (ii) the simulation mode were we can playback the pre-captured data of the dataset as if real sensors were attached to the system. In utilizing this captured data in the simulation mode, we were able to calculate the real energy saving potentials of the described system during the field study as shown in Section 4. The calculations are based upon what would have happened if the system had not been in place.

By detecting the presence and the locomotion of a user in a defined *Symbolic Location* (as shown in Figure 1), the background intelligence can, based on the defined rules, generate the control commands that are further sent to the "adapters" to turn the attached electrical power consumers on and off remotely.

Utilizing the high value of the two dimensional information over only the single locomotion or location information, we built a precise body of rules for each household defining when devices can be turned off safely. The initial set of rules was defined during the setup time of the system by interviewing the residents in combination with knowledge already gathered during the field study in terms of rules defined by other participants. The initial rule set was then extended during the use of the system by the residents to make the system fit their personal needs.

The field study was conducted with each of the 15 participating households for a time period of two weeks. The position of each resident of the household (up to four), in up to two rooms that were further segmented individually in

Symbolic Locations was recorded (mostly kitchen and living-room as the majority of user controllable electrical power consumers were located there). The recording interval was, dependent on the rate of change of the position data, up to 30 samples per second. In addition to the position data, the locomotions of each participant and the power consumption of up to 20 devices were recorded to get a comprehensive dataset for further offline analysis. Again, the recording interval for the locomotion information was dependent on the rate of change and the interval for the electrical power consumers was set to one minute. The field study took place in *Upper Austria* from Dec. 2009 to Dec. 2010 with non scientific but mostly technologically interested people.

4. RESULTS

The empirical results obtained from the data captured during the conducted field study are presented in this Section. The analysis of the data using the simulation capabilities of our implicit energy management system impressively highlight the potential of using an activity and context based approach to reduce power loss due to standby times of electrical power consumers. Table 1 shows the potential energy savings per household during the field study. The highest potentials of saving energy can be identified in consumer electronics and in electric lightning. In these two device categories, implicit energy management is exceedingly effective in frequently reaching a 50% reduction of energy loss.

Analyzing the collected data of the 15 households including the data of the 58 participating persons during the field study (consisting of energy consumption per device, the locomotions of the persons and their time in the defined symbolic locations), it was possible to calculate the absolute potential energy savings. The potential average energy saving over all 15 households in the field study was about *21,5* Watt per hour, respectively ***17%***.

5. CONCLUSION

Within this paper we have presented and evaluated the real-world utilization of the two-dimensional contextual information containing location and locomotion of persons. We let the rubber hit the road by focusing on accessing and utilizing this information in an "out-of-the-lab" setting of a conducted field study within households in terms of implicitly optimizing the energy consumption. We implemented a robust system capable of recognizing the (in-door) location and locomotion information of persons in their homes, without presumably defining the required sensing infrastructure. The opportunistic approach lets us be as flexible and robust as possible by enabling the unobtrusive utilization of on-body and environmental sensor devices to achieve a high degree of acceptance among the residents.

As we did not aim at changing the residents' explicit behavior towards a more energy-aware operation of electronic appliances, but to unobtrusively assist them in their daily living, we have defined a rule-based background intelligence that autonomously controls devices in terms of optimized energy consumption. Input for this background intelligence is the two-dimensional contextual information (location and locomotion) of the users in their homes recognized in an opportunistic way. By utilizing a (user-) defined body of rules, the opportunistic recognition of this information lets us control electrical devices safely, without decreasing the

Potential Energy Saved per Household							
0-01-1102	0-02-1111	0-03-1111	0-04-1110	0-05-1111	0-06-2200	0-07-1102	0-08-1102
15.5%	14.7%	19.3%	23.0%	10.1%	22.2%	36.2%	24.5%
0-09-1111	0-10-1111	0-11-1110	0-12-1111	0-13-2200	0-14-1102	0-15-1111	
21.3%	13.6%	60.8%	8.0%	3.9%	4.8%	13.3%	
Overall						19.4% (stdev: 14.2%)	

Table 1: Potential energy savings in households during the field study using the developed implicit energy management system as described in Section 2 and 3. Outliners of the field study are highlighted in gray. The Household ID in form of x-xx-xxxx encodes with the first number that it was a private household (0), the second number identifies in chronological order the code of the household, and the last four digits show the number of man, woman, boys and girls in the household. The energy saving potential relies on the kind and amount of installed devices in the observed Symbolic Locations.

user comfort. For evaluation purposes we conducted a field study in private households.

We deployed our system in 15 homes (with 58 participating persons), and collected data over two weeks each. We achieved an overall average saving potential of 17% as further offline analysis showed. This is an impressive result, and there could still be further potential to increase the saving for a specific household, since the rule-based part of the background intelligence could be supplementary adapted and improved towards the specific needs and peculiarities of the residents of a particular household.

We showed that it is possible by utilizing, in an opportunistic way, already deployed sensors in smart homes (e.g., smart phones) to infer locomotion and location information in a flexible and robust way. Utilizing this two-dimensional information we implicitly controlled the energy consumers in households. Without affecting or changing the level of living of the residents, it was possible to save, on average, 17% of electrical power. During the short period of two weeks user behavior began to change to a more energy aware behavior as they realized how easy the waste of the scare resource "electrical power" can be avoided resulting in a more efficient and economical usage electrical power. Bringing our approach out in the field can be seen as a small step for the residents of the households due to its unobtrusiveness, but as a large step towards reaching the overall energy saving potentials of 20% on an EU wide scale.

6. ACKNOWLEDGMENTS

The project OPPORTUNITY acknowledges the financial support of the Future and Emerging Technologies (FET) programme within the Seventh Framework Programme for Research of the European Commission, under FET-Open grant number: 225938.

The project POWERSAVER acknowledges the financial support of the Klima- and Energiefonds (Neue Energien 2020) of the Österreichische Forschungsförderungsgesellschaft mbh (FFG) under grant number: 818898.

7. REFERENCES

[1] L. Bao and S. Intille. Activity recognition from user-annotated acceleration data. In A. Ferscha and F. Mattern, editors, *Pervasive Computing*, volume 3001 of *Lecture Notes in Computer Science*, pages 1–17. Springer Berlin / Heidelberg, 2004.

[2] K. Curran, E. Furey, T. Lunney, J. Santos, D. Woods, and A. McCaughey. An evaluation of indoor location determination technologies. *Journal of Location Based Services*, 2011.

[3] C. Harris and V. Cahill. An empirical study of the potential for context-aware power management. In *UbiComp 2007: Ubiquitous Computing*, 2007.

[4] S. Helal, B. Winkler, C. Lee, Y. Kaddoura, L. Ran, C. Giraldo, S. Kuchibhotla, and W. Mann. Enabling location-aware pervasive computing applications for the edlerly. In *Pervasive Computing and Communications*, 2003.

[5] M. Jahn, M. Jentsch, C. R. Prause, F. Pramudianto, A. Al-Akkad, and R. Reiners. The energy aware smart home. *2010 5th International Conference on Future Information Technology*, pages 1–8, 2010.

[6] M. Kurz, G. Hölzl, A. Ferscha, A. Calatroni, D. Roggen, G. Tröster, H. Sagha, R. Chavarriaga, J. del R. Millán, D. Bannach, K. Kunze, and P. Lukowicz. The opportunity framework and data processing ecosystem for opportunistic activity and context recognition. *International Journal of Sensors, Wireless Communications and Control, Special Issue on Autonomic and Opportunistic Communications*, 1, December 2011.

[7] B. Logan, J. Healey, M. Philipose, E. M. Tapia, and S. Intille. A long-term evaluation of sensing modalities for activity recognition. In *9th international conference on Ubiquitous computing*, UbiComp '07, pages 483–500, Berlin, Heidelberg, 2007. Springer-Verlag.

[8] J. Mantyjarvi, J. Himberg, and T. Seppanen. Recognizing human motion with multiple acceleration sensors. In *Systems, Man, and Cybernetics, 2001 IEEE International Conference on*, volume 2, pages 747 –752 vol.2, 2001.

[9] J. Paradiso, P. Dutta, H. Gellersen, and E. Schooler. Guest editors' introduction: Smart energy systems. *IEEE Pervasive Computing*, 10:11–12, January 2011.

[10] D. Salber, A. K. Dey, and G. D. Abowd. The context toolkit: aiding the development of context-enabled applications. In *Proceedings of the SIGCHI conference on Human factors in computing systems: the CHI is the limit*, CHI '99, pages 434–441, New York, NY, USA, 1999. ACM.

[11] E. Tapia, S. Intille, and K. Larson. Activity recognition in the home using simple and ubiquitous sensors. In *Pervasive Computing*, volume 3001 of *Lecture Notes in Computer Science*, pages 158–175. Springer Berlin, 2004.

An Autonomic Resource Provisioning Framework for Mobile Computing Grids

Hariharasudhan Viswanathan, Eun Kyung Lee, Ivan Rodero, and Dario Pompili
NSF Cloud and Autonomic Computing Center
Department of Electrical and Computer Engineering, Rutgers University, New Brunswick, NJ
{hari_viswanathan, eunkyung_lee, irodero, pompili}@cac.rutgers.edu

ABSTRACT

Enabling data- and compute-intensive applications that require real-time in-the-field data collection and processing using mobile platforms is still a significant challenge due to i) the insufficient computing capabilities and unavailability of complete data on individual mobile devices and ii) the prohibitive communication cost and response time involved in offloading data to remote computing resources such as clouds for centralized computation. A novel resource provisioning framework is proposed for organizing the heterogeneous sensing, computing, and communication capabilities of static and mobile devices in the vicinity in order to form an elastic resource pool (a heterogeneous mobile computing grid) that can be harnessed to collectively process massive amounts of locally generated data in parallel. The proposed framework is imparted with autonomic capabilities, namely, self-optimization and self-organization, in order to be energy and uncertainty aware, respectively, in the dynamic mobile environment.

Categories and Subject Descriptors

C.2.4 [**COMPUTER-COMMUNICATION NETWORKS**]: Distributed Systems

Keywords

Mobile grids, autonomic management, uncertainty

1. INTRODUCTION

The computation and communication capabilities of mobile handheld devices such as smart phones, tablets, netbooks, and laptops have improved tremendously due to the advances in microprocessor, storage, and wireless technologies. As more and more of these mobile devices are coupled with in-built as well as external sensors capable of monitoring ambient conditions, acceleration, orientation, gravity, biomedical data (e.g., electrocardiogram, galvanic skin response, oxygen saturation) etc., and Global Positioning System (GPS) receivers, they can provide spatially distributed measurements regarding the environment in their proximity.

In this paper, we present a resource provisioning framework that organizes the heterogeneous sensing, computing, and communication capabilities of static and mobile devices in the vicinity in order to form an *elastic resource pool* – a heterogeneous mobile computing grid. This local computing grid can be harnessed to enable innovative *data- and compute-intensive mobile applications* such as content-based distributed multimedia search and sharing [1], distributed object recognition and tracking, and ubiquitous context-aware health monitoring [7]. The response time, quality, and relevance of such mobile applications, which rely on *real-time in-the-field processing of locally generated data,* can be drastically improved using our envisioned framework. Presently, the primary impediments to real-time in-the-field data processing are, 1) insufficient sensing and computing capabilities on individual mobile devices, which prevents them from producing meaningful results within realistic time bounds *in isolation,* and 2) the prohibitive communication cost and response time involved in enabling such applications using the *wired-grid-computing* and/or *cloud-computing* approaches alone [15] – in which computation and storage are offloaded to remote computing resources on the Internet.

In order to address the research challenges associated with reliable mobile grid coordination and application performance under uncertainty (in terms of device availability due to node mobility and susceptibility to failures), we impart our proposed resource provisioning framework with autonomic capabilities, namely, *self-optimization* and *self-organization*. Applications are made up of one or more workloads, which are usually composed of multiple tasks whose order of execution is specified by a workflow. Workload here refers to compute-intensive mathematical models with different computational, storage, and deadline requirements.

In our solution, the entities of the hybrid grid may at any time play one or more of the following three *logical roles* as shown in Fig. 1(a): i) *service requester,* which places requests for workloads that require additional data and/or computing resources from other devices, ii) *service provider,* which can be a *data provider, resource provider,* or both, and iii) *arbitrator* (also typically known as broker), which processes the requests from the requesters, determines the set of service providers that will provide or process data, and distributes the workload tasks among them. Data providers provide scalar or multimedia data while resource providers lend their computational, storage, and communication resources for processing data. The arbitrator – an additional role played by some of the service providers – is aided by a novel *energy-aware resource allocation engine,* which will distribute the workload tasks optimally among the service providers. This way, we ensure that the data providers do not drain valuable energy. Figure 1(a) depicts the envisioned framework enabling an ubiquitous healthcare application that relies on processing collected biomedical data in-the-field for

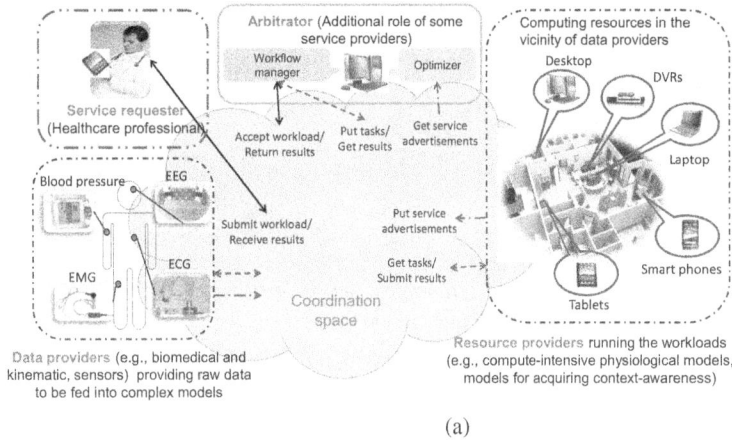

Figure 1: (a) Autonomic resource provisioning framework enabling ubiquitous healthcare; (b) Summary of related work.

Focus	Chu et al. [2]	Giurgiu et al. [8]	Chun et al. [3]	Darby et al. [5]	Costa et al. [4]	Huang et al. [9]	Lima et al. [6]	Jiang et al. [10]	Liao et al. [14]	OURS
Infrastructure										
Mobile					✓		✓	✓	✓	
Static						✓				
Hybrid	✓	✓	✓	✓						✓
Concern										
Energy			✓			✓				✓
Connectivity				✓	✓					✓
Uncertainty					✓					✓
Contribution										
Protocol				✓			✓	✓		
Middleware	✓	✓	✓		✓		✓		✓	✓

real-time physiological monitoring. Workloads in this example scenario include mathematical models for acquiring context awareness that operate on biomedical and kinematic sensor data.

Prior research efforts, summarized in Fig. 1(b), have aimed at integrating mobile devices into the wired-grid and cloud-computing infrastructure mainly as service requesters. In contrast, we exploit mobile devices as service providers and address uncertainty-aware autonomic resource management for ensuring application Quality of Service (QoS) even in highly dynamic and unpredictable environments. Our resource allocation engine relies on long-term statistics regarding the dynamics of the underlying resource pool to protect application performance from the undesired effects of uncertainties. The major contributions of this paper include, 1) a role-based architectural framework for handling service discovery and service request arrivals as well as for task distribution and management, 2) a novel energy-aware resource allocation engine for imparting the self-optimization capability, i.e., for allocating the workload tasks optimally among the computing devices, 3) an innovative mechanisms to estimate the uncertainty (in terms of dynamics and size) in the resource pool for imparting uncertainty-aware self-organization, and 4) a detailed performance analysis of our proposed autonomic resource provisioning framework through experiments on a prototype testbed as well as simulations.

The rest of the paper is organized as follows. In Sect. 2, we present our autonomic resource provisioning framework for mobile grids. In Sect. 3, we describe our experimental methodology and results. Finally, in Sect. 4, we present our conclusions and plans for future work.

2. PROPOSED SOLUTION

Our *role-based architectural framework* facilitates coordination and seamless switching among the three logical roles. The *energy-aware resource allocation engine* and *mechanisms for uncertainty awareness* impart the self-optimization and self-organization capabilities, respectively.

2.1 Role-based Architectural Framework

Service discovery: Service discovery at the arbitrators is achieved through voluntary *service advertisements* from the service providers. Service advertisement from a service provider n includes information about the current position, amount of computing (γ_n^{cpu}, in terms of normalized CPU cycles), memory (γ_n^{mem} [Bytes]), and communication (γ_n^{net} [bps]) resources, the start (t_n^{in}) and end

(t_n^{out}) times of the availability of those resources, and the available battery capacity (e_n^{adv} [Wh]). The arbitrator is aware of the power drawn by the workload tasks of a specific application when running on a specific class of CPU and memory (together given by c_n^{comp} [W]) as well as network (c_n^{net} [W]) resources at each service provider as the information about the different types of devices is known in advance. The arbitrators use the information from service advertisements of the N computing devices to derive the following: $\mathbf{S} = \{s_n\}_{1 \times N}$, where $s_n \in \{1, 0\}$, which conveys whether n is a resource provider or not, and $\mathbf{D} = \{d_n\}_{1 \times N}$, where $d_n \in \{1, 0\}$, which conveys whether n is a data provider or not.

We advocate the use of a distributed arbitrator self-election mechanism similar to the one in [12]. Our self-election mechanism works as follows: each service provider will determine the potential size of its resource pool based on the number of advertisements it has received. Then, all the service providers advertise this number and determine their *rank* in their neighborhood in terms of the potential size of their resource pool. The service providers use a pre-determined rank threshold (which varies depending on the network size and density) to elect themselves as arbitrators.

Workload management: Each arbitrator is composed of two components, namely, *workload manager* and *scheduler/optimizer*, as shown at the top of Fig. 1(a). The workload manager (also called *master*) tracks workload requests, allocates workload tasks among service providers, and aggregates results. The optimizer identifies the number of service providers (also called *workers*) available for the requested duration and determines the optimal distribution of workload tasks among them. The optimizer shares the workload submitted by the data providers among the available service providers based on one of several possible policies. One policy may aim at minimizing the battery drain while another policy may just place emphasis on response time without considering battery drain. Our framework applies to applications exhibiting *data parallelism* (in which data is distributed across different parallel computing nodes that perform the same task) as well as to applications exhibiting *task parallelism* (in which parallel computing nodes may perform different tasks on the same or different data).

2.2 Energy-aware Resource Allocation Engine

Here, we explain our energy-aware resource allocation engine (an optimization problem corresponding to one of the aforementioned policies) for hybrid grids in detail. In the following, we explain the sequence of events happening at one of the arbitrators while similar events happen simultaneously at the other arbitrators in the computing grid. When a service requester needs additional data or computing resources, it submits a service request to the nearest arbitrator and also specifies δ^{max} [h], the maximum duration for which it is ready to wait for a service response. The arbitrator extracts the following information based on the service advertisements: the devices' (service providers') capability, $\boldsymbol{\Gamma}^x = \{\gamma_n^x\}_{1 \times N}$, where $x = cpu, mem, net$; the associated costs, $\mathbf{C}^{comp} = \{c_n^{comp}\}_{1 \times N}$ and $\mathbf{C}^{net} = \{c_n^{net}\}_{1 \times N}$; the devices' availability, $\mathbf{T}^{in} = \{t_n^{in}\}_{1 \times N}$ and $\mathbf{T}^{out} = \{t_n^{out}\}_{1 \times N}$; and their battery status $\mathbf{E}^{adv} = \{e_n^{adv}\}_{1 \times N}$.

The variables that the optimization problem has to find are, $\mathbf{A}$, $\mathbf{U}$, $\boldsymbol{\Delta}^d$, and $\boldsymbol{\Delta}^s$. Matrix $\mathbf{A} = \{a_{ij}\}_{N \times N}$ conveys the associativity of data provider i with service provider j, $\mathbf{U} = \{u_n\}_{1 \times N}$ with $u_n \in \{1, 0\}$ conveys whether a resource provider n is used for computing or not, $\boldsymbol{\Delta}^d = \{\delta_n^d\}_{1 \times N}$ [h] conveys the duration for which the services of each service provider will be used for data collection, and $\boldsymbol{\Delta}^s = \{\delta_n^s\}_{1 \times N}$ [h] conveys the duration for which the resources of each service provider will be used for computation (cpu, mem, and net) and/or for multi-hop communication (net) as a relay node. In this formulation, the *objective* of the optimization problem, given by (1) and (2), is *maximization of minimal residual battery capacity* at all the service providers, $\max \min_n e_n^{res}$ [Wh], while ensuring that the service response is delivered within δ^{max}. This objective maximizes the lifetime of every single service provider and, thus, maintains the heterogeneity of the resource pool for longer periods. The set of service providers and the duration for which each of their capabilities are availed will be determined by considering the trade-offs among the cost e_n^{data} [Wh] (3) for transferring the data locally from data providers to the resource providers, the computational cost e_n^{comp} [Wh] (3) for availing the computational capabilities of the resource providers for servicing the request and for aggregating and generating the final response.

$$\textbf{Maximize}: \quad \min_n e_n^{res}, \tag{1}$$

$$where, \quad e_n^{res} = e_n^{adv} - (e_n^{data} + e_n^{comp}); \tag{2}$$

$$e_n^{data} = \delta_n^d \cdot c_n^{net}; \quad e_n^{comp} = u_n \cdot \delta_n^s \cdot c_n^{comp}. \tag{3}$$

In (2), $e_n^{data} + e_n^{comp}$ is the amount of battery capacity drained at each service provider n. δ_n^d for a service provider n depends on the amount of data it has to transmit (ω [Bytes] as a data provider) or aggregate ($\omega \cdot \sum_{i=1}^N a_{in}$ [Bytes] as a resource provider), and the availed communication capability, given by $\delta_n^d = f(\omega, \gamma_n^{net})$ when $u_n = 0$ and $\delta_n^d = f(\omega \cdot \sum_{i=1}^N a_{in})$ when $u_n = 1$. Here, without any loss of generality, ω is considered to be the problem size of a trivial task and each data provider provides the same amount of data. Function $f()$ monotonically increases as the amount of data to be transmitted or received increases. δ_n^s for a service provider n depends on the amount of data it has to process and the availed computing capabilities specified by γ_n^{cpu} and γ_n^{mem}, given by $\delta_n^s = g(\gamma_n^{cpu}, \gamma_n^{mem}, \omega \cdot \sum_{i=1}^N a_{in})$. Function $g()$ monotonically increases with the amount of data to be processed. The *constraints* to the optimization problem are, $\forall n = 1 \dots N$,

$$s_n \geq u_n; \quad 0 \leq \delta_n^d, \delta_n^s; \tag{4}$$

$$\delta_n^s \leq \min\{t_n^{out}, t^{now} + \delta^{max}\} - \max\{t^{now} + \delta_n^d, t_n^{in}\}; \tag{5}$$

$$\delta_n^d \cdot c_n^{net} + u_n \cdot \delta_n^s \cdot c_n^{comp} \leq e_n^{adv}. \tag{6}$$

Constraint (4) ensures that only a resource provider is chosen to perform the computing. Constraints (5) and (6) ensure that every service provider's advertised availability (duration) and battery limit are not exceeded while satisfying the consumer's deadline for service response.

2.3 Uncertainty Awareness

Inaccurate estimation of the availability (duration) of service provider is a major source of uncertainty that results in a large number of incomplete workload task migrations. The duration of availability specified in the service advertisements is based on the battery drain estimates and may not accurately reflect the duration for which the service provider will be associated with the arbitrator. One or more of the service providers may lose network connectivity to the arbitrator or go offline, i.e., run out of energy due to an unexpected increase in battery drain because of other concurrent compute-intensive critical operations. As the arbitrator is also one of the service providers, this problem holds for arbitrators too.

We advocate the use of multiple arbitrators to avoid a single point of failure. In order to ensure that the unavailability of an arbitrator does not lead to the failure of the entire system, each arbitrator shares with all of its active data and service providers a list of alternate arbitrators – referred to as *proxies* – ranked according to their proximity (primary key) and physical addresses (secondary key). In case of an arbitrator failure, the service providers collaborate with the pre-specified proxy until all active workload tasks end. The arbitrators also share their current state information with their proxies to handle any unexpected failures.

In order to impart the uncertainty-aware self-organization capability to the proposed resource-allocation framework, we designed a mechanism that helps the arbitrator extract the following long-term statistics from the underlying resource pool: the average arrival (joining) rate of service providers ($\widetilde{W}$), the average service provider availability duration ($\widetilde{T}$), and the average number of service providers associated with the arbitrator at any point in time ($\widetilde{N}$). The relationship among these three long-term statistics is given by Little's theorem, $\widetilde{N} = \widetilde{W} \cdot \widetilde{T}$. The arbitrators update continuously these statistics and share at least two of the three aforementioned averages with its proxies. Knowledge of these average statistics helps the arbitrators assess the *churn rate* of service providers. Churn rate is a measure of the number of service providers moving into or out of an arbitrator's resource pool over a specific period of time. Note that the arbitrators need not extract or be aware of the underlying probability distribution of service provider arrivals or of availability durations.

Churn rate of service providers will be different in different geographic location. For example, the churn rate of service providers at a shopping mall is far greater than the one at a coffee shop. Also, at a particular location, the churn rate can vary over time (say, depending on the time of the day). When the churn rate of service providers is high, i.e., the average duration of service providers availability is low, the percentage of migrated workload tasks will be high if the resource-allocation engine does not possess uncertainty awareness. A mismatch between the ground reality and the optimization at the arbitrator occurs when the long-term average of availability duration is not taken into account at the arbitrator and when the durations advertised by the service providers are used as constraints in the optimization problem (presented in the previous subsection). However, our framework with uncertainty awareness achieves a smooth degradation (if any) in QoS (because of the small number of task migrations) when churn rate increases as it effectively exploits the knowledge gathered over time and/or acquired from its predecessors.

3. PERFORMANCE EVALUATION

We have implemented a small-scale prototype of the proposed framework and performed an experimental evaluation. We have also used simulations to show the scalability of the framework be-

Table 1: Heterogeneity of computing devices in the testbed.

	Samsung Galaxy Tab	Motorola Atrix 2	Samsung Galaxy S	LG Optimus	HTC Desire HD	Dell Netbook	Dell Laptop
CPU	1GHz Dual-core ARM	1GHz Dual-core ARM	1GHz ARM	600 MHz ARM	1GHz ARM	1GHz Atom	2GHz Dual-core Intel
Memory (RAM)	1GB	1GB	512MB	512MB	786MB	1GB	2GB
Network	802.11b/g/n, Bluetooth (BT)	2/3/4G, BT, 802.11b/g/n	2/3G, 802.11b/g/n, BT	3G, 802.11b/g, BT	2/3G, 802.11b/g/n, BT	802.11b/g/n, BT	802.11b/g, BT
Battery capacity	28Wh	6.612Wh	5.7Wh	5.7Wh	5.32Wh	49.95Wh	55.5Wh
Workload completion time	150s	300s	390s	590s	340s	100s	35s

yond ten nodes (the size of our testbed). For statistical relevance, we performed multiple trials until we achieved a very small relative confidence interval (less than 10%). First, we present details about our testbed and our experiment methodology. Then, we discuss specific experiment scenarios and the results that demonstrate the autonomic capabilities of our framework.

3.1 Testbed and Experiment Methodology

Heterogeneous devices: The testbed consists of Android- and Linux-based mobile devices with heterogeneous capabilities (summarized in Table 1). In our prototype, communications among the master and workers as well as among the optimizer and workers happen over *Comet Space* [13], a scalable peer-to-peer content-based coordination space developed at the NSF Cloud and Autonomic Computing Center, Rutgers University.

The workload: The mobile application that we used for our experiments is *distributed object recognition*. The service requester (which is also the data provider) submits an image of any object that needs to be recognized while also specifying a deadline. The predominant workload in this application is matrix multiplication and the most fundamental workload task is vector multiplication, which is assigned to the different service providers. Distributed object recognition is representative of a wide range of data-parallel applications that our framework can support. Table 1 shows the time taken by the different mobile devices to complete all the workload tasks of our application when operating in isolation. For near-real-time performance, the delay needs to be in the order of tens of seconds and the numbers clearly motivate the need to divide the tasks among service providers in the vicinity for speed up.

Application profiling: As the objective of the optimization problem is maximization of minimal residual battery capacity, the amount of battery drain in service providers as a result of running workload tasks needs to be estimated and used in decision making. However, the usage of actual Watt-hour (Wh) is unfair to devices with a higher battery capacity. Hence, in order to exploit heterogeneity and to ensure fairness, our prototype uses the residual battery capacity percentage instead of actual Wh values.

In order to ascertain battery drain while running a workload task, first, we ran all the workload tasks of our object recognition application on the individual mobile devices and measured the current drawn in mA (as the voltage drop remains constant) and the total time taken for the workload completion. Then, we determined the average time taken to complete one task. Such a straightforward estimation is possible as object recognition is a data-parallel application whose task (vector multiplication) completion time is not affected by the type of input. Information about task completion time along with the current drawn by the workload tasks and the number of tasks allocated to a service provider helps us calculate the resulting battery drain in Wh. Information about battery current consumption is readily available in most Android-based devices.

3.2 Self-optimization

Competing approaches: To assess the self-optimization capability of our framework, we compare it against two competing approaches: i) *Round-robin*, in which the workload tasks are divided equally among all the available service providers, and ii) *Comet-Cloud* [11], a pull-based task-scheduling mechanism in which the service providers voluntarily pull tasks from the arbitrator, work on them, report the result, and pull the next task to work on. Round-robin is chosen for comparison to show the gains (in terms of application response time and battery drain) that can be achieved by exploiting the heterogeneity in computing capabilities of service providers. CometCloud inherently exploits the heterogeneity in computing capabilities as it schedules tasks on a First-Come-First-Served (FCFS) basis resulting in progressively faster devices completing a correspondingly higher number of tasks over time. It is also robust to service provider failures or loss in connectivity as it is purely pull-based. However, due to lack of self-optimization, there is usually unfair battery drain at the service providers.

Setup: In order to show the superiority in performance of the proposed energy-aware resource allocation engine over the competing approaches under different operational scenarios (in terms of number and combination of service providers), we ascertain and compare the fairness in battery drain when each of the three task-scheduling mechanisms are employed. We use *Jain's fairness index* ranging in [0,1] (1 being the highest and 0 being the lowest) as measure of fairness. The four scenarios in Fig. 2 represent a progressive increase in the scale and the heterogeneity of the underlying service provider pool as well as the problem size (while keeping the deadline constant at 60s). The scaling up is achieved by increasing the resolution of the object's image, which is the input to the object recognition application. In order to determine the amount of battery drain while using the three task-scheduling mechanisms, we simulated 100 consecutive runs (for significant battery drain) of the workload. This procedure is referred to as one trial. We in turn performed multiple trials, each with a different initial condition in terms of available battery capacities in the service providers.

Observations: Figure 2 shows the average fairness in terms of residual battery capacity at the service providers after each trial. Our proposed solution achieves the best performance in terms of fairness in the residual battery capacity as it fully exploits the heterogeneity of the devices in the resource pool to achieve its objective while meeting the user-specified deadline.

3.3 Uncertainty-aware Self-organization

Setup: In order to show the uncertainty-aware self-organization capability of the proposed framework, we performed an experiment to ascertain the gain in terms of reduction in number of workload task migrations that can be achieved by using our framework. The evaluation was carried out under different operational scenarios with different service provider churn rates. The four scenarios

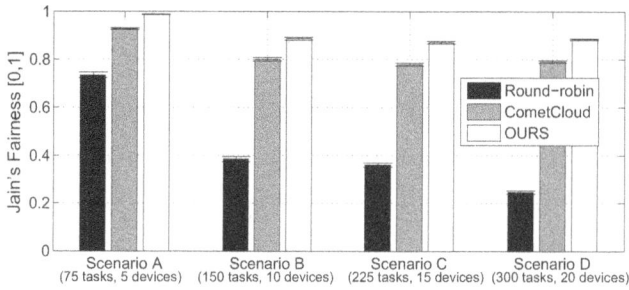

Figure 2: Performance of proposed framework (in terms of fairness) versus CometCloud and round-robin approaches.

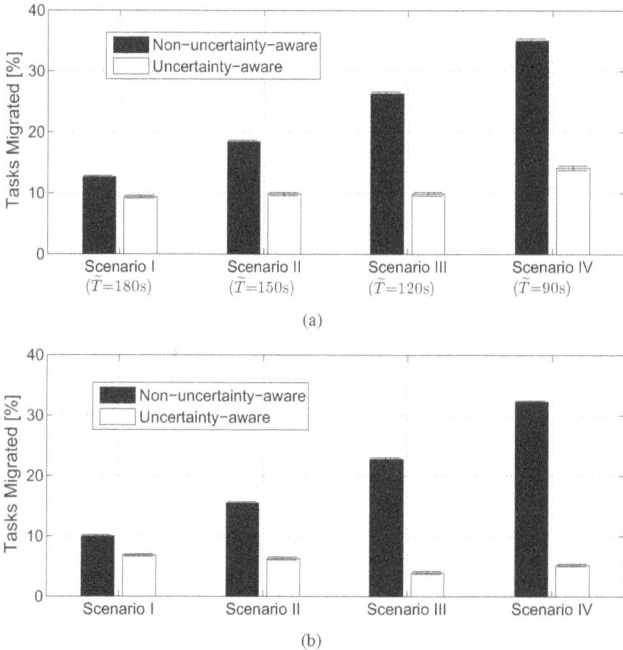

Figure 3: Effectiveness of uncertainty-awareness (in terms of % tasks migrations) when service providers' availability duration follows (a) Normal and (b) Weibull distributions.

(different from the previous ones) in Fig. 3 represent a progressive increase in the churn rate of the underlying resource pool (with a corresponding decrease in average duration of association with the arbitrator). The number (15 in total) and combination of service providers in the mobile grid, the number of workload tasks, and the deadlines remain the same for all the four scenarios.

We used *percentage of migrated workload tasks* to determine the effectiveness of uncertainty awareness. In order to ensure that the uncertainty awareness capability is not dictated by any particular distribution of service-provider-availability duration, it was picked at random based on i) Normal distribution (with mean $\mu = 180, 150, 120, 90s$; and standard deviation $\sigma = 60s$) and then on ii) Weibull distribution (with scale $\lambda = 200, 175, 150, 125$; and shape $k = 4$). Normal distribution is used for its generality while Weibull distribution is the most popular choice amongst statisticians performing reliability (or survivability) analysis.

Observations: Figures 3(a) and (b) show how the arbitrator leverages its knowledge of the long-term average of service provider availability in order to reduce the number of workload task migrations. As the churn rate of service providers increases, i.e., the av-

erage duration of service providers availability decreases, the percentage of migrated workload tasks increases when we use our resource allocation engine "without" uncertainty awareness. When the advertised durations (from service providers) are used as constraints in the optimization problem it leads to a mismatch between the ground reality and the optimization at the arbitrator. However, our framework with uncertainty awareness achieves a smooth degradation (if any) in QoS (because of the small number of task migrations) when churn rate increases as it effectively exploits the knowledge gathered over time. Also, another advantage of uncertainty awareness is that it helps decrease churn rate, especially service provider departures caused by device users opting out of the application due to undesired battery drain.

4. CONCLUSIONS AND FUTURE WORK

We proposed a novel resource-provisioning framework for organizing the heterogeneous sensing, computing, and communication capabilities of static and mobile devices in the vicinity in order to a form a mobile computing grid. We imparted the resource-provisioning framework with autonomic capabilities, namely, self-optimization and self-organization, in order to be energy and uncertainty aware in the dynamic mobile environment. We demonstrated the autonomic capabilities of the framework through experimental evaluation on a prototype testbed. Currently, we are investigating mechanisms for imparting the self-healing capability, i.e., for handling uncertainty arising out of inaccurate estimation of task completion times.

5. REFERENCES

[1] Hyrax: Cloud computing on mobile devices using mapreduce. http://www.dtic.mil/docs/citations/ADA512601.

[2] D. Chu and M. Humphrey. Mobile OGSI.NET: Grid Computing on Mobile Devices. In *Proc. of IEEE/ACM Intl. Workshop on Grid Computing*, Nov. 2004.

[3] B.-G. Chun, S. Ihm, P. Maniatis, M. Naik, and A. Patti. CloneCloud: Elastic Execution between Mobile Device and Cloud. In *Proc. of The European Professional Society on Computer Systems (EuroSys)*, Apr. 2011.

[4] P. Costa, L. Mottola, A. L. Murphy, and G. P. Picco. TeenyLIME: Transiently Shared Tuple Space Middleware for Wireless Sensor Networks. In *Proc. of the Intl. Workshop on Middleware for Sensor Networks (MidSens)*, Nov. 2006.

[5] P. J. Darby and N. F. Tzeng. Peer-to-peer Checkpointing Arrangement for Mobile Grid Computing Systems. In *Proc. of Intl. Conf. on High-Performance Parallel and Distributed Computing (HPDC)*, June 2007.

[6] L. dos S. Lima, A. T. A. Gomes, A. Ziviani, M. Endler, L. F. G. Soares, and B. Schulze. Peer-to-peer Resource Discovery in Mobile Grids. In *Proc. of the Intl. Workshop on Middleware for Grid Computing (MGC)*, Nov. 2005.

[7] D. Estrin and I. Sim. Open mHealth Architecture: An Engine for Health Care Innovation. *Science*, 330(6005):759–760, Nov. 2010.

[8] I. Giurgiu, O. Riva, D. Juric, I. Krivulev, and G. Alonso. Calling the Cloud: Enabling Mobile Phones as Interfaces to Cloud Applications. In *Proc. of the ACM/IFIP/USENIX Intl. Conf. on Middleware (Middleware)*, Nov. 2009.

[9] Y. Huang, S. Mohapatra, and N. Venkatasubramanian. An Energy-efficient Middleware for Supporting Multimedia Services in Mobile Grid Environments. In *Proc. of Information Technology: Coding and Computing (ITCC)*, Apr. 2005.

[10] N. Jiang, C. Schmidt, V. Matossian, and M. Parashar. Enabling Applications in Sensor-based Pervasive Environments. In *Proc. of Broadband Advanced Sensor Networks (BaseNets)*, Oct. 2004.

[11] H. Kim, Y. el Khamra, I. Rodero, S. Jha, and M. Parashar. Autonomic Management of Application Workflows on Hybrid Computing Infrastructure. *Telecommunication Systems*, 19(2-3):75–89, Feb. 2011.

[12] E. K. Lee, H. Viswanathan, and D. Pompili. SILENCE: Distributed Adaptive Sampling for Sensor-based Autonomic Systems. In *Proc. of the Intl. Conf. on Autonomic Computing (ICAC)*, June 2011.

[13] Z. Li and M. Parashar. Comet: A Scalable Coordination Space for Decentralized Distributed Environments. In *Proc. Intl. Workshop on Hot Topics in Peer-to-Peer Systems (HOT-P2P)*, July 2005.

[14] W.-H. Liao, J.-P. Sheu, and Y.-C. Tseng. GRID: A Fully Location-Aware Routing Protocol for Mobile Ad Hoc Networks. *Telecommunication Systems*, 18(1-3):37–60, 2001.

[15] M. Satyanarayanan, P. Bahl, R. Caceres, and N. Davies. The Case for VM-Based Cloudlets in Mobile Computing. *IEEE Pervasive Computing*, 8(4), Oct.-Dec. 2009.

A Self-Tuning Self-Optimizing Approach for Automated Network Anomaly Detection Systems

Dennis Ippoliti
Department of Computer Science
University of Colorado at Colorado Springs
Colorado Springs, CO 80918
dippoliti@aol.com

Xiaobo Zhou
Department of Computer Science
University of Colorado at Colorado Springs
Colorado Springs, CO 80918
xzhou@uccs.edu

ABSTRACT

Parameter tuning in network anomaly detection systems is typically accomplished off-line and in an ad-hoc fashion. For operational deployment in a variety of conditions, it is important but challenging for a system to adaptively tune itself meeting performance goals and constraints. We propose and develop a self-tuning self-optimizing approach for automated network anomaly detection systems. Operators set performance expectations and priorities on a collection of metrics. A controller based on reinforcement learning and neural networks automatically performs control actions to meet expectations according to defined priorities. Tuning is accomplished without requiring direct operator access to system parameters. We examine the approach on AGHSOM anomaly detection system. We validate its effectiveness using a dataset consisting of both live trace and simulated network events. Experimental results show that the approach can self-calibrate its control parameters to meet operator performance requirements. It can self-optimize itself by maximizing individual performance metrics subject to the operator defined constraints. This work is a significant step towards building automated anomaly detection systems.

Categories and Subject Descriptors

C.2 [**Computer-Communication Networks**]: Network Operations; C.4 [**Computer System Organization**]: Performance of Systems

Keywords

network anomaly detection, self-tuning, self-optimizing

1. INTRODUCTION

Anomaly detection is an important step forward in network intrusion detection and defense. They excel at identifying zero-day attacks, previously unknown, or well-disguised attack methods. However despite many years of active research, there are very few practical anomaly detectors in operational use today. While published methods have show promising experimental results, existing anomaly based systems have certain characteristics that make operational deployment challenging and even impractical. One such characteristic is the sensitivity of detection models to the accurate setting of tuning parameters. Generally, anomaly detection algorithms have a set of configurable control parameters. The values assigned to these parameters have a significant impact on the behavior of the model in its current operating environment. In many existing algorithms, those parameters are generally set by researchers directly familiar with the underlying algorithms and are tuned off-line in an ad-hoc fashion, often by trial and error after several experiments in the same environment. It has been found that operational environments have a significant impact on detection results [1, 17]. Once developed, in order for systems to be suitable for operational deployment, they must be able to operate in a wide variety of highly dynamic environments. Control parameters must be tuned for the target environment and then re-tuned as the environment changes. It is unrealistic to expect network operators to have detailed knowledge of every sophisticated detection algorithm. Effective systems must encapsulate the underlying approach such that tuning does not require specific algorithmic knowledge.

Furthermore, because anomaly based systems compare baseline models to the current network behavior, they are subject to concept drift. As normal network behavior evolves, underlying base models must be updated. Recently approaches to accomplish this task adaptively on-line [9]. However, the ability of these adaptive algorithms to correctly distinguish between evolutions in normal behavior and subtle well-disguised attack patterns is also dependent on effective system tuning.

We propose and develop a novel and practical self-tuning self-optimizing controller based on reinforcement learning and neural networks. It acts as an interface between the system operator and the underlying detection algorithm. The performance is a tradeoff between precision, recall, and confidence forwarding. When the detection engine has low confidence in its predictions, the subject events are forwarded for additional processing, operator review, or quarantine. In our approach, operators establish performance objectives and priorities for stated metrics. Feedback is provided to the controller concerning its performance in meeting those objectives. The controller combines this feedback with observations of the current network state and dynamically updates tuning parameters to maximize performance under ever-changing conditions.

Precision and recall are calculated based on the events that are not forwarded, but are classified by the primary detection engine. By using the idea of confidence forwarding we are able to give operators a flexible tool suitable for operational deployment. Our method is generally independent of the underlying detection algorithm as long as that algorithm meets two requirements: 1) It must be tunable via a finite set of control parameters. 2) It must provide some mechanism for determining confidence in its predictions.

Our controller is capable of handling both high-dimensional continuous states and low dimensional continuous action spaces. We accomplish this by using neural-network function approximation to approximate the state-action-value function. We discretize the action space into a computationally manageable set of tuning directions and combine them with a momentum factor to approximate the action space. The overall function is then trained via an on-line Levenberg-Marquardt back-propagation algorithm. Thus, the integrated controller is self-tuning, self-optimizing, and agile as well.

We test the self-tuning self-optimizing controller based on the A-GHSOM detection system [9]. We evaluate its performance using publicly available datasets representing both backbone and subscriber network traffic consisting of live trace and simulated events [18]. Experimental results show the fully implemented model is able to achieve 99% recall and 95% precision while forwarding 21% less traffic than the manual tuned approach.

The main advantages of our approach based on the integration of reinforcement learning and neural networks are as follows:

1. It expands performance flexibility by utilizing the tradeoff between precision, recall, and forwarding to provide security operators the ability to determine performance goals tailored to their environments.

2. It is self-tuning. It does not require direct access to tuning parameters. Based on operator defined goals and priorities, the controller monitors environment and performance and dynamically tunes parameters independently to the used anomaly detection algorithm.

3. It is self-optimizing in that the controller automatically tunes the detection method to maximize the performance according to operator priorities subject to operator defined constraints.

4. It is platform independent. It is able to adapt any parameter tunable detection systems.

2. RELATED WORK

Anomaly detection systems are tuned to achieve optimal operation that is generally considered finding the optimal trade off between false alarm rate and the detection rate. This tradeoff is commonly analyzed using ROC curves [11]. However, it has been identified that using ROC alone has many limitations [2, 4, 7]. To address the limitations of simple ROC analysis, many alternative IDS evaluation methods have been proposed [2, 4, 6, 7]. In all of those methods, it is very hard to accomplish the optimal tuning off line. Even if a reasonable range for the environment variables is known in advance, its exact values are highly dynamic and even small changes in these values can shift the operating point on the ROC curve to an unacceptable tradeoff.

Recently there are a few studies on tuning specific models online [5, 8, 15]. The work in [15] examined the sensitivity of PCA to parameter settings and found that minor changes to the parameter settings increased the false positive rate by a factor of three or more. Himura *et al.* investigated the effect of on-line parameter tuning for the SKETCH algorithm [8]. A method for automatically learning optimal parameter setting and dynamically adapting the learning period was proposed. Fontugne *et al.* described a Hugh transform method for anomaly detection that also automatically adjusts a parameter set in regards to the traffic fluctuations [5].

Zhang *et al.* [17] presented a middleware to correlate functioning and tuning of multiple atomic anomaly detection systems (ADS). They used a reinforcement learning approach to tune ADSes where each individual ADS was considered part of the whole system and adapted tuning based on a global reward signal.

Operator feedback and interaction has been used to tune detection systems on line in [14, 16]. Rehak *et al.* proposed a method of dynamically updating an intrusion detection system by using multiple individually tuned agents and a system of "challenges" [14]. Yu *al.* [16] proposed a rule based tuning IDS that took advantage of the analysis of alarms by the system operators and tuned the model online. Our approach has a number of distinctive merits, which are performance tradeoff flexibility, self-tuning, self-optimizing, and importantly the anomaly detection platform independence.

3. DETECTION PERFORMANCE

Anomaly detectors model network behavior and flag behavior that exceeds some notion of normal. Typically, an alert is generated when an observed behavior exceeds a predefined threshold or tolerance range. This creates the necessity for threshold selection. In general, a larger threshold may cause false negatives, and a smaller threshold may lead to a false positives. The selection of threshold has an direct impact on a systems detection coverage [17].

The tradeoff between detection accuracy and false positive rate is used for evaluating the performance of an anomaly detector as its detection threshold is varied. However, this has been shown to be an ineffective evaluation approach in some situations. Axelson argued that effective intrusion detection systems will maximize both positive predictive value (PPV) and Negative Predictive Value (NPV) [2]. However, when the probability of attack is low, the low attack rate will dominate NPV calculation such that NPV will be high even in cases of low accuracy. Likewise, even low false alarm rates will dominate PPV calculations so that alert logs are flooded with false alarms. We attempt to overcome this situation by using the dynamic metrics of precision, recall, and confidence forwarding metrics that are defined as follows.

$$Precision = \frac{TruePositives}{TruePositives + FalsePositives} \quad (1)$$

$$Recall = \frac{TruePositives}{TruePositives + FalseNegatives} \quad (2)$$

$$Forward = \frac{ConfidenceForwardedEvents}{AllObservedEvents} \quad (3)$$

Precision and recall are commonly used in the field of document retrieval. Maximizing their value allows us to maintain high PPV and NPV while at the same time ensuring we also maintain high overall detection accuracy. Confidence forwarding is the process of identifying predictions with low confidence and forwarding them for additional processing [9]. Utilizing confidence forwarding allows us to maintain high PPV, NPV, and detection accuracy in any operating environment while simultaneously focusing overhead cost to a small subset of predictions.

We explore the concept of confidence forwarding further by first presenting an intuitive discussion of a threshold based anomaly detector. The model considers network events that are observed and represented by description vectors and attempts to sort them into a set of event classes according to a well-defined policy. We use this model to further demonstrate the requirement of confidence forwarding to achieve performance flexibility. The detector is represented by the 4 tuple $\{X, V, C, D\}$.

$X = \{x_1, x_2, ..., x_n\}$ is the set of all possible network events. A network event is the action, state or behavior that we are evaluating to determine if it is malicious or benign. In practice, network events could represent individual packets, packet streams, connections, sessions, etc. Here we use the generic term event.

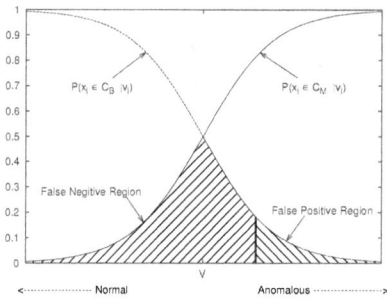

Figure 1: Intuitive tradeoff of false positive and false negative.

C is the set of possible event classes. It is composed of four subsets, C_m, C_b, C_a, and C_n. C_m is the set of all events constituting malicious intent. C_b is the set of all events constituting benign intent. C_a is the set of all events considered anomalous. And C_n is the set of all events considered normal.

V is the set of all possible description vectors $\{v_1, v_2, ..., v_k\}$. Where v_i is a vector of observable values related to x_i and it represents the subset of the global state that the detection system can observe and is aware of. Vector v_i is model dependent and is the input to the core algorithm. In practice this typically includes information collected and aggregated from network logs, packet headers, system logs, statistical analysis, etc. It can be raw data or processed data. Any information that the classifier has access to and can use to make predictions about x_i is contained in v_i.

D is a classification algorithm. P accepts v_i describing event x_i as input and produces a prediction of class membership as output.

Figure 1 illustrates an intuitive tradeoff between false positive and false negative. The X axis represents the degree of normality of a description vector v_i. The two curves represent the probability of class membership of x_i given v_i. The boundary between the two shaded regions represents the decision boundary of the anomaly detector. Events more anomalous than boundary are flagged as alerts. The shaded area represents events that are normal but malicious and therefore generate missed attacks or events that are anomalous but benign and therefore represent false positives. The exact shape of curves and the size of the shaded regions are dependent on the individual detection model, operating environment, traffic patterns, etc. However, this intuitive illustration is based on core anomaly detection assumptions. Generally, researchers develop detection algorithms to minimize the size of the shaded regions and then choose a decision boundary to meet their particular performance objective. While an effective algorithm may be able to reduce the total error region, it is obvious to see that neither sub-region can be further reduced within the total region without increasing its counterpart.

Confidence forwarding expands this model to include three possibilities. We add a second decision boundary and divide the error region into three sub-regions. The added region represents events where we have low confidence in the prediction accuracy of the classifier. We acknowledge that they require additional processing. We consider performance as a tradeoff of three regions and as such we are able to make any two regions arbitrarily small at the expense of the third. This model increases the systems prediction flexibility. Operators can now set specific performance goals for both precision and recall that can be achieved by adapting the confidence region of the prediction model.

4. THE SYSTEM ARCHITECTURE

We develop a framework for a dynamic tuning system by aug-

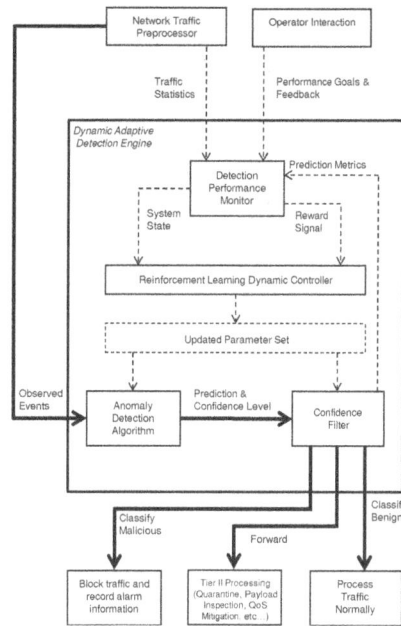

Figure 2: The System Architecture.

menting base detection algorithms with additional components. While we do not require the operator to have any knowledge or understanding of the underlying detection algorithm, we do suppose that performance feedback can be provided. In our work we expect that the operator has some mechanism for providing feedback, but we do not suppose a particular approach. For specific methods of providing feedback see [14, 16]. The detection engine uses this feedback to determine the need for tuning.

Figure 2 illustrates the system architecture. Incoming traffic is passed through a network traffic preprocessor. The preprocessor is to generate traffic statistics used to calculate the network state and to generate the description vectors that are passed to the underlying detection algorithm. The detection algorithm analyzes the input vector according to its design methodology and passes a prediction and confidence level for that prediction to the confidence filter. The confidence filter uses this information to decide whether to process the traffic normally, to forward for secondary processing, or to block the traffic and log an alert. The confidence filter works by comparing the input to two dynamically tuned thresholds, one for alert, one for the absence of alert. If the thresholds are met, the traffic is processed according to the detection algorithms prediction. If thresholds are not met, traffic is flagged for forwarding.

The performance of the detection algorithm and the thresholds of the confidence filter are automatically tuned on line by a reinforcement learning controller. The controller adjusts an augmented parameter set consisting of tunable parameters of the underlying detection algorithm and threshold values of the confidence filter.

As traffic is processed, a performance monitor accepts as input traffic statistics from the network preprocessor, prediction counts from the confidence filter, and performance feedback. It combines the information to generate the system state and reward signal used by the reinforcement learning controller. When the detection engine is operating outside of operator established performance criteria, the controller is used to make adjustments. Based on the system state, the controller generates an updated parameter set. The controller uses the reward signal to learn about the effectiveness of its previous updates and to improve future updates. The detection algorithm and confidence filter then make future predictions based on the updated parameter set. The design and technical details of the reinforcement learning controller are omitted due to space limit.

5. RESULTS AND ASSESSMENT

5.1 Test Dataset and Experiment Setting

We evaluate the proposed and developed self-tuning self-optimizing approach using a mixture of live traces and simulated network traffic. We have built a testing dataset, which consists of a mixture of live trace data and simulated network traffic. It was constructed in three steps. We started with a publicly available trace dataset from the Lawrence Berkeley National Laboratory (LBNL) [18] and performed preprocessing to correct header/payload discrepancies created during packet anonymization. We then processed the dataset through a commercial intrusion detection system Snort to categorize attack vs. normal traffic. Finally, we inserted simulated traffic to ensure adequate coverage of a variety of network attacks.

We use the A-GHSOM intrusion detection system [9] as the testbed to evaluate our developed self-tuning and self-optimizing controller. A-GHSOM is an adaptive growing hierarchical self-organizing map based approach to network anomaly detection. The approach uses dynamic input normalization, threshold based adaptation, and confidence filtering and forwarding. While A-GHSOM has been shown to be effective at intrusion detection, its implementation requires the tuning of several system parameters. We configure the developed controller to self-tune 7 parameters in total, i.e., five A-GHSOM parameters and two confidence filter parameters: one for malicious predictions, and one for benign predictions. We do not directly use the default A-GHSOM confidence threshold. Rather, when the AGHSOM detection engine makes a prediction, it passes a score to the confidence filter. The confidence filter compares the prediction and its confidence score to its relevant threshold and makes a forwarding decision.

5.2 Effect of Operator Priorities

We first evaluate the trained controller's ability to self-tune parameters according to operator priorities without confidence forwarding or performance constraints. We compare self-tuned performance to manually tuned performance. The operator defined performance goals for precision and recall are fixed at 95%. Table 1 gives performance details when the operator defined priorities are adjusted to favor one metric over another, or to favor them equally according to A-GHSOM setting [9]. For the self-tuned parameters, the controller is prioritized to favor the specified metric and tuning decisions were made during runtime.

Metric	Manually Tuned	Prioritize Recall	Prioritize Precision	Prioritize Equally
RECALL	90.61%	92.11%	85.97%	87.15%
PRECISION	70.93%	68.79%	89.23%	86.70%

Table 1: System Performance.

The A-GHSOM detection system is content oblivious. We observe that without confidence forwarding, the performance goals 95% precision and 95% recall are not achievable with tuning alone. However, the controller is able to make tuning decisions capable of increasing performance in the desired metric and is able to equalize performance when both metrics are prioritized equally. For the system to achieve desired performance on all traffic, a portion of the traffic must be selected for additional processing.

5.3 Constrained Self-Optimization

Next, we apply confidence forwarding to achieve the desired performance goals, and examine the impact of self-tuning on constrained self-optimization. We augment the base parameter set with malicious and benign confidence thresholds to focus on the overhead of additional processing of a subset of the testing data. We compare system performance between manual tuning and full self-tuning. In the manually tuned trials, the detection parameters are statically tuned manually and only the confidence thresholds are adjusted by the controller. We evaluate the controller's self-optimizing capability by only adjusting confidence thresholds.

5.3.1 Optimizing Precision Tradeoff

We examine the controller's capability to self-optimize precision as the tradeoff metric. Figure 3 shows performance when recall and forwarding are constrained. Forwarding is constrained to 15% and the recall constraint is adjusted from 90% to 99%. We observe that when the optimization is attempted with manual tuning, the system is not able to achieve constraints. Recall is limited to 94.6% and 19% of evaluated traffic is forwarded. Without the benefit of full self-tuning, the system is unable to successfully shift emphasis from recall to precision and precision, the metric that should absorb the burden of the tradeoff, is uncontrolled. Forwarding is the only recourse to achieve the requested recall goal. With forwarding also constrained, the system does not meet constraints.

However, when full self-tuning is applied, the controller is able to successfully prioritize performance metrics and reduce precision to come much closer to achieving operator objectives. Maximum recall is 97.6% and maximum forwarding is 16.4% only slightly off from requested goals. As precision is reduced, the system becomes less confident in its malicious predictions and attempts to forward them. With forwarding constrained by operator request, both confidence thresholds are reduced over time. This causes many benign predictions with low confidence not to be forwarded. When these predictions are incorrect, recall is reduced. While the fully tuned system is able to perform much closer to the objectives, more forwarding is required to achieve recall performance.

5.3.2 Optimizing Recall Tradeoff

We examine the controller's capability to self-optimize recall as the tradeoff metric. Figure 4 shows results when constraints are precision and forwarding. Forwarding is constrained to 15% and the precision constraint is adjusted from 90% to 99%. When optimization is attempted both with and with out self-tuning, the system is able to approximately meet constraints while at the same time maintaining recall rates above 90%. There is only slight improvement in forward performance by tuning all parameters. In this scenario, the controller constantly attempts to maintain precision and forwarding constraints while making tuning decisions that pass all tradeoff onto recall. We observe that the controller is able to do this very effectively by adapting the benign confidence threshold. In both configurations, the controller significantly reduces the benign confidence threshold therefore ensuring that all benign predictions will be processed and not forwarded. When benign predictions are incorrect, it does not significantly affect the ability to meet constraints. By applying full tuning, we observe tighter overall control and both precision and recall constraints are achieved.

6. CONCLUSIONS

We proposed a self-tuning self-optimizing approach for automated anomaly detection systems. Our model grants security operators the capability to automated performance control without

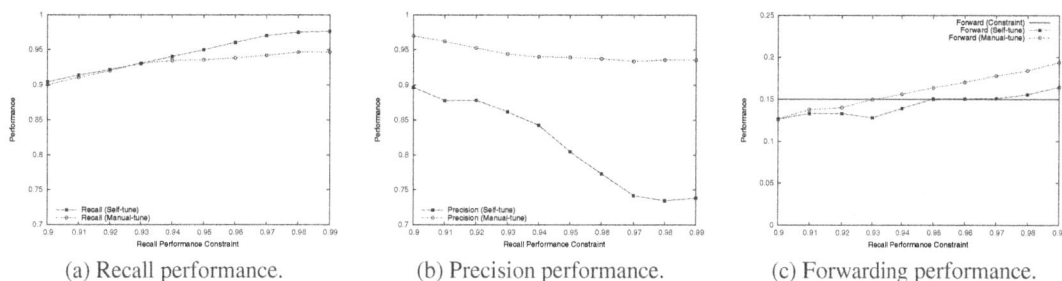

(a) Recall performance.   (b) Precision performance.   (c) Forwarding performance.

Figure 3: Self-optimizing *precision* when forwarding constraint is fixed and recall constraint is adjusted from 0.9 to 0.99.

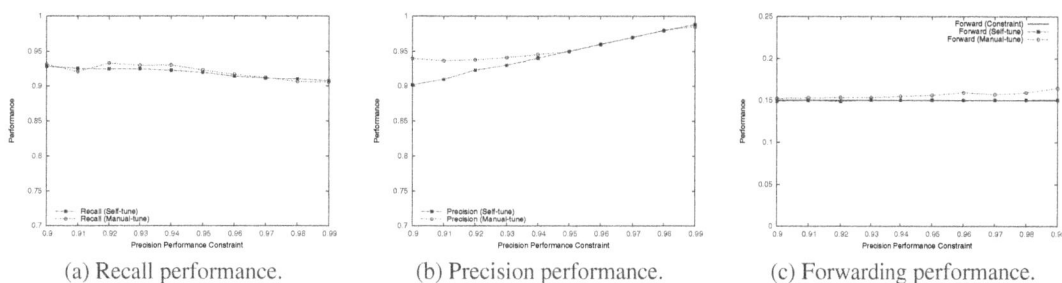

(a) Recall performance.   (b) Precision performance.   (c) Forwarding performance.

Figure 4: Self-optimizing *recall* when forwarding constraint is fixed and precision constraint is adjusted from 0.9 to 0.99.

the requirement of directly accessing the underlying detection algorithm. The reinforcement learning and neural networks based self-tuning self-optimizing controller automatically performs control actions intended to meet expectations according to defined priorities. The reinforcement learning controller is able to learn operating environments and their relationship to tuning parameters. It is then able to self-adapt to operator performance goals and priorities.

Experimental results demonstrate that when operator expectations are not achievable, the controller is able to respond to priority requests and self-tune parameters to place emphases on the desired priority metrics. Results also show that our proposed and developed approach is capable of self-tuning existing detection systems to respond to operator defined priorities for self-optimizing.

Our future study will use other major anomaly detection systems and datasets to evaluate the developed self-tuning and self-optimizing controller for automated anomaly detection.

Acknowledgement

This research was supported in part by NSF CAREER award CNS-0844983.

7. REFERENCES

[1] E. Anceaume, B. Sericola, R. Ludinard, and F. Tronel. Modeling and Evaluating Targeted Attacks in Large Scale Dynamic Systems. In *Proc. IEEE/IFIP Int'l Conference on Dependable Systems and Networks (DSN)*, 2011.

[2] S. Axelsson. The base-rate fallacy and its implications for the difficulty of intrusion detection. In *Proc. ACM Conference on computer and communications security (CCS)*, pages 1-7, 1999.

[3] D. Bolzoni, S. Etalle, and P. Hartel. Panacea: Automating Attack Classification for Anomaly-Based Network Intrusion Detection Systems. In *Proc. International Symposium on Recent Advances in Intrusion Detection (RAID)*, 2009

[4] A. Cardenas, J. Baras, K. Seamon. A framework for the evaluation of intrusion detection systems. In *Proc. IEEE Symposium on Security and Privacy*. 63–77, 2006

[5] R. Fontugne, K. Fekuda. A Hough-transform-based Anomaly Detector with an Adaptive Time Interval. In *Proc. ACM Symposium on Applied Computing (SAC)*, 2011.

[6] J. E. Gaffney, J. W. Ulvila. Evaluation of intrusion detectors: A decision theory approach. In *Proc. IEEE Symposium on Security and Privacy*, pages 50–61, 2001.

[7] G. Gu, P. Fogla, D. Dagon, W. Lee, B. Skoric. Measuring Intrusion detection capability: An information-theoretic approach. In *Proc. ACM Symposium on Information, Computer and Communications Security*, 2006.

[8] Y. Himura, K. Fukuda, K. Cho, H. Esaki An automatic and dynamic parameter tuning of a statistics-based anomaly detection algorithm. In *Proc. IEEE International Conference on Communications*, 2009.

[9] D. Ippoliti, X. Zhou. A-GHSOM: An Adaptive Growing Hierarchical Self Organizing Map for Network Anomaly Detection. In *Proc. IEEE International Conference on Computer Communications and Networks (ICCCN)*, 2010.

[10] K. S. Killourhy and R. A. Maxion. Comparing Anomaly-Detection Algorithms for Keystroke Dynamics. In *Proc. IEEE/IFIP Int'l Conference on Dependable Systems and Networks (DSN)*, 2009.

[11] W. Lee, S. J. Stolfo. A framework for constructing features and models for intrusion detection systems. *ACM Transactions on Information and System Security* (TISSEC), 3(4), 227-261, 2000.

[12] Y. Li, B. Fang, L. Guo and Y. Chen. Network anomaly detection based on TCM-KNN algorithm. In *Proc. of ACM Symposium on Information, Computer and Communications Security*, 2007.

[13] F. Massicotte and Y. Labiche An Analysis of Signature Overlaps in Intrusion Detection Systems. In *Proc. IEEE/IFIP Int'l Conference on Dependable Systems and Networks (DSN)*, 2011.

[14] M. Rehak, E. Staab, V. Fusenig, M. Pechoucek, M. Grill, J. Stiborek, K. Barto, T. Engel. Runtime Monitoring and Dynamic Reconfiguration for Intrusion Detection Systems. In *Proc. International Symposium on Recent Advances in Intrusion Detection (RAID)*, 2009.

[15] H. Ringberg, A. Soule, J. Rexford, C. Diot. Sensitivity of PCA for traffic anomaly detection. In *Proc. ACM SIGMETRICS*, 2007.

[16] Z. Yu, J. Tsai, T. Weigert. An adaptive automatically tuning intrusion detection system. In *ACM Transactions on Autonomous and Adaptive Systems*, 3(3), 2008.

[17] Z. Zhang, H. Shen. M-AID: An adaptive middleware built upon anomaly detectors for intrusion detection and rational response. *ACM Transactions Autonomous and Adaptive Systems*, 4(4), 2009.

[18] *LBNL/ICSI Enterprise Tracing Project*. http://www.icir.org/enterprise-tracing/

Event Correlation for Operations Management of Large Scale IT Systems

Chetan Gupta
HP Labs, CA
chetan.gupta@hp.com

ABSTRACT

Today, many large scale systems IT systems are managed by "Networked Operations Centers"(NOCs). These NOCs are manned by support staff, known as operators. Data in the form of events from various sub-systems in the larger system is sent to the central event console so that the NOC operators can work on problems in the infrastructure before they have a significant impact on the availability and performance of business applications. The challenge for these NOC operators is that of managing the large number of incoming events. In this work, we address the problem of scale by proposing a data-mining technique for automatic event correlation for large scale operations management systems.

Categories and Subject Descriptors

H.4 [**Information Systems Applications**]: Miscellaneous

Keywords

Event Correlation, Event Mining

1. INTRODUCTION

IT Operations Management (IT-OM) is a complicated and labor intensive process. The IT infrastructure of a medium size enterprise may have hundreds of networked systems, running thousands of heterogeneous software components and applications, which together provide the business services required to support the enterprise. Each individual hardware, middleware, and software component reports exceptional conditions as they are detected. These conditions are reported as human readable events. Typically, these events are then streamed to a Network Operations Center (NOC), where operators process these events with the aim of keeping the enterprise systems running smoothly. The large number of events can easily overwhelm the NOC operators and the processing of these IT-OM events is mostly manual and expensive. The challenge then is to create intelligent tools that will automate parts of this process, and

thus bring down the operations management costs and ensure better management of IT resources.

One way to achieve automation is through "event correlation". With event correlation we can replace a set of events with a single "meta correlated event". For instance say we discover that every time *Event A* occurs it is accompanied by *Event B* and *Event C*. This discovery allows us to automatically execute a rule encoding the above. Then, an occurrence of {*Event A, Event B, Event C*} can be replaced by an occurrence of some group label. This would reduce the volume of events that the operator has to process in real time and also provide insight to the operator. Today, current commercial IT-OM systems do use "event correlation" technology to filter and process incoming events and assist in the identification of relevant events. However, these systems require domain experts to recognize the correlations, express these correlation in terms of rules and then maintain the rule-set. This approach leads to significant costs for maintaining an up-to-date rule set and consequently results in little or poorly managed rules. There are topology based correlation services too, but in practice they often suffer from lack of updated topology information.

A solution to this challenge of manually constructing and maintaining correlations is to automate the process of "event correlation". In general, event correlation is a term that is widely used to describe a large set of techniques, such as filtering, suppression, etc. In this paper, we understand *event correlation* to be finding "significant co-occurrence" relationship between event types over the time. We achieve this through techniques from data mining, i.e., from historical data find correlations between events and use them to automatically construct rules to suppress current events.

To make our approach successful we had to address several challenges. The first problem we addressed is of *event typing*. The events that flow into the NOC are verbose and we need to cast them into an event type for ease of analysis. Once the events are types, we use frequent itemset mining [2], for the purpose of discovering correlations. Although, frequent itemset mining is a well understood KDD process, we needed to address the following specific problems that arise in our context (i) define and efficiently compute a construct that is equivalent to a market basket. In the operations management context we call these market baskets, *episodes* [9] (ii) mapping events to these episodes, such that some form of "correctness" is guaranteed (iii) once market baskets (episodes) have been defined, we use traditional frequent itemset mining techniques to find events that are associated together. Once the results of the frequent itemset mining are obtained, the two most important challenges to be overcome are (i) dealing with the large number of noise events that occur in the data and make the distribution of events skewed (ii)presenting a few correlations that can be easily and quickly verified by a domain expert.

The rest of the paper is as follows. We present the related work in Section 2, our approach in Section 3, the experimental results in Section 4, and conclusions in Section 5.

2. RELATED WORK

We need to pre-process data to obtain event types. Some event standard formats have been proposed [1], [11], but they seem to have not become popular across industry. In this paper, we propose a simple and easy to implement event typing approach. Correlation in general is a well studied problem (Refer to [8]), and is studied in time series literature as computing autocorrelation or cross-correlation functions [12]. There has been work in the data mining community on correlation analysis [5] over event data. The applications include predicting certain types of events such as, intrusion detection [6], failures [13], etc. From the perspective of taxonomy for failure prediction [13], our solution belongs to the class of "rule based fault localization techniques to help discover rules in a dynamic systems".

In the data mining community, the problem closest to ours is (sometimes referred to as "episode detection") is the following [9], [7]: Given a set of ordered events, which set of events (ordered or unordered) occur frequently together within a time window. In other words as in our work, correlation is understood to be sets of events that occur together (From the perspective of [9], we are interested in "parallel episodes"). Another variation [3] is to find "correlation rules", where in given predefined sets of objects (could be events), the challenge is to find subsets that are correlated with each other. There has been work in extending these underlying ideas to problems such as motif mining [10] (which finds frequent patterns over time series), etc. In our solution, we extend the basic approach [9] by constructing methods that take into account the large number of noise streams, is able to present a very small number of correlations and adds approximation for efficiency.

RETE based solutions [4] and complex event processing based solutions [1] have been deployed in many systems. Rule based event correlation has been developed and used in industry over decades. Commercial competitive approaches come from HP, IBM, EMC and other such products. These approaches offer very good infrastructures to execute correlation rules. Some of these products have some basic rules that are provided out-of-the-box. However, to the best of our knowledge, most of these industrial products offer little help in discovering event relationships automatically.

3. CORRELATION ANALYSIS

Our solution requires an automated step for determining *event types*. Event types describe the kind of event, or in other words, it describes the event class. Once the events have been typed, the next step is to find correlations on these event types. In our work, we define a correlation over events to be: *Two events A, B are said to be correlated if they occur within a time $\pm T$ of each other*. It is important to note that we look at *sets* of events and not *sequences*.

---

[1]Common Event Expression, http://cee.mitre.org/

This is because in real life systems, events often arrive out of order and hence an analysis based on sequences can be misleading. Generating all such sets of events leads to a large number of sets. In the context of IT-OM, we need to prune this set, such that a "small" number of "strong" correlations are obtained. We begin describing our overall method by first describing event typing.

3.1 Event Typing

Event types are not available in a typical IT OM applications. An attribute for the event type exists in the common event format of many IT management applications, but it is usually not set. Therefore, we need to create surrogate for the missing event types. This is done by decomposing and comparing the event descriptions from historical event logs. In our solution we split the event description into tokens (words), discarding single character tokens. Then for any two event descriptions A, B, we check if at least a fraction k of the tokens at the same position for A, B are identical. If they are they are assigned the same event type, otherwise they are assigned different event types. The event description includes an attribute for the application type. This application attribute is used to narrow the range so that not all events in the history log need to be compared. With this method we achieve 99% coverage and the result is a surrogate event type - a plain integer number.

At the beginning of this step we have all the events from the log in terms of their description and some other details. After this step, we obtain a data set D, where each element is an event type and that event's time of occurrence. In the next step, we create "episodes" over this set D.

3.2 Episode Creation

As we mentioned before we use *frequent itemset mining* [2] to discover correlations. Traditional frequent itemset mining is performed over market basket data, where a market basket is defined as a set of items bought together. In the IT OM context we need an equivalent concept, but since the events are arriving continuously, this requires us to introduce a concept called an *episode* [9]. Before we explain the concept of an episode in detail, we would like to introduce some notation. We use e_A, e_B to denote a particular instance of event A and B respectively. To address a specific instance (say k^{th}) for reference, we might use $e_{A,k}$. The time of occurrence of e_A, e_B, is denoted by T_{e_A} and T_{e_B} respectively.

The intuition behind performing an frequent itemset analysis is that the events that are associated with each other, would occur "close" to each other in time. Then, the purpose of the episode creation step is to create sets such that all events that occur close to each other are in the same set. Such a set is called an *Episode*. For the sake of precision, we introduce some definitions:

DEFINITION 1. *Two events e_A, e_B are said to be adjacent to each other if $|T_{e_A} - T_{e_B}| \leq T_W$, where T_W is some user defined episode size.*

DEFINITION 2. *An episode, E_{e_A}, corresponding to the event e_A is a collection of all events that are adjacent to e_A.*

For discovering frequent itemsets, if we were to maintain precise episodes corresponding to occurrence of each event, it would lead to computing a large number of episodes with redundant information. To overcome this problem, we introduce an approximated method of episode creation:

1. Divide the overall time range into 2 series of windows:

$(0..2*T_W), [2*T_W..4*T_W), \ldots, [2k*T_W..2(k+1)*T_W)$

$(T..3*T_W), [3*T_W..5*T_W), \ldots, [(2k+1)*T_W..(2k+3)*T_W)$

. Each of these windows is considered an *Episode*.

2. Once this is done, every event is placed into a window in both series. For example if $T_W = 15$ and $T_{e_A} = 40$, then the two windows associated with this event are [30..60) and [15..45).

With this approach, all other events in the two windows into which an event e_A is placed are considered events to be adjacent to e_A. This windowing mechanism is obviously approximate, but it reduces the number of episodes. For example, if $T_w = 15$ *minutes*, the maximum number of episodes would be 96 in a day and in most practical cases, this number would be much smaller than the number of events received in a day. Although, the window mechanism is approximate, we can say something about its accuracy:

LEMMA 1. *1. Every event adjacent to an event e_A is in one of the two episodes corresponding to event e_A.*

2. Not every event in episodes corresponding to e_A is adjacent to e_A, but there is no event e_B in an episode of e_A, such that $|T_{e_A} - T_{e_B}| \geq 2 * T_W$.

3. The correct span of an episode corresponding to an event e_A is T_W, whereas the total span (both episodes combined) with our approach is $\frac{3}{2}T_W$.

The proofs of the above are straightforward, hence we skip them. For creating episodes, we could have used any other alternative scheme, wherein, we take window with some other span and shift that window by some margin. But, our scheme is optimal in the following sense:

LEMMA 2. *There is no other set of two series of windows, such that all the events adjacent to an events are in one of two episodes and the bounds on the window size are tighter than $|T_{e_A} - T_{e_B}| \leq 2 * T_W$.*

Now that we have defined episodes, we describe the process of finding correlations over these episodes.

3.3 Frequent Itemset Mining for Discovering Correlations

Our goal is to find correlations among events. These correlations are discovered in the form of frequent itemsets. The logic of this as explained before is simple, i.e., if we find that a particular set of events occurs together very frequently and is "strongly correlated", than we can replace that set of events with a meta-event, thus achieving *event reduction*. We use the *A-priori* algorithm [2], where the requirement in finding frequent itemsets is to specify a minimum threshold value S_{min} for *Support*. (Support for an itemset A is defined as the percentage of episodes, that contain a A, and is denoted as $|A|$). We specify $S_{min} = 2\%$. The reason for this is that for all IT-OM data sets that we tested, there is a large spike in the number of itemsets when we move from 2% support threshold to a 1% support threshold. We do not

Table 1: Distribution of event types in a selection of Operations Management Data. The data shows a substantial skew.

Support	< 10	10 − 100	100 − 750	> 1000
Number	938	198	57	6

go into the details of frequent itemset mining, since this is a well known approach [5].

As is typical with frequent itemset mining, the number of frequent itemsets obtained is large (typically in 1000s) and needs to be pruned so that they can be easily verified by domain experts. Furthermore, we want the pruned set to satisfy the following:

1. The events in any frequent itemsets should be "strongly" correlated.

2. The set of correlations (in terms of frequent itemsets) presented to the domain expert should be small, and each frequent itemset should be "independent" of every other frequent itemset. This is important so that a domain expert can quickly verify the correlations found. We have found that in an industrial setting, the ability of a domain expert to verify the associations is critical.

3. The verified correlations should be able to serve the primary purpose of this approach, i.e., to reduce the number of events. If possible they should help in root cause analysis.

In other words, we want a small set of strong, verifiable correlations, that would help us reduce the number of events. (Note that it is sufficient for us to discover the correlations as itemsets ($\{A, B\}$)rather than traditional rules ($A \to B$).)

3.4 Pruning

The mechanism we use for pruning is by controlling the *h-confidence* measure [14]. The *h-confidence* for an itemset $\{e_1, e_2, \ldots, e_n\}$ is defined as:

$$h\text{-}confidence(\{e_1, e_2, \ldots, e_n\}) = \frac{|e_1 \cap e_2 \cap \ldots \cap e_n|}{\max\{|e_1|, |e_2|, \ldots, |e_n|\}} \quad (1)$$

Where, $|e_1 \cap e_2 \cap \ldots \cap e_n|$, is the number of time the events $\{e_1, e_2, \ldots, e_n\}$ occur together in a dataset D, and $|e_i|$ is the number of times the event e_i occurs in D.

The h-confidence measure helps us identify *cross-support* patterns and also "strongly correlated" patterns. Cross support patterns are those patterns that are artifact of data skew. In Table 1, where we have tabulated the distribution of event types for OM data for a time slice of data. The table shows the support of various items obtained through frequent itemset mining, clearly showing a substantial skew in distribution (Most items (938) have support less than 10, but there are a few items (6) that have more than support greater than 1000). In such a scenario, if the support threshold s_{min} is set too high, it will eliminate patterns with low support, and if the support threshold is kept too low, many spurious patterns that relate a high-frequency patterns with low-frequency patterns are obtained. A threshold on h-confidence helps removes the cross support patterns since the denominator is a maximum of the supports of the individual events. If an event is a noise event and occurs

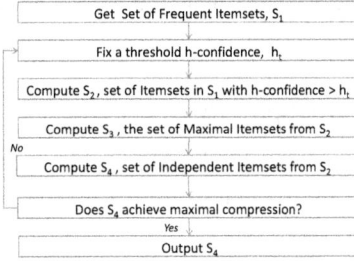

```
┌─────────────────────────────────────────────────┐
│        Get  Set of Frequent Itemsets, S₁         │
└─────────────────────────────────────────────────┘
                      ↓
┌─────────────────────────────────────────────────┐
│        Fix a threshold h-confidence, hₜ          │
└─────────────────────────────────────────────────┘
                      ↓
┌─────────────────────────────────────────────────┐
│  Compute S₂, set of Itemsets in S₁ with h-confidence > hₜ │
└─────────────────────────────────────────────────┘
                      ↓
┌─────────────────────────────────────────────────┐
│   Compute S₃, the set of Maximal Itemsets from S₂ │
└─────────────────────────────────────────────────┘
  No                  ↓
┌─────────────────────────────────────────────────┐
│   Compute S₄, set of Independent Itemsets from S₂ │
└─────────────────────────────────────────────────┘
                      ↓
┌─────────────────────────────────────────────────┐
│     Does S₄ achieve maximal compression?         │
└─────────────────────────────────────────────────┘
                Yes   ↓
┌─────────────────────────────────────────────────┐
│                 Output S₄                        │
└─────────────────────────────────────────────────┘
```

Figure 1: Figure depicting the overall process for obtaining the final rule set

very frequently, its support will be large and as a result the h-confidence will be small.

Another advantage of h-confidence is that it ensures that the events contained in the itemsets are strongly associated with each other. Suppose that h-confidence of an itemset i_1 is $p\%$, then if one of the items is present in an episode, then there is at least a $p\%$ chance the rest of the items in the itemset are also present in the episode. Such strongly associated patterns are called *hyperclique patterns*. In OM, where there are large number of very disparate event types, events that form a clique are *very* desirable from a perspective of human verifiability.

Now we discuss how to obtain a small set of useful itemsets with the help of h-confidence. Suppose we start with a set of frequent itemsets S_1 obtained as a result of frequent itemset mining: (i) Following this, we start with a small value for h-confidence h_1, and find all itemsets above this threshold to obtain $S_{2,h1}$. (ii) We then obtain *maximal itemsets* $S_{3,h1}$ from $S_{2,h1}$ (Maximal itemsets are those itemsets such that no proper subset of them is a frequent itemset). (iii) We then check to see if all our itemsets in $S_{3,h1}$ are *independent* (We will define this in the next paragraph) of each other. If not, we slowly raise the h-confidence till we obtain a set $S_{4,h1}$ such that all itemsets in it are independent. (iv) Then we compute the compression, say C_{h1} achieved by $S_{4,h1}$. Compression is defined as: $\sum_{i \in S} |N_i|(1 - \frac{1}{l_i})|i|$, where, i is some itemset in set S, N_i is the number of times it occurs and l_i is the length of i, or in other words, the number of events in the itemset. The term $\frac{l_i - 1}{l_i}$ is the ratio of space saved to the original space required when a set of events is replaced by a single event. (v) Once this is done we repeat with a new value for h-confidence h_2 by raising the threshold. Again we obtain itemsets $S_{2,h2}$, $S_{3,h2}$, and so on, and compute a compression obtained C_{h2}. In this way we explore the space of itemsets obtained by small increments in the h-confidence and choose the itemset that achieves maximal compression. The overall flow is shown in Figure 1.

We choose to represent frequent itemsets as maximal itemsets, since it reduces the number of itemsets as desired by us and maximal hence longer itemsets will offer us more compression. Domain experts also prefer itemsets containing a larger number of events. In their experience, if a subset of set of itemsets occurs along with its superset, than the superset has more semantic meaning. Independent itemsets make it easier for verification the semantics of an itemset. By independence we mean that every itemset forms a clique, or specifically: *A set of itemsets is independent if no two members, say i_1, i_2 share an event, or $i_1 \cap i_2 = \phi$*. If the

itemsets were not independent, all the links between different sets have to be manually verified. Such large number of linkages can quickly overwhelm a humans ability to for manual verification.

In Figure 2 we have plotted the compression as a function of h-confidence for several OM data sets. All of figures have an inverted parabola shape. The curve shows that if we make small increments in the value of threshold for h-confidence, we can hope to obtain at-least a local optimal value for compression. Note that, the curve is not always a smooth parabola, and there is a danger of being stuck in a local optima, if we stop when the compression value goes down after continuously going up. In other words we assume that we have reached the right hand side of the parabola. Hence, for an optimal solution we should make small increments in the threshold till we reach zero compression. This process can be expensive hence we do a simple (and non-optimal) search for the h-confidence value that gives us the highest compression). Once the value of compression starts to go down, we test two more increments of h-confidence. If for both the increments the compression goes down we stop, otherwise we continue increasing the value of h-confidence, till we have reached the right hand side of the parabola.

4. EXPERIMENTS

We tested our solution with customer event data from Customer X Managed Services platform (we can't disclose the customer due to confidentiality). This data represents events from multiple customers where Customer X Managed Service monitors the availability and performance of the IT infrastructure. Each customer of Customer X can have one or more management servers that send their data to customer X. The multiple customers of Customer X are geographically dispersed and the applications that are monitored are of various kinds. For episode creation we took the episode size to be 30 minutes. This was in consultation with domain experts who believe that two events that are typically correlated occur within half an hour of each other.

We took this actual propriety data over several months from Customer X and created various projections of it to arrive at the data sets. We present results on five such sets:(i)*Data Set 1*: A slice of eight month data. (ii)*Data Set 2*: Eight month data, but only for one management server. This provide a "long" history for a good subset of the managed environment. (iii) *Data Set 3*: Two month of data, for certain customer, for the whole managed environment. (iv) *Data Set 4*: One month of data, for the whole managed environment of one customer. This gives a comprehensive view of the data from all managed servers for a reasonable expanse of time.*Data Set 5*: Just one day of data of a completely different customer from the first data set. This means we have totally different kind of events.

For the experimental setup, as a first step we created episodes as discussed in the previous section. Once the episodes are created we divide the episodes into a test set and a training set. The test set contained 75% of randomly picked episodes and the training set contained the rest. Once the training set is obtained, we performed the set of steps discussed earlier and drawn in Figure 1 on the training set. Once the final results are obtained we checked for compression and ease of verifiability on the test set.

The first thing we verified for, is compression. For example,if the itemset found by our approach is $\{e_A, e_B\}$. We

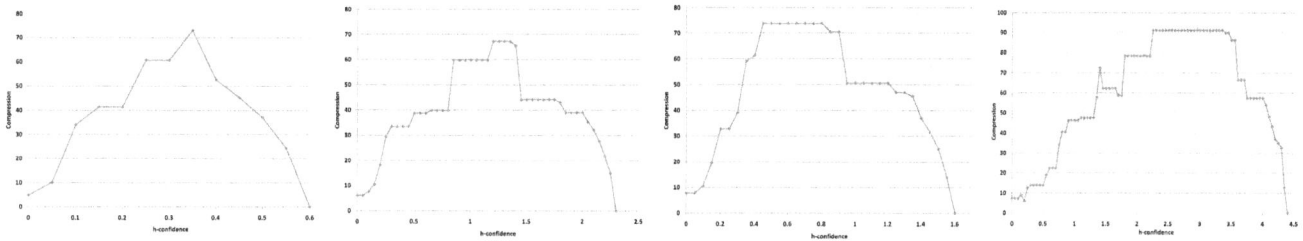

Figure 2: Compression achieved as a function of h-confidence

Data Set	Compression
1	12.4%
2	19.9%
3	11.2%
4	15.3%
5	7.5%

Table 2: Compression achieved for the five data sets

Data Set	Itemsets
1	15
2	16
3	15
4	17
5	4

Table 3: Number of itemsets obtained for the three data sets

Acknowledgments

We would like to acknowledge Stefan Bergstein, Abhay Mehta and Song Wang for very helpful discussions.

replace the occurrence of $\{e_A, e_B\}$ with some event e_* in all episodes. Hence the number of elements in the episode is reduced by 1 (more generally by $e_l - 1$, where e_l is the number of items in the itemset). Let $l_{old}(i_a)$ be the number of events in an episode i_a before replacement and $l_{new}(i_a)$ be the new length after replacement. Then the total compression achieved is $100 * \frac{\sum_{i \in S} l_{old}(i) - \sum_{i \in S} l_{new}(i)}{\sum_{i \in S} l_{old}(i)}$. We have tabulated the compression achieved for the three data sets in Table 2. It can be seen that we achieve reasonable compression ($> 10\%$ as per domain expertise) for four out of five data sets.

The second thing we verified for was the ability of the itemsets to be quickly verified by humans. In this regard, we checked for two things, the number of itemsets and whether the itemsets were independent or not. The independence is in-built into our design, hence is always achieved. In Table 3, we have tabulated the number of frequent itemsets obtained by our method for the five data sets. All the numbers are less than 25, which is desirable.

5. CONCLUSIONS AND FUTURE WORK

In this paper we have provided a solution to the problem of event correlation for IT Operations Management. A highlight of our approach is: *Our approach allows us to obtain such a curve, and hence we obtain the set of frequent itemsets, without manually setting a value for h-confidence.* Hence, we do not artificially set any thresholds except for a the minimum support threshold. The fact that there is no manual tuning for a threshold value frees the NOC operator, who typically does not understand data-mining, from trying to fiddle with the algorithm.

Increasingly, as we learn to manage large systems, we will need to develop technologies that can handle event data. Events are generally *typed*, which means that every event is assigned a type and we mine data over event types. The most basic form of mining is that of finding correlations. In future work, we aim to add forecasting to our framework.

6. REFERENCES

[1] J. Agrawal, Y. Diao, D. Gyllstrom, and N. Immerman. Efficient pattern matching over event streams. In *ACM SIGMOD*, pages 147–160, 2008.

[2] R. Agrawal, T. Imielinski, and A. Swami. Mining association rules between sets of items in large databases. In *ACM SIGMOD*, pages 207–216, 1993.

[3] S. Brin, R. Motwani, and C. Silverstein. Beyond market baskets: Generalizing association rules to correlations. In *ACM SIGMOD*, 1997.

[4] C. Forgy. A fast algorithm for the many pattern/many object pattern match problem. *Artificial Intelligences*, 19(1):17–37, 1982.

[5] J. Han, H. Cheng, and D. X. andů Xifeng Yan. Frequent pattern mining: Current status and future directions. *Data Mining and Knowledge Discovery*, 15:55–86, 2007.

[6] K. Julisch and M. Dacier. Mining intrusion detection alarms for actionable knowledge. In *Proc. of the eighth ACM SIGKDD*, pages 366–375, 2002.

[7] M. Klemettinen, H. Mannila, and H. Toivonen. Rule discovery in telecommunication alarmdata. *J. Netw. Syst. Manage.*, 7(4):395–423, 1999.

[8] H. O. Lancaster. *The Chi-squared Distribution.* John Wiley & Sons, New York, 1969.

[9] H. Mannila, H. Toivonen, and A. Verkamo. Discovery of frequent episodes in event sequences. *Data Mining and Knowledge Discovery*, 1:259–289, 1997.

[10] P. Patel, E. Keogh, J. Lin, and S. Lonardi. Mining motifs in massive time series databases. In *IEEE ICDM*, 2003.

[11] C.-S. Perng, D. Thoenen, G. Grabarnik, S. Ma, and J. Hellerstein. Data-driven validation, completion and construction of event relationship networks. In *In Proceedings of KDD*, 2003.

[12] R. H. Shumway and D. Stoffer. *Series Analysis and Its Applications.* Springer, New York, 2nd edition, 2006.

[13] M. Steinder and A. S. Sethi. A survey of fault localization techniques in computer networks. *Sci. Comput. Program.*, 53(2):165–194, 2004.

[14] H. Xiong, P.-N. Tan, and V. Kumar. Mining strong affinity association patterns in data sets with skewed support distribution. In *IEEE ICDM 2003*, pages 387–394, Nov. 2003.

PowerTracer: Tracing Requests in Multi-tier Services to Diagnose Energy Inefficiency

Gang Lu, Jianfeng Zhan
State Key Lab. of Computer Sys. and Arch.
Institute of Computing Tech.
Chinese Academy of Sciences
{lugang,jfzhan}@ncic.ac.cn

Lin Yuan
Institute of Computing Tech.
Chinese Academy of Sciences
{yuanlin}@ncic.ac.cn

Haining Wang
The College of William and Mary
Williamsburg, VA 23187, USA
hnw@cs.wm.edu

Chuliang Weng
Advanced System Lab
Shanghai Jiao Tong University, Shanghai, China
weng-cl@cs.sjtu.edu.cn

ABSTRACT

As energy has become one of the key operating costs in running a data center and power waste commonly exists, it is essential to reduce energy inefficiency inside data centers. In this paper, we develop an innovative framework called *PowerTracer*, for diagnosing energy-inefficiency. Inside the framework, we first present a resource tracing method based on request tracing in multi-tier services of black boxes. Then, we propose a generalized methodology of applying a request tracing approach for energy-inefficiency diagnosis in multi-tier service systems. With insights into service performance and resource consumption of individual requests, we develop a bottleneck diagnosis tool that pinpoints the root causes of energy inefficiency. We implement the prototype and conduct experiments to validate its effectiveness.

Categories and Subject Descriptors

C.4 [**Performance of Systems**]: Power cost; D.2.5 [**Software Engineering**]: Testing and Debugging

Keywords

Multi-tier web server, request tracing, diagnosing energy inefficiency, saving power

1. INTRODUCTION

To date energy cost has been a major part of the total cost of ownership (TCO) of a data center. With the continuing decrease of hardware prices, the portion of energy cost will grow even larger in the near future. Thus, energy efficiency has become a top priority for data center administrators. However, energy inefficiency—a running state in which a computing system consumes power in a sub-optimal manner—is not uncommon in data centers. There are various causes of energy inefficiency, ranging from inappropri-

ate architectures to system misconfigurations. The focus of this work is on the development of innovative techniques to diagnose energy inefficiency mainly caused by inappropriate power management strategies and system misconfigurations.

In this paper, we propose a generalized framework of applying a request tracing approach for energy inefficiency diagnosis. Our request tracing approach traces user requests or jobs of interest traversing across services or job execution frameworks to diagnose energy inefficiency in multi-tier service platforms. Through kernel instrumentation, our request tracing tool accurately profiles the major activities of requests, in terms of *major causal path patterns* (in short, patterns) that represent *repeatedly executed* causal paths and account for significant fractions out of all requests. Then, our tool can measure the server-side latency, and even the service time of each tier in different patterns. Meanwhile, the request tracing tool with the capability of tracing requests' resource consumption can collect resource consumption information of individual requests and then analyze resource consumption features in various forms, such as features in each tier and features of each pattern. Thus, we can understand the role of each tier in serving different requests and figure out the causes of energy inefficiency with the help of power metering.

We design and implement a working prototype of the proposed framework, called *PowerTracer*. To trace the behaviors of request services, we use PreciseTracer [13], a precise request tracing mechanism, and further enhance it with the capability of collecting and analyzing resource consumption. We name the enhanced tool as ResourceTracer[1]. We conduct extensive experiments on a three-tier platform to validate the effectiveness of PowerTracer. For diagnosing energy inefficiency, we use several case studies to demonstrate the efficacy of PowerTracer, including state-of-the-art DVFS control policy—SimpleDVS [7], state-of-the-practice DVFS control policy—OnDemand [9], and the DVFS control policy that leverages the *average* service time of each tier without major causal path patterns. Resource tracing is also used to reveal the characteristics of resource consumption in multi-tier services. Our experimental results show

---

[1]The source code can be downloaded from http://prof.ict.ac.cn/DCBenchmarks.

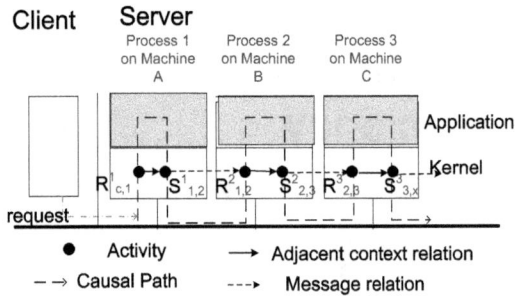

Figure 1: Activities with causal relations in the kernel [13].

that PowerTrace is able to locate the root causes of energy inefficiency.

The remindar of the paper is structured as follows. Section 2 describes the system architecture of PowerTracer and its basic working mechanisms. Section 3 summarizes the implementation of the major componets in PowerTracer. Section 4 presents the experimental results. Finally, Section 5 draws a conclusion.

2. SYSTEM DESIGN

In this section, we first brief the online request tracing approach in multi-tier services and then detail the way of applying it in PowerTracer. We assume that the target service applications run in a multi-tier architecture, and services are replicated or distributed on a cluster of servers [12].

2.1 Online Request Tracing

As shown in Fig. 1, a request triggers a series of *interaction activities* in the OS kernel or shared libraries, e.g. sending or receiving messages. Those activities happen under specific contexts (processes or kernel threads) of different components. We record an activity of sending a message as $S_{i,j}^i$, which indicates a process i sends a message to a process j. We record an activity of receiving a message as $R_{i,j}^j$, which indicates a process j receives a message from a process i. Activity types of interest include: *BEGIN, END, SEND*, and *RECEIVE*. The SEND and RECEIVE activities are those of sending and receiving messages. A BEGIN activity marks the start of servicing a new request, while an END activity marks the end of servicing a request.

When an individual request is serviced, a series of activities that have causal or happened-before relationship constitute a causal path. For each individual request, there exists a causal path. For a request, the server-side latency can be defined as the time difference between the timestamp of the BEGIN activity and that of the END activity in its corresponding causal path. The service time of each tier can be defined as the accumulated processing time between SEND activities and RECEIVE activities. For each tier, its role in serving a request can be measured in terms of service time percentage, which is the ratio of service time of the tier to the server-side latency.

After correlating those activity logs into causal paths, we classify the causal paths into different *patterns*. A pattern is a theme of recurring causal request paths with common characteristics. For a certain multi-tier service, causal path patterns are supposed to remain relatively stable. The patterns of past request paths can be used to predict the portions and characteristics of upcoming request path patterns. Usually, the method of classifying causal paths into pat-

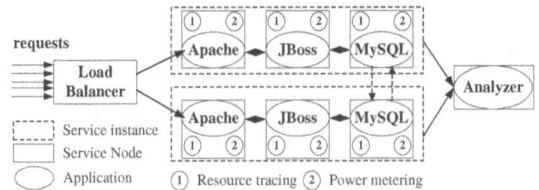

Figure 2: The architecture of PowerTracer.

terns is agile; and we can conduct the classification based on path shapes, server-side latencies, and resource consumptions. PowerTracer provides two different ways of classifying causal paths into different patterns. One uses a k-means clustering method [6] to classify causal paths based on the size of the first message sent by a client. Note that the size of the first packet, which includes different URL segments for different requests, has a linear relationship with the length of request URLs, and the length of the URL likely reflects the depth of the service and the complexity of the work to be performed. The other employs a multi-dimension k-means clustering algorithm. The distance metric is a function of the string-edit-distance of two paths, which denotes the difference of graphs of two causal paths, and the resource consumption deltas of two paths, which include deltas of the CPU jiffies, memory page faults, disk R/W sizes, and net I/O sizes. We observe that the first method behaves more deterministic and faster, strongly implying that URL length is positively correlated with the service depth and the complexity of services. For the latter, it is hard to decide the optimizing parameters and usually the number of patterns is much bigger than the former. Therefore, we use the first method to classify paths into causal patterns in our evaluation.

For each pattern, we compute the average server-side latency and the average service time of each tier. In addition, by counting the number of BEGIN activities, which mark the beginning of serving new requests, we can derive the current load level of the services. We use a four-tuple <pattern ID, the average server-side latency of pattern ID, the average service time per tier, the current load> to represent the online performance data of a pattern in a multi-tier service.

2.2 Diagnosing Energy Inefficiency

PowerTracer consists of three modules: ResourceTracer, power metering, and Analyzer, as shown in Fig. 2. The general method of diagnosing energy-inefficiency is to trace request and monitor performance. The power metering module, which is responsible for collecting power consumption of each node, is simple and straightforward. We use a latest commercial power analyzer to measure the power consumption. The detailed descriptions of ResourceTracer and Analyzer are given as follows.

2.2.1 ResourceTracer

Most existing request tracing approaches can only figure out latencies of requests. Some tools, such as Magpie [4] developed by Microsoft Research, can profile request resource consumption in multi-tier service systems. Unfortunately, these tools work in white boxes, that is to say, source code of target systems is needed for instrumentation. As an online request tracing tool for multi-tier services of black boxes, PreciseTracer only measures latencies.

To profile request resource consumption of each request, we develop a new tool *ResourceTracer* by extending Precise-Tracer. What makes ResourceTracer different from Precise-Tracer is that it records resource consumption information besides latencies, such as CPU time, memory page faults, disk R/Ws, and net I/Os. These microcosmic statistics help to capture the features of resource consumption behaviors of each request. Moreover, ResourceTracer also monitors resource utilization of individual physical nodes, providing a macro-scope in the status of the servers.

2.2.2 Analyzer

The Analyzer module analyzes request casual paths generated by resource tracing. The core component is *Classifier*, which is responsible for classifying a large variety of causal paths into different patterns, and extracting online performance data and resource consumption for main patterns according to their fractions.

The stage of classifying causal paths addresses the following two problems: first, it is difficult to leverage each individual causal path from massive request traces as guidelines for diagnosing energy inefficiency or DVFS modulation; second, causal paths are different and the overall statistics of performance information (e.g., the average server-side latency used in [7]) of all paths hide the diversity of patterns. Analyzer characterizes online performance data of different patterns at different tiers, and provides insights into subtle influences induced by different system configurations or power management strategies, disclosing the sources of energy inefficiency.

3. SYSTEM IMPLEMENTATION

Through online request tracing, ResourceTracer records all service logs and periodically reports the resource status. Based on the resource logs, Analyzer can unveil the top N patterns, which is responsible for diagnosing energy inefficiency.

ResourceTracer instruments the OS kernel activities using SystemTap [1] and utilizes the same correlation algorithm as PreciseTracer. It records resource consumption information, such as CPU time, memory page faults, disk R/Ws, and net I/Os. These resource profiling jobs are fulfilled through SystemTap probes, like ioblock, netdev, and vm.pagefault probes. The probes are instrumented into kernel events we concern. ResourceTracer profiles resource consumption of certain processes or threads, ignoring the information that is unrelated to serving requests. Note that resource tracing for individual requests must satisfy the assumption that a single execution entity (a process or a kernel thread) of each component can only serve one request in a certain period. For serving each individual request, the execution entities of the components cooperate through sending or receiving messages via a reliable communication protocol, like TCP. The overhead of request tracing has been proved to be minor in both throughput and average response time in [11]. In addition, ResourceTracer also monitors resource utilizations of each physical node by a coarse-grain resource accounting, like */proc* in Linux systems.

4. EVALUATION

We use three different kinds of three-tier web applications RUBiS, RUBBoS, and TPC-W to evaluate the efficacy of our approach for diagnosing energy inefficiency. RUBiS is

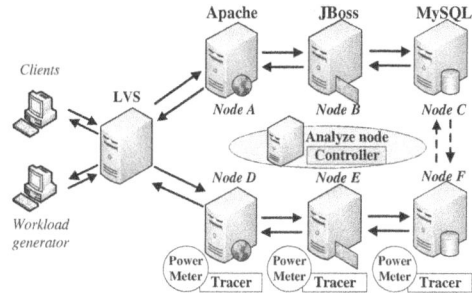

Figure 3: The deployment diagram of three-tier platform.

Table 1: Experiment deployment.

Nodes	Total cores	Available frequencies(GHz)
A & B	2	1.0, 1.8, 2.0, 2.2
C & D	8	0.8, 1.1, 1.6, 2.3
E & F	16	1.6, 1.7, 1.8, 2.0, 2.1, 2.2, 2.4

a three-tier auction site prototype modeled after eBay.com and developed by Rice University. RUBBoS is a bulletin board benchmark modeled after an online news forum like Slashdot, also developed by Rice University. TPC-W is a transactional web e-commerce benchmark that simulates the activities of a business oriented transactional web server.

4.1 Experimental Setup

Our testbed is a heterogeneous ten-node platform composed of Linux-OS blade servers. In the following experiments, we deploy one or two service instances, each of which includes an Apache server, a JBOSS Server, and a MySQL database server on the testbed as shown in Fig. 3. Table 1 lists the available cores and frequencies.

4.2 Case Studies of Diagnosing Energy Inefficiency

We conduct three case studies of diagnosing energy inefficiency with PowerTracer. The experiments are run on the mixed workload of RUBiS with 500 clients. The three-tier services are deployed on Nodes A, B, and C in Fig. 3. Each workload includes three stages, of which the up ramp time, runtime session, and down ramp time are set to 5, 300, and 5 seconds, respectively. For control systems, the control period is set to 6 seconds. For PowerTracer, the sampling period is 6 seconds. During each sampling period, Power-Tracer collects the performance data only for one second.

4.2.1 SimpleDVS

The SimpleDVS DVFS control algorithm presented by Horvath *et al.* [7] takes CPU utilization as the indicator in determining which server's clock frequency should be scaled, and implements a feedback controller based on the DVS mechanism. The scaling policy of SimpleDVS is that stepping down the clock frequency of the server with the maximum CPU utilization if the latency is below a lower threshold and stepping up the clock frequency of the server with the minimum CPU utilization if the latency is above an upper threshold. For SimpleDVS, we set the latency threshold, UP (the upper latency threshold coefficient), and LP (the lower latency threshold coefficient) to 16.35 milliseconds, 1.2, and 0.8, respectively. The parameters are configured based on our experiences presented in [2].

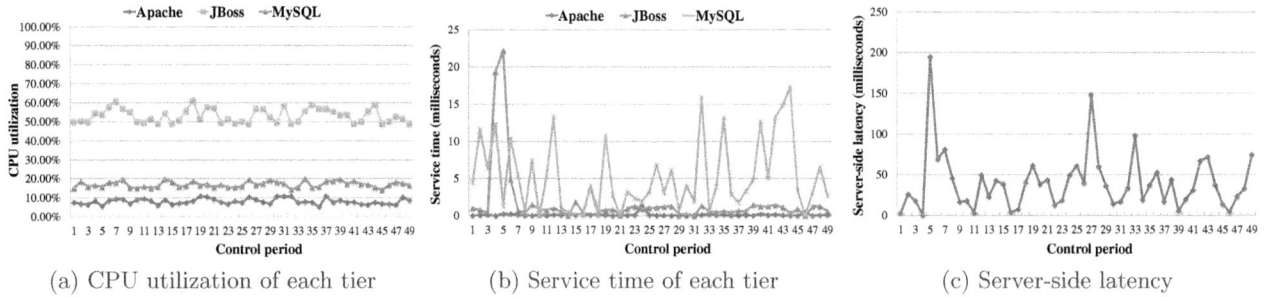

(a) CPU utilization of each tier   (b) Service time of each tier   (c) Server-side latency

Figure 4: Experiment results of the target system equipped with simpleDVS.

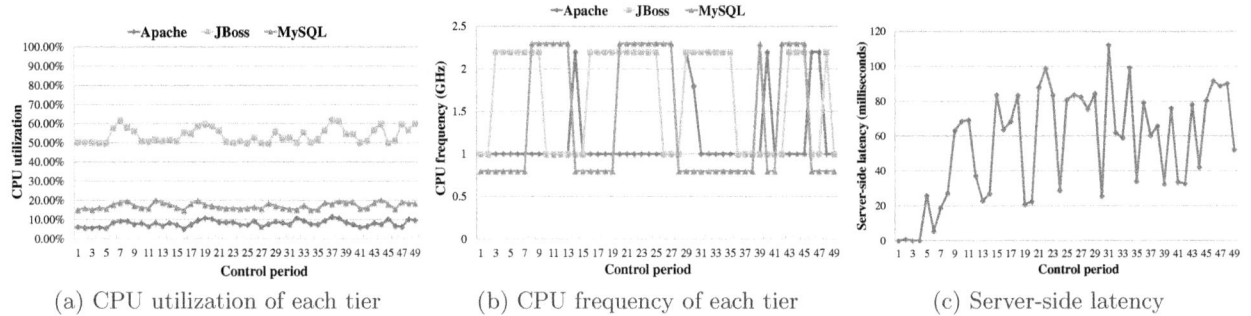

(a) CPU utilization of each tier   (b) CPU frequency of each tier   (c) Server-side latency

Figure 5: Experiment results of the target system equipped with Ondemand.

Through online resource tracing, we obtain performance results, which are shown in Fig. 4. We can see that at most of the time the CPU utilization of each tier has an approximate relationship of *JBoss > MySQL > Apache* and the service time of each tier has the relationship of *MySQL > JBoss > Apache*, indicating that the service time of each tier is not consistent with its CPU utilization. Thus, it is not optimal to use SimpleDVS by scaling clock frequency of the server, which has the maximum or minimum CPU utilization to affect the server-side latency.

4.2.2 Ondemand governor

The Ondemand governor, the most effective power management policy offered by Linux kernel, can vary CPU frequency based on CPU utilization. Fig. 5 shows that the CPU utilization of each tier, the CPU frequency of each node, and the server-side latency are dynamically changed in different control periods, respectively, due to the use of Ondemand governor.

Fig. 5(c) shows that the server-side latency of the service equipped with Ondemand is higher than that of SimpleDVS. At most of the time, the server-side latency of the service equipped Ondemand is higher than 50 milliseconds, while the server-side latency of the service equipped with SimpleDVS is lower than 50 milliseconds. Meanwhile, at most of the time, the CPU utilization of each tier with Ondemand is higher than that of SimpleDVS. Our additional experiment results in [2] also show that the service with Ondemand consumes more power than that of SimpleDVS. These observations demonstrate that the lack of the coordination of DVFS control actions on each node is the root cause of energy inefficiency of Ondemand.

4.2.3 AverageDVS

We implement a DVFS control policy that leverages the *average* service time of each tier without major causal path patterns, called *AverageDVS*. It uses the average server-side latency as the direct indication of scaling servers' CPU frequencies.

Fig. 6 shows the server-side latencies of the top two patterns, pattern 1 and pattern 2, and the average server-side latency of all paths, respectively. The causal paths of pattern 1 and pattern 2 take up 40.19% and 13.88% of all causal paths, respectively. Even under the control of AverageDVS, the two patterns perform very differently, and hence we cannot choose an accurate DVFS control policy without classifying main causal path patterns. Moreover, in Fig. 6(b), the server-side latency of AverageDVS is on average bigger than that of SimpleDVS shown in Fig. 4(c). We can infer that using the average server-side latency as the scaling condition is the root cause of energy inefficiency of AverageDVS.

4.3 Resource tracing

The workloads of this set of experiments are generated by RUBiS. The up ramp time, run session, and down ramp time are set to 5 seconds, 300 seconds, and 5 seconds, respectively. We deploy a service instance on a three-node platform composed of Nodes A, B and C, as shown in Fig. 3.

Energy inefficiency can also be caused by system misconfiguration or inappropriate deployment. To pinpoint system misconfigurations, we need to analyze resource information obtained through resource tracing in multi-tier services. Fig. 7(a) shows that the CPU utilization in the MySQL tier is the highest and that of the JBoss tier ranks second. Thus, we should pay more attention on database deployment and configuration. Fig. 7(b) shows that the disk read/write time of the JBoss and MySQL tiers are two or three times as that of the Apache tier. This is because the Java virtual machine and plugins in JBoss increase the disk R/Ws, and MySQL handles a large number of transactions that frequently access the database files. Since the disk R/Ws consume much more power, power-saving and high-performance disks are needed for the JBoss and MySQL tiers. Fig. 7(c) shows that as for networking performance, more attention should be paid for the Apache tier. In general, if services run in

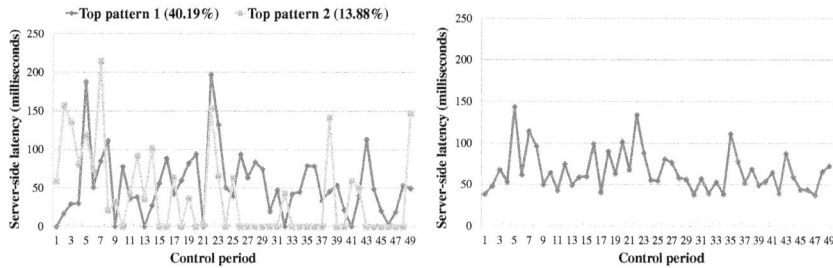

(a) Server-side latencies of the top two patterns

(b) Server-side latency

Figure 6: Experiment results of the target system equipped with AverageDVS.

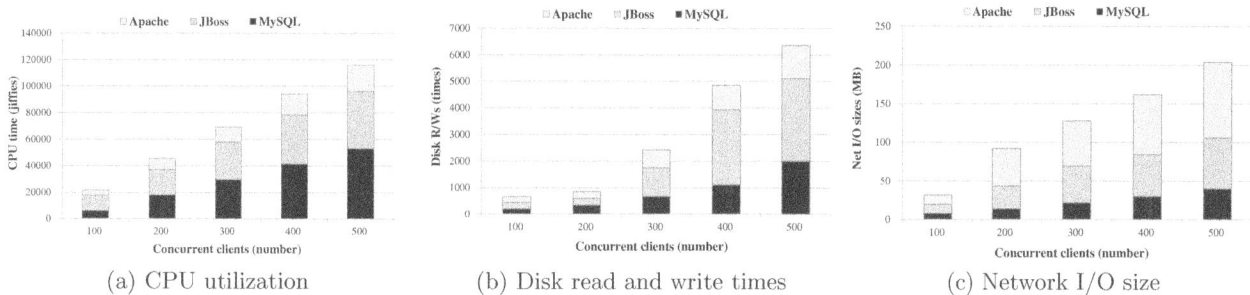

(a) CPU utilization

(b) Disk read and write times

(c) Network I/O size

Figure 7: The resource consumption of all requests for each tier.

abnormal states, we should use resource tracing methods to diagnose the cause of abnormalities.

5. CONCLUSIONS AND FUTURE WORK

In this paper, we have proposed a generalized framework of applying a request tracing approach for energy-inefficiency diagnosis in multi-tier service systems. Our request tracing tool can characterize major causal path patterns in serving different requests. It also records server-side latency, especially the service time of each tier in different patterns, and resource consumption information, providing guidelines for diagnosing energy inefficiency. We have developed a prototype and conducted extensive experiments on a threetier platform. The experimental results demonstrate that our framework can uncover the root causes of existing energy inefficiency, including wrong assumptions, lack of coordination, and adopting average policies.

The purpose of diagnosing energy inefficiency is to improve power savings. We are building an efficient power saving tool using individual server-side latencies of the top N patterns as the main metric to scale servers' clocks. We believe it will lead to much more power savings. Moreover, in most of commercial servers, CPU is the only energy proportional component, and our work is also confined by this limitation. Barroso et al. [5] showed that four components, including CPU, DRAM, disk, and network switches, are the main sources of power consumption in data centers. Existing accurate DVFS policies can play a more important role in power saving when they are extended to the other system components. In addition, we plan to apply the request tracing approach for dynamic cluster reconfiguration [7] [10], as it will also benefit from accurate performance monitoring.

6. ACKNOWLEDGEMENTS

We are very grateful to anonymous reviewers. This work is supported by the NSFC project (Grant No.60933003) and the Chinese 973 project (Grant No.2011CB302500).

7. REFERENCES

[1] Systemtap simplifies the gathering of information about the running linux system. http://sourceware.org/systemtap.

[2] Powertracer: Tracing requests in multi-tier services to diagnose energy inefficiency. *Technical Report*, 2011.

[3] M. K. Aguilera, J. C. Mogul, J. L. Wiener, P. Reynolds, and A. Muthitacharoen. Performance debugging for distributed systems of black boxes. *SIGOPS Oper. Syst. Rev.*, 37:74–89, Oct. 2003.

[4] P. Barham, A. Donnelly, R. Isaacs, and R. Mortier. Using magpie for request extraction and workload modelling. In *OSDI*, 2004.

[5] L. Barroso and U. Holzle. The case for energy-proportional computing. *Computer*, 40(12):33 –37, dec. 2007.

[6] J. A. Hartigan and M. A. Wong. Dynamic voltage scaling in multitier web servers with end-to-end delay control. *Applied Statistics*, 28(1):100 –108, 1979.

[7] T. Horvath, T. Abdelzaher, K. Skadron, and X. Liu. Dynamic voltage scaling in multitier web servers with end-to-end delay control. *Computers, IEEE Transactions on*, 56(4):444 –458, April 2007.

[8] J. Leverich and C. Kozyrakis. On the energy (in)efficiency of hadoop clusters. *SIGOPS Oper. Syst. Rev.*, 44:61–65, March 2010.

[9] V. Pallipadi and A. Starikovskiy. The ondemand governor: past, present and future. In *OLS*, 2006.

[10] K. Rajamani and C. Lefurgy. On evaluating request-distribution schemes for saving energy in server clusters. In *ISPASS*, 2003.

[11] B. Sang, J. Zhan, G. Lu, H. Wang, D. Xu, L. Wang, and Z. Zhang. Precise, scalable, and online request tracing for multi-tier services of black boxes. *Parallel and Distributed Systems, IEEE Transactions on*, PP(99):1, 2011.

[12] B. Urgaonkar, G. Pacifici, P. Shenoy, M. Spreitzer, and A. Tantawi. An analytical model for multi-tier internet services and its applications. *SIGMETRICS Perform. Eval. Rev.*, 33:291–302, June 2005.

[13] Z. Zhang, J. Zhan, Y. Li, L. Wang, D. Meng, and B. Sang. Precise request tracing and performance debugging for multi-tier services of black boxes. In *DSN*, 2009.

Automated Machine Learning for Autonomic Computing

Subutai Ahmad

Numenta

sahmad@numenta.com

ABSTRACT

We are witnessing an explosion in the amount of data generated. Every server, device, and system is able to generate a stream of information that is both valuable and ever changing. It is becoming insufficient to simply store the data for later analysis and modeling. Instead there is a growing need to stream data to adaptive models and take instant action. This type of online system imposes hard constraints that the field of machine learning has not addressed. The systems must be highly automated, automatically adapt to changing statistics, deal with temporal data, and work well across a wide range of inputs. In this talk I will go over these issues and how they impact adaptive systems. I will describe a new technology for streaming analytics and illustrate how this technology works in a practical product called Grok. Using Grok I will show how streaming analytics can be appropriate for applications such as predictive maintenance, server capacity planning and cluster health monitoring. As the number of data sources increases, adaptive streaming solutions will play an increasingly important role in the future of autonomic computing.

Categories and Subject Descriptors

C.0 [**Computer Systems Organization**]: General

Keywords

Machine Learning, Autonomic Computing, Streaming Analytics, Learning

BIO

Subutai Ahmad brings experience in real time systems, computer vision and machine learning. At Numenta Subutai oversees technology and product development. Prior to Numenta, Subutai served as VP Engineering at YesVideo, Inc. He helped grow YesVideo from a three-person start-up to a leader in automated digital media authoring. YesVideo's real time video analysis systems have been deployed internationally on a variety of platforms: large scale distributed clusters, retail minilabs, and set-top boxes. Subutai holds a Bachelor's degree in Computer Science from Cornell University, and a PhD in Computer Science from the University of Illinois at Urbana-Champaign.

Budget-Based Control for Interactive Services with Adaptive Execution

Yuxiong He[1]   Zihao Ye[2]   Qiang Fu[2]   Sameh Elnikety[1]

[1]Microsoft Research Redmond
Redmond, WA, USA

[2]Microsoft Research Asia
Peking, China

ABSTRACT

We study the problem of managing a class of interactive services to meet a response time target while achieving high service quality. We focus here on interactive services that support adaptive execution, such as web search engines and finance servers. With adaptive execution, when a request receives more processing time, its result improves, posing new challenges and opportunities for resource management.

We propose a new budget-based control model for interactive services with adaptive execution. The budget represents the amount of resources assigned to all pending requests. The budget-based control model consists of two components: (1) a hybrid control mechanism, which combines adaptive and integral controllers and controls the budget in order to meet the response time target with small steady-state error, fast settling time and little runtime overhead, and (2) an optimization procedure, which takes advantage of adaptive execution to maximize the total response quality of all pending requests under a given budget.

We implement and evaluate the budget-based control model experimentally in Microsoft Bing, a commercial web search engine. The experimental results show that it achieves more accurate control of mean response time and higher response quality than traditional static and dynamic admission control techniques that control the queue length. We also apply the model to a finance server that estimates option prices, and conduct a simulation study. The simulation results show large benefits for budget-based control. For example, under the same response time and quality requirements, the budget-based model accommodates double the system throughput compared to a traditional queue-based control model.

Categories and Subject Descriptors: C.4
[Performance of Systems]: *Reliability, availability, and serviceability*

Keywords:
feedback control; partial execution; adaptive control; scheduling algorithms; optimization; web search; response time; interactive services

1. INTRODUCTION

Interactive services such as web search, web content servers, finance servers and online gaming serve millions of customers using thousands of servers. The SLA of these services often

specifies stringent response time requirements. The most common metrics include mean and high-percentile response time. Long response times are not acceptable because they cause user dissatisfaction and revenue loss [21]. In addition to response time requirements, interactive services need to achieve high result quality. For example, a web search engine should return the most relevant web pages to user queries; a finance server needs to estimate price of the finance derivatives with small estimation error. Designing interactive services to meet their response time and quality requirement is an important and challenging problem.

To meet response time requirements, a common approach is to limit the length of the incoming request queue: when the queue is full, new requests are dropped upon arrival. Intuitively, the bounded queue length provides bounded waiting time that potentially leads to a desired response time target. However, such a static admission-control approach [22] leads to several undesirable situations which result in the failure to meet a response time target or in degraded quality. If the queue limit is too small, available resources become underutilized and response quality is degraded. A large queue limit, on the other hand, may result in violating response time requirements. Determining the appropriate static queue length limit is challenging in data center environments since systems change: the incoming load fluctuates over time; software updates and hardware upgrades affect request service demand; and service SLAs change to reflect the evolving business requirements. Moreover, while a well-designed interactive service should not be persistently overloaded, transient periods of overload are often inevitable. The load increase at the server that leads to a transient period of overload is often difficult to predict [3]. These factors suggest the need for self-managed systems that can adapt to the changes and meet response time and quality requirements.

An intuitive way to offer a response time guarantee in a changing environment is to apply feedback control. Feedback control has been widely used to achieve performance guarantees in many applications [5, 6]. Prior work [8, 9, 20, 23, 24] adjusts the queue length limit dynamically (or equivalently the buffer size or request drop rate) according to the feedback on response time: when the measured response time is higher than the target response time, the queue length limit is decreased; when response time is lower than that the target, the limit is increased. This type of dynamic admission control is effective for the classic "binary" request model: The server either processes the request returning a complete response or drops it with a null response. We call this model *binary* because the scheduler has a binary decision to make: either accept or reject the request.

In contrast to the binary request model, many online services support adaptive execution: a request may have several partial results with different qualities depending on the amount of received processing time. The request has a quality function that maps the received processing time to a corresponding response quality; the response quality often improves with more processing time. Many important applications follow the adaptive model, including the following: (1) Web search: A web search engine receives requests from clients and returns the matching webpages within a short deadline. For a web query, there are multiple acceptable answers, and more processing time allows the search engine to match and rank more webpages online, providing progressively better responses. (2) Finance servers: Traders interactively submit requests to estimate the price of financial derivatives. A finance server executes a computation, such as Monte Carlo based pricing algorithms, and the server can trade-off more processing time for smaller error between the estimated price and the real price.

Applying feedback control to adaptive interactive services is challenging. In addition to accepting or rejecting a request, the scheduler can execute requests partially: it needs to assign some processing time to each request based for example on request quality function or on system load. The goal is to meet the response time target and to provide high response quality. Existing approaches for the binary request model are not suitable here: they do not consider partial execution of requests, and therefore some queries are fully served while the others are rejected. Although traditional approaches may still meet the response time target; they result, however, in large degradation in the service quality, and they bring inconsistent user experience as some requests receive no service.

We exploit the problem of scheduling interactive requests with adaptive execution to meet the response time target while achieving high response quality. We introduce a budget-based control optimization model where the budget is defined as the total execution time (or amount of resources) for all pending requests. The model consists of two components: a feedback control mechanism to adapt the budget so the system can meet its desired response time, and an optimization procedure that schedules requests within the provided budget. The optimization procedure assigns the execution time of individual requests based on their service demands and quality profiles to improve their total response quality.

For interactive services, the control mechanism should adapt to the changing workload quickly and accurately while being simple enough with little runtime overhead. We develop a hybrid control mechanism combining adaptive and integral control to achieve this objective. Given the complexity of real systems, it is often hard to quantify the transfer function between system input and output in a changing environment. Therefore, we adopt a linear quadratic (LQ) adaptive control mechanism, which performs recursive linear regression to capture system behavior and uses an LQ optimal controller to compute the control output. However, frequent regression evaluation is too expensive for interactive services since each request takes on average only 20 ms of execution time. In addition, the pure LQ adaptive control cannot eliminate steady-state error. We, therefore, perform regression evaluation for adaptive control only at coarse-grain intervals, and within a coarse-grain interval, we apply integral control to adjust the control output, reducing both runtime overhead and steady-state error.

The budget-based control model applies the optimization procedure to exploit adaptive execution. With adaptive execution, a request can be partially processed, and a quality function maps the received processing time to the response quality. We develop two optimization procedures for two types of scheduling scenarios: (1) clairvoyant scheduling: the scheduler knows request service demand at their arrival, and (2) nonclairvoyant scheduling: the scheduler does not know request service demand until the request completes. The optimization procedure assigns processing time to pending requests using the budget determined by the control mechanism to improve the response quality.

We assess the benefits of the budget-based control model through system implementation and experimental evaluation as well as through a simulation study.

We show that the budget-based control model is feasible in practice, and we implement and evaluate it experimentally in Microsoft Bing, a large commercial web search engine. We employ hybrid control combining adaptive and integral controllers to meet the target mean response time with small steady-state error, fast settling time and little runtime overhead. The hybrid controller adjusts the budget. We measure the quality profile of Bing search requests and exploit the concavity of the quality profile to design an optimization procedure to schedule requests. The experimental results show significant benefits of using budget-based control over controlling the queue limit statically or dynamically. In particular, budget-based control meets the desired response time target and achieves high result quality. Moreover, since many commercial applications specify SLA using high percentile response time, we also apply the budget-based model to control the 90-percentile response time for web search and show its effectiveness.

We also evaluate the budget-based control model with a different optimization procedure in a finance server. We build a simulator that models a finance server using Monte Carlo methods to evaluate option prices. Here each request is a task to estimate the price of a financial option, and the response quality is measured by the price estimation error: the smaller the estimation error, the better the result quality. Our results show that, to meet the same mean response time target, the budget-based control model reduces the estimation error and improves response quality compared to the queue-based control model. In particular, to achieve the same target quality, the budget-based control model doubles the system throughput while satisfying the target mean response time.

The contributions of this paper are as follows: (1) We propose the budget-based control model for interactive services with adaptive execution. (2) We introduce a hybrid control mechanism suitable for interactive services, which combines adaptive and integral control to meet response time requirements. We also introduce two optimization procedures to improve response quality for clairvoyant and nonclairvoyant scheduling environments. (3) We show how to implement budget-based control in modern servers as used in Bing. (4) We evaluate the benefits of budget-based control experimentally, using real server software and workload in Bing. (5) We conduct a simulation study to evaluate budget-based control in a finance server.

The paper is organized as follows. Section 2 discusses adaptive execution and presents the measured quality profile from Bing. Section 3 describes the budget-based control model, and its two components: the control mechanism and the optimization procedure. Section 4 describes the implementation and experimental evaluation results in Bing. Section 5 describes the simulation results in a finance server. Section 6 discusses related work and Section 7 shows our conclusions.

2. Adaptive Execution

Adaptive execution is the flexibility of trading more resources for better results. Examples include estimation computations in which better estimates are obtained with more processing. For example in a finance server, Monte Carlo methods compute option pricing to find better answers with more processing.

With adaptive execution, the relationship between the quality of the result and the used amount of computational resources is quantified by request quality function. A quality function $f: R \rightarrow R$ maps the request completion ratio (processing time / service demand) to a quality value gained by executing the request. Quality functions of different applications can have different shapes. We observe that the quality functions are usually monotonically non-decreasing: result quality stays the same or improves with more processing. Moreover, many best-effort applications exhibit concave quality profiles due to the effects of diminishing returns.

To demonstrate the quality profile for a real application, we measure the response quality profile in Bing using $200K$ queries from a production trace and present it in Figure 1. Each request is a web search query for a set of keywords. The search engine scans its inverted index looking for webpages that match the requested keywords and ranks the matching webpages. The more time the server spends on matching and ranking the webpages from the inverted index, the better the results. The response includes a set of links to the top webpages matching the keywords specified by the user query. The response quality compares the set of webpages returned in the test to a golden set of base results (as explained in Section 4). The x-axis of Figure 1 is request completion ratio; the y-axis is the average response quality. The figure demonstrates that the quality profile of Bing search is monotonically increasing and concave: the concavity comes from the effect of diminishing returns. The inverted index lists important (e.g., popular) webpages first; therefore webpages matched earlier are more likely to rank higher and contribute more to total response quality.

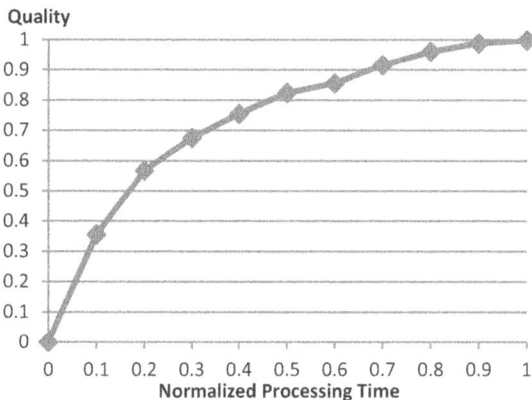

Figure 1. Measured quality profile in Bing search.

A scheduler can exploit adaptive execution and request quality profile to improve the response quality. Without adaptive execution, a scheduler can either execute a request fully or reject it. In contrast, adaptive execution opens the possibility of partial processing in which some requests can be processed half-way returning an approximated result, which is a favorable trade-off in many situations.

3. Budget-based Control Model

This section presents the budget-based model for interactive services with adaptive execution. The budget is defined as the total processing time (or total amount of resources) we plan to allocate to all pending requests. The budget-based control model consists of two components: (1) the control mechanism, which applies feedback control to adjust the budget to meet the response time target, and (2) the optimization procedure, which is a scheduling algorithm using adaptive execution to maximize total response quality at a given target. The budget-based model divides the two main goals of the system, meeting response time target and achieving high quality, into the control mechanism and optimization procedure respectively, so each component has a clear design goal and responsibility. This section elaborates the design and features of the control mechanism and optimization procedure.

3.1 Control Mechanism

The control mechanism takes the observed response time as feedback and determines the budget value in order to meet the response time target. There are several approaches to design such a controller. We present a hybrid controller, combining adaptive and integral controller, which offers accurate and light-weight control of interactive services to meet their response time requirements. Our experimental results show that such hybrid control combines the benefits of adaptive and integral control: It meets the response time target with small steady-state error, fast settling time and little runtime overhead, outperforming the adaptive controller alone and integral controller alone. This section first gives a brief description of the integral and adaptive controllers then it introduces the hybrid controller.

3.1.1 Integral Control

Integral control is a simple and well-known control mechanism, adjusting the value of control variable based on the difference between the observed output and the reference output. The control function is expressed as follows:

$$u(k) = u(k - 1) + K_I e(k)$$

Here k represents time steps; $u(k)$ is the output of the integral controller (which is also the control variable of the system) at time step k. The tracking error $e(k)$ is the difference between the observed system output and the reference output, i.e., $e(k) = y_{\text{ref}}(k) - y(k - 1)$. The controller parameter K_I defines the ratio of control change to the control error. In our system, the control variable u is the budget, and the output y is the metric such as mean response time, or the 90-percentile response time.

Integral control has two main advantages. First, it has zero steady-state error, which allows systems to meet their desired SLA. Second, it is computationally efficient, which is an important property in interactive systems, The integral controller incurs almost negligible system overhead allowing recalculating the budget with each request arrival or departure.

Integral control has its limitation: Its response is relatively slow. For example, when the workload has a big change, it will track the change slowly, producing a large deviation initially. Integral control is usually combined with another control mechanism to overcome this limitation.

3.1.2 Adaptive Control

We consider a linear quadratic adaptive controller [15] with two parts: a model estimator and a linear quadratic optimal controller.

The Model Estimator. The model estimator uses the prior behavior of the system to predict the current system model. More precisely, it uses a number of prior control input and output values to predict their relationship using a Recursive Least Square (RLS) model estimation. In our problem, adaptive control predicts the relationship between the budget and response time using a linear function. The order of the regression model (i.e., the number of prior data points used for predicting the system model) indicates a tradeoff between the estimation precision and computational overhead. With a larger order, the estimation is generally more precise, however, the regression computation incurs a higher computation overhead.

Linear Quadratic (LQ) Optimal Controller. The primary control objective is to make the system output track the desired SLA with small error. It is also desirable to avoid large changes to the control variables. These two goals are achieved by minimizing the quadratic cost function F defined as follows for linear quadratic optimal control:

$$F = |W(y_{est}(k+1) - y_{ref}(k+1))|^2 + |Q(u(k) - u(k-1))|^2$$

Here $y_{est}(k+1)$ denotes the estimated system output from the estimator, $y_{ref}(k+1)$ denotes the reference output for the step $k+1$, and $u(k)$ and $u(k-1)$ are the control variables (or system inputs) at time step k and step $k-1$, respectively. Moreover, W is a positive weighting parameter on the tracking errors, and Q is a positive weighting parameter to penalize large changes in the control variable. The relative magnitude of W and Q trades off between tracking accuracy and smaller changes in the control variable. The value of the control variable $u(k)$ that minimizes F can be obtained by setting the derivative $\partial F/\partial u(k) = 0$.

Next we turn to the advantages of adaptive control. Interactive services are complex systems: they use heterogeneous hardware crossing different data centers and generations of software and hardware components; the workload fluctuates over time; software updates and hardware upgrades affects the request service demand. More fundamentally, when an interactive service supports adaptive execution, requests can be partially processed. Therefore, it is hard to quantify the transfer function between the control variable (in our case, it is the budget) and the response time. This makes adaptive controller a good choice: it captures the system behavior by modeling the correlation between budget and response time using the recent data points. The RLS-based model estimator identifies the changes in the system behavior, and the controller adjusts the control output and adapts the system correspondingly.

There are limitations of adaptive control. (1) It is computationally expensive for interactive services. Given a regression order N, i.e., the estimator uses the latest N data points (i.e., control input, control output), it requires $O(N^3)$ arithmetic operations at each time step to compute the prediction model online. Our measurements indicate that it takes about 2.2 ms on our server when $N = 10$. The average service demand of a request is around 20 ms. If adaptive control is applied on every request, it introduces fairly large overhead to the system. (2) The LQ adaptive controller, similar to a proportional controller, incurs steady-state errors. More specifically, if we set Q to 0, the LQ has the form of a proportional controller which can't guarantee the small steady-state errors.

3.1.3 Hybrid Control

We develop a hybrid controller to combine the integral and adaptive control: it runs adaptive control periodically in a coarse-grain time interval to learn the system model and adjust the control output, the budget. Within the fine-grain interval, the hybrid controller uses integral control for the execution of each request to perform fine-grain adjustment of the control output. This combination reduces the computation overhead and the steady-state error. The block diagram of the hybrid controller is shown in Figure 2.

The hybrid controller uses both integral and adaptive control. If we use integral control only, we may have slow response for tracking changes in workload or system environment. Adding adaptive control allows learning the system model according to the recent system behavior. We cannot, however, afford the runtime overhead of using adaptive control for each request and there will be a steady-state error. Using integral control complements adaptive control, since integral control runtime overhead is almost negligible and it eliminates the steady-state error to meet the response time target. The adaptive part of the hybrid controller helps to adapt the system to large changes.

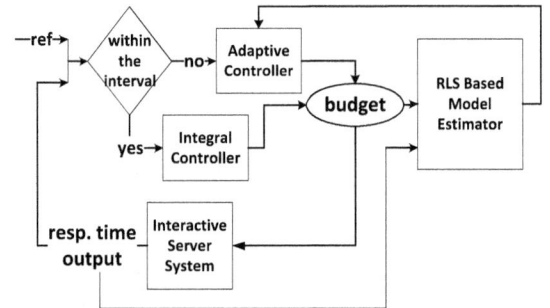

Figure 2: Hybrid Control Block Diagram.

Comparing the hybrid controller with a classic PI controller, the parameter of the P controller is fixed and difficult to tune for different loads and configurations, while the adaptive control of the hybrid controller adapts the system on different hardware configurations and workload regions automatically.

3.2 Optimization Procedure

The optimization procedure is a scheduling algorithm that takes a resource budget and a set of pending requests as inputs, and assigns a portion of the budget to each request with the objective of maximizing total response quality. The design of the optimization procedure depends on the request quality profile, service demand, and other application specific constraints. We do not intend to enumerate all optimization procedures to cover all scenarios. Rather, we focus on concave quality profiles as they are popular in practice due to the iterative nature of many best-effort applications and the effect of diminishing return. We introduce two optimization procedures for clairvoyant and nonclairvoyant scheduling environment respectively. This section presents how these two optimization procedures work and they are evaluated in Section 4 and 5. For other quality profiles and application specific constraints, one can develop and employ a tailored optimization procedure.

3.2.1 Optimization for Clairvoyant Scheduling

This section describes an optimization procedure with known request service demand and concave quality profile. An example is the finance server that uses Monte Carlo methods to evaluate option prices (Section 5). This optimization procedure maximizes the response quality of the pending requests under a given budget.

Figure 3 presents the optimization procedure. The budget is defined as the amount of processing time available for all ready requests. The optimization procedure decides the assigned processing time of each request in the ready queue by solving the optimization problem defined at MaxQuality. MaxQuality maximizes the total quality of requests based on the budget, request demand and quality profile. Since all constraints in the MaxQuality are linear and its objective is to maximize the summation of concave functions, MaxQuality is a convex optimization problem and can be solved using convex solvers such as CVS [1]. MaxQuality produces a solution that maximizes the total quality of all pending requests with a given budget.

Without compromising the total response quality, we can further reduce response time by applying MinMRT after MaxQuality. MinMRT sorts the requests in the ascending order of the assigned processing time. It is well known that given a batch of jobs, running the shortest job first produces a schedule with the smallest mean response time [17]. Here by performing MinMRT after MaxQuality, the scheduler further minimizes the response time in the set of solutions that maximize the total quality. This also benefits the response quality: given the same budget, MinMRT reduces the mean response time; thus given the same mean response time target, MinMRT relaxes the budget and leads to higher quality.

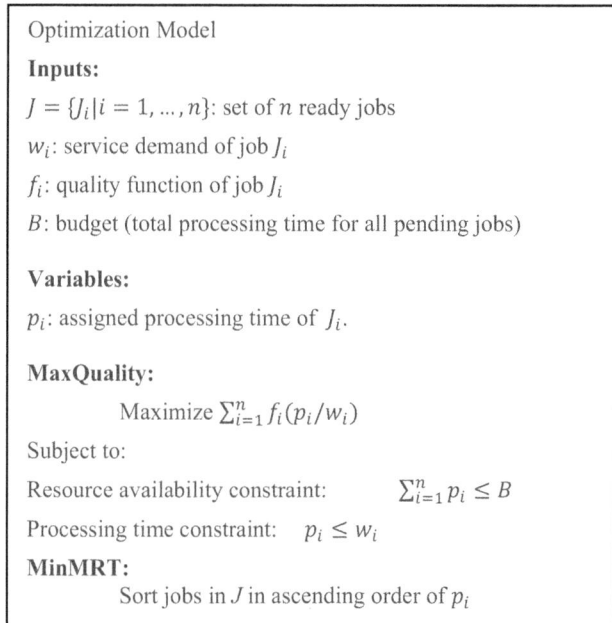

Optimization Model

Inputs:

$J = \{J_i | i = 1, ..., n\}$: set of n ready jobs

w_i: service demand of job J_i

f_i: quality function of job J_i

B: budget (total processing time for all pending jobs)

Variables:

p_i: assigned processing time of J_i.

MaxQuality:

$$\text{Maximize } \sum_{i=1}^{n} f_i(p_i/w_i)$$

Subject to:

Resource availability constraint: $\quad \sum_{i=1}^{n} p_i \leq B$

Processing time constraint: $\quad p_i \leq w_i$

MinMRT:

$$\text{Sort jobs in } J \text{ in ascending order of } p_i$$

Figure 3: Optimization procedure for clairvoyant scheduling.

The optimization procedure performs local optimization on the set of pending requests and the available budget. When there is new request arrival or budget change, we can repeat the optimization procedure with the updated request information.

3.2.2 Optimization for Nonclairvoyant Scheduling

This section describes an optimization procedure assuming requests have unknown request service demands and have concave quality profile. An example application is the index server at Bing (Section 4). Besides meeting response time and quality requirement, Bing server has two additional requirements: (1) It is often hard to know the exact quality profile of each request. The scheduler uses an expected quality profile (as shown in Figure 1) for all requests. (2) Context switching is expensive because of cache warm-up; it may take a few hundred

microseconds to more than a millisecond [2]. Since the mean service demand of Bing requests is only about 20 ms, the scheduler should execute each request only once, rather than suspending the request and resuming it later.

Figure 4 shows the pseudo-code of the optimization procedure EqResv. The budget is defined as the amount of processing time available for all pending requests. The input does not include request service demand because it is unknown at request arrival. EqResv is a heuristic algorithm to improve total response quality of ready requests under a given budget.

EqResv processes requests in the FIFO order and it decides the assigned processing time of the first job in the FIFO queue based on the load and the budget. In order to improve total response quality, when requests are competing for resources, a scheduler prefers running the part of requests with higher quality gain. Given a concave quality profile, the early portion of processing request has higher gain than its later portion. Therefore, the key idea of EqResv is to prevent jobs at the beginning of the queue from consuming the entire budget and starving later requests so each request has a fair opportunity to be processed (at least for its early portion). To achieve this goal, EqResv applies two techniques. (1) Equi-Partitioning (EQ): When the system is heavily loaded, EqResv performs EQ to reserve a fair share of processing time for waiting requests (in Line 2). With a concave quality function, giving each job the same amount of processing time maximizes the overall quality. (2) Reservation (RESV): In a lightly loaded case, EqResv performs RESV to reserve the expected service demand for the queuing requests and allocates the remaining time to the current running job (in Line 3)[1]. RESV gives the long requests a chance to finish if they will not impact short ones.

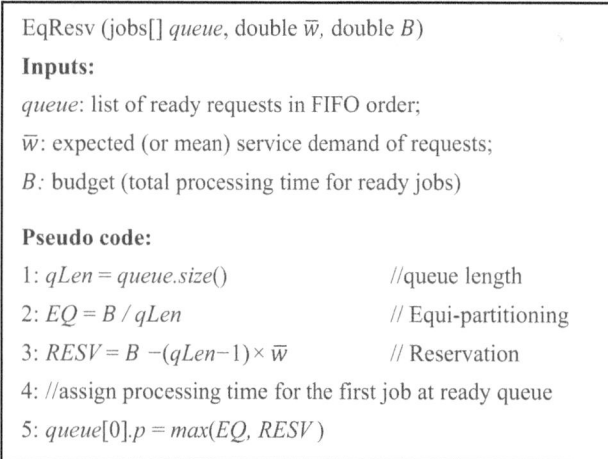

EqResv (jobs[] *queue*, double $\bar{w}$, double B)

Inputs:

queue: list of ready requests in FIFO order;

$\bar{w}$: expected (or mean) service demand of requests;

B: budget (total processing time for ready jobs)

Pseudo code:

```
1: qLen = queue.size()              //queue length
2: EQ = B / qLen                    // Equi-partitioning
3: RESV = B −(qLen−1)× w̄          // Reservation
4: //assign processing time for the first job at ready queue
5: queue[0].p = max(EQ, RESV )
```

Figure 4: Optimization procedure for nonclairvoyant scheduling.

EqResv does not need a load threshold to decide if it should use the result from EQ or RESV. During light load, we want to estimate the processing time using RESV, and its processing time is larger than the one produced by EQ. During heavy load, we want to use EQ, and its processing time is larger than the one

---

[1] Service demand of individual request is unknown but expected or mean service demand of requests can be obtained through offline measurement or online approximation.

produced by RESV. Therefore, selecting the larger between these two gives the assigned processing time (in Line 5).

4. Implementation and Evaluation in Bing

This section presents the implementation and evaluation of the budget-based control model in Microsoft Bing web search engine.

4.1 Application Overview

Bing is a large commercial web search engine from Microsoft. We focus on the index serving part (interactive processing), which serves user queries online to return the best matching webpages. Notably, the index serving part is different from the web crawler and index builder (batch processing) which processes crawled webpages to generate the inverted index offline.

The index serving system of Bing accepts user queries, and it forwards the queries to index servers when the query's results do not exist in the cache. Each index server manages a small portion of the inverted index and therefore becomes responsible for a set of web pages. The index server searches its inverted index for all webpages that match the query, ranks these webpages, and returns the top N webpages that match the query. The index server supports adaptive execution: the result quality improves with the increased number of webpages examined and ranked. Moreover, the response quality profile is concave as shown in Figure 1. In Bing, we want to limit the mean response time of the index server as part of the web search SLA requirements for important commercial reasons. These factors make the index server a good candidate to apply the budget-based control model.

4.2 Implementation

The web index is partitioned among many index servers. We use our approach to control each index server so that each individual server can satisfy the target mean response time while returning high quality results. The original index server works as follows. Newly arrived requests join the waiting queue. The waiting queue has a length limit: when the queue is full, new requests are dropped. There are a number of worker threads and each worker thread processes one request at a time. The number of workers is equal to the number of cores in the system. When a worker thread completes a request, it gets a new query from the head of the waiting queue and starts to process it. To process a query, the worker searches the inverted index and obtains a list of matching webpages to the search keywords. It then ranks the matching webpages in a loop, which we call index ranking loop. This loop is the most time consuming part of the query processing. After ranking all matched webpages, the worker returns the top N matched results and completes the query.

Our implementation at index server includes three parts to apply budget-based control.

(1) We enable adaptive execution of requests using early termination. We add a termination condition in the ranking loop, so that when a request uses up its assigned processing time, the request is terminated early.

(2) We add the optimization procedure from Figure 4 to dynamically assign processing time to requests based on the budget. The optimization procedure is extended to multicore servers by changing the queue length value (qLen) to reflect the expected queue length for each core.

(3) We implement the hybrid controller consisting of the model estimator and linear quadratic optimal controller to adjust the budget based on mean response time. The mean response time is computed online as a moving average $MRT = (1 - \alpha) \times MRT +$ $\alpha \times r_i$, where r_i is the response time of the last processed request i and α is a constant multiplier. We use $\alpha = 0.05$ in our implementation.

To compare the budget-based control to the traditional dynamic approaches, we also implement queue-based control and integrate it in the index server. It applies the same hybrid controller in Section 3 to adjust the queue length limit based on the mean response time. When the queue is full, the newly arrived requests are dropped. When the queue length limit decreases due to control decision, the overflowed requests are also dropped.

In the remainder of this section, we compare these three implementations of the index server:

- OriginalIS: original implementation of index server
- BudgetIS: index server using budget-based control
- QueueIS: index server using queue-based control.

4.3 Experimental Setup

Performance Metrics: The primary goal to control an interactive system is to meet the response time target and to achieve high response quality. The index server has an SLA requirement on the average response time and response quality. The request response time is the duration between when request arrives to the index server and when the response is sent back; the server sends responses to all requests including the dropped ones. Our experiments use 35 ms as our target mean response time, and we control the server to make the mean response time at or below the target. We also tried several other mean response time targets and the results are similar.

To compute the quality of a response of a web search query, we compare returned webpages in the response to the webpages in the base results of the query when it is processed completely. We use proportional quality, which gives each of the top N webpages the same weight. For example, when $N=10$ and there are 8 matches between the response and the base results, the quality is 8/10. Proportional quality is one way to measure the response quality. We also used other quality metrics, such as assigning higher weights to higher ranking webpages; the experimental results are similar we, therefore, present the proportional quality only.

Other important measures include classic metrics for evaluating controllers, such as settling time and steady-state error. Settling time is the time from the change in the workload to when the measured output is sufficiently close to its new steady-state value. Shorter settling time is desired. Moreover, the control mechanism should be computationally efficient without incurring high overhead.

Workload and Hardware: Our evaluation includes an index server that answers queries and a client that replays queries from a trace file. We use a query trace with 200,000 actual user queries from production to drive the experiments. We run the system by issuing queries following a Poisson distribution in an open-loop system. We vary system load by changing the arrival rate expressed as QPS (queries per second). The index server searches its local index and returns the top 10 matching results to the client. The index server for our evaluation has a six core Intel 64-bit Xeon processor (3.33 GHz) and 24 GB main memory.

Controller Configurations: The hybrid controller uses adaptive control to adjust the budget at every 10 queries and applies integral control at every step with $K_I = 1$. The order of the RLS-based model estimator is 10. The weight parameters of the linear quadratic controller have values Q=0.5 and W=0.5.

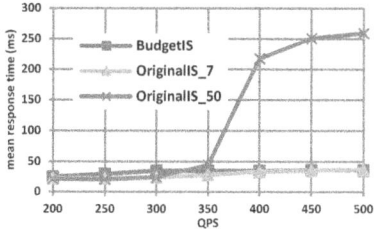

Figure 5: Mean response time for BudgetIS and OriginalIS.

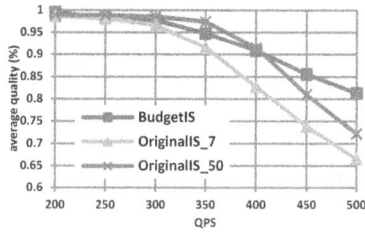

Figure 6: Average quality for BudgetIS and OriginalIS.

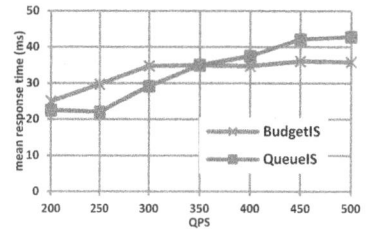

Figure 7: Mean response time for BudgetIS and QueueIS.

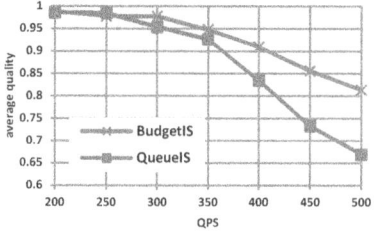

Figure 8: Average quality for BudgetIS and QueueIS.

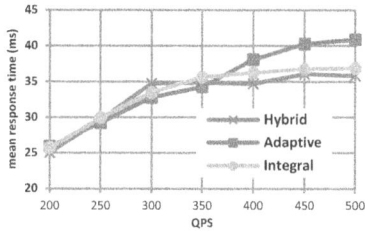

Figure 9: Mean resp. time for different control mechanisms

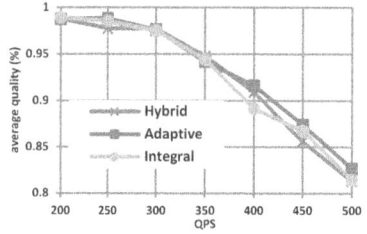

Figure 10: Average quality for different control mechanisms.

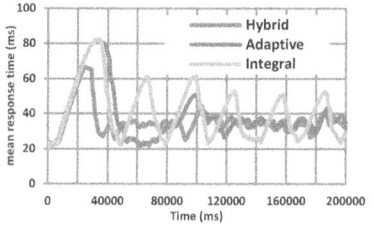

Figure 11: Transient behavior.

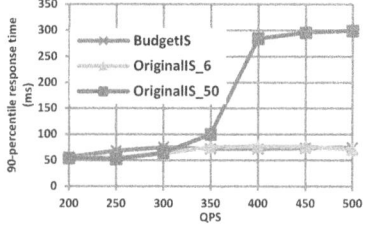

Figure 12: P90 response time for BudgetIS and OriginalIS.

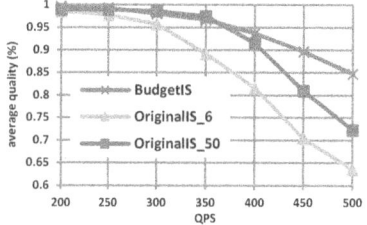

Figure 13: Average quality for BudgetIS and OriginalIS.

Experiments: We conduct the following four sets of experiments and present their results in the remaider of this section.

(1) Comparing budget control to static queue: we compare the budget-based control model (BudgetIS) to the original index server that has a static limit on the queue length (OriginalIS).

(2) Control variables: we compare BudgetIS that uses budget as control variable to QueueIS that uses queue length.

(3) Control mechanisms: we evaluate the impact of integral, adaptive, and hybrid control mechanisms.

(4) Controlling high-percentile response time: we apply budget-based control to meet a 90-percentile response time target.

4.4 Comparing Budget Control to Static Queue

This experiment compares BudgetIS to the static approach of having a fixed queue length. We use two fixed queue length values 7 and 50 (corresponding to OriginalIS_7 and OriginalIS_50 respectively) to demonstrate the effect of different queue lengths. Figures 5 and 6 show the mean response time and quality results for the three implementations: their x-axis represents the load expressed as the request arrival rate, varying from 200 to 500 QPS, which covers the operational range of the workload. The y-axis is the mean response time and average response quality, respectively.

The results show that for static approach, different queue lengths represent a tradeoff between mean response time and average response quality. With shorter queue length, the mean response time decreases and the quality degrades too. OriginalIS_7 meets the response time target, but its quality degrades even at light and moderate load; OriginalIS_50 obtains higher quality but its mean

response time at high load is significantly higher than the target. It indicates that there is no single queue length value that meets both the response time and quality requirement.

Figure 5 shows that BudgetIS successfully bounds the request mean response time to the 35 ms target with tracking error less than 1 ms. Moreover, Figure 6 shows that BudgetIS also improves response quality at high load. In particular, the response quality of OriginalIS_7 and OriginalIS_50 drops more sharply at high load and OriginalIS_50 exceeds the response time target, while BudgetIS offers higher quality. BudgetIS achieves this by assigning request processing time dynamically exploiting request quality profile to improve the total response quality. For example at 450 QPS, BudgetIS terminates 32% queries early with partial results and no queries are dropped, while OriginalIS_7 drops 25% queries and these queries have quality 0.

This experiment demonstrates that (1) Using a fixed queue length cannot meet response time requirements with high response quality, and (2) The budget-based model accurately controls the mean response time to match the SLA target and uses partial evaluation to improve the request response quality.

4.5 Control Variables: Budget vs. Queue Length

This experiment compares QueueIS, which controls the length of the waiting job queue, to BudgetIS, which controls the budget. Figures 7 and 8 show the mean response time and quality comparison for the two approaches. Both approaches can bound request mean response time at high load, however, QueueIS incurs bigger errors tracking the response time target and has worse quality at high load.

111

QueueIS incurs bigger tracking error than BudgetIS for two factors. (1) QueueIS uses queue length as control input, which is an integer value with the smallest change of incrementing or decrementing by one; the discrete values of the control input may not be able to meet the control target precisely. (2) In BudgetIS, changes in the budget value are immediately reflected on the queries' processing times, since the system assigns query processing time according to the budget. However, in QueueIS, changes of the queue length take effect only after a period of time, since queue length won't affect response time of the queries before the queue becomes full. Such a delay between control input and output can also cause reduced control accuracy.

QueueIS produces lower quality than BudgetIS at high load because QueueIS drops queries to meet the response time target while BudgetIS processes queries partially. Given a concave quality profile, partially executing queries with similar processing time achieves higher average quality than executing some queries fully while dropping the others.

4.6 Comparing Control Mechanisms

This section shows that the hybrid control mechanism which combines integral and adaptive control outperforms either integral control alone or adaptive control alone. Hybrid control offers small steady-state errors, small settling time and is computationally efficient. Adaptive and integral control offer a subset of these properties rather than all of them.

In this experiment, all the evaluated systems use the budget as the control variable with the same optimization procedure but different control mechanisms.

Figure 9 and 10 show mean response time and average quality for the different control mechanisms with the system load. We discuss each of them below.

Adaptive controller. The adaptive controller exceeds the mean response time target of 35 ms at high load. It uses the RLS model estimator to predict system behavior and its control law is close to proportional control: its accuracy is sensitive to workload variation and the control law cannot eliminate steady-state errors. Moreover, running model estimation of adaptive control before executing every request introduces a considerable amount of computational overhead (about 2.2 ms of overhead for every query with average service demand of 20 ms). This not only increases the mean response time of requests but also becomes the noise factor that the control law cannot remove from its steady-state error. Therefore, using adaptive controller alone cannot bound mean response time effectively.

Integral controller. The integral controller controls the mean response time effectively with tracking errors less than 2.5 ms. However, it has a long settling time. Figure 11 compares the transient state behavior of integral controllers to the hybrid and adaptive controllers. In this experiment, we first launch queries at 200 QPS; then we double the load to 400 QPS. The figure shows that hybrid controller has the shortest settling time. As for the integral controller, it has slower responsiveness to the workload change, with large settling time. Due to its slow responsiveness, the integral controller does not meet all the desired properties.

Hybrid controller. The hybrid controller has the best characteristics among the three control mechanisms: the smallest steady-state error, highest response quality, and the shortest settling time. It uses the adaptive controller in a coarse-grain manner to detect large changes and responds quickly; it uses the integral controller in a fine-grain manner to reduce steady-state

error and reduce computation overhead. The hybrid controller combines the advantage of adaptive and integral controller.

4.7 Controlling High-Percentile Response Time

High-percentile response time is another important and common SLA requirement for interactive services. This section shows that the budget-based model meets the high percentile response time target. This experiment is conducted on Bing index server with a 90-percentile response target of 75 ms, i.e., 90% requests must have response time of 75 ms or less. We use the last 1000 queries' 90-percentile value as the current observed value in a moving window of recent requests and we adjust the budget based on the difference between the observed and the target 90-percentile response time.

Figure 12 and 13 show the 90-percentile response time and average response quality for BudgetIS, OriginalIS_6 and OriginalIS_50. The results are similar as in Section 4.4. BudgetIS effectively meets the 90-percentile response target while OriginalIS_50 incurs very high response time at heavy load and OriginalIS_6 suffers from quality loss at light and moderate load. The quality of both versions of OriginalIS is lower than BudgetIS at heavy load due to request dropping. Again, the benefits of BudgetIS come from adopting partial results and exploiting the concave quality profile. This experiment demonstrates that the budget-based model is not limited to controlling mean response time; it can be extended to meet other SLA for adaptive interactive services.

5. Finance Server

Section 4 evaluates the budget-based control model for nonclairvoyant scheduling where request service demand is unknown. This section evaluates it for clairvoyant scheduling. We build a simulator to model a finance server where request service demand is known. We show that budget-based control model outperforms the queue-based model: under the same load, the budget-based control model produces higher response quality and under the same quality requirement, it achieves higher throughput.

5.1 Application Overview

Banks and fund management companies evaluate thousands of financial derivatives every day. Traders and analysts submit requests to value the derivatives, and they make trading decisions online based on the returned results. At the backend, there are many servers that perform quantitative analysis on various financial products. This section presents an option pricing server that uses Monte Carlo methods to price complex path-dependent options. Monte Carlo methods are widely used for analyzing complex derivatives that are difficult to value using other techniques such as Black-Scholes and lattice-based computations [16]. Monte Carlo methods are computationally intensive and rely on repeated random sampling to compute the results. Such a finance server is a good candidate for budget-based control: (1) tasks are time-bounded: traders often wait for no more than a few seconds to get the results and perform online trading and (2) tasks are adaptive: with more processing time, the price estimation error reduces and result quality improves.

5.2 Performance Metric and Quality Profile

The result quality is measured by a statistical metric called standard error of mean (SEM), which is the standard deviation of the sample mean to the population mean [4]. It indicates how well the sample mean estimates the population mean. The SEM value

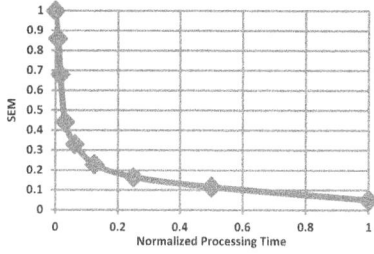

Figure 14: Error profile.

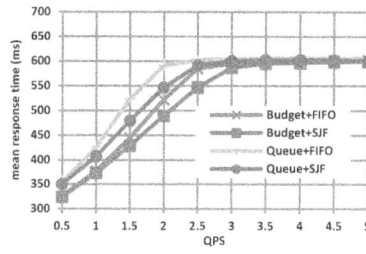

Figure 15: Mean resp. time comparison.

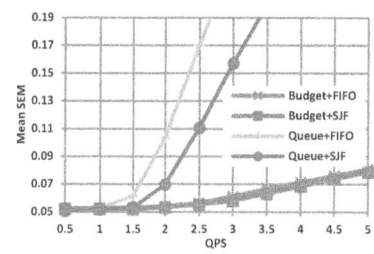

Figure 16: Mean SEM comparison.

is calculated as the population standard deviation [2] divided by the square root of the sample size n, i.e., $SEM = \delta/\sqrt{n}$. The smaller SEM is, the closer the estimated price is to the real price.

Figure 14 shows the request error profile[3] with the normalized processing time, which is the ratio of request processing time to its full service demand. Here we set the SEM target to 0.05: when a request's SEM reaches 0.05, we consider it fully evaluated. When the number of samples increases along with the processing time, SEM decreases, which indicates the increase of the result quality. Moreover, the error profile is convex; when we compute more samples, the additional reduction on error for adding a sample gets smaller. Here minimizing SEM with a convex error profile is equivalent to maximizing quality with a concave quality profile. Smaller SEM indicates better quality.

Request service demand is known because it depends on two input values of the option, namely (1) the total duration and (2) period value, and the target SEM, which are all known at request arrival.

5.3 Experimental Setup

In the simulation study, requests arrive following a Poisson process, and their service demands follow an exponential distribution with an average of 300 ms. The desired mean response time is 600 ms. We implement and compare two control models: budget-based and queue-based control. Moreover, since request service demand is known at request arrival, we also apply the shortest job first (SJF) technique [17] to reduce mean response time. So in total, we evaluate four schemes:

- Budget+FIFO: budget-based model with optimization procedure in Figure 3 with MaxQuality only (and without MinMRT). The requests are processed in FIFO order.
- Budget+SJF: budget-based model with optimization procedure in Figure 3 with both MaxQuality and MinMRT. The requests with smaller assigned processing time are processed earlier.
- Queue+FIFO: queue-based model serving requests in FIFO order and dropping a new request when the queue is full.
- Queue+SJF: queue-based model serving requests using SJF ordering and dropping the longest request when queue is full.

5.4 Performance Evaluation

Figure 15 and 16 show the mean response time and SEM of the four schemes with the varying load expressed as QPS or user

requests per second. All schemes effectively bound mean response time at 600 ms or below, but budget-based schemes produce much smaller SEM and thus higher quality. For example, to keep $SEM \leq 0.1$, the maximum throughput which the queue-based approach sustains is less than 2.5 QPS while budget-based approach can sustain more than 5 QPS, which doubles the throughput. We now look into more details of the results.

From Figure 15, all schemes effectively bound the mean response time under 600 ms. SJF helps to reduce mean response time at moderate load: both Budget+SJF and Queue+SJF exhibit lower response time than their corresponding FIFO versions at load 1.5-2.5 QPS. At light load, SJF is similar to FIFO because most jobs don't wait and mean response time is close to mean service demand. At heavy load, again, SJF is similar to FIFO because response time is controlled around the 600 ms target value.

There are three observations from Figure 16. (1) Budget-based schemes show much lower error and thus higher quality than queue-based schemes because they use adaptive execution to achieve partial results and use quality profile to optimize the assigned processing time of requests for higher quality. (2) Queue+SJF achieves higher quality than Queue+FIFO because given the same queue length, SJF helps to reduce the mean response time; thus given the same mean response time, Queue-SJF may allow longer queue length than Queue-FIFO, which results in less dropped queries and higher quality. (3) The quality difference of Budget-SFJ and Budget-FIFO is very small. This seems to be inconsistent with observation (2), but it does not. Using optimization procedure MaxQuality at Figure 3, when requests have concave quality profile and they are competing for resources, long requests are likely to be cut to prevent them from starving the short requests. Therefore, at heavy load, requests tend to obtain nearly equal processing time such that using FIFO or SJF results in similar orderings, making little difference.

6. Related Work

Feedback control theory has been widely used to achieve performance guarantees in computer systems with many applications such as multimedia streaming, real-time computing, transaction processing, embedded systems, and many others [5, 6]. In this section we focus on server systems using feedback control to meet response time guarantees, and applications that use adaptive executions.

Controlling server systems with response time requirements. The prior works along this line focus on three scenarios.

(1) Control for relative response time. For example, Adbelzaher et al. [7] build a feedback control loop for an Apache web server that enforces desired relative response time among different service classes via connection scheduling and process reallocation.

(2) Control elastic resources. In these prior works [8, 9, 25, 26, 27], systems acquire and release resources in response to dynamic workload to meet response time target. There are various types of

---

[2] The population standard deviation is often unknown in practice. As a conventional technique, we estimate SEM using the sample standard deviation divided by the square root of the sample size.

[3] When total processing time of a request is 0, SEM value is undefined and can be arbitrarily large. To compute mean SEM of requests including the unprocessed ones, we set the unprocessed request with quality 1 (a small value in favor of queue-based model since it is likely to drop more requests.)

resources to adapt: For example, adding or removing a storage node [27], altering CPU allocation [25], changing processing speed through dynamic voltage and frequency scaling [26].

(3) Control to prevent overloading. While a well-designed system should not be persistently overloaded, transient periods of overload are often inevitable, since the load is external to the server system and requests arrive according to a stochastic process, leading to transient overload and underload periods at the server. Such transient periods are inevitable and difficult to predict [3]. Many prior works [20, 23, 24] apply feedback control to cope with transient overload, deciding when to drop requests in order to meet response time target.

The above prior work [7, 8, 9, 20, 23, 24, 25, 26, 27] uses control theory to achieve response time guarantees, however, none of them consider adaptive execution of requests. Like many prior work [18, 19] on admission control, they either serve a request in full or reject a request completely. Our budget-based model is designed for applications with partial evaluation and it optimizes the scheduling based on request quality profiles.

Adaptive execution. Employing adaptive execution and approximate computations is an active area of research. Web content adaptation [10, 11] offers different versions of the content for the same request. Loop perforation [12] offers compiler and runtime support for adaptive execution and has been applied to audio and video codecs. Baek and Chilimbi [13] develop a general framework to support approximated computation of different applications to trade quality for lower energy.

These prior works [10, 11, 12, 13] offer important insights on how to adapt execution for different applications. They focus on adaptive execution mechanism that enables individual requests to produce partial results. They do not, however, consider server environments where multiple requests are competing for resources with response time and quality targets.

Control systems with content adaptation. The closest prior work to ours is controlling web servers that support content adaptation, which is a form of adaptive execution. Abdelzaher and Bhatti [14] propose to resolve the overloading problem of web servers by adapting web content to load conditions. To meet the desired server utilization, they control the ratio between the requests offering degraded content versus all the requests. Although this work uses adaptive execution to meet their control target, it has important differences from our work: they do not consider maximizing overall response quality for all requests as a goal, and they do not consider request quality profiles to improve the scheduling decision. We develop the budget-based model as a general approach for interactive services supporting adaptive execution. With an appropriate optimization procedure, it is applicable to web servers with content adaptation.

7. Conclusions

This paper presents the budget-based control model for interactive services with adaptive execution to meet a response time target while achieving high service quality. The budget-based model consists of two components: (1) a hybrid control mechanism that adapts the budget so as to meet the response time target accurately and quickly, and (2) an optimization procedure that improves the total response quality using adaptive execution. We assess the benefits of the budget-based control model through system implementation and experimental evaluation on a commercial search engine as well as through a simulation study of a finance server. Both the experimental and simulation results show that the budget-based model achieves more accurate control of mean

response time with higher response quality than the traditional static and dynamic approaches that do not consider adaptive execution.

8. References

[1] J. Hiriart-Urruty and C. Lemar´echal. Convex Analysis and Minimization Algorithms, I and II. 305 and 306. 1993.

[2] C. Li, C. Ding, and K. Shen. Quantifying the cost of context switch. ECS, 2007.

[3] B. Schroeder and M. Harchol-Balter. Web servers under overload: How scheduling can help. ACM Trans. on Internet Tech. 2006.

[4] http://en.wikipedia.org/wiki/Standard_error.

[5] J. L. Hellerstein, Y. Diao, S. Parekh, and D. M. Tilbury. Feedback Control of Computing Systems. 2004.

[6] T. Abdelzaher, Y. Diao, J. L. Hellerstein, C. Lu, and X. Zhu. Introduction to control theory and its application to computing systems. Performance Modeling and Engineering. 2008.

[7] C. Lu, T.F. Abdelzaher, J. Stankovic, and S. Son. A feedback control approach for guaranteeing relative delays in web servers. RTAS, 2001.

[8] L. Sha, X. Liu, Y. Lu, and T. Abdelzaher. Queuing model based network server performance control. RTSS, 2002.

[9] X. Liu, R. Zheng, J. Heo, Q. Wang, and L. Sha. Timing performance control in web server systems utilizing server internal state information. ICAS/ICNS, 2005.

[10] A. Fox, S. D. Gribble, Y. Chawathe, and E. A. Brewer. Adapting to network and client variation using infrastructural process proxies: lessons and perspectives. Personal Communications, IEEE. 1998.

[11] Y. Chen. Detecting web page structure for adaptive viewing on small form factor devices. WWW, 2003.

[12] H. Hoffmann, S. Sidiroglou, M. Carbin, S. Misailovic, A. Agarwal, and M. C. Rinard. Dynamic knobs for responsive power-aware computing. ASPLOS, 2011.

[13] W. Baek and T. M. Chilimbi. Green: A framework for supporting energy-conscious programming using controlled approximation. PLDI, 2010.

[14] T. F. Abdelzaher and N. Bhatti. Web content adaptation to improve server overload behavior. WWW, 1999.

[15] J. Yao, X. Liu, M. Yuan, and Z. Gu. Online adaptive utilization control for real-time embedded multiprocessor systems. CODES+ISSS, 2008.

[16] R. Reitano. Introduction to Quantitative Finance: A Math Tool Kit. 2010.

[17] I. Adan and J. Resing. Queueing Theory. 2001.

[18] R. Gullapalli, C. Muthusamy, and V. Babu. Control systems application in java based enterprise and cloud environments – a survey. Journal of ACSA, 2011.

[19] C. A. Yfoulis, and A. Gounaris. Honoring SLAs on Cloud Computing Services: A Control Perspective. ECC, 2009.

[20] X. Liu, J. Heo, L. Sha, and X. Zhu. Queueing-model-based adaptive control of multi-tiered web applications. IEEE Trans. on Network and Service Management, 2008.

[21] J. Hamilton. Blog article at http://perspectives.mvdirona.com/ 2009/10/31/thecostoflatency.aspx, 2009.

[22] W. Szpankowski. Bounds for queue lengths in a contention packet broadcast system. IEEE Trans. on Comm., 1986.

[23] H. Chen and P. Mohapatra, Session-based overload control in QoS-aware web servers. INFOCOM, 2002.

[24] L Cherkasova and P. Phaal, Session-based admission control: a mechanism for peak load management of commercial web sites. IEEE Trans. Comput., 2002.

[25] R Wang, Dara M. Kusic, N. Kandasamy, A distributed control framework for performance management of virtualized computing environments. ICAC, 2010.

[26] J. Leite, D. Kusic, D. Mosse, Stochastic approximation control of power and tardiness in a three-tier web-hosting cluster. ICAC, 2010.

[27] H. C. Lim, S. Babu, and J. S. Chase. Automated Control for Elastic Storage. ICAC, 2010.

On the Design of Decentralized Control Architectures for Workload Consolidation in Large-Scale Server Clusters

Rui Wang
ECE Department
Drexel University
Philadelphia, PA 19104, USA
rui.wang@drexel.edu

Nagarajan Kandasamy
ECE Department
Drexel University
Philadelphia, PA 19104, USA
kandasamy@drexel.edu

ABSTRACT

This paper develops a fully decentralized control architecture to address the workload consolidation problem in large-scale server clusters wherein the cluster's processing capacity is dynamically tuned to satisfy the service level agreements (SLAs) associated with the incoming workload while consolidating the workload onto the fewest number of servers. In a decentralized setting, this problem is decomposed into simpler subproblems, each of which is mapped to a server and solved by a controller assigned to that server. Though control loops on different servers run independently of each other, they are implicitly coupled via the shared high-level performance goal and interactions between controllers may result in undesired system behavior such as SLA violations and frequent switching of cores on and off. Using the proposed architecture as the reference, we analyze how the organization of individual controllers within the control structure affects its overall performance for large clusters of up to thousand servers. Our studies indicate that the control structure, when organized as a causal system in which a precedence relation exists among the individual controllers, achieves a high degree of SLA satisfaction (> 98%) while significantly reducing the corresponding switching cost.

Categories and Subject Descriptors

C.4 [**Performance of systems**]: Design studies, modeling techniques, fault tolerance

General Terms

Algorithms, Performance, Management, Reliability

Keywords

Workload consolidation, receding horizon control, decentralized control, team decision theory

1. INTRODUCTION

In the context of data center operations, virtualization technology enables *workload consolidation* wherein a single server plat-form can be shared among multiple operating systems and software applications using virtual machines (VMs). Resources such as CPU, memory, and disk space can be allocated to VMs as needed, based on the currently prevailing workload demand, rather than statically, based simply on the peak workload demand. During periods of light workload, data center operators can consolidate multiple workloads onto fewer servers to increase server utilization. Power consumption costs can then be decreased by switching off unneeded servers. Newer multi-core architectures such as Intel's Nehalem offer even more flexible power management options such as the ability to dynamically turn individual processor/cores within the package (as well as the entire package) on or off.

Routine system management tasks such as workload consolidation and power management can be automated by formulating them as online control problems in terms of performance metrics [6, 7]. Various control techniques have been used to solve the resulting problems, including classical proportional-integral-derivative control, multiple-input multiple-output control, and optimal control. In terms of implementation, a fully centralized controller, though offering the best performance, is impractical in large-scale systems. A hierarchical implementation improves scalability by imposing a decentralized control structure on the problem. For example, in a two-level hierarchical scheme, a supervisory controller directs high-level commands aimed at satisfying system-wide service level agreement (SLA) goals to a set of lower-level controllers. These commands act as operating constraints on each local controller which then tries to optimize the performance of the component (subsystem) under its control using a specific cost function while satisfying these constraints. Though hierarchical schemes improve scalability, the supervisor's design becomes increasingly complex and computationally expensive when it has to coordinate interactions between large numbers of low-level controllers.

For a large-scale system comprising hundreds of servers, a fully decentralized or distributed control scheme has the potential to be highly scalable. Problem permitting, the system-wide SLA goal is decomposed into a set of simpler subproblems and each subproblem is mapped to an underlying system component—say, a server in this case. Controllers, implemented within each component, optimize their respective subproblems in independent fashion while satisfying the requisite local constraints. Though they operate independently without the need for a centralized coordinator, coupling between the controllers arises from the shared performance objective (the common task) of satisfying the SLA goals set for the overall system. Compared to centralized and hierarchical schemes, the use of decentralized control for performance management is not as well studied in the literature. Our paper makes two contributions in this area: (1) design of a fully decentralized control structure to address the workload consolidation problem in a large-scale cluster;

(2) an analysis of how interactions between independent controllers affect overall system behavior.

The problem of interest is to dynamically tune the cluster's processing capacity to cover the incoming workload intensity at any given time by powering processor cores on/off as needed and consolidating the workload on the fewest number of servers (thereby managing power consumption as well). The SLA is to maintain the response times of the services hosted by the cluster under the set points. We develop the solution within a *receding horizon control (RHC)* framework in which the current control action is obtained by solving on-line, at each control instant, a finite horizon open-loop optimal control problem using the system's current state as the initial state. The first part of the optimal control sequence is then applied to the system and the procedure repeated for future control steps. In a decentralized setting, the centralized RHC problem is decomposed into simpler subproblems and controllers, implemented locally within each server, independently solve their respective subproblems such that performance goals for the overall system are satisfied. Each controller decides two distinct actions.

- A low-level control action that dynamically tunes the CPU share, representing the processing rate, provided to the VMs hosted on the server based on the local system state and workload intensity such that the SLA goals are guaranteed.

- Since the per-VM CPU share is constantly tuned, servers have spare CPU capacity available during periods of light workload. The controller, therefore, observes the cluster's aggregate processing capacity at the current time, predicts the incoming global workload, and implements a high-level switching policy to decide whether to turn the entire processor package on or off.

If the overall control structure behaves in a desired and meaningful way, then at any given time the aggregate processing capacity of the cluster will be tuned—due to individual controllers deciding the number of operational cores on their respective servers—to satisfy the SLA requirements of the incoming workload. This in turn will consolidate the workload on the fewest number of servers and increase server utilization.

Using the above-described decentralized RHC architecture as our reference, we analyze how interactions between the independently running control loops affect system behavior, especially as its size increases and more controllers are added to the mix. Recall that these control loops are coupled via the shared high-level cost function and so local decisions made by one controller, in terms of switching cores on/off, affect similar actions taken by other controllers in the system. This may induce undesired oscillations, in both time (frequent switching by a single controller) and in space (frequent switching activity affecting multiple controllers), when provisioning cores. So, the organization of individual controllers within the system and the underlying information structure play a decisive role in determining control performance. If at time instant k, each controller receives (or estimates) some information $z_i(k)$ and controls the decision variable $u_i(k)$, we analyze two organizational structures:

- *Static teams*: The information $z_i(k)$ is only the function of some random variable but is independent of what other members have done during that time instant. So, there is no explicit causal relation between the control and information of different members.

- *Dynamic teams*: The estimation of $z_i(k)$ and the control decision of a controller are dependent on the actions of the other members during the time instant k, implying that an ordered precedence (or causal) relationship exists among the team members.[1]

We investigate the control framework's behavior via detailed simulations for system sizes up to a thousand servers, in which servers host multiple online services and process a time-varying workload.[2] Performance is measured in terms of the percentage of requests meeting their SLA requirements, the number of operational cores, and the switching activity (how often are cores turned on or off). For the workload traces used in our studies, the proposed control architecture achieves a high degree of SLA satisfaction (> 95 %) under both static and dynamic teams of controllers, while keeping, on average, about 70% of the cores active over a ten hour period. Dynamic teams achieve a slightly higher degree of SLA satisfaction (> 98%) while reducing the corresponding switching activity by up to 58% when compared to static ones. We also show that the workload consolidation problem, as formulated in this paper, supports an information structure that enables the reduction of the dynamic-team problem to a static one: since the team agrees in advance on the specific control law used, each member can deduce the actions taken by other team members without explicit exchange of messages. Finally, the control architecture is scalable and allows for the dynamic addition and removal of servers during system operation while maintaining overall performance.

The paper is organized as follows. Section 2 describes the system model used in our simulation studies. Section 3 develops the decentralized RHC structure in a top-down fashion and Section 4 analyzes its performance. Section 5 discusses related work in the area of workload consolidation and power/performance management of virtualized systems and Section 6 concludes the paper.

2. THE SYSTEM MODEL

Figure 1 shows the system model assumed in this paper: a two-tier architecture offering multiple online services using front-end application servers and back-end databases. These services are enabled by *enterprise applications*, defined broadly as any software which simultaneously provides services to a large number of users over a computer network. For example, Figure 1 shows an application tier comprising three types of heterogeneous servers, each hosting multiple VMs dedicated to one of three services termed as Gold, Silver, and Bronze. VMs residing on different servers but supporting the same application form a *virtual computing cluster*. A Type 1 server has eight cores, offering a total CPU capacity of 18 GHz, while a Type 2 or Type 3 server has four cores, offering a CPU capacity of 9 GHz. We focus on workload consolidation within the application tier only, since in most cases the application layer requires many more CPUs than the database layer for each online service [1].

The system is subjected to a highly variable workload in which request arrivals change quite significantly within a short time period. The incoming workload to the three services, Λ, is dispatched as local workloads, λ, to VMs within the corresponding virtual computing cluster in weighted round-robin fashion with the weights being proportional to the VMs' CPU shares. Since a VM's CPU

---

[1]The terms, "static" and "dynamic" teams, were introduced in a paper on team decision theory by Ho and Chu [8].

[2]To ensure that the simulated system's behavior closely mimics that of a real cluster, the dynamical models for the enterprise applications used in the simulations (Trade6, RUBBoS and RUBiS) are obtained by profiling their behavior on actual server hardware, and these models are subjected to realistic workload traces that exhibit significant variability and burstiness in request arrival rates.

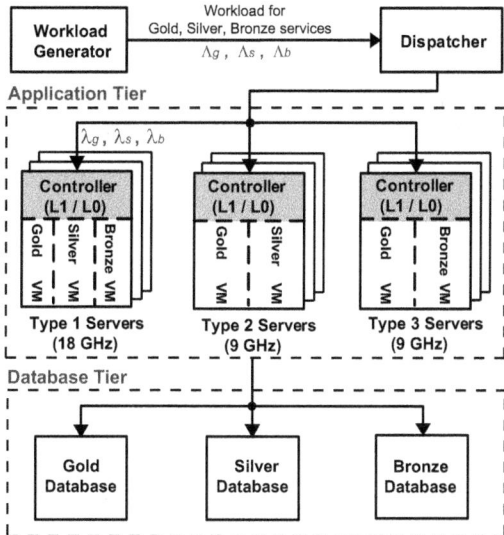

Figure 1: The system architecture hosting the online services. Local controllers on each server decide both the CPU share to assign to VMs under their control within the application tier as well as the number of processing cores to operate. Here, Λ is the incoming workload to the cluster and λ is the workload dispatched to an individual server. The subscripts g, s, and b, denote the Gold, Silver, and Bronze services, respectively.

share reflects the processing capacity, the larger the CPU share, the more requests that VM will receive. Given a certain CPU share, the response time achieved by a VM for an incoming request arrival rate λ can be estimated using basic results from queuing theory [10]. Assuming that requests arrive as per a Poisson process in which the interarrival times are iid exponential random variables with mean $1/\lambda$ and that μ is the average rate at which the VM can process requests such that the service times are iid exponential random variables with mean $1/\mu$, then when $\lambda < \mu$, the system is stable and the average time t spent by requests within the VM is

$$t = \frac{1}{\mu - \lambda}. \qquad (1)$$

When $\lambda > \mu$, the system is unstable and the number of queued requests will grow steadily without bound; these requests are considered as having timed out. Moreover, as (1) shows, there is a nonlinear relationship between the arrival and processing rates, and the achieved response time: given a constant λ, the same amount of increase (or decrease) in μ could cause a small decrease (or a dramatic increase) in t. This nonlinearity poses a challenge when allocating CPU shares to guarantee the desired response times.

Recent processor architectures such as the Intel's Nehalem support an additional power management state—the so called C6 state—that allows the operating system to idle any core in the package such that the core consumes approximately zero Watts. Furthermore, if all cores are placed in the C6 state, the package itself can be idled (the PC6 state), saving additional power. In our system model, controllers manage the overall power consumed by the cluster during each time step k by making decisions local to their servers: (1) if the server is deemed unnecessary, place the entire processor package in an idle state, and the server is denoted as *idle*; or (2) if the server is needed to process the incoming workload, minimize the CPU capacity offered to its VMs by idling unneeded cores, and the server is denoted as *active*. Though the C6 and PC6 states allow for fine-grain power management, idling cores incurs some switching cost. To enter the C6 state, for example, the core caches must

be flushed, the pipeline state saved to static RAM, the core clocks turned off, and the gate transistors turned on, and the entire process must be reversed to turn the core back on. This switching activity increases power consumption and so it must be minimized to achieve best overall system performance.

Returning to Figure 1, each controller is dedicated to manage one physical application server. A dispatcher periodically broadcasts to the controllers the system's global information in terms of the global request rate Λ and the total number of active servers. A controller then decides: (1) the number of operational cores on its server and (2) the CPU share (in MHz) to provide to local VMs executing on these cores, thereby affecting the parameter μ in (1), such that the system-wide SLAs are met. The CPU share decisions are also transferred to the dispatcher to update the weights in the round-robin dispatching scheme. Note that to tune the CPU share in a meaningful fashion, the controller requires dynamical models that estimate the processing rates achieved by the applications (hosted within the VM) as a function of CPU share. Section 4 details the profiling experiments used to obtain the models for the enterprise applications used in our study.

3. CONTROL ARCHITECTURE

The system-wide control problem of meeting SLAs of the services while consolidating them on the fewest number of operating servers is decomposed into multiple of simpler subproblems and each one is assigned to a server (controller). Given multiple subsystems whose local cost functions are quadratic and whose dynamics and operating constraints are uncoupled, having each controller independently optimize its local cost function can achieve the global optimal, that is the summation of the local costs recovers the centralized cost [4, 5]. A controller has two control levels termed L1 and L0, each with the following responsibilities:

L1 level: During each time step, the controller obtains information regarding the global workload and the number of active servers in the cluster, and decides if the server is needed to handle the estimated workload. If not, the entire processor package is placed in the idle state, reducing the number of active cores in the cluster.

L0 level: If the high-level switching decision is to keep the server active, this level optimizes the per-VM CPU shares to accommodate the local workload λ dispatched to the server while idling unused cores. This guarantees SLA requirements while minimizing the corresponding use of CPU capacity which also contributes to power savings.

Since the L0 levels dynamically tune the CPU share of VMs with respect to the time-varying workload, servers have spare processing capacity available during periods of light load. Therefore, the L1 levels are able to make switching decisions aimed at reducing power consumption by idling servers not needed and consolidating the workload on to fewer servers. The control laws governing the L1 level are simplified to provide high-level solutions that the lower control level can refine further. Specifically, the L1 level estimates the global workload over a prediction horizon and decides only to operate/idle the server such that the cluster possesses enough aggregate processing capacity to satisfy the workload, leaving the assignment of CPU shares to the L0 level if the server is active.

The rest of this section describes how control laws for the L1 and L0 levels are synthesized.

3.1 Estimating the Workload

The control algorithms are developed within the RHC framework where we solve a multi-objective optimization problem that maximizes the performance goal over a given time horizon, and then periodically roll this horizon forward [11]. This technique uses a dynamical model to predict the system's behavior over the time horizon, requiring that the environment variables—inputs to the model—be predicted as well. We use Holt's linear exponential smoothing (LES) filter at both the L1 and L0 levels to predict the environment variables of interest for each control step: the global request rate Λ and local request rate λ [12]. As an example, during time step k, the estimated value of λ for a one-step prediction horizon is obtained as follows.

$$\tilde{\lambda}(k) = \bar{\lambda}(k) + b(k), \tag{2}$$

$$\bar{\lambda}(k) = \alpha \cdot \lambda(k)$$
$$+ (1 - \alpha) \cdot [\bar{\lambda}(k-1) + b(k-1)], \text{ and} \tag{3}$$

$$b(k) = \beta \cdot [\bar{\lambda}(k) - \bar{\lambda}(k-1)]$$
$$+ (1 - \beta) \cdot b(k-1). \tag{4}$$

Here, α and β are smoothing constants, $\bar{\lambda}(k)$ denotes the estimate up to time step k, and $b(k)$ captures the linear trend present in the time series. The estimation error recorded during time step k is

$$e(k) = \lambda(k) - \tilde{\lambda}(k-1), \tag{5}$$

and the variance $\sigma(k)$ is dynamically calculated based on past mismatches between the actual and observed values. To ensure that the prediction $\hat{\lambda}(k)$ adequately covers any variability in the actual value $\lambda(k)$ with high probability, we finally compute it as

$$\hat{\lambda}(k) = \tilde{\lambda}(k) + \gamma \cdot \sigma(k). \tag{6}$$

Since the forecasting errors $e(\cdot)$ obey a normal distribution, if γ is set to 2 or 3, $\hat{\lambda}(k)$ would statistically cover variations in the actual value 97.8% or 99.9% of the time, respectively.

3.2 Switching Scheme at the L1 Level

At the beginning of control step k, irrespective of the server state, the L1 level decides whether the server should be active or idle during this step. Let

$$\mu = m \cdot c, \tag{7}$$

where c is a VM's CPU share and m is the mapping factor which maps c to the corresponding processing rate μ for the supported service. (The profiling experiments used to obtain the m are described in Section 4.) Plugging (7) into (1), we get

$$\frac{1}{m \cdot c - \lambda} = t. \tag{8}$$

As per the performance requirement, a single VM aims to offer enough CPU share $c(k)$, based on the predicted (local) request arrival rate $\hat{\lambda}(k)$ to guarantee that the response time t satisfies the SLA set point $\bar{t}$, as:

$$\frac{1}{m \cdot c(k) - \hat{\lambda}(k)} \leq \bar{t}. \tag{9}$$

That is,

$$m \cdot c(k) \geq \hat{\lambda}(k) + \frac{1}{\bar{t}}. \tag{10}$$

So, from the local controller's perspective, all VMs belonging to one virtual computing cluster (i.e., residing in different servers but supporting one service) should satisfy the sum of (10) as:

$$m \sum c(k) \geq \sum \hat{\lambda}(k) + \sum \frac{1}{\bar{t}}. \tag{11}$$

Figure 2 shows the three types of heterogeneous servers assumed in our setup, with the subscripts $i = \{1, 2, 3\}$ denoting the specific

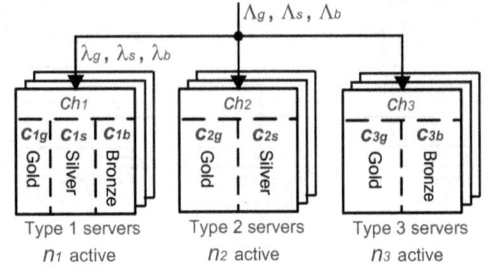

Figure 2: The types of heterogeneous servers assumed in our setup, based on their CPU capacities and services supported.

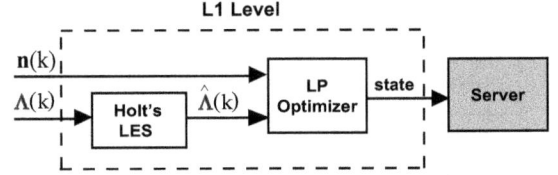

Figure 3: Schematic of the L1 control level that decides if a server should be active or idled.

server type, and from each controller's viewpoint, $n_i(k)$ represents the current number of active servers belonging to type i (excluding the local server under its control). Figure 3 summarizes the L1 control level. Once the global arrival rate, $\hat{\Lambda}(k)$, is predicted by the LES filter, the controller determines whether the number of active servers $\mathbf{n}(k)$ within all three types offer enough processing capacity by seeking a solution to the following linear programming (LP) optimization problem in terms of $c_{ij}(k)$:[3]

$$\min_{c_{ij}(k)} 0 \tag{12}$$

subject to

$$\begin{cases} c_{lij} \leq c_{ij}(k) \leq c_{uij} \\ \sum_j c_{ij}(k) \leq c_{hi} \\ m_j \sum_i [n_i(k) \cdot c_{ij}(k)] \geq \hat{\Lambda}_j(k) + \frac{\sum_i n_i(k)}{\bar{t}_j} \end{cases} \tag{13}$$

In (12) the objective function is set to 0, meaning our only concern lies in satisfying the constraints listed in (13). Here, c_{ig}, c_{is}, and c_{ib} denote feasible solutions for CPU shares of the Gold, Silver, and Bronze VMs residing in type i servers (not necessarily the optimal solutions which will be computed by the lower control level); c_{lij} and c_{uij} represent lower and upper bounds on each VM's share; c_{hi} represents the maximum CPU capacity offered by a type i server; and m_j represents the mapping factor for the jth service. The final constraint in (13) implies that the aggregate capacity offered by the active servers must satisfy the desired response time $\bar{t}_i$.

If the above LP problem has at least one feasible solution indicating the current number of active servers $\mathbf{n}(k)$ is sufficient, this local server is idled until the beginning of next time step (meaning all its cores are idled during time step k). However, if no solution is found, meaning the number of servers is insufficient, the server is placed in an active state and the L0 level is executed.

---

[3]The subscript $j = \{g, s, b\}$ represents the Gold, Silver and Bronze services. So, c_{ij} denotes the CPU share of the VM residing within a sever of type i and hosting application j.

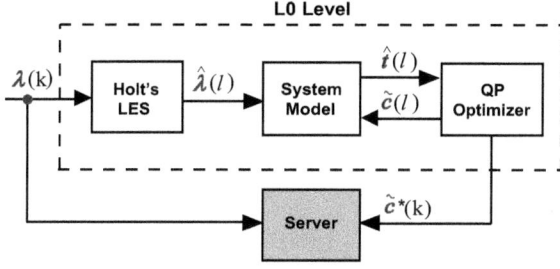

Figure 4: Schematic of the L0 control level that decides the CPU share to provide to VMs under its control.

3.3 Resource Allocation at the L0 Level

If the L1 level decides that the server should be active during step k, the L0 level is called immediately to optimize the per-VM CPU share, so that the server can meet the desired response times $\bar{\mathbf{t}}$ with respect to the local request arrival rate $\lambda(k)$ while using as little CPU $\mathbf{c}(k)$ as possible. It then activates the requisite number of cores and idles the rest until the beginning of next step $k + 1$.

Figure 4 shows the RHC scheme where at the start of step k, the local request arrival rate λ is estimated as $\hat{\lambda}$ over a time horizon of h steps. Based on $\hat{\lambda}$ and the system model captured by (1), a quadratic programming (QP) optimizer finds an optimal sequence of control actions $\{\tilde{\mathbf{c}}(l)|l \in [k, k+h-1]\}$ representing CPU shares to VMs within the horizon. Then, only the first control action in the chosen sequence, $\tilde{\mathbf{c}}^*(k)$, is applied to the server and the rest are discarded. The process is repeated at the start of step $k + 1$ when new information becomes available. The RHC scheme within the L0 level uses a one-step prediction horizon.

Take a server supporting all three services as an example. The L0 goal is specified in terms of response times to be achieved while simultaneously reducing the CPU share of VMs. So, the objective function poses this problem as one of maintaining both vectors $\mathbf{t}(k)$ and $\mathbf{c}(k)$ near their set points $\bar{\mathbf{t}}$ and $\bar{\mathbf{c}}$ during the control step k as

$$\min_{\mathbf{t}(k),\mathbf{c}(k)} \quad [\frac{1}{\mathbf{t}(k)} - \frac{1}{\bar{\mathbf{t}}}]^T \cdot \mathbf{P} \cdot [\frac{1}{\mathbf{t}(k)} - \frac{1}{\bar{\mathbf{t}}}]$$
$$+ [\mathbf{c}(k) - \bar{\mathbf{c}}]^T \cdot \mathbf{Q} \cdot [\mathbf{c}(k) - \bar{\mathbf{c}}], \quad (14)$$

where $\mathbf{P} = p \cdot \text{diag}(p_g, p_s, p_b)$ and $\mathbf{Q} = q \cdot \mathbf{I}_3$; p and q are weights reflecting the tradeoff between response time and CPU share; and p_g, p_s, and p_b are weights reflecting the relative priorities among the Gold, Silver, and Bronze services, respectively. We define

$$\mathbf{R} = \hat{\lambda}(k) + \frac{1}{\mathbf{t}}, \quad (15)$$

and by plugging (8) and (15) into (14) we get a standard QP problem in terms of the control input vector $\mathbf{c}(k)$ as

$$\min_{\mathbf{c}(k)} \quad \mathbf{c}(k)^T \cdot (\mathbf{m}^T \cdot \mathbf{P} \cdot \mathbf{m} + \mathbf{Q}) \cdot \mathbf{c}(k)$$
$$- 2(\mathbf{R}^T \cdot \mathbf{P} \cdot \mathbf{m} + \bar{\mathbf{c}}^T \cdot \mathbf{Q}) \cdot \mathbf{c}(k)$$
$$+ \mathbf{R}^T \cdot \mathbf{P} \cdot \mathbf{R} + \bar{\mathbf{c}}^T \cdot \mathbf{Q} \cdot \bar{\mathbf{c}}. \quad (16)$$

The L0 level must also consider the upper and lower bound, $\mathbf{c}_l$ and $\mathbf{c}_u$, respectively, on the per-VM CPU share, and the overall CPU share provided to VMs within a server must not exceed the maximum available CPU capacity c_h. So, (16) is subject to the following constraints:

$$\begin{cases} \mathbf{c}_l \leq \mathbf{c}(k) \leq \mathbf{c}_u \\ \Sigma \mathbf{c}(k) \leq c_h. \end{cases} \quad (17)$$

Solving (16) and (17), the controller obtains the optimal control vector $\tilde{\mathbf{c}}^*(k)$ and applies it to the VMs under its control. This information is communicated to the dispatcher which then distributes incoming requests to VMs based on the assigned CPU shares.

3.4 The Decentralized Control Structures

Though the L1 and L0 loops within individual controllers run independently of each other, these control loops are implicitly coupled via the shared task of consolidating the incoming workload while meeting SLA goals. So, local decisions made by a controller such as being active or idle affect decisions made by other controllers in the system. These interactions may induce undesired behavior such as frequent switching of cores and processor packages. So, the organization of individual controllers and the underlying information structure greatly influence the performance of the control structure. This paper studies two such organizational structures: static teams and dynamic teams of controllers.

Static Teams: Controllers are logically grouped into N teams as shown in Figure 5(a) where each team comprises a mix of server types. Controllers use the same control period T_s. Members of the same team execute simultaneously, while members belonging to two immediate teams have their starting times staggered by $dt = T_s/N$. At the start of a team's control step k, the same global information in terms of the observed global request rate $\mathbf{\Lambda}(k)$ and the number of active servers in the whole cluster $\mathbf{n}(k)$ is broadcast—in this example, by the dispatcher—to all members in this team. Each member i also observes its local request rate $\lambda_i(k)$ and forms the information set $z_i(k) = \{\mathbf{\Lambda}(k), \mathbf{n}(k), \lambda_i(k)\}$ needed to make its control decision $u_i(k)$, where $u_i(k)$ indicates being active or idle (as in L1) and if active, what is the optimal CPU share $\tilde{\mathbf{c}}^*(k)$ to the local VMs (as in L0). The members execute simultaneously and independently, and their decisions are not causally related because when each member starts its L1 loop, $\mathbf{n}(k)$ is not updated to consider the decisions made by other members.

Dynamic Teams: Controller i's observation $z_i(k)$ and its decision $u_i(k)$ during control step k incorporate the decisions of other team members during the same control step—which does not require member i to wait for other members to transmit their decisions to it prior to deciding $u_i(k)$. Consider Figure 5(b) in which dashed arrows show the ordered precedence (causal) relationship that we impose on controllers within a team. Since each member knows its position within the precedence graph and since the team can agree in advance on the control law used by each member at both the L1 and L0 levels, the structure has the property that member i can always deduce the decisions of its predecessors. As a specific example, consider decisions taken by member 3 within team 2. This member has access to two pieces of information as it relates to the overall team structure: the number of active servers in other teams (excluding its own) which is broadcast by the dispatcher, and the number of predecessors (no matter if they are active or idle) within its team as well as the server types of these predecessors. So, it can independently compute $\mathbf{n_3}(k)$ as simply a sum of the above information items and execute its L1 loop to check if $\mathbf{n_3}(k)$ servers can offer enough CPU capacity to accommodate the estimated workload, assuming that members 1 and 2 are both active (because they would have decided to be active if needed). If $\mathbf{n_3}(k)$ is sufficient, member 3 stays idle during step k; and if not, it stays active. Similarly, member 4 simultaneously decides its active/idle state assuming that members 1, 2, and 3 are active, and so on.

The above discussion implies that even when organized as dynamic teams, controllers can be developed as *non-communicating agents* wherein the ith controller within a team independently obtains $z_i(k) = \{\mathbf{\Lambda}(k), \mathbf{n_i}(k), \lambda_i(k)\}$, uses the causal relation among

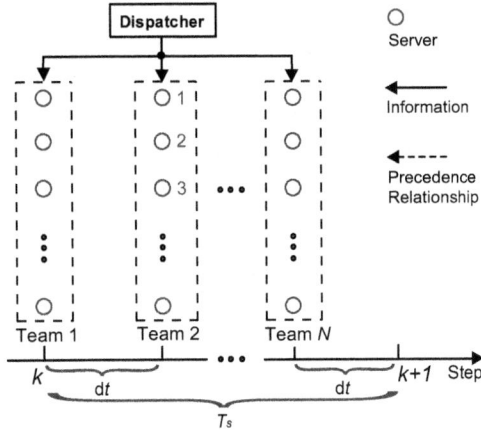

(a) Static teams of controllers.

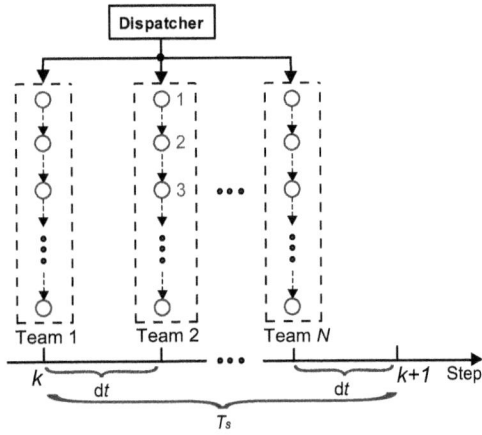

(b) Dynamic teams of controllers.

Figure 5: Two possible organizational structures for decentralized control. In static teams of controllers, the information observed or estimated by each controller at time k is independent of what other team members have done during that time step. In dynamic teams, the observations and control decisions of a controller during time step k incorporate the actions of other controllers during that time step.

team members to deduce the actions taken by its predecessors, and uses this information to decide $u_i(k)$. This scheme minimizes the messaging overhead incurred by the control structure.

4. PERFORMANCE ANALYSIS

Since our studies target large cluster sizes of up to thousand servers, the performance of the control structure is evaluated via simulations. However, the dynamical models for the software applications used in the simulations are generated by profiling their behavior on actual server hardware, ensuring that the simulated system's behavior closely mimics that of a real cluster. The control performance is measured in terms of SLA satisfaction, average number of operational cores, and switching activity.

4.1 System Parameters

The control period T_s of each controller is set to two minutes and the cluster is divided into 24 teams, each comprising multiple heterogeneous servers, so that the stagger time dt between two consecutive teams is five seconds for asynchronous operation. When predicting the incoming arrival rate $\hat{\Lambda}$, controllers overestimate the

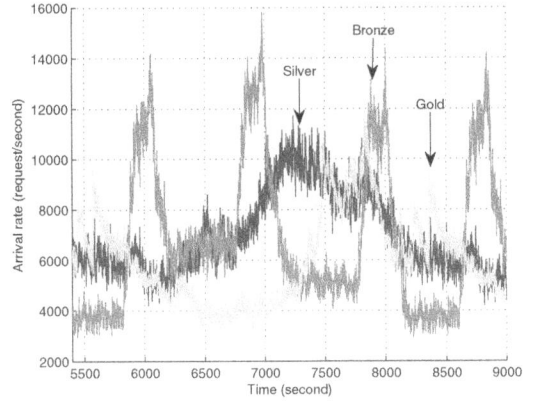

Figure 6: A portion of the workload provided to the Gold, Silver, and Bronze services.

Table 1: The arrival rates accommodated by VMs for each of the three services as function of CPU share.

App	1.5 GHz	2 GHz	3 GHz	4 GHz	5 GHz
Trade6	30 req/s	40 req/s	65 req/s	85 req/s	115 req/s
RUBBoS	20 req/s	25 req/s	45 req/s	65 req/s	90 req/s
RUBiS	20 req/s	25 req/s	40 req/s	55 req/s	65 req/s

value by 2σ so that the predictions will cover any variability in the actual arrival rate 97.8% of the time. The overestimation also guarantees that the achieved response time $\mathbf{t}$ will be maintained lower than the set point $\bar{t}$ most of the time, which is just what the SLA requires. In the objective function described in (14), the weights p and q are set to 100 and 1 respectively, thereby prioritizing response times over assigning lower CPU shares; and the weights p_g, p_s, and p_b are set to 1, equally prioritizing all three services. Our simulations also take into account the dead time involved in changing CPU shares.[4]

Figure 6 shows a portion of a 10-hour long workload trace, synthesized such that request rates vary significantly within short time periods.[5] Also, for a given cluster size, the peak workload that can be handled is determined via an appropriate capacity planning process (which is not shown in the paper due to space limitations).

4.2 Building the Application Models

We assume that the cluster hosts three online services, enabled by corresponding enterprise applications hosted within VMs. In our study, the Gold service is enabled by Trade6, a stock-trading benchmark which allows users to browse, buy, and sell stocks; the Silver service is enabled by RUBBoS, a bulletin board application that allows users to browse stories and post comments, and the Bronze service is enabled by RUBiS, an auction site that allows users to browse for items, bid, and post comments. Dynamical models corresponding to application behavior, in terms of the response times achieved by a VM as a function of CPU share, arrival rate, and workload mix, are obtained by profiling these application on an actual server platform. Virtualization of the server is enabled by VMware's ESX Server running a Linux RedHat kernel.

Table 1 summarizes the arrival rates accommodated by a VM

---

[4]If VMWare's virtualization technology is used, measurements indicate it takes about three seconds after issuing the command to actually affect the change in CPU share.

[5]The degree of SLA satisfaction remained qualitatively similar for simulations performed using other workload traces; the power savings achieved, of course, depends on the intensity of the specific workload used.

Table 2: Performance of static teams in terms of SLA satisfactions, number of active cores, and switching activity per server.

Sim #	Cluster Size (Type 1/2/3 Servers)	Servers per Team	Controller Exe Time (second)			SLA Satisfaction (%)			♯ of Cores Active (%)	Switches per Server
			Compute	Implement	Total	Gold	Silver	Bronze		
1	30 (15/8/7)	1 or 2				97.19	97.52	96.74	62.87	51.10
2	100 (50/25/25)	4 or 5	0.016	3.0	3.016	97.33	96.25	96.01	65.73	86.13
3	500 (250/125/125)	20 or 25				96.70	96.06	97.71	68.04	103.28
4	1000 (500/250/250)	40 or 50				96.18	95.23	97.58	68.11	105.40

for each of the Gold, Silver, and Bronze services as a function of CPU share. We explain the profiling method that generated this information using an example. Consider the case where the VM hosting Trade6 is provided a fixed CPU share of 3 GHz. Requests are then sent to the VM with an increasing arrival rate to generate the corresponding response times. As long as the arrival rate is below 65 req/s, we observe that the VM achieves a relatively steady response time (below 200 ms). However, if the arrival rate exceeds 65 req/s, the response time increases dramatically from around 200 ms to thousands of ms. This jump indicates an unstable system in which the arrival rate has exceeded the VM's processing rate. So, we conclude that a 3 GHz VM can accommodate approximately 65 req/s before queuing instability occurs. If the VM's CPU share is further constrained, say to 2 GHz, the maximum arrival rate it can handle is constrained to about 40 req/s.

From Table 1, the mapping factors m_g, m_s, m_b that relate a VM's CPU share to a corresponding processing rate (see (7)) are determined as 22.5, 17.9, and 13.2, respectively, for the three services. The SLAs for the services, $\bar{t}_g$, $\bar{t}_s$, and $\bar{t}_b$ are set as 200 ms, 300 ms, and 400 ms, respectively, corresponding to the stable response times achieved by the VMs under test.

4.3 Static Teams of Controllers

Table 2 summarizes the system performance when controllers are organized as static teams. For example, Simulation #2 assumes a cluster of 100 servers, 50 servers of Type 1, and 25 servers each of Types 2 and 3. Servers are organized into 24 teams, each with four or five heterogeneous servers. Each local controller executes independently, taking 0.016 seconds to run the L1 and L0 algorithms. Taking also the dead time of 3 seconds into account the total execution time is 3.016 second, an overhead of 2.51% with respect to the two-minute control period. The degree of SLA satisfaction is high (> 96%); on average, 65% of the total number of cores are active; and a server is switched between active and idle states an average of 86 times during a simulation run of ten hours.

We also test cluster sizes of 30, 500, and 1000 servers by amplifying the workload magnitude appropriately. As shown in Table 2, SLA satisfaction is below the expected value of 97.8% in all cases and individual servers are switched on/off more often as the system grows.[6] When multiple servers in a static team execute simultaneously and independently of each other, they observe the same external environment and system state, and make the same switching decisions. For example, suppose the global request rate for a service increases at some time step. Each member will observe this happening at exactly the same time and since controllers do not communicate with each other, each will activate cores to consume the increased workload. Since there is now excess capacity in the system, the SLA satisfaction will improve (> 97.8%). However, since all members have made the same decision, the cluster's ca-

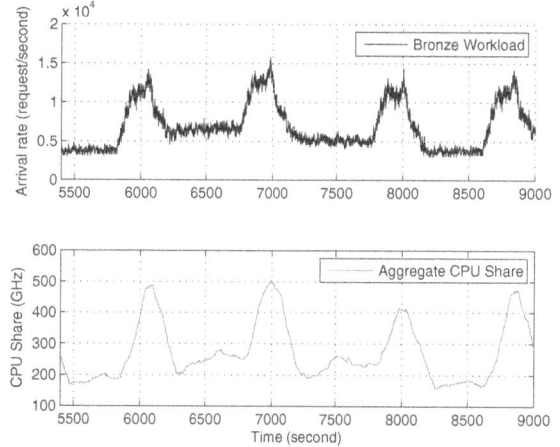

Figure 7: The global Bronze workload and the corresponding aggregate CPU share provided to the Bronze virtual computing cluster during a one-hour period.

pacity may be a lot higher than necessary and during the next time step, the members will compensate for this situation by switching off cores, and the cycle may repeat itself. If on the other hand, team members estimate that the global request rate will drop and that their cores are not needed, then a whole set of cores may be idled simultaneously, causing a large drop in cluster capacity and resulting in a corresponding drop in SLA satisfaction (<97.8 %).

4.4 Dynamic Teams of Controllers

Organizing controllers into static teams has some shortcomings: reduced SLA satisfaction and increased switching activity. We hope to improve system performance by organizing controllers as dynamic teams. Assuming a cluster size of 100 servers, Figure 7 shows the performance of the Bronze virtual cluster over a one-hour period of a simulation run in terms of the aggregate CPU share provided to the Bronze workload. Though the workload intensity is very bursty, the CPU capacity covers this variability very well for the following reason. Since the starting times are staggered as per Figure 5, a team executes every $dt = 5$ seconds and so the control structure can respond quickly even to workload variations that occur over very short time periods. (The same concept applies to static teams as well.)

Compared to their static counterparts, dynamic teams achieve a higher degree of SLA satisfaction (>97.65%) while reducing the corresponding switching activity, by up to 58% for large clusters, as shown in Table 3. Since the observation and control decision made by member i consider actions taken by other members during the same time step, from this member's perspective, if it deduces that the predecessors will switch on enough cores to cover the incoming workload, then i does not need to switch on the package. This reduces switching activity significantly and since the cluster capacity does not fluctuate as much, SLAs are maintained at a high level.

---

[6]Since we overestimate the predicted arrival rate to cover any variability in the actual arrival rate 97.8% of the time, it is reasonable to expect a properly organized control structure to satisfy the SLA requirements of at least 97.8% of the incoming requests.

Table 3: Performance of dynamic teams in terms of SLA satisfactions, number of active cores, and switching activity per server.

Sim ♯	Cluster Size	Servers per Team	Controller Exe Time (second)			SLA Satisfaction (%)			♯ of Cores Active (%)	Switches per Server
			Compute	Implement	Total	Gold	Silver	Bronze		
5	30	1 or 2				98.22	98.98	99.12	63.50	44.27
6	100	4 or 5	0.016	3.0	3.016	98.64	99.09	98.25	61.74	43.90
7	500	20 or 25				98.73	98.90	97.65	61.98	43.71
8	1000	40 or 50				98.72	98.85	97.68	61.97	43.85

Table 4: Performance of a centralized RHC scheme.

Sim ♯	Cluster Size	Controller Exe Time (second)			SLA Satisfaction (%)			♯ of Cores Active (%)	Switches per Server
		Compute	Implement	Total	Gold	Silver	Bronze		
9	30	0.706	3.0	3.706	97.04	99.24	99.71	60.77	47.67
10	100	6.294	3.0	9.294	96.02	97.70	96.59	58.92	43.48
11	500	24.365	3.0	27.365	93.71	94.13	93.55	57.54	39.66
12	1000	64.480	3.0	67.480	87.57	86.23	88.71	57.42	34.31

Table 5: Fault tolerance capabilities of the distributed control scheme.

Sim ♯	Cluster Size	♯ of Faults	SLA Satisfaction (%)			♯ of Cores Active (%)	Switches per Server
			Gold	Silver	Bronze		
6	100	0	98.64	99.09	98.25	61.74	43.90
13	100	3	98.63	99.08	98.64	61.78	43.83
14	100	10	98.36	99.07	98.15	62.06	43.90

We now compare the performance of the dynamic distributed architecture with a centralized RHC scheme (whose synthesis is shown in the Appendix) that uses the same control parameters detailed in Section 4.1. The centralized controller has an advantage is that it has access to all the system information and is more likely to make an optimal decision. A major disadvantage, however, is that unlike distributed control in which multiple controllers are staggered to execute at different times so that workload variations can be observed and handled immediately, the centralized controller only executes once every two minutes, reacting slowly to bursty workload. One possible solution is to reduce the control period, but it cannot be too short since it is desirable that the controller's execution time consume a very small percentage of the control period. Also, as the system grows, the time needed to obtain an optimal solution increases exponentially, as shown in Table 4, and when the decision is finally made after this time (for example, 64.48 seconds for a 1000-server cluster), the "optimal" solution is outdated and is no longer optimal. For a small system comprising 30 servers, the centralized scheme offers comparable performance to distributed ones. However, as system size increases, due to the increased computation time the outdated solution does not match the dynamically changing workload and the SLA drops to around 87% for a system with 1000 servers. The centralized scheme consistently uses fewer cores than the distributed one since it has access to all the system information and therefore can better allocate CPU resources.

Finally, the distributed control architecture is quite flexible in that it can easily accommodate the addition or removal of servers during system operation without any change to the architecture itself. From a local controller's viewpoint, there is no difference between an idle server, one removed by the operator, or one that has crashed, since the only information needed for the controller to make its decision is the global workload and the total number of active servers of each type. Likewise, adding a new server or integrating a previously failed one into the cluster has the same effect as activating a previously idle server. In Simulation #13 shown in Table 5, $Host_{21}$ crashes 1.5 hours into the simulation run and recovers after six hours; $Host_{44}$ crashes three hours into the run and

never recovers; and $Host_{70}$ is removed from the system during hour five and replaced with a new server at hour seven. Simulation #14 tests an even worse situation where 10 of the 100 servers crash at various time steps with 3 of them never recovering. By comparing the data to Simulation #6, a fault-free run of the system, we can see the performance remains statistically unaffected, confirming that the control scheme tolerates these failures seamlessly.

4.5 Sensitivity Analysis

Table 6 discuss the effects of tuning the following key control parameters on performance assuming dynamic teams of controllers:
(1) The *factor* γ. This factor can be tuned in (6) to overestimate the predicted values for the incoming workload. For instance, if $\gamma = 3$, the predicted arrival rate $\hat{\lambda}$ would statistically cover variability in the actual rate λ with 99.9% confidence; the L1 level becomes more conservative when idling servers to save power and the L0 level becomes more generous when assigning per-VM CPU shares. When compared to Simulation #6 in which $\gamma = 2$, Simulation #15 confirms that increasing γ increases the degree of SLA satisfactions (e.g., 100% for the Bronze service) at the expense of keeping more cores active, from 61.74% to 72.34%.

(2) The *weighting factors*. The factors in (14) offer an effective way to balance the achieved response times and corresponding power consumption by tuning factors p and q, as well as to prioritize the various services by tuning p_g, p_s, and p_b. For example, in Simulation #16, the Gold and Silver workload intensities are amplified to 1.5 times that of the original intensities. As a result, the cluster may not possess enough CPU capacity to satisfy all three services during the period of heavy load and the SLA satisfaction drops across the board (92.29% for Gold, 89.09% for Silver, and 97.62% for Bronze). In Simulation #17, p_g, p_s, and p_b are set to 10, 5, 1, respectively, prioritizing the Gold service much more than Bronze in case of insufficient CPU capacity. As expected, the SLA satisfaction of the Gold service jumps to 98.04%, while that of the Bronze drops to 88.87%.

In addition to the above knobs, other parameters can be tuned to affect system performance as well, such as the control period

Table 6: The effect of tuning key control parameters on overall system performance.

Sim ♯	Cluster Size	factor γ	Gold/Silver/Bronze Workload Amplifier	factors $p_g/p_s/p_b$	SLA Satisfaction (%) Gold	Silver	Bronze	♯ of Cores Active (%)	Switches per Server
6	100	2	1/1/1	1/1/1	98.64	99.09	98.25	61.74	43.90
15	100	3	1/1/1	1/1/1	99.91	100.00	100.00	72.34	40.43
16	100	2	1.5/1.5/1	1/1/1	92.29	89.09	97.62	85.05	27.59
17	100	2	1.5/1.5/1	10/5/1	98.04	94.99	88.87	84.83	27.59

Table 7: Execution time overhead incurred by the controller as a function of the number of supported services and server types.

Test ♯	♯ of Services	Server Types	♯ of Servers in Each Type	Computing Time (second) L1	L0	Total
1	3	3	14/5/5	0.0106	0.0053	0.0159
2	5	5	100/.../100	0.0151	0.0059	0.0210
3	10	10	100/.../100	0.0183	0.0093	0.0276

and the stagger time between teams of controllers. With convenient tuning options available, the system operator is free to choose whatever is best for the operational goals.

4.6 Computational Complexity

Our design reduces the computational overhead incurred by the controller by having the L1 level make only switching decisions, and as per (12) and (13), the running time of L1 algorithm depends only on the number of services supported on the system and the types of servers in the cluster. The L0 level is only responsible for local CPU-share allocation and as per (16) and (17), its running time is determined only by the number of services supported on the local server. Table 7 shows some representative results. Test #3 assumes a large-scale cluster supporting ten different services using ten server types; the total execution time incurred by each controller is just 0.0276 seconds, taking 0.023% of the two-minute control period. These results validate the excellent scalability of the distributed control scheme.

5. RELATED WORK

This section places our work within the larger context of related research into power/performance management of server clusters. This paper extends the current state of the art is this area in the following aspects. First, we describe the design of a fully distributed control structure without a centralized coordinator to address the workload consolidation problem. Then we study how interactions between independent controllers as well as specific controller organizations within this control structure affect system behavior.

A number of centralized control architectures have been proposed to tackle the power/performance management problem in server clusters. For example, Kusic et al. [9] propose a two-level lookahead controller to manage a virtualized cluster by dynamically provisioning VM and CPU resources. Wang et al. [18] design a centralized controller to reduce the power consumed by a virtualized server while achieving the specified SLA. This controller is only able to manage VMs residing within a single server. Meng et al. [13] propose a provisioning method to consolidate multiple VMs as per their cumulative capacity needs, so that resource utilization can be improved while guaranteeing SLAs. This method focuses on relatively high-level resource provisioning over a long timescale (the timescale of interest is in hours), whereas our work considers resource allocation in which the fine tuning happens over a much shorter time period in the order of few seconds. A common problem faced by centralized control architectures is their limited scalability; as the number of applications/VMs/servers in the sys-

tem grows, the complexity of the control problem increases exponentially, leading to very long controller execution times and making centralized designs intractable.

Recently, hierarchical control architectures have been proposed to manage large-scale computing systems. The authors of [17] present a three-level control structure for power management of data centers. However, as its goal is to drive the power consumption to a desired set point, this architecture can only be applied to applications which allow for degraded performance. The authors also do not directly address the workload consolidation problem in that under utilized servers are not turned off to save power. By contrast, our structure offers tuning knobs to affect a tradeoff between power and performance, and unused servers are idled for further power efficiency. The authors in [15] propose a two-level hierarchical control framework for workload consolidation in virtualized environments: fully distributed controllers that independently optimize the CPU share provided to VMs under their control, so that the system-wide CPU capacity is appropriately tuned to the incoming workload intensity; and a supervisory controller that reduces power consumption during periods of light workload by consolidating the workload on to fewer VMs and shutting down extra servers. Tesauro [14] describes how reinforcement learning (RL) can be implemented within a two-level control architecture to manage the SLA of a non-virtualized computing environment by allocating servers among multiple applications. This paper does not consider the issue of power management. However, to learn an optimal or sub-optimal policy, the RL technique requires a large amount of training data and incurs a long learning time. Additionally, if a major change (such as adding new server types or modifying the SLA) occurs in the system, the RL policy needs to be retrained. The distributed control structure proposed here can accommodate such changes easily without major modifications to the structure itself; these changes can be reflected in our system by modifying parameter values in the appropriate local controllers.

In terms of research into fully decentralized control structures, Das et al. [3] demonstrate a multi-agent approach to manage power and performance in data centers by switching servers off during light workload. However, as they use an off-line model building approach to empirically measure the response time as a function of different numbers of clients and servers powered on, the approach is only feasible for small-scale systems. The authors in [16] use distributed model-predictive controllers to manage the performance of computing system, but reducing energy consumption is out of their scope. Chen et al. [2] propose an integrated solution with multiple controllers to manage application performance, as well as power and cooling in a virtualized data center comprising twenty servers. However, the scalability of the approach when managing larger numbers of servers is not evaluated.

To summarize, decentralized decision making in the context of real-time control of large-scale systems is an emerging research topic within the autonomic computing community. We believe that the control framework developed and analyzed here is an important step in this direction, especially in characterizing and controlling inter-controller interactions.

6. CONCLUSION

This paper has developed a fully decentralized control architecture to address the workload consolidation problem in server clusters wherein the processing capacity is dynamically tuned to satisfy the SLAs associated with the incoming workload while consolidating the workload on the fewest number of servers. The centralized RHC problem is decomposed into simpler subproblems and controllers, implemented locally within each server, independently solve their respective subproblems such that the performance goals for the overall system are satisfied. We use two organizational structures based on static and dynamic teams of controllers and analyze how interactions among independently running control loops affect system behavior. Simulation studies for system sizes up to a thousand servers show that the control architecture achieves a high degree of SLA satisfaction (> 95 %) under both static and dynamic teams of controllers, while keeping, on average, about 70% of the cores active over a ten hour period. Dynamic teams achieve a higher degree of SLA satisfaction (> 98%) while significantly reducing switching activity when compared to static ones. We also show that the workload consolidation problem supports an information structure that enables the reduction of the dynamic-team problem to a static one.

7. REFERENCES

[1] T. Atwood. Right architecture for the right workload: The application tier. Technical report, Sun Microsystems Report, Products, Jul. 2004.

[2] Y. Chen, D. Gmach, C. Hyser, Z. Wang, C. Bash, C. Hoover, and S. Singhal. Integrated management of application performance, power and cooling in data centers. In *Network Operations and Mgmt. Symposium*, 2010.

[3] R. Das, J. O. Kephart, C. Lefurgy, G. Tesauro, D. W. Levine, and H. Chan. Autonomic multi-agent management of power and performance in data centers. In *Conf. Autonomous agents and multiagent systems*, 2008.

[4] W. B. Dunbar and R. M. Murray. Distributed receding horizon control for multi-vehicle formation stabilization. *Automatica*, 42(4):549–558, 2006.

[5] A. Guez, I. Rusnak, and I. B. Kana. Multiple objectives optimization approach to adaptive and learning control. *Intl. Journal of Control*, 56(2):469–482, September 1992.

[6] J. Hellerstein, S. Singhal, and Q. Wang. Research challenges in control engineering of computing systems. *IEEE Trans. Network & Service Mgmt.*, 6(4):206–211, Dec. 2009.

[7] J. L. Hellerstein, Y. Diao, S. Parekh, and D. M. Tilbury. *Feedback Control of Computing Systems*. Wiley-IEEE Press, 2004.

[8] Y.-C. Ho and K.-C. Chu. Team decision theory and information structures in optimal control problems–Part I. *Automatic Control, IEEE Transactions on*, 17(1):15 – 22, Feb. 1972.

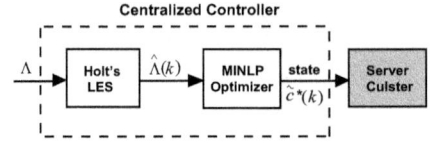

Figure 8: Schematic of the centralized controller.

[9] D. Kusic, J. Kephart, J. Hanson, N. Kandasamy, and G. Jiang. Power and performance management of virtualized computing environments via lookahead control. *Cluster Computing*, 12:1–15, 2009.

[10] A. Leon-Garcia. *Probability, statistics, and random processes for electrical engineering*. Prentice Hall, 2008.

[11] J. M. Maciejowski. *Predictive Control with Constraints*. Prentice Hall, London, 2002.

[12] S. G. Makridakis, S. C. Wheelwright, and R. J. Hyndman. *Forecasting: methods and applications*. Wiley, 1998.

[13] X. Meng, C. Isci, J. Kephart, L. Zhang, E. Bouillet, and D. Pendarakis. Efficient resource provisioning in compute clouds via VM multiplexing. In *Intl Conf. on Autonomic computing*, New York, NY, USA, 2010.

[14] G. Tesauro. Reinforcement learning in autonomic computing: A manifesto and case studies. *IEEE Internet Computing*, 11:22–30, 2007.

[15] R. Wang and N. Kandasamy. Workload consolidation in virtualized computing systems via hierarchical control. *Intel Technology Journal*, 16, June 2012.

[16] R. Wang, D. M. Kusic, and N. Kandasamy. A distributed control framework for performance management of virtualized computing environments. In *Intl. Conf. on Autonomic computing*, 2010.

[17] X. Wang, M. Chen, C. Lefurgy, and T. Keller. Ship: Scalable hierarchical power control for large-scale data centers. In *Intl. Conf. on Parallel Architectures and Compilation Techniques*, sept. 2009.

[18] Y. Wang, X. Wang, M. Chen, and X. Zhu. Power-efficient response time guarantees for virtualized enterprise servers. In *Real-Time Systems Symp.*, 2008.

APPENDIX

The centralized RHC scheme, shown in Figure 8, aims to satisfy response times while minimizing the number of active cores. It is posed as the following mixed-integer nonlinear programming (MINLP) problem in terms of $c_{ij}(k)$ and $n_i(k)$:

$$\min_{n_i(k)} \quad \sum_i ch_i \cdot n_i(k) \qquad (18)$$

subject to

$$\begin{cases} c_{lij} \le c_{ij}(k) \le c_{uij} \\ \sum_j c_{ij}(k) \le c_{hi} \\ m_j \sum_i [n_i(k) \cdot c_{ij}(k)] - \dfrac{\sum_i n_i(k)}{\bar{t}_j} \ge \hat{\Lambda}_j(k) \\ 0 \le n_i(k) \le N_i \end{cases} \qquad (19)$$

Here, the variables i, j, ch_i, c_{lij}, c_{uij}, m_j, $\bar{t}_j$, and $\hat{\Lambda}_j(k)$ are the same as those in (13); $c_{ij}(k)$ denotes the CPU share of VM_j in type i, and n_i represent the number of active servers during step k, with N_i being the total number of servers in type i. Since power consumption depends on operating frequency, $\sum_{i=1}^{3} ch_i \cdot n_i(k)$ approximates the power consumed by the active hosts.

Transactional Auto Scaler:
Elastic Scaling of In-Memory Transactional Data Grids

Diego Didona, Paolo Romano
I.S.T./INESC-ID, Lisbon, Portugal

Sebastiano Peluso, Francesco Quaglia
Sapienza, Università di Roma, Italy

ABSTRACT

In this paper we introduce TAS (Transactional Auto Scaler), a system for automating elastic-scaling of in-memory transactional data grids, such as NoSQL data stores or Distributed Transactional Memories. Applications of TAS range from on-line self-optimization of in-production applications to automatic generation of QoS/cost driven elastic scaling policies, and support for what-if analysis on the scalability of transactional applications.

The key innovation at the core of TAS is a novel performance forecasting methodology that relies on the joint usage of analytical modeling and machine-learning. By exploiting these two, classically competing, methodologies in a synergic fashion, TAS achieves the best of the two worlds, namely high extrapolation power and good accuracy even when faced with complex workloads deployed over public cloud infrastructures.

We demonstrate the accuracy and feasibility of TAS via an extensive experimental study based on a fully fledged prototype implementation, integrated with a popular open-source transactional in-memory data store (Red Hat's Infinispan), and industry-standard benchmarks generating a breadth of heterogeneous workloads.

Categories and Subject Descriptors

C.4 [**Computer Systems Organization**]: Performance of Systems—
Modeling techniques,Measurement techniques,Performance attributes

Keywords

Analytical Models, Performance Evaluation, Autonomic Provisioning, Distributed Software Transactional Memory

1. INTRODUCTION

Context. The advent of commercial cloud computing platforms has led to the proliferation of a new generation of in-memory, transactional data platforms, often referred to as NoSQL data grids. This new breed of distributed transactional platforms (that includes products such as Red Hat's Infinispan, Oracle's Coherence and Apache Cassandra [19]) is designed from the ground up to meet the elasticity requirements imposed by the pay-as-you-go cost model

at the basis of the cloud computing paradigm. By relying on a simple data model (key-value vs relational), employing efficient mechanisms to achieve data durability (in-memory replication vs disk-based logging) and dynamically resizing the cluster on top of which they are deployed, these platforms allow non-expert users to provision a cluster of virtually any size within minutes.This gives tremendous power to the average user, while placing a major burden on her shoulders. Removing the classic capacity planning process from the loop means in fact shifting the non-trivial responsibility of determining a good cluster configuration to the non-expert user [26].

Motivations. Unfortunately, forecasting the scalability trends of real-life, complex applications deployed on distributed transactional platforms is an extremely challenging task. In fact, as the number of nodes in the system grows, the performance of these platforms exhibits strong non-linear behaviors. Such behaviors are imputable to the simultaneous, and often inter-dependent, effects of contention affecting both physical (computational, memory, network) and logical (conflicting data accesses by concurrent transactions) resources.

These effects are visible in Figure 1, which shows results obtained by running two transactional benchmarking frameworks on top of the Infinispan data grid platform [25]: Radargun[1] and TPC-C[2][35]. We deployed Infinispan over a private cluster encompassing a variable number of nodes and ran benchmarks generating heterogeneous workloads for what concerns the number of (read/write) operations executed within each transaction, the percentage of read-only transactions, the number of items in the whole dataset, as well as the size of the individual objects manipulated by each operation.

As shown in Figure 1a, the scalability trends (in terms of the maximum throughput) for the three considered workloads are quite heterogeneous. The TPC-C benchmark scales almost linearly and the plots in Figure 1b and Figure 1c show that scalability is hindered by a steady increase of contention at both network and data (i.e., lock) levels. This leads to a corresponding increase of the network round trip time (RTT) and of the transaction abort probability. On the other hand the two Radargun workloads clearly demonstrate how the effects of high contention levels on logical and physical resources can lead to strongly non-linear scalability trends.

Contributions. In this paper, we present Transactional Auto Scaler (TAS), a system that introduces a novel performance prediction methodology based on the joint usage of analytical and machine

---

[1]http://sourceforge.net/apps/trac/radargun/wiki/WikiStart
[2]TPC-C is designed to operate on a relational database, hence we implemented a porting running directly on top of a key-value store such as Infinispan.

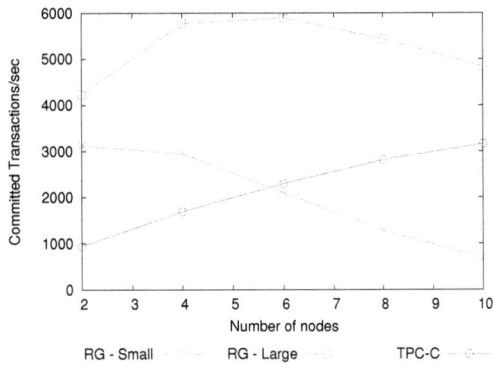

(a) Throughput (committed transactions per second)

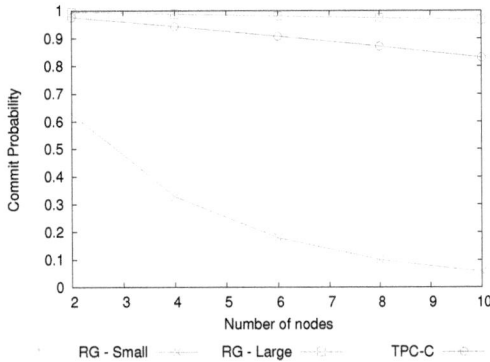

(b) Transaction commit probability

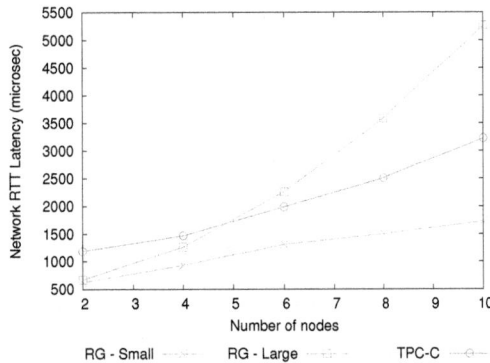

(c) Round-trip network latency

Figure 1: Performance analysis of different data grid applications.

learning (statistical) models. The analytical model (AM) employed by TAS exploits knowledge of the dynamics of the concurrency control/replication algorithm to forecast the effects of data contention using a white-box approach. On the other hand, TAS exploits black-box, machine-learning (ML) methods to forecast the impact on performance due to shifts in the utilization of system level resources (e.g,. CPU and network) imputable to variations of the system's scale.

The synergic usage of AM and ML techniques allows TAS to take the best of these two, typically competing, worlds. On the one hand, the black-box nature of ML spares from the burden of explicitly modeling the interactions with system resources that would be otherwise needed using white-box, analytical models. This is not only a time-consuming and error-prone task given the complexity

of current hardware architectures. It would also constrain the portability of our system (to a specific infrastructural instance), as well as its practical viability in virtualized Cloud environments where users have little or no knowledge of the underlying infrastructure.

On the other hand, analytical modeling allows to address two well known drawbacks of ML, namely its limited extrapolation power (i.e., the ability to predict scenarios that have not been previously observed) and lengthy training phase [5]. By exploiting *a priori* knowledge of the dynamics of data consistency mechanisms, AMs can achieve good forecasting accuracy even when operating in still unexplored regions of the parameters' space. Further, by narrowing the scope of the problem tackled via ML techniques, AM allows to reduce the dimensionality of the ML input features' space, leading to a consequent reduction of the training phase duration [5].

While the hybrid AM/ML methodology presented in this paper can be applied to a plethora of alternative replication/concurrency control mechanisms, one of the main contributions of this paper is the design of an innovative analytical performance model that targets the replication/concurrency control mechanisms used in Infinispan. Similarly to other recent transactional data grids, e.g., [6, 19], Infinispan opts for guaranteeing a weaker consistency semantics than classic serializability.Specifically, Infinispan ensures Repeatable Read [2] by using an encounter time based write locking strategy and Two-Phase Commit.

One of the key innovative elements of the analytical performance model presented in this paper consists in the methodology introduced to characterize the probability distribution of transactions' access to data items. In fact, existing white-box models of transactional systems [8, 10, 28] rely on strong approximations on the data accesses distribution, e.g., uniformly distributed accesses on one or more sets of data items of fixed cardinality, which require complex and time-consuming workload characterization studies in order to derive the parameters characterizing the data access distributions. Conversely, in the presented model, we capture the dynamics of the application's data access patterns via a novel abstraction, which we call *Application Contention Factor* (ACF). ACF exploits queuing theory arguments and a series of lock-related statistics measured in (and dependent on) the current workload/system configuration, in order to derive, in a totally automatic fashion, a probabilistic model of the application's data access pattern that is independent of both the current level of parallelism (e.g., number of concurrently active threads/nodes) and the utilization of physical resources (e.g., CPU or network).

We demonstrate the viability and high accuracy of the proposed solution via a large scale evaluation study using both a private cluster and public cloud infrastructures (Amazon EC2), and relying on benchmarks that generate a breadth of heterogeneous workloads for what concerns contention on both logical and physical resources. The results also highlight that the overhead introduced by TAS' monitoring system is negligible, and that the time required to solve the performance forecasting model is on the order of at most a few hundreds of milliseconds on commodity hardware.

The remainder of this paper is structured as follows. In Section 2 we discuss related research. The target data grid architecture of the TAS system is described in Section 3. Section 4 presents the forecasting methodology that we integrated in TAS, and Section 5 validates it via an extensive experimental study. Finally, Section 6 concludes this paper.

2. RELATED WORK

The present work is related to the literature on performance modeling and prediction for transactional systems. This includes performance models for traditional database systems and related concurrency control mechanisms (see, e.g., [28, 21, 34, 1]), approaches targeting more recent Software Transactional Memory architectures (see, e.g., [11]), and solutions dealing with distributed/replicated transaction processing systems, such as [8]. With respect to these approaches, TAS presents two key differences: i) it relies on analytical modeling only for capturing data contention dynamics, whereas it relies on black-box statistical methods to model the effects of contention on physical resources; ii) from an analytical modeling perspective, in TAS we introduce a novel abstraction (ACF) that allows to concisely characterize and effectively reason about arbitrary transactional data access patterns.

Our work has also relationships with systems that rely solely on ML techniques to automate resource provisioning both in transactional [7, 15, 27, 33] and non-transactional application domains, such as MapReduce [17] and VM sizing [30]. As it will be shown in Section 5, the joint usage of AM and ML, which represents one of the key innovative characteristics of TAS, allows enhancing the extrapolation power and reducing the training time of pure ML-based performance predictors.

Control theory techniques are also at the basis of several works in the area of self-tuning of application performance. These solutions often assume a linear performance model, which is possibly updated adaptively as the system moves from one operating point to another. For example, first-order autoregressive models are used to manage CPU allocation for Web servers [31]. Linear multi-input-multi-output (MIMO) models have been applied to manage different kinds of resources in multi-tier applications [23], as well as to allocate CPU resource for minimizing the interference between VMs deployed on the same physical node [22]. Compared to these adaptive linear models, the continuous non-linear models used by TAS to forecast both the logical and physical contention can accurately capture the system's entire behavior and allow optimized resource allocation over the entire operating space.

3. SYSTEM ARCHITECTURE

The architecture of TAS is depicted in Figure 2. Incoming transactions are dispatched by a front-end load-balancer towards the set of nodes composing the data grid. Periodically, statistics concerning load and resource utilization across the set of nodes in the data grid are gathered by a, so called, *aggregator* module.

Aggregated statistics are then fed to the *load predictor*, which serves the twofold purpose of forecasting future workload volumes and characteristics (e.g., ratio between read-only and update transactions, average number of read/write operations for read-only/update transactions), as well as detecting relevant workload shifts. The current TAS prototype relies on the Kalman filter algorithm [32] for load forecasting, and on the CUSUM [9] algorithm for distinguishing, in a robust manner, actual workload shifts from transient statistical fluctuations. Similar techniques have been employed in prior systems for automatic resource provisioning [7, 15], and have been shown to enhance the stability of the auto-scaling process.

The key innovative point of TAS, which represents the focus of this paper, is the methodology employed for predicting the performance of transactional applications when varying the number of nodes of the underlying data grid. More in detail, the *performance predictor* employed by TAS takes as input the workload characteristics (as output by the load predictor and/or aggregator) and the platform scale (i.e., the number of nodes to be used by the data grid), and outputs predictions on several key performance indicators (KPIs), including average response time, maximum sustainable throughput, transaction abort probability. As shown in Figure

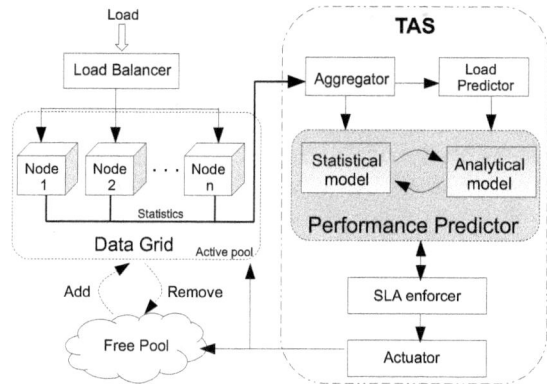

Figure 2: TAS reference architecture.

2, TAS relies on the joint usage of a white-box AM (to forecast the effects of data contention) and black-box ML techniques (to forecast the effects of contention on physical resources). A detailed description of the proposed performance forecasting methodology will be provided in Section 4.

The component in charge of querying the performance predictor is the *SLA enforcer*, which identifies the optimal platform configuration (in terms of number of nodes) on the basis of user-specified SLA and cost constraints. Our current prototype supports elastic-scaling policies that take into account constraints on cost, average response time and throughput. However, given that the performance predictor can forecast a number of additional KPIs (such as commit probability, or response time of read-only vs update transactions), our system lends itself to support more complex optimization policies involving constraints on additional performance metrics.

Finally, the *actuator* reconfigures the system by adding or removing (virtual) servers from the data grid. In order to maximize portability, TAS relies on δ-cloud[3], an abstraction layer which exposes a uniform API to automate provisioning of resources from heterogeneous IaaS providers (such as Amazon EC2, OpenNebula, RackSpace). The addition/removal of nodes needs of course to be coordinated also at the data grid level (not only at the IaaS level). To this end, TAS assumes the availability of APIs to request the join/departure of nodes from the data grid, which is a feature commonly supported by modern NoSQL data stores, such as Infinispan.

3.1 Infinispan Overview

As already mentioned, we selected as target platform for TAS a popular open source in-memory NoSQL data grid, namely Infinispan, which is developed by JBoss/Red Hat. At the time of writing, Infinispan is the reference NoSQL data platform and clustering technology for the JBoss AS, a mainstream open source J2EE application server. As TAS employs a white-box analytical model for capturing the effects of data contention on system's performance, in the following we provide an overview of the main mechanisms employed by Infinispan to ensure transactional consistency.

Infinispan exposes a key-value store data model, and maintains data entirely in-memory relying on replication as its primary mechanism to ensure fault-tolerance and data durability.

As other recent NoSQL platforms, Infinispan opts for weakening consistency in order to maximize performance. Specifically, it does not ensure serializability [3], but only guarantees the Repeatable Read ANSI/ISO isolation level [2]. More in detail, Infinispan implements a non-serializable variant of the multi-version concur-

---

[3]δCloud, http://http://deltacloud.apache.org/

rency control algorithm, which never blocks or aborts a transaction upon a read operation, and relies on an encounter-time locking strategy to detect write-write conflicts. Write locks are first acquired locally during the transaction execution phase, which does not entail any interaction with remote nodes. At commit time, Two Phase Commit (2PC) [3] is executed. During the first phase (also called prepare phase), lock acquisition is attempted at all replicas, in order to detect conflicts with transactions concurrently executing on other nodes, as well as for guaranteeing transaction atomicity. If the lock acquisition phase is successful on all nodes, the transaction originator broadcasts a commit message, in order to apply the transaction's modifications on the remote nodes, and then it commits locally.

In presence of conflicting, concurrent transactions, however, the lock acquisition phase (taking place either during the local transaction execution or during the prepare phase) may fail due to the occurrence of (possibly distributed) deadlocks. Deadlocks are detected using a simple, user-tunable, timeout based approach. In this paper, we consider the scenario in which the timeout on deadlock detection is set to 0, which is a typical approach for state of the art transactional memories [13] to achieve deadlock freedom. In fact, distributed deadlocks represent a major threat to system scalability, as highlighted by the seminal work in [16] and confirmed by our experimental results.

4. PERFORMANCE PREDICTOR

This section describes the performance prediction methodology employed by TAS. In Section 4.1, we introduce the analytical model used to capture data contention among transactions. Next, in Section 4.2, we present the machine learning based approach used to forecast the effects of contention on physical resources. Finally, in Section 4.3, we describe how to couple the two approaches.

4.1 Analytical Model

Our analytical model uses mean-value analysis techniques to forecast the probability of transaction commit, the mean transaction duration, and the maximum system throughput. This allows supporting what-if analysis on parameters like the degree of parallelism (number of nodes and possibly number of threads) in the system or shifts of workload characteristics, such as changes of the transactions' data access patterns.

The model treats the number of nodes in the system (denoted as ν) and the number of threads processing transactions at each node (denoted as θ) as input parameters. For the sake of simplicity, we will assume these nodes to be homogeneous in terms of computational power and available RAM, and distinguish only two classes of transactions, namely read-only vs update transactions. A discussion on how to extend the model and relax these assumptions will be provided in Section 4.1.4.

We denote with λ_{Tx} the mean arrival rate of transactions, and with w the percentage of update transactions, which perform, on average, a number N_l of write operations before requesting to commit. Note that, at this abstraction level, any operation that updates the state of the key-value store, e.g., put or remove operations, is considered a write operation. We say that a transaction is "local" to a node if it was activated on that node. Otherwise, we say that it is "remote".

We do not model explicitly the issuing of read operations, as the concurrency control of Infinispan ensures that these are never blocked and can never induce an abort. However, we denote with $T_{localRO}$, resp. $T_{localWR}$, the average time to execute a read-only, resp. update, transaction, namely since its beginning till the time in which it requests to commit, assuming that it does not abort earlier due to lock contention (in case it is a write transaction).

We denote with T_{prep} the mean time for the transaction coordinator to complete the first phase of 2PC, which includes broadcasting the prepare message, acquiring locks at all replicas, and gathering their replies. Note that the value of T_{prep} (and, in principle, also of $T_{localWR}/T_{localRO}$) can vary as the system scale changes, as an effect of the shift of the level of contention on physical resources (network in primis, but also CPU and memory). As these phenomena are captured in TAS via machine-learning techniques (described in Section 4.2), the analytical model treats T_{prep} and $T_{localWR}/T_{localRO}$ simply as input parameters.

Finally, we assume that the system is stable, with the meaning that i) all the parameters are defined to be either long-run averages or steady-state quantities and ii) the arrival rate of transactions does not exceed the service rate.

4.1.1 Data Access Pattern Characterization

In order to compute the response time for a transaction, we need first to obtain the probability that it experiences local or remote lock contention, that is whether it requires a lock currently held by another transaction. Note that in the modeled concurrency control algorithm, lock contention leads to an abort of the transaction, hence the probability of lock contention, P_{lock}, and of transaction abort, P_a, coincide.

As in other AMs of locking [34, 11], in order to derive the lock contention probability we model each data item as a server that receives locking requests at an average rate λ_{lock}, and which takes an average time T_H before completing the "service of a lock request" (i.e., freeing the lock) . This level of abstraction allows to approximate the probability of experiencing lock contention upon issuing a write operation on a given data item with the utilization of the corresponding server (namely, the percentage of time the server is busy serving a lock request), which is computable as $U = \lambda_{lock}T_H$ [18] (assuming $\lambda_{lock}T_H < 1$).

The key innovative element of our AM is that it does not rely on any a priori knowledge about the probability of a write operation to insist on a specific datum. Existing techniques, in fact, assume uniformly distributed accesses on one [11] (or more [28]) set(s) of data items of cardinality D (where D is assumed to be a priori known) and compute the probability of lock contention on any of the data items simply as:

$$P_{lock} = \frac{1}{D}\lambda_{lock}T_H \qquad (1)$$

Unfortunately, the assumption on the uniformity of the data access patterns strongly limit the employment of these models in complex applications, especially if these exhibit dynamic shifts in the data access distributions. We overcome these limitations by introducing a powerful abstraction that allows the on-line characterization of the application data access pattern in a lightweight and pragmatical manner. We call this abstraction *Application Contention Factor* (ACF) and define it as:

$$ACF = \frac{P_{lock}}{\lambda_{lock}T_H} \qquad (2)$$

ACF has two attractive features that make it an ideal candidate to characterize the data access patterns of complex transactional applications:

1. It is computable on-line, on the basis of the values of P_{lock}, λ_{lock} and T_H measured in the current platform configuration. By Eq. 1, it is possible to see that $\frac{1}{ACF}$ can be alternatively interpreted as the size D of an "equivalent" dataset

accessed with uniform probability. Here, equivalent means that, if the application had generated a uniform access pattern over a dataset of size $D = \frac{1}{ACF}$, it would have incurred in the same contention probability experienced during its actual execution (in which it generated arbitrary, non-uniform access patterns).

2. As we will show in Section 5, even for applications with arbitrary, complex data access patterns (such as in TPC-C, whose access pattern is very hard to model analytically), ACF is an invariant with respect to the arrival rate, degree of concurrency in the system (i.e., number of nodes/threads generating transactions) and physical hardware infrastructure (e.g., private cluster vs public cloud platform).

The ACF abstraction represents the foundation on top of which we built the AM of the lock contention dynamics, to be discussed shortly. This model allows to predict the contention probability that would be experienced by an application in presence of different scenarios of workloads (captured by shifts of λ_{lock} or ACF), as well as of different levels of contention on physical resources (that would lead to changes of the execution time of the various phases of the transaction life-cycle, captured by shifts of T_H).

4.1.2 Lock Contention Model

Denoting with λ_{lock}^l, respectively λ_{lock}^r, the lock request rate generated by local, respectively remote transactions, on a given node, we can compute them as:

$$\lambda_{lock}^l = \frac{\lambda_{Tx} \cdot w \cdot \tilde{N}_l}{\nu}, \quad \lambda_{lock}^r = \tilde{N}_r \cdot \lambda_{Tx} \cdot w \cdot \frac{\nu - 1}{\nu} \cdot P_p$$

where we have denoted with P_p the probability for a transaction to reach the prepare phase (i.e., not to abort earlier), and with $\tilde{N}_l$, respectively $\tilde{N}_r$, the number of locks successfully acquired on average by local, respectively remote, transactions, regardless of whether they abort or commit.

When a transaction executes locally, it can experience lock contention (and therefore abort) both with other local transactions and remote ones. By using Eq. 1, we can therefore compute the probability of abort during local transaction execution, P_a^l, as:

$$P_a^l = P_{lock}^l = (\lambda_{lock}^l + \lambda_{lock}^r) \cdot ACF \cdot T_H \qquad (3)$$

The probability P_a^r for a remote transaction T to experience contention upon any lock request issued during its prepare phase with a transaction T' on any node of the data grid can be instead approximated by considering exclusively the probability for T to contend with T' on the node $\nu_{T'}$ that generated the latter transaction. In fact, if T were to contend with T' at a node different from $\nu_{T'}$, then, with very high probability, T would experience lock contention with T' also when trying to complete its prepare phase on $\nu_{T'}$. As a consequence we can compute P_a^r as:

$$P_a^r = \lambda_{lock}^l \cdot ACF \cdot T_H^l$$

where T_H^l denotes the mean lock hold time for a local transaction. Thanks to this approximation, we can consider the remote abort probabilities for a transaction on different nodes as independent.

By the above probabilities, we can compute the probability that i) a transaction reaches its prepare phase (P_p), ii) successfully completes its prepare phase on all the $N-1$ remote nodes (P_{coher}), and iii) commits (P_c):

$$
\begin{aligned}
P_p &= (1 - P_a^l)^{N_l} \\
P_{coher} &= (1 - P_a^r)^{N_l \cdot (\nu - 1)} \\
P_c &= P_p \cdot P_{coher}
\end{aligned}
$$

We can now compute the mean number of locks successfully acquired by a transaction, $\tilde{N}_l$, taking into account that it can abort during its execution:

$$\tilde{N}_l = P_p \cdot N_l + \sum_{i=1}^{N_l} P_a^l \cdot (1 - P_a^l)^{i-1} \cdot (i - 1)$$

In order to compute $\tilde{N}_r$ we use a similar reasoning:

$$\tilde{N}_r = (1 - P_a^\dagger)^{N_l} \cdot N_l + \sum_{i=1}^{N_l} P_a^\dagger \cdot (1 - P_a^\dagger)^{i-1} \cdot (i - 1)$$

with the exception that in this case we estimate the probability to incur in lock contention taking into account that there cannot be remote contention between two transactions originated by the same node:

$$P_a^\dagger = (\lambda_{lock}^l + \lambda_{lock}^r \cdot \frac{(\nu - 2)}{(\nu - 1)}) \cdot ACF \cdot T_H^\dagger$$

Where we denoted with $T_H^\dagger$ the average lock holding time of the transactions with which it is possible to experience contention during the prepare phase, which we estimate as:

$$T_H^\dagger = \frac{\lambda_{lock}^l \cdot T_H^l + \lambda_{lock}^r \cdot \frac{(\nu - 2)}{(\nu - 1)} \cdot T_H^r}{\lambda_{lock}^l + \lambda_{lock}^r \cdot \frac{(\nu - 2)}{(\nu - 1)}}$$

In order to compute the aforementioned probabilities, we need to obtain the mean holding time for a lock. To this end let us define as $G(i)$ the sum of the lock hold time over i consecutive lock requests (recalling that we are assuming that the average time between two lock requests is equal to $\frac{T_{localWR}}{N_l}$):

$$G(i) = \sum_{i=1}^{N_l} \frac{T_{localWR}}{N_l} \cdot i$$

We can then compute the local lock hold time as the weighted average of three different lock holding times, referring to the case that a transaction aborts locally (H_l^{la}), remotely (H_l^{ra}) or successfully completes (H_l^c):

$$
\begin{aligned}
T_H^l &= H_l^{la} + H_l^{ra} + H_l^c \\
H_l^{la} &= \sum_{i=2}^{N_l} P_a^l \cdot (1 - P_a^l)^{i-1} \cdot \frac{G(i-1)}{i-1} \\
H_l^{ra} &= P_p \cdot (1 - P_{Coher}) \cdot [T_{prep} + \frac{G(N_l)}{N_l}] \\
H_l^c &= P_p \cdot P_{Coher} \cdot [T_{prep} + \frac{G(N_l)}{N_l}]
\end{aligned}
$$

Let us now compute the remote lock hold time, T_h^r. We neglect the lock holding times for transactions that abort while acquiring a lock on a remote node, as in this case locks are acquired consecutively (without executing any business logic between two lock requests). On the other hand, if a remote transaction succeeds in acquiring all its locks, then it holds them until it receives either a commit or an abort message from the coordinator. Therefore we compute T_h^r as:

$$T_h^r = (1 - P_a^\dagger)^{N_l} \cdot [T_{prep} + (1 - P_a^r)^{N_l \cdot (\nu - 2)} \cdot T_{com}]$$

where $(1 - P_a^\dagger)^{N_l}$ represents the probability for a remote transaction T executing its prepare phase at node n to successfully acquire all the locks it requests on n, and $(1 - P_a^r)^{N_l \cdot (\nu - 2)}$ represents the probability for T to successfully acquire its remote locks on the remaining $\nu - 2$ nodes.

Given that an update transaction can terminate its execution (either aborting or committing) in three different phases, its mean service time, denoted as T^W, can be expressed as:

$$T^W = T_c + T_a^l + T_a^r$$

where

$$T_c = P_c \cdot (T_{localWR} + T_{prep} + T_{comm})$$

$$T_a^l = \sum_{i=1}^{N_l} [T_{roll} + (\frac{T_{localWR}}{N_l} \cdot i)] \cdot P_a^l \cdot (1 - P_a^l)^{i-1}$$

$$T_a^r = P_p \cdot (1 - P_{coher}) \cdot (T_{localWR} + T_{prep})$$

Considering also read-only transaction, the average service time of a transaction, denoted as T, is:

$$T = w \cdot T^W + (1 - w) \cdot T^{localRO} \qquad (4)$$

4.1.3 AM Resolution and Predicted KPIs

As in previous analytical models of transactional data contention [34, 12], also our model exhibits a mutual dependency between the abort probabilities and other parameters, such as the mean hold time. Prior art copes with this issue by using an iterative scheme in which abort probabilities are first initialized to zero. Next, the depending parameters are computed, and, on the basis of their values, a new set of abort probabilities is obtained and used in the next iteration; the process continues till the relative difference between the abort probabilities at two subsequent iterations becomes smaller than a given threshold.

It is known [34] that this iterative solution technique can suffer from convergence problems at high contention rates. We tackle this issue by adopting a binary search in the bi-dimensional space $[0, 1] \times [0, 1]$ associated with the abort probabilities (local and remote), which is guaranteed to converge at a desired precision $\epsilon \in (0, 1]$ after a number of steps $n \leq 1 + \lceil log_2\epsilon \rceil$. This analysis was confirmed by our evaluation study, reported in Section 5, for which we set $\epsilon = 0.001$ and observed convergence in at most 11 iterations.

Once obtained the commit probability and the average transaction service time, the model can be employed to compute additional KPIs typically employed in SLA definition, such as maximum system throughput or percentiles on response times.

The maximum throughput can be computed by exploiting Little's law [20] in an iterative fashion. At the first step of the iteration, an upper-bound on system throughput is provided as input to the model, which is computed by assuming no conflicts and that all threads in the system constantly execute transactions. This corresponds to setting:

$$\lambda = \frac{\nu\theta}{w \cdot (T_{localWR} + T_{prep} + T_{comm}) + (1 - w) \cdot T_{localRO}}$$

At each step, a new value of λ is fed in input to the model, replacing the denominator of the above equation with the value of T (see Eq. 4) computed in the previous iteration, till convergence to the desired precision is reached.

In order to compute response time percentiles, it is possible to model each data grid node as a $G/G/\theta$ queuing system, i.e., a queue with θ servers subjected to arbitrary service and arrival rate distributions. One can then exploit the Köllerström's approximation [4] for the waiting time distribution of $G/G/\theta$ queues in the heavy-traffic case, namely when the queue utilization $\rho \simeq 1$. This result states that the approximate distribution of the waiting time, w, of a

$G/G/\theta$ queue in heavy traffic is exponential and is given by:

$$P(w \leq t) \simeq 1 - e^{-\frac{2(1/\lambda - T_s)}{\sigma_u^2 + \frac{\sigma_b^2}{\theta^2}}t}$$

where σ_u is the inter-arrival time variance, σ_b^2 is the service time variance (both measurable at run-time, as done in other systems for automated resource provisioning, such as [27]), λ is the request arrival rate, and T_s is the average service time. The above formula can hence be used to compute the maximum arrival rate λ such that the response time is less than a given threshold y with probability k.

4.1.4 Extensions of the AM

The presented model lends itself to be extended in several directions. In the following we briefly overview some of the most interesting possible extensions.

Mix-aware modeling: extending our approach to account for multiple transaction classes having different characteristics (for instance in terms of data access pattern or duration of local execution) would require two main steps.

1. Extracting a characterization of the different transactional classes, including per-class information on ACF, abort probability, mean number of locks requested per transaction and local execution time, and of the ratio of each class in the mix. Identification of different transactional classes can be performed in a transparent way using classic clustering techniques, such as the one used, e.g., in [15].

2. Specializing the analytical model to forecast the contention probability (and depending statistics, such as throughput) per transaction-class. This result can be achieved in a relatively simple way by employing a methodology, similar to the one proposed in [34], in which the transaction conflict probability is computed taking into account the data access patterns (in our case captured by the ACF) of each single transaction class.

Heterogeneous platforms: as in prior approaches for automated resource provisioning for the Cloud [27, 26], heterogeneous platforms can be handled by using simple multiplication factors between servers depending on their hardware characteristics. For example, Amazon EC2 offers various instances (small, medium, large, etc.), each equipped with different hardware resources. Via a preliminary benchmarking study (using synthetic workloads, as in [26], or, whether possible, directly the target application, as in [27]), it is easy to determine scaling factors relating the performance achieved when deploying the application on different type of instances. For example, a medium instance performs 1.5 times better than a small instance, or a large instance provides 2x the throughput of a small instance. These scaling factors can then be applied to forecast the values of the parameters associated with the duration of local transaction execution, namely $T_{localRO}$ and $T_{localWR}$, when deploying the application on a different instance type.

4.2 Machine-Learning-Based Modeling

TAS relies on black-box, machine-learning-based modeling techniques to forecast the impact on performance due to shifts of the level of contention on physical resources depending on workload's fluctuations or to the re-sizing of the data grid. Developing white-box models capable of capturing accurately the effects on performance due to contention on hardware resources can in fact be

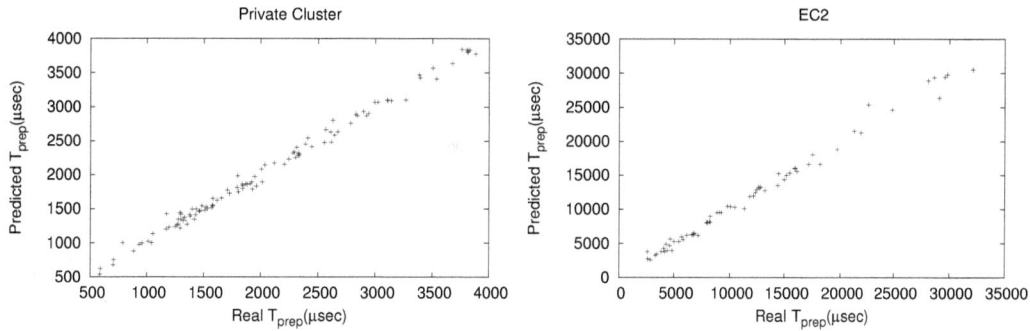

Figure 3: Accuracy of the machine-learning based T_{prep} predictions on the private cluster (left) and on EC2 (right).

very complex (or even non-feasible, especially in virtualized cloud infrastructures), given the difficulty to gain access to detailed information on the exact dynamics of hardware-level components.

In TAS we exploit the availability of a complementary white-box model to formulate the machine-learning based forecasting problem in a way that differs significantly from traditional, pure black-box approaches. Conventional machine learning based techniques, e.g., [26], try to forecast some performance metric p_2 in an unknown system configuration c_2, given the performance level p_1 and the demand of physical resources d_1 in the current configuration c_1. In TAS, instead, the analytical model can provide the machine learner with valuable estimates of the demand of physical resources d_2 in the target configuration c_2. Specifically, we use the analytical model to forecast what will be, in the target configuration c_2, the rate of transactions that will initiate a 2PC scheme (once reached their commit phase) as well as the percentage of CPU time consumed by the threads in charge of processing local transactions.

As already mentioned, contention on physical resources can have a direct impact on the execution time of two key phases of transactions' execution, namely the duration of the local transaction processing phase, denoted as $T_{localWR}$ and $T_{localRO}$, and the network latency incurred in by transactions while executing the 2PC protocol, denoted as T_{prep}. We are here faced with a non-linear regression problem, in which we want to learn the value of continuous functions defined on multivariate domains. Given the nature of the problem, we used, as machine learner, Cubist, a decision-tree regressor that approximates non-linear multivariate functions by means of piece-wise linear approximations. Analogously to classic decision tree based classifiers, such as C4.5 and ID3 [24], Cubist builds decision trees choosing the branching attribute such that the resulting split maximizes the normalized information gain. However, unlike C4.5 and ID3, which contain elements in a finite discrete domain (i.e., the predicted class) as leaves of the decision tree, Cubist places a multivariate linear model at each leaf.

In order to build an initial knowledge base to train the machine learner, TAS relies on a suite of synthetic benchmarks that generate heterogeneous transactional workloads in terms of mean size of messages, memory footprint at each node and network load (number of transactions that activate 2PC per second). Additional details on the criteria used to perform feature selection are provided, for space constraints, in [14]. During the initial, off-line, training phase, the benchmark suite injects workload while varying the size of the cluster and the number of threads concurrently processing local transactions at each node. In our experiments we found that using a simple uniform sampling strategy allowed to achieve rather quickly (in about one hour) a satisfactory coverage of the parame-

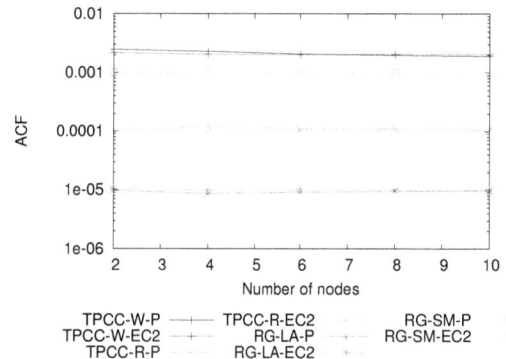

Figure 4: ACF for heterogeneous benchmarks.

ters' space, which is the reason why we did not decide to integrate more advanced sampling mechanisms, like adaptive sampling [29].

Once deployed on a data grid, the statistical gathering system of TAS periodically collects new samples of the workload and performance of the system. This allows to support periodic re-training of the machine learner and to incorporate in its knowledge base profiling data specific to the target user level applications.

4.3 AM and ML Coupling

By the above discussion, it is clear that the AM and the ML are tightly intertwined: the AM relies on the predictions of the ML to obtain the values of T_{prep} and $T_{localWR}/T_{localRO}$ as input; the ML, on the other hand, uses as one of the input features of its model the transaction throughput forecast by the AM, which represents an estimate on the level of resource contention in the target configuration.

For simplicity, the current prototype solves this problem by using the following fixed point iterative solution, which, in our experiments, has never shown convergence problems: the AM is initialized with the current values of T_{prep} and $T_{localWR}/T_{localRO}$, it outputs the estimated throughput in the target configuration, and provides it as input feature to the ML to obtain a new value of T_{prep} and $T_{localWR}/T_{localRO}$. The process is repeated till the requested precision is reached. Note that, also in this case, we may have employed a binary search technique analogous to the one described in Section 4.1.3. Such a technique provides stronger convergence properties, at the cost of a higher complexity since, in this scenario, it would need to operate on a three-dimensional space.

5. VALIDATION

In this section we report the results of an experimental study

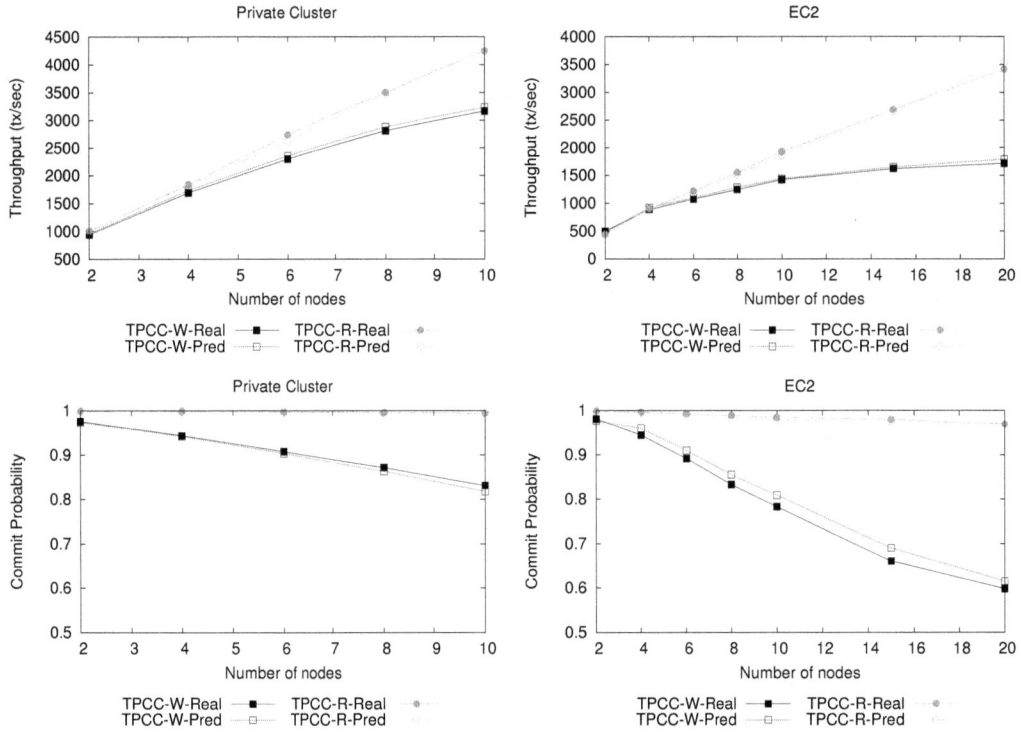

Figure 5: Validation using the TPC-C benchmark.

aimed at evaluating the accuracy and viability of TAS. Before presenting the results, we describe the workloads and experimental platforms used in our study.

Workloads. We consider two well-known benchmarks, already mentioned in Section 1, namely TPC-C and Radargun. The former is a standard benchmark for OLTP systems, which portrays the activities of a wholesale supplier and generates mixes of read-only and update transactions with strongly skewed access patterns and heterogeneous durations. Radargun, instead, is a benchmarking framework specifically designed to test the performance of distributed, transactional key-value stores. The workloads generated by Radargun are simpler and less diverse than TPC-C's ones, but have the advantage of being very easily tunable, thus allowing assessing the accuracy of TAS in a wider range of workload settings.

For TPC-C we consider two different workload scenarios. The first, which we denote as TPCC-R, is a read dominated workload (containing 90% read-only transactions) that generates reduced contention on both physical and data resources as the scale of the cluster grows. The second (TPCC-W) includes around 50% of update transactions and generates a high data contention level.

For Radargun we also consider two workloads, denoted as RG-LA and RG-SM. Both workloads generate uniform data access patterns, but RG-LA performs, in each transaction, a single put operation over a set of 100K data items, yielding a very low contention rate. RG-SM, instead, updates in each transaction 10 data items selected over a set of cardinality 1K, thus generating a very high contention probability. We decided to use the Radargun workloads in our evaluation study because their data access patterns are particularly simple and easily predictable, thus allowing us to validate the correctness and semantics of the ACF abstraction.

Experimental Platforms. We use, as experimental test-beds for this study, both a private cluster and Amazon EC2. The private

cluster is composed of 10 servers equipped with two 2.13 GHz Quad-Core Intel(R) Xeon(R) processors and 8 GB of RAM and interconnected via a private Gigabit Ethernet. For EC2 we used up to 20 Extra Large Instances, which are equipped with 15GB of RAM and 4 virtual cores with 2 EC2 Compute Units each.

ML validation. We start by assessing the accuracy of the machine learners built using the synthetic benchmarking suite described in Section 4.2. We focus on the forecasting of T_{prep}, since in all the explored settings we observed negligible shifts of the value of $T_{localRO}/T_{localWR}$ in face of changes of the cluster size. This is due to the fact that, in the considered settings, the system bottleneck is consistently the network rather than the CPU.

In order to evaluate the accuracy of the machine learning model in isolation (i.e., decoupling it from the analytical model), in this experiment we provide the machine learners with the correct guess of the target throughput. The scatter-plots in Figure 3 report the results of 10-fold cross validation, highlighting that, on both the private cluster and on EC2, the ML attains a high prediction accuracy. Specifically, the correlation factor was around 99% in both cases, with an average absolute error equal to 500 micro-seconds for EC2 and around 60 micro-seconds for the private cluster. Note that, in practice, the relative error is similar on both platforms, since, on EC2, the maximum value of T_{prep} is around 10 times greater than the maximum T_{prep} value on the private cluster.

ACF validation. In Figure 4 we report the ACFs obtained when running both the TPC-C and Radargun workloads on EC2 and on the private cluster (note that we tag the curves obtained on the private cluster with the suffix "-P"). The plots confirm our finding, namely that, once fixed an application workload, the ACF represents an invariant across platforms of different scale, even when deployed on infrastructures of different nature (private vs public). It is noteworthy to highlight that the ACF value is equal to 1E-5,

132

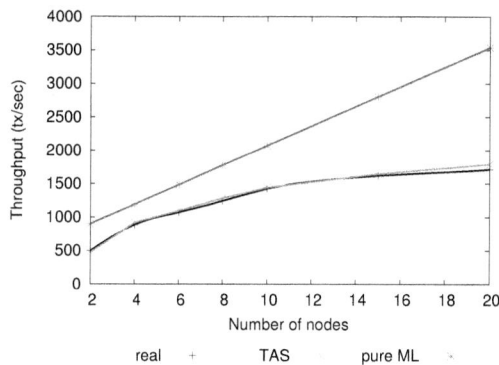

Figure 6: Comparing TAS with a pure ML approach.

resp. 1E-3, for the workloads RG-LA, resp. RG-SM. We recall that these workloads generate uniform accesses to datasets of size 100K, resp. 1K, items. Therefore, these results confirm that ACF can be interpreted as the inverse of the size of an equivalent, uniformly accessed, dataset.

AM/ML validation. Let us now evaluate the accuracy of the final performance predictions output by TAS when jointly using the AM and the ML. We use as KPIs the maximum throughput and commit probability. We report in Figure 5 the forecasts for the TPC-C workloads. For space constraints, we cannot include the plots for Radargun, however they show analogous trends. The experimental data demonstrate the ability of TAS to predict with high accuracy not only the maximum transaction throughput, but also important intermediate statistics such as commit probability. More in detail, TAS achieves a remarkable average relative error (defined as $|real - prediction|/real$) on the predicted throughput of 2%, with a maximum of 3.5%.

Comparison with a pure ML approach. We conclude by comparing the accuracy of TAS with that of a pure ML-based solution, namely the approach at the basis of several recent works in the area of elastic scaling [7, 15]. To this end, we trained Cubist on the TPCC-R workload, varying the number of nodes from 2 to 20 and the incoming load from 100 requests per second until reaching the maximum throughput. The input features for the ML included CPU, memory and network utilization, the percentage of update transactions and the mean number of locks they request, the transaction arrival rate, number of nodes and active threads per node. As in the previous evaluation study, we use maximum throughput as the output variable. These experiments were performed using Amazon EC2.

As test dataset, we use TPCC-W, which, we recall, generates a significantly higher data contention level with respect to TPCC-R. Further, unlike TPCC-R, TPCC-W exhibits a non-linear scalability trend. As expected [7], in these conditions, the pure ML-based approach manifests its limits in terms of reduced extrapolation power. In fact, the plots in Figure 6 clearly highlight that the pure ML-based solution tends to mimic the linear scalability trend that it observed during its training phase. As a consequence, it blunders when faced with workloads, like the TPCC-W, that i) have previously unobserved input characteristics, and ii) exhibit significantly different performance trends. This problem might be, to some extent, addressed by increasing the coverage of the training phase. However, achieving a good accuracy across a wide range of workloads may require a prohibitive increase of the ML training time. In fact, data contention dynamics in a (distributed) transactional sys-

tem are influenced by a wide range of parameters [12, 3], and it is well known that the training time of ML techniques grows exponentially with the number of input features (the, so called, curse of dimensionality problem [5]).

The AM employed by TAS, on the other hand, can exploit the *a priori* knowledge on the dynamics of data consistency mechanisms to achieve a higher extrapolation power. Further, it allows to narrow the scope of (and hence to simplify) the problem tackled via ML techniques, reducing the dimensionality of the ML input features' space and, consequently, the duration of the training phase.

As a final remark, it is noteworthy to highlight that, in all our experiments, the performance attained with or without the monitoring framework were indistinguishable. Also, the time required to instantiate and solve a TAS query is on the order of a few hundreds of milliseconds, highlighting the practical viability of the proposed solution to support on-line what-if analysis and automate elastic scaling.

6. CONCLUSIONS AND FUTURE WORK

In this paper we introduced TAS (Transactional Auto Scaler), a system designed to accurately predict the performance achievable by applications executing on top of transactional in-memory data grids, in face of changes of the scale of the system.

TAS relies on a novel hybrid forecasting methodology that jointly utilizes analytical modeling and machine learning techniques according to a divide-and-conquer approach: availability of precise knowledge of the concurrency control scheme/replication protocol is exploited to derive a white-box analytical model of data contention; black-block statistical techniques are instead used to capture the effects of contention on physical resources (CPU, memory, network) while avoiding explicit modeling of the interactions with system resources, which is not only complex and time consuming given the complexity of current hardware architectures, but is also normally non-viable in virtualized Cloud environments where users have little or no knowledge of the underlying infrastructure.

We demonstrated the viability and high accuracy of the proposed solution via an extensive validation study based on industry standard benchmarks deployed both on a private cluster and on a public cloud infrastructure (Amazon EC2).

Future work will be aimed at integrating analytical models for different concurrency control schemes in TAS and in extending TAS' lightweight data access pattern characterization to encompass also the case of partially replicated data sets.

Acknowledgment

This work has been partially supported by national funds through FCT – Fundação para a Ciência e a Tecnologia, under projects PTDC/EIA-EIA/102496/2008 and PEst-OE/EEI/LA0021/2011, by the Cloud-TM project (co-financed by the European Commission through the contract no. 57784) and by COST Action IC1001 EuroTM.

7. REFERENCES

[1] M. Bennani and D. Menasce. Resource allocation for autonomic data centers using analytic performance models. In *Proc. of the International Conference on Autonomic Computing (ICAC)*, 2005.

[2] H. Berenson, P. Bernstein, J. Gray, J. Melton, E. O'Neil, and P. O'Neil. A critique of ansi sql isolation levels. In *Proc. of the ACM SIGMOD International Conference on Management of Data*, 1995.

[3] P. A. Bernstein, V. Hadzilacos, and N. Goodman. *Concurrency control and recovery in database systems.* 1986.

[4] U. N. Bhat, M. Shalaby, and M. J. Fischer. Approximation techniques in the solution of queueing problems. *Naval Research Logistics Quarterly*, 1979.

[5] C. M. Bishop. *Pattern Recognition and Machine Learning (Information Science and Statistics).* 2007.

[6] F. Chang, J. Dean, S. Ghemawat, W. C. Hsieh, D. A. Wallach, M. Burrows, T. Chandra, A. Fikes, and R. E. Gruber. Bigtable: a distributed storage system for structured data. In *Proc. of the USENIX Symposium on Operating Systems Design and Implementation (OSDI)*, 2006.

[7] J. Chen, G. Soundararajan, and C. Amza. Autonomic provisioning of backend databases in dynamic content web servers. In *Proc. of the International Conference on Autonomic Computing (ICAC)*, 2006.

[8] B. Ciciani, D. M. Dias, and P. S. Yu. Analysis of replication in distributed database systems. *IEEE Transactions on Knowledge and Data Engineering*, 2(2), 1990.

[9] Y. Dai, Y. Luo, Z. Li, and Z. Wang. A new adaptive cusum control chart for detecting the multivariate process mean. *Quality and Reliability Engineering International*, 27(7), 2011.

[10] P. di Sanzo, B. Ciciani, F. Quaglia, and P. Romano. A performance model of multi-version concurrency control. In *Proc. of the International Symposium on Modeling, Analysis and Simulation of Computer and Telecommunication Systems (MASCOTS)*, 2008.

[11] P. di Sanzo, B. Ciciani, F. Quaglia, and P. Romano. Analytical modelling of commit-time-locking algorithms for software transactional memories. In *Proc. of the International Computer Measurement Group Conference (CMG)*, 2010.

[12] P. di Sanzo, R. Palmieri, B. Ciciani, F. Quaglia, and P. Romano. Analytical modeling of lock-based concurrency control with arbitrary transaction data access patterns. In *Proc. of WOSP/SIPEW International Conference on Performance Engineering (ICPE)*, 2010.

[13] D. Dice, O. Shalev, and N. Shavit. Transactional locking ii. In *Proc. of the International Symposium on Distributed Computing (DISC)*, 2006.

[14] D. Didona, P. Romano, S. Peluso, and F. Quaglia. Transactional auto scaler: Elastic scaling of in-memory transactional data grids. Technical Report 50/2011, INESC-ID, December 2011.

[15] S. Ghanbari, G. Soundararajan, J. Chen, and C. Amza. Adaptive learning of metric correlations for temperature-aware database provisioning. In *Proc. of the International Conference on Autonomic Computing (ICAC)*, 2007.

[16] J. Gray, P. Helland, P. O'Neil, and D. Shasha. The dangers of replication and a solution. In *Proc. of the ACM SIGMOD International Conference on Management of Data*, 1996.

[17] H. Herodotou, F. Dong, and S. Babu. No one (cluster) size fits all: automatic cluster sizing for data-intensive analytics. In *Proc. of the ACM Symposium on Cloud Computing (SOCC)*, 2011.

[18] L. Kleinrock. *Theory, Volume 1, Queueing Systems.* 1975.

[19] A. Lakshman and P. Malik. Cassandra: a decentralized structured storage system. *SIGOPS Operating System Review*, 44, 2010.

[20] J. D. C. Little. A proof for the queuing formula: L= λ w. *Operations Research*, 9(3), 1961.

[21] D. A. Menascé and T. Nakanishi. Performance evaluation of a two-phase commit based protocol for ddbs. In *Proc. of the ACM SIGACT-SIGMOD symposium on Principles of Database Systems (PODS)*, 1982.

[22] R. Nathuji, A. Kansal, and A. Ghaffarkhah. Q-clouds: managing performance interference effects for qos-aware clouds. In *Proc. of the ACM European Conference on Computer Systems (EuroSys)*, 2010.

[23] P. Padala, K.-Y. Hou, K. G. Shin, X. Zhu, M. Uysal, Z. Wang, S. Singhal, and A. Merchant. Automated control of multiple virtualized resources. In *Proc. of the ACM European conference on Computer Systems (EuroSys)*, 2009.

[24] J. R. Quinlan. *C4.5: Programs for Machine Learning.* 1993.

[25] Red Hat / JBoss. JBoss Infinispan. http://www.jboss.org/infinispan.

[26] Z. Shen, S. Subbiah, X. Gu, and J. Wilkes. Cloudscale: elastic resource scaling for multi-tenant cloud systems. In *Proc. of the ACM Symposium on Cloud Computing (SOCC)*, 2011.

[27] R. Singh, U. Sharma, E. Cecchet, and P. Shenoy. Autonomic mix-aware provisioning for non-stationary data center workloads. In *Proc. of the International Conference on Autonomic Computing (ICAC)*, 2010.

[28] Y. C. Tay, N. Goodman, and R. Suri. Locking performance in centralized databases. *ACM Transactions on Database Systems*, 10, 1985.

[29] S. Thompson. *Sampling.* 2002.

[30] L. Wang, J. Xu, M. Zhao, Y. Tu, and J. A. B. Fortes. Fuzzy modeling based resource management for virtualized database systems. In *Proc. of the International Symposium on Modeling, Analysis and Simulation of Computer and Telecommunication Systems (MASCOTS)*, 2011.

[31] Z. Wang, X. Zhu, and S. Singhal. Utilization and slo-based control for dynamic sizing of resource partitions. In *Proc. of IFIP/IEEE Distributed Systems: Operations and Management (DSOM)*, 2005.

[32] G. Welch and G. Bishop. An introduction to the kalman filter. Technical report, 1995.

[33] P. Xiong, Y. Chi, S. Zhu, J. Tatemura, C. Pu, and H. Hacigümüş. Activesla: a profit-oriented admission control framework for database-as-a-service providers. In *Proc. of the ACM Symposium on Cloud Computing (SOCC)*, 2011.

[34] P. S. Yu, D. M. Dias, and S. S. Lavenberg. On the analytical modeling of database concurrency control. *Journal of the ACM (JACM)*, 40, 1993.

[35] Transaction Processing Performance Council. *TPC Benchmark^{TM} C, Standard Specification, Revision 5.1.* Transaction Processing Perfomance Council, 2002.

Adaptive Green Hosting[†]

Nan Deng
The Ohio State University
dengn@cse.ohio-state.edu

Christopher Stewart
The Ohio State University
cstewart@cse.ohio-state.edu

Daniel Gmach
Hewlett Packard Labs
daniel.gmach@hp.com

Martin Arlitt
Hewlett Packard Labs
martin.arlitt@hp.com

Jaimie Kelley
The Ohio State University
kelley.530@osu.edu

ABSTRACT

The growing carbon footprint of Web hosting centers contributes to climate change and could harm the public's perception of Web hosts and Internet services. A pioneering cadre of Web hosts, called *green hosts*, lower their footprints by cutting into their profit margins to buy carbon offsets. This paper argues that an adaptive approach to buying carbon offsets can increase a green host's total profit by exploiting daily, bursty patterns in Internet service workloads. We make the case in three steps. First, we present a realistic, geographically distributed service that meets strict SLAs while using green hosts to lower its carbon footprint. We show that the service routes requests between competing hosts differently depending on its request arrival rate and on how many carbon offsets each host provides. Second, we use empirical traces of request arrivals to compute how many carbon offsets a host should provide to maximize its profit. We find that diurnal fluctuations and bursty surges interrupted long contiguous periods where the best carbon offset policy held steady, leading us to propose a reactive approach. For certain hosts, our approach can triple the profit compared to a fixed approach used in practice. Third, we simulate 9 services with diverse carbon footprint goals that distribute their workloads across 11 Web hosts worldwide. We use real data on the location of Web hosts and their provided carbon offset policies to show that adaptive green hosting can increase profit by 152% for one of today's larger green hosts.

Categories and Subject Descriptors

C.4 [**computer systems organization**]: performance of systems; H.1 [**information systems**]: models and principles

Keywords

system management, green computing, web hosting, datacenter, renewable energy, performance and cost models, autonomic

[†] *Supported in part by NSF EAGER grant CNS-1230776.*

1. INTRODUCTION

Web hosting centers, or datacenters, provide fast servers at low cost for Internet services ranging from search engines to e-commerce sites. Their success has changed the world, but their growing carbon footprint is a concern. By 2020, the annual carbon footprint of hosting centers worldwide is expected to exceed the footprint of the entire Netherlands [27]. Such a large footprint would add to climate change and put Web hosts at risk of costly, punitive regulations. Web hosts can slow the growth of their carbon footprint by using less electricity from coal and other dirty energy sources. There are two ways to do this: 1) use less energy per hosted service and 2) use energy from clean sources in place of energy from dirty sources. The first approach, using less energy, not only reduces carbon footprint, it also reduces the cost of Web hosting and has been widely studied [9, 32, 34, 36]. The second approach, using cleaner energy, can reduce or even eliminate carbon footprints, but typically increases energy costs. Green hosts[1] —an emerging cadre of Web hosts that invest in costly, clean energy while maintaining low prices—must host more services than traditional hosts to profit from their investment. This paper helps green hosts invest efficiently, buying clean energy only if it will bring in new customers and increase profit.

We propose *adaptive green hosting*, the hosting center's response to geographically distributed Internet services [28, 31, 32, 46]. Such services meet their cost, SLA, and carbon footprint goals by routing their workload to hosts that offer either 1) low carbon footprints, 2) high performance, or 3) a little bit of both. Our key insight is that a green host can entice a service to route workload to it by providing more carbon offsets. In this paper, we use the term *carbon offset* to represent a unit of clean energy that can replace a unit of dirty energy, both measured in Joules. Carbon offsets can be produced by on-site solar panels, power received from local wind farms, or renewable energy credits (RECs) purchased via energy markets. In adaptive green hosting, Web hosts set the ratio of carbon offsets to dirty energy, henceforth the *offset ratio*, by observing their profit from each hosted service under various settings over time. Where geographically distributed Internet services look for hosts with good offsetting policies, adaptive green hosting sets policies to entice service providers to use them.

Adaptive green hosting contrasts with the approach most widely used in practice today, fixed offset ratios. In choosing a fixed offset ratio, today's green hosts try to meet the carbon footprint goals

---

[1]The term "green Web host", instead of green datacenter, is widely used in popular press and on business websites [4, 22, 35]. In this paper, we follow this precedent.

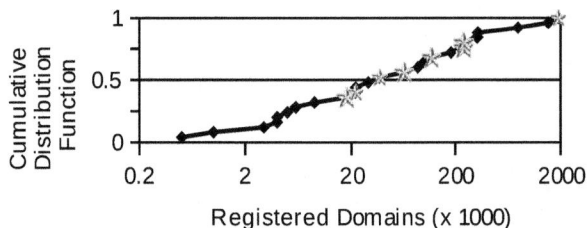

Figure 1: A niche market for green hosting. Each point represents 1 Web host. The X-axis is the number of A-type DNS records registered to the host. Stars indicate green hosts.

of their hosted services. However, meeting this threshold does not ensure that a green host will receive a service's workload. Instead, a service may route its workload across multiple hosts, mixing resources that differ in performance and offset ratios. This latter approach exploits fungible carbon offsets. The service needs only ensure that the weighted sum of their carbon footprint across all hosts meets their goals.

We compare fixed versus adaptive offset ratios using a geographically distributed service proposed in prior work [28]. The service chooses between 3 international Web hosts. We show that daily and bursty workload patterns alone can change the service's routing policies, suggesting that fixed offset ratios do not always maximize a green host's profit. At times, a fixed offset ratio causes green hosts to buy too many offsets (wasting money). At other times, it causes green hosts to buy too few offsets (losing customers). Our proposed adaptive approach can increase profit by 152% for one of today's larger green hosts. This paper makes the following contributions:

1. We present a new problem that intersects autonomic and green computing: Adaptive management of carbon offsets in shared web hosting centers.

2. We show that a green host's profit from an investment in clean energy is affected by the workload patterns of hosted services.

3. We propose a reactive approach to set the offset ratio that increases profit across diverse workloads and carbon footprint goals.

The remainder of this paper is as follows. Section 2 describes the state of the art in green hosting and discusses prior systems research on adapting to changing workloads. Section 3 overviews adaptive green hosting and defends its key premise: Time-varying workload changes can affect the yield of a given offset ratio. Section 4 computes a host's best offset ratio across real traces with diurnal and bursty patterns and proposes a reactive approach to set the offset ratio. Section 5 studies adaptive green hosting across multiple, geographically distributed services, showing that adaptive green hosting increases profits compared to an aggressive fixed offset ratio. Section 6 concludes by framing these results in the broader context of green and autonomic computing.

2. RELATED WORK

This paper models a green host's profit under adaptive and fixed carbon offset to dirty energy ratios, advancing the state of the art. Our models study how carbon-aware services react as green hosts increase their offset ratios, extending recent research on carbon awareness. Finally, we propose a reactive approach to set offset ratios, adding to a large body of work in workload adaptation. In this section, we outline related work in these areas.

State of the Art in Green Hosting: AISO [4], HostGator [22], Green Geeks, and GreenQloud [19] reflect a growing cadre of green hosts that hope to profit from their investments in clean energy. AISO, the eldest of these green hosts, was founded in 1997 but its customer base began to grow rapidly in 2002, increasing by 60% through 2008 [45]. AISO's growth marks the start of an ongoing boom in green hosting. HostGator [22], a green host based in windy Texas and founded in 2002, is now one of the largest low-cost Web hosts in the world, hosting over 1.8 million domain names. While AISO buys solar panels to invest in clean energy, HostGator buys renewable energy credits from local wind farms. The latter approach, using renewable energy credits, allows HostGator to support offset ratios greater than 100% by buying multiple credits for every joule used. HostGator in particular offsets 130% of the dirty energy used to power its servers. Green Geeks offset 300%.

Green hosting firms are targeting a small but growing market, Internet service providers that want show their commitment to the environment. Most people worldwide (83%) say that they prefer green products when they do not cost more than non-green alternatives [21], perhaps reflecting conspicuous altruism [20]. Similar results show that CIOs (61%) and system managers (71%) are willing to support green hosts if prices, response times, and throughput are the same [8, 23].

Figure 1 provides evidence of the growth. We plot registrations on the domain name services (DNS) of Web hosts, a rough but widely used metric to size Web hosts. Hosts with more authoritative (A-type) DNS records likely support more services. Using Domain Tools [12], we counted the DNS records of 200 Web hosts returned from online searches, plotting the 25 largest. In this group, there were 8 hosts that mentioned clean energy investments on their public Web pages (green hosts) and 17 traditional hosts that did not. We also controlled for price and hosting features. Each host offered hosting plans below $5, a 99.9% uptime guarantee, and unlimited network data transfer. Most green hosts in our study were above the median in terms of registered domains with 2.9 times more A-type records than traditional hosts on average.

Research on Carbon-Aware Services: With the boom in green hosting, some services now consider their carbon footprint when choosing between Web hosts. These services, called geographically distributed services, can use many hosts worldwide. Le et al. [28] studied services that capped their carbon footprints either by cap-and-trade, cap-and-pay, or absolutely capped policies. Their key insight was that a central load balancer could route requests between green and dirty Web hosts to maintain a low carbon footprint while meeting SLAs. Liu et al. [31, 32] provided a model to assess a Web host's performance to carbon footprint efficiency. They use weighted linear models to find the best host, proposing a scalable algorithm to do so. Zhang et al. [46] studied services that tried to minimize the carbon footprint of certain requests within a fixed budget. This approach reflects a common practice where large companies outsource a small portion of their operation to a green host, often for conspicuous altruism [4, 20]. Ren et al. [38] also discuss the costs of going green.

Internet services can also consider their carbon footprint by deciding when, if ever, to process requests. A service can drop requests and turn off machines to use less dirty energy. Blink [39] proposed a key-value storage service that transferred popular keys away from nodes that were turned off during intermittent clean energy outages. The challenge was to serve as many read and write requests as possible using only resources powered by clean energy. Li et al. [29] turned off processor cores to increase the ratio of renewable energy to dirty energy on a system. Similarly, Gmach et

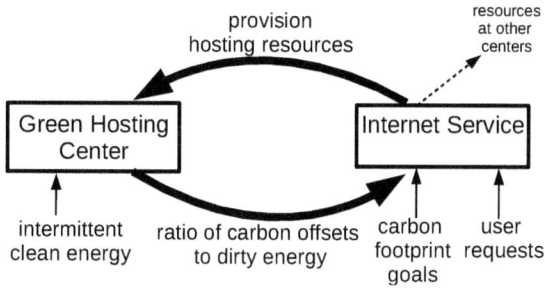

Figure 2: Adaptive green hosting for Internet services that lease resources on demand.

al. [16, 17] found that server-power capping and consolidation to power servers under low renewable-energy production can enable renewable powered services, albeit with a performance cost. Stewart et al. [42] was among the first to explore these problems, "showing that datacenters must use costly batteries or grid ties to make up for below-threshold renewable-energy production."

Workload Adaptation: It is well known that Web hosts support dynamic workloads that exhibit daily [5, 40], bursty [7], and nonstationary patterns [40]. Control theory solutions are now widely used in research and practice. Abdelzaher et al. [3] provides a good primer on such techniques, covering resource and admission controllers, sensors, and reactive and predictive techniques. There has been too much work in this area to list here. Our work adds to the field by considering a new metric, the offset ratio.

3. MAKING THE CASE FOR AN ADAPTIVE APPROACH

Given the boom in green hosting, we believe future Web hosts will compete by offering fast, cheap, and *green* resources to nimble cloud-based services. We propose adaptive green hosting, a new control loop based on carbon offset ratios (shown in Figure 2). Hosts adapt their offset ratios for each hosted service in response to changes in the availability of carbon offsets and request arrival patterns. We define a *carbon offset policy* as a vector where each element indicates the offset ratio assigned to each hosted service. This section makes the case for an adaptive approach by showing that fixed policies yield below optimal profits even when carbon offsets are always available at a fixed price and hosted services have fixed carbon-footprint goals.

3.1 Motivating Example

Consider Ecosia [13], a simple Internet service that provides a wrapper to Bing's search APIs and uses ad revenue to 1) offset Bing's estimated footprint and 2) invest in a rainforest protection program. Rather than spending its ad revenue on carbon offsets for the servers that host its homepage, CSS style sheets, and CGI scripts, Ecosia uses green hosts, bundling the costs of carbon offsets with hosting expenses. Ecosia commits to a carbon neutral footprint for its servers [13], i.e. 100% offset ratio. That is, Ecosia must be able to attribute 1 carbon offset for every joule of dirty energy used to power its servers. Every month these servers support more than 15 million unique searches that must complete quickly or else Ecosia will lose users [2].

For this example, we assume that Ecosia can send search requests that originate in the East Coast of the US to a Web host in either 1) the Eastern US, 2) the Western US, or 3) Europe. This setup mimics prior work [11, 28]. The hosts differ only in their network latency and carbon offsets per joule. The eastern host has

the lowest network latency (41ms round trip on average), then the western host (80ms), and finally the European host (121ms). Each host leases cloud instances that can service a request in 1.6ms, supporting up to 600 requests per second (RPS). However, successful requests must complete within 150ms, including network latency, queuing delay, and service time. The expected successful requests from each datacenter is shown below, using an modified M/M/1 queuing model [25].

$$\text{Eastern US Host} \qquad v_0 = \frac{(0.150 - 0.041)}{\frac{1}{(600 - \lambda_0)}} \qquad (1)$$

$$\text{Western US Host} \qquad v_1 = \frac{(0.150 - 0.080)}{\frac{1}{(600 - \lambda_0)}} \qquad (2)$$

$$\text{European Host} \qquad v_2 = \frac{(0.150 - 0.121)}{\frac{1}{(600 - \lambda_0)}} \qquad (3)$$

Here, λ_0 reflects the request arrival rate at time 0. The eastern host offers no carbon offsets, the western host is carbon neutral, and finally the European host buys 2 offsets for every joule it uses. In other words, the hosts have offset ratios of 0%, 100%, and 200% respectively.

Ecosia wants to use as few cloud instances as possible while ensuring 1) all arriving requests complete successfully and 2) carbon footprint goals are met. Cloud instances are leased hourly. We assume that at every 1-hour interval t, Ecosia knows its request arrival rate for that interval, e.g., $\lambda_t = 120$ requests per second. With the request arrival rate, we can compute how many requests each instance can complete successfully (i.e., $v_0 = 51, v_1 = 38, v_2 = 16$ under $\lambda_t = 120$ RPS). Knowing the offset ratio for each instance (i.e., $c_0 = 0\%, c_1 = 100\%, c_2 = 200\%$) and Ecosia's goal of being carbon neutral ($C = 100\%$), we can compute the Ecosia's optimal workload distribution, i.e., the vector $X = <x_0, x_1, \cdots, x_i>$ where each element reflects how many instances (an integer) Ecosia leases from each host i. The formal optimization model is:

$$\text{Minimize} \sum_{i=0}^{n} x_i^{(t)} \qquad (4)$$

$$\text{Subject to} \frac{\sum_{i=0}^{n} E_i c_i^{(t)} x_i^{(t)}}{\sum E_i x_i^{(t)}} \geq C \qquad (5)$$

$$\text{and} \sum_{i=0}^{n} v_i x_i^{(t)} \geq \lambda \qquad (6)$$

$$\text{and} \forall_i (x_i \in \mathbb{Z}) \qquad (7)$$

The goal is to minimize the total number of instances used. The first constraint keeps Ecosia's servers within a target carbon footprint (C). To be carbon neutral, Ecosia would set $C = 0$. Assuming green hosts and traditional hosts differ only in their offset ratio, we uniformly set the energy per instance coefficient (E_i) to 100wH. The second constraint requires enough instances to process incoming requests (λ_t) within SLA.

Integer programming solvers can find near optimal workload distributions for Ecosia [28, 31, 46]. We used LP solve, an open source solver commonly bundled with Linux platforms [33]. Under 120 RPS, Ecosia would use 4 instances from the host in western US only. Even though the host in eastern US can successfully complete 1.3X more requests per instance, the lack of carbon offsets forces Ecosia to use other hosts.

Under adaptive green hosting, the eastern host could buy carbon offsets specifically to attract Ecosia's workload. The carbon-offset

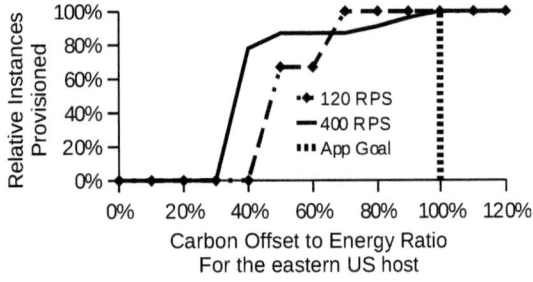

Figure 3: Carbon-offset elasticity for the eastern US host. The y-axis shows instances provisioned on the host relative to the maximum setting, i.e., $\frac{\eta_{east}(X) - \eta_{east}(K)}{\eta_{east}(K)}$ where K maximizes η_{east}. Ecosia routes requests differently across offset ratios (x-axis). Under 120 requests per second (RPS), $\eta_{east}(K)$ equals 3 instances. Under 400 RPS, it equals 23 instances.

elasticity (η) captures a host's workload as a function of carbon offsets assigned (ζ) to a target service. The carbon-offset elasticity tells us if a host can increase its workload by giving a target service more offsets per joule of dirty energy. These offsets can be bought as renewable energy credits, transferred from another service, or pulled from on-site sources. Because energy is fungible, this is an accounting problem. Below, we show the optimization formula for carbon offset elasticity for a single service. Equation 9 projects Equation 5 to a single host that considers the marginal gain by changing its offset ratio (Equation 10).

$$\eta_j(\zeta) = x_j : \text{Minimize} \sum_i^n x_i^{(t)} \tag{8}$$

$$\text{Subject to} \frac{\sum_{i=1}^n c^{(t)} x_i^{(t)} + \zeta x_0^{(t)}}{\sum x_i^{(t)}} \geq C \tag{9}$$

$$\text{and} \sum_{i=0}^n v_i x_i^{(t)} \geq \lambda \tag{10}$$

For N discrete settings of ζ, we can compute a host's carbon offset elasticity for a model-driven service by solving N integer programming problems. *Throughout this paper, we use this key insight to assess the yield of clean energy investments for a host.*

Figure 3 shows the carbon-offset elasticity for the eastern host. The result highlights a unique aspect of clean energy: it is fungible. Even though Ecosia managers want their service to be carbon neutral, they will lease instances from a host that offsets less than 100% of its carbon footprint if other hosts offset more than 100%. In this example, the eastern host benefited. Under 120 RPS, if the eastern US host were to offset just 50% of its carbon footprint, the best workload distribution used only eastern US and European instances. If the eastern host were to offset 70% of its carbon footprint, the best workload distribution used 1 European and 3 eastern US instances, matching the the number of instances used if the host were to offset 100% (carbon neutral).

The carbon elasticity changes when Ecosia's request arrival rate rises to 400 RPS. Under 70% carbon offset ratio, European instances detracted 13% of the workload that would be sent to the eastern US host if it were carbon neutral. In fact, under 400 RPS, the eastern host leases the same number of instances under a 50% offset ratio as it does at the 70% offset ratio. This shows that a static carbon offset policy chosen under 1 request arrival rate can be below optimal when the request rate changes. Note, this finding does not require that Ecosia managers change their carbon footprint

Table 1: A summary of all outcomes for the workload distribution found via integer programming solution for carbon-capped and performance-oriented services.

Conditions	Hosts chosen
$c_{BP} \geq C$	East
$\forall_i lp_i(\lambda) \in Z$ and	East, West, or Euro
$\sum v_i \cdot [lp_i(\lambda) - \lfloor (lp_i(\lambda)) \rfloor] \leq 2v_{sp}$	East, West, or Euro
$\sum v_i \cdot [lp_i(\lambda) - \lfloor (lp_i(\lambda)) \rfloor] > 2v_{west}$ and $\sum v_i \cdot [lp_i(\lambda) - \lfloor (lp_i(\lambda)) \rfloor] \leq v_{east}$	East, West Euro, $Euro_\infty$
$\sum v_i \cdot [lp_i(\lambda) - \lfloor (lp_i(\lambda)) \rfloor] > 2 * v_{east}$ and $\sum v_i \cdot [lp_i(\lambda) - \lfloor (lp_i(\lambda)) \rfloor] \leq v_{east} + v_{euro}$	East, West Euro, $Euro_\infty$

goals or relax their SLA, nor does it require that carbon offsets become more or less available. Also, we observe that the elasticity function grew slowly after 40% offset, raising the question, "does a 15% increase in leased instances justify a 60% increase in the offset ratio?" We address this question Section 4.

3.2 Generalizing the Example

The relative throughput and offset ratios of the hosts in our example capture a practical region of the workload distribution problem for carbon aware services. The general problem is an integer programming problem; each service assigns an integer ($ip_i \in \mathbb{Z}$) to n-tuples (v_i, c_i) reflecting the instances leased from each host. The ideal solution is not limited by the integer requirement and finds a solution equal to the linear programming solution ($lp_i \in \mathbb{R}$). We constrain this space of problems with the following assumption: a service will consider only 1 host that doesn't meet its carbon footprint goals, the best performing host. Our assumption builds from the intuition that workload distribution involves some management costs that will deter managers from choosing poor performing hosts that offer too few offsets to meet a service's goals. We call services that follow this assumption performance oriented.

We claim that any carbon-capped and performance-oriented service will lease instances from only 1) its best performing host, 2) its best performing host that meets carbon footprint goals (i.e., second best performing host), or 3) the host offers an offset ratio that exceeds the service's footprint goals and combines with the best performing host to yield highest performance per instance achievable while meeting footprint goals (exploiting fungible offsets). These properties correspond to the eastern US, western US, and European hosts in the Ecosia example. Changing the absolute throughput and offset ratios of a service's hosts will change the proportions with which each host is selected. However, our claim is that any host used by a carbon capped service will have (in the limit) at least one of the 3 properties above.

We prove this claim by considering all possible outcomes of the optimization model. Table 1 provides a summary of our proof.

Outcome #1: The best performing host offers an offset ratio that exceeds the service's carbon footprint goals. The service uses instances from only the eastern US host.

Outcome #2: The linear programming solution returns only integer values. With only 2 constraints, an n-host linear programming solution chooses between only 3 hosts [43]. The service picks instances from either only the western US host or some linear combination of the eastern US and European hosts, whichever provides the best performance per instance. The outcomes here are restricted by our prior assumption that each service considers at most 1 dirty host. We leave to future work an extension of this analysis for services that can use more than 1 dirty host. For such services, any mix of dirty and green hosts could be the most efficient, which would make computing the η function more complex.

Outcome #3: The linear programming solution uses fractional instances to process fewer than $2v_{west}$ requests. Here, the integer programming solution replaces the fractional instances with whole instances. The western US host represents the most efficient way to do this, since, by definition, it offers the greatest performance among hosts that meet carbon footprint goals.

Outcome #4: The linear programming solution uses fractional instances to process fewer than v_{east} requests. Here, we rely on the performance-oriented assumption. The service either provisions (more than 2) instances from only the western US host, or it mixes instances with the eastern US host and some other host that exceeds its footprint goals. The service must use either the eastern US host or the western US host because no other host offers fewer offsets than the western US host and exceeds its throughput. As the Europoean host's offset ratio goes to infinity, we can show that it becomes the host that the eastern US host is combined with. Thus, we denote it as $euro_\infty$ in Table 1.

Outcome #5: The linear programming solution uses fractional instances to process fewer than $v_{east} + v_{euro}$ requests. This outcome combines instances from Outcome #3 and #4. Finally, we note that the linear programming solution would not process more fractional requests than $v_{east} + v_{euro}$.

4. ADAPTING TO REAL WORKLOADS

Section 3 described an Internet service that divided user requests among competing hosts to 1) be carbon neutral and 2) keep its costs low. Hosts received a portion of the service's requests, depending on their cost to throughput ratio, carbon footprint, and the rate at which user requests arrived. This example showed that, as request rates change over time, green hosts that use fixed offset ratios will sometimes lower their profit by buying too many (spending more than needed) or too few offsets (losing customers).

This section shows that green hosts can increase profit derived from a service by eschewing fixed offset ratios in favor of an adaptive approach. Prior research on adapting to workload changes has focused on how services should provision instances to maximize throughput [3], minimize costs [15, 32], and meet carbon goals [28, 31, 46]. In this section, we focus on how *hosts* should set their offset ratio (e.g., by buying RECs) to maximize their profit for a service. Like prior work, this function depends on the service's request rate, cost models, and carbon footprint goals. However, unlike prior work, this function also depends on the performance and offset ratios of other hosts.

We revisit our example service from Section 3. This time, we use a trace from a real enterprise service to capture changing request rates. For each 1-hour window in the traces, we compute carbon offset ratios that maximize profit for the eastern, western, and European hosts. We study 1) how many times the best carbon offset ratio changes, 2) how quickly it changes, and 3) how much it changes. Our results prompted us to create a reactive approach that adapts the offset ratio based on recent history. We begin by presenting a formal profit model for green hosting.

4.1 Profit Model

Web hosting centers that adopt a cloud computing model earn money by leasing virtual resources over a fixed period of time [6]. A leasable resource is called an instance. Hosts profit when they earn more money per leased resource than they spend buying, maintaining, and powering them (captured in Equation 11).

$$P = I \cdot p \cdot R - \frac{StartupCosts}{T} \qquad (11)$$

In the above equation, profit P is a function of instances leased (I), revenue per instance (R), the percentage of revenue turned into profit considering only operational costs (p), and amortized startup costs (where T captures the host's expected lifetime). We assume $I \geq 1$. In most places, clean energy costs more than dirty energy, so green hosts will have higher operational costs. They must lease more instances to profit from this investment.

$$P(c) = \eta(c) \cdot p \cdot R - c \cdot E \cdot cost_{co2e} \cdot S - \frac{StartupCosts}{T} \qquad (12)$$

$$P(c) = \eta(c) \cdot p \cdot R - c \cdot E \cdot cost_{co2e} \cdot \lceil \frac{\eta(c)}{S} \rceil S - \frac{StartupCosts}{T} \qquad (13)$$

Equation 12 adds the cost of carbon offsets ($cost_{co2e}$), energy per instance (E), the granularity of energy data (measured in instances) (S), and the ratio of carbon offsets to joules (c). These factors make green hosting less profitable than traditional Web hosting. The equation also shows the effect of carbon offset elasticity ($\eta(c)$) in increasing the amount of instances leased. Green hosts can profit by investing in clean energy only when the carbon offset elasticity leads to increased revenue. Equation 13 shows the full profit model when $\eta(c)$ can exceed S.

In practice, green hosts invest in clean energy with caution, trying to keep the risk of losing money low. Here, we formalize a risk aware approach commonly used in practice [14, 26]. The idea is to cap how much money is invested in clean energy so that a small increase in leased instances yields profit.

Low Risk Green Hosting: *The maximum ratio of carbon offsets to dirty energy (c_{max}) is capped, such that $c_{max} \leq \frac{pR}{E \cdot cost_{co2e} \cdot |S|}$. Where S is the set of leasable instances receiving the offsets. Plugging c_{max} into Equation 12, we see that it allows a host to recoup costs when increasing the offset ratio from 0 to c_{max} yields only 1 leased instance (the worst case).*

Theorem: A green host that invests with the above low-risk approach should choose the smallest c that maximizes $\eta(c)$ in order to maximize profit. Here, we provide a short proof. First, we observe that a host's costs are linear in c, provided $E > 0$ and $cost_{co2e} > 0$. If $\eta(c + \epsilon) = \eta(c)$, then costs under $c + \epsilon$ would exceed costs under c, meaning lower total profit. Thus, the smallest c is a necessary condition. Second, we prove by contradiction that η must be maximized.

$$Hypothesis: Assume P(c_1) > P(c_2) \text{ where } \eta(c_1) < \eta(c_2) \qquad (14)$$

$$WLOG: StartupCosts = 0 \qquad (15)$$

$$Substitution: P(c_1) = \eta(c_1)pR - c_1 Ecost_{co2e}|S| \qquad (16)$$

$$Substitution: P(c_2) = \eta(c_2)pR - c_2 Ecost_{co2e}|S| \qquad (17)$$

$$WLOG: Assume c_1 = 0 \qquad (18)$$

$$Substitution: \eta(0)pR > \eta(c_2)pR - c_2 Ecost_{co2e}|S| \qquad (19)$$

$$Algebra: \frac{c_2 Ecost_{co2e}|S|}{pR} > \eta(c_2) - \eta(0) \qquad (20)$$

$$WLOG: Assume \eta(c_2) - \eta(0) = 1 \qquad (21)$$

$$WLOG: Assume c_2 = c_{max} \text{ i.e., as large as possible} \qquad (22)$$

$$Contradiction: \frac{|S|}{|S|} > 1 \qquad (23)$$

Finally, we used both public data and local tests to calibrate a realistic c_{max}. Table 2 shows inputs to our profit model and their

Table 2: Values used to estimate c_{max} for this study.

Public Data		
variable	value	source
R	\$0.085	Amazon EC2 [1]
p	4%	Amazon's EBITDA [44]
$cost_{co2e}$	\$0.0045	Renewable energy credits online [18]
Local Tests		
variable	value	source
E	23Kj	ARM Marvel processor + SSD
S	32	Tripp Lite PDU with power display

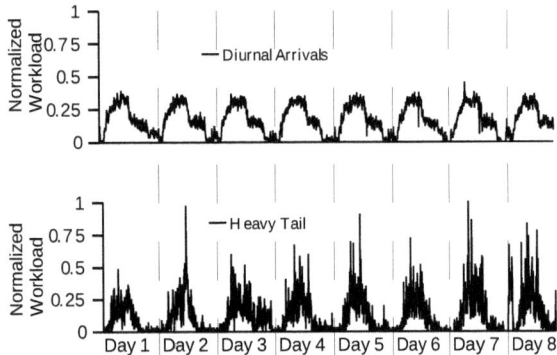

Figure 4: Request rates for a modern enterprise application, code-named VDR [40]. VDR is used in six continents. The plots show requests rates at 2 servers hosted in the Americas. The first plot compiles arriving requests for both servers, capturing diurnal patterns. The second plot shows request rates for a request type with fast response times, likely static content. In the second plot, requests arrive according to a heavy tail.

source. Our local setup uses a small cluster of ARM processor devices with attached SSD storage. These devices host Apache on Linux, supporting up to 600 requests per second throughput. These results match findings from prior work [30, 37]. The peak power from our ARM nodes is 5.5W; multiplying by 3,600 seconds provides our value for the hourly energy usage of an instance. We also consider a PUE of 1.2. Most (81%) power distribution units (PDU) used at the rack level in today's datacenter include LCD displays and network access for energy data [41]. Our PDU can support 32 instances. Note, the PDU is a good level to assign carbon offsets since energy data is easy to acquire. Assigning carbon offsets at higher levels in the power delivery system increase the size of S, diluting the amount of carbon offsets that can be purchased with low risk [10]. Filling these values into our model, we set $c_{max} = 300\%$ for all studies in the remainder of this paper.

4.2 Trace-driven Study

We used empirical traces of request rates and carbon prices to study the most profitable carbon offset ratios for green hosts over time. Recall, in Section 3, we computed η for the eastern host using a constant request rate and the default offset ratios of the western US and European hosts. In this section, we compute η for T timestamped request rates and offset ratios. Assuming low risk investing, the output reduces to a vector of T carbon offset ratios for each host, where the tth setting reflects the smallest ratio c_t that maximizes $\eta_t(c_t)$ given the request rate λ_t. Our final assessment of profit uses our model to combine results from all T time steps.

Figure 4 shows two normalized request rate traces taken from an HP service used across the world [40]. These traces cover approx. 8 days and capture diurnal patterns in the request rate. Both traces were normalized to produce about 1.5 million requests per

day (about 175 RPS). They differ in the distribution of request rates within a day. The top trace matches the distribution of all arriving requests. Its 99th percentile of request rates is 1.5X larger than the 99th percentile of an exponential distribution with the same mean. In other words, the top trace has a tail that is only slightly heavier than an exponential distribution. The bottom trace captures the arriving requests for 1 request type. The 99th percentile of request rates in this trace is 5X larger than the 99th percentile of a normal distribution with the same mean. In other words, the bottom trace has a tail that is much "heavier" than an exponential distribution. Such heavy tails are a well studied in Internet services [5, 7].

We also studied the effect of changing carbon prices by discounting c_{max} and default offset ratios. We used a trace of the daily market price for carbon offsets from iPath Global Carbon [24]. Our trace ranged from Feb. 8, 2012 through Feb. 14, 2012. The resulting daily, relative prices were 1.08, 1.08, 1.03, 0.98, 0.97, 0.94, and 1. Market prices often track wholesale prices well.

Study Results: We used the iterative method described in Section 3 to compute carbon offset elasticities for each host, workload, and time step. We chose 31 discrete values for the offset ratio, using multiples of 10% from 0 to 300%. For every 1-hour time step, we used the request rate (λ_t) from either the diurnal or heavy tail traces above to compute how many instances a host would provision if it set its offset ratio to one of the above discrete values. We assume that the other hosts keep their default offset ratio.

Table 3 shows how the best carbon offset ratio changed over time under 1) the diurnal workload with fixed carbon prices, 2) the heavy tail workload with fixed carbon prices, and 3) the heavy tail workload with changing carbon prices. In total we computed 1,674 offset elasticities (3 hosts x 3 workloads x 186 hours).

To maximize profit across each studied workload, every host needed to use at least 3 different offset-ratio settings. The hosts used fewer settings (below 4) under the diurnal workload than under the heavy tail traces. We explain these results by highlighting a key aspect of the integer programming (IP) outcomes outlined in Section 3: Linear programming (outcomes #1 and 2) provide the best solution modulo the request rate. When the request rate is larger than $v_{east} + v_{euro}$, a host should set its offset ratio to maximize its usage under the linear programming solution. For the eastern and western US hosts, this setting is very close to the service's carbon footprint goal. For the European host, this setting is the smallest setting that ensures the following $k * v_{east} + v_{euro} > v_{west}$ where k in $\mathbb{R}$ is the number of eastern US instances sponsored by the European host's fungible offsets. However, when the request rate falls below $v_{east} + v_{euro}$ (outcomes #3–5), the best settings change depending on the IP solution.

In our example, $v_{east} + v_{euro}$ equals 67 RPS and the average arrival rate is 175 RPS. The distribution of request rates in the diurnal workload is close to exponential, meaning the median request rate is close to the average rate. Indeed only 18% of the 1-hour intervals under the diurnal had request rate below 67 RPS. The offset ratio found under the linear programming solution was chosen of 90% of the time for all hosts. Heavy tail distributions do not share this property. Instead, short workload bursts make the average rate larger than the median. Despite having the same arrival rate, the heavy tail distribution shows request rates below 67 RPS 45% of the time. More generally, we can not claim that all heavy tail workloads on all cloud platforms will include some intervals where $\lambda_t < v_{east} + v_{euro}$. However, for a given average arrival rate, a high variance, heavy tail distribution is more likely than an exponential distribution to include such intervals.

Table 3: Data on the best carbon offset ratios in our study.
Metric: Number of Ratios Chosen ($|\bar{c}| : c \in \bar{c}$ iff $\exists t \, \forall k \, P_t(c) \geq P_t(k)$)
What to look for: Numbers greater than 1 suggest that fixed policies yield below optimal profit.

Workload	Eastern	Western	European
Diurnal	4 settings	3	3
Heavy tail	5	4	5
Heavy tail and market carbon prices	7	8	5

Metric: Expected Contiguity of 2nd Most Frequent Setting (Ex($|L|$: $\forall$ 1 $\in$ L $C_l = k \wedge$ (l+1) $\in$ L)
What to look for: Large numbers suggest carbon offset ratios are stable.

Workload	Eastern	Western	European
Diurnal	1.60 hours	1.75	1.23
Heavy tail	1.65	3.00	4.05
Heavy tail and market carbon prices	2.05	2.75	8.86

Metric: Absolute distance from 1st
What to look for: Large numbers reflect the magnitude of profits lost by static hosts. Minimum value is 10% and maximum is 300%.

Workload	Eastern	Western	European
Diurnal	100%	100%	200%
Heavy tail	100%	50%	190%
Heavy tail and market carbon prices	100%	100%	100%

Second, we observe that offset ratios change slowly. In particular, we observe several long contiguous periods under the second most frequent policy, even under the diurnal workload. Several last longer than 4 hours. We note that this correlated behavior is well explained by low request rates 1) at night and 2) between bursty periods. The average period of contiguity rounds up to 2 hours in all but 1 of the study traces. Finally, we also observe that the absolute distance between the second most frequent and most frequent ratio are far apart, simply setting the offset ratio to the larger of the two can waste a lot of money.

Table 4: Accuracy of reactive and tail-aware reactive approaches. Shown for the western US host.
Metric: Accuracy ($\sum_n \frac{I(C_n = Pred(n))}{n}$))

Web host	Mode	Reactive	Tail Aware
Diurnal	97%	95%	97%
Heavy tail	66%	65%	70%
Heavy tail w/ Carbon market	79%	73%	80%

4.3 A Reactive Approach

Since our trace-driven approach revealed that the best offset ratio held for long contiguous periods, we implemented a reactive approach to set the carbon offset ratio. We assume that Internet services tell each host what their ideal offset ratio was for the previous hour. Given that the service can monitor its request arrival rate, it can compute this offset directly using the approach described in Section 3.

Our reactive approach considers the history of a service's ideal offset ratio. When the ideal ratios over the last 2 hours match, we change the offset ratio to the matching value. Otherwise, we assign the ratio to the statistical mode. The latter works well under diurnal workloads where the most frequent ratio occurs 97% of the time. The former helps with heavy tailed workloads where the ratio changes for several hours at time.

Our full approach also exploits heavy tailed contiguous periods in the offset ratio. We scan the history of results for patterns indicating that a contiguous period of length l has a large probability of

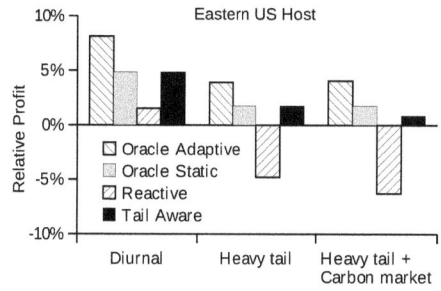

(a) Eastern US Host

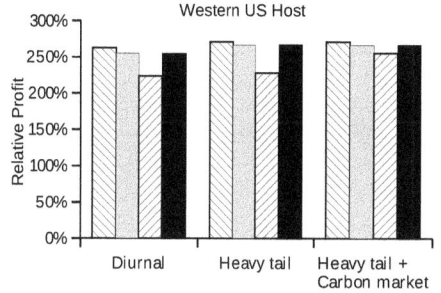

(b) Western US Host

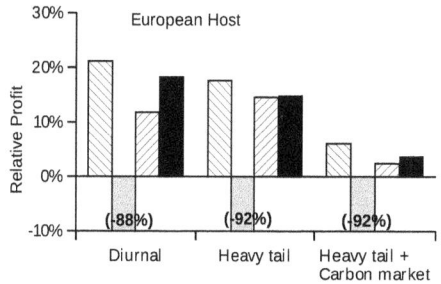

(c) European Host

Figure 5: Profit of east, west, and European hosts from the Ecosia example using real workload traces. All results are reported relative to the profit under the over-offsetting approach.

leading to a period of length $l + k$. If such patterns are found, our reactive policy returns to the mode after the $l + k$ interval. Table 4 shows the accuracy of our full, *tail-aware* approach in predicting the ideal offset ratio compared to using the mode or our base approach for the western US host. Our full approach makes the most accurate predictions in all cases, a property that holds across all studied hosts.

Results: We compare our reactive approach to an oracle-driven adaptive approach that sets the offset ratio to the value that maximizes profit for the upcoming interval (called *oracle adaptive*). We also compare against an oracle-driven fixed-setting approach that sets the offset ratio to the value that most frequently maximized profit throughout the trace (i.e., the statistical mode for the whole trace). These approaches use advanced knowledge that would be unavailable in a deployed system, but they are useful in demonstrating how well our reactive approach works. We also compare against the *over offsetting* approach which sets offset ratio to c_{max}. The idea behind this approach is that increasing the offset ratio will only increase η (which is not true). We make this over-offsetting approach our baseline.

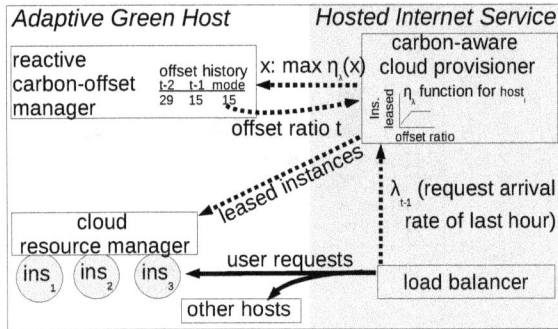

Figure 6: Our setup for adaptive green hosting. Dotted lines reflect data that is transmitted at every cloud provisioning interval (e.g., hourly). Solid lines reflect real time actions.

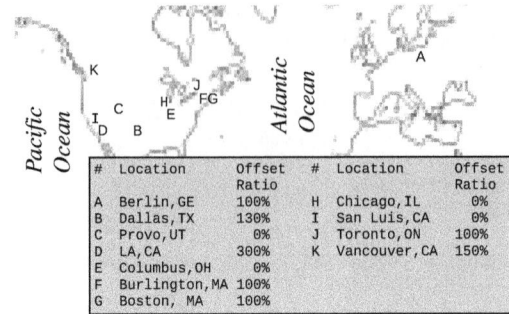

Figure 7: Where the shared Web hosts in our case studies live. We chose 11 of the largest Web hosts (green and traditional) using domain tools and online searches. Unintentionally, our results include hosts in North America and Europe only.

Figure 5 shows the profit achieved under the different carbon offsetting strategies. We highlight results from each host individually.

1. The eastern US host provides the best performance. If it raises its offset ratio about 100%, Ecosia would provision all instances on it. However, this may result in buying too many offsets. Generally, the profit loss from buying too many offsets, under low-risk investing, is lower than the loss from buying too few offsets. Thus, our base reactive approach which can under provision resources after noisy fluctuations in the ideal offset ratio is less profitable than the over-offsetting approach. Our tail-aware approach avoids losing money due noisy fluctuations by preemptively moving back to the mode when heavy tailed periods expire. We observe that small, short term changes in the ideal offset ratio can affect achieved profit.

2. The western US host sits in the middle. If the eastern host offers no carbon offsets, Ecosia often chooses the western host as a second option. However, since carbon offsets are fungible, if the western host increases its offsets to c_{max}, Ecosia will use the western host only so it can offset instances on the eastern host. Over-offsetting performs poorly. Comparing only the other approaches, the results are similar to the eastern US host.

3. The European host provides qualitatively different results. This host must offer high offset ratios (near c_{max}) to entice Ecosia to use it in combination with the eastern US host. It is most often best for this host to set an offset ratio of 0% to avoid wasting money on instances that won't be provisioned. However, for long periods in the middle of the day, the European host is best served by an offset ratio above 200%. Recall from Figure 3 that under high requests rates the European datacenter can reduce the offsets needed to provision eastern US instances. The mode is the wrong metric for this datacenter because the lost profit in the middle of the day far outweighs the cost of over offsetting. Our full approach is comparable to the optimal adaptive approach for this host.

5. CASE STUDIES ON SHARED HOSTS

Figure 6 details adaptive green hosting. At every provisioning interval, the hosted service uses recently observed data on its request arrival rate to compute the offset ratios that would maximize instances leased from each host (Section 3). The adaptive green hosts keeps a history of such data, and uses it to set its offset ratio for the next interval (Section 4). The hosted service then tries to maximize throughput within a carbon budget based on each host's performance and offset ratio by balancing its workload across hosts. In Section 4, we studied the effect of adaptive offset ratio on one service, finding that green hosts can increase profit by adapting

their offset ratio to the service's daily and bursty workload patterns. This section studies hosts that support many services.

5.1 Setup

We used our VDR traces to simulate 9 Ecosia services. Each service used a load balancer to route requests to either: 1) its best performing host, 2) the best performing host that met its carbon footprint goals, or 3) a host that offered a high offset ratio. We defined these services such that the best performing host mapped to one of the large Web hosts described in Figure 1.

Each service placed its load balancer at the best performing host and set its carbon footprint goal to the offset ratio of the fastest green host. When the load balancer sent requests to a remote host, the penalty was 1 round trip network delay (as in the queuing models in Section 3). We modeled delay between hosts using: 1) distance in miles between the other hosts and the nearest host, 2) speed of light, 3) a slowdown coefficient, and 4) TCP processing overhead. We calibrated the slowdown coefficient with regression tests on ping results between a laptop in Columbus, OH and servers deployed in London, UK, Frankfurt, GE, Berkeley, CA, St. Louis, MO, and Rochester, NY. We set the coefficient to 2.4.

Figure 7 plots the cities where each Web host's servers resided. The legend in the figure shows the carbon offset to dirty energy ratio offered by each host. We collected this data from public websites. There are 11 hosts listed, each is labeled with a letter to hide its identity. The two hosts offering the most carbon offsets (D and K) do not provide the highest throughput for any service.

Table 5 shows the set up for each service's load balancer and its carbon footprint goal. Two hosts (B and K) that offered offset ratios greater than 100% were used by services with diverse carbon footprint goals. Also, one well located carbon-neutral host (J) supported diverse footprint goals. Specifically, host B supported 7 services with the following goals: 100%, 100%, 130%, 130%, 130%, 130%, and 150%. Host J supported 3 services with the following goals: 100%, 100%, and 130%. Finally, host K supports 6 servies with the following goals: 150%, 130%, 130%, 130%, 130%, and 130%. We used the heavy tailed VDR trace for each service (Figure 4). The price of carbon offsets was fixed. The maximum throughput of each node was 600 requests per second.

At the top of every hour, our tail-aware reactive approach collected the ideal offset ratio for each service during the previous hour. We set the offset ratio for each service individually. Total profit for a host was the sum of profit from each hosted service. We compared this approach to the fixed offset policies commonly used in practice: 100%, 150%, 200%, and 300%. Here again, we call 300% the over offsetting approach and used it as our baseline.

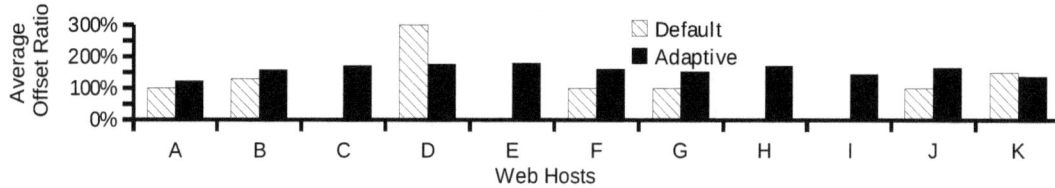

Figure 9: Average offset ratio recommended by adaptive green offsetting for each host in our setup.

Table 5: The configuration of each service's load balancer in our setup. The leftmost columns show the service number and its footprint goal. The rightmost columns label which hosts the service routes requests to.

#	footprint goal	Best performing	Best performing + meets goals	Many Offsets
1	100%	E	J	B
2	150%	C	K	D
3	100%	H	J	B
4	130%	A	B	K
5	130%	J	B	K
6	130%	F	B	K
7	150%	I	K	D
8	130%	G	B	K
9	130%	B	K	D

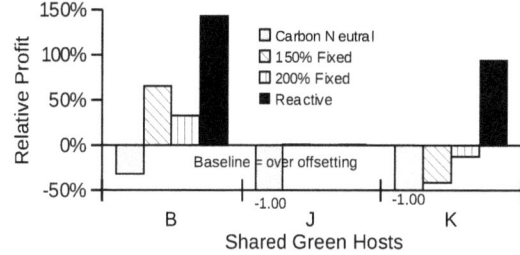

Figure 10: Relative profit of the shared green hosts when services provision according to a different optimization model [46]. Each host's profit per service under the over offsetting policy was $6.33, $5.50, and $4.83 respectively.

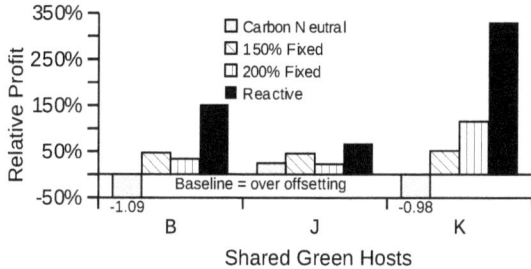

Figure 8: Relative profit of the shared green hosts (B, J, and K). Each host's profit per service under the over offsetting policy was $2.17, $7.66, and $1.5 respectively. We used the VDR request trace with heavy tail arrival patterns (7.8 days). The over offsetting policy sets a fixed offset ratio of 300%. Recall, only hosts B, J, and K were shared by services with diverse footprint goals.

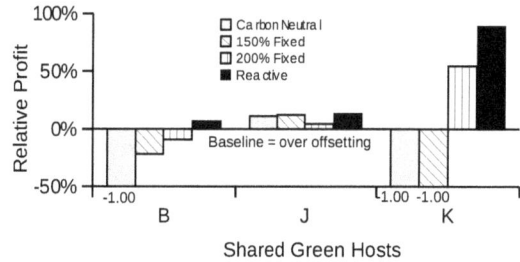

Figure 11: Relative profit of the shared green hosts when services can choose to buy carbon offset directly. Each host's profit per service under the over offsetting policy was $1.71, $2, and $0.66.

5.2 Shared Hosting Results

Figure 8 shows the relative profit increase from our *adaptive green hosting approach*. Our approach consistently outperformed the over offsetting approach, increasing profit by at least 68% in each case. Our gains were lowest (68%) for host J because its hosted services saw a wide difference in the offset ratio between their best performing hosts (0%) and host J (100%). Any investment in carbon offsets offered high yield. Indeed, the profit per service under the over offsetting policy ($7.66) was 2–4 times larger than the other hosts. Here, our approach increases profit by adapting to workload changes in services. We also run the same experiment on diurnal traces mentioned in Section 4. The relative profit increase for host B, J and K are 105%, 69% and 236% respectively.

We also compared two approaches commonly used in practice: over offsetting and carbon-neutral green hosting. Host B and K gain the most from over offsetting because they were in competition against other green hosts. Host J preferred a carbon neutral approach. First, our approach adapted to each host's environment, consistently outperfoming both approaches.

Is Adaptive Green Hosting Really Green? Adaptive green hosting increases profit in two ways. First, it helps green hosts buy

carbon offsets with low risk, allowing them to make bold investments (up to c_{max}) to bring in customers. Second, it helps green hosts avoid wasting money on too many offsets. This latter benefit could actually make hosts less green than they are today. Figure 9 shows the suggested average offset ratio of adaptive green hosting in our setup. The average offset ratio increased for 10 of the 11 hosts. Only host D, which offered a ratio of 300%, had a lower average offset ratio than its default. Because green hosts reflect a minority of web hosts in general, adaptive green hosting is likely to suggest increased investment in clean energy.

Can Adaptive Green Hosting be Applied to Different Service Models? The services that we have studied so far have been based on minimizing instances (cost) within carbon and throughput constraints [28]. However, recent work has explored alternative models. Zhang et al. [46] proposed a model that maximizes renewable energy usage within cost and throughput constraints. Our approach to create carbon offset elasticity models can be applied to this service model also. We modified our setup to allow services #1, 2 and 3 to use this service model. Figure 10 shows the results. Services in this model tend to route a few requests to the greenest datacenter. Host J (which offers on 100% offset ratio by default) suffers the most. Over offsetting helps this host the most. Hosts B and K can adapt not only to supporting diverse carbon footprint goals but even to diverse service models. Our adaptive approach increases relative profit by more than 100 percentage points for both hosts.

Is Adaptive Green Hosting Useful when Services by Offsets Directly? Instead of using green hosts, services could buy offsets directly, removing the need to route requests across multiple data-centers. As discussed in Section 3, services that adopt this approach lose economic benefits from bundling hosting and offsetting costs. Nonetheless, we can compute the carbon-offset elasticity for these services by treating carbon markets as a special Web host that offers many offsets and zero throughput. We divided $cost_{co2e}$ by the price of an EC2 instance and used the result (approx. 8000%) as the offset ratio for the special, carbon-market host. We added this host as a fourth choice to every service in our setup. Some services used this host, reducing the profit per service for the shared hosts. However, as shown in Figure 11, our adaptive approach still provided the most profit for shared green hosts, increasing profit by at least 7% compared to the over offsetting approach.

6. CONCLUSION

Green hosts invest in clean energy while keeping their prices low and competitive. These hosts profit from their investment by hosting more Internet services than their traditional counterparts; it is possible that they can tap into a niche market to accomplish this. Today's green hosts adopt ad-hoc policies for investing in clean energy, e.g., by buying as much clean energy as possible within a fixed budget. This paper showed that such fixed policies yield below optimal profit when the hosted Internet services support diurnal and bursty workloads and when the hosted services have diverse carbon footprint goals. We proposed a new research agenda: *adaptive green hosting*, where hosts invest in clean energy based on prior or predicted yield. We proposed a first-cut reactive solution that exploits heavier-than-exponential tails in Internet service workloads. Our reactive approach improves profit for existing green hosts and tends to urge hosts to increase their investments in clean energy. Future work will improve upon our approach by considering more complex interplay between SLAs and carbon footprint goals, heterogeneous energy efficiency and carbon efficiency among hosts, and in depth workload prediction approaches.

7. REFERENCES

[1] Amazon elastic compute cloud. http://aws.amazon.com/ec2/pricing/.
[2] Ecosia - number of daily searches. http://ecosia.org/statistics.php.
[3] T. Abdelzaher, J. Stankovic, C. Lu, R. Zhang, and Y. Lu. Feedback performance control in software services. *Control Systems, IEEE*, 23(3), 2003.
[4] Aiso.net: Web hosting as nature intended. http://aiso.net.
[5] M. Arlitt and C. Williamson. Web server workload characterization: The search for invariants. In *SIGMETRICS*.
[6] L. Barroso and U. Holzle. *The Datacenter as a Computer – An Introduction to to the Design of Warehouse-Scale Machines*. Morgan and Claypool Publishers, 2009.
[7] A. Bestavros and M. Crovella. Self-similarity in world wide web traffic: Evidence and possible causes. In *Sigmetrics*, 1995.
[8] J. Chattaway. Rackspace green survey. In *Rackspace Hosting White Paper*, June 2008.
[9] G. Chen, W. He, J. Liu, S. Nath, L. Rigas, L. Xiao, and F. Zhao. Energy-aware server provisioning and load dispatching for connection-intensive internet services. In *USENIX NSDI*, Apr. 2008.
[10] N. Deng and C. Stewart. Concentrating renewable energy in grid-tied datacenters. In *International Symposium on Sustainable Systems and Technology (ISSST)*, May 2011.
[11] N. Deng, C. Stewart, D. Gmach, and M. Arlitt. Policy and mechanism for carbon-aware cloud applications. In *NOMS*, Apr. 2012.
[12] Domain Tools.
[13] Ecosia - the green search. http://www.ecosia.org/.

[14] Eileen, OWC.net. Personal communication. http://owc.net.
[15] A. Gandhi, Y. Chen, D. Gmach, M. Arlitt, and M. Marwah. Minimizing data center sla violations and power consumption via hybrid resource provisioning. In *IGCC*, 2011.
[16] D. Gmach, Y. Chen, A. Shah, J. Rolia, C. Bash, T. Christian, and R. Sharma. Profiling sustainability of data centers. In *ISSST*, 2010.
[17] D. Gmach, J. Rolia, C. Bash, Y. Chen, T. Christian, A. Shah, R. Sharma, and Z. Wang. Capacity planning and power management to exploit sustainable energy. In *International Conference on Network and Services Management*, Oct. 2010.
[18] GoodEnergy. http://www.goodenergy.com, 2012.
[19] Greenqloud- the worlds first truly green compute cloud. http://www.greenqloud.com.
[20] V. Griskevicius, J. M. Tybur, and B. Van den Bergh. Going green to be seen: status, reputation, and conspicuous conservation. *J Pers Soc Psychol*, 98(3):392–404, 2010.
[21] N. Holdings. The nielsen global online environmental survey, 2011.
[22] Hostgator: Web hosting services. http://hostgator.com.
[23] P. Inc. Going green:sustainable growth strategies. www.pwc.com/en_GX/gx/technology/pdf/going-green.pdf, 2011.
[24] ipath global carbon etn. http://www.ipathetn.com/product/GRN/.
[25] R. Jain. *The Art of Computer Systems Performance Analysis*. John Wiley and Sons, 1991.
[26] James Packard, Emerson Inc. Personal communication. http://emerson-datacenter.com.
[27] J. Kaplan, W. Forrest, and N. Kindler. Revolutionizing data center energy efficiency. McKinsey and Company, 2008.
[28] K. Le, O. Bilgir, R. Bianchini, M. Martonosi, and T. D. Nguyen. Capping the brown energy consumption of internet services at low cost. In *International Green Computing Conference*, Aug. 2010.
[29] C. Li, W. Zhang, C. Cho, and T. Li. Solarcore: Solar energy driven multi-core architecture power management. In *HPCA*, Feb. 2011.
[30] K. Lim, P. Ranganathan, J. Chang, C. Patel, T. Mudge, and S. Reinhardt. Understanding and designing new server architectures for emerging warehouse-computing environments. In *ISCA*, 2008.
[31] Z. Liu, M. Lin, A. Wierman, S. Low, and L. Andrew. Geographical load balancing with renewables. In *Greenmetrics*, June 2011.
[32] Z. Liu, M. Lin, A. Wierman, S. Low, and L. Andrew. Greening geographical load balancing. In *ACM SIGMETRICS*, June 2011.
[33] LPSolve. http://www.lpsolve.com.
[34] D. Meisner, B. Gold, and T. Wenisch. Powernap: Eliminating server idle power. In *ASPLOS*, Mar. 2009.
[35] M. Ontkush. Plethora of options for green web hosting. www.treehugger.com, 2007.
[36] R. Raghavendra, P. Ranganathan, V. Talwar, Z. Wang, and X. Zhu. No power struggles: Coordinated multi-level power management for the data center. In *ASPLOS*, Mar. 2008.
[37] P. Ranganathan and P. Leech. Simulating complex enterprise workloads using utilization traces. In *ASPLOS*, Mar. 2007.
[38] C. Ren, D. Wang, B. Urgaonkar, and A. Sivasubramaniam. Carbon-aware energy capacity planning for datacenters. In *MASCOTS*, Aug. 2012.
[39] N. Sharma, S. Barker, D. Irwin, and P. Shenoy. Blink: managing server clusters on intermittent power. In *ASPLOS*, Mar. 2011.
[40] C. Stewart, T. Kelly, and A. Zhang. Exploiting nonstationarity for performance prediction. In *EuroSys Conf.*, Mar. 2007.
[41] C. Stewart and J. Li. Power provisioning for diverse datacenter workloads. In *Workshop on Energy Efficient Design*, June 2011.
[42] C. Stewart and K. Shen. Some joules are more precious than others: Managing renewable energy in the datacenter. In *Workshop on Power Aware Computing and Systems(HotPower)*, Sept. 2009.
[43] M. J. Todd. The many facets of linear programming. *Mathematical Programming*, 91(3), Feb. 2002.
[44] Trefis Team. Amazon kills it in cloud computing but it wont budge the stock price.
[45] The AMD Opteron Processor Helps AISO. www.vmware.com.
[46] Y. Zhang, Y. Wang, and X. Wang. Greenware: Greening cloud-scale data centers to maximize the use of renewable energy. In *Middleware*, Dec. 2011.

Dynamic Energy-Aware Capacity Provisioning for Cloud Computing Environments

Qi Zhang
University of Waterloo
Waterloo, ON, Canada
q8zhang@uwaterloo.ca

Mohamed Faten Zhani
University of Waterloo
Waterloo, ON, Canada
mfzhani@uwaterloo.ca

Shuo Zhang
National University of Defense
Technology
Changsha, Hunan, China
zhangshuo@nudt.edu.cn

Quanyan Zhu
University of Illinois at
Urbana-Champaign, USA
zhu31@illinois.edu

Raouf Boutaba
University of Waterloo
Waterloo, ON, Canada
Pohang University of Science
and Technology (POSTECH)
Pohang 790-784, Korea
rboutaba@uwaterloo.ca

Joseph L. Hellerstein
Google, Inc.
Seattle, Washington, USA
jlh@google.com

ABSTRACT

Data centers have recently gained significant popularity as a cost-effective platform for hosting large-scale service applications. While large data centers enjoy economies of scale by amortizing initial capital investment over large number of machines, they also incur tremendous energy cost in terms of power distribution and cooling. An effective approach for saving energy in data centers is to adjust dynamically the data center capacity by turning off unused machines. However, this dynamic capacity provisioning problem is known to be challenging as it requires a careful understanding of the resource demand characteristics as well as considerations to various cost factors, including task scheduling delay, machine reconfiguration cost and electricity price fluctuation.

In this paper, we provide a control-theoretic solution to the dynamic capacity provisioning problem that minimizes the total energy cost while meeting the performance objective in terms of task scheduling delay. Specifically, we model this problem as a constrained discrete-time optimal control problem, and use *Model Predictive Control* (MPC) to find the optimal control policy. Through extensive analysis and simulation using real workload traces from Google's compute clusters, we show that our proposed framework can achieve significant reduction in energy cost, while maintaining an acceptable average scheduling delay for individual tasks.

Categories and Subject Descriptors

C.4 [**Performance of Systems**]: Modeling techniques; I.2.8 [**Problem Solving, Control Methods, and Search**]:

Control Theory; I.6.3 [**Simulation and Modeling**]: Applications

General Terms

Management, Performance, Experimentation

Keywords

Cloud Computing; Resource Management; Energy Management; Model Predictive Control

1. INTRODUCTION

Data centers today are home to a vast number and a variety of applications with diverse resource demands and performance objectives. Typically, a cloud application can be divided into one or more tasks executed in one or more containers (e.g., virtual machines (VMs)). At run time, schedulers are responsible for assigning tasks to machines. In today's reality, production data centers such as Google's cloud backend often execute tremendous number (e.g., millions) of tasks on a daily basis [27]. Such extremely large-scale workload hosted by data centers not only consumes significant storage and computing power, but also huge amounts of energy. In practice, the operational expenditure on energy not only comes from running physical machines, but also from cooling down the entire data center. It has been reported that energy consumption accounts for more than 12% of monthly operational expenditures of a typical data center [5]. For large companies like Google, a 3% reduction in energy cost can translate into over a million dollars in cost savings [19]. On the other hand, governmental agencies continue to implement standards and regulations to promote energy-efficient (i.e., "Green") computing [1]. Motivated by these observations, cutting down electricity cost has become a primary concern of today's data center operators.

In the research literature, a large body of recent work tries to improve energy efficiency of data centers. A plethora of techniques have been proposed to tackle different aspects of the problem, including the control of power distribution systems [20], cooling systems [8], computer hardware [25], software components such as virtualization [24] and load-balancing algorithms [11, 15]. It is known that one of the most effective approach for reducing energy cost is to dynamically adjust the data center capacity by turning off unused machines, or to set them to a power-saving (e.g., "sleep") state. This is supported by the evidence that an idle machine can consume as much as 60% of the power when the machine is fully utilized [11, 15, 17]. Unsurprisingly, a number of efforts are trying to leverage this fact to save energy using techniques such as VM consolidation [24] and migration [23]. However, these studies have mainly focused on improving the utilization of clusters by improving the "bin-packing" algorithm for VM scheduling. In a production data center where resource requests for tasks can arrive dynamically over time, deciding the number of machines to be switched off is not only affected by the efficiency of the scheduling algorithm, but also time-dependent characteristics of resource demand. While over-provisioning the data center capacity can lead to sub-optimal energy savings, under-provisioning the data center capacity can cause significant performance penalty in terms of scheduling delay, which is the time a task has to wait before it is scheduled on a machine. A high scheduling delay can significantly hurt the performance of some services that must be scheduled as soon as possible to satisfy end user requests (e.g., user-facing applications). On the other hand, tasks in production data centers often desire multiple types of resources, such as CPU, memory, disk and network bandwidth. In this context, devising a dynamic capacity provisioning mechanism that considers demand for multiple types of resources becomes a challenging problem. Furthermore, there are reconfiguration costs associated with switching on and off machines. In particular, turning on and off a machine often consumes large amount of energy due to saving and loading system states to memory and disk [18]. When turning off a machine with running tasks, it is necessary to consider the performance penalty due to migrating (or terminating) the tasks on the machine. Therefore, the reconfiguration cost due to server switching should be considered as well. Finally, another aspect often neglected in the existing literature is the electricity price. For example, it is known that in many regions of the U.S., the price of electricity can change depending on the time of the day. Electricity price is thus another factor that should be considered when making capacity adjustment decisions.

In this paper, we present a solution to the dynamic capacity provisioning problem with the goal of minimizing total energy cost while maintaining an acceptable task scheduling delay. Different from existing works on server capacity provisioning problem, we formulate the problem as a convex optimization problem that considers multiple resource types and fluctuating electricity prices. We then analyze the optimality condition of this problem and design a *Model Predictive Control* (MPC) algorithm that adjusts the number of servers to track the optimality condition while taking into account switching costs of machines. Through analysis and simulation using real workload traces from Google's compute clusters, we show our proposed solution is capable of achieving significant energy savings while minimizing SLA violations in terms of task scheduling delay.

The remainder of the paper is organized as follows. Section 2 presents a survey of related work in the research literature. In Section 3, we present an analysis of real workload

traces for one of Google's production compute clusters and illustrate the benefits of our approach. Section 4 describes the architecture of our proposed system. In Section 5, we present our demand prediction model and control algorithm. In Section 6, we provide our detailed formulation for the optimal control problem and present our solution based on the MPC framework. In Section 7, we evaluate our proposed system using Google workload traces, and demonstrate the benefits under various parameter settings. Finally, we draw our conclusions in Section 8.

2. RELATED WORK

Much effort has been made to achieve energy savings in data centers. Dynamic capacity provisioning is one of the most promising solutions to reduce energy cost that consists of dynamically turning on and off data center servers. For instance, motivated by the time-dependent variation of the number of users and TCP connections in Windows live messenger login servers, Chen et al. [11] have derived a framework for dynamic server provisioning and load dispatching. They have proposed a technique to evaluate the number of needed servers based on the predicted load in terms of users' login rate and active TCP connections. The load dispatching algorithm ensures that incoming requests are distributed among the servers. However, their framework does not consider the cost of switching on and off machines. Guenter et al. [16] have proposed another automated server provisioning and load dispatching system based on the predicted demand while considering the cost of transitioning servers between different power states (e.g., "on", "off", "hibernate"). This cost depends on the transition time, the energy cost and the long-term reliability of the server. Different from our work, they analyze the number of requests that can be satisfied instead of request scheduling delay. Furthermore, the multi-dimensional aspect of resource demand and fluctuations of electricity prices are not considered in their work.

Kusic et al. [18] have proposed a dynamic resource provisioning framework for virtualized server environments based on lookahead control. The framework minimizes power consumption by adjusting the number of physical and virtual machines. It also estimates the CPU share and the workload directed to every virtual machine. In addition, their controller manages to maximize the number of transactions that satisfy Service Level Agreement (SLA) in terms of average response time while taking into account the cost of turning on and off the machines. However, they mainly consider the performance of application servers rather than the scheduling of VMs. Furthermore, time-dependent variations of electricity prices are not considered in their framework. Abbasi et al. [7] have proposed a thermal-aware server provisioning technique and a workload distribution algorithm. In this approach, active servers are selected using heuristics in a way that minimizes cooling and computing energy cost. The workload distribution algorithm ensures that servers' utilizations do not exceed a threshold in order to satisfy SLA defined in terms of average response time. However, their approach does not consider switching cost of machines.

There is also a large body of work that applies control theory to achieve energy savings in data centers. Fu et al. [15] have proposed a control-theoretic thermal balancing that reduces temperature differences among servers. Hence, the controller acts on the utilization of each processor in order to reduce or increase its temperature. Model predictive control

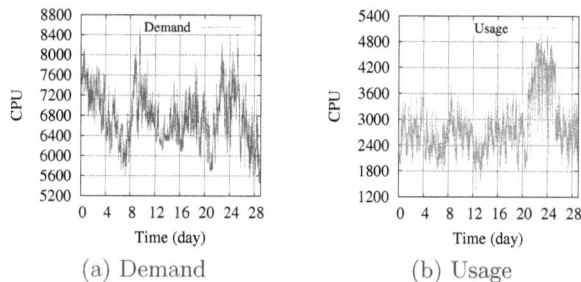

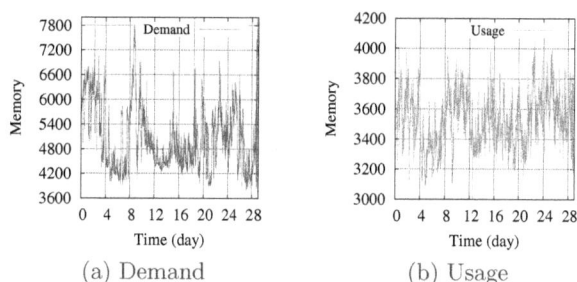

(a) Demand

(b) Usage

Figure 1: Total CPU demand and usage (29 days).

(a) Demand

(b) Usage

Figure 2: Total memory demand and usage (29 days).

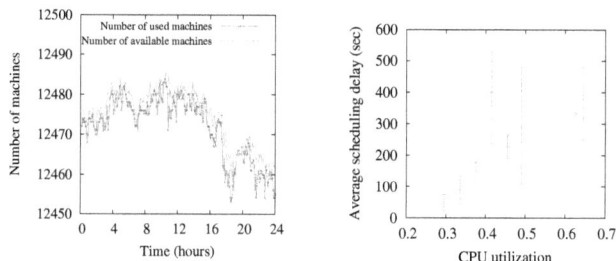

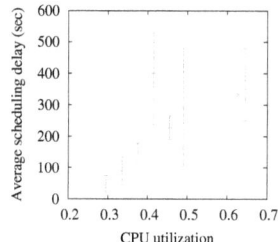

Figure 3: Number of machines available and used in the cluster.

Figure 4: Average task scheduling delay vs. Resource utilization.

is used by Wang et al. [26] to reduce the total power consumption of a cluster by tuning CPU frequency level for the processor of each server. However, most of previous work has focused on capacity provisioning from a service provider perspective, i.e., provisioning server capacities (e.g., number of web servers) to accommodate end user requests. Existing solutions to this problem rely on queuing-theoretic models that consider only a single type of resource (mainly CPU). In contrast, our approach investigates the problem from the cloud provider's perspective, where resource demand and usage are multi-dimensional. Our solution considers resource usage and capacity for multiple resource types, such as CPU and memory. Furthermore, none of the existing work has considered additional factors such as the fluctuating electricity prices. Our approach is also lightweight and independent of the scheduling algorithm, making it more suitable for practical implementation.

3. WORKLOAD ANALYSIS

To motivate the problem and justify our solution approach, we have conducted an analysis of workload traces for a production compute cluster at Google [4] consisting of approximately 12,000 machines. The dataset was released on November 29, 2011. The workload traces contain scheduling events as well as resource demand and usage records for a total of 672,003 jobs and 25,462,157 tasks over a time span of 29 days. Specifically, a *job* is an application that consists of one or more tasks. Each task is scheduled on a single physical machine. When a job is submitted, the user can specify the maximum allowed resource *demand* for each task in terms of required CPU, memory and disk size. At run time, the *usage* of a task measures the actual consumption of each type of resources. The current Google cluster traces provide task

demand and usage for CPU, memory and disk [1]. The usage of each type of resource is reported at 5 minute intervals. Our current analysis mainly focuses on CPU and memory, as they are typically scarce compared to disk. However, we believe it is straightforward to extend our approach to consider other resources such as disk space.

In addition to resource demand, the user can also specify a scheduling class, a priority and placement constraints for each task. The scheduling class captures the type of the task (e.g., user-facing or batch). The priority determines the importance of each task. The task placement constraints specify additional scheduling constraints concerning the machine configurations, such as processor architecture of the physical machine [21]. To simplify, we do not consider the scheduling class, priority and task placement constraints in our model. The analysis of these factors is left for future work.

We first plot the total demand and usage for both CPU and memory over the entire duration. The results are shown in Figure 1 and 2 respectively. The total usage at a given time is computed by summing up the resource usage of all the running tasks at that time. On the other hand, the total demand at a given time is determined by total resource requirement by all the tasks in the system, including the tasks that are waiting to be scheduled. From Figure 1 and 2, it can be observed that both usage and demand for each type of resource can fluctuate significantly over time. Figure 3 shows the number of machines available and used in the cluster. Specifically, a machine is available if it can be turned on to execute tasks. A machine is used if there is at least one task running on it. Figure 3 shows that the capacity of this cluster is not adjusted based on resource demand, as the number of used machines is almost equal to the number of available machines. Combining the observations from Figure 1, 2 and 3, it is evident that a large number of machines can be turned off to save energy. For instance, we estimated that a perfect energy saving schedule where the provisioned capacity exactly matches the current demand can achieve about 22% and 17% percent resource reduction for CPU and memory, respectively, compared to provisioning capacity according to the peak demand. This indicates that there is great potential for energy savings in this compute cluster using dynamic capacity provisioning.

However, while turning off active machines can reduce total energy consumption, turning off too many machines can also hurt task performance in terms of scheduling delay. Classic queuing theory indicates that task scheduling delay

---

[1]Note that the values reported in Google cluster traces were normalized between 0 and 1.

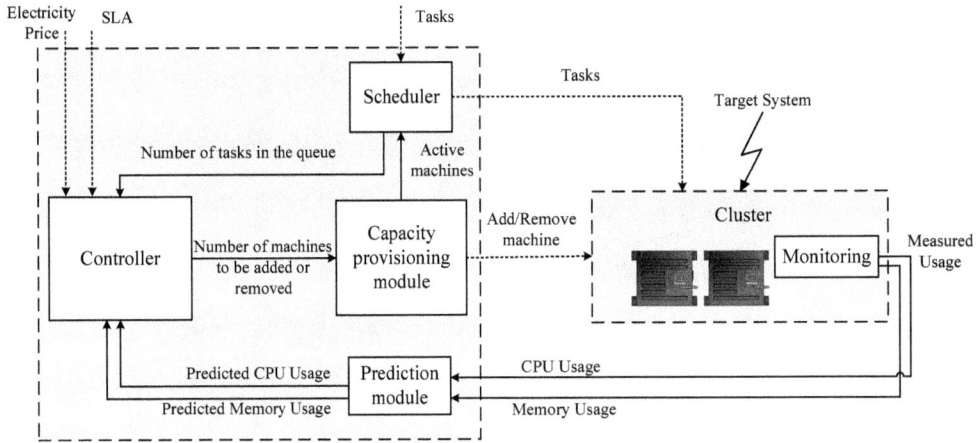

Figure 5: System architecture.

grows exponentially with resource utilization. To quantify this effect, we analyzed the relationship between scheduling delay experienced by each task and the average utilization of the bottleneck resource (e.g., CPU) while the task is waiting to be scheduled. We then plotted the average task scheduling delay as a function of the utilization of the bottleneck resource, as shown in Figure 4. The error bar in this diagram represents the standard deviation of task scheduling delay with average utilization at each given value. Indeed, we found that there is a direct relationship between task scheduling delay and resource utilization. We also modeled the relationship through curve fitting. It seems that both a linear function (i.e., $d = a \cdot U + b$) or a delay function for $M/M/1$ queuing model (i.e., $d = a \cdot \frac{U}{1-U} + b$)) can fit the curve well. Similar observations have been reported in recent work [27][21].

The above observations suggest that while the benefits of dynamic capacity provisioning is apparent for production data center environments, designing an effective dynamic capacity provisioning scheme is challenging, as it involves finding an optimal tradeoff between energy savings and scheduling delay. Furthermore, turning off active machines may require killing or migrating tasks running on these machines, which will introduce an additional performance penalty. The goal of this paper is to provide a solution to this dynamic capacity provisioning problem that finds the optimal trade-off between energy savings and the cost of reconfigurations, including cost of turning on and off machines and killing/migrating tasks.

4. SYSTEM ARCHITECTURE

Our proposed system architecture is depicted in Figure 5. It consists of the following components:

- *The scheduler* is responsible for assigning incoming tasks to active machines in the cluster. It also reports the average number of tasks in the queue during each control period to help the controller make informed decisions.

- *The monitoring module* is responsible for collecting CPU and memory usage statistics of every machine in the cluster. The monitoring is performed periodically.

- *The prediction module* receives statistics about the usage of all resources (CPU and memory) in the cluster and predicts the future usage for all of them.

- *The controller* implements a MPC algorithm that controls the number of machines based on the predicted usage of the cluster and taking into account the reconfiguration cost.

- *The capacity provisioning module* gathers the status information of machines from the controller, and decides which machines in particular should be added or removed. It then provides the scheduler with the list of active machines.

It is worth mentioning that different schedulers may adopt different resource allocation schemes. For example, in a public cloud environment such as Amazon EC2, it is necessary to schedule tasks according to their resource demand (e.g., VM size). However, since the actual resource usage of each task can be much lower than the demand, many advanced schedulers adjust dynamically resource allocation based on task usage [22]. Even though our framework is applicable to both scenarios, in this work, we use the latter case for illustration, not only because it is more general, but also because it reflects the behavior of Google cluster schedulers. In particular, Google's schedulers intentionally over-commit resources on each machine [3]. Finally, as an initial effort towards solving this problem, we currently consider that all the machines in the cluster are homogenous and with identical resource capacities. It is part of our future work to extend our model to consider machine heterogeneity (e.g., multiple generations of machines [21]).

In the following sections, we will describe the design of each component in details.

5. USAGE PREDICTION

In this section, we describe our model for predicting usage of each resource type. We used *the Auto-Regressive Integrated Moving Average* (ARIMA) model [9] to predict the time series G_k^r which represents the usage of resource type r in all the machines at time k. For convenience, we drop the superscript r and we write simply G_k in this section.

5.1 One-step Prediction

Knowing the last n observations of G_k, i.e., $G_{k-n+1},\dots G_k$, we want to predict G_{k+1}, which is the expected usage at time $k+1$ predicted at time k. The time series G_k follows an ARMA(n,q) model if it is stationary and if for every k:

$$G_{k+1} = \phi_0 G_k + .. + \phi_{n-1} G_{k-n+1}$$
$$+\epsilon_{k+1} + \theta_0 \epsilon_k + .. + \theta_{q-1} \epsilon_{k+1-q}, \qquad (1)$$

where the ϕ_i and θ_j are constants estimated from available data. The terms ϵ_k are error terms which are assumed to be independent, identically distributed samples from a normal distribution with zero mean and finite variance σ^2. The parameters n and q are the number of lags used by the model (i.e., the number of last measured values of the usage) and the number of error terms respectively. Equation (1) can also be written in a concise form as:

$$G_{k+1} = \sum_{i=0}^{n-1} \phi_i L^i G_k + \epsilon_{k+1} + (\sum_{i=0}^{q-1} \theta_i L^i)\epsilon_k, \qquad (2)$$

where L is the backward shift operator defined as follows: $L^i G_k = G_{k-i}$. We point out that AR and MA models are special cases of the ARMA model when $q = 0$ or $n = 0$.

The ARMA model fitting procedure assumes that the data are stationary. If the time series exhibits variations, we use differencing operation in order to make it stationary. It is defined by:

$$(1-L)G_k = G_k - G_{k-1}. \qquad (3)$$

It can be shown that a polynomial trend of degree k is reduced to a constant by differencing k times, that is, by applying the operator $(1-L)^k y(t)$. An ARIMA(n,d,q) model is an ARMA(n,q) model that has been differenced d times. Thus, the ARIMA(n,d,q) can be given by:

$$\left(1 - \sum_{i=0}^{n-1} \phi_i L^i\right)(1-L)^d G_k = \left(1 + \sum_{i=0}^{q-1} \theta_i L^i\right)\epsilon_k \qquad (4)$$

5.2 Multi-step Prediction

In our model, we aim to predict future resource usage over a time window $H \in \mathbb{N}^+$. This requires predicting resource usage $h \in \mathbb{N}^+$ steps ahead from an end-of-sample G_k for all $1 \leq h \leq H$. Let $G_{k+h|k}$ denote the hth step prediction of G_k knowing the last n observations, i.e., $G_{k-n+1},\dots G_k$. Thus, we aim to predict $G_{k+1|k}, G_{k+2|k}, \dots, G_{k+h|k}$. The multi-step prediction is obtained by iterating the one-step ahead prediction. The hth step prediction $G_{k+h|k}$ is given by:

$$G_{k+h|k} = f(G_{k+h-n|k}, \dots, G_{k+h-i|k}, \dots, G_{k+h-1|k}), \qquad (5)$$

where $G_{k-i|k} = G_{k-i} \,\forall i \in [0,n]$, the function f is the prediction model, n is the number of lags used by the model and h is the prediction step. Table 1 illustrates how one-step prediction is iterated to obtain multi-step predictions.

6. CONTROLLER DESIGN

We formally describe the dynamic capacity provisioning problem in this section. We assume the cluster consists of $M_k \in \mathbb{N}^+$ homogeneous machines at time k. The number of machines in the cluster can change due to machine failure and recovery. We assume each machine has $d \in \mathbb{N}$ types of resources. For example, a physical machine provides CPU, memory and disk. Let $R = \{1, 2, \dots, d\}$ denote the set of

Table 1: Example of multi-step prediction ($n = 3$).

Prediction step	Inputs of the model	Output
1	$G_{k-2|k}, G_{k-1|k}, G_{k|k}$	$G_{k+1|k}$
2	$G_{k-1|k}, G_{k|k}, G_{k+1|k}$	$G_{k+2|k}$
3	$G_{k|k}, G_{k+1|k}, G_{k+2|k}$	$G_{k+3|k}$
4	$G_{k+1|k}, G_{k+2|k}, G_{k+3|k}$	$G_{k+4|k}$

resource types. Denote by $C^r \in \mathbb{R}^+$ the capacity for resource type $r \in R$ of a single machine.

To model the system dynamics, we divide time into intervals of equal duration. We assume reconfiguration happens at the beginning of each time interval. At interval $k \in \mathbb{N}^+$, the measured usage for resource type r in the cluster is denoted by G_k^r. Let x_k denote the number of active machines. Denote by $u_k \in \mathbb{R}$ the change in the number of active machines. A positive value of u_k means more machines will be turned on, whereas a negative value of u_k means some active machines will be powered off. Therefore, we have the following simple state equation that calculates the number of active machines at time $k + 1$:

$$x_{k+1} = x_k + u_k. \qquad (6)$$

Our objective is to control the number of machines in order to reduce the total operational cost in terms of energy consumption and penalty due to violating the SLA, while taking into consideration the cost of dynamic reconfiguration. In what follows, we describe how to model each of the cost factors in details.

6.1 Modeling SLA penalty cost

In our model, the SLA is expressed in terms of an upper bound $\bar{d}$ on the average task scheduling delay. Thus, in order to meet the SLA, the average task scheduling delay d_k at time k should not exceed $\bar{d}$. As suggested in Section 3, the average task scheduling delay is correlated with the cluster resources' utilization, and more particularly with the utilization of the bottleneck resource. Therefore, we define the *bottleneck resource* $b \in R$ at time $k \in \mathbb{N}^+$ as the resource that has the highest utilization. In our model, the utilization of resource $r \in R$ in the cluster at time $k \in \mathbb{N}^+$ is given by:

$$U_k^r = \frac{G_k^r}{x_k C^r}. \qquad (7)$$

Therefore, the utilization of the bottleneck resource b can be calculated as:

$$U_k^b = \max_{r \in R} \{U_k^r\}. \qquad (8)$$

Then the average scheduling delay at time $k \in \mathbb{N}$ can be expressed as:

$$d_k = q_b(U_k^b), \qquad (9)$$

where $q_b(U_k^b)$ denotes the average latency given current utilization U_k^b for the bottleneck resource b. The function $q_b(\cdot)$ can be obtained using various techniques, such as queue theoretic models, or directly from empirical measurements as described in Section 3.

We adopt a simple penalty cost model for SLA violation. Specifically, if the delay bound is violated, then there will be a SLA penalty cost P_k^{SLA} proportional to the degree of violation. Therefore, the penalty function $P_k^{SLA}(\cdot)$ can be rewritten as:

$$P_k^{SLA}(U_k^b) = N_k p^{SLA}(q(U_k^b) - \bar{d})^+, \tag{10}$$

where p^{SLA} represents the unit penalty cost for violating the delay upperbound, and N_k is the weight factor representing the severity of the violation at time k (e.g., N_k can be the number of requests in the scheduling queue at time k).

6.2 Modeling the total energy cost

In the research literature, it is known that the total energy consumption of a physical machine can be estimated by a linear function of CPU, memory and disk usage [16, 7, 11, 14]. Thus, the energy consumption of a machine at time k can be expressed as:

$$e_k = E_{idle} + \sum_{r \in R} \alpha^r U_k^r. \tag{11}$$

Let p_k^{power} denote the electricity price at time k. Then, for a given number of machines x_k, the total energy cost P_k^{power} at time k can be expressed as

$$
\begin{aligned}
P_k^{power}(x_k) &= p_k^{power} x_k e_k \\
&= p_k^{power} x_k (E_{idle} + \sum_{r \in R} \alpha^r \frac{G^r}{x_k C^r}).
\end{aligned} \tag{12}
$$

6.3 Formulation of the optimization problem

As mentioned previously, our objective is to control the number of servers so as to minimize the total operational cost, which is the sum of SLA penalty cost $P_k^{SLA}(U_k^b)$ and energy cost $P_k^{power}(x_k)$. At the same time, we need to ensure that the number of active machines in the cluster must not exceed M_k, the total number of physical machines in the cluster. This can be formulated by the following optimization problem:

$$
\min_{x_k \in \mathbb{R}^+} N_k p^{SLA} \left(q \left(\max_{r \in R} \left\{ \frac{G^r}{x_k C^r} \right\} \right) - \bar{d} \right)^+
$$
$$
+ p_k^{power} x_k \left(E_{idle} + \sum_{r \in R} \alpha^r \frac{G^r}{x_k C^r} \right) \tag{13}
$$

$$\text{s.t. } 0 \leq x_k \leq M_k,$$

where $(x)^+ = \max(x, 0)$. Notice that $p_k^{power} x_k \cdot \sum_{r \in R} \alpha^r \frac{G^r}{x_k C^r}$ does not depend on x_k at time k, thus it can be omitted in the optimization formulation. In addition, define $w_k = \max_r \{ \frac{G_k^r}{C^r} \}$, we can further simplify the problem to:

$$\min_{0 \leq x_k \leq M_k} N_k p^{SLA} \left(q \left(\frac{w_k}{x_k} \right) - \bar{d} \right)^+ + p_k^{power} x_k E_{idle}. \tag{14}$$

Assuming that $q(\frac{w_k}{x_k})$ is a decreasing function of x_k (namely, the average queuing delay decreases as the number of machines increases), we can see that the optimal solution x_k^* of this problem satisfies $x_k^* \leq \frac{w_k}{q^{-1}(\bar{d})}$, since if $x_k^* \geq \frac{w_k}{q^{-1}(\bar{d})}$, $(q(\frac{w_k}{x_k}) - \bar{d})^+ = 0$, in this case we can decrease x_k^* to $\frac{w_k}{q^{-1}(\bar{d})}$ to reduce energy cost while maintaining $(q(\frac{w_k}{x_k}) - \bar{d})^+ = 0$. Therefore, we can further simplify the problem to:

$$\min_{0 \leq x_k \leq \frac{w_k}{q^{-1}(\bar{d})}} N_k p^{SLA}(q(\frac{w_k}{x_k}) - \bar{d}) + p_k^{power} x_k E_{idle} \tag{15}$$

In order to solve this optimization problem, we use the Karush-Kuhn-Tucker (KKT) approach [10]. The Lagrangian function is

$$
\begin{aligned}
L(x_k, \gamma) = & N_k p^{SLA} \left(q \left(\frac{w_k}{x_k} \right) - \bar{d} \right) + p_k^{power} x_k E_{idle} \\
& + \gamma(x_k - \frac{w_k}{q^{-1}(\bar{d})}) + \mu(0 - x_k).
\end{aligned} \tag{16}
$$

The KKT conditions are:

$$\frac{dL}{dx} = p_k^{power} E_{idle} - N_k p^{SLA} w_k \frac{dq\left(\frac{w_k}{x_k}\right)}{dx} \left(\frac{1}{x_k^2}\right) + \gamma - \mu = 0,$$

$$\mu x_k = 0,$$

$$\gamma(\frac{w_k}{q^{-1}(\bar{d})} - x_k) = 0,$$

$$0 \leq x_k \leq \frac{w_k}{q^{-1}(\bar{d})}, \quad \mu, \gamma \geq 0.$$

We need to consider three cases: (1) $\gamma > 0$, (2) $\mu > 0$, and (3) $\gamma = 0$ and $\mu = 0$. The first two cases correspond to boundary conditions whether $x_k^* = \frac{w_k}{q^{-1}(\bar{d})}$ or $x_k^* = 0$. In the third case, assuming $q(\cdot)$ is convex and differentiable, we can solve x_k^* using the first condition. For instance, $q(U) = a \cdot \frac{U}{1-U} + b$ (which is the case for $M/M/1$ queuing model), we can obtain

$$x_k^* = w_k + \sqrt{\frac{N_k p^{SLA} a w_k}{p_k^{power} E_{idle}}}. \tag{17}$$

The above equation reveals many insights. First, the optimal number of servers x_k^* depends mainly on the cluster utilization, which is captured by the variable w_k. Second, x_k^* is also dependent on the electricity price and the SLA violations. In particular, it increases either when the electricity price drops down or when the SLA penalty cost rises. Therefore, it can be seen that equation (17) tries to strike a balance between saving electricity cost and SLA penalty cost in a dynamic manner.

6.4 Capacity provisioning module

The capacity provisioning module takes as input the number of machines that should be added or removed from the cluster, and determines which machine should be turned on or off. The decision of switching on a particular machine can be made based on different criteria such as its usage and its location in the cluster. However, choosing which machine to power off is more complicated since some tasks could be running on it. Thus, more criteria should be considered such as the number of running tasks on the machine, their priorities, the cost of migrating or killing those tasks as well as the resource usage in the machine. For simplicity, define c_t as the cost for migrating (or terminating) the task t, depending on the scheduling policy applied to task t. For example, if task t is an interactive task such as a web server, it is better to migrate the server to another machine to minimize the service down time. On the other hand, if the task t belongs to a MapReduce job, it is more cost-effective to simply terminate the task and restart it on a different machine [12]. We define the cost of powering off a particular machine i, $1 \leq i \leq M_k$ at time k as

$$c_k^i = \sum_{t \in S_k^i} c_t, \tag{18}$$

Algorithm 1 MPC Algorithm for DCP
91: Provide initial state x_k, $k \leftarrow 0$
92: **loop**
93:     At the end of control period k:
94:     Predict $N_{k+h|k}$, $w_{k+h|k}$, $p^{power}_{k+h|k}$ for time $h \in \{1, H\}$
95:     Solve tracking problem to obtain $u(k + h|k)$ for horizons $h \in \{0, \cdots, H\}$
96:     Perform the reconfiguration using the capacity provisioning module according to $u(k|k)$
97:     $k \leftarrow k + 1$
98: **end loop**

where S^i_k denotes the set of tasks running on the machine i at time $k \in \mathbb{N}$. It is clear that c^i_k increases with the number of tasks and their costs. Consequently, the capacity provisioning module turns off machines having the lowest cost c^i_k.

6.5 Designing the MPC controller

The goal of our controller is to adjust the number of machines to minimize the violation of KKT conditions, while taking into consideration the reconfiguration cost. As N_k, w_k, p^{power}_k can change over time, we adopt the well-known MPC framework to design an online controller for this problem. The MPC algorithm is illustrated by Algorithm 1. It can be intuitively described as follows: At time k, the prediction module is responsible for predicting the future values of N_k, w_k, p^{power}_k for a prediction window H. The controller will then solve an optimal control problem that will determine the optimal decisions for the entire window H. As only the first step is required, the controller will only carry out the first control decision. The procedure will repeat at the beginning of every time interval k, $k + 1$, and so on.

More formally, we can define $N_{k+h|k}, w_{k+h|k}, p^{power}_{k+h|k}$ as the values of N_k, w_k, p^{power}_k predicted for time $k + h$, given the historical values up to time k. We also define

$$e_{k+h|k} = x_{k+h|k} - x^*_{k+h|k}, \tag{19}$$

as the *tracking error* at time k, the objective of the controller is to solve the following program:

$$\min_{u_k \in \mathbb{R}} J_k = \sum_{h=1}^{H} Q(e_{k+h|k})^2 + R(u_{k+h|k})^2 \tag{20}$$

$$\text{s. t. } x_{k+h+1|k} = x_{k+h|k} + u_{k+h|k}, \qquad \forall 0 \leq h \leq H - 1$$

$$e_{k+h|k} = x_{k+h|k} - x^*_{k+h|k}, \qquad \forall 1 \leq h \leq H$$

$$0 \leq x_{k+h|k} \leq N, \qquad \forall 1 \leq h \leq H$$

where H is the horizon of interest. The first term represents the tracking error, the second term represents the *control penalty*. The tracking error aims to reduce the error between the actual and the optimal number of machines. The second term is the control penalty which takes into account the cost of adding or removing machines. Thus, J_k can be interpreted as a *plan of action* for next H time intervals. Q and R are weight factors that will control the stability and convergence rate of the controller. If Q is much bigger than R, then the controller will place a higher weight on maximizing power savings and adjust number of servers aggressively. On the other hand, if R is large compared to Q, then the controller will adjust the capacity less aggressively to minimize reconfiguration cost. A standard way to determine the

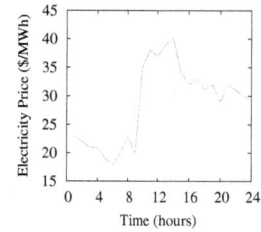

Figure 6: Electricity price of Houston, TX over 24 hours.

values of Q and R is to normalize both terms. In our case, we normalize them by converting both terms into monetary cost. Define $\bar{r} = \frac{1}{2}(c^{avg,on} + c^{avg,off})$ where $c^{avg,on}$ and $c^{avg,off}$ are the average cost for turning on and off servers, respectively. Similarly, we define $\bar{q} = \frac{1}{2}(c^{avg}_{over} + c^{avg}_{under})$ where c^{avg}_{over} is average cost introduced per machine due to provisioning, and c^{avg}_{under} is average cost introduced per machine due to underprovisining, respectively. Even though it is possible to compute analytically the values of $c^{avg,on}$, $c^{avg,off}$, c^{avg}_{over}, c^{avg}_{under}, it is more practical to estimate their values through empirical measurement. Notice that we set $\bar{q}$ and $\bar{r}$ to the average penalty cost of both positive and negative errors, because in practice, the number of occurrences of both positive and negative errors will likely to be the same, if the capacity provisioned by our controller only fluctuates within a fixed range. Finally, although we can set $(Q, R) = (\bar{q}^2, \bar{r}^2)$ to ensure both terms are in the unit of $dollar^2$, to simplify our model, we set $(Q, R) = (1, \frac{\bar{r}^2}{\bar{q}^2})$ in our experiment so that we only need to control R to achieve different trade-offs between solution optimality and reconfiguration cost.

7. EXPERIMENTAL EVALUATION

We have implemented our system shown in Figure 5 and evaluated the quality of our solution using trace-driven simulations. In our experiment, we set the CPU and memory capacity of each machine to 1. This represents a majority of machines in the Google cluster[2]. In our simulation we implemented a greedy First-Fit (FF) scheduling algorithm, which is used by many cloud computing platforms such as Eucalyptus [2]. In our simulations, we set E_{idle} to 200 Watts, α^r to 121 and 0 for CPU and memory, respectively, similar to the values used in [18]. For electricity price, we used the electricity prices for the city of Houston, Texas, obtained from a publicly available source [6]. Figure 6 shows the fluctuation of electricity price over a duration of 24 hours. It can be observed that the electricity price is generally higher during day time. The fluctuation sometimes can be as large as 20% compared to the average electricity price over the 24 hours. Finally, we set $\bar{d}$ to 10 seconds as an upperbound on task scheduling delay.

7.1 Prediction performance

In our first experiment, we assess the performance of the multi-step prediction for resource usages. We first describe the prediction procedure and the performance criteria. Then

---

[2] The values of CPU and memory capacity reported in Google traces were normalized to the configuration of the largest machine.

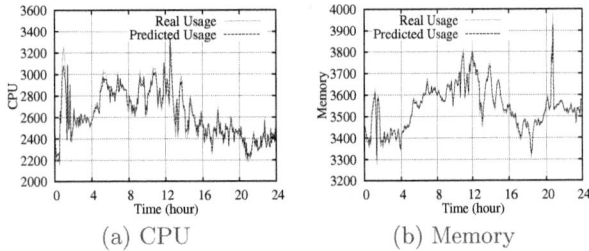

Figure 7: Prediction of resource usage in the Google cluster - one-step prediction - ARIMA(2, 1, 1).

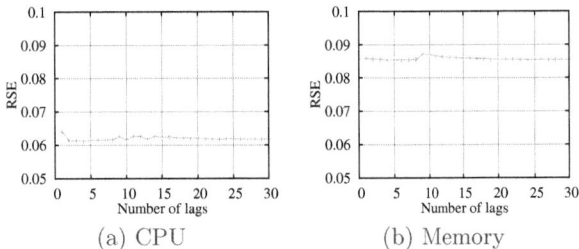

Figure 8: Effect of the number of lags on usage prediction - One-step prediction ($h = 1$).

we study the effect of the number of lags and the prediction horizon on the prediction accuracy.

To evaluate the quality of our prediction technique, the available traces (e.g., measured CPU or memory usage) are divided into a *training data set* and a *validation data set*. Training data are used to identify the model parameters n, d, q and the coefficient ϕ_i and θ_j. For given n and q, the coefficients ϕ_i, $i \leq n$ and θ_j, $j \leq q$ are estimated using the RPS toolkit [13]. The validation data set is then used to assess the accuracy of the prediction model. The performance metric used to evaluate the prediction accuracy is *the relative squared error* (RSE). It is calculated for every prediction step h as:

$$RSE_h = \frac{\sum_{k=1}^{T} \left[G_k - G_{k+h|k} \right]^2}{\sum_{k=1}^{T} \left[G_k - \mu \right]^2} \quad (21)$$

where T is the size of the validation data set and μ is the average of G_k over the T time intervals. The advantage of the RSE_h is that it neither depends on the used scale nor on the size of data. Having the RSE_h lower than 1 means that the predictor is outperforming the use of the average of the data as prediction for G_k ($G_{k+h|h} = \mu$). In addition, the smaller is the RSE_h, the more accurate is the prediction. The RSE can also be seen as the ratio of the mean squared error divided by the variance of validation data set.

Since our model exploits the predicted usage of the cluster in terms of CPU and memory to proactively add and remove servers, we assess the prediction model accuracy. We applied the ARIMA model to the real data collected at the Google cluster and we evaluated the effect of the number of lags used as input for the prediction model (n) and the effect of the prediction horizon (h) on the multi-step squared error (RSE_h). Memory and CPU usage are measured every five minutes. Hence, a one-step prediction is equivalent to predict the cluster usage in the next five minutes.

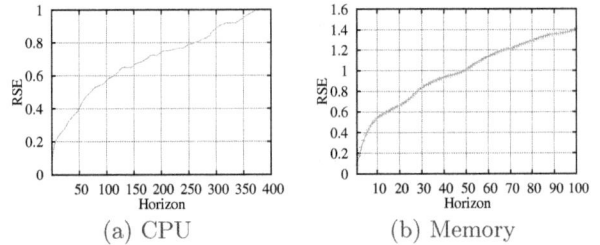

Figure 9: Performance of multi-step prediction - ARIMA(2, 1, 1).

Figure 7 shows the one-step prediction of the CPU and memory usage compared to the real usage. The graph shows that the predicted values are always close to the real ones even during peaks. The prediction relative squared error RSE_1 is close to zero which proves that the ARIMA(2,1,1) provides an accurate prediction of the usage either for CPU ($RSE_1 \approx 0.062$) or memory ($RSE_1 \approx 0.086$).

Figure 8 depicts the effect of increasing the number of lags used in the ARIMA model to predict CPU and memory usage. Regarding CPU usage prediction (Figure 8(a)), it is apparent from the results that starting from the second lag ($n = 2$), the prediction error becomes stable around $RSE_1 \approx 0.062$. If we now turn to memory usage prediction, Figure 8(b) shows the prediction error remains almost stable regardless of the number of lags used for the ARIMA model ($RSE_1 \approx 0.086$). Consequently, there is no improvement of the prediction performance beyond two lags ($n = 2$). This result is interesting since a small number of lags reduces the ARIMA model complexity and allows to implement it online with minimal overhead and high accuracy.

We also conducted more experiments to examine the impact of the horizon h on the prediction performance. Since using more than two lags does not reduce the prediction error, we only considered two lags as input for the ARIMA model (i.e., $n = 2$). As expected, when we increase the prediction horizon, the prediction error grows for both CPU and memory usage (Figure 9). What is interesting in these results is that the error remains small ($RSE_h \leq 1$) for multiple prediction steps. In particular, the prediction error RSE_h remains below 1 for 400 steps ahead (≈ 33 hour) for CPU usage and for 50 steps ahead (≈ 250 min) for memory usage. We also mention that increasing the number of error terms (q) for the ARIMA model does not improve the prediction performance. In summary, these results suggest that we can apply ARIMA(2,1,1) using two lags to predict 12 steps ahead (equivalent to one hour), and this ensures that the prediction error does not exceed 0.3 and 0.5 for CPU and memory, respectively (Figure 9).

7.2 Controller performance

We conducted several experiments to evaluate the performance of our controller. In our experiment, we set the control frequency to once every 5 minutes to match Google's Cluster measurements frequency [4]. Typically, a high control frequency implies fast response to demand fluctuations. However, it also incurs a high computational overhead. However, we found the computational overhead of both demand prediction algorithm and controller to be almost negligible, thus, once every 5 minutes is a reasonable control frequency.

(a) CPU   (b) Memory

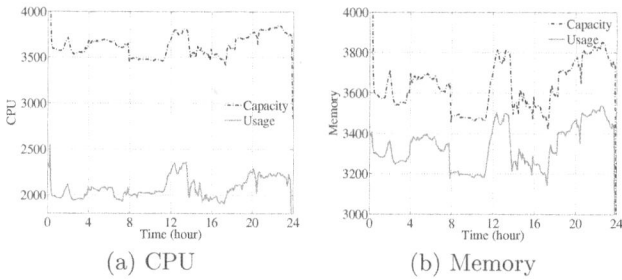

Figure 10: Capacity vs. Usage over 24 hours (R=0.1).

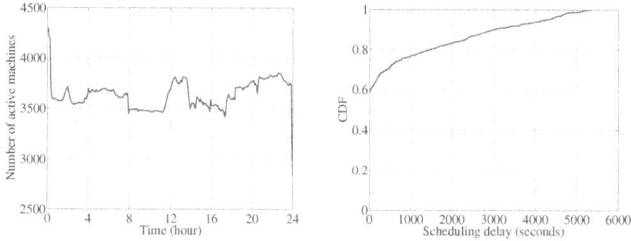

Figure 11: Number of machines over 24 hours (R=0.1).

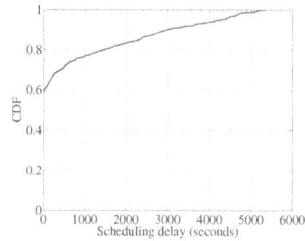

Figure 12: Average scheduling delay over 24 hours (R=0.1).

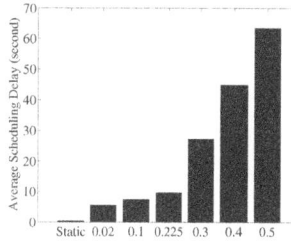

Figure 13: Average Queuing Delay.

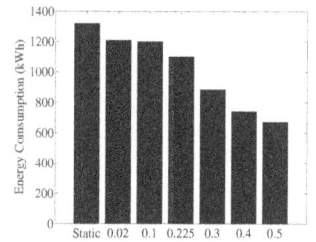

Figure 14: Energy Consumption.

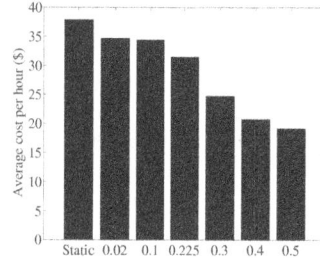

Figure 15: Average cost per hour.

Lastly, we set $Q = 1$ in our experiments. Thus, the reconfiguration cost can be controlled by properly adjusting the value of R.

In our experiments, we first evaluated the response of our system to usage fluctuation. The number of active servers provisioned over the 24-hour duration is shown in Figure 11 (for $R = 0.1$). Figure 10 show the capacity and the usage of the cluster. It can be observed that the controller adjusts the number of servers dynamically in reaction to usage fluctuation, while avoiding rapid change in the number of active machines. The cumulative distribution function of task scheduling delay is shown in Figure 12. It can be seen that more than 60% of tasks are scheduled immediately.

We performed several other experiments for comparison purpose. In the first experiment, the number of machines is provisioned statically according to peak usage (i.e., 4100 machines). In the remaining experiments, we applied our controller using different values of R. Figures 13 and 14 show the corresponding average scheduling delay and energy consumption for different values of R compared to the static provisioning. It can be observed that the static provisioning achieves the lowest scheduling delay since it significantly overprovisions the cluster capacity. On the other hand, dynamic provisioning with $R = 0.5$ causes a significant scheduling delay although it allows to reduce the energy consumption (up to 50%). Furthermore, setting R to a small value (e.g., 0.02) does not achieve significant energy reduction. Through experiments, we found that setting $R = 0.225$ achieves our desired SLA objective of keeping the average scheduling delay around 10 seconds while reducing the energy consumption by 18.5%. Figure 15 shows the actual energy cost per hour, taking into consideration the fluctuation of the electricity price. It can be seen that our dynamic capacity provisioning mechanism reduces 7 dollars per hour

in energy costs, which implies 20% reduction in energy cost, while achieving the desired scheduling delay (for $R = 0.225$). Furthermore, depending on the desired average scheduling delay (Figure 13), our proposed approach can reduce total operational cost by about $18.5 - 50\%$ (Figure 15).

8. CONCLUSION

Data centers have become a cost-effective infrastructure for data storage and hosting large-scale service applications. However, large data centers today consume significant amounts of energy. This not only rises the operational expenses of cloud providers, but also raises environmental concerns with regard to minimizing carbon footprint. In this paper, we mitigate this concern by designing a dynamic capacity provisioning system that controls the number of active servers in the data center according to (1) demand fluctuation, (2) variability in energy prices and (3) the cost of dynamic capacity reconfiguration. Our solution is based on the well-established Model Predictive Control framework, and aims to find a good trade-off between energy savings and capacity reconfiguration cost. Simulations using real traces obtained from a production Google compute clusters demonstrate our approach achieves considerable amount of reduction in energy cost. As such, we believe our approach represents an initial step towards building a full-fledged capacity management framework for cloud data centers.

There are several promising directions we can pursue in the future. First, our current approach assumes that machines are homogenous. While this is applicable to many situations (cloud providers often buy large quantities of identical machines in bulk), recent literature suggests that production data centers often consists of multiple types (sometimes multiple generations) of machines. Extending our current solution to handle machine heterogeneity requires careful consideration of scheduling capability of each type of machine. Another interesting problem is to understand the interplay between the scheduler and the capacity controller.

We believe it is possible to further reduce the cost of energy consumption and reconfiguration (i.e., task preemption and migration cost) if the scheduler and the capacity controller can cooperate tightly at a fine-grained level (e.g., interaction of server consolidation algorithms with our capacity controller).

Acknowledgment

This work was supported in part by a Google Research Award, by the Natural Science and Engineering Council of Canada (NSERC) SAVI Research Network, and by the World Class University (WCU) Program under the Korea Science and Engineering Foundation funded by the Ministry of Education, Science and Technology (Project No. R31-2008-000-10100-0).

9. REFERENCES

[1] Energy star computers specification - feb. 14, 2012. http://www.energystar.gov/ia/partners/prod_development/revisions/downloads/computer/ES_Computers-_Draft_1_Version_6.0_Specification.pdf.

[2] Eucalyptus community. http://open.eucalyptus.com/.

[3] Google cluster-usage traces: format + schema. http://googleclusterdata.googlecode.com/files/Google%20cluster-usage%20traces%20-%20format%20%2B%20schema%20%282011.10.27%20external%29.pdf.

[4] Googleclusterdata - traces of google workloads. http://code.google.com/p/googleclusterdata/.

[5] Technology research - Gartner Inc. http://www.gartner.com/it/page.jsp?id=1442113.

[6] U.S. Energy Information Administration (EIA). http://www.eia.gov/.

[7] Z. Abbasi, G. Varsamopoulos, and S. K. S. Gupta. Thermal aware server provisioning and workload distribution for Internet data centers. In *Proceedings of the ACM International Symposium on High Performance Distributed Computing (HPDC)*, 2010.

[8] C. Bash, C. Patel, and R. Sharma. Dynamic thermal management of air cooled data centers. In *IEEE Intersociety Conference on the Thermal and Thermomechanical Phenomena in Electronics Systems (ITHERM)*, 2006.

[9] G. E. P. Box, G. M. Jenkins, and G. C. Reinsel. *Time Series Analysis, Forecasting, and Control*. Prentice-Hall, third edition, 1994.

[10] S. Boyd and L. Vandenberghe. *Convex Optimization*. Cambridge University Press, New York, USA, 2004.

[11] G. Chen, W. He, J. Liu, S. Nath, L. Rigas, L. Xiao, and F. Zhao. Energy-aware server provisioning and load dispatching for connection-intensive Internet services. In *USENIX Symposium on Networked Systems Design and Implementation (NSDI)*, 2008.

[12] J. Dean and S. Ghemawat. MapReduce: Simplified data processing on large clusters. *Communications of the ACM*, 51(1), 2008.

[13] P. A. Dinda. Design, implementation, and performance of an extensible toolkit for resource prediction in distributed systems. *IEEE Trans. Parallel Distrib. Syst.*, 17, February 2006.

[14] X. Fan, W.-D. Weber, and L. A. Barroso. Power provisioning for a warehouse-sized computer. In *Proceedings of the annual international symposium on Computer architecture (ISCA)*, 2007.

[15] Y. Fu, C. Lu, and H. Wang. Robust control-theoretic thermal balancing for server clusters. In *IEEE International Symposium on Parallel Distributed Processing (IPDPS)*, April 2010.

[16] B. Guenter, N. Jain, and C. Williams. Managing cost, performance, and reliability tradeoffs for energy-aware server provisioning. In *IEEE INFOCOM*, April 2011.

[17] A. Gulati, A. Holler, M. Ji, G. Shanmuganathan, C. Waldspurger, and X. Zhu. VMware distributed resource management: Design, implementation, and lessons learned. In *VMware Technical Journal*, 2012.

[18] D. Kusic, J. O. Kephart, J. E. Hanson, N. Kandasamy, and G. Jiang. Power and performance management of virtualized computing environments via lookahead control. In *Proceedings of the International Conference on Autonomic Computing (ICAC)*, 2008.

[19] A. Qureshi, R. Weber, H. Balakrishnan, J. Guttag, and B. Maggs. Cutting the electric bill for Internet-scale systems. In *ACM SIGCOMM Computer Communication Review*, volume 39, 2009.

[20] R. Raghavendra, P. Ranganathan, V. Talwar, Z. Wang, and X. Zhu. No power struggles: Coordinated multi-level power management for the data center. In *ACM SIGARCH Computer Architecture News*, volume 36. ACM, 2008.

[21] B. Sharma, V. Chudnovsky, J. Hellerstein, R. Rifaat, and C. Das. Modeling and synthesizing task placement constraints in google compute clusters. In *Proceedings of ACM Symposium on Cloud Computing*, 2011.

[22] Z. Shen, S. Subbiah, X. Gu, and J. Wilkes. Cloudscale: Elastic resource scaling for multi-tenant cloud systems. In *Proceedings of the ACM Symposium on Cloud Computing*, 2011.

[23] A. Verma, P. Ahuja, and A. Neogi. pMapper: power and migration cost aware application placement in virtualized systems. In *ACM/IFIP/USENIX Middleware*, 2008.

[24] A. Verma, G. Dasgupta, T. Nayak, P. De, and R. Kothari. Server workload analysis for power minimization using consolidation. In *Proceedings of the conference on USENIX Annual technical conference*. USENIX Association, 2009.

[25] G. von Laszewski, L. Wang, A. Younge, and X. He. Power-aware scheduling of virtual machines in DVFS-enabled clusters. In *IEEE International Conference on Cluster Computing and Workshops (CLUSTER)*, 2009.

[26] X. Wang and M. Chen. Cluster-level feedback power control for performance optimization. In *IEEE International Symposium on High Performance Computer Architecture (HPCA)*, February 2008.

[27] Q. Zhang, J. Hellerstein, and R. Boutaba. Characterizing task usage shapes in Google's compute clusters. In *Workshop on Large Scale Distributed Systems and Middleware (LADIS)*, 2011.

VESPA: Multi-Layered Self-Protection for Cloud Resources

Aurélien Wailly
Orange Labs, France
aurelien.wailly@orange.com

Marc Lacoste
Orange Labs, France
marc.lacoste@orange.com

Hervé Debar
Télécom SudParis, France
herve.debar@telecom-
sudparis.eu

ABSTRACT

Self-protection has recently raised growing interest as possible element of answer to the cloud computing infrastructure protection challenge. Faced with multiple threats and heterogeneous defense mechanisms, the autonomic approach proposes simpler, stronger, and more efficient cloud security management. Yet, previous solutions fall at the last hurdle as they overlook key features of the cloud, by lack of flexible security policies, cross-layered defense, multiple control granularities, and open security architectures. This paper presents VESPA, a self-protection architecture for cloud infrastructures overcoming such limitations. VESPA is policy-based, and regulates security at two levels, both within and across infrastructure layers. Flexible coordination between self-protection loops allows enforcing a rich spectrum of security strategies such as cross-layer detection and reaction. A multi-plane extensible architecture also enables simple integration of commodity detection and reaction components. Evaluation of a VESPA implementation shows that the design is applicable for effective and flexible self-protection of cloud infrastructures.

Categories and Subject Descriptors

D.4.7 [**Operating Systems**]: Organization and Design—*Distributed Systems*; D.4.6 [**Operating Systems**]: Security and Protection

Keywords

Self-Protection, Autonomic Computing, Cloud Security, IaaS

1. INTRODUCTION

Security is currently viewed as one of the main adoption stoppers to cloud computing. Sheer system complexity leaves the door open to many types of threats coming both from the outside and from the inside [4]. Intrusions, malware and other rootkits, or security policy-violations of curious or malicious administrators are just but a few. This problem is particularly acute at the very cloud foundation: the infrastructure-level cloud model, or IaaS (*Infrastructure-as-a-Service*).

To master mushrooming heterogeneity and vulnerabilities, *self-protection* is a promising next step for stronger security management of such infrastructures, e.g., to fight intrusions [7]. Automated capabilities of detection and reaction to threats also bring well-known benefits such as lighter administration, lower incident response times, or reduced error-rates.

A self-protected IaaS infrastructure should take into account three main features of cloud environments: (1) *multi-layering*; (2) *multi-laterality*; and (3) *openness*. This means that: (1) a cloud infrastructure is composed of many independent software layers with their specific security mechanisms, while attacks may target several layers; (2) a cloud involves multiple organizations with their own security objectives, calling for flexible policies and monitoring granularities for security management; (3) clouds are increasingly evolving towards interoperability with other clouds or third-party IT systems, making a closed-world vision of security not adequate. From those features may in turn be derived a set of key design principles for a self-protection cloud architecture:

[**P1**] **Policy-based self-protection:** the architecture should be a refinement of a well-defined security adaptation model based on policies. This approach has well-known benefits to increase self-management adaptability and extensibility [18].

[**P2**] **Cross-layer defense:** detection and reaction should not be performed within a single software layer, but may also span several layers. Benefits include greater accuracy of the security response by capturing the global picture of an attack.

[**P3**] **Multiple self-protection loops**: several control loops of variable level of granularity should be defined and coordinated. A single loop has insufficient flexibility for supervision perimeter and does not enable trade-offs for response optimality.

[**P4**] **Open architecture:** multiple detection and reaction strategies and mechanisms – notably heterogeneous off-the-shelf security components – should be easily integrated in the architecture, to mitigate both known and unknown threats.

Substantial prior work has attempted to build systems fulfilling one or several of those principles, in terms of policy management frameworks, self-protecting distributed systems, protection mechanisms for virtual machines (VMs) and for the virtualization layer, or traditional Intrusion Detection and Prevention Systems (IDPS) and anti-malware tools. Yet, those solutions always seem to fall short of addressing one principle or more. For instance, despite quite extensive models, generic policy frameworks usually little address security or cloud environments. Most of the time, policies are not very granular, and multi-layered defense is not addressed. Existing cloud protection mechanisms are either detection- or reaction-oriented, but rarely both. Similarly, they tackle cross-layering or

Systems	Principle fulfilled?			
	P1	P2	P3	P4
Policy frameworks	yes	no	no	yes
Self-protection frameworks	no	no	no	some
Protecting VMs	some	yes	no	no
Hypervisor defense	no	a few	no	no
IDPS/anti-malware techniques	no	no	a few	yes

Table 1: Principle coverage by some classes of existing systems.

have flexible policies, but not both. Integration with outside systems also remains difficult. Legacy IDPS are more open, but often without a well-formalized adaptation model. Overall, multiple loops are almost always ignored.

To overcome those limitations, this paper presents an architecture and framework based on the previous design principles for building self-defending IaaS infrastructures. Our system called VESPA (Virtual Environments Self-Protecting Architecture) regulates protection of IaaS resources through several coordinated autonomic security loops which monitor the different infrastructure layers. The result is a very flexible approach for self-protection of IaaS resources.

The main features of VESPA are the following: (1) *policy-based security adaptation* based on a self-protection model capturing symmetrically and flexibly both detection and reaction phases; (2) *two-level tuning of security policies* according to security contexts both inside a software layer and across layers; (3) *flexible orchestration* of layer-level *self-protection loops* using system-wide knowledge to allow a rich spectrum of overall infrastructure self-protection strategies; and (4) a *layered, extensible architecture* allowing simple integration of commodity detection and reaction components thanks to an agent-based mediation plane abstracting away security component heterogeneity.

The VESPA framework was implemented over a KVM-based IaaS infrastructure and applied to perform dynamic VM confinement. Experimental results show that VESPA enables to achieve effective and yet flexible IaaS self-protection, with reasonable performance overheads.

The rest of this paper is organized as follows. After reviewing related work (Section 2), we present the VESPA self-protection model and architecture (Section 3). Finally, we present a deployment scenario and evaluation results (Section 4).

2. RELATED WORK

Self-protection has been addressed from several perspectives, with a large body of related work. Table 1 gives a coverage estimation of principles P1–P4 for the most relevant classes of systems.
Policy frameworks. Several generic policy management frameworks [5, 19] have been proposed to automate context-aware system and network adaptations. They are generally built around well-documented, extensible information models. If some of them address security for traditional IT systems [5], overall policy-driven security automation remains at an early stage for the cloud [9, 16]. Few frameworks address multi-layered defense or multiple loops. A notable exception is the FOCALE architecture [19] that shares similarities with our work, e.g., the use of a mediation layer to abstract security component heterogeneity. Multiple loops are also supported, but with different adaptation models: FOCALE features an outer loop enabling context-aware adaptation of each component of a main control loop, while VESPA is based on a hierarchical composition of autonomic managers. However, FOCALE does not seem easy to implement, nor to have been applied to the cloud.

Self-protection frameworks. A number of self-defending systems [1, 6, 13] have also been explored. Principle coverage is broadly similar to policy frameworks, although some projects like RootSense [13] investigate cross-layer security, or support multiple security algorithms. Like VESPA, RootSense defines a layered security achitecture. However, the RootSense design is more oriented towards detection (reaction being only the last stage), while VESPA is balanced between detection and reaction (performed symmetrically by dedicated agents). Similarly, the self-protection architecture of [6] defines a 2-level architecture. Introspection and control interfaces directly derive from the use of a component-based model. However, security mechanisms for detection and reaction remain implicit. By contrast, VESPA makes them appear as an explicit security management plane, which increases flexibility to include third-party security components in the system.
Protecting VMs. Virtual machine introspection [15] sparked a whole stream of research to use the capabilities of the hypervisor (Virtual Machine Monitor or VMM) to monitor VM behaviors. Different alternatives were proposed to place the monitoring component: embedded in the VM, in the VMM, or in an "out-of-VM" appliance. A few systems tackled the well-known "semantic" gap issue by comparing monitoring information gathered from different layers [10, 11]. These attempts, mostly focused on detection, only provided very simple remediation policies [10], and architectures hardly compatible with legacy anti-malware software. Several reaction mechanisms were also investigated (mainly firewalls [17]), but with little self-protecting features or flexible security policies.
Hypervisor defense. One layer below, a variety of techniques aim to protect the VMM from subversion, with special attention to kernel exploitation through poorly confined faulty device drivers. One can mention: trusted computing architectures [2] providing strong VMM code integrity guarantees; sandboxing [8] controlling communications between driver and device, kernel, or user space; virtualization [20] to strengthen isolation; or language techniques [23] to detect safety violations. Unfortunately: solutions remained limited to pure integrity checking [2, 23] or containment [8, 20], without actions to sanitize the kernel; in general, security policies were not well separated from interception mechanisms, and thus difficult to manage; and security mechanisms required extensive code rewriting, and thus hard to apply to legacy hypervisors.
Detecting intrusions and malware. Finally, generic IDPS and anti-malware tools [3, 22] may also be viewed as providing some form of self-protection, to detect both known and unknown attacks. Those systems are usually based on a single control loop, with some attempts at cross-layering [22] to detect elusive malwares. Architectures are fairly open to allow selection and composition of several detection algorithms to improve accuracy. However, in most cases, they have been little applied to the cloud.

3. VESPA DESIGN

3.1 Design Principles

VESPA is built around four guiding principles:
[P1] Policy-based self-protection. This principle addresses the heterogeneity, multi-layering, and multi-laterality cloud challenges. The policy-driven paradigm has successfully demonstrated its power and generality to increase adaptability in self-management [18]. For self-protection, this means defining and enforcing a richer set of security strategies [12].
[P2] Cross-layer defense. This principle tackles the multi-layering challenge. This means that events detected in one layer may trigger reactions in other layers. Conversely, a reaction may be launched based on events aggregated from several layers. The cross-layer

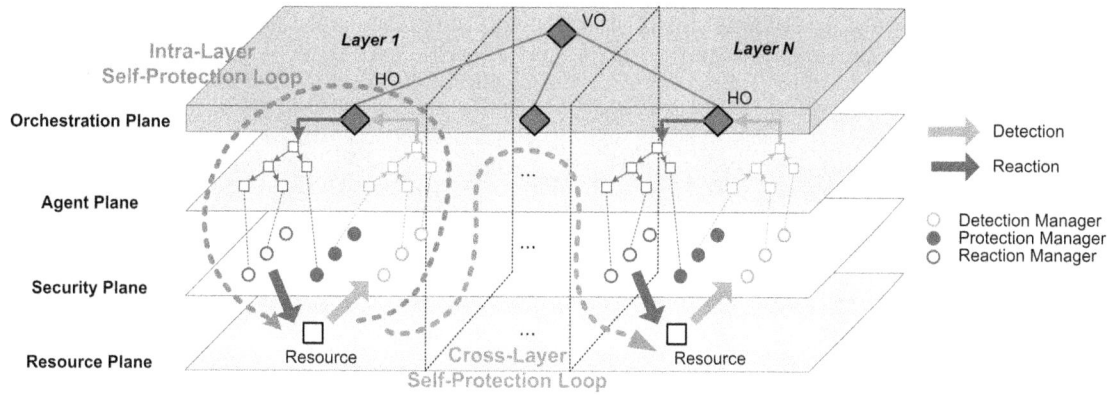

Figure 1: VESPA Self-Protection Architecture.

approach also improves security by helping to capture the overall extent of an attack, often not limited to a single layer, and to better respond to it.

[P3] Multiple self-protection loops. This principle addresses the multi-laterality challenge by considering self-protection over multi-decisional and reaction paths. A simple decision can generate several reactions, extending monitoring granularity. Multiple stages of decision are also possible. Different scope levels for security supervision may thus be defined and coordinated, and degrees of optimality chosen for the response [14].

[P4] Open architecture. This principle addresses the openness and heterogeneity challenges. Several types of detection and reaction strategies should easily be integrated and flexibly composed in the security architecture. The design should notably allow to integrate simply heterogeneous off-the-shelf security components, for strong mitigation of both known and unknown threats. This also increases interoperability between security components across clouds.

3.2 VESPA System Architecture Overview

IaaS infrastructures group resources into *layers* according to the virtualization level. VESPA considers security management orthogonally to layers. Self-protection is achieved through a set of autonomic loops operating over a number of components organized into four distinct *planes*, as shown in Figure 1.

At the bottom, the *Resource Plane* contains the IaaS *resources* to be monitored and protected, i.e., managed elements.

Above, the *Security plane* contains commodity detection and reaction components that deliver security services such as monitoring of resource behavior and/or state (e.g., an IDS), or control of resource behavior and/or state (e.g., a firewall). The APIs of those components are usually vendor-specific.

Still above, the *Agent Plane* abstracts away security component heterogeneity by defining a mediation layer between security services and decision-making elements. This plane is built from two hierarchies of *agents*, one for detection, and another for reaction.

A *leaf agent (LA)* is an adapter between the VESPA framework and the security components to translate vendor-specific APIs into a normalized format both for detection and reaction. It enables to plug-in third-party security components within the framework. LAs cover directly design principle P4, by defining an open and generic interface for framework integration of and interoperability with off-the-shelf security components. LA APIs are usually close to the ones of security components, tending to make agents highly specific. The other extreme is to have generic agents abstracting away widely used security libraries.

Higher-level agents are in charge either of alert correlation or of reaction policy refinement. Thus agents enable a granular level of security supervision over underlying resources.

Finally, at the top, the *Orchestration Plane* contains the decision-making logic. It is composed of two types of autonomic managers called *orchestrators*: *Horizontal Orchestrators (HOs)* perform layer-level security adaptation; *Vertical Orchestrator (VOs)* are in charge of cross-layer security management.

VESPA made the choice of a layered architecture for security supervision, while ad hoc cross-layer controls are also possible. The VESPA design allows simpler, more flexible integration of unknown security components. Indeed, in current cloud infrastructures hand-crafted integration is usually required. A well-formalized architecture may decrease such complexity.

3.3 VESPA Model

We now present the design of each plane of the architecture.

Resource Model. IaaS *resources* are categorized according to two orthogonal criteria. A *layer* defines the location of the resource in a cloud stack. Three separate layers are identified: *physical machines* running a *hypervisor*, in turn executing *virtual machines (VMs)*. The *view* abstraction captures a broad class of resources: *computing*, *networking* or *storage*.

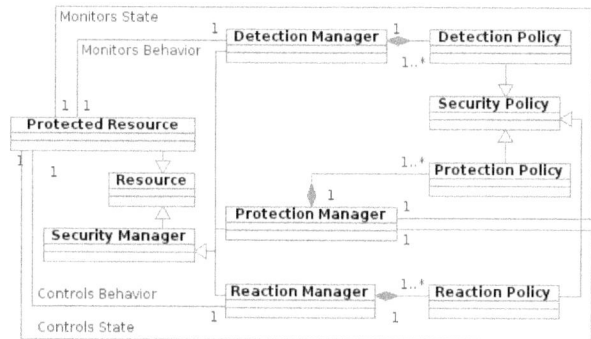

Figure 2: Security Model.

Security Model. *Protected Resources (PR)* are the critical assets of the infrastructure to defend (see Figure 2). The main considered threats target the *VM layer*: a malicious VM may fool the IaaS VM placement strategy to become co-located on the same physical server as the target VM. A side-channel attack breaking VMM isolation may then be used to steal or corrupt information from the infiltrated VM. Attacks on the *hypervisor layer* are also relevant: a VM "escapes" from VMM isolation and takes full control of the hypervisor. Possible attack vectors include misconfigurations, or malicious or poorly confined device drivers in the hypervisor. Attacks against the *physical layer* such as DMA attacks on devices or traditional physical network security threats are also considered.

Security supervision of PRs is performed by *Security Managers (SM)*. This may mean: (1) monitoring resource behavior through a *Detection Manager (DM)*, e.g., an Intrusion Detection System (IDS); (2) modifying resource behavior through a *Reaction Manager (RM)*, e.g., a firewall; or (3) monitoring and modifying the resource internal state with a *Protection Manager (PM)*, e.g., a file system integrity checker. Those security components are typically off-the-shelf, accessible only via vendor-specific APIs. All SM behaviors are governed by *security policies*.

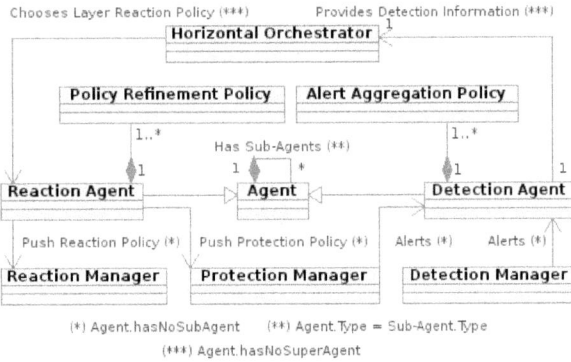

Figure 3: Agent Model.

Agent Model. *Agents* perform security context aggregation from low-level security events gathered from detection mechanisms (DM/PM) to a high-level risk assessment able to guide the decision process (see Figure 3). They also realize reaction policy refinement from the high-level response chosen after the decision to low-level policies which can be enforced by reaction mechanisms (RM/PM).

Detection works as follows: a DM or PM notifies its associated *Detection Agent (DA)* of security-sensitive events. Each DA then applies an *Alert Aggregation Policy* to correlate collected information from sub-agents before sending them to its parent agent. When reaching the root detection agent, security context information is transmitted to the orchestration plane through the HO.

The reaction process is symmetrical: after choosing a layer-specific reaction policy, the HO sends it to the root *Reaction Agent (RA)*. Each RA will apply a *Policy Refinement Policy* to fine-tune the selected response, before sending it to chosen sub-agents for enforcement. When reaching a leaf reaction agent, reaction and/or protection policies are pushed towards the corresponding managers in the security plane.

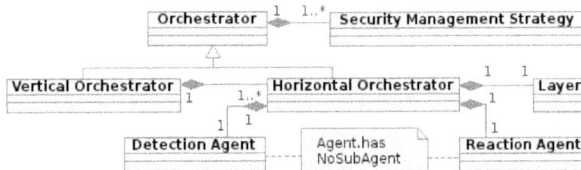

Figure 4: Orchestration Model.

Orchestration Model. Each IaaS layer contains a HO providing a layer view of security management. The HO is a simple autonomic security manager performing a reflex, local response to threats on layer resources. The HO gathers the overall layer security context information from the root DA (see Figure 4). The HO *Security Management Strategy* allows it to choose the best layer-level reaction policy, then dispatched to the root RA for enforcement.

The HO may also apply decisions coming from the VO. The latter orchestrator realizes higher-level, wider spectrum security reactions. The VO coordinates layer-level decisions to provide a consistent, cross-layer response to detected threats. The VO *Security Management Strategy* contains administrator-defined policies on alert feedbacks to trigger or not a cross-layer response. It also allows the VO to choose the overall reaction policy, which is then pushed down to the relevant layers for enforcement by their HOs.

Such loop composition may induce interferences between heterogeneous technologies in the security plane (e.g., resource contention, predictibility issues) – and thus requires careful component orchestration. Security management strategies govern decision-making at each level, and may serve to address a particular type of interference. For instance, we plan to perform integration testing between security components to detect policy conflicts and define the right resolution strategies. Learning and prediction schemes should also help to build knowledge, but remain to be explored.

4. EXPERIMENTS AND RESULTS

A Case Study. We now illustrate how the VESPA framework may be deployed in practice to automate and coordinate security management between IaaS layers. We explore *dynamic VM quarantine*: several VMs suspected to be compromised are isolated temporarily, and migrated to a secured zone for cleaning. If remediation succeeds, VMs may be migrated back in their original environment, and confinement lifted.

Figure 5 shows a simple VESPA instantiation on a typical IaaS infrastructure. A specific host (not shown on the Figure), strongly isolated and trusted, is dedicated to quarantine management. On each host, the hypervisor contains two reaction components: a *firewall* to control strictly inter-VM communications; and a *migration manager* to handle VM migration to the quarantine host. *User VMs (UVMs)* are VM instances protected by VESPA. A UVM contains an *anti-virus* to analyze and sanitize infections within the VM. An *Administrative VM (AVM)* realizes the VESPA orchestration plane.

Consider a user watching a movie streamed from an untrusted source: a virus is detected a few seconds after the video started. The UVM anti-virus alerts the AVM, which selects a security response. Several types of reactions may be chosen and combined: (1) isolate the infected VM to prevent the virus from spreading by cutting its network connections through the firewall; (2) move the UVM to the quarantine host, anticipating virus propagation over unusual channels (e.g., hypercalls) through the migration manager; (3) analyze and clean possible infection vectors by invoking the anti-virus. Upon success, next steps are to migrate back the UVM to the original host, and restore network connections.

Figure 5 shows the different VESPA components to protect the video stream. Three levels of self-protection may be achieved: (1) within the VM layer, with only the anti-virus for VM analysis and cleaning; (2) cross-layer, with the hypervisor firewall to isolate the VM; and (3) cross-layer, including also the migration manager to move the VM to the quarantine zone.

Response Time. We analyzed the VESPA self-protection overhead in terms of overall loop latency for the different security adaptations of the case study. Results are shown in Table 2. In reaction (1), walking the hierarchy of framework entities during detection is fast (0.15s) compared to the effective cleaning operation (5.53s), which involves scanning memory and files. For reaction (2), adding layer interaction increases response time by only 13% while providing network isolation. Reaction (3) takes about 37 s, which is acceptable to contain infections that are not acute. The major part (90%) of this latency comes from migrating to and from the quarantine host. Reaction (2) may be a good trade-off between strong security and low latency, as response time falls to only 6s.

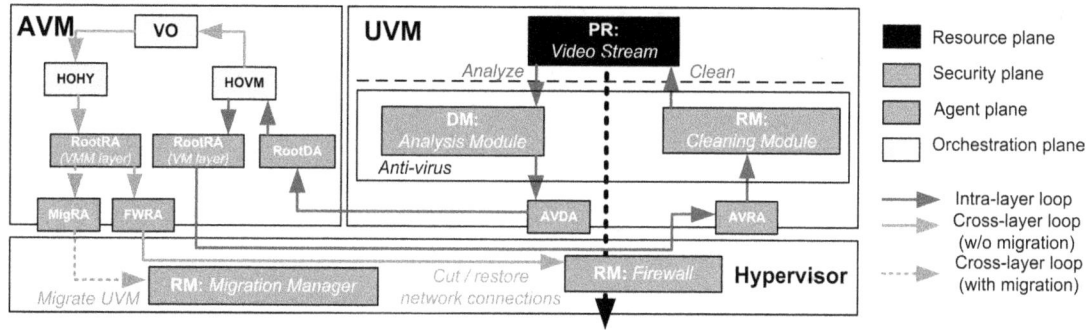

Figure 5: Realizing Flexible VM Quarantine with VESPA.

Phase	(1) Intra-Layer	(2) Cross-Layer (w/o Migration)	(3) Cross-Layer (with Migration)
Detection	0.15	0.16	0.17
Decision	0.14	0.32	0.37
Disconnect	-	0.20	0.20
Migration	-	-	14.91
Cleaning	5.53	5.72	5.98
Migration	-	-	15.23
Reconnect	-	0.20	0.20
Total	5.82	6.60	37.06

Table 2: End-to-End Self-Protection Latencies (in s).

Other Benchmarks. VESPA self-protection capabilities were also evaluated in terms intrusivity and resilience. Detailed results are not presented here for lack of space. The idea is to disturb the system by an attack, and see how fast the system recovers to a steady state, and with which performance impact (bandwidth). Measured recovery time is $\sim 60s$, with a drop in bandwidth of $\sim 16\%$. Thus, VESPA enables effective self-protection of a cloud infrastructure with reasonable performance overhead. VESPA openness should also be assessed. To date, adequate quantitative benchmarks are still under investigation. A first next step will be to implement agents for different classes of off-the-shelf security components (e.g., IDS, anti-virus, firewall) to evaluate qualitatively integration easiness of existing security technologies within VESPA.

5. NEXT STEPS

Future work includes clarifying the smarts needed in the agents by defining a richer set of policies (e.g., detection, policy refinement, reaction) to extend currently implemented ECA rules.

VESPA is also being refined to address hypervisor-level self-protection [21]: automated monitoring and sanitization of device driver I/Os is a big step towards strengthening IaaS security, as such drivers are generally the weakest point of hypervisors.

VESPA will finally be extended to provide self-protection for the inter-cloud setting: as heterogeneous clouds become federated in a single multi-lateral infrastructure, placement of security mechanisms will no longer be only a vertical, layer-oriented issue. It will also be a horizontal design challenge between multiple security domains in the network and system security architecture, challenge to which self-protection may bring answers.

Acknowledgements

We thank the anonymous reviewers for their insightful comments. This work was supported by the OpenCloudWare project, funded by the French Fonds national pour la Société Numérique (FSN).

6. REFERENCES

[1] Y. Al-Nashif, A. Kumar, S. Hariri, G. Qu, Y. Luo, and F. Szidarovsky. Multi-Level Intrusion Detection System (ML-IDS). In *International Conference on Autonomic Computing (ICAC)*, 2008.

[2] A. M. Azab et al. HyperSentry: Enabling Stealthy In-Context Measurement of Hypervisor Integrity. In *ACM Conference on Computer and Communications Security (CCS)*, 2010.

[3] A. Baliga, L. Iftode, and X. Chen. Automated Containment of Rootkits Attacks. *Computers & Security*, 27:323–334, 2008.

[4] Cloud Security Alliance. Top Threats To Cloud Computing, 2011. http://www.cloudsecurityalliance.org/topthreats.html.

[5] N. Damianou, N. Dulay, E. Lupu, and M. Sloman. The Ponder Policy Specification Language. In *International Workshop on Policies for Distributed Systems and Networks (POLICY)*, 2001.

[6] N. De Palma, D. Hagimont, F. Boyer, and L. Broto. Self-Protection in a Clustered Distributed System. *Parallel and Distributed Systems, IEEE Transactions on*, 23(2):330–336, 2012.

[7] D. Frincke, A. Wespi, and D. Zamboni. From Intrusion Detection to Self-Protection. *Comput. Netw.*, 51:1233–1238, April 2007.

[8] V. Ganapathy et al. The Design and Implementation of Microdrivers. In *International Conference on Architectural Support for Programming Languages and Operating Systems (ASPLOS)*, 2008.

[9] R. He, M. Lacoste, and J. Leneutre. ASPF: A Policy Administration Framework for Self-Protection of Large-Scale Systems. *IARIA International Journal On Advances in Security*, 3(3–4):104–122, 2010.

[10] A. Ibrahim, J. Hamlyn-Harris, J. Grundy, and M. Almorsy. CloudSec: A Security Monitoring Appliance for Virtual Machines in the IaaS Cloud Model. In *International Conference on Network and Systems (NSS)*, 2011.

[11] X. Jiang, X. Wang, and D. Xu. Stealthy Malware Detection through VMM-Based "Out-of-the-Box" Semantic View Reconstruction. *ACM Trans. Inf. Syst. Secur.*, 13:1–28, 2010.

[12] J. Kephart and W. Walsh. An Artificial Intelligence Perspective on Autonomic Computing Policies. In *Fifth IEEE International Workshop on Policies for Distributed Systems and Networks (POLICY)*, 2004.

[13] R. Koller et al. Anatomy of a Real-Time Intrusion Prevention System. In *International Conference on Autonomic Computing (ICAC)*, 2008.

[14] O. Mola and M. Bauer. Towards Cloud Management by Autonomic Manager Collaboration. *International Journal of Communications, Network and System Sciences*, 4(12):790–802, 2011.

[15] K. Nance, M. Bishop, and B. Hay. Virtual Machine Introspection: Observation or Interference? *IEEE Security and Privacy*, 6:32–37, September 2008.

[16] ObjectSecurity. OpenPMF White Paper, 2011. www.openpmf.org.

[17] R. Sailer et al. Building a MAC-Based Security Architecture for the Xen Open-Source Hypervisor. In *Annual Computer Security Applications Conference (ACSAC)*, 2005.

[18] J. Strassner. *Policy-Based Network Management: Solutions for the Next Generation*. Morgan Kaufman, 2003.

[19] J. Strassner et al. The Design of a New Context-Aware Policy Model for Autonomic Networking. In *International Conference on Autonomic Computing (ICAC)*, 2008.

[20] L. Tan et al. iKernel: Isolating Buggy and Malicious Device Drivers Using Hardware Virtualization Support. In *International Symposium on Dependable, Autonomic and Secure Computing (DASC)*, 2007.

[21] A. Wailly, M. Lacoste, and H. Debar. KungFuVisor: Enabling Hypervisor Self-Defense. In *EUROSYS Doctoral Workshop (EURODW)*, 2012.

[22] Y.-M. Wang, D. Beck, B. Vo, and C. Verbowski. Detecting Stealth Software with Strider GhostBuster. In *International Conference on Dependable Systems and Networks (DSN)*, 2005.

[23] Z. Wang and X. Jiang. HyperSafe: A Lightweight Approach to Provide Lifetime Hypervisor Control-Flow Integrity. In *IEEE Symposium on Security and Privacy*, 2010.

Usage Patterns in Multi-tenant Data Centers: a Temporal Perspective

Robert Birke
IBM Research Zurich Lab
Rüschlikon, Switzerland
bir@zurich.ibm.com

Lydia Y. Chen
IBM Research Zurich Lab
Rüschlikon, Switzerland
yic@zurich.ibm.com

Evgenia Smirni
College of William and Mary
Williamsburg, VA, USA
esmirni@cs.wm.edu

ABSTRACT

Data centers, hosted either on-site or by a third party, have become a dominant computing platform. Here, we focus on the usage patterns of in-production data centers that are hosted by a third party and serve several corporate customers. We characterize the data center workload and concentrate especially on the temporal evolution of utilization of basic resource components. We especially focus on the autonomic aspect of this characterization as it can be used to identify how loads across components change in order to identify conditions that can trigger resource reallocation toward better workload management. To this end, we focus on the resource demands of six distinct corporate customers on two specific data centers, highlight the workload diversity across these customers, and especially focus on how resources are used in time scales that range from minutes to days, weeks, and months. This study fills an important gap in our understanding on how data center resources are used and provides helpful insights for the development of autonomous resource management in multi-tenant data centers.

Categories and Subject Descriptors

C.4 [**Computer Systems Organization**]: Performance of Systems

General Terms

Measurement, Performance

Keywords

Data centers, performance, workload characterization

1. INTRODUCTION

Data centers are nowadays ubiquitous and have become a commonplace computing platform for corporations as well as individuals, providing a diverse array of services. Data centers may be universal and prevalent, but so are their administrative challenges that include how to best use them, as well as how to optimize their power and cooling costs. The sheer diversity of customer demands (e.g., one may expect very different needs and performance expectations between individual users of cloud-based data centers versus corporate customers) make data center administration challenging and without clear solutions. Studying the workload that typical data centers experience can provide many useful insights for the better usage of data centers, for the design of autonomic management policies for various resources, even for more efficient power and/or cooling management policies.

Most of existing data center studies can be roughly classified as those that focus on power and thermal management [4–7], capacity planning and resource provisioning [11–13], and traffic engineering [1, 2, 8–10]. The above works either aim at a specific architectural component (e.g., network) or evaluate resource provisioning via simulation or via small scale prototypes at a laboratory setting. To the best of our knowledge, there is very little information on *how exactly* corporate data centers are used by clients, how their workload demands change across time, and how customer demands on different resources fluctuate across time. In this paper we fill this gap by providing the first very detailed resource allocation study that considers two specific data centers and focuses on the usage patterns of several corporate customers across different time scales.

In our previous work [3], we present a workload characterization study of corporate data centers consisting of several thousand servers that are geographically dispersed across the entire globe. The collected data represent the evolution of cloud workload in a time span of 24 months and give a view on how data center workloads evolve across different enterprises, countries, even continents. The focus of [3] is on the time evolution and seasonal characteristics of resource demands from a capacity planning viewpoint. The holistic view that is adopted in [3] gives an excellent perspective for an economics analysis but does not shed any light into the interdependency of workloads that are collocated within the same datacenters, how specific enterprises utilize specific data center resources, or how the demands on the various resources are correlated.

In this study, we select two specific data centers, which host multiple enterprises from the data set collected by Birke et al. [3]. One is a "small" data center that consists of 393 servers and hosts service applications from three enterprises and the other one is a "large" datacenter that consists of 3681 servers and hosts more than 10 enterprises. Here, we focus

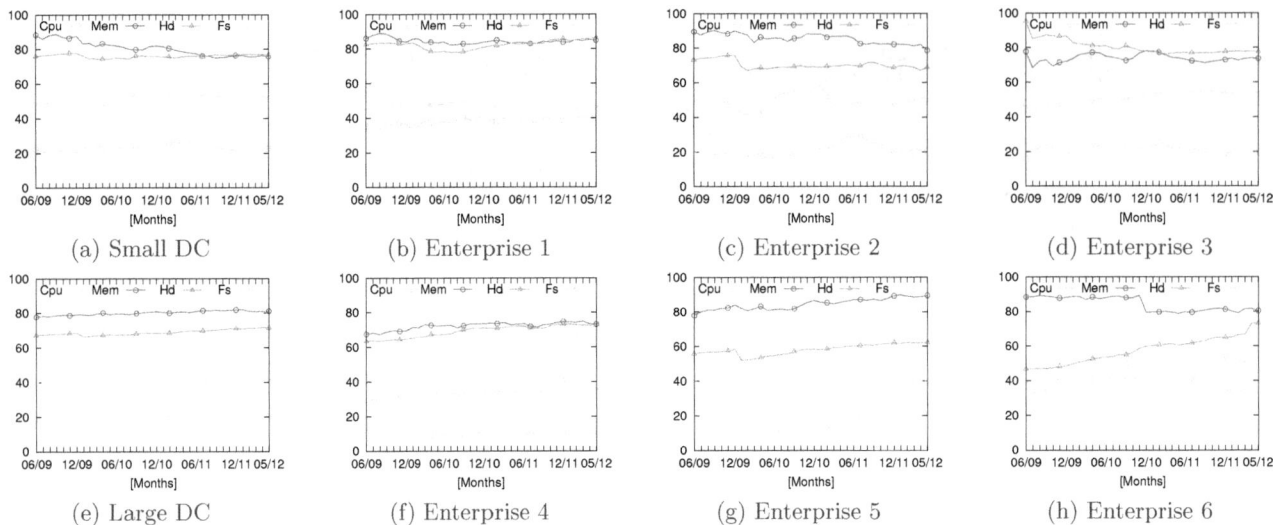

| (a) Small DC | (b) Enterprise 1 | (c) Enterprise 2 | (d) Enterprise 3 |

| (e) Large DC | (f) Enterprise 4 | (g) Enterprise 5 | (h) Enterprise 6 |

Figure 1: Time series of resource utilizations of monthly averages over three years. Note that memory, disk, and file system values correspond to space utilization.

on how specific enterprises use specific data centers. We adopt a per-enterprise view and concentrate on how six different enterprises, three from each data center, utilize each center's resources. While we give an overview of resource utilization for CPU, disk, memory, and file system, we especially focus on the per-server CPU utilization by each enterprise. We illustrate the importance of the granularity of the observation by showing the per day utilizations of the servers used by each enterprise across a time period of one month and then we focus on a random weekday and a weekend day to further untangle utilization patterns but at a much finer time granularity.

The presented study aims at characterizing the workload diversity by looking at how specific enterprises utilize data center resources across time. We especially focus on CPU utilizations because we find that CPUs are consistently under utilized. This characterization can be incorporated in the design of autonomic solutions for workload consolidation and load balancing in today's data centers. Beyond that, this characterization could be further used in combination with temperature/cooling information for better power management in data centers, but we believe that it can be primarily used in the design of autonomic policies for data center resource allocation.

Despite the fact that this study is based on a very rich data set that reveals how corporate data centers use data center resources, it does not provide any information on the type of applications that different enterprises use or on the response times of these applications. Nevertheless, from the utilization values across the different servers and across time, one could speculate about the effects of over provisioning as well as the efficacy of designing better autonomic policies for workload consolidation and resource management in today's data centers.

2. MULTI-TENANT DATACENTERS

We collect resource utilization statistics from several thousands of servers from two in-production data centers. These systems are used by different industries, including banking,

Table 1: Overview of resource utilization by different enterprises.

Small DC	CPU		Memory		Disk		File Sys.	
	mean	std	mean	std	mean	std	mean	std
All	23.53	23.17	78.17	9.93	76.03	22.34	51.55	20.62
Ent 1	38.22	23.15	84.18	9.51	82.37	19.63	47.39	15.60
Ent 2	21.64	21.24	84.33	6.61	69.08	23.15	48.54	20.23
Ent 3	20.73	22.86	73.70	11.16	77.86	21.93	53.25	21.22

Large DC	CPU		Memory		Disk		File Sys.	
	mean	std	mean	std	mean	std	mean	std
All	20.82	23.84	80.33	10.52	68.89	26.08	40.15	19.82
Ent 4	10.56	14.02	72.80	5.67	70.05	28.00	33.88	18.64
Ent 5	16.10	20.75	85.37	9.47	58.09	26.08	38.14	20.96
Ent 6	37.81	27.89	83.12	13.63	60.34	25.74	43.32	18.95

pharmaceutical, IT, consulting, and retail industries. The collected samples contain a rich set of representative server statistics reflecting the current practices of resource management in corporate data centers and contain mainly resource utilizations.

The average utilization values over base periods are collected via prevailing utilities such as vmstat and df. All data is stored in a database and aggregated into different time scales ranging from one minute to one month. For each timescale only a fixed number of the most recent records is kept. Consequently, recent data is available at a higher time resolution than older data in order for the database to maintain an upper limit of the space footprint per server. In particular, we consider fine grained 15-minute data on Wednesday, May 23, 2012 and Sunday, May 27, 2012. In most cases, we focus on the comparison between Wednesday and Sunday, i.e., the workload difference between a working day and a weekend day.

We focus on the basic physical resources per server: CPU, network, memory, disk, and file system statistics that are collected in units of resource utilization which is just a percentage value. Since a server can have multiple disks, the disk utilization is defined by the sum of all used space divided by sum of all disk sizes. The file system includes both local and remote data storage, which can be on the media

162

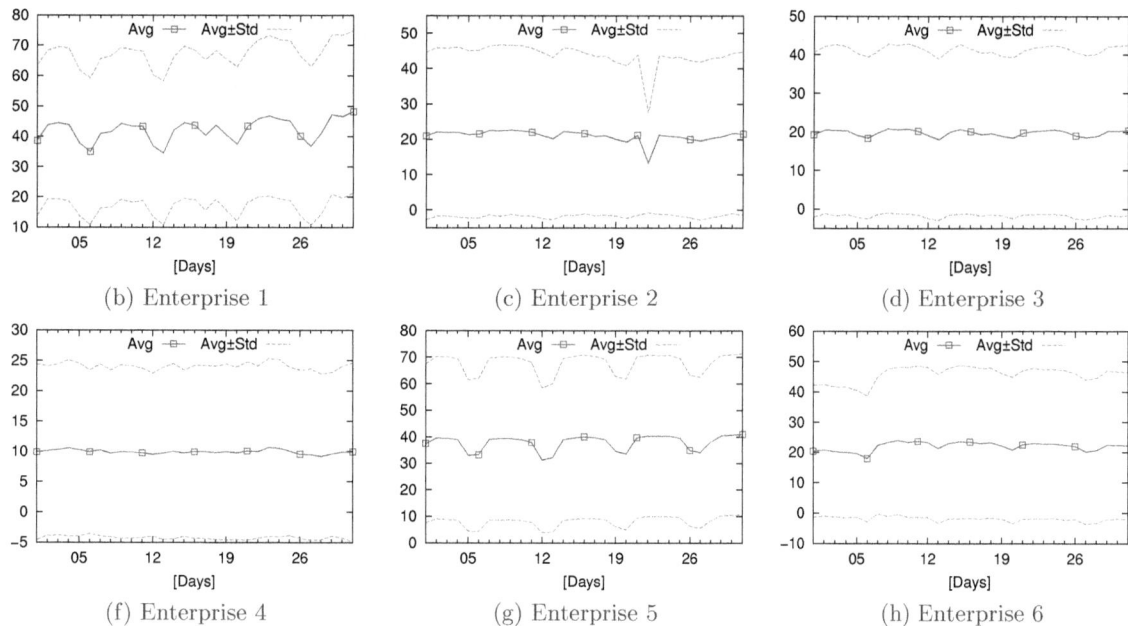

Figure 2: Time series of daily CPU utilization over during the entire month of May 2012.

of disks and memory. Similar to the disk, when there are multiple file systems, the utilization is computed from the sum of all used space divided the sum of all file system sizes. The CPU utilization is defined by the percentage of time the CPU is active over an observation period. Utilization values of memory, disk, and file system are defined by the volume usage, i.e., used space divided by the total available space.

2.1 Evolution of resource demands

Before focusing on how the workload evolves across time, we present some aggregate measures in Table 1. The table presents the mean and standard deviation of utilization values of the servers used by the six selected enterprises across an observation period of three years, and gives a per enterprise view, as well as a per data center view. Note that across all resource utilization values, standard deviations are significant, especially in light of the fact that utilizations values are bounded between 0 and 100.

We also present how the workload diversity evolves across the observation time. We depict the time series of monthly utilization across three years for all resources in Fig. 1. The utilization evolution for most of resources and across all enterprises are rather stable albeit with a slightly increasing trend, which indicates that the growth of demand of a particular resource is greater than the growth of its supply. A decreasing trend indicates the opposite, i.e., the growth of supply is greater than the demand. Dips in the time series correspond to hardware/software upgrades. In general, Fig. 1 consistently shows that the CPU is the *least* utilized resource across all datacenters and across all enterprises. In the following, we further investigate how CPUs are utilized by the various data centers.

2.2 CPU Load Balancing

In Figure 2 we illustrate the time series of daily average CPU utilization for the six enterprises across the entire month of May 2012. On this figure we also plot the stan-

dard deviation of the average server utilization. Notice that the number of servers that are assigned to each enterprise range from 130 to 1380, therefore the significant standard deviation can be viewed as a strong indication of very unbalanced utilization values across servers, which is a consistent trend across all enterprises. The figure also illustrates another interesting behavior: there are clear daily patterns, i.e., weekends can be clearly seen across most enterprises (see the distinct dips in the plots for enterprises 1, 3, 5, and 6). Weekend utilizations can be as low as ten percentage points comparing to working day utilizations. Enterprises 2 and 4 have a more even utilization pattern across time, with only slight ripples in their averages across time.

Motivated by these observations, we now turn to the time series of CPU utilizations calculated every 15 minutes. We focus on one representative week day, Wednesday May 23, and one representative weekend day, Sunday May 27. Figure 3 illustrates the average utilizations together with the standard deviation. On each graph, we plot data for Wednesday and Sunday. The figure clearly illustrates that there are severe utilization imbalances across servers within 15-minute time periods. In addition, it shows that some enterprises utilize the CPUs during weekdays very differently from the weekends (e.g., look in Figures 3(a) and 3(e) where there is a significant change in values, especially during mid-day) while some others have a quite similar usage on both Wednesday and Sunday. Across several enterprises, we also observe a slightly spiky pattern at the beginning of each hour. This pattern is consistent across most graphs in Figure 3 and is especially prominent during off-peak hours. Close observation on the data and on what CPU does during these periods shows that this is due to the scheduling of batch jobs on the hour, commonly done via a cron utility. In addition, the figure illustrates the tendency to schedule batch jobs during off-peak hours. In general, we observe clear load unbalances across enterprises and at the same time similar practices in resource usage across time and across all enterprises.

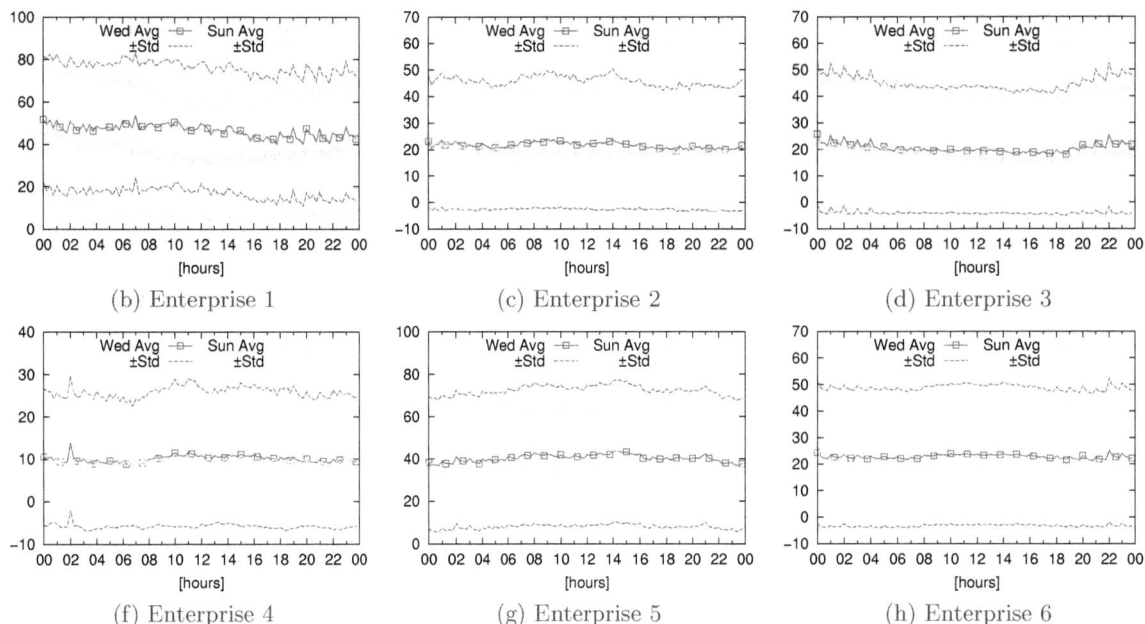

Figure 3: Time series of 15-minute CPU utilization during a representative workday (Wednesday, May 23 2012) and during a representative weekend day (Sunday, May 27 2012).

2.3 The Impact of Time Scales

To illustrate fluctuations of resource demands across time and also across servers, we also present the daily utilizations for 21 representative days, namely May 2012 for the six enterprises, see Fig. 4. In the interest of a clearer presentation, we present heatmaps that illustrate the CPU utilization levels for only a subset of the servers used by each enterprise, namely only for 50 servers which are mapped on the y-axis of each graph.[1] The x-axis corresponds to the specific days within the selected 31-day period, (i.e., the entire May). The y-axis corresponds to the server identification number. We note that despite the fact that we only show daily utilizations for 50 servers, the patterns shown are representative. Dark colors in the figure correspond to high utilization values, while light colors to low utilizations.

Fig. 4 clearly shows that across all enterprises, there are well defined cyclic patterns that correspond to week- and weekend- days, see for example the illustration of three vertical lighter regions that signify weekend (lighter) loads across all enterprises. In addition, a striking similarity across all enterprises is that there is a clear load unbalancing, as shown by the presence of multiple colors/shades as well as the fact that some servers are mostly always highly loaded, even during low weekend cycles. The graph illustrates opportunities for power savings, e.g., see Fig. 4(e) as well as load balancing to improve system usage. Overall, these graphs can be used to demonstrate the current state-of-the-practice and can be used to evaluate the need of new load balancing or consolidation techniques.

Figure 5 selects a single day, Wednesday, May 23 2012, and zooms into the utilization of the same set of selected CPUs as in Figure 4 but looking at utilizations at 15-minute time periods. This new figure allows us to see more clearly fluctuations in utilization on the selected CPUs during a 24 hours period. Observe that in most of enterprises, there is a surge in utilizations on the first 15-minute period of every hour. In addition, it appears that load is not steady across time but could fluctuate significantly.

Figure 6 selects the exact same servers as in Figure 5 but plots 15-minute utilizations for a typical weekend day. For some enterprises there is a dramatic drop in utilizations (see for example enterprise 6) comparing to the typical working day, while for some others (e.g., enterprises 2, 4, and 5) the reduction in utilization is only moderate. In general, comparing Figures 4, 5, and 6, we observe that there are dramatic load imbalances both across servers and across time, pointing to excellent opportunities for intelligent workload consolidation and improved load balancing. This observation, in addition to the fact that CPUs tend to be lowly utilized, should drive the development of more effective workload management in data centers.

3. SUMMARY

In this paper, we characterize workloads collected from two data centers, each of which host multiple enterprises, for the span of three years. We report on the utilization of four resources, i.e., CPU, memory, disk, and file system, but focus mainly on the CPU utilizations across different time scales. We show the workload diversity, long-term evolution, CPU load balancing, and discuss the needs for developing autonomous resource management at different time scales. This study can be used as a baseline against which autonomic policies for data center management can be evaluated. In future work we also intend to do a similar study for storage and memory resources and also measure the resource correlation in data centers, trying to understand whether resource provisioning should be bundled.

---

[1]Each enterprise uses different number of servers, with the majority of them using more than 130 servers, which unfortunately results in an illegible heat map.

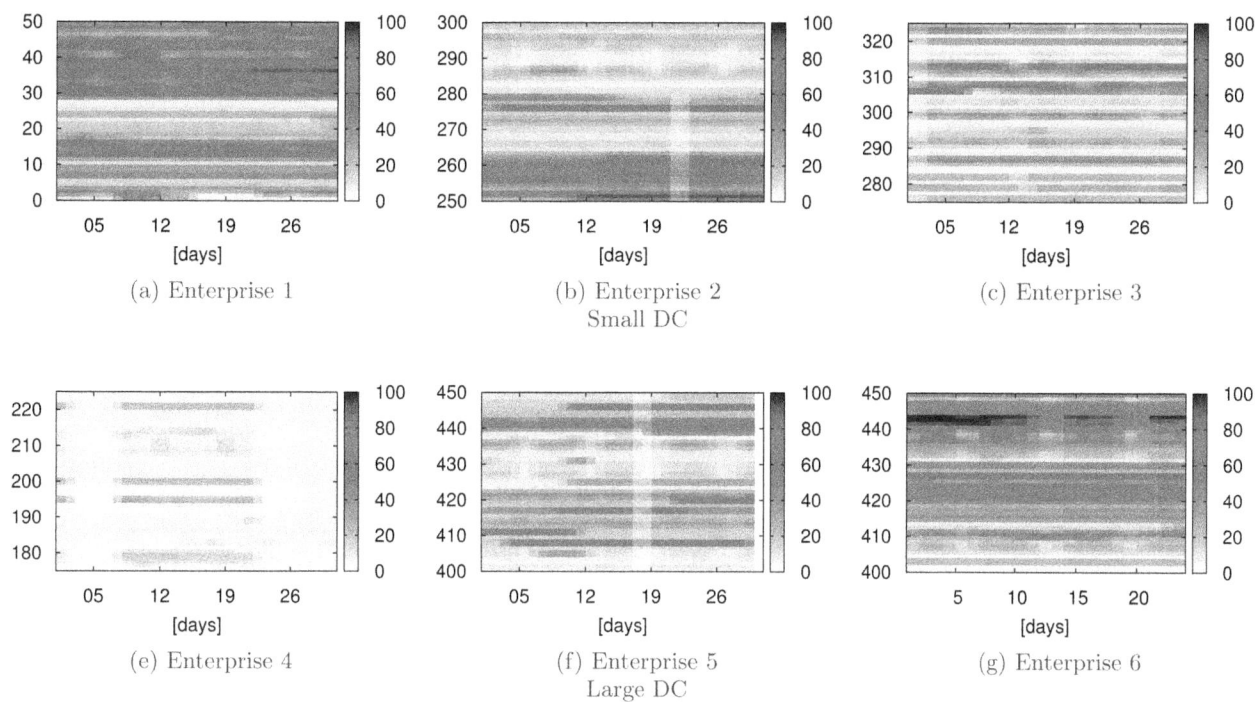

Figure 4: CPU daily utilization of different industries for May 2012.

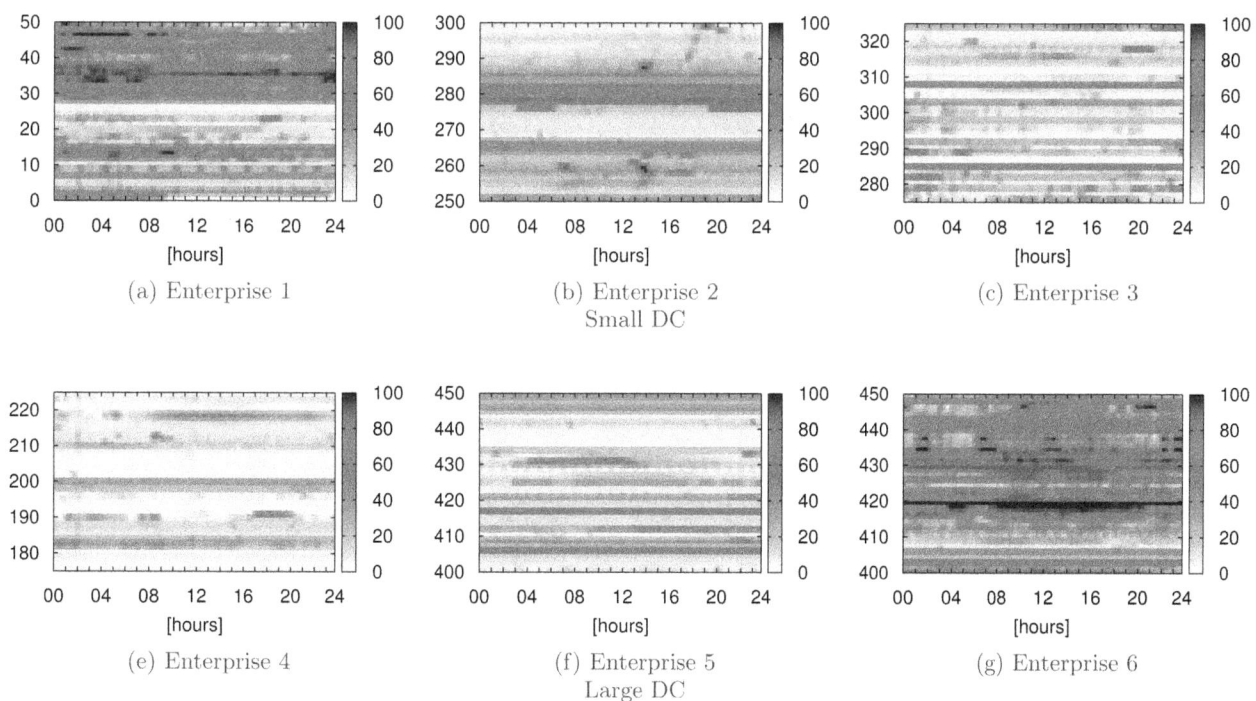

Figure 5: CPU utilizations for 15-minute time periods for a typical working day (Wednesday, May 23, 2012).

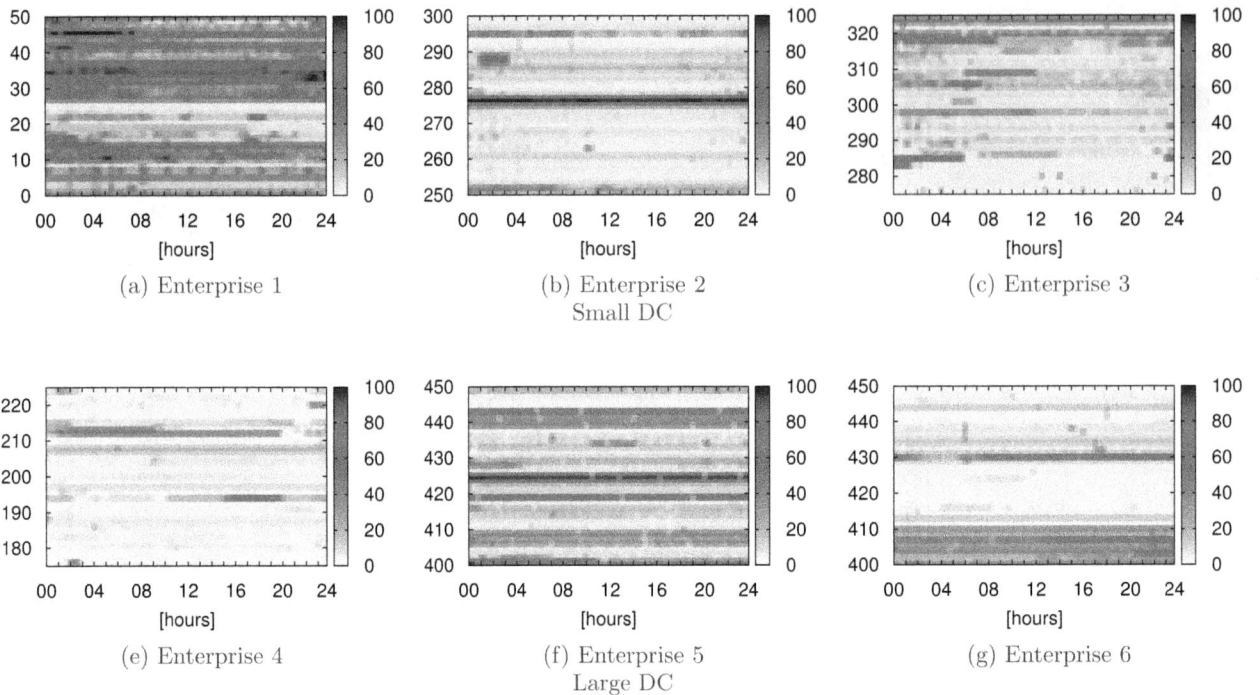

Figure 6: CPU utilizations for 15-minute time periods for a typical weekend day (Sunday, May 27, 2012).

Acknowledgments

We thank Nishi Gupta for granting us access to the data and share our insights with the scientific community. Part of this work has been done while Evgenia Smirni was on sabbatical leave at IBM Research, Zurich Lab. Evgenia Smirni is partially supported by NSF grants CCF-0937925 and CCF-1218758.

4. REFERENCES

[1] M. Al-Fares, A. Loukissas, and A. Vahdat. A scalable, commodity data center network architecture. In *SIGCOMM*, pages 63–74, 2008.

[2] T. Benson, A. Akella, and D. A. Maltz. Network traffic characteristics of data centers in the wild. In *Internet Measurement Conference*, pages 267–280, 2010.

[3] R. Birke, L. Y. Chen, and E. Smirni. Data centers in the cloud: A large scale performance study. In *Proceedings of IEEE CLOUD*, pages 336–343, 2012.

[4] G. Chen, W. He, J. Liu, S. Nath, L. Rigas, L. Xiao, and F. Zhao. Energy-aware server provisioning and load dispatching for connection-intensive internet services. In *NSDI*, pages 337–350, 2008.

[5] Y. Chen, A. Das, W. Qin, A. Sivasubramaniam, Q. Wang, and N. Gautam. Managing server energy and operational costs in hosting centers. In *SIGMETRICS*, pages 303–314, 2005.

[6] N. El-Sayed, I. A. Stefanovici, G. Amvrosiadis, A. A. Hwang, and B. Schroeder. Temperature management in data centers: why some (might) like it hot. In *SIGMETRICS*, pages 163–174, 2012.

[7] S. Govindan, J. Choi, B. Urgaonkar, A. Sivasubramaniam, and A. Baldini. Statistical profiling-based techniques for effective power provisioning in data centers. In *EuroSys*, pages 317–330, 2009.

[8] C. Guo, H. Wu, K. Tan, L. Shi, Y. Zhang, and S. Lu. Dcell: a scalable and fault-tolerant network structure for data centers. In *SIGCOMM*, pages 75–86, 2008.

[9] D. Halperin, S. Kandula, J. Padhye, P. Bahl, and D. Wetherall. Augmenting data center networks with multi-gigabit wireless links. In *SIGCOMM*, pages 38–49, 2011.

[10] B. Heller, S. Seetharaman, P. Mahadevan, Y. Yiakoumis, P. Sharma, S. Banerjee, and N. McKeown. Elastictree: Saving energy in data center networks. In *NSDI*, pages 249–264, 2010.

[11] M. Kutare, G. Eisenhauer, C. Wang, K. Schwan, V. Talwar, and M. W. Matthew. Monalytics: online monitoring and analytics for managing large scale data centers. In *Proceeding of the 7th international conference on Autonomic computing*.

[12] R. Singh, U. Sharma, E. Cecchet, and P. Shenoy. Autonomic mix-aware provisioning for non-stationary data center workloads. In *International Conference on Autonomic Computing (ICAC)*, pages 21–30, 2010.

[13] X. Zhu, D. Young, B. J. Watson, Z. Wang, J. Rolia, S. Singhal, B. McKee, C. Hyser, D. Gmach, R. Gardner, T. Christian, and L. Cherkasova. 1000 islands: an integrated approach to resource management for virtualized data centers. *Cluster Computing*, 12(1):45–57, 2009.

Toward Fast Eventual Consistency with Performance Guarantees

Feng Yan
College of William and Mary
Williamsburg, VA, USA
fyan@cs.wm.edu

Alma Riska
EMC Corporation
Cambridge, MA, USA
alma.riska@emc.com

Evgenia Smirni
College of William and Mary
Williamsburg, VA, USA
esmirni@cs.wm.edu

ABSTRACT

Systems have adopted the notion of *eventual consistency* which means that the targeted redundancy of data in the system is reached *asynchronously*, i.e., outside of the critical path of user traffic, so that performance of user traffic is impacted minimally. Here, we propose a scheduling framework that makes decisions about when to schedule the asynchronous tasks associated with new or updated data such that they are completed as soon as possible without violating user traffic quality targets. At the heart of the framework lies a learning methodology that extracts the characteristics of idle periods and infers the average amount of work to be filled during periods of idleness so that asynchronous tasks are completed transparently to the user. Extensive trace-driven evaluation shows the effectiveness and robustness of the proposed framework when compared to common practices.

Categories and Subject Descriptors

C.4 [**Computer Systems Organization**]: Performance of Systems

General Terms

Performance, Algorithms

Keywords

performance, workload characterization, idle periods, eventual consistency, user traffic, storage systems

1. INTRODUCTION

In distributed storage systems, it is expected that data is distributed across multiple nodes and geographic locations. Yet, as new data arrives in the system, from the performance perspective, it is not as efficient for the system to propagate the data to the various locations in real time, because the impact on end user performance (now including also WAN transfers) may be significant. A solution is for the system to distribute the data across the locations asynchronously [1, 2, 3]. As a result, the data reaches its expected locations *eventually* as systems strive to achieve *eventual data consistency* [4, 5, 6].

ICAC'12, September 18–20, 2012, San Jose, California, USA.
Copyright 2012 ACM 978-1-4503-1520-3/12/09 ...$15.00.

Eventual consistency [4, 7, 5, 3] assures that if no new updates are made to a data object, then eventually all copies of the object data get updated. The inconsistency window affects data reliability since data loss may occur while the targeted redundancy is not reached immediately. Here, we denote the node in the distributed system that receives the new data as the "active" node and the nodes that would receive replicas (or parts of the data) asynchronously "inactive nodes". Data may arrive in any node in the system, which means that any node can be an active or inactive node.

When new data arrives, it is acknowledged and processed by the active node and then distributed to the nodes that should receive it. Data either is replicated in multiple locations or it is stripped, coded, and distributed in different locations (erasure coding). When the redundant data is sent out from the active node over the network, it can be delayed depending on the distance between the nodes and the amount of data being transferred. The inactive node that receives it, buffers it in cache before committing it to a storage device. Buffering is required as the inactive node may be serving its own user traffic, and the goal is to not impact its performance. If the inactive node processes such data immediately upon arrival then its user performance impact may be severe.

It is clear that the inconsistency window has three parts: the time it takes to send out the data from the active node, the time to transfer the data over the network, and the time to commit the data on the storage devices of the inactive node. Eventual consistency for each piece of data is achieved when *all* inactive nodes that should have received a copy or fragment of the data have done so successfully. From the perspective of modeling and without loss of generality, the problem of modeling the duration of inconsistency window can be simplified to that of a single active node and a single inactive node.

The issue with the asynchronous traffic is that it impacts system performance regardless of how carefully it is scheduled because often IO tasks are not *instantaneously* preemptable [8]. Judicious scheduling of asynchronous tasks that is done as quickly as possible so that system is less vulnerable for losing data, while user traffic is not affected, is challenging. There are two methods that are widely used to schedule background work in storage systems. The first one is *Aggressive* scheduling that schedules replication work immediately and without any consideration for user traffic. The second one is *Utilization-guided* scheduling that uses system utilization as guidance and schedules the replication work only when the system utilization is low in order to minimally affect user traffic. Other complicated mechanisms exist [9], but require to modify control protocols and user applications.

In this paper, we focus on how to schedule the asynchronous tasks that distribute data across different locations such that performance in the active and inactive nodes meets predefined quality of service goals. The scheduling parameters for the asynchronous tasks are determined and updated continuously at the individual node level as the characteristics of the workload they are serving change. Such parameters are exchanged between the nodes so that the speed of data transfer is synchronized. Our scheduling policy learns changes of workload, capturing the available idleness that can be used to serve the asynchronous updates. We utilize the histogram of idle periods as in [10] to determine when to start and stop servicing the tasks without violating performance goals. Our framework is used at the disk level, and it is orthogonal to the sophisticated upper level policies and specific applications, because idleness is observed as the outcome of interaction of policies with applications. Extensive experimentation demonstrates the robustness of our framework, which performs orders of magnitude faster than the common practice of Utilization-based scheduling and very comparably to an Aggressive policy, while respecting user performance target.

2. ASYNCHRONOUS UPDATE SCHEDULING FRAMEWORK

Here, we propose a learning-based framework for scheduling asynchronous updates. We first introduce the basic premise of the learning-based scheduling. Then we propose a more aggressive variation of the scheduling mechanism for the purpose of achieving an even faster response time for asynchronous tasks.

2.1 Learning-based Scheduling with Performance Guarantees

We first describe an algorithmic framework that schedules asynchronous updates with performance guarantees for user traffic. This algorithmic framework estimates the performance impact of asynchronous updates. It determines the most effective schedule by examining when and for how long to schedule asynchronous updates during idle periods in storage devices, such that the trade-off between performance degradation and timely asynchronous updates meets system quality targets.

One could argue that starting the asynchronous updates immediately after the storage device becomes idle is most efficient. However, the stochastic nature of idleness and the non-instantaneously preemptive nature of tasks in storage devices may cause delays to user requests when the asynchronous tasks are served. In storage systems, it is common to idle wait for some time before starting a "background" task to avoid utilizing the very short idle periods for any background activities [11]. In addition, [12] suggests that limiting the amount of time that the system serves background tasks further limits the performance impact on user traffic. The framework in [10] computes both the *idle wait* I and the duration T of the time to serve background jobs as a function of past workload (i.e., the stochastic characteristics of past idle periods). We use here this (I, T) tuple for scheduling asynchronous updates during idle periods and essentially treat asynchronous updates as background tasks.

Central to the calculation of I and T is the Cumulative Distribution Histogram (CDH) of idle intervals. In addition to the CDH, the framework also uses the user-provided average performance degradation target D, which is defined as the allowed average relative delay of an IO operation due to asynchronous updates and can be computed from the (I, T) scheduling pair and other information such as average user response time.

The first target is for the scheduling of asynchronous updates (e.g., replica WRITEs) to remain transparent to the user, which is measured by the performance degradation D introduced earlier. To find the qualified scheduling pair (I, T), we scan the CDH of idle periods length for (I, T) pairs that do not violate the target D. A pair (I, T) guarantees the performance target D if

$$D \geq \frac{W_{(I,T)}}{RT_{w/o\ BG}}, \qquad (1)$$

where $RT_{w/o\ BG}$ is monitored and $W_{(I,T)}$ is the average IO wait due to serving replica WRITEs using the scheduling parameters (I, T). For the details on computing $W_{(I,T)}$, we direct the interested readers to [13].

The second scheduling target is to complete all replica WRITEs. Here we define the average replication work amount *target* B_W and the average amount of replica work B_{BG} given a pair (I, T) for a performance target D. Both are measured in units of time. For details on computing B_W and B_{BG}, we direct the interested readers to [13]. Among all (I, T) scheduling pairs that can meet performance target, we choose only the one that can also meet the amount of replication work target ($B_{BG} >= B_W$) so that no replication work starves. There might be multiple pairs that qualify for meeting both the target D and target B_W. In this case, we select the one with the smallest I. If there are multiple pairs with the smallest I, we choose the one with the largest T so we schedule as aggressively as possible, ensuring that replication work finishes as fast as possible.

2.2 Learning-based+ Scheduling

Here we provide a more aggressive variation of the scheduling mechanism described above. The standard approach above only schedules for at most T units time for each idle interval longer than I. If there are still asynchronous tasks to complete upon T elapsing, the system does not schedule, even if there is still available idleness. For this reason we consider the above scheduling policy as being strictly non-work-conserving, guided by both I and T.

Here we are proposing a more aggressive and less non-work-conserving policy by relaxing the condition on T. Specifically, after scheduling asynchronous tasks for T time units and the system remains idle with additional asynchronous work outstanding, then the policy is changed to wait another I time units and re-start scheduling for another T time units. This is done repeatedly until there is no more asynchronous work to be served or the system becomes busy. This variation ensures that the very long idle intervals are utilized more if there are asynchronous tasks waiting for completion. It does not change the behavior for the short idle intervals, where the potential for delays to user traffic is higher. However, since the goal is to serve as fast as possible all asynchronous tasks, then by allowing the long idle intervals (that are only a few) to be utilized more if there is work to be done, we achieve a faster response time for asynchronous tasks.

3. EXPERIMENTAL EVALUATION

In this section, we evaluate the proposed scheduling framework via trace-driven simulations. First, we introduce the traces that are used to drive the experiments. Then we compare our method with common practice methods in terms of the inconsistent window, performance impact, and the amount of buffer space required to store all incoming data updates at the inactive (i.e., destination) nodes before committing them on persistent storage.

We use storage system traces made available through the SNIA IOTTA repository [14] collected by Microsoft and published by the Microsoft Research Cambridge (MSR) [15]. Table 1 presents an overview of various statistical measures for four traces[1]. The

---

[1]The Microsoft IOTTA repository has a much larger number of

Trace	Duration (hour)	Utilization (%)	Average Arrival Rate (1/ms)	Average Service Rate (1/ms)	Average Response Time (ms)	Idle Length Average (ms)	CV	R/W ratio
usr0	168	1.07	0.0012	0.1203	8.94	805.36	1.74	0.11
mds0	168	0.52	0.0007	0.1412	7.21	1404.16	1.93	0.03
ts0	168	0.61	0.0008	0.1455	7.06	1150.20	1.74	0.04
web0	168	0.72	0.0010	0.1468	7.12	959.72	2.11	0.13

Table 1: General trace information. ms stands for millisecond.

usr0 trace is obtained from a user file server, the mds0 trace comes from a media server, the ts0 trace is collected from a terminal server, and the web0 trace is captured in the Web/SQL server. Each trace has a duration of one week (168 hours) and represents a wide range of common traffic patterns. From the table, we can see that these systems show very low utilization, which suggests that good opportunities exist for serving background work, such as asynchronous tasks. The relatively substantial Coefficient of Variation (C.V., which is a normalized measure of dispersion, defined as the ratio of the standard deviation to the mean) suggests that using idleness may be challenging because scheduling too much background work during small idle periods may cause performance degradation. During large idle periods, scheduling too little background work may waste idleness and slow down the synchronization speed. We also note these traces are WRITE dominant workloads for which the asynchronous data updates through the system play a very important role.

3.1 Experimental Scenarios

We apply our scheduling framework for both active and inactive nodes and focus on minimizing the delays experienced at these nodes. We do not limit the buffer space, contending that the faster we complete the synchronization of data, the less buffer is needed. We also assume that there is no packet loss in the network and that the network delay is exponentially distributed with an average of 100 ms (i.e., the average delay for intercontinental round trip communication).

In our experiments, we use three different pairs of traces to evaluate our framework under 3 different workload combinations, i.e., (usr0-active, mds0-inactive), (mds0-active, ts0-inactive) and (ts0-active, web0-inactive). For each workload combination, we divide the available traces into seven portions or time windows, each corresponding to a full day workload (i.e., recall that the traces are 7 days long). During learning we update the histogram of idle periods length, the average arrival and service rate of WRITE, the average arrival and service rate of all IO. Our framework uses these monitored parameters to compute the (I, T) scheduling parameters. The learning procedure of our framework occurs during one full time window and the learning results apply on the next time window. This means that we run our framework once a day and update the scheduling parameters accordingly. We run the experiments across all six time windows (the first day/time window is used only for learning), but due to the limited space, we only show results of one time window as an example.

In our experiments we evaluate the following solutions for achieving eventual consistency: the fully work-conservative approach (we label it as Aggressive) that starts to serve the asynchronous tasks as soon as the node becomes idle. The Utilization-based policy monitors the utilization of the system for the past 10 minutes, and if it increases above a threshold (the threshold is chosen as the average utilization during a long period, e.g., one day), then no asyn-

chronous tasks are scheduled. If utilization drops below the threshold, then asynchronous tasks are scheduled aggressively, i.e., as soon as the node becomes idle. Note that we use 10 minutes as the measurement window for the utilization-based approach because the utilization is a statistical parameter and if the window is set too small (e.g., 1 min), then swift changes are used for predicting near future; if set too large (e.g., 1 hour), the synchronization speed is too slow and there is always backlog. The above two policies are evaluated as baseline versions to compare with the two scheduling versions of our framework, the basic Learning-based non-work-conserving version and the Leaning-Based+ less non-work-conserving variant introduced in Section 2.1.

Note that the Utilization-based approach is not work-conserving but is widely used in systems today, in an effort to limit the unpredictable performance impact that an Aggressive approach would have during periods of high utilization. Our experiments show that *all* alternative methodologies have an unpredictable impact on node performance and that only our Learning-based methods consistently maintain user-performance guarantees.

3.2 Delay on Achieving Eventual Consistency

Our initial experiments evaluate the total time, on the average, to propagate the new data or updates from the active node to the inactive node. Obviously, the faster the propagation of WRITEs, i.e., the smaller the inconsistency window, the more robust and resilient the system is. During the inconsistency window, the system has stale data in inactive nodes, which is detrimental to applications [1, 2]. We provide the results of the experiments on the duration of the inconsistency window in Figure 1, Since our framework relies on the knowledge of various scheduling parameters including the CDH of idle intervals, we compute the (I, T) scheduling pair based on system measurements in the previous time interval (an entire day). Results are plotted for different user performance targets (in %) as captured in the x-axis. For different performance targets, there are different scheduling parameters for our framework and consequently, different results. However the results for the baseline approaches are independent of such goals and their corresponding results do not change across the x-axis.

The Aggressive approach performs best with regard to how fast the WRITEs propagate through the distributed system, because it represents the *only* work-conserving policy that we are evaluating here. However, as we show in the next subsection, it also causes the largest, possibly unbounded delays in user performance. As a result, in systems today, it is rarely used, but we include it here to use its performance with regard to the length of the inconsistency window as a baseline of the possible minimum. The closer other policies come to this approach without sacrificing performance, the more resilient they are.

The Utilization-based policy makes scheduling decisions based on the monitored utilization levels in the immediate past. Because of the strong oscillations in the short-term utilization, it behaves as a very conservative policy that does not take take advantage of the

traces than what we show here. We have selected only these four traces as representatives.

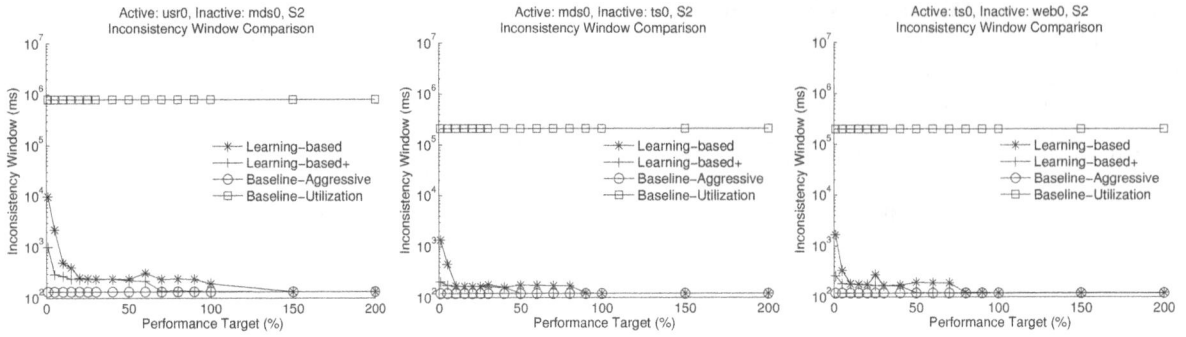

Figure 1: Inconsistency Window comparison between different scheduling for various active-inactive pairs.

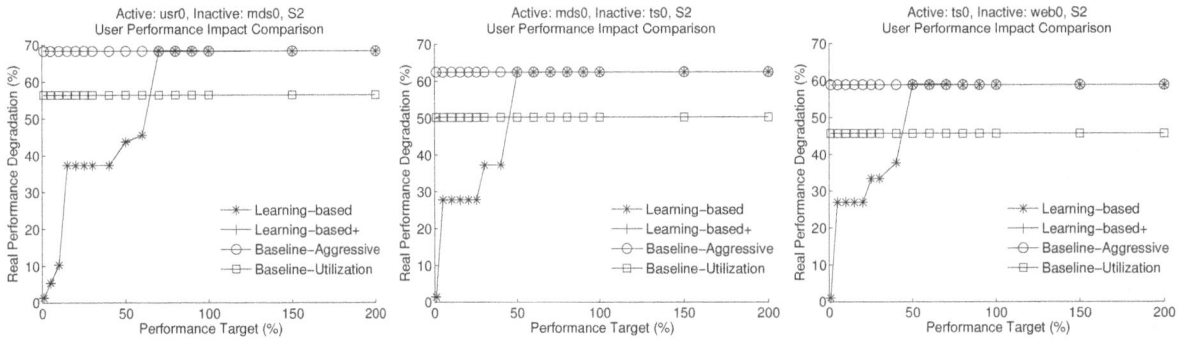

Figure 2: User performance impact comparison between different scheduling for various active-inactive pairs.

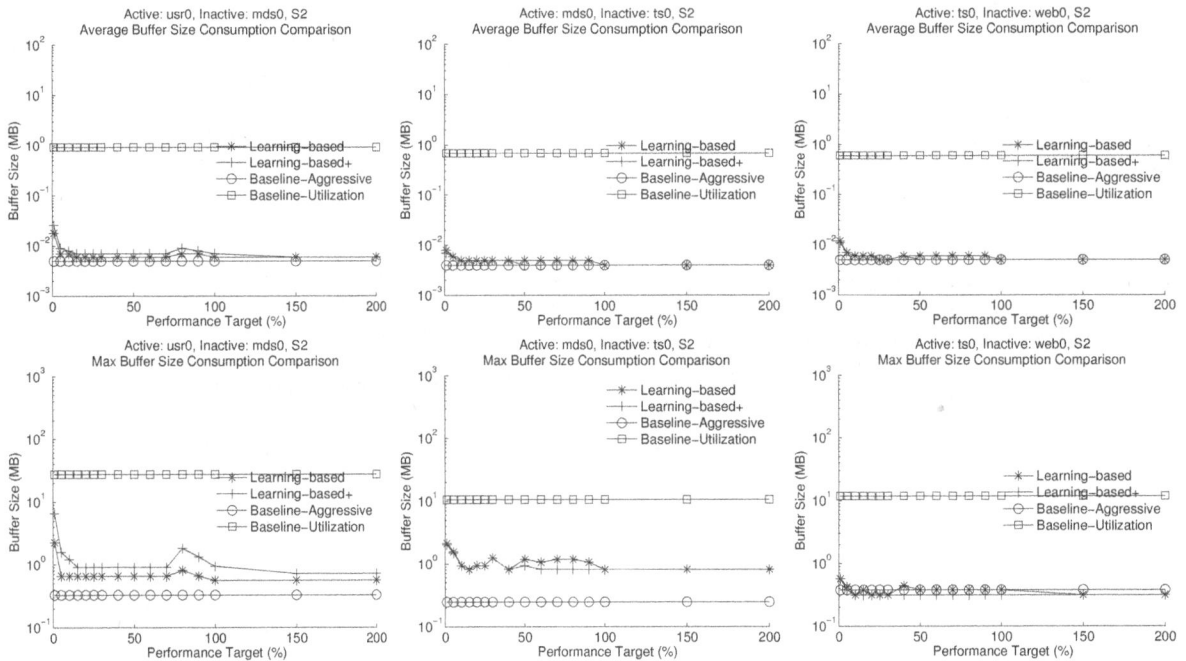

Figure 3: Buffer consumption comparison between different scheduling for various active-inactive pairs. Both Average (first row) and Max (second row) Buffer consumption are provided.

available idleness. The inconsistency window is orders of magnitude higher than the other alternative policies.

The curves corresponding to our framework, dynamically change as the target performance goal changes. As expected, for systems

that are more sensitive to performance and where the target is low, eventual consistency is achieved at a slower pace than when the performance target is less stringent. Our scheduling converges to the Aggressive scheduling as the performance target increases to the performance degradation caused by the Aggressive approach. Note that the looser the performance target, the smaller the value of I, which indicates how non-work-conserving the policy is (i.e., $I = 0$ and large T corresponds to a work-conserving policy). As expected Learning-based+ achieves eventual consistency faster than the basic Learning-based approach and converges faster to the Aggressive scheduling.

The main observation from Figure 1 is that our framework (also its versions) performs comparable to the Aggressive policy for any performance target (excluding the very small and impractical ones 1-5%). The Utilization-based approach is orders of magnitude worse, and as we show later, for much higher performance degradation.

3.3 Impact on User Performance

As discussed above, the time it takes to propagate the WRITE traffic and achieve eventual consistency is highly dependent on how much the user performance is degraded. Recall that serving the IO replicas as background work delays foreground user requests that arrive while the system serves replica updates because IO tasks are not *instantaneously* preemptable. Here, we focus on how the various approaches perform with respect to foreground task degradation, measured as the percentage of the average user response time increase in presence of asynchronous tasks. We show the results in Figure 2, where we still use the performance target (in %) as index of the x-axis and plot the *actual* performance degradation measured in simulations (in %) in the y-axis.

As expected, the Aggressive policy performs very poorly with regard to the actual user degradation in the system. The average user response time increases beyond 60%, despite the fact that the asynchronous replica work is modest. The Utilization-based policy proves to be really ineffective, because although it results in very slow eventual consistency, it still penalizes user performance significantly, which attests to the inefficiency of making decisions based on short-term learning. We believe that not only the short-term learning is ineffective, but also the metric of utilization itself as a guide to scheduling asynchronous tasks, despite the fact that it is widely used in practice.

Our framework, on the other hand, adapts its decisions to the system quality targets striking a good balance between system user performance and replica completion speed. The results in Figure 2 confirm using long learning periods are more robust and effective than shorter learning periods as used in the Utilization-based policy.

3.4 Buffer Space Requirements

Since there is no perfect synchronization between the speed that the active node sends its updates with the speed that the inactive node processes them, there is a clear need for buffering at the inactive node to temporarily store the incoming replica WRITEs. Although we do not limit buffer availability here, as to be able to assess the maximum buffer requirement for each of the evaluated approaches, in real systems the buffer space is limited. Therefore, buffer size is preferred to be as small as possible. We show the required buffer size for the various policies in Figure 3. The x-axis in the graphs of Figure 3 is the performance degradation target (%) and y-axis is the required buffer space (in MB).

The Utilization-based policy demands the largest buffer space since under that policy the replica WRITEs accumulate for a long time before being served. The Aggressive policy requires the least buffer space because it serves the incoming asynchronous tasks the fastest. The buffer space under our scheduling policies depends on the performance target. The smaller the performance target, the larger the buffer space. Yet, as expected it converges to the Aggressive policy buffer requirements for higher performance tar-

gets. Note, that there are cases when our framework consumes less maximum buffer space than the Aggressive policy. This is because the Aggressive policy causes often the WRITEs to arrive in large batches at the inactive node, while our framework smooths out this bursty behavior for sending out *almost* equal number of WRITEs every idle interval.

4. CONCLUSIONS

In this paper, we presented a framework that facilitates the efficient synchronization of data distribution in the background for quick eventual data consistency, common in distributed storage systems, with user performance guarantees. The framework learns the idleness characteristics dynamically and determines how fast the data can be sent or received without violating performance goals. The results presented here support our claim that learning the characteristics of idle periods, is crucial to the effectiveness of the two learning-based approaches. Also, since the captured traces from live systems show that the workload does not change drastically across time, learning over long periods, as we do in our framework (a whole day) results not only on a more resilient approach, but is also computationally inexpensive. Our framework introduces only a small overhead on the system for monitoring and storing the results. System gains are nevertheless of orders of magnitude favorable regarding eventual consistency speed, user performance impact and buffer requirement, which is critical for the availability, reliability, and performance of large scale distributed systems.

Acknowledgments

This work is supported by NSF grants CCF-0937925 and CCF-1218758. The authors thank Microsoft Research for publishing the enterprise traces used in this work.

5. REFERENCES

[1] L. Gao, M. Dahlin, A. Nayate, J. Zheng, and A. Iyengar, "Application specific data replication for edge services," in *WWW*, 2003, pp. 449–460.

[2] B. F. Cooper, R. Ramakrishnan, U. Srivastava, A. Silberstein, P. Bohannon, H.-A. Jacobsen, N. Puz, D. Weaver, and R. Yerneni, "Pnuts: Yahoo!'s hosted data serving platform," *PVLDB*, vol. 1, no. 2, pp. 1277–1288, 2008.

[3] A. Singh, P. Fonseca, P. Kuznetsov, R. Rodrigues, and P. Maniatis, "Zeno: Eventually consistent byzantine-fault tolerance," in *NSDI*, 2009, pp. 169–184.

[4] W. Vogels, "Eventually consistent," *ACM Queue*, vol. 6, no. 6, pp. 14–19, 2008.

[5] E. Anderson, X. Li, A. Merchant, M. A. Shah, K. Smathers, J. Tucek, M. Uysal, and J. J. Wylie, "Efficient eventual consistency in pahoehoe, an erasure-coded key-blob archive," in *DSN*, 2010, pp. 181–190.

[6] H. Wada, A. Fekete, L. Zhao, K. Lee, and A. Liu, "Data consistency properties and the trade-offs in commercial cloud storage: the consumers' perspective," in *CIDR*, 2011, pp. 134–143.

[7] G. DeCandia, D. Hastorun, M. Jampani, G. Kakulapati, A. Lakshman, A. Pilchin, S. Sivasubramanian, P. Vosshall, and W. Vogels, "Dynamo: amazon's highly available key-value store," in *SOSP*, 2007, pp. 205–220.

[8] V. Prabhakaran, A. C. Arpaci-Dusseau, and R. H. Arpaci-Dusseau, "Analysis and evolution of journaling file systems," in *USENIX Annual Technical Conference, General Track*, 2005, pp. 105–120.

[9] P. Padala, K.-Y. Hou, K. G. Shin, X. Zhu, M. Uysal, Z. Wang, S. Singhal, and A. Merchant, "Automated control of multiple virtualized resources," in *EuroSys*, 2009, pp. 13–26.

[10] N. Mi, A. Riska, X. Li, E. Smirni, and E. Riedel, "Restrained utilization of idleness for transparent scheduling of background tasks," in *Proceedings of the Eleventh International Joint Conference on Measurement and Modeling of Computer Systems, SIGMETRICS/Performance*, 2009, pp. 205–216.

[11] L. Eggert and J. Touch, "Idletime scheduling with preemption intervals," in *In Proceedings of the 20th ACM Symposium on Operating Systems Principles (SOSP)*, 2005, pp. 249–262.

[12] R. A. Golding, P. B. II, C. Staelin, T. Sullivan, and J. Wilkes, "Idleness is not sloth," in *USENIX Winter*, 1995, pp. 201–212.

[13] F. Yan, A. Riska, and E. Smirni, "Fast eventual consistency with performance guarantees for distributed storage," in *DCPerf*, 2012.

[14] "SNIA IOTTA repository." [Online]. Available: http://iotta.snia.org/traces

[15] D. Narayanan, A. Donnelly, and A. I. T. Rowstron, "Write off-loading: Practical power management for enterprise storage," in *FAST*, 2008, pp. 253–267.

Optimal Autoscaling in a IaaS Cloud

Hamoun Ghanbari
Dept. of Computer Science
York University
Toronto, Canada
hamoun@cse.yorku.ca

Bradley Simmons
Dept. of Computer Science
York University
Toronto, Canada
bsimmons@yorku.ca

Marin Litoiu
Dept. of Computer Science
York University
Toronto, Canada
mlitoiu@yorku.ca

Cornel Barna
Dept. of Computer Science
York University
Toronto, Canada
cornel@cse.yorku.ca

Gabriel Iszlai
Centre for Advanced Studies
IBM Toronto Lab
Toronto, Canada
giszlai@ca.ibm.com

ABSTRACT

An application provider leases resources (i.e., virtual machine instances) of variable configurations from a IaaS provider over some lease duration (typically one hour). The application provider (i.e., consumer) would like to minimize their cost while meeting all service level obligations (SLOs). The mechanism of adding and removing resources at runtime is referred to as autoscaling. The process of autoscaling is automated through the use of a management component referred to as an autoscaler. This paper introduces a novel autoscaling approach in which both cloud and application dynamics are modeled in the context of a stochastic, model predictive control problem. The approach exploits trade-off between satisfying performance related objectives for the consumer's application while minimizing their cost. Simulation results are presented demonstrating the efficacy of this new approach.

Categories and Subject Descriptors

I.6 [**Simulation and Modelling**]: Model Development; C.4 [**Computer Systems Organization**]: Performance of Systems

Keywords

Application, Cloud, Autoscaling, Cost, Performance, Model Predictive Control, Optimization

1. INTRODUCTION

A *cloud* represents an ultra large-scale system focused on the delivery of computational power (specifically storage, network, and computation, and high-level services on top of these), in an *on-demand* fashion, to a consumer community. At the infrastructure as a service (IaaS) layer of the layered-cloud architecture, the cloud provider partitions physical resources into various configurations of virtualized memory, CPU and disk, a virtual machine instance (VMI), and offers them to consumers, at variable prices for a lease period (typically one hour).[1]

An *elasticity policy* [5] governs how and when resources are added to and/or removed from a cloud application. An *autoscaler* is a component of a management framework that is responsible for implementing an application's elasticity policy. In terms of autoscaling an application on the cloud, the current *state-of-the-art* involves specifying rules to implement the elasticity policy for an application server tier. These rules may or may not implicitly minimize the application provider's cost. Further, a single VMI configuration is typically considered (per tier).

This paper introduces a new approach to autoscaling that utilizes a stochastic model predictive control (MPC) technique to facilitate effective resource acquisition and releases meeting the service level objectives of the application provider while minimizing their cost. This technique accounts for the delay in resource provisioning times (due to the stochastic nature of the IaaS provider's infrastructure), the stochastic nature of workloads and does not waste instances (i.e., retains instances for the full duration of their lease).

The remainder of the paper is structured as follows. Section 2 describes the problem. Section 3 maps the problem to an optimal control one. In Section 4 we provide a solution to the formulated control problem using stochastic MPC. Section 5 presents a brief description of case study where the technique is applied for a simulated cloud consumer. In Section 6 we discuss the related work and in Section 7 we provide our conclusion on the topic.

2. PROBLEM DEFINITION

In general, the task of the autoscaler is to implement the elasticity policy of the application provider. The elasticity policy is guided by the values of a set of monitored and/or computed metrics. Let y_k denote a column vector of these

---

[1]Each configuration is associated with its own specification and cost (e.g., m1.small on Amazon Elastic Compute Cloud).

metrics at discrete time instant k:

$$y_k = \begin{bmatrix} y_k^1 \\ \vdots \\ y_k^j \end{bmatrix}$$

The approach to autoscaling being introduced in this paper focuses on two goals: satisfying the application provider's objectives[2] (as defined in terms of this set of metrics) and optimizing for the cost incurred by resource usage[3].

A IaaS provider offers several VMI configurations for lease. A configuration represents a specific allocation of CPU, memory, network bandwidth and storage. VMIs are purchased on behalf of the application provider by the autoscaler (i.e. composed of possibly several IaaS providers) in various configurations and over some lease duration (typically one hour). The leasing model can be generally divided into four categories: (i) **immediate reservation**: where resources are processed right away or rejected. (ii) **in-advance reservation**: where resources must be available at specified time. Often an up-front fixed price charge is required to initiate a reservation and a discounted rate is charged for the instances throughout the duration of the reservation. (iii) **best effort reservation**: where request are queued and serviced accordingly. (iv) **auction based reservation**: where customers bid for some number of a particular configuration and should the dynamically adjusted resource price be less than the bid price, the resources are allocated.

In all cases the IaaS provider offers a set of possible VMI configurations each associated with a set of `time interval` and `price` tuples. Launching a VMI for this configuration is billed based on the reservation mechanism at the specified price. Note that, in general, the outcome of a reservation action in the cloud is non-deterministic, and it is not the case that a reservation action always succeeds. For example: immediate and in-advance reservations fail, prices in auction-based reservations are non-deterministic, and in best effort reservations resource may not be provisioned in a timely manner.

To formalize the notion of a reservation action we do the following. Assume that κ_k is the reservation action at time k, and the amount of resource to be used from the cloud is denoted by ϑ_k. The cost to the application provider for using resources depends on the reservation actions performed during application lifetime $(\kappa_0, ..., \kappa_N)$, where application lifetime is denoted by N. An autoscaler seeks to choose a sequence of optimal reservation actions $(\kappa_0^*, ..., \kappa_N^*)$ that minimizes the long term resource cost[4], $\sum_{k=1}^{N} \lambda(\kappa_k)$, where $\lambda(\kappa_k)$ denotes the cost of reservations made at time k.

3. OPTIMAL CONTROL FORMULATION

In this work, the objectives of the autoscaler are: guiding

performance metrics to a desired region and the minimization of the application provider's cost. However, upon closer scrutiny, it can be observed that these two set of objectives conflict.

An optimal control approach searches for a solution that finds a good trade-off between a set of goals. In optimal control, the desired behaviour of a system is represented by a single cost function, J, which captures factors of interest over a long horizon of time. More formally, the cost function J that includes the actual cost of resources and the (virtual or actual) cost of deviation from desired performance objectives over the whole period that the application provider leases VMIs from the cloud, can be specified as follows:

$$J((\kappa_0, ..., \kappa_{N-1})) = E\left[\sum_{k=0}^{N-1} (\Phi(y_k) + \gamma\lambda(\kappa_k))\right] \quad (1)$$

where N is the lifetime of cloud usage for a specific application provider (i.e., customer), $E[...]$ denotes the expected value (in statistical sense), $\Phi(y_k)$ is the virtual (or actual) cost associated with deviation from desired objectives defined in terms of performance metrics, and γ is a coefficient that adjusts the trade-off between performance objectives and cost.[5]

Notice that we took the expected value over the cost function due to stochastic effects of software and the cloud. In other words, although the expression representing the stage cost[6] does not seem to have a random component, the underlying system that drives y_k is stochastic.

The idea of optimal control is that by minimizing this cost function over a long horizon, we penalize the *greedy* and *reactive* reservation actions. A greedy reservation action only minimizes the current stage cost, ignoring the effect of current resource reservations κ_k on future performance except for y_{k+1}. This results in a lower cost for the present stage, due to under-reservation; however, this misjudgment drives the system to a sub-optimal future state that is difficult to recover from, incurring very high long-term cost. A reactive reservation action tries to minimize long-term penalty and cost, but it tries to do so only through reservation actions in current or relatively near future states. That is, since it is not able to trade-off the penalty of subsequent steps with the resource cost of current step it will incur sub-optimal resource costs.

In a feedback-based scheme, at any given time instant the controller (i.e., the autoscaler) makes its decisions (i.e., to add/remove resources) based on the information available from the system up to that time and the information deduced and maintained by the controller itself. More precisely, at each time step k this information can be summarized in a collection of variables which we call the *state vector* denoted by x_k. We will discuss the choice of variables to be included in this state vector later; however, the assumption is that it contains enough information so that the controller can make a decision based on it alone.

Our autoscaler attempts to find a proper reservation action κ_k at any given time k based on the current system state x_k. A stationary reservation *policy* denoted by ϕ suggests such a reservation action at any given time, k, based

---

[2]These objectives might take different forms, such as (i) minimization, (ii) regulation, (i) and maximization of certain performance metrics. For example, it is usually desirable to minimize response time of web applications, regulate hardware utilization around certain value, and maximize systems throughput.

[3]The cost incurred for an amount of computation, storage, or network usage in cloud, is not only a function of resources used but also the strategy used to reserve those resources.

[4]This is done while trying to satisfy performance metrics over time (as discussed earlier).

[5]In case Φ represents an actual cost or penalty comparable to resource cost γ is considered 1.

[6]Stage cost refers to the cost for each time increment, k.

on system state as follows:

$$\kappa_k = \phi(x_k)$$

In [5] we investigated the efficiency of an autoscaler where ϕ was composed of a set of user defined rules, and described the issue of finding the optimal policy and state definitions which was not addressed by the technique. The next section introduces our new approach to autoscaling that harnesses model-predictive control technique to address the optimality issue.

4. PROPOSED SOLUTION

In optimal control techniques there exist numerous ways to obtain the optimal policy ϕ^* such that the cost function is minimized:

$$\phi^*(x) = \text{argmin}_\phi J(\phi(x)) \tag{2}$$

To find a computationally tractable solution, these techniques require that the following conditions are satisfied: (i) the relation between controllable inputs (here κ_k) and terms of the cost function J (here y_k) should be formulated in certain formats such as linear state-space and (ii) the controller cost function (here including resource cost $\lambda(\kappa_k)$ and performance violation cost $\Phi(y_k)$) should be expressed in certain formats such as quadratic or convex.

Model. Regarding item (i), the relation between performance metrics y_k and the used resource ϑ_k over time has been thoroughly investigated in the queuing theory and performance modeling literature. There are several ways to describe the transient effect of resources on well-known performance metrics. For example, it has been shown that transient response time of a simple homogenous c-server cluster[7] handling transactional workload where service demands do not depend on the queue lengths, can be modeled as a simple linear difference equation:

$$\begin{aligned}
\mu_k &= \sum_{i=1}^{c} \mu_k^i \\
q_{k+1} &= q_k + (w_k - \mu_k).T \\
r_{k+1} &= (1 + q_k)/\mu_k
\end{aligned} \tag{3}$$

where μ_k is the aggregate cluster service rate, w_k is arrival rate of the workload, q_k is the number requests in queues of servers, and r_k is the response time at time k.

Since the service rate of each instance depends on the hardware specification of the instance, one can expect the aggregate service rate to be described in terms of the instance quantity vector ϑ_k:

$$\mu_k = \sum_{i=1}^{c} \mu_k^i = \rho \vartheta_k^T \tag{4}$$

where ϑ_k represents a vector of the currently obtained quantity of each resource type from the set of the cloud provider's available resource types G [8] and ρ is the vector of service rates[9] for different types of resource.

Item (i) also implies that one has to model the dynamics of the reservation rules as explained in subsection 2. In this paper we targeted modelling the delay in delivery of running instances[10], and the finite property of lease durations. For example, lets assume that an instance has an associated delay of D minutes and a single lease duration of T minutes. We then model the lifecycle of resource delivery using a graph of nodes, each node representing the number of each type of resource in each minute of *delivery* and *usage*.[11] As time passes, the resources pass through graph nodes, and while they are in usage nodes they affect the performance. A flow model of this form can be represented as an equation of the form:

$$\begin{aligned}
X_{k+1} &= AX_k + B\kappa_k \\
\vartheta_{k+1} &= CX_k
\end{aligned} \tag{5}$$

where X is $m \times n$ matrix to represent the nodes ($m = T + D$ and $n = |G|$), and $A_{m,m}$, $B_{m,n}$, and $C_{1,m}$ have the form[12]:

$$A_{m,m} = \begin{pmatrix} 0 & \cdots & 0 \\ 1 & \cdots & 0 \\ \vdots & \ddots & \vdots \\ 0 & \cdots & 1 \end{pmatrix}, B_{m,n} = \begin{pmatrix} 1 \\ 0 \\ \vdots \\ 0 \end{pmatrix}, C_{1,m} = \begin{pmatrix} \mathbf{0}_{1,D} & \mathbf{1}_{1,T} \end{pmatrix}$$

and κ_k is a $1 \times n$ vector of reservation amounts of resources. In the rest of this paper, we use a combined form of equations 3 and 5 in a state-space format as a model:

$$\begin{aligned}
x_{k+1} &= f(x_k, \kappa_k, w_k) \\
y_k &= g(x_k)
\end{aligned} \tag{6}$$

where workload w_k is a random term, κ_k is control variable, and x_k includes μ_k, q_k, ϑ_k, and X_k:

$$x_k = \begin{bmatrix} \mu_k \\ q_k \\ \vartheta_k \\ X_k \end{bmatrix}$$

Also our experiments only focus on response time, so we take the vector of metrics of interest as:

$$y_k = [r_k]$$

Cost function. Regarding item (ii), it is usually possible to find a convex stage penalty function $\Phi(y_k)$ for a performance violation, based on the type of the performance objective (i.e. minimization, maximization, or regulation). For example for minimization one can use quadratic form $\Phi(y_k) = y_k^T Q y_k$, while using $\Phi(y_k) = (y_k - \bar{y}_k)^T Q (y_k - \bar{y}_k)$ for regulation, where Q is a user defined matrix of coefficients.

Control Algorithm. The approach used to minimize the cost function has to (i) take into account the disturbances w_k by considering that an outcome of an action is non-deterministic and computing the expected value (i.e., $E[...]$) over a long horizon of time and (ii) be tractable in terms of computational complexity.

---

[7]c is the number of servers in the cluster.

[8]G can be understood to represent the set of possible VMI configurations offered by a IaaS provider.

[9]This can be derived from specifications such as virtual compute units specified by the cloud provider.

[10]Here, delay refers to a sum of delays specifically: the delay involved in resource delivery, the delay associated with boot-up, the delay associated with running the initial installation scripts, and the delay associated with the initial warm-up.

[11]A similar approach is used in inventory control and supply chain management.

[12]This form represents a simple chain of nodes which was our flow model in this paper.

In the stochastic MPC approach, both of these items are dealt with. One converts the stochastic planning problem into several step-by-step optimizations, and each optimization takes place on arrival at each new state by taking the current observed state as an initial point of planning. Further, in each optimization, the planning is only done for a limited number of steps ahead which is referred to as the *lookahead horizon* and denoted by N'; thus reducing the number of steps involved in optimization from $N - k$ to N' (i.e., this assumes that $N' << N - k$). It is also assumed that the remaining cost from N' to N can be estimated using a simple cost-to-go function $\hat{V}(x_{k+N'})$ which approximates the accumulated cost from the edge of the lookahead horizon (i.e. $k + N'$) to the end of problem N (here application lifetime). This prevents the plan from ending up in an unrecoverable state at the edge of the lookahead horizon. In general, planning over a lookahead horizon inhibits the planner from making reactive or greedy decisions, and that is the essence of predictive control.

The stochastic property of the system is also dealt with during the planning phase. We use the *certainly equivalent control* (CEC) approach to reduce the impact of disturbances. In CEC, at each time step k, process disturbances $\{w_j\}_{j \geq k}$ are fixed at a deterministic value (e.g., their conditional mean) $\overline{w}_j(x_j, u_j) = E[w_k|x_j, u_j]$ which in the simplest case can be considered to be zero. Then, at each step, a perfect information, deterministic optimal control problem with limited horizon is solved once, and the control value to be applied is derived[13]; everything is repeated once a new observation is available. Our adapted version of CEC is presented in algorithm 1.

5. CASE STUDY

We simulated an application provider (i.e., a cloud consumer) that uses purchased VMIs of multiple configurations to build a web server cluster to handle transactional workloads. Both computing cluster and application users were simulated as network of queues. There were two goals: minimization of average response time (i.e., an objective on a metric) and minimization of resource cost.

The input to the simulator at each step is a set of reservation actions (in terms of VMIs of different configurations), the number of users using the system, and the service time per request. The output of the simulator at each step is the average response times and throughput for users, and utilization of each server. To resemble a real system, the queue length of each server is considered a hidden parameter. Different VMI configurations are simulated based on their specified *virtual processing units*. Presently, Amazon EC2 offers eleven alternative configurations for lease. Prices were taken according to the hourly rates advertised for on-demand instances. The workload used was a 21 hour excerpt of the FIFA'98 workload [2], day 42.

Application model. We used equation 3 as the model of the environment. Here, ϑ_k denotes a vector of quantities of each VMI configuration class and has 11 elements since we are considering the 11 VMI configuration of Amazon EC2. The service rate μ was assumed to be dependent solely on the VMI configuration and was discovered by performing a least-squares method on data obtained from offline simulations.

Algorithm 1: CEC implementation of MPC.

input : system model f, violation penalty function Φ, resource cost function λ, trade-off coefficient γ, current system state x_0 (i.e. estimated queue lengths, already reserved resources) , process disturbance mean $\overline{w}_j$, approximate cost-to-go function $\hat{V}$

output : optimal reservation action sequence $\{\kappa_k^*\}$

1   initialize: $x_k = x_0$
2   **while** *application uses the cloud* **do**
3   take k as current time
4   given x_k, at each time k solve the (planning) problem

$$\text{minimize} \quad \sum_{j=k}^{k+N'} (\Phi(y_j) + \gamma\lambda(\kappa_j)) + \hat{V}(x_{k+N'})$$

$$\text{subject to} \quad x_{j+1} = f(x_j, \kappa_j, \overline{w}_j(x_j, \vartheta_j))$$
$$y_j = g(x_j) , \; y_j \in \mathcal{Y},$$
$$\text{for } j = k, ..., k + N' - 1$$

5   take solution $\tilde{\kappa}_j, ..., \tilde{\kappa}_{j+N'}$ as *plan of action* for next N' steps
6   take the first reservation action in plan of action (i.e. $\tilde{\kappa}_j$) as κ_k and apply it
7   if κ_k was successful update x_{k+1} (i.e. $\vartheta_{k+1},...$) with the obtained resources
8   estimate unobserved portion of x_k (queue lengths) and update x_{k+1}

Estimation. The queue length is estimated at simulation time on-the-fly using a Kalman estimator.[14] The estimation is iterative; the estimate is updated once a new response time measurement is available from the simulator.

Cost function. Here, we assumed that the performance penalty function has a quadratic form for minimizing response time. The stage resource cost function λ was built based on the hourly lease rates of EC2 instances multiplied by the reservation vector κ_k. The lower and upper limit on the number of purchased instances specified by EC2, was imposed as an input constraint and the fact that queue length cannot be negative was imposed as a constraint on state. Trade-off coefficient γ was lowered in favor of a response time guarantee.

Challenges. During formulation of the problem, we encountered two issues regarding formulation of the problem into convex format: (i) The first issue was the fact that number of purchased instances is integer in nature rather than real and cannot be asserted in convex form, and (ii) that, unlike what we expected from equation 4, response time in the simulated heterogeneous server cluster was highly affected by the server that had the minimum virtual processing unit. Modelling this effect similar to equation 4, while preserving linear affine form is impossible.

To alleviate the above issues, we first solved the optimization problem in terms of virtual compute units reservation (as opposed to VMI configurations), and then use a mapping function $\mathbb{R} \to \mathbb{N}$ to choose the best choice of VMI configuration for the obtained sub-optimal compute unit to purchase. The mapping function considers the current formation of the

---

[13]In original MPC this value is the first value of the planning sequence.

[14]Kalman estimator is an optimal state estimator for linear models.

cluster and penalizes choosing a relatively small instance in a cluster of large ones. It basically pushes the system towards using homogeneous instance types, with minimum price per compute unit.

Assessment. We ran several tests to asses the effectiveness of the approach in autoscaling on the simulated cloud. The aspects we tested are as follows: (i) The effect of lookahead horizon (N') on the control cost J for different Cloud dynamics. (ii) The trade-off between resource cost and QoS violation penalty by performing optimization for a different value of γ. (iii) Effectiveness of the approach for different Cloud reservation dynamics (i.e. different resource delivery delay and lease interval). (iv) Time complexity of a MPC step based on prediction horizon. Due to shortage of space, we cannot report the result, however, the result was consistent with MPC literature.

6. RELATED WORK

There is a substantial amount of work on applying optimal control to management of software systems and the associated hardware infrastructure. Classical optimal control has been employed in processor power management [9, 12], QoS adaptation in web servers [1], and load balancing [6, 8, 10]. The approaches used by these various proposals are referred to as classical linear proportional-integral-derivative (PID) or Linear-Quadratic-Gaussian (LQG) control. In fact, LQG uses an analytical solution of an optimal control problem[15] (like the one we targeted in equation 2) but when several limitations are applied to the problem.

MPC has already been used in web server power management (by controlling the CPU frequency) [3, 7], QoS management (using number of sessions as a handle) [11], and network throughput maximization (by controlling the disk cached data) [4]. The main differentiators of the problem we targeted with existing problems are: (i) number of possible actions which in our case was very high (i.e. order of resource type times quantity), (ii) the effect of choices is both delayed and long lasting, thus we were not able to use a small lookahead horizon, (iii) we could not calculate the actual expected value of cost over noise (w_j) distribution because of explosion of states resulting from (i) and (ii), and (iv) we had to use a new technique for modelling lease durations and delivery delay that was not used in the above proposals.

7. CONCLUSION AND FUTURE WORK

This paper has presented a novel autoscaling approach that exploits the trade-off between satisfying performance related objectives for a consumer's application while minimizing their cost. Autoscaling was formulated as a stochastic MPC problem, in which both cloud and application dynamics were modeled. Cost functions were formulated based on objectives of the application. The associated problem was solved using a convex optimization solver. This technique accounts for the delay in resource provisioning and the stochastic nature of workloads.

Future work will proceed along several paths: (i) extending the reservation model to include auction-based reservations, (ii) utilizing more sophisticated software models such as layered and tiered performance models, (iii) studying the

impact of the model accuracy on the efficiency of the controller and (iv) expanding the context of control from the case of managing one application to the case of managing a set of applications with different resource constraints and performance objectives.

8. REFERENCES

[1] T. F. Abdelzaher, K. G. Shin, and N. Bhatti. Performance guarantees for web server end-systems: A control-theoretical approach. *IEEE Transactions on Parallel and Distributed Systems*, pages 80–96, 2002.

[2] M. Arlitt and T. Jin. A workload characterization study of the 1998 world cup web site. *Network, IEEE*, 14(3):30 –37, may. 2000.

[3] J. Bai and S. Abdelwahed. Efficient algorithms for performance management of computing systems. In *Fourth International Workshop on Feedback Control Implementation and Design in Computing Systems and Networks FeBID*. IEEE, 2009.

[4] V. Bhat, M. Parashar, et al. Enabling self-managing applications using model-based online control strategies. In *2006 IEEE International Conference on Autonomic Computing*, pages 15–24. IEEE, 2006.

[5] H. Ghanbari, B. Simmons, M. Litoiu, and G. Iszlai. Exploring alternative approaches to implement an elasticity policy. In *Proceedings of the 4th IEEE International Conference on Cloud Computing*, Washington DC, USA, 2011. IEEE.

[6] J. Hellerstein, Y. Diao, S. Parekh, and D. Tilbury. *Feedback control of computing systems*. Wiley Online Library, 2004.

[7] N. Kandasamy, S. Abdelwahed, and J. P. Hayes. Self-optimization in computer systems via online control: Application to power management. In *First International Conference on Autonomic Computing (ICAC'04)*, pages 54–61, New York, New York, May 2007. IEEE Computer Society.

[8] C. Lu, G. Alvarez, and J. Wilkes. Aqueduct: online data migration with performance guarantees. In *Proceedings of the Conference on File and Storage Technologies*, pages 219–230. USENIX Association, 2002.

[9] Z. Lu, J. Hein, M. Humphrey, M. Stan, J. Lach, and K. Skadron. Control-theoretic dynamic frequency and voltage scaling for multimedia workloads. In *Proceedings of the 2002 international conference on Compilers, architecture, and synthesis for embedded systems*, pages 156–163. ACM, 2002.

[10] S. Parekh, N. Gandhi, J. Hellerstein, D. Tilbury, T. Jayram, and J. Bigus. Using control theory to achieve service level objectives in performance management. *Real-Time Systems*, 23(1):127–141, 2002.

[11] T. Patikirikorala, L. Wang, A. Colman, and J. Han. Hammerstein-Wiener nonlinear model based predictive control for relative QoS performance and resource management of software systems. *Control Engineering Practice*, 20(1):49 – 61, 2012.

[12] V. Sharma, A. Thomas, T. Abdelzaher, K. Skadron, and Z. Lu. Power-aware QoS management in Web servers. In *Real-Time Systems Symposium, 2003. RTSS 2003. 24th IEEE*, pages 63–72. IEEE, 2003.

---

[15]This solution called LQ optimal gain is obtained by directly solving the associated Riccatti equation

High Efficiency at Web Scale

Eitan Frachtenberg
Facebook

etc@fb.com

ABSTRACT

Every day, over half a billion people log in to Facebook to communicate with their contacts. They exchange more than 300 million photos and more than 3 billion likes and comments each day. And almost every day, Facebook releases new code with new features and products to all these users. This staggering amount of information and processing is served from dozens of clusters in four geographical regions. The keys to operating successfully at this almost incomprehensibly large scale are efficiency and automation. Efficiency starts at the hundreds Facebook engineers and the processes they use to develop, test, and deploy code; it continues with scalable models of distributing and constantly monitoring the software on tens of thousands of servers on a daily basis; and ends at the very hardware and datacenters that serves this data, bringing capital and operational expenditures down to make the economic model viable. Automation is the leverage behind each of these relatively few engineers. It lets them focus on quick iteration and experimentation, catching problems early and solving many automatically. This talk will describe the challenges of developing and operating a product that serves a significant percentage of the worldwide internet population. Through several examples, we will see how efficiency and automation drive and enable operation at Web scale.

Categories and Subject Descriptors

C.0 [**Computer Systems Organization**]: General

Keywords

Efficiency, Web, Automation, Scale

BIO

Eitan Frachtenberg is a Research Scientist at Facebook, where he focuses on power-efficient computing at scale. Prior to Facebook, He held research positions at Microsoft, Powerset, and Los Alamos National Laboratory. His research interests include scalable and parallel computing, performance evaluation and optimization, and parallel job scheduling. Eitan holds a Ph.D degree in Computer Science from the Hebrew University in Jerusalem, Israel.

3-Dimensional Root Cause Diagnosis via Co-analysis

Ziming Zheng
Department of Computer
Science
Illinois Institute of Technology
zzheng11@iit.edu

Zhiling Lan
Department of Computer
Science
Illinois Institute of Technology
lan@iit.edu

Li Yu
Department of Computer
Science
Illinois Institute of Technology
lyu17@iit.edu

Terry Jones
Oak Ridge National
Laboratory
Oak Ridge, TN 37831
trjones@ornl.gov

ABSTRACT

With the growth of system size and complexity, reliability has become a major concern for large-scale systems. Upon the occurrence of failure, system administrators typically trace the events in Reliability, Availability, and Serviceability (RAS) logs for root cause diagnosis. However, RAS log only contains limited diagnosis information. Moreover, the manual processing is time-consuming, error-prone, and not scalable. To address the problem, in this paper we present an automated root cause diagnosis mechanism for large-scale HPC systems. Our mechanism examines multiple logs to provide a 3-D fine-grained root cause analysis. Here, 3-D means that our analysis will pinpoint the failure layer, the time, and the location of the event that causes the problem.

We evaluate our mechanism by means of real logs collected from a production IBM Blue Gene/P system at Oak Ridge National Laboratory. It successfully identifies failure layer information for the failures during 23-month period. Furthermore, it effectively identifies the triggering events with time and location information, even when the triggering events occur hundreds of hours before the resulting failures.

Categories and Subject Descriptors

D.2.5 [**Software Engineering**]: Testing and Debugging—*Diagnostics*; B.8.1 [**Performance and Reliability**]: Reliability, Testing, and Fault-Tolerance

General Terms

Reliability

Keywords

Diagnosis, Co-Analysis, Large-scale System

1. INTRODUCTION

1.1 Motivation

Recognizing the growing impact of failures on today's production HPC systems and the projected trends for the systems of tomorrow, resilience is identified as a critical challenge, among the other three challenges (power, concurrency, and memory/storage), for extreme-scale computing [16]. Root cause diagnosis plays a critical role for improving system resilience. Studies have shown that the average failure repair time ranges from a couple of hours to nearly 100 hours in production systems due to complications of various root causes [24, 31]. A timely and accurate diagnosis can significantly reduce failure repair time, thereby reducing the loss of processing cycles and maintenance cost [9].

Nevertheless, root cause diagnosis becomes increasingly challenging as systems continue to increase in scale and complexity. Despite of considerable studies on fault diagnosis, it remains an open problem, in particular on large-scale systems composed of hundreds of thousands of components. We identify two major issues with existing approaches. First, *existing works mainly focus on a single data source*, e.g., RAS (Reliability, Availability, and Serviceability) log [32, 23] or performance log [18], to trace fault-related information. The problem is that a single data source typically contains only limited information about the system and its operating environment, and consequently the information is inadequate to identify the actual root causes in many circumstances [24, 9, 35, 25]. Second, *most studies provide coarse-grained diagnosis* such as pinpointing the faulty node [32, 18] or suspicious events [7, 29]. There are many cases where such a coarse-grained root cause identification is not sufficient for effective fault management. For example, system managers are unable to assign appropriate recovery mechanism without knowing failure layer information [8, 9]; more detailed location information of the problematic component is essential for hardware replacement, especially given that a node may associate with number of hardware devices [9]; and accurate time information is necessary to understand time-delayed effects [23].

In this paper we present a novel root cause diagnosis mechanism for large-scale HPC systems. Distinguishing from existing studies, *our method has two distinct features*. First, it synthesizes fault related information from multiple data sources, rather than relying on one specific system log. In this study we examine three system logs, i.e., RAS log, job log, and environmental log. Here RAS log lists the fault related events, job log records job execution information, and environmental log typically provides numeric status values from the underlying hardware devices, such as temperatures, clock frequency, fan speeds, and voltages. They are representative system logs that are commonly collected on HPC systems. For instance, IBM Blue Gene comes with a dedicated monitoring and logging system to collect these logs [17]; the OVIS monitoring tool developed from Sandia National Lab can collect these data on various large-scale clusters [3, 33]. Co-analysis of these logs can not only help us to understand the failure impact on different layers, but also assist us to pinpoint the root causes of failures. Second, it provides three dimensional fine-grained root cause information. Here, three dimension means that our root cause analysis can identify the failure layer (i.e., hardware, system software, or application), the time and the location of the events that cause the failures.

1.2 Technical Challenges

Before presenting our detailed method, we list key challenges in the design of the proposed 3-D diagnosis mechanism.

- *Data volume.* Due to the tremendous system size, data collected for analysis are characterized by their huge volume [24]. These data generally often contain noises and redundant records. Hence, it is difficult to extract important diagnosis information from a large amount of data.

- *Data diversity.* As a single log alone does not contain sufficient information for failure analysis, we have to study multiple logs generated from multiple sources. However, these logs often have different formats and contexts, thereby making them hard to integrate.

- *System complexity.* Due to the complicated error propagation among components in different layers, it is difficult to distinguish the failure layer information [8, 34]. Furthermore, due to the lack of priori knowledge of system structure and component dependencies, it is infeasible to apply the well-known techniques based on causality graphs or dependency graphs for failure layer identification on large-scale systems [11, 4, 21].

- *Long latency.* For large-scale systems, triggering event may occur far away from the resulting fatal event, and as such a large amount of data may be recorded between the triggering event and its resulting failure event [7, 10, 20]. Hence, static and fixed approach is infeasible due to the long latency.

1.3 Paper Contribution

To address the above challenges, our design is based on co-analysis of multiple system logs, and it contains four interrelated steps as shown in Figure 1. First, *preprocessing* tackles the challenge of data volume by significantly reducing the amount of data for following data analysis. It removes redundant records and noises from raw logs and extracts important information for subsequent analysis. Second, to address the second challenge — data diversity, *information*

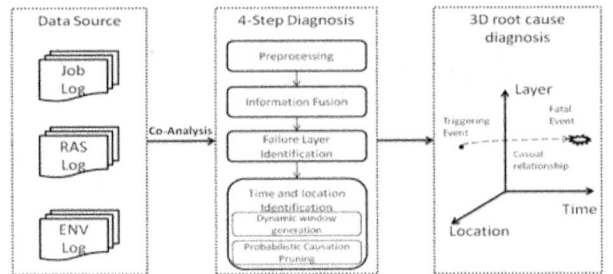

Figure 1: Overview of our root cause diagnosis mechanism.

fusion is utilized to synthesize the information from RAS log, job log and environmental log. Third, *layer identification* narrows down the search space by locating the layer (i.e., application, system software, or hardware) where the failure is generated. This step aims to address the third challenge — system complexity— by co-analyzing multiple logs on different layers, rather than analyzing the problem at each layer separately. Finally, *time and location identification* pinpoints the triggering event via dynamic tracing window and probabilistic causality pruning. The key feature of dynamic tracing window is that it can trace back to the triggering event that occurred days or even weeks ahead of the resulting failure, which is infeasible by using conventional fixed window methods. Hence, this step tackles the fourth challenge listed above, i.e., long latency.

We evaluate our methodology by means of real logs collected from a production IBM Blue Gene/P system at Oak Ridge National Laboratory. Our method is capable of classifying the root causes of fatal events into three layers. Furthermore, it successfully identifies the triggering events for these fatal events, even in case that the trigger event occurs several weeks before the resulting failure. For example, it pinpoints a trigger event as an unstable current output in a faulty power module, which was reported 452 hours before the resulting failure. While our case studies are contributed to failure diagnosis in Blue Gene/P system, we believe our diagnosis methodology can discover more root cause information for variety HPC systems since it uses representative system logs.

1.4 Paper Outline

The rest of the paper is organized as follows. A brief discussion of related works is presented in Section 2. In Section 3, we provide background information about the Blue Gene/P system at Oak Ridge National Laboratory, and three system logs collected from this machine. In Section 4 we present the detailed description of our methodology. Section 5 discusses the case studies. Finally, we conclude the paper in Section 6.

2. RELATED WORK

To mitigate the impact of failures, increasing attention has been dedicated for automated root cause identification. Existing works mainly focus on node level fault localization [22, 18, 32, 13] and parallel programm debugging [11, 6, 4]. For example, the *nodeinfo* algorithm compares the frequency of message terms in each node to localize the faulty nodes [32]. In [18], PCA and ICA based methods are adopted to extract important features from system and application performance metric, and cell-based outlier detection is used to pinpoint the abnormal nodes. In [13], peer comparison diagnosis approach compares the I/O related metrics to identify the faulty node across I/O servers. In terms of parallel programm debugging, both [4] and [22] analyze the function call traces to identify the trace that is most different from others and pinpoint the suspect functions. In [11], DMTracker compares the frequency of data movement on process chain to identify abnormal data movements in MPI program. These methods generally analyze specific jobs or assume similar workloads. Our proposed method can work with them to identify the notorious jobs and workloads, then trigger the proper debugging progress. Meanwhile, our method can recognize faults unrelated to the applications such as hardware problem, thus avoid unnecessary debugging overhead.

In distributed systems, common solutions for diagnosis include fault propagation models (FPM) [15, 6] and trace comparison [5, 30]. These solutions typically assume that the system can be perturbed. Nevertheless, instrumentation is often prohibitive in production HPC systems [23]. Thus it is difficult to generate and maintain an accurate model, especially given the unprecedented system size and dynamic workload.

Statistical analysis is widely adopted to identify the symptoms associated with the failure. In [29], the message is highlighted for system administrator if it has more instances in the log than the expected value for computer system in normal status. In [20], GIZA infrastructure is designed to use several statistical data mining techniques to troubleshoot the problems in IPTV systems. In [7], Pearson correlation is adopted to extract relevant events from the system logs, and tupling heuristic method is used to construct the episode in event sequence. Distinguished from these studies, this paper not only uses correlation analysis, but also studies the job log and environmental log for triggering events identification. Furthermore, we use the probabilistic causation based method to screen off false triggering events.

Considerable research has demonstrates the effectiveness of co-analysis of multiple data sources [25, 18, 35]. For example, both [25] and [18] collect the data from OS level and application level for anomaly analysis. In [2], fine-grained events generated by kernel, middleware and application components are monitored to construct concise workload models. In our previous work [35], we present a co-analysis method to study RAS logs and systemwide job logs in Blue Gene/P system. In this paper, we extend [35] by integrating the environmental data for root cause diagnosis.

Research in this paper is inspired by the work of Oliner [23]. In [23], Oliner et.al. present a Structure-of-Influence Graph (SIG) to isolate system misbehavior [23]. They calculate the anomaly signal in each component and use statistical correlation with time-delayed effect to identify the potential faulty components. Our work fundamentally distinguishes from Oliner's work in three key aspects. First, their work mainly focused on analyzing RAS events for root cause analysis. However, RAS logs only contain limited information, which is inadequate in understanding failures and system behaviors [24]. Our work integrates the RAS information with job log and environmental data to understand the underlying system operating environment and the impact of failures on multiple layers. Second, we explore different methods to provide three dimensional fine-grained root cause information. Especially, our study considers much larger range of

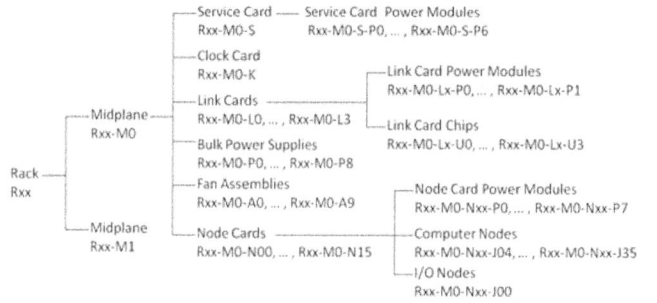

Figure 2: The hierarchy of hardware components and naming convention in *Eugene*.

time delay between the triggering event and the resulting fatal event, which may vary from seconds to days [10].

3. BACKGROUND

In this section, we briefly describe Blue Gene/P and the system logs used in our experiments.

3.1 Eugene: Blue Gene/P System at ORNL

Eugene is a 2-rack Blue Gene/P system laid in two rows (i.e., R0 to R1). The system consists of 8,192 compute nodes with a total number of 32,768 cores, offering a peak performance of 27.9 TFlops [1]. In Eugene, each rack has two midplanes (i.e., M0 to M1), which consists of 16 node cards, 4 link cards, 1 service card, 1 clock card, 9 bulk power supplies, and 10 fan assemblies. In each node card, there are 32 compute nodes connected into a 3D torus for communication, which are served by 1 I/O node and 8 power modules. In each link card, there are 6 link card chips and 2 power modules. The service card is served by 7 power modules. In summary, there are 12 types of hardware components in each midplane. Figure 2 illustrates the hardware components and their hierarchical relationship in the *Eugene* machine.

In Blue Gene/P, a dedicated CMCS (Core Monitoring and Control System) is responsible for system monitoring and error checking. It acquires specific software and hardware information directly through the dedicated control network. Monitored information is stored in a back-end DB2 repository. Three logs generated by CMCS in *Eugene* during the three-month period (i.e., from 2009-11-05 to 2010-02-05) are used in this study, and they are environmental data, RAS log and job log.

3.2 Environmental data

On Blue Gene/P, the environmental monitors read status information from the cards monitored and store the data in the environmental database in a frequency of every 300 seconds. The environmental data are stored in 12 tables, each of which represents one type of hardware components in *Eugene* (see Figure 2). For each hardware component, the sensors collect several environmental features such as temperature, current, and voltage. The total number of features used in our experiments is 3214. An example of environmental data is shown in Figure 3.

3.3 RAS Log

On Blue Gene/P, RAS records are generated when CMCS notices special events (e.g., when abnormal readings are

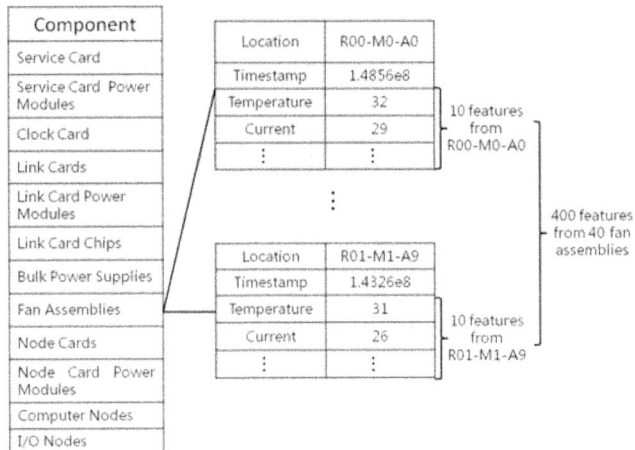

Figure 3: Environmental data is stored in 12 tables corresponding to 12 types of hardware components. Here we show an example from fan assemblies. In *Eugene*, there are 40 fan assemblies, and 10 features collected from each location, resulting in 400 features in total.

encountered) from compute nodes, I/O nodes, and various networks. The entries in the RAS log include hard errors, soft errors, machine checks, and software problems [17]. An example of RAS events is shown in Table 1.

Items	Content
RECID	2457581
MSG_ID	MMCS_0101
COMPONENT	MMCS
SUBCOMPONENT	MMCS_OPERATIONS
ERRCODE	BGPMASTER_STARTED
SEVERITY	INFO
EVENT_TIME	2009-09-09-10.28.03.006954
FLAGS	DefaultControlEventListener
LOCATION	R00-M1-N1
SERIALNUMBER	44V4173YL11K8021017
MESSAGE	BGPMaster has been started. ⋯

Table 1: RAS data from *Eugene*

- *RECID* is the sequence number for an event record in the log, which is increased when a new record is added to the log.

- *MSG_ID* indicates the source of the message.

- *COMPONENT* is the software component detecting and reporting the event. The COMPONENT could be APPLICATION, KERNEL, MC, MMCS, BAREMETAL, CARD, or DIAGS.

- *SUBCOMPONENT* indicates the functional area that generated the message for each component.

- *ERRCODE* identifies the fine-grained event type information.

- *SEVERITY* can be DEBUG, TRACE, INFO, WARNING ERROR and FATAL, with increasing severity.

- *EVENT_TIME* specifies the start time of event.

- *LOCATION* refers to the location where the event occurs.

- *MESSAGE* is a brief overview of the event condition.

3.4 Job Log

The job log of *Eugene* is collected by CMCS as well. An example of job information from the *Eugene* job log is shown in Table 2.

Items	Content
JOB_ID	7
EXECUTABLE	mpirun.26838.bgpsn
START_TIME	2007-10-18-21.51.16.627593
END_TIME	2007-10-18-21.51.21.789395
LOCATION	R01-M0-N12-128
USERNAME	bgpadmin

Table 2: Job log from *Eugene*

- *JOB_ID* is the sequence number for a job.

- *EXECUTABLE* indicates the directory and the name of executable file.

- *START_TIME* is the time when the job starts to run on the nodes.

- *END_TIME* is the time when the job exits. The job could be finished or interrupted by a failure.

- *LOCATION* refers to the location of the execution.

- *USERNAME* is the user name.

4. METHODOLOGY

4.1 Preprocessing

Raw logs cannot be directly used because they generally contain redundant records and noisy data. As a result, preprocessing is applied on raw logs to generate clean logs as well as to extract important information before further analysis [35]. Given that different system logs have different formats and characteristics, in this study, we apply different preprocessing mechanisms on them. Specifically, we apply wavelet transformation, temporal-spatial filtering, and categorization tree on environmental log, RAS log, and job log respectively.

With regard to environmental data, preprocessing has two main goals. First, as most features contain noisy signals, it is essential to filter out the noise and to extract key tendencies of signals. Second, it is critical to identify the timestamps of the abrupt change points, which generally indicate more diagnosis related information than stable signals. In signal processing, wavelet transformation [28] is a popular tool to serve these two purposes. The wavelet transform decomposes the original data into approximation coefficients and detail coefficients. The key tendencies are stored in the approximate coefficients, while the information of abrupt change points are stored in the detail coefficients. An example of wavelet transformation based preprocessing on environmental data is shown in Figure 4.

RAS log typically contains large volume of redundant records, and temporal-spatial filtering is a widely adopted method

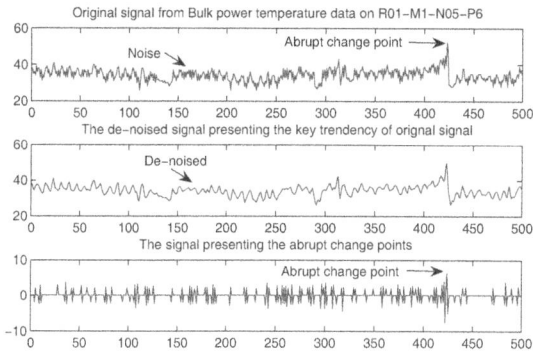

Figure 4: The wavelet based preprocessing of Bulk power temperature data on R01-M1-N05-P6.

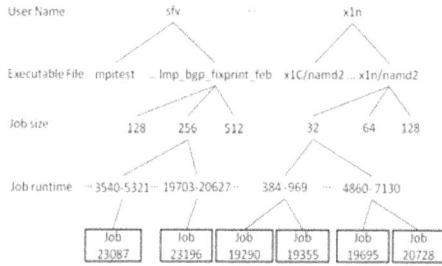

Figure 5: Job categorization tree.

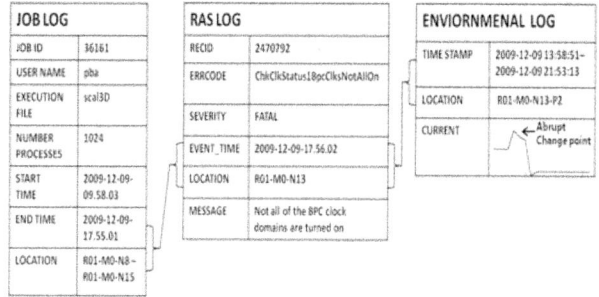

Figure 6: An example of information fusion.

for removing its redundant data [24, 35]. The filtering method presented in our previous work is used for preprocessing RAS log [34]. Distinguishing from other temporal-spatial filtering methods [24, 19], our filtering method is capable of preserving important diagnostic information, such as event start time, event end time, and event locations.

With regard to job log, the execution history of user jobs with the similar characters can provide important information for diagnosis. As a result, the purpose of job log preprocessing is to group the jobs via analyzing their principle characters. In particular, we develop a categorization tree based method to group the jobs. We first divide job records into high-level classifications based on user names, and then further group jobs into subcategories based on executable files, job sizes, and job runtimes.

As shown in Table 2, user names, executable files, and job sizes can be directly obtained from the job log. In terms of job runtimes, further processing is needed for data discretization. The observation on job runtimes is that the jobs from the same buggy application are usually interrupted after the similar execution periods [35]. As a result, we use DBSCAN clustering algorithm [12] to divide the job runtimes into different groups. DBSCAN is a density-based algorithm which identifies the clusters based on estimation of the density distribution. One advantage of DBSCAN is that we do not need to know the number of clusters at the beginning of the process. After DBSCAN clustering, the ranges of job runtimes are depicted on the lowest category level of the categorization tree. An example of job categorization tree is shown in Figure 5.

4.2 Information Fusion

After preprocessing, information fusion is applied to integrate multiple logs. For the purpose of failure diagnosis, we consider the RAS fatal events as the central events and connect them with the interrupted jobs and the subset of environmental features related to the fatal events. Formally speaking, for each fatal event F, information fusion generates a 3-tuple $< F, J_F, E_F >$, where J_F is the set of jobs interrupted by F and E_F is the subset of environmental features that are informative in depicting F.

In terms of job log, we can directly identify the job interruptions by matching the corresponding $Event\_Time$ and $Location$ attributes of the fatal events and jobs. In terms of environmental log, a simple strategy using time and location matching is infeasible. Time delay is common between hardware sensor readings and RAS recording because of the different collection mechanisms. For instance, the records in RAS log and job log are collected by event-driven mechanism, whereas environmental log is periodically collected in every 300 seconds. Furthermore, with regard to location dimension, there are 12 types of hardware components with different location granularities in the environmental log (see Figure 2), which is inconsistent with the location information in RAS log.

To address these issues, we develop an algorithm to extract environmental features that are close to the fatal event in both time and location dimensions (see Algorithm 1). In the time dimension, a time window W is assigned to cover the values of features in $[T_F - W, T_F + W]$, where T_F is the start time of fatal event F. Due to the possible interval caused by delay between hardware sensor readings and RAS recordings, we set W as long as one hour to capture the main tendencies of the environmental features nearby T_F. In the location dimension, for each type of hardware component listed in Figure 2, our algorithm identifies the specific components sharing the least common ancestor (LCA) with the fatal event. For example, if the location of fatal event L_F is R01-M0-N13-J23, all the node card power modules from R01-M0-N13-P0 to R01-M0-N13-P7 are examined in our algorithm as they share LCA R01-M0-N13 with L_F.

Note that Algorithm 1 only keeps the environmental features with abrupt change points, which are more informative in depicting fatal events than the other features.

An example of information fusion is presented in Figure 6. A BPC clock fatal event was reported in a computer code. It interrupted job 36161. There are six environmental features

Algorithm 1 Information fusion between RAS log and environmental log

---

Let T_F and L_F be the time and location of fatal event F in RAS log.
Let L_e be the location of environmental feature e.
$E_F \leftarrow \emptyset$
for each component C **do**
  if $L_e \in LCA(C, L_F)$ **then**
    if e has abrupt change point in $[T_F - W, T_F + W]$
    then
      $E_F \leftarrow E_F \bigcup e$ in C
    end if
  end if
end for

---

associated with it, one of which is the output current from the node card power module.

4.3 Failure Layer Identification

In this study, we distinguish the source of failure into three different layers, i.e., application, system software, and hardware. Application failures denote the fatal events introduced by users, such as buggy codes or user operation mistakes. System software failures denote the fatal events that are generated from system software like the operating system or middleware. Examples include kernel panic and network packet error. Hardware failures denote the fatal events originated from hardware facilities, such as power module or link card. Note that the accurate failure layer information is not provided by the failure logs directly in many cases [35, 32]

To identify failure layer, our method examines failures of the same type. With regard to application failure, the key rationale is that users tend to resubmit their problematic job upon job interrupt, thereby resulting in a series of failure events [35]. Specifically, we compare the jobs interrupted by the failures of the same type and identify the application failure if the interrupted jobs show similar characters, e.g., user names, executable files, job sizes, and job runtimes. In this study, we use the categorization tree (see Figure 5) to measure job similarity score $JS(i, j)$ between job i and job j. If two jobs are grouped in the same category at the lowest level, i.e., with the same user, executable file, job size and job runtime, they are considered as extremely similar jobs with score of 3. On the other hand, if two jobs have different executable files, job sizes, and job runtimes, they have a score of 0.

Based on the pairwise value of $JS(i, j)$, we further analyze all the interrupted jobs caused by the same type of fatal events together. Suppose there are n jobs interrupted by a specific type of fatal events, we define the overall job similarity score JSA as follows.

$$JSA = \frac{\sum_{i=1}^{n} \max_{j=1:n, j \neq i} JS(i, j)}{3n} \quad (1)$$

While application failure usually leads to high JSA, JSA alone cannot be used to distinguish between application failure and system failure. For example, when a hardware failure occurs, a scheduler may keep assigning the failed node to the interrupted job [35], which can also lead to a high score of JSA. To avoid misclassification, our method also examines location information for layer identification. A fatal event is considered as application failure if both of the following conditions are satisfied (1) JSA is close to 1.0 and (2) there exist two associated interrupted jobs which exhibit the highest similarity score of 3, but have different locations.

To distinguish hardware failures, our key rationale is that hardware failures of the same type generally show similar waveforms of environmental features from the corresponding hardware component. Specifically, for each fatal event, our method compares the environmental features associated with it and the failures of the same type. In this study, the normalized cross-correlation [23] is adopted to measure the similarity of environmental features. For a pair of time series of environmental feature $x(t)$ and $y(t)$, the normalized cross-correlation $ES(x, y)$ is defined as

$$ES(x, y) = \frac{E[(x(t) - \mu_x)(y(t + \tau) - \mu_y)]}{\sigma_x \sigma_y} \quad (2)$$

where μ_x and μ_y are the mean values of $x(t)$ and $y(t)$, σ_x and σ_y are the standard deviations of $x(t)$ and $y(t)$, and τ is the time-lag. In this study, we calculate $ES(x, y)$ only if both $x(t)$ and $y(t)$ have abrupt change points. τ is decided by the time difference between the abrupt change points in $x(t)$ and $y(t)$.

Suppose n fatal events of the same type are reported before F, we extract the matched features associated with all the $n+1$ events (i.e., F and n fatal events of the same type). For example, if the temperature feature from fan assemblies is identified to be associated with all the events, this feature is identified as a matched feature. Suppose there are m matched features, for each feature we calculate the similarity score between the F and the n fatal events of the same type. We then select the feature exhibiting the highest value on average to calculate the overall environmental feature similarity score ESA as follows,

$$ESA = \max_{j=1:m} \left(\frac{\sum_{i=1}^{n} |ES(f_{Fj}, f_{ij})|}{n} \right) \quad (3)$$

where f_{ij} is the ith feature associated with the jth event, and f_{Fj} is the ith feature associated with the fatal event F. We classify a fatal event as hardware failure if its ESA is close to 1.0.

For a fatal event, which is not application failure or hardware failure, we classify it as a system software failure. Note that system software failure may also introduces high JSA score if it only interrupts jobs from single user. However, as one system software failure usually interrupts multiple jobs from different users, the JSA of system software failure is generally lower than JSA of application failure.

4.4 Time and Location Identification

To pinpoint the time and location of root cause, our method aims at identifying the triggering event. To this end, our method analyzes the failures of the same type and their precursor events. In particular, our strategy consists two parts: *dynamic window generation* to dynamically set the time interval preceding the fatal event for diagnosing, and *probabilistic causality pruning* to find the precursor event causing the fatal event based on correlation analysis and probabilistic causality analysis.

4.4.1 Dynamic Window Generation

Existing studies mainly use a fixed time window before

Algorithm 2 Dynamic window generation for hardware failure and system software failure

---
Let $F_1, F_2, \cdots, F_n$ be n fatal events of the same type.
Let T_{F_i} and L_{F_i} be the time and location of fatal event F.
Let A_i be the adjacent fatal event of F_i, $L_{A_i} = L_{F_i}$, $T_{A_i} < T_{F_i}$. Let C_{A_i} be the failure type of A_i.
for i=1:n **do**
    $W_{F_i} \leftarrow T_{F_i} - T_{A_i}$
end for
Split RAS log by $\max(W_{F_i})$
for i=1:n **do**
    if $lift(C_{A_i}, F) > 1$ **then**
        $W_{F_i} \leftarrow W_{F_i} + W_{A_i}$
    end if
end for
return W_{F_i}

---

the fatal events for diagnosing (e.g., a couple of hours) [7, 20, 29]. Nevertheless, such a static and fixed approach is not effective since the time delay between the triggering event and the resulting fatal event may vary from seconds to days [10]. To address this issue, we develop a dynamic window generation scheme where the tracing window is dynamically tuned based on event correlation analysis.

With regard to hardware failures and system software failures, the window size is dynamically adapted based on the time interval between two *adjacent* fatal events. Two fatal events A and B are adjacent if they are reported at the same location, and no other fatal event occurring between them at the same location. Further, the time window will be dynamically extended if two adjacent fatal events have different event types but show positive correlation (see Algorithm 2). Here the correlation between event A and B is measured by *lift* [34, 27] as follows.

$$lift(A, B) = \frac{P(AB)}{P(A)P(B)} \quad (4)$$

To estimate the probabilities $P(A)$, $P(B)$, and $P(AB)$, we split the RAS log into different slices by the maximum size of the time window. Suppose there are n windows, in which m windows contain event A, k windows contain event B, and r windows contain both A and B, then $P(A) = m/n$, $P(A) = k/n$, and $P(AB) = r/n$. If *lift* is greater than 1.0, A and B are positively correlated, which generally indicates causal relationship between A and B. As a result, we extend the time window between A and B for further analysis.

In terms of application failure, the window size is decided by job execution time. In other words, all the events occurring between the job start time and the fatal event time are covered in the time window.

4.4.2 *Probabilistic Causation Pruning*

To pinpoint the triggering event, our method first determines a list of candidate events within the tracing-back window via correlation analysis, and then identify the event by applying probabilistic causality analysis. The list of candidate events is determined as follows. First, our method finds out potential triggering events based on the failure layer information. In terms of application failures, it finds out the precursor events associating with the same job as the fatal

Table 3: JSA scores of all the 59 fatal events. It is clearly shown that JSA is a good metric to distinguish application failures from other failures.

JSA	0-0.2	0.2-0.5	0.5-0.7	0.7-0.8	0.8-1
Application	0%	0%	0%	23%	77%
Hardware	76%	24%	0%	0%	0%
System software	13%	58%	29%	0%	0%

Table 4: ESA scores of all the 59 fatal events. It is clearly shown that ESA is a good metric to distinguish hardware failures from other failures.

ESA	0-0.2	0.2-0.5	0.5-0.7	0.7-0.8	0.8-1
Application	100%	0%	0%	0%	0%
Hardware	0%	0%	0%	24%	76%
System software	93%	7%	0%	0%	0%

event. In terms of hardware failures, it identifies the precursor events exhibiting similar waveforms of environmental features as the fatal event. In terms of system software failures, we collect the events from the culprit nodes where the interrupted job is executed. Next, our method selects the events positively correlated with the fatal event, i.e., its *lift* with the fatal event is greater than 1.0.

Next, our method explores probabilistic causality to identify the actual triggering event by removing other false triggering events from the candidate list. Here false triggering event indicates the event sharing common cause of fatal event [14]. For example, in our case study, a kernel problem causes the network error, and finally leads to the network failure. While the network error event shows positive correlation with the resulting failure, it is not the triggering event. Based on probabilistic causality theory [26], we determine the actual triggering event as follows. Suppose both A and B are candidate events, our method sorts them based on their time stamps. If the ordering of A and B is not fixed, both A and B are kept as actual triggering event. If A always occurs before B and the occurrence of B does not raise the probability of F, i.e., $P(F|AB) \leq P(F|A\bar{B})$, then B is removed as the false triggering event. Note that the clocks in HPC systems are synchronized, so we can use event ordering here.

We can further validate the triggering event by comparing the job similarity or environmental feature similarity between the potential triggering event and the resulting fatal event. The high similarity score generally indicates true triggering event.

5. CASE STUDIES

In this section, we present case studies of using our diagnosis method on real system logs collected from a production Blue Gene/P system at Oak Ridge National Lab. The details of these system logs are described in Section 3.

5.1 Failure Layer Identification

During the 23-month period, there are 219 fatal events. To verify our layer identification, we get the layer information from experts and split these events into training set and testing set. The training set consists of 7 hardware failures, 36 system software failures, and 16 application failures. We examine job similarity scores (JSA) and environmental fea-

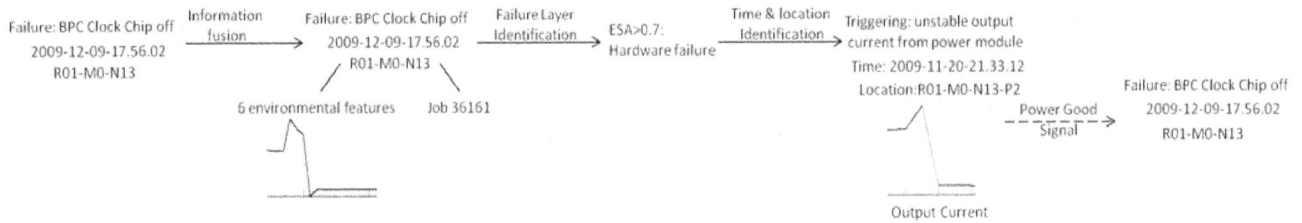

Figure 7: Diagnosis of BPC clock chip failure from hardware layer. The root cause is due to the unstable current output in the power module, which is reported 452 hours before the resulting failure.

ture similarity scores (ESA) of the fatal events in training set in Table 3 and 4. Based on the results from training, we classifying the failure layers in testing set, which consists of 13 hardware failures, 127 system software failures, and 20 application failures.

As shown in Table 3, in training set, JSA is a good metric to distinguish application failures from hardware failures because 100% application failures show $JSA > 0.7$ and 100% hardware failures show $JSA < 0.5$. However, JSA may lead to misclassification of system software failures because 27% system software failures with $JSA > 0.5$. This is because the scheduler may keep assigning failed nodes to a series of similar jobs [35]. Nevertheless, our mechanism cooperates the location information with the job similarity score for application failure identification, thus avoids misclassification of system software failures.

As shown in Table 4, in training set, 100% hardware failures show high environmental feature similarity score, i.e., $ESA > 0.7$. Meanwhile, all of system software failures and application failures have $ESA < 0.7$. As a result, ESA does a good job of distinguishing hardware failures from other failures.

Based on the training results, 0.7 of JSA and ESA are used to classify failure layers in testing set. In terms of application failure and hardware failure, our mechanism achieves 100% accuracy for all the 33 failures. In terms of system software failures, we successfully classify 87.4% failures. There are 16 failures with $JSA > 0.7$. However, the jobs interrupted by these 16 failures are reported from the same locations. By cooperating the location information, our mechanism avoids classification of them as application failures.

5.2 Time and Location Identification

Our mechanism analyzes the triggering events for the 219 fatal events. Here we list four case studies to illustrate the effectiveness of our time and location identification mechanism.

5.2.1 Hardware Failure

On December 9th 2009, a BPC clock failure *BpcClksNotAllOn* is reported in node card R01-M0-N13. The message shows that not all of the BPC clocks are turned on. As shown in Figure 7, our information fusion step identifies the interrupted job 36161 and 6 associated environmental features, such as output current and node card voltage. In failure layer identification step, this fatal event is classified as a hardware failure because $ESA > 0.7$.

In time and location identification step, dynamic window generation mechanism obtains the maximum time window of 656.7 hours. Then probabilistic causation pruning identi-

fies two types of events with positive correlation with BPC clock chip failure, namely node power error and card power error. Next, the card power error is removed as a false triggering event because it always occurs after the node power error and does not raise the probability of BPC clock chip failures. Finally, the node power error from power module R01-M0-N13-P2 is identified as the triggering event. This type of error was continually reported 14 times and the earliest one occurred 452 hours before the resulting BPC clock chip failure.

Both triggering event and the BPC clock failure associate the environmental feature of output current from power module R01-M0-N13-P2. As a result, we believe the unstable output current is the root cause. This conclusion is consistent with the knowledge from hardware experts. When the power module cannot maintain proper outputs, a power good signal will be generated. When the BPC clock chip receives this signal, it will automatically shut down, thus lead to the occurrence of BPC clock chip failure.

5.2.2 Application failure

On June 2th 2009, a fatal event *bg_code_oom* is reported in R01-M0-N11-J00, which indicates an out of memory failure. As shown in Figure 8, our information fusion mechanism identifies the interrupted job 27487, which has executable file *pstg2r.x*. In failure layer identification step, this fatal event is classified as a application failure because $JSA > 0.7$ and there exist two associated interrupted jobs with highest similarity score but from different locations.

In time and location identification step, our dynamic window generation mechanism obtains the time window up to 707 hours. Then probabilistic causation pruning mechanism identifies the trigger event as an error of insufficient memory introduced by *pstg2r.x*, which was reported 669.7 hours before the resulting failure.

Obviously, it necessary to analyze the memory related functions in *pstg2r.x* for debugging. While debugging is outside of our study, our mechanism still provides useful information. The results from information fusion show a successful execution from the executable file *pstg1r.x*. As a result, user can compare the difference between these two versions to identify the potential bugs.

5.2.3 System Software Failure

On February 20th 2008, a torus sender failure is reported in 16 I/O nodes. The message shows that data was sent in torus network but not received. As shown in Figure 9, our information fusion mechanism identifies that the interrupted job 8406. In failure layer identification step, this fatal event

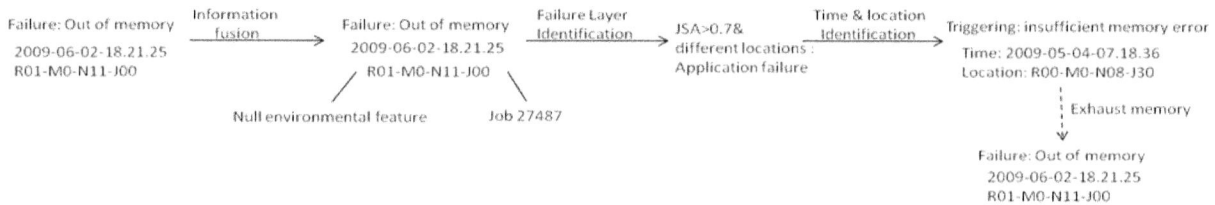

Figure 8: Diagnosis of out of memory failure from application layer. The root cause is an application bug that exceeds the limits of memory, which is reported 669.7 hours before the resulting failure.

is classified as a system software failure because $ESA < 0.2$ and $JSA < 0.5$.

In time and location identification step, dynamic window generation mechanism generates the maximum time window of 42.6 hours. Then probabilistic causation pruning identifies three types of events showing positive correlation with the torus sender failure, namely torus receiver warning, torus sender retransmission, and invalid memory address error.

While torus receiver warning and torus sender retransmission seem like more related to the torus sender failure based on the contexts, these two events are identified as false triggering events because they do not increase the probability of torus sender failure if invalid memory address error occurs. Finally, invalid memory address error is identified as the triggering event. This error was from Linux kernel, which was reported 42.3 hours before the resulting failure. When the receiver tried to receive the packet from torus network, it accessed invalid memory address thus dropped the data, which finally leaded to the occurrence of torus sender failure.

To diagnose torus sender failure, system administrators executed 135 testing programs in 506 hours. Our automated diagnosis method can significantly reduce the diagnosis overhead, thereby reducing the impact of failure on system resilience.

5.2.4 Rare Failure

While our methodology assumes multiple failures with the same type have occurred in history, it still can provide partial diagnosis information for rare failure via co-analysis. For example, on July 22nd 2009, a new failure bg_code_panic is reported, which indicates a kernel panic. Because it is a new failure, we can neither calculate the JSA/ESA nor adopt probabilistic causation analysis. To address the issue of rare failure, we simply use information fusion and dynamic window generation mechanisms. Our information fusion identifies that the bg_code_panic failure interrupted job 29780. In dynamic window generation step, we identify a machine check error from DDR controller, which is associated with the same job 29780 as the failure. As a result, the memory related operations in job 29780 are suspicious triggering event for further analysis.

6. CONCLUSIONS

In this paper, we have presented an automated mechanism for root cause diagnosis in HPC systems. Distinguishing from existing studies, our work effectively integrates information from multiple logs, and provides three dimensional fine-grained diagnosis information. Our case studies on a production Blue Gene/P system have demonstrated the effectiveness of our mechanism in terms of discovering failure

layer information and triggering events with time and location information.

As a part of our future work, we plan to further test this diagnosis mechanism on more production HPC systems, including Cray XT5 and general HPC clusters.

7. ACKNOWLEDGMENTS

The work at Illinois Institute of Technology was supported in part by US National Science Foundation grants CNS-0834514, CNS-0720549. The work at ORNL was supported in part by the Office of Advanced Scientific Computing Research, Office of Science, U.S. Department of Energy, under Contract DE-AC02-06CH11357.

8. REFERENCES

[1] S. Alam, R. Barrett, M. Bast, M. Fahey, J. Kuehn, C. McCurdy, J. Rogers, P. Roth, R. Sankaran, J. Vetter, P. Worley, and W. Yu. Early evaluation of IBM BlueGene/P. *Proc. of Supercomputing*, 2008.

[2] P. Barham, A. Donnelly, R. Isaacs, and R. Mortier. Using magpie for request extraction and workload modelling. In *Proceedings of OSDI*, 2004.

[3] J. Brandt, A. Gentile, C. Houf, J. Mayo, P. Pebay, D. Roe, D. Thompson, and M. Wong. OVIS 3.2 user's guide. *SAND 2010-7109, Sandia National Laboratories*, October 2010.

[4] G. Bronevetsky, I. Laguna, S. Bagchi, R. Bronis, D. Ahn, and M. Schulz. AutomaDeD: Automata-based debugging for dissimilar parallel tasks. In *Proceedings of DSN*, 2010.

[5] M. Chen, E. Kiciman, E. Fratkin, A. Fox, and E. Brewer. Pinpoint: problem determination in large, dynamic Internet services. In *Proceedings of DSN*, 2002.

[6] T. Chilimbi, B. Liblit, K. Mehra, A. Nori, and K. Vaswani. Holmes: Effective statistical debugging via efficient path profiling. In *Proceedings of ICSE*, 2009.

[7] E. Chuah, S. Kuo, P. Hiew, W. Tjhi, G. Lee, J. Hammond, M. Michalewicz, T. Hung, and J. Browne. Diagnosing the root-causes of failures from cluster log files. In *Proceedings of HiPC*, 2010.

[8] N. DeBardeleben, J. Laros, J. Daly, S. Scott, C. Engelmann, and B. Harrod. High-end computing resilience: Analysis of issues facing the HEC community and path-forward for research and development. *White Paper*, 2009.

[9] N. Desai, R. Bradshaw, C. Lueninghoener, A. Cherry, S. Coghlan, and W. Scullin. Petascale system

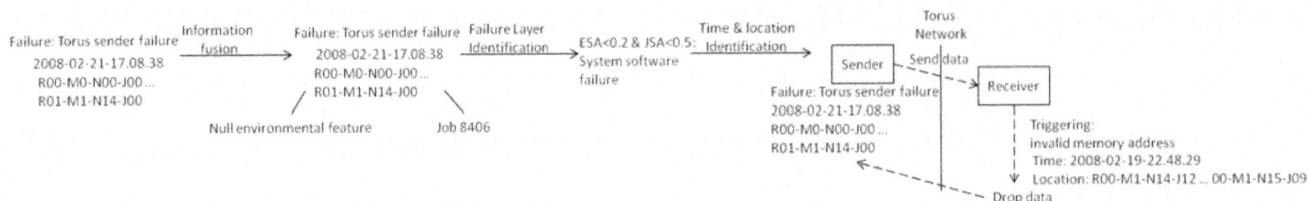

Figure 9: Diagnosis of torus sender failure from system software layer. The triggering event is the invalid memory address error from torus receiver, which is reported 42.3 hours before the resulting failure.

management experiences. In *Proceedings of LISA*, 2008.

[10] A. Gainaru, F. Cappello, F. J., and S. Trausan. Adaptive event prediction strategy with dynamic time window for large-scale HPC systems. In *Proceedings of SLAML*, 2011.

[11] Q. Gao, F. Qin, and D. Panda. DMTracker: Finding bugs in large-scale parallel programs by detecting anomaly in data movements. In *Proceedings of Supercomputing*, 2006.

[12] J. Han and M. Kamber. *Data Mining:Concepts and Techniques*. Morgan Kaufmann, 2000.

[13] M. Kasick, J. Tan, R. Gandhi, and P. Narasimhan. Black-box problem diagnosis in parallel file systems. In *Proceedings of FAST*, 2010.

[14] M. Khan, H. Le, H. Ahmadi, T. Abdelzaher, and J. Han. Dustminer: troubleshooting interactive complexity bugs in sensor networks. In *Proceedings of SenSys*, 2008.

[15] E. Kiciman and A. Fox. Detecting application-level failures in component-based internet services. *IEEE Trans. Neural Networks*, 16(5):1027–1041, 2005.

[16] P. Kogge and et al. Exascale computing study: Technology challenges in achieving exascale systems. *White Paper*, 2008.

[17] G. Lakner and G. Mullen-Schultz. IBM BlueGene solution: System administration. *IBM Redbook*, 2007.

[18] Z. Lan, Z. Zheng, and Y. Li. Toward automated anomaly identification in large-scale systems. *IEEE Trans. on Parallel and Distributed Systems*, 21(2):174–187, 2010.

[19] Y. Liang, Y. Zhang, A. Sivasubramanium, R. Sahoo, J. Moreia, and M. Gupta. Filtering failure logs for a BlueGene/L prototype. In *Proceedings of DSN*, 2005.

[20] A. Mahimkar, Z. Ge, A. Shaikh, J. Wang, J. Yates, Y. Zhang, and Q. Zhao. Towards automated performance diagnosis in a large IPTV network. In *Proceedings of SIGCOMM*, 2009.

[21] N. Maruyama and S. Matsuoka. Model-based fault localization: Finding behavioral outliers in large-scale computing systems. *New Generation Comput*, 28:237–255, 2010.

[22] A. Mirgorodskiy, N. Maruyama, and B. Miller. Problem diagnosis in large-scale computing environments. In *Proceedings of Supercomputing*, 2006.

[23] A. Oliner, A. Kulkarni, and A. Aiken. Using correlated surprise to infer shared influence. In *Proceedings of DSN*, 2010.

[24] A. Oliner and J. Stearley. What supercomputers say: A study of five system logs. In *Proceedings of DSN*, 2007.

[25] X. Pan, J. Tan, S. Kalvulya, R. Gandhi, and P. Narasimhan. Blind men and the elephant: Piecing together hadoop for diagnosis. In *Proceedings of ISSRE*, 2009.

[26] J. Pearl. *Causality: Models, Reasoning, and Inference*. Cambridge University Press, 2000.

[27] A. Pecchia, D. Cotroneo, Z. Kalbarczyk, and R. Iyer. Improving log-based field failure data analysis of multi-node computing systems. In *Proceedings of DSN*, 2011.

[28] X. Rao, H. Wang, D. Shi, Z. Chen, H. Cai, and Q. Zhou. Identifying faults in large-scale distributed systems by filtering noisy error logs. In *Proceedings of DSNW*, 2011.

[29] S. Sabato, E. Yomtov, and A. Tsherniak. Analyzing system logs: A new view of what's important. In *USENIX SysML workshop*, 2007.

[30] R. Sambasivan, A. Zheng, M. Rosa, E. Krevat, S. Whitman, M. Stroucken, W. Wang, L. Xu, and G. Ganger. Diagnosing performance changes by comparing request flows. In *Proceedings of NSDI*, 2011.

[31] B. Schroeder and G. Gibson. A large-scale study of failures in high-performance computing systems. In *Proceedings of DSN*, 2006.

[32] J. Stearley and A. Oliner. Bad words: Finding faults in spirit's syslogs. In *Proceedings of the Workshop on Resiliency in High Performance Computing*, 2008.

[33] L. Yu, Z. Zheng, Z. Lan, T. Jones, J. Brandt, and A. Gentile. Filtering log data: Finding the needles in the haystack. In *Proceedings of DSN*, 2012.

[34] Z. Zheng, Z. Lan, B. Park, and A. Geist. System log pre-processing to improve failure prediction. In *Proceedings of DSN*, 2009.

[35] Z. Zheng, L. Yu, W. Tang, Z. Lan, R. Gupta, N. Desai, S. Coghlan, and D. Buettner. Co-analysis of RAS log and job log on Blue Gene/P. In *Proceedings of IPDPS*, 2011.

UBL: *U*nsupervised *B*ehavior *L*earning for Predicting Performance Anomalies in Virtualized Cloud Systems

Daniel J. Dean, Hiep Nguyen, Xiaohui Gu
Department of Computer Science
North Carolina State University
{djdean2,hcnguye3}@ncsu.edu, gu@csc.ncsu.edu

ABSTRACT

Infrastructure-as-a-Service (IaaS) clouds are prone to performance anomalies due to their complex nature. Although previous work has shown the effectiveness of using statistical learning to detect performance anomalies, existing schemes often assume labelled training data, which requires significant human effort and can only handle previously known anomalies. We present an *U*nsupervised *B*ehavior *L*earning (UBL) system for IaaS cloud computing infrastructures. UBL leverages Self-Organizing Maps to capture emergent system behaviors and predict unknown anomalies. For scalability, UBL uses residual resources in the cloud infrastructure for behavior learning and anomaly prediction with little add-on cost. We have implemented a prototype of the UBL system on top of the Xen platform and conducted extensive experiments using a range of distributed systems. Our results show that UBL can predict performance anomalies with high accuracy and achieve sufficient lead time for automatic anomaly prevention. UBL supports large-scale infrastructure-wide behavior learning with negligible overhead.

Categories and Subject Descriptors

C.4 [**Performance of Systems**]: Reliability, availability, and serviceability

General Terms

Reliability, Management, Experimentation

Keywords

Unsupervised System Behavior Learning, Cloud Computing, Anomaly Prediction

1. INTRODUCTION

Infrastructure-as-a-Service (IaaS) cloud infrastructures [1] allow users to lease resources in a pay-as-you-go fashion. Due to its inherent complexity and sharing nature, the cloud system is prone to performance anomalies due to various reasons such as resource contentions, software bugs, or hardware failures. It is a daunting

task for system administrators to manually keep track of the execution status of tens of thousands of virtual machines (VMs) all the time. Moreover, delayed anomaly detection can cause long service level objective (SLO) violation time, which is often associated with a large financial penalty. Thus, it is highly desirable to provide automatic anomaly prediction techniques that can forecast whether a system will enter an anomalous state and trigger proper preventive actions to steer the system away from the anomalous state.

It is challenging to achieve efficient anomaly management for large-scale IaaS cloud infrastructures. First, applications running inside the cloud often appear as black-box to the cloud service provider. Therefore, it is impractical to apply previous white-box or grey-box anomaly detection techniques (e.g., [7]) which require application instrumentation. Second, a large-scale cloud infrastructure often runs thousands of applications concurrently. The anomaly management scheme itself must be light-weight and should operate in an online fashion. Third, it is difficult, if not totally impossible, to obtain *labelled* training data (i.e., measurement samples associated with normal or abnormal labels) from production cloud systems. As a result, it is hard to apply previous supervised learning techniques [15, 17, 33] for monitoring production cloud systems. More importantly, supervised learning techniques can only detect previously known anomalies.

In this paper, we present the design and implementation of an *U*nsupervised *B*ehavior *L*earning (UBL) system for virtualized cloud computing infrastructures. UBL does not require any labelled training data, allowing it capture *emergent* system behaviors. This makes it possible for UBL to predict both known anomalies and *unknown* anomalies. UBL employs a set of continuous VM behavior learning modules to capture the patterns of normal operations of all application VMs. To avoid manual data labeling and capture emergent system behaviors, UBL leverages an unsupervised learning method called the Self Organizing Map (SOM) [24]. We chose the SOM because it is capable of capturing complex system behaviors while being computationally less expensive than comparable approaches such as k-nearest neighbor [32]. To predict anomalies, UBL looks for early deviations from normal system behaviors. UBL only relies on system-level metrics that can be easily acquired via the hypervisor or guest OS to achieve black-box anomaly prediction.

For scalability, UBL takes a *decentralized* and *virtualized* learning approach that leverages *residual* resources in the cloud infrastructure for behavior learning and anomaly prediction. It encapsulates the behavior analysis program within a set of special *learning VMs*. We then use the Xen credit scheduler [8] to enforce the learning VM to only use residual resources without affecting other co-located application VMs. We can also easily migrate the learning VM between different hosts using live VM migrations [14] to utilize time-varying residual resources on different hosts.

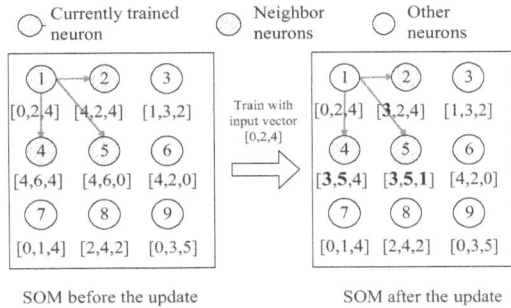

Figure 1: SOM training process.

Specially, this paper makes the following contributions:

- We show how to use the SOM learning technique to achieve efficient unsupervised system behavior learning.

- We describe how to leverage the system behavior model along with the node neighborhood area size analysis to predict emergent system anomalies and infer anomaly causes.

- We present a virtualized system behavior learning scheme that leverages the virtualization technology to efficiently and safely harvest residual resources in the cloud to achieve scalable online system behavior learning and anomaly prediction with little add-on cost.

We have implemented a prototype of UBL on top of the Xen platform [8]. We have deployed and tested UBL on the NCSU's virtual computing lab (VCL) [6] that operates in a similar way as Amazon EC2 [1]. We conducted extensive experiments using a range of real distributed systems: 1) RUBiS, an online auction benchmark [4], 2) IBM System S, a commercial stream processing system [18], and 3) Hadoop, an open source implementation of MapReduce framework [2]. Our experimental results show that UBL can predict a range of performance anomalies with 5.9-87.7% higher true positive rates and 3.3-84.5% lower false alarm rates than other alternative schemes. UBL can achieve sufficient lead time in most cases for the system to take just-in-time preventative actions [34]. Our prototype implementation shows that UBL is feasible and imposes negligible overhead for the cloud system.

The remainder of the paper is organized as follows. Section 2 presents the design details of UBL. Section 3 presents the experimental evaluation. Section 4 compares our work with related work. Finally, Section 5 concludes this paper.

2. SYSTEM DESIGN

In this section, we present the design details of the UBL system. We first describe our continuous runtime system behavior learning scheme. We then present our unsupervised anomaly prediction algorithm that can raise advance alerts about both known and unknown anomalies. Next, we present our decentralized learning framework to achieve scalable and low-cost cloud infrastructure behavior learning.

2.1 Online System Behavior Learning

It is a challenging task to achieve efficient online system behavior learning for large-scale cloud computing infrastructures. The learning scheme first needs to achieve scalability, which can induce behavior models for a large number of application components on-the-fly without imposing excessive learning overhead. Furthermore, system metric measurements for real world distributed applications are often fluctuating due to dynamic workloads or measurement noises, which requires a robust learning scheme. We chose to use the SOM learning technique in this work to achieve scalable and efficient system behavior learning.

The SOM maps a high dimensional input space into a low dimensional map space (usually two dimensions) while preserving the topological properties of the original input space (i.e., two similar samples will be projected to close positions in the map). Thus, the SOM can handle multi-variant system behavior learning well without missing any representative behaviors. Specially, we collect a vector of measurements $D(t) = [x_1, x_2, ..., x_n]$ continuously for each VM, where x_i denotes one system-level metrics (e.g., CPU, memory, disk I/O, or network traffic), and use the measurement vectors as inputs to train SOMs. UBL can dynamically induce a SOM for each VM to capture the VM's behaviors.

A SOM is composed of a set of neurons arranged in a lattice, illustrated by Figure 1. Each neuron is associated with a weight vector and a coordinate in the map. Weight vectors should be the same length as the measurement vectors (i.e., $D(t)$), which are dynamically updated based on the values of the measurement vectors in the training data. UBL uses SOMs to model system behaviors in two different phases: learning and mapping. We first describe the learning phase. We will present the mapping phase in detail in the next subsection.

During learning, the SOM uses a competitive learning process to adjust the weight vectors of different neurons. The competitive learning process works by comparing the Euclidean distance of the input measurement vector to each neuron's weight vector in the map. The neuron with the smallest Euclidian distance is selected as the currently trained neuron. For example, Figure 1 shows a map consisting of 9 neurons being trained with an input measurement vector of [0,2,4]. We first calculate the Euclidean distance to every neuron. Neuron 1 is selected as the currently trained neuron because it has the smallest Euclidean distance to the measurement vector. That neuron's values along with its neighbor neurons are then updated. In this example, we define our neighborhood to be the neurons in a radius of $r = 1$. Striped neurons (neurons 2, 4, and 5) are the neurons in neuron 1's neighborhood. The general formula for updating the weight vector of a given neuron at time t is given in Equation 1. We use $W(t)$ and $D(t)$ to define the weight vector and the input vector at time instance t, respectively. $N(v, t)$ denotes the neighborhood function (e.g., a Gaussian function) which depends on the lattice distance to a neighbor neuron v. $L(t)$ denotes a learning coefficient that can be applied to modify how much each weight vector is changed as learning proceeds.

$$W(t + 1) = W(t) + N(v, t)L(t)(D(t) - W(t)) \qquad (1)$$

Figure 1 illustrates the learning process using Equation 1 with a learning coefficient of 1 and a neighborhood function of $\frac{1}{4}$. We use a simple function here to illustrate the learning process, but more complex neighborhood functions are used in non-trivial applications, which we discuss further in Section 3. For example, neuron 2 has a weight vector of [4,2,4] and the input vector is [0,2,4]. Taking the difference between the input vector and the weight vector gives a value of [-4,0,0] which is then multiplied by 1 and $\frac{1}{4}$. This gives value of [-1,0,0] which is then added to the initial weight of [4,2,4] to give a final updated value of [3,2,4] to neuron 2. All updated values are shown in bold. The intuition behind this approach is to make the currently trained neuron and the neurons in its neighborhood converge to the input space.

When each input vector has been used to update the map multiple times (e.g., 10 in our experiments), learning is complete. At this point, the weight vectors of neurons represent a generalization of the whole measurement vector space. Thus, the SOM can capture the *normal* system behaviors under different workloads. We define this phase to be the *bootstrap* learning phase. UBL also supports incremental updates which can continuously adjust the SOM with new measurement vectors. However, too many incremental updates may degrade the quality of the SOM as all weight vectors may converge to a small number of vector values. This can happen when the system starts to process a completely different new workload. In this case, we can re-bootstrap the SOM with new measurement data to maintain the quality of the SOM.

When applying the SOM to learning real system behaviors, we found that UBL needs to address several metric pre-precessing problems in order to achieve efficiency. First, different system metric values can have very different ranges in their raw form. For example, the MEM_USAGE metric ranges from 0 to 2048, while the CPU_USAGE metric expressed as a utilization percentage from 0 to 100. This is problematic for our map as large data ranges would require a large number of neurons. To address this problem, we normalize all metric values to the range [0,100] by looking at the maximum value of each metric in the learning data. We chose to normalize our values this way because we found using the absolute maximum possible value sometimes produced distorted normalized values that distribute within a small range. For example, during normal operation, the observed network traffic should be much less than the maximum traffic possible. Normalizing to the maximum possible value would mean the network traffic value would only cover a small range.

During online operation, some measurement values might exceed the maximum value in the training data. This will cause some normalized metric values to be greater than 100. However, we found this does not cause an unexpected result. By doing this, we can significantly reduce the number of neurons needed for covering the whole measurement space while still capturing the patterns of the system behavior. We also filter constant metric values which have no effect on our system to further decrease the memory footprint for storing the training data. Second, some real system metric values (e.g., memory usage in Hadoop) are highly fluctuating. We might induce a map with poor quality using the raw monitoring data. To address the problem, we apply k-point moving average filter to smooth the raw monitoring data. The length of k represents the degree of smoothing, which computes an average value for the current value with the k metric values before the current value.

Determining how to properly configure and initialize the map is critical for the performance of SOM. We first need to decide the size of the map we should use for modeling a VM's behavior. We found a matrix topology based map with dimensions 32x32 consisting of 1024 total neurons works well for all the applications we tested. As values have been normalized to [0,100], we initialize each weight vector element to a random value between 0 and 100. We found random initialization to be necessary because initializing the weight vectors to a set of known values causes the produced map to be heavily biased towards the known values. This decreases the ability of the map to predict unknown values.

Due to the randomness used in weight vector initialization, we found the random vectors generated in some maps would only represent a subset of the training data values. This caused only a small portion of neurons to be trained, which in turn led to a poor quality map. To address this problem, we use K-fold cross validation as part of our learning phase, which works as follows. The training data is first partitioned into K parts denoted by $D_1, \cdots, D_K$. The validation process takes K rounds to complete. In round i, $1 \leq i \leq K$, D_i is selected to be the testing data while the other $(K-1)$ parts $D_1, \cdots, D_{i-1}, D_{i+1}, \cdots, D_K$ are used as the training data.

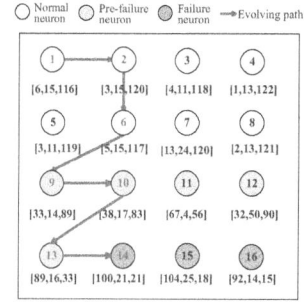

Figure 2: An example path showing the system evolution from normal to failure.

We collect various correct and incorrect classification statistics to compute the accuracy of each map. Since UBL is designed to be unsupervised, we only use unlabeled *normal* data to train the map. UBL relies on the SLO feedback from the application or some external SLO monitoring tool [11] to select normal data. Suppose N_{fp} is the number of false positives, when UBL raised an alarm yet no anomaly was found. N_{fn} is the number of false negatives, when UBL failed to raise an alarm but the current sample was an anomaly. N_{tp} is the number of true positives, when UBL raised an alarm and there was an anomaly. N_{tn} is the number of true negatives, when UBL did not raise an alarm and the current sample was normal. Since our training data are all normal data, $N_{fn} = N_{tp} = 0$. The accuracy metric for each map is calculated using the standard way as follows:

$$A = \frac{N_{tn} + N_{tp}}{N_{tn} + N_{fp} + N_{fn} + N_{tp}} \quad (2)$$

The cross validation module selects the map with the best accuracy as the final trained map. We use the same Gaussian neighborhood function and the same constant learning coefficient among all datasets. We also conducted sensitivity experiments to show how those parameter values affect the performance of UBL. We will present those results in Section 3.

2.2 Unsupervised Anomaly Prediction

Performance anomalies, such as SLO violations, in distributed systems often manifest as anomalous changes in system-level metrics. Faults do not always cause a SLO failure immediately. Instead there is a time window from when the fault occurs to the actual time of failure. Therefore, at any given time, a system can be thought to be operating in one of three states: normal, pre-failure, or failure. Additionally, the system typically first enters the pre-failure state before entering the failure state. Since the SOM is able to maintain the topological properties of the measurement samples, we can observe when the system enters the pre-failure state and moves to the failure state. Figure 2 shows an example using a real system failure where the failing system follows a path through the SOM over time. UBL can raise an advanced alarm when the system leaves the normal state but has not yet entered the failure state.

To decide the system state represented by each neuron, UBL calculates a neighborhood area size for each neuron in the SOM. As mentioned in Section 2.1, when neurons in the SOM are updated with training data, we also adjust the weight vectors of their neighboring neurons. After learning, frequently trained neurons will have modified the weight vector values of their neighboring neurons with the same input measurement vectors. As a result, the weight vectors of the neurons that are frequently trained will look similar to the weight vectors of their neighboring neurons.

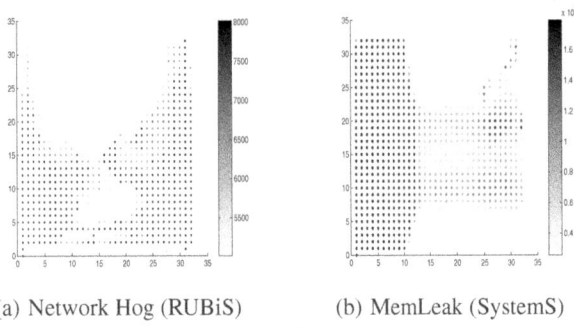

(a) Network Hog (RUBiS)   (b) MemLeak (SystemS)

Figure 3: Grey-scale visualization of the SOM models for the RUBiS with the Network Hog fault and System S with the MemLeak fault. Darker neurons have larger neighborhood area sizes while lighter neurons have smaller neighborhood area sizes.

Since systems are usually in the normal state, neurons representing the normal state will be more frequently trained than the neurons representing the pre-failure or failure states. Thus, we will have clusters of neurons representing different normal system behaviors. We calculate a neighborhood area size value for each neuron by examining the immediate neighbors of each neuron. As our lattice topology is a two-dimensional grid, this means we examine the top, left, right, and bottom neighbors. We calculate the Manhattan distance between two neurons N_i, N_j with weight vectors $W_i = [w_{1,i}, \cdots, w_{k,i}]$, $W_j = [w_{1,j}, \cdots, w_{k,j}]$ respectively, as follows:

$$M(N_i, N_j) = \sum_{l=1}^{k} |w_{l,i} - w_{l,j}| \qquad (3)$$

We define the neighborhood area size for a neuron N_i as the sum of Manhattan distance between the neuron N_i and its top, left, right and bottom immediate neighbors denoted by N_T, N_L, N_R and N_B, as follows:

$$S(N_i) = \sum_{X \in \{N_T, N_L, N_R, N_B\}} M(N_i, X) \qquad (4)$$

UBL determines if a neuron is normal or anomalous by looking at the neighborhood area size of that neuron. If the neighborhood area size is small, we know that the neuron we have mapped to is in a tight cluster of neurons, meaning the neuron is normal. On the other hand, if a neuron maps to a neuron with a large neighborhood area value, we know that the neuron is not close to other neurons, and thus, probably anomalous. For example, in Figure 2, the calculated neighborhood area size for neuron 6 (a normal neuron) of would be the sum of the differences to neighbors 2,5,7, and 10, which is 102. The neighborhood area size of neuron 10 (a pre-failure neuron), on the other hand, is the sum to neighbors 6, 9, 14, and 11, which is 280.

Figure 3 shows two maps after bootstrap learning has completed: one is for the RUBiS web server with a network hog bug and the other is for one faulty component in System S including a memory leak bug. We use gray-scale visualization to illustrate the behavior patterns. Darker neurons represent anomalous behaviors while lighter neurons represent normal behaviors. Once learning is complete, we can clearly see different systems present distinct behavior patterns that can be captured by the SOM.

During application runtime, we map each measurement vector to a neuron using the same Euclidean distance metric as the learning phase. We look at the neighborhood area size of the mapped

neuron. If the neighborhood area size is below the threshold for the map, that means the sample has mapped to a neuron which is close to many other neurons. We consider this sample to be a normal sample and do not raise an alarm. However, if the sample maps to a neuron with an area value greater than or equal to our threshold value, this sample represents something we rarely see during learning. We consider this type of sample to be anomalous. Transient fluctuations in system metrics due to noise can still be present even after data smoothing. Those momentary fluctuations may be mapped to anomalous neurons, although it would be incorrect to raise an alarm in this case. As a result, we raise an alarm only when the system identifies three consecutive anomalous samples.

Determining a neighborhood area size threshold to differentiate normal and anomalous neurons is integral to the accuracy of the UBL system. If the threshold is set too high, we cannot raise an alarm early enough and may miss some anomalies. Alternatively, if we set the threshold too low, we might raise too many alarms, including false alarms. Additionally, neighborhood area size values vary from map to map depending on the range of values in the dataset. To address this issue, we set the threshold value based on a percentile instead of a fixed value. We sort all calculated neighborhood area size values and set the threshold value to be the value at a selected percentile. We found a percentile value of 85% is able to achieve good results across all datasets in our experiments. We further examine the effect of the threshold on accuracy in Section 3.

2.3 Anomaly Cause Inference

Determining the root cause of an anomaly is a highly non-trivial task. UBL is able to ameliorate this task by giving a hint as to what metrics are the top contributors to an anomaly. While this does not directly identify the root cause of the anomaly, it provides a clue of where to start looking. As the SOM preserves the topological properties of the measurement space, UBL can use this information to identify the faulty metric causing an anomaly. The basic idea is to look at the difference between anomalous neurons and normal neurons, and output the metrics that differ most as faulty metrics. Specifically, when we map a measurement sample to an anomalous neuron, we calculate the Euclidean distance from the mapped anomalous neuron to a set of nearby normal neurons. Here, it is necessary to avoid comparing with anomalous neighbor neurons as they represent unknown states and therefore may give incorrect anomaly cause hints. We examine the neighborhood area value for each neuron first. If it is above our threshold, we ignore it and move on to the next neuron in our neighborhood. If no normal neuron is found in the anomalous neuron's neighborhood, we expand our distance calculation to include more neurons in the map. In order to ensure we get a good representation of normal metrics, we select Q normal nearby neurons (e.g., Q = 5 in our experiments).

Once a set of normal neurons has been found, we calculate difference between the individual metric values of each normal neuron and those of the anomalous neuron. As the change can be positive or negative, we take the absolute value of the calculated difference. We then sort the metric differences from the highest to the lowest to determine a ranking order. After this process completes, we will have Q metric ranking lists. Finally, we examine the ranking orders of each of the Q rankings to determine a final order. To do this, we use majority voting. Each list votes for which metric it had identified as having the largest difference in values. We then output the metric with the most votes as the first ranked metric, the metric that has the 2nd most is the second ranked metric, and so on. Ties indicate no consensus could be reached and we output the metric that happens to come first in the output list construction. While we have found ties to be rare, a potential refinement of this approach would be to use the total difference of each metric to break ties. As an example, suppose three ranking lists rank CPU usage as the top anomaly cause but two other ranking lists rank Memory usage as the top cause. We will output CPU usage as the top anomaly cause as it has been ranked the top anomaly cause by a majority.

2.4 Decentralized Behavior Learning

Based on the monitoring results of a production cloud infrastructure, we observe that many hosts have less than 100% resource utilization. UBL leverages these *residual* resources to perform behavior learning as background tasks that are co-located with different application VMs (foreground tasks) on distributed hosts. Through this, we can achieve scalable infrastructure-wide behavior learning with minimum add-on cost. Our approach is particularly amenable for energy saving since a large portion of energy consumption is wasted in machine's idle state. To avoid affecting the foreground tasks, UBL takes advantage of the isolation provided by *Xen* to encapsulate itself within a special *learning VM*. We then use weight-based priority scheduling provided by the Xen platform to ensure the learning VM has a minimal effect on the foreground workload. Specifically, we assign a very low weight (e.g., 8) to all learning VMs which causes them to yield resources to the foreground application VMs.

UBL monitors the residual resources on each host by aggregating the resource consumption of all the VMs running on the host. If we find the available residual resources are insufficient, we employ live migration to move the learning VM to a host with sufficient residual resources. UBL maintains a resource demand signature for each learning VM and the residual resource signature for each host [19]. UBL finds a suitable host for migrating the learning VM by matching the resource demand signature of the learning VM with the residual resource signature of the host. We define a host to be overloaded when the total resource consumption of the host exceeds a certain threshold (e.g., > 90%). In this case, we relocate all the learning VMs running on that host to the hosts with suitable residual resources.

3. EXPERIMENTAL EVALUATION

We have implemented a prototype of UBL on top of the Xen platform and conducted extensive experiments using three benchmark systems: the RUBiS multi-tier online auction web application (EJB version) [4], IBM System S data stream processing system [18], and the Hadoop MapReduce framework [2]. We begin by describing our evaluation methodology. We then present our results.

3.1 Evaluation Methodology

Our experiments were conducted on the Virtual Computing Lab (VCL) infrastructure [6] which operates in a similar way as Amazon EC2 [1]. Each VCL host has a dual-core Xeon 3.0GHz CPU and 4GB memory, and runs 64bit CentOS 5.2 with Xen 3.0.3. The guest VMs also run 64bit CentOS 5.2 .

UBL monitors VMs' resource demands from domain 0, using the `libxenstat` and `libvirt` libraries to collect resource usage information (e.g., CPU usage, memory allocation, network I/O, disk I/O) for both domain 0 and guest VMs. UBL also uses a small memory monitoring daemon within each VM to get memory usage statistics (through the /proc interface in Linux). The sampling interval is 1 second.

We have chosen three benchmark systems to evaluate UBL in order to demonstrate the agnosticism necessary for such a system to be used in the real world. Moreover, UBL can handle dynamic applications processing time-varying workloads. To demonstrate this,

we drive all the benchmark applications using dynamic workload intensity observed in real world online services. We injected faults at different times while the system was under dynamic workload. Each experiment duration varies slightly but all last about one hour. Fault injections also vary slightly depending on the fault type but all last between 1 and 5 minutes. For each fault injection, we repeated the experiment 30 to 40 times. We now describe all the systems and fault injections in detail as follows.

RUBiS online auction benchmark: We used the three-tier online auction benchmark system RUBiS (EJB version) with one web server, two application servers, and one database server. In order to evaluate our system under workloads with realistic time variations, we used a client workload generator that emulates the workload intensity observed in the NASA web server trace beginning at 00:00:00 July 1, 1995 from the IRCache Internet traffic archive [5] to modulate the request rate of our RUBiS benchmark. The client workload generator also tracks the response time of the HTTP requests it made. A SLO violation is marked if the average request response time is larger than a pre-defined threshold (e.g., 100ms).

We injected the following faults in RUBiS: 1) *Memleak*: we start a memory-intensive program in the VM running the database server; 2) *CpuLeak*: a CPU-bound program with gradually increasing CPU consumptions competes CPU with the database server inside the same VM; and 3) *NetHog*: we use httperf [3] tool to send a large number of http requests to the web server.

IBM System S: We used the IBM System S that is a commercial high-performance data stream processing system. Each System S application consists of a set of inter-connected processing elements (PEs). We measured the average per-tuple processing time. A SLO violation is marked if the average processing time is larger than a pre-defined threshold (e.g., 20ms). In order to evaluate our system under dynamic workloads with realistic time variations, we used the workload intensity observed in the ClarkNet web server trace beginning at 1995-08-28:00.00 from the IRCache Internet traffic archive [5] to modulate the data arrival rate.

For System S, we injected the following faults: 1)*MemLeak*: we start a memory-intensive program in one randomly selected PE; 2) *CpuHog*: a CPU-bound program competes CPU with one randomly selected PE within the same VM; and 3) *Bottleneck*: we make one PE the bottleneck in the application by setting a low CPU cap for the VM running the PE.

Hadoop: We run Hadoop sorting application that is one of the sample applications provided by the Hadoop distribution. We measure the progress score of the job through Hadoop API. A SLO violation is marked when the job does not make any progress (i.e., 0 progress score increase). We use 3 VMs for Map tasks and 6 VMs for Reduce tasks. The number of map slots on each VM running map tasks is set to 2, and the number of Reduce slots on each VM running reduce tasks is set to 1. We use this configuration because the reduce task requires much more disk and memory space than the map task in the sorting application. Since this is a small Hadoop cluster, the JobTracker and NameNode are very light-weight. We colocate them together with the first reduce VM. The data size we process is 12GB, which is generated using the RandomWriter application.

For Hadoop, we injected two types of faults into all the VMs running the map tasks: 1) *MemLeak*: we injected a memory leak bug into all the map tasks, which repeatedly allocates certain memory from the heap without releasing; and 2) *CpuHog*: we injected an infinite loop bug into all the map tasks.

We evaluate the anomaly prediction accuracy using the standard *receiver operating characteristic* (ROC) curves. ROC curves can effectively show the tradeoff between the true positive rate (A_T)

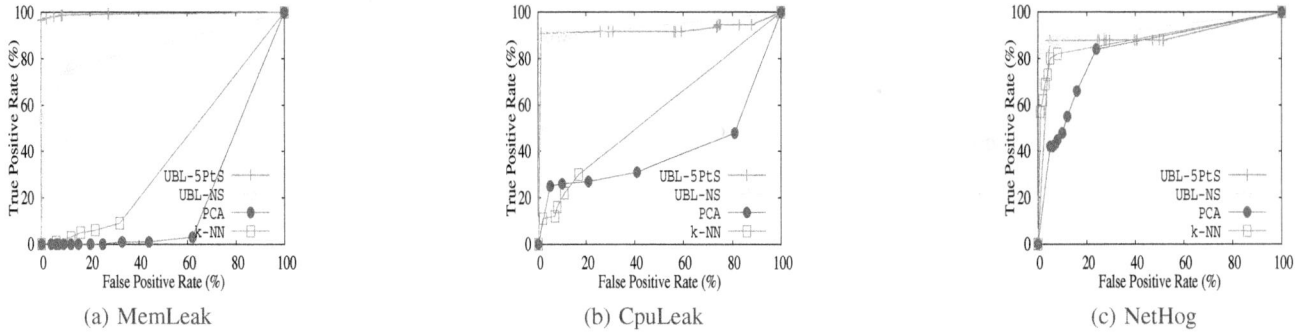

(a) MemLeak

(b) CpuLeak

(c) NetHog

Figure 4: Performance anomaly prediction accuracy comparison for RUBiS under different faults.

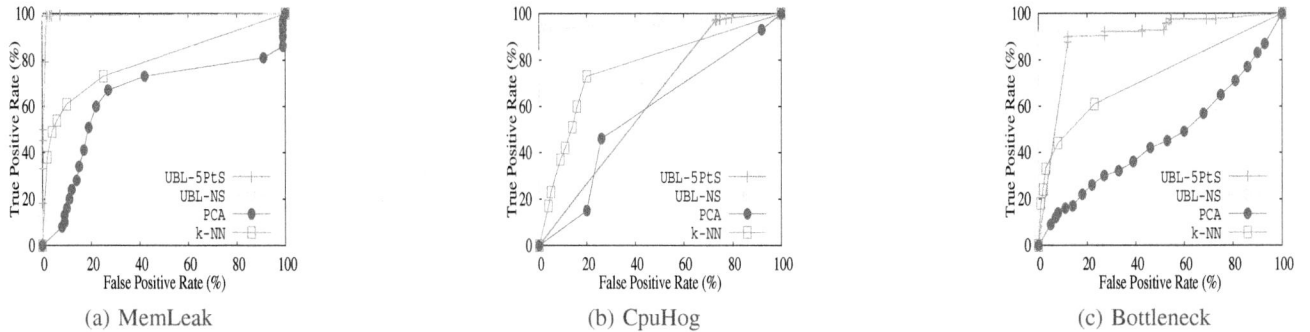

(a) MemLeak

(b) CpuHog

(c) Bottleneck

Figure 5: Performance anomaly prediction accuracy comparison for IBM System S under different faults.

and the false positive rate (A_F) for a prediction model. We use standard *true positive rate* A_T and *false positive rate* A_F metrics given in equation 5. The N_{tp}, N_{fp}, N_{tn}, and N_{fn} values are the same as those described in Section 2.

$$A_T = \frac{N_{tp}}{N_{tp} + N_{fn}}, A_F = \frac{N_{fp}}{N_{fp} + N_{tn}} \qquad (5)$$

We say the prediction model makes a true positive prediction if it raises an anomaly alert at time t_1 and the anomaly indeed happens at time t_2, $t_1 < t_2 < t_1 + W$, where W denotes the upper-bound of the anomaly pending time.[1]. Otherwise, we say the prediction model fails to make a correct prediction. If the predictor raises an alert and the predicted anomaly does not happen within the $t_1 + W$, we say that the prediction model raises a false alarm. We further evaluate the prediction capability of UBL using *achieved lead time*, which we define to be the amount of lead time we give prior to a SLO violation occurring. For example, if we raise an alarm at time t and the actual SLO violation occurs at time $t+20$ seconds, we have achieved a lead time of 20 seconds.

For comparison, we also implemented a set of commonly used unsupervised learning schemes: 1) the *PCA* scheme uses principle component analysis to identify normal and anomalous samples [26]; and 2) the *k-NN* scheme calculates a k-nearest neighbor distance for each measurement sample to identify normal and anomalous samples [32]. Different from UBL, both PCA and k-NN models need to be trained with both normal and anomalous data. In contrast, UBL does not require the training data to con-

---

[1]We have determined an appropriate anomaly pending time upperbound W for each dataset by manually examining the fault injection time to the SLO violation time. For example, if a fault is injected at time $t = 20$ and a SLO violation is observed at time $t = 30$, our window size would be 10.

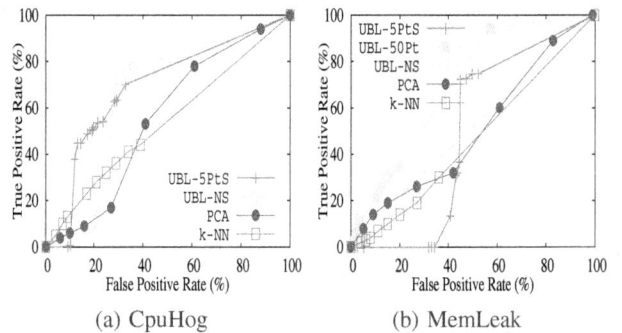

(a) CpuHog

(b) MemLeak

Figure 6: Performance anomaly prediction accuracy comparison for Hadoop under different faults.

tain anomalous data. We use *UBL-NS* to denote the UBL scheme without applying any data smoothing. We use *UBL-kPtS* to represent the UBL scheme using the k-point moving average smoothing. Through experimentation, we have defined our map to be 32x32 nodes, the neighborhood of each node to have a radius of 4, the learning factor to be a constant 0.7, and the neighborhood function to be a Gaussian function. We use 3-fold cross validation to select the best map among three randomly initialized map. We have also conducted sensitivity study experiments on those parameters, which will be presented in the next subsection.

3.2 Results and Analysis

3.2.1 Prediction Accuracy Results

We now present the anomaly prediction accuracy comparison results. We acquire the ROC curves for the UBL schemes by ad-

(a) RUBiS

(b) System S

(c) Hadoop

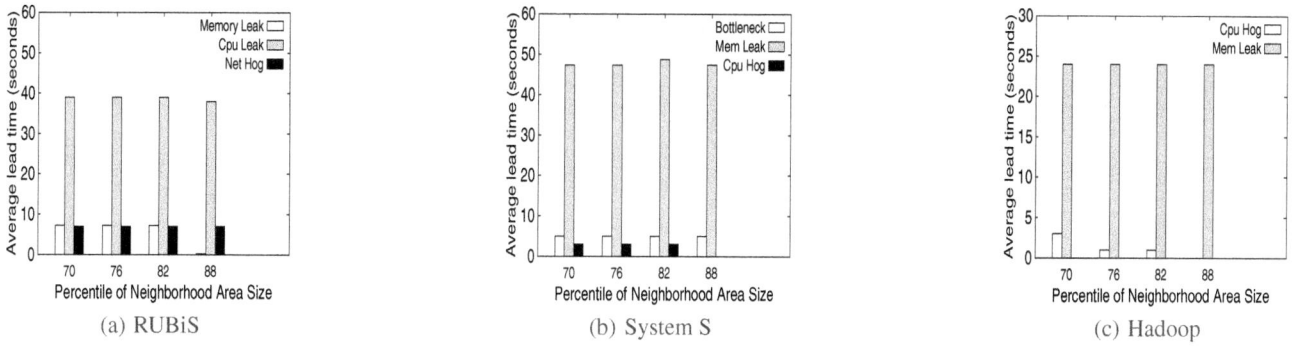

Figure 7: The achieved lead time by the UBL anomaly prediction model.

justing the neighborhood area size percentile threshold (i.e., 70'th percentile to 98'th percentile). For PCA, we obtain the ROC curves by adjusting the variance threshold. The ROC curves of k-NN is calculated by adjusting the $k'th$ nearest neighbor distance threshold.

We begin with the results of our RUBiS experiments. Figure 4 shows the ROC curves for the RUBiS systems under three different faults. The memory leak dataset was our best RUBiS dataset, we were able to achieve a high true positive rate of 97% with a very low false positive rate of 2%. This is consistent with what we expected as the memory leak manifests gradually and slowly. Conversely, we see our worst results from our NetHog dataset, achieving a 87% maximum true positive rate with a corresponding 4.7% false positive rate. This is also consistent with what we expected since the NetHog fault manifests more quickly than the other two faults. In all cases, UBL consistently outperforms PCA and k-NN with higher true positive rates and lower false positive rates.

We can see the positive effect of smoothing by looking at the Memleak dataset. Due to the gradual nature of this fault, smoothing allows us to achieve approximately 20% higher true positive rates with corresponding false positive rates. This is expected as the RUBiS dataset contains quite some transient noises. Additionally, due to the gradual manifestation time of the fault, we do not smooth out any pre-failure symptoms. Therefore, we see a marked improvement between the smoothed and non-smoothed data.

Figure 5 shows the prediction accuracy results for the IBM System S application under different faults. The results show that UBL is able to achieve higher prediction accuracy than the other schemes in all cases. The best result we were able to achieve was a 98% true positive rate along with a 1.7% false positive rate in the memory leak dataset. The worst results we achieved were in the CPU Hog dataset, with a 93% true positive rate and a 0.5% false positive rate. This is expected as CPU spikes are more difficult to predict due to the rapid onset of the fault. Similarly, the Bottleneck fault is also hard to predict as the time from fault to failure is also short. The System S dataset has relatively less noise than the RUBiS datasets, so the high accuracy results are expected. Additionally, the Bottleneck and CPU Hog datasets are harder to predict than the Memleak dataset, while our results for these datasets are good, they are lower than Memleak as expected.

It is interesting to observe smoothing does not always help achieve better accuracy. In the Bottleneck and CPU Hog datasets, the best results we achieve are those without any smoothing. This is due to two reasons. First, both faults manifest very quickly. Second, System S datasets are inherently not very noisy. When we apply smoothing, even 5-point smoothing, we sometimes smooth out those critical pre-anomaly symptoms. When this happens, our model

is unable to raise an alarm appropriately, leading to lower accuracy than without smoothing.

We now present the results of our Hadoop experiments shown by Figure 6. The MemLeak dataset was able to achieve the highest overall true positive rate due to the gradual nature of the fault. Hadoop is our noisiest dataset, which explains for the high false positive rates observed in these datasets. As expected, the rapid onset time of the CpuHog fault means the overall true positive rate we could achieve here was lower than the gradual memory leak dataset. As we can see, smoothing helps the MemLeak dataset, reducing the overall noise of the dataset while preserving the pre-failure symptoms. We show an additional curve to illustrate this point. Conversely, while smoothing reduced the noise of the CpuHog dataset, reducing the overall false positive rate, it also smoothed out pre-failure symptoms leading to a lower true positive rate as well. In both cases, UBL still can achieve better prediction accuracy than PCA and k-NN.

3.2.2 Lead Time Results

Figure 7 shows the average lead times achieved by UBL for RUBiS, System S, and Hadoop, respectively. The results shown only consider the lead time achieved for cases determined to be true positive results. We first discuss the RUBiS lead time results. We were closest to the maximum achievable lead time in the CpuLeak dataset. We achieved an average lead time of 38 seconds, with a maximum lead time of 40 seconds. The memory leak results for this dataset were the worst results we saw. We achieved an average lead time of only 7 seconds, with a maximum lead time of 50 seconds. This can be explained by variations in the data. The workload and background noise of the system caused the metrics to approach unknown levels only when the system was close to the anomaly state.

We next discuss the lead time we were able to achieve for the System S datasets. Here, we were able to achieve an average lead time of 47 seconds for the memory leak dataset with a maximum lead time possible of 50 seconds. While the lead time is lower for the CpuHog dataset, we achieved an average lead time of 3 seconds, with a maximum possible lead time of 4 seconds. Similarly, we achieved a lead time of 5 seconds in the Bottleneck dataset, with a maximum lead time of 6 seconds possible. The memory leak dataset had the best lead time because it was a gradual change with little memory fluctuation. The CpuHog and BottleNeck datasets had much shorter manifestation durations, and thus our system had little time to predict the anomaly, however we still are able to achieve results close to the maximum possible lead time.

Finally, we present the average lead time we are able to achieve in the Hadoop experiments in. The average lead time we were able to achieve in the memory leak dataset was 24 seconds. Here the

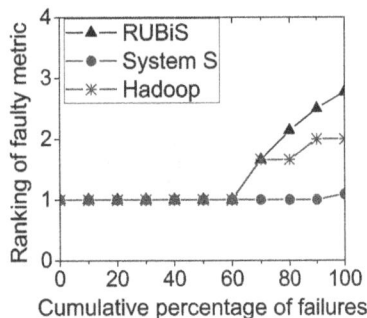

Figure 8: Ranking results of the faulty metrics in different failure instances. The Y axis is the faulty metric rank as determined by UBL while the X axis represents the total number of faults observed.

maximum lead time possible was 25 seconds. In this case, UBL is able to quickly determine the pattern is not normal and raise an early alarm. In contrast, the CpuHog lead time is lower, but as before this is due to the rapid onset time. We achieved an average lead time of 3 seconds with a maximum possible lead time of 4 seconds.

All in all, UBL can achieve close to maximum possible lead time for different faults tested in our experiments. Our previous study [34] shows that we can take local anomaly prevention actions such as VM resource scaling within one second and more costly anomaly preventions such as live VM migration within 10 to 30 seconds. Thus, the lead time achieved by UBL is sufficient in most cases for the cloud system to provide automatic anomaly preventions.

3.2.3 Anomaly Cause Inference Results

We now present our anomaly cause inference results shown by Figure 8. We consider the faulty metric to be the metrics most closely associated with a given failure. For example, for the MemLeak datasets, we consider the memory metric as the faulty metric. The figure shows the ranking of the faulty metric in the rank list output by UBL. As the Figure shows, UBL can correctly rank the faulty metric as top ranked metric in most failure cases. These results indicate UBL is able to preserve the topological properties of the input measurement space and is useful for diagnosis as well as prediction. In datasets where noise is less of an issue, such as System S, UBL achieves near perfect ranking results.

3.2.4 Scalability Results

To demonstrate the benefit of using the decentralized approach, we first measure the CPU load and power consumption of centralized system behavior learning approach. We run 25 learning VMs on five physical hosts, each of which runs five VMs. This experiment is conducted on a small cluster in our lab since VCL hosts are not equipped with power meters. Each host has a quad-core Xeon 2.53GHz processor, 8GB memory and 1Gbps network bandwidth, and runs CentOS 5.5 64 bit with Xen 3.4.3. In each physical host, we pin down Domain 0 to one core and run all learning VMs on three other cores, each VM is configured with one virtual core.

Figure 9 shows the total CPU consumption and energy consumption of the 25 VMs using 6000 data samples. The X-axis shows different numbers of learning VMs in the training state (the rest are in the prediction state). The left Y-axis shows the total CPU consumption and the right Y-axis shows the total energy consumption. We find that in all three schemes (PCA, k-NN, UBL), the learning VMs in the training state are CPU-greedy. The total CPU

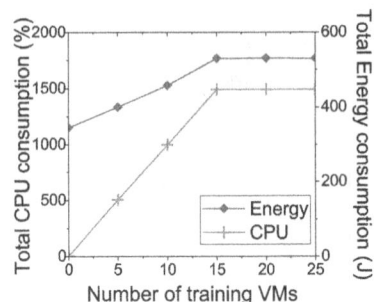

Figure 9: CPU load of 25 learning VMs running on 15 cores.

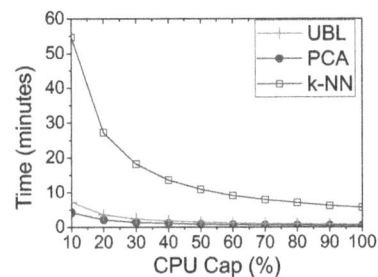

Figure 10: Training time comparison.

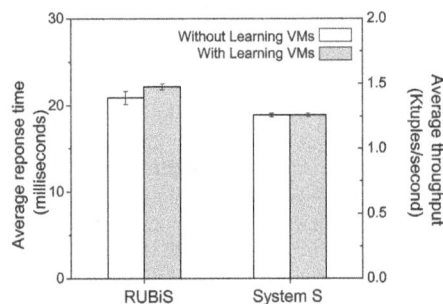

Figure 11: Learning VM impact to co-located application VMs.

consumption and energy consumption exhibits linear growth according to the number of learning VMs in the training state. Since there are a total of 15 cores on 5 hosts, the total CPU consumption cannot exceed 1500%. This experiment shows that the centralized learning approach will not be scalable.

Figure 10 shows the training time using 6000 data samples when varying the CPU cap of the learning VM on the HGCC host. We see that the training time of UBL is similar to PCA and much faster compared to k-NN. This is expected since k-NN has higher computation complexity than PCA and UBL. We also find that the training time of UBL decreases linearly as the CPU cap increases, from 7 minutes to 42 seconds. This motivates our idea of leveraging residual resources with migration to achieve fast system learning with low cost. Additionally, this demonstrates that even with few resources available, UBL training time is reasonable.

We now examine the impact of learning VMs to the performance of co-located application VMs. We set up a small cluster in which we run both RUBiS and System S. We use the Xen credit scheduler to set the scheduling weight of the application VMs to 256 and the weight of the learning VM to 8. Figure 11 shows the performance of the RUBiS and System S with and without the presence of learning VMs. We observe that with the presence of learning VMs, the average response time of RUBiS and the throughput of System S

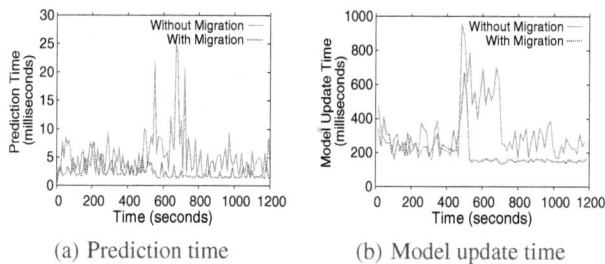

(a) Prediction time   (b) Model update time

Figure 12: Prediction time and model update time of UBL.

System Modules	CPU cost
VM monitoring (8 attributes)	1.33±0.09 ms
3-fold cross validation (6000 samples)	42 ± 1 sec
SOM model updating	245±54.9 ms
Anomaly prediction	2.4±2.6 ms

Table 1: UBL System overhead measurements.

	Accuracy (NetHog)	Accuracy (Memleak)
Map 25x25	97%	93%
Map 32x32	**98%**	**92.8%**
Map 40x40	97.1%	93.3%
Neighborhood size 3	98.6%	93.6%
Neighborhood size 4	**98.5%**	**92.8%**
Neighborhood size 5	97.6%	92.5%
Gaussian function height 7	98.2%	92.9%
Gaussian function height 10	**98.5%**	**92.8%**
Gaussian function height 13	98.9%	93.8%

Table 2: Sensitivity experiment results for the NetHog fault in RUBiS and MemLeak fault in System S.

have little difference compared to the case that the learning VMs are not present. The results show that the learning VMs have little impact to the performance of the co-located application VMs.

Figure 12 shows the benefit of using learning VM migration to maintain the prediction time and online model update time. Since we require the learning VMs to always yield to foreground applications, the performance of the learning VMs will be affected when the foreground applications use up the resources. The results show that, from time 450 to 700, the prediction time and the model update time increase because residual resources are low. By migrating the learning VMs to another physical host with more resources, the performance of UBL is preserved.

Finally, we evaluate the overhead of the UBL system. Table 1 lists the CPU cost of each key module in our system. The VM monitoring module runs within Domain 0 of each host and collects eight resource attributes per second. Each collection takes about 1.3 milliseconds. 3-fold cross validation is the most time-consuming operation, taking about 42 seconds. However, this step is only used during bootstrap learning phase. Incremental SOM updates take about 245 milliseconds for every 30 new data samples. Anomaly prediction takes about 2.4 milliseconds. During the normal execution, the learning VM imposes less than 1% CPU load and UBL consumes less than 16MB of memory. Overall, the overhead measurements show that UBL is light-weight, which makes it practical for online system anomaly management.

3.2.5 *Sensitivity Study*

We have conducted sensitivity experiments to study how UBL performs under different key parameter settings. Due to space limitation, we only show a subset of our results in Table 2. The accu-

racy values are calculated using Equation 2. We observe that UBL is not very sensitive to different parameter values and is able to achieve accuracy values which differ by less than 1% in most cases. The map size parameter has the potential to affect the accuracy of the system if it is set too low. For example, a 5x5 map is too small to effectively capture the overall pattern of the system. Additionally, if the map size is too large, the learning time becomes long. We have found map sizes in the range we list are able to give good results for all datasets we tested.

4. RELATED WORK

The idea of using machine learning methods to detect and predict anomalies, faults, and failures has been of great interest to the research community in recent years. Broadly, these approaches can be classified into supervised approaches and unsupervised approaches. Supervised approaches rely on labelled training data to accurately identify previously known anomalies. Unsupervised approaches do not require labelled training data to find problems, but generally are less accurate than supervised approaches, looking for a broader range of problems. These approaches can be further divided into detection schemes and prediction schemes. Detection schemes identify failures at the moment of failure, while prediction schemes try to predict a failure before it happens.

Supervised anomaly prediction. The most closely related work to ours is Tiresias [36], which also addresses the black-box failure prediction problem in distributed systems. Tiresias relies on external anomaly detectors to create anomaly vectors. The system then applies Dispersion Frame Technique (DFT) prediction heuristics on the anomaly vectors for anomaly prediction. Gu et al. [20] integrate Markov feature value prediction with naive Bayesian classification to predict performance anomalies. Tan et al. [33] use a hierarchical clustering technique to discover different execution contexts of a dynamic system but build context-aware prediction models to improve prediction accuracy. Different from UBL, the above works need labelled normal and failure data in the training data and do not provide anomaly cause inference. In contrast, UBL does not require any data labeling, which allows UBL to predict both known and unknown performance anomalies.

Supervised anomaly detection. Cohen et al. [16] use clustering over labelled failure data to extract failure signatures, which can be used to detect recurrent problems. Powers et al. [27] study different statistical learning methods to find the approaches that can detect performance violations in an enterprise system. Bhatia et al. [9] develop sketches of system events, which are then visualized for diagnosis by an expert. The Fa system [17] uses anomaly-based clustering to achieve automatic failure diagnosis for query processing systems. Cha et al. [12] use a signature based approach along with a bloom filter for malware detection. Bodik et al. [10] use signatures along with feature selection and a regression model to detect performance anomalies. In contrast, our approach focuses on predicting unknown anomalies and does not require prior knowledge about different failure instances.

Unsupervised anomaly detection. Previous work has proposed model-driven approach to performance anomaly detection. For example, Stewart et al. [31] instrument the OS to gather data and profile system performance using queuing models. Shen et al. [29] use a reference based approach to detect performance anomalies by looking at how metrics differ from the ideal case. Stewart et al. [30] use a transaction mix model to predict the performance given a certain workload, and hence can detect the anomaly if the observed performance is different with the predicted performance. Compared to UBL, those model-driven approaches typically require extensive model calibration using offline profiling and need to make certain assumptions about the workload type (e.g, transactions) and user request arrival patterns. In contrast, UBL is application-agnostic and does not require extensive application profiling. Cherkasova et al. [13] build regression-based transaction models and application performance signatures to provide a solution for anomaly detection considering system changes. Different from UBL, this model is designed to consider a single metric. Wang et al. [35] have used entropy based approaches to quantify the metric distribution and detect anomalies using signal processing and spike detection. Similarly, Jiang et al. [22] detect failures by looking at the entropy of clustered system metric relationships. Makanju et al. [25] assign entropy scores to event log data to detect anomalies. WAP5 [28] detects the bottleneck in distributed systems by analyzing message traces to infer the causal structure and timing of communication within these systems. Kasick et al. [23] use peer comparison to determine the root cause of a problem in a distributed environment. Jiang et al. [21] employ linear regression models to extract invariants and then track their changes to detect the anomaly in transaction systems. In contrast to the above approaches, UBL can predict future anomalies as opposed to detecting anomalies at the moment of failure. Moreover, UBL is broader in scope, designed to learn system behavior for a variety of uses. We show anomaly prediction as one of the uses of UBL.

5. CONCLUSION

In this paper, we have presented UBL, a novel black-box unsupervised behavior learning and anomaly prediction system for IaaS clouds. UBL leverages the Self-Organizing Map (SOM) learning technique to capture dynamic system behaviors without any human intervention. Based on the induced behavior model, UBL can predict previously unknown performance anomalies and provides hints for anomaly causes. UBL achieves scalable behavior learning by virtualizing and distributing the learning tasks among distributed hosts. We have implemented a prototype of UBL on top of the Xen platform and conducted extensive experiments using real world distributed systems running inside a production cloud infrastructure. Our results show that UBL can achieve high prediction accuracy with up to 98% true positive rate and 1.7% false positive rate, and raise advance alarms with up to 47 seconds lead time. UBL is lightweight, which makes it practical for large-scale cloud computing infrastructures.

6. ACKNOWLEDGMENT

This work was sponsored in part by NSF CNS0915567 grant, NSF CNS0915861 grant, NSF CAREER Award CNS1149445, U.S. Army Research Office (ARO) under grant W911NF-10-1-0273, IBM Faculty Awards and Google Research Awards. Any opinions expressed in this paper are those of the authors and do not necessarily reflect the views of NSF, ARO, or U.S. Government. The authors would like to thank the anonymous reviewers for their insightful comments as well as Zhiming Shen, Yongmin Tan, and Kamal Kc for their help.

7. REFERENCES

[1] Amazon elastic compute cloud. http://aws.amazon.com/ec2/.
[2] Apache Hadoop System. http://hadoop.apache.org/core/.
[3] Httperf. http://code.google.com/p/httperf/.
[4] RUBiS: Rice University Bidding System. http://rubis.ow2.org.
[5] The IRCache Project. http://www.ircache.net/.
[6] Virtual computing lab. http://vcl.ncsu.edu/.
[7] P. Barham, A. Donnelly, R. Isaacs, and R. Mortier. Using magpie for request extraction and workload modelling. In *Proc. of OSDI*, 2004.
[8] P. Barham and et al. Xen and the Art of Virtualization. In *Proc. of SOSP*, 2003.
[9] S. Bhatia, A. Kumar, M. E. Fiuczynski, and L. Peterson. Lightweight, high-resolution monitoring for troubleshooting production systems. In *Proc. of OSDI*, 2008.
[10] P. Bodik, M. Goldszmidt, and A. Fox. Hilighter: Automatically building robust signatures of performance behavior for small- and large-scale systems. In *Proc. of SysML*, 2008.
[11] D. Breitgand, M. B.-Yehuda, M. Factor, H. Kolodner, V. Kravtsov, and D. Pelleg. NAP: a building block for remediating performance bottlenecks via black box network analysis. In *Proc. ICAC*, 2009.
[12] S. K. Cha, I. Moraru, J. Jang, J. Truelove, D. Brumley, and D. G. Andersen. Splitscreen: enabling efficient, distributed malware detection. In *Proc. of NSDI*, 2010.
[13] L. Cherkasova, K. Ozonat, N. Mi, J. Symons, and E. Smirni. Anomaly? application change? or workload change? In *Proc. of DSN*, 2008.
[14] C. Clark, K. Fraser, S. Hand, J. G. Hansen, E. Jul, C. Limpach, I. Pratt, and A. Warfield. Live migration of virtual machines. In *Proc. of NSDI*, 2005.
[15] I. Cohen, M. Goldszmidt, T. Kelly, J. Symons, and J. S. Chase. Correlating Instrumentation Data to System States: A Building Block for Automated Diagnosis and Control. In *Proc. of OSDI*, 2004.
[16] I. Cohen, S. Zhang, M. Goldszmidt, J. Symons, T. Kelly, and A. Fox. Capturing, indexing, clustering, and retrieving system history. In *Proc. of SOSP*, 2005.
[17] S. Duan, S. Babu, and K. Munagala. Fa: A system for automating failure diagnosis. In *Proc. of ICDE*, 2009.
[18] B. Gedik, H. Andrade, K.-L. Wu, P. S. Yu, and M. Doo. SPADE: the system s declarative stream processing engine. In *Proc. of SIGMOD*, 2008.
[19] Z. Gong and X. Gu. PAC: Pattern-driven Application Consolidation for Efficient Cloud Computing. In *Proc. of MASCOTS*, 2010.
[20] X. Gu and H. Wang. Online anomaly prediction for robust cluster systems. In *Proc. of ICDE*, 2009.
[21] G. Jiang, H. Chen, and K. Yoshihira. Discovering likely invariants of distributed transaction systems for autonomic system management. In *Proc. of ICAC*, 2006.
[22] M. Jiang, M. Munawar, T. Reidemeister, and P. A. S. Ward. Automatic fault detection and diagnosis in complex software systems by information-theoretic monitoring. In *Proc. of DSN*, 2009.
[23] M. P. Kasick, J. Tan, R. Gandhi, and P. Narasimhan. Black-box problem diagnosis in parallel file systems. In *Proc. of FAST*, 2010.
[24] T. Kohonen, M. R. Schroeder, and T. S. Huang, editors. *Self-Organizing Maps*. Springer, 3rd edition, 2001.
[25] A. Makanju, A. N. Zincir-Heywood, and E. E. Milios. Fast entropy based alert detection in super computer. In *Proc. of DSN*, 2010.
[26] I. T. Olliffe. *Principal Component Analysis*. Springer-Verlag, 2002.
[27] R. Powers, M. Goldszmidt, and I. Cohen. Short term performance forecasting in enterprise systems. In *Proc. of KDD*, 2005.
[28] P. Reynolds, J. Wiener, J. Mogul, M. Aguilera, and A. Vahdat. Wap5: black-box performance debugging for wide-area systems. In *Proc. of WWW*, 2006.
[29] K. Shen, C. Stewart, C. Li, and X. Li. Reference-driven performance anomaly identification. In *Proc. of SIGMETRICS*, 2009.
[30] C. Stewart, T. Kelly, and A. Zhang. Exploiting nonstationarity for performance prediction. In *Proc. of Eurosys*, 2007.
[31] C. Stewart and K. Shen. Performance modeling and system management for multi-component online service. In *Proc. of NSDI*, 2005.
[32] P.-N. Tan, M. Steinbach, and V. Kumar. *Introduction to Data Mining*. Addison Wesley, 2005.
[33] Y. Tan, X. Gu, and H. Wang. Adaptive system anomaly prediction for large-scale hosting infrastructures. In *Proc. of PODC*, 2010.
[34] Y. Tan, H. Nguyen, Z. Shen, X. Gu, C. Venkatramani, and D. Rajan. PREPARE: Predictive Performance Anomaly Prevention for Virtualized Cloud Systems. In *Proc. of ICDCS*, 2012.
[35] C. Wang, V. Talwar, K. Schwan, and P. Ranganathan. Online detection of utility cloud anomalies using metric distributions. In *Proc. of NOMS*, 2010.
[36] A. W. Williams, S. M. Pertet, and P. Narasimah. Tiresias: Black-box failure prediction in distributed systems. In *Proc. of IPDPS*, 2007.

Evaluating Compressive Sampling Strategies for Performance Monitoring of Data Centers

Tingshan Huang
ECE Department
Drexel University
Philadelphia, PA 19104, USA
th423@drexel.edu

Nagarajan Kandasamy
ECE Department
Drexel University
Philadelphia, PA 19104, USA
kandasamy@drexel.edu

Harish Sethu
ECE Department
Drexel University
Philadelphia, PA 19104, USA
sethu@drexel.edu

ABSTRACT

Performance monitoring of data centers provides vital information for dynamic resource provisioning, fault diagnosis, and capacity planning decisions. Online monitoring, however, incurs a variety of costs—the very act of monitoring a system interferes with its performance, and if the information is transmitted to a monitoring station for analysis and logging, this consumes network bandwidth and disk space. This paper proposes a low-cost monitoring solution using compressive sampling—a technique that allows certain classes of signals to be recovered from the original measurements using far fewer samples than traditional approaches—and evaluates its ability to measure typical parameters or signals generated in a data-center setting using a testbed comprising the Trade6 enterprise application. Experiments indicate that by using the compressive sampling mechanism, the recovered signal adequately preserves the spikes and other abrupt changes present in the original. The results, therefore, open up the possibility of using low-cost compressive sampling techniques to detect performance bottlenecks and anomalies in data centers that manifest themselves as abrupt changes exceeding operator-defined threshold values in the underlying signals.

Categories and Subject Descriptors

C.4 [**Performance of systems**]: Design studies, modeling techniques, fault tolerance

General Terms

Algorithms, Performance, Management, Reliability

Keywords

Performance management, online monitoring, compressive sampling

1. INTRODUCTION

Online performance monitoring of both the IT infrastructure as well as the physical facility is vital to ensuring the effective and ef-

ficient operation of data centers [5,9]. Examples of monitoring solutions include the Tivoli Monitoring software from IBM for the IT infrastructure [10] and the Data Center Environmental Edge from HP that monitors temperature, humidity, and state of the power network within the data center. The monitored information has a variety of uses. It drives real-time performance management decisions such as dynamic provisioning of IT resources to match the incoming workload, detection and mitigation of performance-related hotspots/bottlenecks, and fault diagnosis. In the case of intermittent problems that are hard to isolate, browsing back through historical data can help identify and localize recurring problems affecting the same portion of the IT infrastructure at different times. The information also drives decisions of a longer-term nature: intelligent capacity planning that identifies resources that are over-utilized (under-utilized) and aims to improve overall facility utilization by adding (removing) appropriate resources.

We consider a server cluster wherein software-based sensors embedded within the IT infrastructure measure various performance-related parameters associated with the cluster—high-level metrics such as response time and throughput as well as low-level metrics such as processor utilization, I/O activity (disk reads and writes), and network activity (packets sent and received). The information collected by the sensors is transmitted over a network to a monitoring station for data analysis and visualization. Online monitoring, however, incurs a variety of costs. First, the very act of monitoring an application interferes with its performance; if sensing-related code is merged with the application code, this change may interfere with the timing characteristics of the application or if sensors execute as separate processes, they contend for CPU resources along with the original application. Transmitting the monitored data over a network consumes bandwidth. Finally, logging the data for future use (such as analysis aimed at capacity planning) consumes disk space. So, when monitoring a large-scale computing system, it is desirable to minimize the above-described costs, which is the focus of this paper.[1]

Traditional methods of sampling signals use Shannon's theorem: the sampling rate must be at least twice the signal bandwidth to capture all the information content present in the signal. The theory of compressive sampling, a recent development in signal processing, states, however, that we can recover a certain class of signals from the original measurements using far fewer samples than techniques that use Shannon's theorem [2–4, 7]. Compressive sampling contends that many natural signals are sparse in that they have concise representations when expressed in the proper basis. This property is used to capture the useful information content embedded in the

---

[1]A preliminary version of this paper appeared as a poster in the IEEE/IFIP Network Operations and Management Symposium (NOMS), 2012.

signal and condense it into a small amount of data. In other words, one can acquire these signals from the underlying system directly in a compressed form. From a viewpoint of reducing the costs associated with online monitoring, compressive sampling allows for a very simple sensing strategy; rather than tailoring the sensing scheme to the specific signal being measured, a signal-independent strategy such as randomized sampling can be used, significantly reducing the intrusion of monitoring on application performance. Also, since signals are acquired directly in compressive form, the network bandwidth required to transmit these few samples to the monitoring station is reduced, and so is the hard-disk space required to store them. When operators wish to analyze the original signal, there is a way to use numerical optimization to reconstruct the full-length signal from the sample set.

This paper investigates the feasibility of using compressive sampling to measure signals typically generated in an enterprise-level data center and compares data sampling, encoding, and recovery strategies. We use IBM's Trade6 benchmark, a stock-trading service which allows users to browse, buy, and sell stocks, as our testbed and subject it to a self-similar workload while measuring these signals: response time, CPU utilization, and disk I/O activity in terms of sectors read and written. The measurements are acquired directly in terms of fewer number of samples by encoding the data in an appropriate representation basis. For our experiments, we choose four representation bases—the Fourier basis, and the Haar, Daubechies-2, and Daubechies-4 wavelet bases—to determine the sparsity or conciseness of the data when encoded in each of the basis functions. At the monitoring station, the process of recovering the original signal from these samples is posed as a linear programming problem and solved as such. We assess the quality of the reconstructed signal using two performance metrics: relative error that captures the normalized error between the original and reconstructed signals, and receiver operating characteristics (ROC) that characterizes the number of spikes that can be detected using the reconstructed signal.

A major benefit offered by compressive sampling in the context of data center operations is reducing the overhead of generating, storing, and using performance log files for offline analysis tasks such as capacity planning, bottleneck detection, and long-term trend forecasting. When analyzing the data, if the operator wishes to detect performance-related bottlenecks or anomalies that manifest themselves as spikes or abrupt changes in the signal exceeding some nominal threshold value, then the signal reconstructed via compressive sampling must preserve the spikes observed in the original trace. This performance is quantified by the ROC curve and in this regard compressive sampling performs quite well for all signals considered in this paper. By selecting the threshold value appropriately, a hit rate of 93% can be achieved with a false alarm rate of only 0.1%, using about 30% of the samples from the original signals. The results reported in the paper open up the possibility of using compressive sampling as a low-cost online monitoring tool in data centers, especially for anomaly detection and long-term capacity planning.

The paper is organized as follows. Section 2 describes our experimental testbed. Section 3 discusses the compressive sampling of signals generated by the testbed and Section 4 presents experimental results evaluating the performance of this sampling scheme in recovering the original signals. Section 5 discusses related work and Section 6 concludes the paper.

2. EXPERIMENTAL SETUP

Fig. 1 shows the computing system used in our experiments, comprising three servers networked via a gigabit switch. The sys-

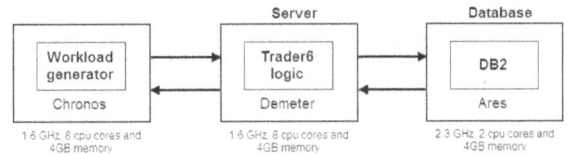

Figure 1: The overall system architecture hosting the Trade6 service.

tem for server hosts IBM's Trade6 benchmark, a stock-trading application which allows users to browse, buy, and sell stocks. So, users can perform dynamic content retrieval as well as transaction commitments, requiring database reads and writes, respectively. The application logic for Trade6 resides within the IBM WebSphere Application Server, which in turn is hosted by the virtual machine on the server `Demeter` within the application tier. Virtualization of this system is enabled by VMWare's ESX Server 3.5 running a Linux RedHat kernel. The operating system on the virtual machine is the SUSE Enterprise Linux Server Edition. The database component is DB2 which is hosted on the server `Ares` running SUSE Enterprise Linux. The database maintains 10,000 user accounts and information for 20,000 stocks.

We use Httperf, an open-loop workload generator, to send a mix of browse, buy, and sell requests to the Trade6 application [11]. Based on available evidence on web access traffic patterns [6], the workload follows a self-similar distribution as shown in Fig. 2(a), with an arrival rate of 100 requests per second with a 50/50 mix of buy to browse transactions. Every 100 milliseconds, we measure the average end-to-end response time incurred by the requests (*response_time*). At the database tier, we collect data every 30 seconds corresponding to CPU utilization (*cpu_util*), and the number of disk sectors read and written (*read_activity* and *write_activity*). Fig. 2(b) shows a sample set of parameters/signals collected during an experimental run of the system.

3. COMPRESSIVE SAMPLING OF SYSTEM PARAMETERS

This section describes how to acquire the signals of interest from the testbed directly in a compressed form. First, we familiarize the reader with the two key conditions underlying compressive sampling: sparsity and incoherence. The first condition applies to the signals themselves and the second condition affects the way we sample these signals. We then discuss how the original signal can be recovered from a small set of samples.

3.1 Sparse Representation of Signals

Assume that the data to be sampled $\mathbf{d}$ is a vector of length N and its representation in some basis B is $\mathbf{x}$. In other words, $d(t) = \sum_{i=1}^{N} x_i b_i(t) = B\mathbf{x}$, where $B = [b_1, b_2, \ldots, b_N]$. For example, if B is selected to be the Fourier basis, the elements of the vector $\mathbf{x}$ are Fourier coefficients corresponding to the signal $\mathbf{d}$. Also, if at most S entries in $\mathbf{x}$ are nonzero, then $\mathbf{x}$ is called an S−sparse vector and $\mathbf{d}$ is said to be sparsely represented in the basis B.

Using the data collected from our testbed, we now aim to find a basis B in which this data can be most concisely represented. We consider the following four basis functions: the Fourier basis, the Haar wavelet basis, the Daubechies-2 (or db2) wavelet basis, and the Daubechies-4 (or db4) wavelet basis [14]. The waveforms corresponding to these functions are shown in Fig. 3. These four bases are common for time-frequency analysis on time series data:

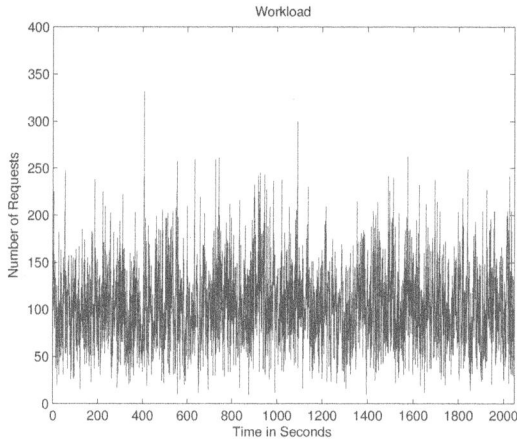

(a)

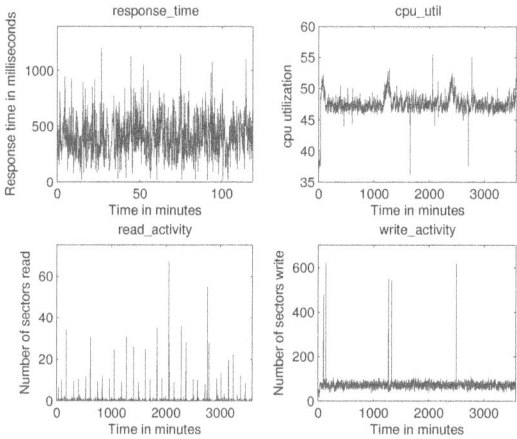

(b)

Figure 2: (a) The self-similar workload presented to the computing system shown in Fig. 1; (b) the various signals collected from the system during an experimental run.

Fourier basis is the traditional tool for analyzing the frequency characteristics of a signal while wavelet bases show signal characteristics in both time and frequency domains. Considering the advantages of using wavelets to capture sharp or abrupt changes in the signal, we focus on three commonly used wavelets: the Haar, the simplest wavelet that captures discontinuities in the data; db2, a more complex waveform with more similarity to the data collected from the testbed; and db4, a wavelet that also shows similarity with our data but has a longer waveform, leading to better frequency resolution. A full introduction to the waveforms corresponding to these wavelets may be found in [13].

We analyze the above-described basis functions in terms of how concisely they encode the data collected from our system. We first perform a signal transform on each data set to find the corresponding coefficients within the chosen basis and arrange them in decreasing order of their magnitude. Then, we use only the first n coefficients, $1 \leq n \leq N$, set all the other coefficients to 0, and reconstruct a new signal $\tilde{\mathbf{d}}(n)$. A relative-error metric captures the difference between the original and reconstructed signals as

$$e(n) = \frac{\|\tilde{\mathbf{d}}(n) - \mathbf{d}\|}{\|\mathbf{d}\|}. \tag{1}$$

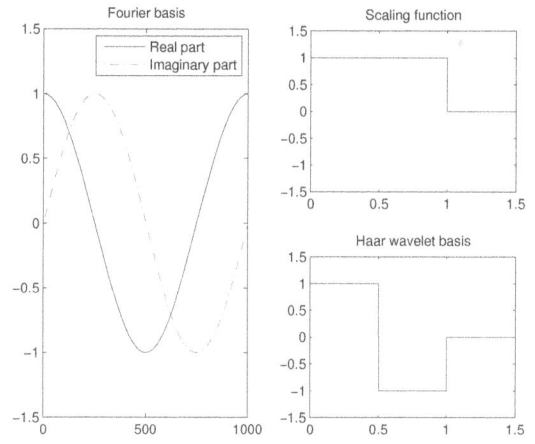

(a) The Fourier and Haar wavelet basis functions.

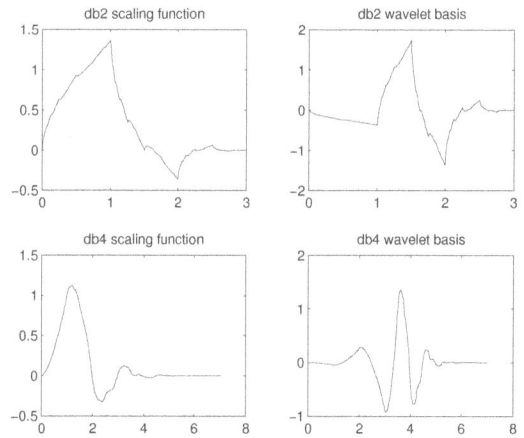

(b) The Daubechies-2 and Daubechies-4 basis functions.

Figure 3: The waveforms corresponding to the four basis functions considered in this paper.

Finally, we examine how this relative error changes as the value of n is increased. For each set of data, we repeat the analysis for each of the four basis functions. The basis in which the relative error decreases to zero fastest represents the signal most concisely.

Fig 4 shows that the relative error, when using the Haar wavelet, decays most quickly for *cpu_util* and *read_activity* signals and that the representations of *response_activity* and *write_activity* are not sparse enough within any of the selected bases. The relative error achieved by the Fourier basis is the worst, especially for the *read_activity* and *cpu_activity* signals. This is because these data sets exhibit marked discontinuities with numerous spikes, and thus their representation in the Fourier basis is less concise than those in other bases. For the same reason, we find that the Haar and db2 wavelets represent *cpu_util* and *read_activity* quite concisely. Note that *read_activity* is the sparsest signal in that it requires the smallest percentage of the coefficients to reconstruct the signal within a small relative error, achieving relative error of less than 0.1% when using only 18% coefficients in Haar wavelet basis; *cpu_util* is also sparse since it can be reconstructed with relative error around 2% using 25% of the coefficients under all bases except for Fourier; for the *response_time* and *write_activity* signals, we find that more than 50% of the coefficients are needed to reconstruct them with small

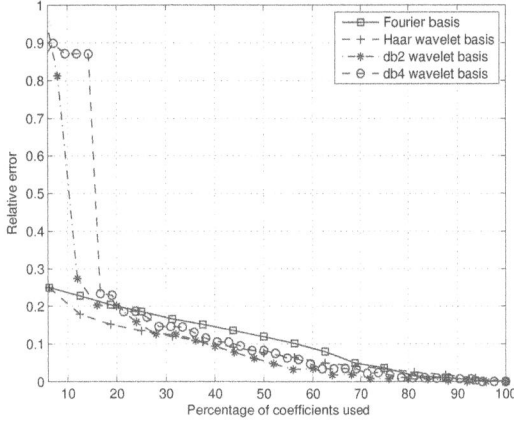

(a) Relative error for the *response_time* signal.

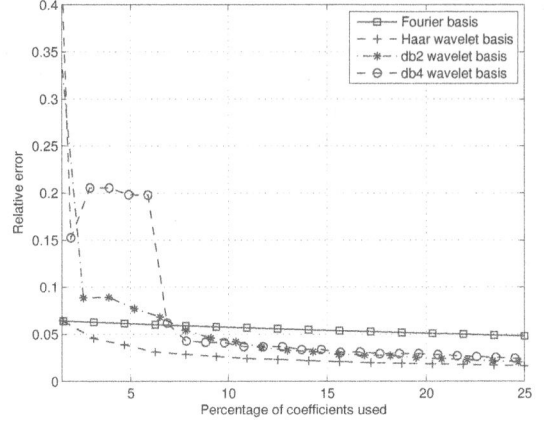

(b) Relative error for the *cpu_util* signal.

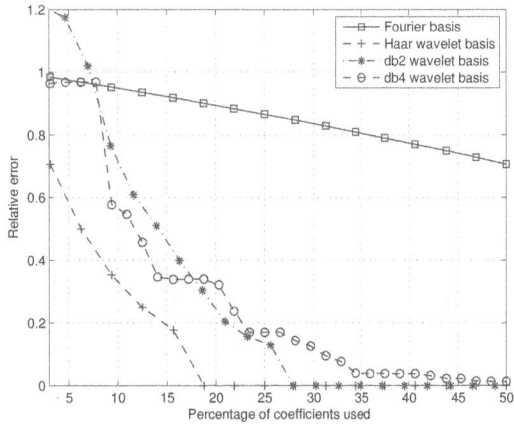

(c) Relative error for the *read_activity* signal.

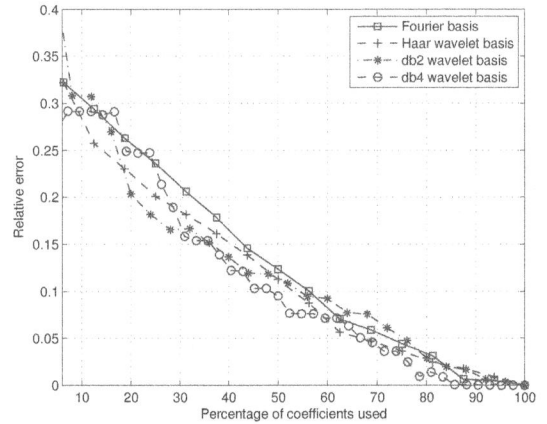

(d) Relative error for the *write_activity* signal.

Figure 4: Plots showing the change in relative error for the *response_time*, *cpu_util*, *read_activity* and *write_activity* signals as a function of the percentage of coefficients used during reconstruction.

Table 1: Percentage of coefficients needed to maintain the relative error within 5%.

Data	Haar	db2	db4	Fourier
response_time	62.5%	51.6%	58.9%	68.8%
cpu_data	2.7%	8.4%	7.5%	21.8%
read_data	19.9%	27.0%	33.9%	99.1%
write_data	66.4%	75.4%	66.6%	72.4%

relative error of 5%, irrespective of the basis. Table 1 summarizes the percentage of coefficients needed to maintain the relative error within 5% for each of the bases.

Section 4 quantifies the effect of using the different bases, in terms of relative error, when the original signal is reconstructed using the samples obtained via compressive sampling. We also use another metric, ROC, in Section 4 to characterize the number of spikes that can be detected in the reconstructed signal.

3.2 Incoherent Sampling of the Signal

Given two N-dimensional bases Ψ and Φ, the coherence between these bases is defined as the largest coherence between any two basis vectors in Ψ and Φ, and is given by

$$\mu(\Psi, \Phi) = \sqrt{N} \max_{1 \leq k, j \leq N} |\langle \phi_k, \psi_j \rangle|, \quad (2)$$

where $\langle \phi_k, \psi_j \rangle$ is the dot product of vectors ϕ_k and ψ_j.

Usually, the coherence between two bases lies in the range of $\left[1, \sqrt{N}\right]$ and when the value of coherence is small we consider the two bases to be uncorrelated or incoherent. When the sensing basis and the representation basis have a small coherence value, and thus uncorrelated, then a signal that is represented as a spike in one basis will be represented as a spread-out waveform in the other. For example, the Dirac delta basis and Fourier basis have a coherence of one; a signal shown as a spike in the Dirac basis is spread out when represented using the Fourier basis. This property allows us to capture the complete information present in the original data using a small number of samples obtained by incoherent sampling.

As a sampling strategy to collect measurements from our testbed, we choose Gaussian random matrices that have a low coherence of $\sqrt{2 \log N}$ relative to any representation matrix with high probability. Table 2 shows the average coherence between an $M \times N$ Gaussian sensing basis and the various representation bases of interest where N is the length of the input data and M is the desired number of samples. As expected, the coherence values are quite low.

Table 2: Average coherence between an $M \times N$ random Gaussian sensing basis and the different representation bases when $N = 2048$.

Representation basis	Haar	db2	db4	Fourier
$M = 0.1N$	3.67	4.81	4.77	4.82
$M = 0.3N$	3.81	5.05	5.04	5.07
$M = 0.5N$	3.90	5.11	5.12	5.10

To collect M samples, we generate an $M \times N$ Gaussian random matrix G as the underlying sampling matrix. Elements in the matrix are independently chosen from a standard Gaussian distribution and the rows are orthonormalized such that the rows have unit norm and are orthogonal to each other. To obtain the samples from the input data, we simply multiply this matrix G by the vector of data $\mathbf{d}$.

For example, assume the data to be sampled is an 8×1 vector

$$\mathbf{d} = \begin{pmatrix} B_{1,1} & B_{1,2} & \cdots & B_{1,8} \\ B_{2,1} & B_{2,2} & \cdots & B_{2,8} \\ \vdots & \vdots & \ddots & \vdots \\ B_{8,1} & B_{8,2} & \cdots & B_{8,8} \end{pmatrix} \begin{pmatrix} x_1 \\ x_2 \\ \vdots \\ x_8 \end{pmatrix} = B \times \mathbf{x},$$

where B is an 8×8 matrix corresponding to the Haar wavelet basis and $\mathbf{x}$ is the representation of $\mathbf{d}$ in the Haar basis. Suppose we wish to obtain a 4×1 vector of samples $\mathbf{y}$. The data is multiplied with a Gaussian matrix G such that

$$\mathbf{y} = \begin{pmatrix} G_{1,1} & G_{1,2} & \cdots & G_{1,8} \\ G_{2,1} & G_{2,2} & \cdots & G_{2,8} \\ G_{3,1} & G_{3,2} & \cdots & G_{3,8} \\ G_{4,1} & G_{4,2} & \cdots & G_{4,8} \end{pmatrix} \begin{pmatrix} d_1 \\ d_2 \\ \vdots \\ d_8 \end{pmatrix}$$

$$= G \times \mathbf{d} = G \times B \times \mathbf{x} = A \times \mathbf{x},$$

where $A = G \times B$ is a 4×8 matrix.

Fig. 5 shows the implementation of compressive sampling in our system in which the incoming signal $\mathbf{d}$ is acquired directly in a compressed form $\mathbf{y}$. When a new data item $d(t)$ arrives at time t, it is multiplied by the entries in the sampling matrix $G(j,t)$, $j = 1, \ldots, M$, and the partial products are accumulated into $y(j)$. After a period of length $N \times T$, where T is the sampling period, the current values of $y(j)$ are sent out as the M samples and then reset back to zero. Effectively, $y(j) = \sum_{j=1}^{M} G(j,t)d(t)$, where $t = 1, \ldots, N$, and thus $\mathbf{y} = G \times \mathbf{d}$.

3.3 Recovering the Original Signal

The process of incoherent sampling gives us a set of values $\mathbf{y} = G \times \mathbf{d} = G \times B \times \mathbf{x} = A\mathbf{x}$, where $A = G \times B$. To reconstruct the original data $\mathbf{d}$, we must solve this inverse problem: given a vector $\mathbf{y}$ of length M and matrix A of size $M \times N$ where $M \ll N$, find a sparse vector $\tilde{\mathbf{x}}$ of length N such that $\mathbf{y} = A\tilde{\mathbf{x}}$. In other words, we are looking for $\tilde{\mathbf{x}}$ as a solution to

$$\min_{\mathbf{b} \in \mathcal{R}} \ \|\mathbf{b}\|_{l_0} \quad \text{subject to: } \mathbf{y} = A\mathbf{b}, \tag{3}$$

where $\|\mathbf{b}\|_{l_0}$ is the number of nonzero entries in $\mathbf{b}$. This problem is under-constrained since the matrix A has more columns than rows; there are infinitely many candidate signals $\mathbf{b}$ for which $A\mathbf{b} = \mathbf{y}$. The problem of minimizing the l_0 norm is a computationally expensive nonlinear optimization problem. So, one of the following classes of reconstruction algorithms is typically used for computational efficiency: basis pursuit and iterative algorithms based on hard thresholding pursuit.

The basis pursuit technique solves the problem in (3) by minimizing the l_1 norm, which is the linear programming problem posed

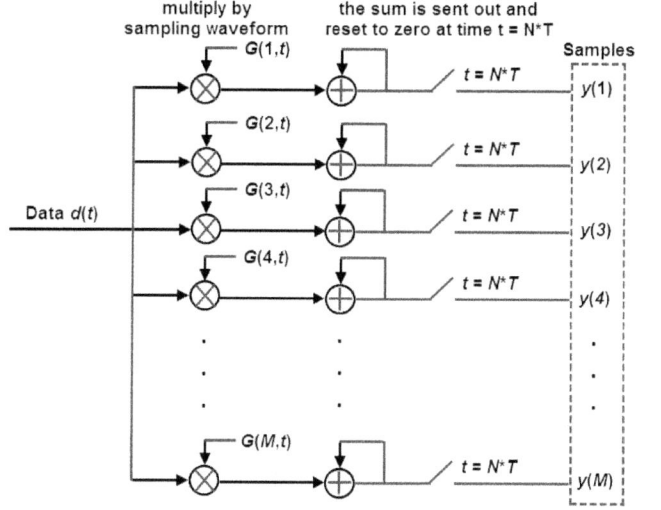

Figure 5: Implementation of compressive sampling in our system that takes N data items over a time period as input and returns M samples.

as follows:

$$\min_{\mathbf{b} \in \mathcal{R}} \ \|\mathbf{b}\|_{l_1} \quad \text{subject to: } \mathbf{y} = A\mathbf{b}. \tag{4}$$

Reconstruction of the original signal using (4) is considered to be exact with probability exceeding $1 - \delta$, where δ is a very small constant, if the number of samples

$$M \geq C\mu(\Psi, \Phi)^2 S \log \frac{N}{\delta}, \tag{5}$$

where C is some positive constant [1]. The direct consequence of (5) is that when the coherence between the representation and sensing bases, μ, as well as the sparsity metric, S, is small, we need only a few samples to recover the original signal exactly with high probability.

In iterative algorithms, the problem in (3) is solved by iteratively selecting an sparse vector $\mathbf{b}$ based on the previous selection. In our work, we use a method termed the hard thresholding pursuit previously proposed by Foucart [8]. Let the initial value of the vector be $\mathbf{b} = \mathbf{0}$ and let the S–sparse vector selected at step n be $\mathbf{b}^n$, the iteration scheme involves two steps:

$$I^{n+1} = \{\text{Indices of S largest entries in } \mathbf{b}^n + A^*(\mathbf{y} - A\mathbf{b}^n)\}$$

$$\mathbf{b}^{n+1} = \arg\min\{\|\mathbf{y} - A\mathbf{b}\|_2, \ \text{supp}(b) \subseteq I^{n+1}\}$$

The iterations continue until $I^{n+1} = I^n$. This algorithm has been validated to perform faster than other threshold-based methods such as orthogonal matching pursuit.

4. PERFORMANCE EVALUATION

This section evaluates the performance of compressive sampling in recovering the various signals obtained from the testbed using the Fourier basis and the Haar, db2, and db4 wavelet bases. The goal of these experiments is to determine the most suitable representation basis to use when reconstructing the original signal.

4.1 Performance Metrics

We use the following metrics to assess the quality of the signal recovered from its sampled form.

Relative error. This metric (defined in Section 3.1) expresses the normalized error between the original and recovered signals.

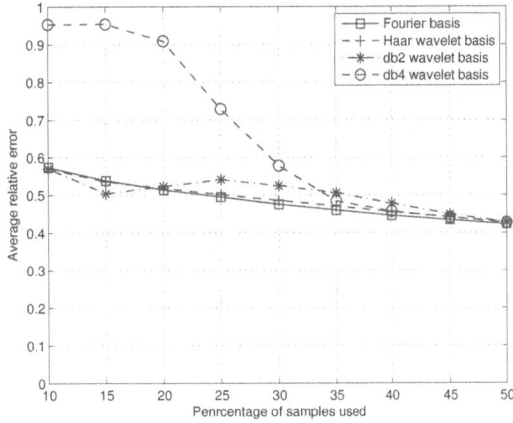

(a) Relative error achieved by the recovered *response_time* signal.

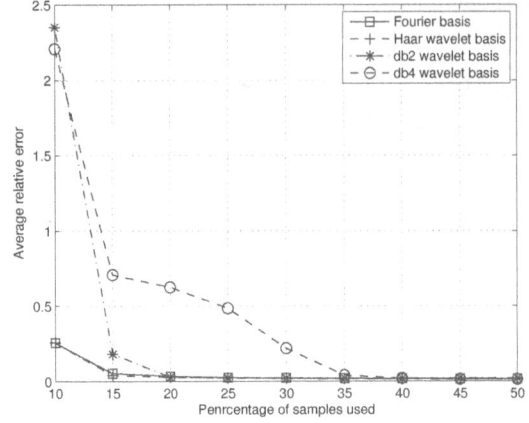

(b) Relative error achieved by the recovered *cpu_util* signal.

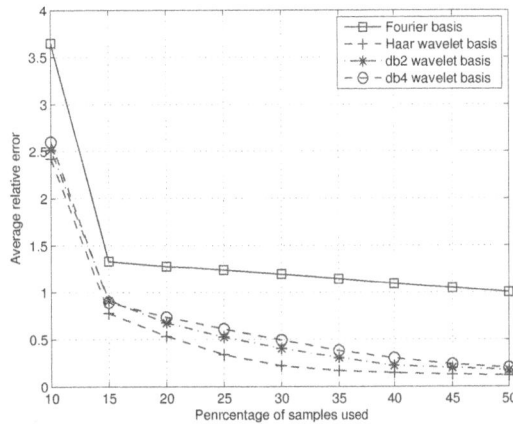

(c) Relative error achieved by the recovered *read_activity* signal.

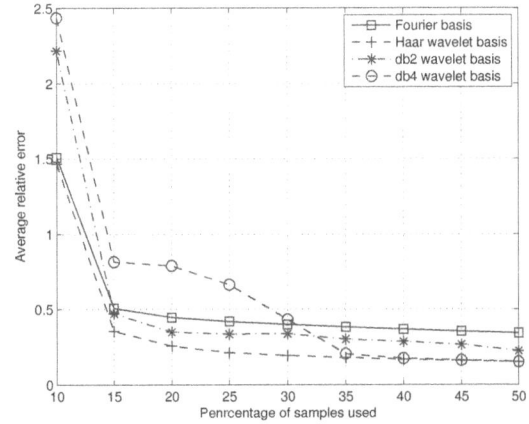

(d) Relative error achieved by the recovered *write_activity* signal.

Figure 6: The relative error achieved by the recovered signals as a function of the number of samples used during the reconstruction.

Receiver operating characteristic (ROC). Considering the number of spikes present in the *cpu_util*, *read_activity*, and *write_activity* data sets, we use the ROC metric to characterize the number of spikes that can be detected using the reconstructed signal. We define a hit as follows: at time t within the original and recovered signals, a spike occurring in the recovered signal matches a similar spike in the original signal. We define a false alarm as follows: at time t, a spike occurring in the recovered signal has no match in the original signal. The ROC plots the hit rate against the false alarm rate. The ROC becomes relevant in situations in which it may not be essential for compressive sampling to recover the original signal exactly, such as when the operator is mainly interested in detecting performance bottlenecks, hot spots, or anomalies affecting the computing system, some of which manifest themselves as spikes or abrupt changes in the signals being monitored.

4.2 Characterizing Signal Recovery via Relative Error

Figure 6 summarizes the relative errors achieved by the various representation bases when recovering the signals as a function of the percentage of samples used. Figure 6(a) shows the relative error achieved when reconstructing the *response_time* signal. Even when 50% of the samples are used, the relative error is over 40% for all the bases. This result is expected since, as shown in Fig. 4(a), none of the bases can concisely represent the signal in terms of the number of required coefficients. For example, we find that at least 50% of the coefficients are needed in the db2 basis to capture most of the signal energy, and so the sparsity of the signal in db2 basis is more than $0.5N$, where N is the length of the signal. According to (5), we require $4 \times S \times \mu^2 (\Phi, \Psi)$ samples for exact reconstruction. For example, when using the db2 wavelet as the representation basis Ψ, the coherence $\mu (\Phi, \Psi)$ is around 5.1 (from Table 2) and to reconstruct *response_time* exactly, we need around $4 \times 0.5N \times 5.1^2 = 52.02N$ samples—a sample size fifty times larger than the original data. When *response_time* is represented using the other bases, the sample size required for exact reconstruction is even larger. This demonstrates why compressive sampling is not very effective on data sets that cannot be represented as a sparse vector within a certain basis.

Figure 6(b) summarizes the relative error achieved by the recovered *cpu_util* signal; when 20% of the samples are used, the relative error is less than 4% using the wavelet bases. The signal is quite sparse and when represented in any of the wavelet bases, *cpu_util* can be reconstructed with less than 5% relative error using at most 20% of the wavelet coefficients. Furthermore, if we approximate the sparsity of *cpu_util* in the Haar wavelet basis by

0.02N and use 3.67 as the coherence value, then we require about $4 \times 0.02N \times 3.67^2 = 1.13N$ samples for exact signal reconstruction with high probability. However, we find a better result from our experiment: when 15% of the samples are used, the relative error corresponding to each of the three wavelet bases falls below 3%.

Figure 6(c) shows that when 50% of the samples are used, the relative error achieved by the reconstructed *read_activity* signal is around 20% under the wavelet bases. The relative error never falls below 100% when the Fourier basis is used, implying that this basis is not suitable for the compressive sampling of *read_activity*. Figure 6(d) summarizes the relative error achieved for the *write_activity* signal. Under the db4 or Haar wavelets, the relative error falls below 25% when about 35% of the samples are used. Conversely, even when 50% of the samples are used, the relative error is around 25% for the db2 wavelet basis and 40% for the Fourier basis. The result for the Fourier basis is as expected. Figure 4 indicates that a very large percentage of the Fourier coefficients are needed to maintain a 5% relative error and the coherence between our sampling waveform and the Fourier basis is about 5.1 (from Table 2). We find that the sparsity of *write_activity* under the Fourier basis is about 0.75N and for an exact signal recovery, we need a sample size $4 \times 0.75N \times 5.1^2 = 78.03N$; that is, even a sample set the same size as the original data is not sufficient for reconstruction. So, *write_activity* is not appropriate for compressive sampling using the Fourier basis. We find similar results with the Haar, db2, and db4 wavelet bases as well. As discussed in Section 3.1, more than 70% of coefficients are necessary to maintain a 5% relative error using these bases; the sparsity of *write_activity* when represented in these bases is at least $S = 0.7N$. Since the coherence between the Gaussian sampling matrix and the Haar, db2, or db4 bases is at least 3.67 (from Table 2), the sample size required for exact recovery has to be $4 \times 0.7N \times 3.67^2 = 37.71N$. As a result, we can conclude that *write_activity* is less appropriate for compressive sampling using the Haar, db2, or db4 bases—at least for exact recovery.

We summarize the results as follows: for the data sets considered in this paper, the Haar wavelet basis achieves, on average, the best performance in terms of the relative error metric. The Fourier basis performs well for *response_time* and *cpu_util*, but is the worst for *read_activity* and *write_activity* signals. If the Haar wavelet is used as the representation basis, the basis vector for the *cpu_util* signal is sparser than those for the *response_time*, *read_activity* and *write_activity* signals. Fig. 7 shows the performance of the Haar basis as the sample size is varied; when 30% of the samples are used, the relative error is nearly 2.5% for the recovered *cpu_util* signal. For the *read_activity* and *write_activity* signals, however, we require at least 50% of the samples to lower the relative error to 15% and the relative error for the *response_time* signal is almost 43% even if we use 50% of the samples.

4.3 Characterizing Signal Recovery via Receiver Operating Characteristics

As noted earlier in the paper, there are situations in which it is not essential for compressive sampling to recover the original signal exactly. If the operator is mainly interested in detecting performance bottlenecks, hot spots, or anomalies affecting the computing system that manifest themselves as spikes or abrupt changes in the signals being monitored, it is more important that the reconstructed signal preserve these characteristics.

Fig. 8 shows the original and recovered signals for *write_activity*, *cpu_util*, and *read_activity*, overlayed on each other. The signals are mostly limited to narrow bands of values and compressive sampling does an adequate job of reconstruction using about 30% of the

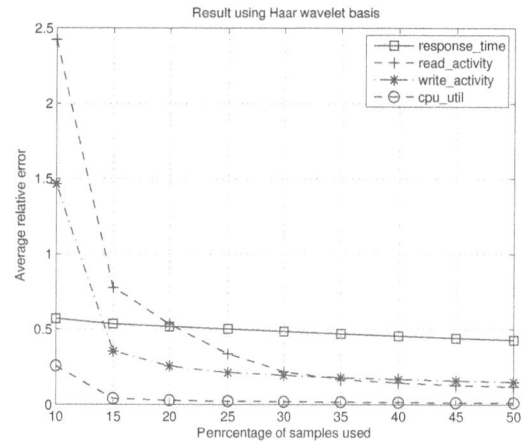

Figure 7: The relative error achieved by the Haar wavelet basis for the various data sets as a function of the number of samples used for signal reconstruction.

Table 3: False alarm and hit rates associated with different threshold levels for the reconstructed *write_activity* and *cpu_util* signals.

Data	read_activity	write_activity	cpu_util
Threshold level	6	132	43.8%
False alarm rate	0.05	0.05%	0.05%
Hit rate	94.64	97.59%	93.96%

original signal when using Haar wavelet basis even though the relative error are larger than 15% for *read_activity* and *write_activity*. More importantly, the recovered signal preserves the spikes found in the original quite well, preserving the abrupt bursts in the *read_activity* and *write_activity* signals, and sudden (steep) decreases in *cpu_util*. Figs. 9(a), 9(b) and 9(c) graph the ROC curves for the *read_activity*, *write_activity* and *cpu_util* signals reconstructed under the different representation bases. The plots are generated using 30% of the samples from the original *write_activity*, *write_activity* and *cpu_util* signals, respectively. We change the threshold level that defines a spike, and for each threshold obtain and plot a pair of values: the hit rate and the corresponding false alarm rate.

Table 3 lists the false alarm rates and hit rates with their corresponding threshold-level settings for the reconstructed *read_activity*, *write_activity* and *cpu_util* signals. The original signals were encoded using the Haar wavelet basis. The performance, in terms of ROC, indicates that compressive sampling still helps to reconstruct the spikes of interest. For example, from the viewpoint of detecting anomalies affecting *write_activity*, a hit rate of more than 95% can be achieved with a corresponding false alarm rate of less than 0.1% by setting the threshold to about 132 sectors written.

Generally, both the false alarm rate and the hit rate should decrease as the threshold is increased since fewer false spikes occur in the reconstructed signal. However, we see in Fig. 9(a) that the hit rate corresponding to the db2 basis increases as the threshold is increased whereas the corresponding false alarm decreases from 0.2% to 0.05%. We see a similar result as well for the db4 basis in Fig. 9(b) and for all the bases in Fig. 9(c). To explain this unusual result, we examine the reconstructed signal for the *read_activity* when using db2 in conjunction with the original signal (shown in the overlay plot in Fig. 10). We find that spikes larger than 7 in the *read_activity* signal are all detected but under-estimated in the reconstructed signal, i.e., the reconstructed spikes match those in

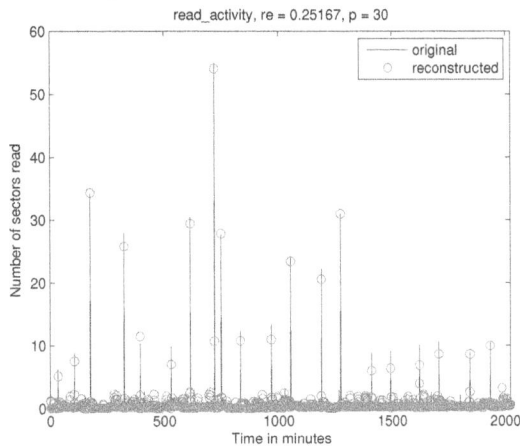

(a) Overlay of the original and recovered *read_activity* signals.

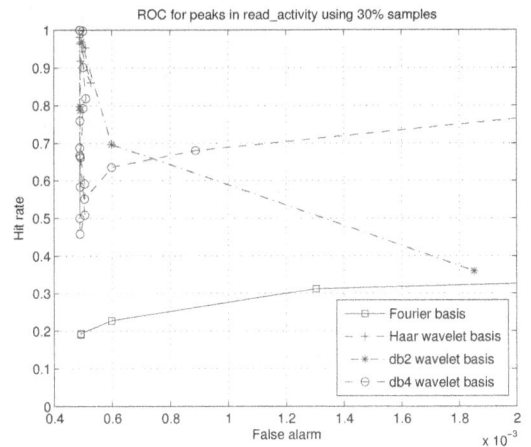

(b) Overlay of the original and recovered *write_activity* signals.

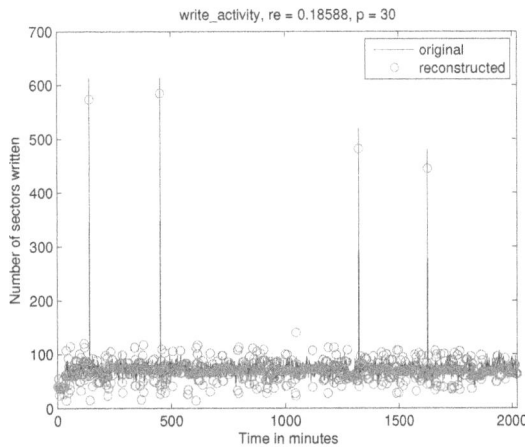

(c) Overlay of the original and recovered *cpu_util* signals.

Figure 8: Overlay plots comparing the recovered *read_activity*, *write_activity* and *cpu_util* signals using Haar wavelet basis with the originals. Compressive sampling preserves the spikes present in the original signals quite well.

the original signal but have smaller values. Besides, we find that smaller spikes in the original signal within the range [1, 7] are

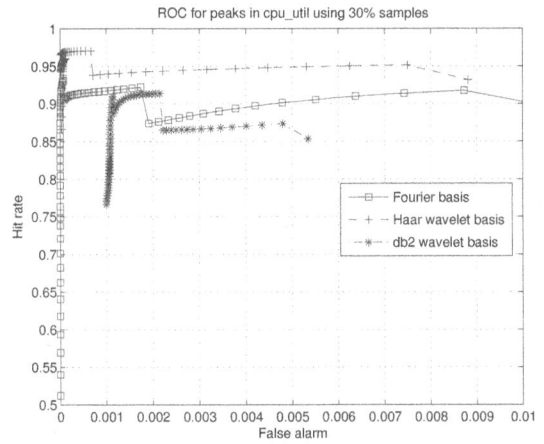

(a) ROC curve generated by the recovered *read_activity* signal.

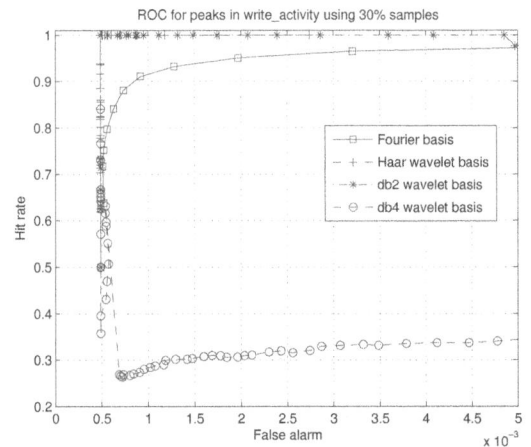

(b) ROC curve generated by the recovered *write_activity* signal.

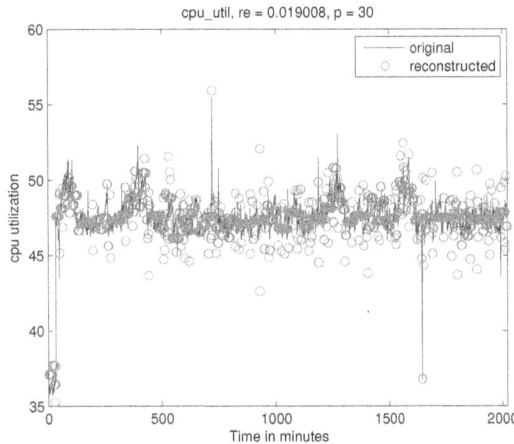

(c) ROC curve generated by the recovered *cpu_util* signal.

Figure 9: Plots showing the ROC curves for the read_activity, write_activity and cpu_util signals reconstructed under the four representation bases.

not detected and there are small spikes in the reconstructed signal without a match in the original signal. For these reasons, as the threshold is increased within the [1, 7] range the number of de-

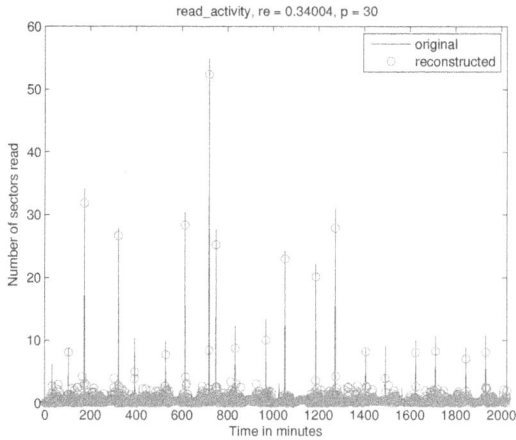

Figure 10: Overlay plot comparing the recovered *read_activity* signal using db2 wavelet basis with the original. Spikes present in the original signals are underestimated in the reconstructed signal.

Table 4: Execution Time (in milliseconds) for the incoherent sampling process as a function of sample size N.

Percentage of Samples	10%	20%	30%
$N = 1024$	0.14	0.29	0.38
$N = 2048$	0.52	0.96	1.40
$N = 4096$	1.90	3.90	5.50

Table 5: Execution Time (in seconds) incurred by the signal recovery process as a function of sample size N.

Percentage of Samples	10%	20%	30%
$N = 1024$	0.3	0.3	0.6
$N = 2048$	0.9	1.8	1.9
$N = 4096$	5.1	9.1	11.7

tected spikes that are above the threshold stays the same, whereas the number of spikes above the threshold in the original signal decreases. As a result, the hit rate increases. Furthermore, as the threshold increases within this range, there are fewer reconstructed spikes above the threshold without a match in the original and the false alarm decreases as expected. The unusual trend in the other plots can be explained similarly. This explanation also shows the importance of selecting both the proper basis for compressive sampling and threshold values to detect anomalies.

4.4 Computational Complexity

We quantify the execution-time overhead incurred by both the sampling and signal recovery processes as a function of sample size. The algorithms were implemented in MATLAB and executed on a server equipped with an AMD Athlon II 3.0 GHz processor. For presentation purposes, we denote the length of original data to be sampled as N; the length of compressed samples as M; and the average execution time incurred by the sampling and recovery processes as $t_s(N, M)$ and $t_r(N, M)$, respectively.

The execution time for incoherent sampling is summarized in Table 4 as a function of sample size. Generally, this process is not time-consuming: when $N = 4096$ (corresponding to approximately 48 hours of monitoring time in the case of *cpu_util*, *read_activity*, and *write_activity* signals) and when we wish to compress this data to 30% of its original size (or $M/N \times 100\% = 30\%$) the running

time is about 6 ms. The average value for $t_s(N, 2M)/t_s(N, M)$ is 1.99 and the average value for $t_r(N, 3M)/t_r(N, M)$ is 2.77, which indicates that the execution time grows sublinearly with M. Assume the execution time for the sampling and the recovery to be exponential with N as the exponent,

$$t_s(N, M) = c_s \times N_s^r,$$

$$t_r(N, M) = c_r \times N_r^r,$$

where the values for c_s and c_r depend on M. Then the value for order r_s and r_r can be calculated by

$$c_s = \frac{\log(t_s(2N, M)) - \log(t_s(N, M))}{\log(2)}.$$

$$c_r = \frac{\log(t_r(2N, M)) - \log(t_r(N, M))}{\log(2)}.$$

From Table 4, we find the average value for order c_s is 1.89, indicating that the running time grows sublinearly with N^2. Since the running time increases linearly as M/N increases and quadruples as N is doubled, the computational complexity associated with incoherent sampling is $O(N^2 M)$. In our implementation, the process of incoherent sampling is simply the multiplication of an $M \times N$ matrix with an $N \times 1$ vector, and the complexity is actually $M \times (N \times \text{multiplication} + (N - 1) \times \text{addition}) = O(NM)$.

The algorithm used for the signal recovery is a recent iterative algorithm termed Hard Thresholding Pursuit proposed by Foucart [8]. Table 5 lists the execution times incurred by the recovery algorithm as a function of N. The average value for $t_r(N, 2M)/t_r(N, M)$ is 1.59 and for $t_r(N, 3M)/t_r(N, M)$, it is 2.14, indicating that the running time grows sublinearly with M; the average value for order c_r is 2.22, showing that the running time grows linearly with N^2. Therefore, the computational complexity associated with the signal recovery process is $O(N^2 M)$.

5. RELATED WORK

To the best of our knowledge compressive sampling has not been perviously studied as a technique for monitoring the performance of enterprise computing systems. It has recently been validated for monitoring fine-grained processor performance [12] and for the detection of Internet traffic anomalies [15].

Tuma et al. study the applicability of compressive sampling to fine-grained monitoring of processor performance and propose the method as a means of simplifying the complex processes of sensing and transferring signals related to micro-architecture performance [12]. The authors evaluate the performance of compressive sampling on signals representing one or more micro-architectural counters within a processor core, and show that compressive sampling can recover these signals if one can identify the bases in which the signals can be sparsely represented. Their approach bears some similarity to our work, but the measurements are obtained from hardware counters inside various micro-architectural components of the processor and the evaluation is limited to a signal-to-noise (SNR) metric—same as the relative error metric used in this paper. Our data is obtained from a server platform and includes both high-level performance metrics (response time) as well as low-level ones (CPU utilization and disk I/O activity). We also evaluate compressive sampling in terms of the ROC metric to evaluate how well spikes can be recovered within the reconstructed signal. Besides, rather than using traditional algorithms such as Orthogonal Matching Pursuit for signal recovery as in [12], we use a faster iterative Hard Thresholding Pursuit algorithm originally proposed in [8].

In the area of computer network monitoring, Zhang *et al.* use the spatial-temporal compressive sampling framework for traffic matrix interpolation [15]. This technique uses an algorithm called sparsity regularized matrix factorization that uses both the global low-rank property of traffic in a network and spatio-temporal properties of the local traffic, and the authors focus on building a model that includes both spatial and temporal properties of the underlying traffic matrix. They claim that the normal component of the traffic matrix can be captured via a low-rank matrix, and try to determine a low-rank matrix that best estimates the original traffic matrix. Their work shows that over 90% of the missing values in traffic matrix can be inferred with reasonable accuracy using compressive sampling.

Finally, it could be argued that any number of existing compression algorithms, especially lossless ones such as `bzip2` and `DEFLATE`, could be used to condense the information monitored at the data center before writing to disk. However, massive data acquisition followed by compression is extremely wasteful of computing and memory resources. Compressive sampling, on the other hand, enables us to acquire data directly in compressed form.

6. CONCLUSIONS

This paper has proposed and evaluated a low-cost monitoring solution for data centers based on the concept of compressive sampling that allows certain classes of signals to be recovered from the original measurements using far fewer samples than traditional approaches. Using the Trade6 application as our testbed, we showed how to acquire measurements corresponding to response time, CPU utilization, and disk I/O activity directly in a compressed form, and how to reconstruct the full-length signal at the monitoring station using a few number of samples. We have experimented with four different basis functions to determine the conciseness of the data when encoded in each of these functions and assessed the resulting quality of the reconstructed signal. The performance of compressive sampling is quite promising in terms of the ROC—the recovered signal adequately preserves the spikes and other abrupt changes present in the original signal. By selecting the threshold value appropriately, a hit rate of 93% can be achieved with a false alarm rate of less than 0.1%.

Acknowledgments

This work was partially funded by the Office of Naval Research (ONR) through grant number N00014-10-1-0625.

7. REFERENCES

[1] E. J. Candès and J. Romberg. Sparsity and incoherence in compressive sampling. *Inverse Prob.*, 23(3):969–985, 2007.

[2] E. J. Candès, J. Romberg, and T. Tao. Robust uncertainty principles: Exact signal reconstruction from highly incomplete frequency information. *IEEE Trans. Inform. Theory*, 52(2):489–509, 2006.

[3] E. J. Candès and T. Tao. Near optimal signal recovery from random projections: Universal coding strategies? *IEEE Trans. Inform. Theory*, 52(12):5406–5425, 2006.

[4] E. J. Candès and M. B. Wakin. An introduction to compressive sampling. *IEEE Signal Proc. Mag.*, 25(2):21–30, 2008.

[5] L. Cherkasova, K. Ozonat, N. Mi, J. Symons, and E. Smirni. Automated anomaly detection and performance modeling of enterprise applications. *ACM Trans. Comput. Syst.*, 27:6:1–6:32, Nov. 2009.

[6] M. E. Crovella and A. Bestavros. Self-similarity in world wide web traffic: Evidence and possible causes. *IEEE Trans. Networking*, 5(6):835–846, 1997.

[7] D. Donoho. Compressed sensing. *IEEE Trans. Inform. Theory*, 52(4):1289–1306, 2006.

[8] S. Foucart. Hard thresholding pursuit: An algorithm for compressive sensing. *preprint*, 2010.

[9] M. Kutare et al. Monalytics: Online monitoring and analytics for managing large scale data centers. *Proc. ACM ICAC*, 2010.

[10] G. Lanfranchi, P. D. Peruta, A. Perrone, and D. Calvanese. Toward a new landscape of systems management in an autonomic computing environment. *IBM Systems Journal*, 42(1):119–128, 2003.

[11] D. Mosberger and T. Jin. httperf: A tool for measuring web server performance. *Perf. Eval. Review*, 26:31–37, 1998.

[12] T. Tuma, S. Rooney, and P. Hurley. On the applicability of compressive sampling in fine grained processor performance monitoring. *Proc. IEEE Int'l Conf. on Engineering of Complex Computer Systems*, pages 210–219, 2009.

[13] J. S. Walker. *A Primer on Wavelets and their Scientific Applications*. Chapman and Hall, 2 edition, 2008.

[14] G. G. Walter and X. Shen. *Wavelets and Other Orthogonal Systems*. CRC Press, 2 edition, 2000.

[15] Y. Zhang, M. Roughan, W. Willinger, and L. Qiu. Spatio-temporal compressive sensing and internet traffic matrices. *Proc. ACM SIGCOMM*, pages 267–278, 2009.

Author Index